JOHN M. CULBERTSON
Professor of Economics
University of Wisconsin

money and banking

McGraw-Hill Book Company
New York St. Louis San Francisco Düsseldorf Johannesburg
Kuala Lumpur London Mexico Montreal New Delhi Panama
Rio de Janeiro Singapore Sydney Toronto

This book was set in Melior by Black Dot, Inc., and printed and bound by Kingsport Press, Inc.
The designer was Paula Tuerk; the drawings were done by Vantage Art, Inc. The editors were Jack R. Crutchfield and James R. Belser. Matt Martino supervised production.

MONEY AND BANKING

Library of Congress Catalog Card Number 78-39066

07-014899-6

5 6 7 8 9 0 K P K P 7 9 8 7 6 5 4 3

TO

Jo, John, Lynn, and Amy

To limit the total amount of paper issued, and to resort for this purpose, whenever the temptation to borrow is strong, to some effectual principle of restriction; in no case, however, materially to diminish the sum in circulation, but to let it vibrate only within certain limits; to afford a slow and cautious extension of it, as the general trade of the kingdom enlarges itself; to allow of some special, though temporary, encrease in the event of any extraordinary alarm or difficulty, as the best means of preventing a great demand at home for guineas; and to lean to the side of diminution, in the case of gold going abroad, and of the general exchanges continuing long unfavourable; this seems to be the true policy of the directors of an institution circumstanced like that of the Bank of England. To suffer either the solicitations of merchants, or the wishes of government, to determine the measure of the bank issues, is unquestionably to adopt a very false principle of conduct.

Henry Thornton, *An Enquiry into the Nature and Effects of the Paper Credit of Great Britain*, 1802

contents

preface

This is a textbook for the undergraduate course in money and banking. It treats the usual subjects of the course at a level suited to the student who has had only the introductory course in economics. The approach taken here uses theory as a framework for explaining experience and evaluating policy; it should be useful both in courses emphasizing theory and in those looking more to practical applications.

While the topics and level of discussion are conventional, the treatment differs in some important respects from what has prevailed in money and banking textbooks. The 1960s were a time of rapid change in monetary theory and rich as well in innovations of practice. Of the material that had become traditional in money and banking textbooks, a good deal had by the end of the 1960s become obsolete or irrelevant, or had been disclosed as erroneous. The subject now needs a thoroughgoing reinterpretation.

At the present time we are able to give students a version of money and banking in which the evaluation of monetary policy and interpretation of the course of events actually apply the material covered in the theory section of the book. We are also able to introduce students to many new ideas developed during the past decade, and fortunately for the length of the course, we can drop or deemphasize some old ones that seem unimportant or erroneous.

In addition to integrating theory with practice, we can interpret many important new developments: the genesis of SDRs, the two-tier gold system, Eurodollar borrowing, short-run swings in CDs, and new ideas on monetary theory and optimal decision rules for stabilization policy. Some years ago, the view was spreading that money and banking had become an obsolete subject. It rather seems now, happily for those of us who teach it, an important course, even an exciting one, dealing with ideas and institutions that conspicuously shaped the 1960s and that will go far to define our economic success in the 1970s.

Several of the book's chapters can be omitted without substantial loss of continuity: Chap. 4, Theory of Investment and Intermediation; Chap. 15, Total Demand, Inflation, and Unemployment; Chap. 19, United States Monetary Policy before the Federal Reserve; Chap. 22, Fiscal Policy; Chap. 23, Debt Management and Liquidity Policy; and Chap. 24, The Future of Monetary Policy. If an instructor wished to do so, he could omit Chap. 12, The Keynesian Theory: Monetary

Theory in the 1940s and 1950s. Omission of some of these chapters will permit the book to be adapted to courses with various emphases and different degrees of reliance on other source materials.

For their most helpful comments on earlier versions of the manuscript, I am much indebted to Professors David Meiselman of Macalester College and Jack McCroskey of the University of Denver. I wish also to thank Mrs. Phyllis Nelson for her secretarial assistance.

JOHN M. CULBERTSON

money and banking

JOHN M. CULBERTSON
Professor of Economics
University of Wisconsin

money and banking

McGraw-Hill Book Company
New York St. Louis San Francisco Düsseldorf Johannesburg Kuala Lumpur London Mexico Montreal New Delhi Panama Rio de Janeiro Singapore Sydney Toronto

This book was set in Melior by Black Dot, Inc., and printed and bound by Kingsport Press, Inc.
The designer was Paula Tuerk; the drawings were done by Vantage Art, Inc. The editors were Jack R. Crutchfield and James R. Belser. Matt Martino supervised production.

MONEY AND BANKING

Library of Congress Catalog Card Number 78-39066

07-014899-6

5 6 7 8 9 0 K P K P 7 9 8 7 6 5 4 3

TO

Jo, John, Lynn, and Amy

To limit the total amount of paper issued, and to resort for this purpose, whenever the temptation to borrow is strong, to some effectual principle of restriction; in no case, however, materially to diminish the sum in circulation, but to let it vibrate only within certain limits; to afford a slow and cautious extension of it, as the general trade of the kingdom enlarges itself; to allow of some special, though temporary, encrease in the event of any extraordinary alarm or difficulty, as the best means of preventing a great demand at home for guineas; and to lean to the side of diminution, in the case of gold going abroad, and of the general exchanges continuing long unfavourable; this seems to be the true policy of the directors of an institution circumstanced like that of the Bank of England. To suffer either the solicitations of merchants, or the wishes of government, to determine the measure of the bank issues, is unquestionably to adopt a very false principle of conduct.

Henry Thornton, *An Enquiry into the Nature and Effects of the Paper Credit of Great Britain*, 1802

contents

preface

This is a textbook for the undergraduate course in money and banking. It treats the usual subjects of the course at a level suited to the student who has had only the introductory course in economics. The approach taken here uses theory as a framework for explaining experience and evaluating policy; it should be useful both in courses emphasizing theory and in those looking more to practical applications.

While the topics and level of discussion are conventional, the treatment differs in some important respects from what has prevailed in money and banking textbooks. The 1960s were a time of rapid change in monetary theory and rich as well in innovations of practice. Of the material that had become traditional in money and banking textbooks, a good deal had by the end of the 1960s become obsolete or irrelevant, or had been disclosed as erroneous. The subject now needs a thoroughgoing reinterpretation.

At the present time we are able to give students a version of money and banking in which the evaluation of monetary policy and interpretation of the course of events actually apply the material covered in the theory section of the book. We are also able to introduce students to many new ideas developed during the past decade, and fortunately for the length of the course, we can drop or deemphasize some old ones that seem unimportant or erroneous.

In addition to integrating theory with practice, we can interpret many important new developments: the genesis of SDRs, the two-tier gold system, Eurodollar borrowing, short-run swings in CDs, and new ideas on monetary theory and optimal decision rules for stabilization policy. Some years ago, the view was spreading that money and banking had become an obsolete subject. It rather seems now, happily for those of us who teach it, an important course, even an exciting one, dealing with ideas and institutions that conspicuously shaped the 1960s and that will go far to define our economic success in the 1970s.

Several of the book's chapters can be omitted without substantial loss of continuity: Chap. 4, Theory of Investment and Intermediation; Chap. 15, Total Demand, Inflation, and Unemployment; Chap. 19, United States Monetary Policy before the Federal Reserve; Chap. 22, Fiscal Policy; Chap. 23, Debt Management and Liquidity Policy; and Chap. 24, The Future of Monetary Policy. If an instructor wished to do so, he could omit Chap. 12, The Keynesian Theory: Monetary

Theory in the 1940s and 1950s. Omission of some of these chapters will permit the book to be adapted to courses with various emphases and different degrees of reliance on other source materials.

For their most helpful comments on earlier versions of the manuscript, I am much indebted to Professors David Meiselman of Macalester College and Jack McCroskey of the University of Denver. I wish also to thank Mrs. Phyllis Nelson for her secretarial assistance.

JOHN M. CULBERTSON

money and banking

Pat Schwind

PART 1

money and the financial system

1 introduction

Economics is divided into two branches: microeconomics and macroeconomics. Microeconomics deals with the allocation of resources among competing uses and the division of output among the members of the economy. This aspect of the performance of the economy governs its efficiency. Thus it affects the standard of living that the economy can provide. "Economic development" and the rate of improvement in the standard of living depend on the rate of increase in the efficiency of the economy.

Where do money, banking, and finance fit into this picture? Economic efficiency derives from specialization and division of labor, which require efficient facilities for making exchanges. Complex systems of exchange require the use of money as a medium of exchange and a measure of value. Thus, the efficiency of a modern economy can be achieved only with the aid of an effective monetary system.

The efficiency of a modern economy also requires the use of a large amount of machinery and capital goods. The effectiveness of a society in accumulating capital goods depends on its institutions for encouraging saving and causing the savings to be invested in productive capital goods. An important difference between high-income and low-income nations is that the latter have not developed the institutions required to build up a stock of productive capital goods. These institutions—banks, savings institutions, capital markets, and money markets—constitute the financial system of the economy. An efficient productive system and a high standard of living require an effective financial system.

The monetary and financial system plays an even more dominating role in the other branch of economics. Macroeconomics deals with total demand, inflation and deflation, unemployment, and economic stagnation. When total demand for the output of the economy grows too rapidly and becomes excessive, this causes inflation, which leads to a complex set of economic and political difficulties. On the other hand, when total demand grows too slowly and becomes deficient this leads to recession or depression, to large unemployment, and in some cases to a decline in the price level. The Great Depression of the 1930s illustrates the catastrophic effects of a large decline in total demand.

Financial factors, and especially the performance of the nation's monetary system and its monetary policy, are a major determinant of the behavior of its total demand. Serious episodes of inflation or depression seem always to have involved misbehavior of the monetary system. In the course in money and banking, our assignment is to go into detail, especially with regard to the monetary and financial factors affecting business conditions. In the process of doing so, we deal with topics that are of great interest in their own right: interest rates, conditions of credit availability, foreign exchange rates, international capital flows, and the international monetary system. These topics are seldom absent from the front page of the newspaper.

Policy Problems to Which Money and Banking Are Relevant

In the United States and most other countries, banks and financial institutions are heavily regulated and supervised by the government. Many issues arise as to the effects of these policies and how they might be made more conducive to economic efficiency and stability. The ideas we discuss in money and banking provide the basis for evaluating different positions on these policy issues.

Money and banking relate to many important problems and issues of macroeconomic policy: evaluation and improvement of monetary and fiscal policy, policy toward interest rates and "tight money," policy toward inflation and toward wages and prices, the balance of payments, the international monetary system, and the international position and value of the dollar. Monetary theory provides the framework within which we can understand these policy issues and form meaningful judgments about them.

These policy issues, of course, concern us all as participants in the economy and as voters. The continued leadership and even the survival of our society depends on its ability to deal with these crucial policy problems. This, in turn, depends upon the voters' choice as to who is to make the controlling decisions. Thus, ultimately, the success of our society depends upon the knowledge and understanding of its voters—not a new idea, but one with special importance in our subject area.

The subjects with which we deal also are crucially important for business policy. They underlie analysis of business conditions and economic prospects, interest rates and financial markets, and international financial developments.

The Method and Tools of Money and Banking

To our knowledge of natural phenomena, the scientific method has brought a revolution in beliefs and in man's control over his environment, and in the effectiveness of his "policies." When his subject is himself, in "social science," man has less success with the scientific method. Doubtless one reason for this is our lack of objectivity in matters affecting human interests and images. It has been said that the reason social scientists do not more often find the truth is that they are not usually looking for it. In terms of tools, economics suffers from the inability to conduct the experiments that are so important to the natural scientist. We must somehow find the truth through objective interpretation of the facts of history.

The task of economics is not to fill an admitted void in people's knowledge but rather, which is more difficult, somehow to distinguish truth from error in a welter of emotionally held and politically involved beliefs. The basic logic of our efforts to do this involves three elements: (1) Statement of propositions and theories in definite, quantitative, testable form. (2) Testing of propositions and theories against the data of experience, making maximum possible use of statistical techniques. (3) Continually revising and integrating theory in the light of these tests.

Systematic testing of economic theory by statistical methods, or "econometrics," is quite new. Most such studies have been done within the past 10 or 15 years. These exploratory studies have not been entirely successful in distinguishing truth from error. The implications of statistical studies have also become a matter of uncertainty and dispute. Nevertheless, this body of work makes it possible to give the student of today a treatment of money and banking that is more of a science than would have been possible even a decade ago. We shall refer to empirical studies relating to our subject, pointing out the areas in which these studies have not resolved differences of opinion. Later economists will no doubt overcome some of these difficulties.

Agenda

The remaining chapters of Part 1 of this book lay necessary groundwork for later discussion of specific topics. The functions and significance of the monetary and financial system are treated in Chap. 2. Chapter 3 reviews the concepts in terms of which our subject is formulated, giving a quantitative review of the performance of the United States economy. The theoretical framework of investment decisions is covered in Chap. 4. Chapter 5 gives a factual picture of the financial flows through the United States economy and the organizations and institutions of the financial system.

Part 2 of the book then discusses banking and central banking. The theoretical core of the book is Part 3, which deals with explanation of the monetary system, behavior of total demand, interest rates, and change in the price level. International aspects of the financial system and their relation to monetary policy are dealt with in Part 4. Finally, Part 5 applies this theoretical and factual material to the problem of stabilization policy. It deals with standards for policy evaluation, the role of policy in the past performance of the economy, and suggestions for improving policy in the future.

SUMMARY

1. The financial system contributes to growth in economic efficiency and improvement in the standard of living by facilitating the accumulation of capital and its effective allocation to particular uses.

2. Inflation, on the one hand, and depression and unemployment, on the other hand, to an important degree reflect misbehavior of the monetary system and monetary policy.

3. The effectiveness of a nation thus depends upon its financial system and its monetary policies. To define institutions and policies that will produce the desired performance requires knowledge and theory.

4. Although unsettled questions remain, economics in recent decades has greatly increased our information on the monetary and financial system. It also has developed new methods of formulating and validating economic theories, which may add importantly to knowledge in the coming decades.

QUESTIONS FOR REVIEW AND DISCUSSION

1. What is the subject of microeconomics and of macroeconomics? Discuss the role of the monetary and financial system in each of these branches of economics.

2. Explain how the effectiveness of the financial system affects the standard of living. Give some hypothetical examples of cases in which the performance of the financial system promotes increases in economic efficiency, and others of performance that impedes improvement in the efficiency of the economy.

3. Discuss major policy problems to which the subject of money and banking is relevant.

4. Spell out the logic of the method used in economics as a social science. Contrast this with the method that applies in a field of the arts.

2

the functions and side effects of money

The puzzlement and disagreement caused by money seems to reflect the uniqueness of this institution. This makes it difficult to think about money—as we usually think—by analogy. As a basis for later detailed consideration of the supply of and demand for money, we review here the factors that give rise to the development of money, that endow the monetary system with important side effects, and that make the choice of a monetary system and the behavior of the money supply an optional and politically determined element in the economic system. These ideas constitute the foundation of monetary theory.

Money and Economic Efficiency

The improvement in economic efficiency of the past 200 years, which underlies modern civilization, depended on a great increase in specialization and division of labor. The modern economy's efficiency requires men to spend their lives as heart surgeons, computer specialists, cancer researchers, and production engineers. The rise in economic efficiency was based on the great increase in scientific and technological knowledge, but knowledge cannot be continually improved, or even maintained, except by a specialization that permits men to spend their professional lives working in a limited area. The modern world could not survive without economic specialization.

A high degree of specialization, in turn, requires efficient institutions for making exchanges. The heart surgeon or the computer specialist cannot live on what he produces. He depends upon complex facilities for exchange to obtain the particular consumer goods that he needs and wants. Great factories cannot exist without an enormous network of exchange to bring to them their raw materials and to distribute their products throughout the nation and the world. Modern civilization depends upon economic efficiency, which depends upon specialization, which depends upon efficient exchange. The next step brings us to our particular subject. Efficient exchange requires the use of money.

Limitations of barter exchange

In the absence of money, goods must be exchanged directly for one another, in "barter" exchange. This is technically inefficient in an economy with more than a few goods, for two reasons. First, a prospective trader could not expect to find someone else whose desired transaction was the mirror image of his own (for instance, a bushel of wheat for a red necktie). Such "double coincidence of wants" would be a rarity in an economy including many goods. Lacking this, a person with a good to exchange would have to take what he could get from whoever wanted to acquire this good, in the hope through a chain of transactions of finally getting what he wanted. This would be very wasteful of time and effort, and would make a really complex economy impossible. Can you imagine running a university, a modern hospital, and an automobile factory on the basis of barter exchange?

The other aspect of the inefficiency of barter is that it gives rise to an unworkable multiplicity of prices. In a barter system, prices of goods are quoted in terms of other goods. Each good potentially has a price quoted in terms of every other good. Thus, excluding the price of each good in terms of itself (which is always unity) a system with n goods has $n \times n - 1$ barter prices. This is no problem in an economy with three goods and, thus, six barter prices. But a 100,000-good system—still a very small economy—generates 9,999,900,000 prices. To keep records and plan rationally in a complex economy would be impossible because of the multiplicity of barter prices. Imagine keeping the books of General Motors Corporation in terms of such barter prices.

Taking together these two considerations—the inefficiency of barter exchange and the multiplicity of barter prices—a specialized and complex economy could not develop under a barter system. Modern civilization and the development of modern knowledge are contingent on the invention of money.

The gain in efficiency from using money

The kind of social invention that is required to break through the inefficiency of barter exchange is an obvious one. The discovery has been made in many societies. If everyone who wants to "sell" something will exchange it for any good X, the problem is solved. Then one can exchange any good for any other good in only two transactions. To get rid of a basket of tomatoes and acquire a bottle of beer, one simply sells his tomatoes for X. Since everyone is selling everything for X, he knows that he can "spend" the X for beer. Breaking the exchange into two components, a "sale" for money and a "purchase" with money disposes of the onerous requirement of double coincidence of wants or of a lengthy chain of exchanges in default of it.

A money is thus easy to invent. All it requires is the adoption of a social convention, a matter of usage: general agreement to use good X for this function. For the efficiency of the arrangement depends on general use of a particular good as the medium of exchange. It is this specialization of function that yields the increase in efficiency.

This convention also cures the multiplicity of barter prices. When we exchange any other good for good X, this naturally generates a price stated in terms of X. Prices of all other goods, thus, are quoted in terms of X and need be stated only in terms of X. The 100,000-good system now has only 99,999 prices, rather than 9,999,900,000. These are the prices of all other goods stated in terms of X (the price of X stated in terms of itself being 1). There is only one price per good, which is the optimal arrangement for conveying the needed information.

What is required to break through the barrier to economic specialization and efficiency imposed by the inefficiency of barter exchange is thus only the social convention of settling upon any one good to serve as the medium of exchange and as the unit in terms of which prices are stated. While some moneys in the long run prove to serve better than others—a point to which we return below—the adoption of *any* good as money will cure the inefficiency of barter exchange. Be it tobacco, rum, wampum, playing cards, cattle, gold, beaver skins, cigarettes, curiously shaped stones, or any of the other things that have served as money, the difficulties of barter exchange are solved. For this achievement does not depend upon *what* is designated as money, but only on general agreement to use *the same thing* as money.

The things that have served as money in various societies are diverse. Rum, tobacco, gold, and paper notes—these are in most respects very different things: one cannot drink tobacco or smoke gold. In serving as the medium of exchange, however, each performs the same function in the society. "Money," thus, is a concept that is based upon the function of a good, on a particular use to which it is put, and not upon its other characteristics. We are familiar with other functional concepts: fuel, clothing, and beverage. Money is the same kind of concept.

Objective definition of the medium of exchange

An objective characterization of the operation of money can be given by recording the exchanges actually made in an economy, as in the illustrative exchange matrix of Fig. 2-1. This shows that when people relinquish V, W, Y, and Z they do not exchange them for anything but X.[1] Similarly, when people acquire V, W, Y, and Z, they do not acquire them with anything but X. Clearly, X is serving as the medium of exchange, and this is a perfectly objective and measurable function. Other things may be very similar to X

[1]This approach is from Robert Clower, "A Reconsideration of the Microfoundations of Monetary Theory," *West. Econ. J.* **6:** 1-8(1967).

	V	W	X	Y	Z
V	O	O	+	O	O
W	O	O	+	O	O
X	+	+	+	+	+
Y	O	O	+	O	O
Z	O	O	+	O	O

Fig. 2-1 Exchange Matrix

in some respects, but with reference to its operation as a medium of exchange it stands in a class by itself.

In an economy habituated to a medium of exchange, commonly, other goods can be acquired *only* with money. In the United States, you can walk into any store and acquire anything with dollars, which are our medium of exchange. But if you took another good to the store and tried to make a barter exchange, you probably would not get far. In a money economy, thus, one not only *may* sell his goods for money and buy with money, but he *must* operate in this way.

While the difficulties of barter exchange can be overcome by agreeing upon anything whatever as money, the choice of one thing as money rather than another has important side effects. Indeed, monetary theory largely involves an exploration of these side effects.

Desirable characteristics of money

To serve efficiently as money, a good must have characteristics that are easy to define but hard to find in actual goods. If the money is to serve for small transactions, it must be divisible, a characteristic not met, for example, by cattle as money. If the good is too valuable, the quantity needed to make a minor payment will be so small that it cannot be easily handled. This was always a difficulty with gold. On the other hand, for money to be used for large payments it must be rather valuable. To make a large payment in silver was something of a moving operation.

The money also should be readily recognizable and not easily counterfeited. Moreover, it should be quite standardized, a condition met by metals of a certified degree of fineness. An interesting side effect of the use of an agricultural product as money without standardization of quality was a tendency to degrade the quality of the product. If a pound of tobacco has a fixed value as money irrespective of its quality, there is an incentive to produce low quality tobacco. When tobacco served as money in Virginia, it became necessary finally to impose grading standards to prevent continual deterioration in quality.

The most efficient commodity moneys were coins. Ideally, these were standardized, easily recognizable, difficult to counterfeit, and issued in convenient denominations. But the practice often deviated from the ideal. Hard-pressed monarchs debased their coinage by reducing the amount of metal in a coin without adjusting its nominal value. Coins were "clipped" and "sweated," small amounts of metal being removed from each coin and sold as metal, leaving the coins weighing less than their official or nominal amount. Moreover, normal wear and tear reduces the amount of metal in each coin, and those in circulation for a long period come to contain considerably less than their full value in metal. Lastly, coins whose value was proportional to their weight could not really be convenient for both large and small transactions unless they included coins made from a number of metals of widely different value by weight.

A final consideration is the cost of commodity money. A significant amount of real resources were used up in mining gold and silver and coining them. This can be avoided by using paper money, which costs very little to produce. But this saving of resources introduces some new problems. The amount of the commodity money is limited by its cost of production. If paper notes have a value as money far in excess of their cost of production, how is the amount of them to be limited and controlled?

Side Effects of Money

Very important side effects of the use of money are the existence of a "price level" and the possibility of inflation and deflation. In a pure barter economy, where each good has a price quoted in terms of each other good, what can we mean by the price level? The price level means the level of prices of all other things measured in terms of a single unit of value, or measured in terms of money. Whenever we refer to the price level we can alternatively refer to the "value of money." Since prices are quoted in terms of money, an increase in the price level means that it takes more money to buy other things or that the value of money has declined. Obviously, there cannot be a value of money if there is no money. Neither can there be a price level unless there is a money in terms of which prices are quoted.

The nonmonetary economy, thus, cannot have inflation or deflation. The reason for this relates to the symmetry of rates of exchange in the barter economy. If the price of oats in terms of pigs is 30 bu per pig, the price of pigs in terms of oats is 1/30 pig per bu. If the relative value of pigs increases, this is deflation if one is looking at it from a pigs point of view but inflation from an oats point of view. If people look at the exchange ratio equally from both points of view, the change in relative values is not interpreted as either inflation or deflation, just a change in relative values.

We noted that the efficiency of money in reducing the number of prices in the economy [from $n(n-1)$ to $n-1$] derives from the practice of quoting prices only in terms of money. Directly attached to this very productive innovation, thus, is the side effect of conferring on the value of whatever serves as money a special status. Prices quoted in terms of money become the focus of people's behavior. Their calculations, plans, expectations, and contracts focus on money prices. Realizing the potential efficiency of the simplification of the price system from the use of money requires this. But, then, all of these calculations, plans, expectations, and contracts are disturbed if there is a change in the value of money or in the general price level.

Would an increase in the value of silver have a devastating effect upon an economy? Not ordinarily, no more than an increase in the price of beans or Burgundy. But if silver served as the money of the economy, an increase in its value would be a crucially important event. This would mean a reduction in the general price level. Borrowers would have to repay money worth more than what they borrowed, and some would be unable to do so. People may respond to declining prices by waiting to buy when prices are lower, and the cut in their spending may cause prices to decline further. The reductions in spending and in prices will lead to production cutbacks, layoffs, and rising unemployment. A change in the value of money can be a very disturbing influence on the economy.

Once a monetary unit, such as the dollar, is firmly established as the unit in which plans are made and contracts are drawn, it is not surprising that the economy will be disrupted if changes occur in the value of money. When contracts are drawn for future delivery of tons of coal or bushels of wheat, we do not contemplate that when the time comes for delivery we shall find that the ton and the bushel have declined by one-tenth. If this happened, the buyer would be damaged and the seller benefited. The effectiveness of planning and the rationality of relations among individuals and businesses in the economy would be disrupted.

In practice, many more contracts are denominated in (defined in units of) dollars than of tons or bushels, and change in the value of money *does* importantly affect the operation of the economy. This is especially true where the change in the value of money occurs at a rapid rate and where it comes as a surprise, so that no allowance had been made for it when making plans and contracts.

Adverse effects of changes in the price level

One adverse side effect of the existence of money thus is that the value of the money can change over time. An increase in the value of money means the same thing as a reduction in average prices of other things, the prices being stated in terms of money, and the reverse. Thus inflation, an increase in the price level, is a reduction in the value of money, while deflation, a decrease in the price level, involves an increase in the value of money.

The significance of such side effects of money can be indicated by reviewing the major ways in which they affect the performance of the economy:

1. Change in the price level causes economic plans and contracts not to work out as they had been planned by their makers. Insofar as the plans and contracts are a part of a rational system of production and distribution of goods and services, this disruption hurts the efficiency of the economy.

2. When price-level change comes to be expected, people divert their time and effort from the production of goods and services to efforts to beat the inflation or deflation—or to avoid being beaten by it. But these activities do not add to total output or contribute to raising the standard of living. By thus diverting the economy's human resources from fruitful to sterile activities, changes in the price level adversely affect economic efficiency and the standard of living.

3. Inflation or reduction in the value of money causes direct and immediate damage to creditors—lenders, holders of government bonds, and members of pension systems with benefits defined in dollar terms. In terms of direct effects, it benefits debtors—farmers with large mortgages, businesses financed with debt and holding real assets, and speculators in physical assets. Deflation, of course, has the opposite effects. The existence of price-level change thus tends to polarize people into debtor and creditor groups, focused on their own immediate interests. This encourages political animosities and class-oriented legislation. It reduces the probability of achieving reasoned discussion of economic policy and effective government action. Such debtor-creditor polarization has been a significant influence in the economic and political history of the United States.

4. The economy is intimately tied into the social and political system. The effectiveness of this complex system depends on the acceptance and confidence it enjoys. Events that undermine belief in the reasonableness and equity of the system thus may importantly damage its performance. Inflation or deflation, with their irrational damages to some and benefits to others, undermine belief in the equity of the system—and not without justification. When the monetary system and other aspects of economic policy are directly controlled by the government, as is true in the modern world, this may seem to make the inequity worse, since it is attributed not to inexorable fate but to misdeeds of government. The affront is yet further compounded when the government is a large borrower from the public—the usual case—and then causes an inflation that permits it to repay its debt and pay its interest in money that is depreciated in value. This may, not without merit, be viewed as a kind of legalized theft by the government from its more trusting citizens.

5. Inflation is very unpopular with people who find that their money will not buy as much as in the past, some of whom may be placed in severe want by this state of affairs. Under pressure from those damaged by rising prices, government commonly uses its power in an effort to hold prices down by imposing some form of price controls. But prohibiting increases in prices when demand for goods is rising means that there are not enough goods to go around at the official prices. This creates new problems with evasion of the price controls, "black markets," and an absolute unavailability of goods to the less favored buyers. So the attempt to solve the symptoms of the inflation problem creates a new set of problems. When goods are not effectively rationed by prices and cannot be bought at their legal prices, the price controls send a false set of signals to producers and can seriously reduce the efficiency of the economy. Similarly, inflation-caused restrictions on foreign transactions may disrupt patterns of international trade and lead to the development of inefficient industries.

6. Finally, change in the price level impedes the accumulation of capital goods, upon which increase in economic efficiency depends. Efficient financing of capital goods requires the use of debt securities and of contracts for the lending and repayment of money. But if the value of money is rising so that the borrower must pay in dollars more valuable than he borrowed, this kind of financing becomes onerous to the borrower unless the rate of interest is very low or even is negative. On the other hand, when prices are rising and repayment is made in cheaper dollars, the lender is damaged unless the rate of interest is so high as to more than compensate for the decline in the value of money. But the required very high or very low interest rates cannot feasibly be brought about, in part because of legal and institutional restrictions and in part because there is not that much certainty or agreement as to the rate at which the price level is going to change. If debt securities cannot be used efficiently to finance the building of houses, factories, and new machinery, then fewer of these will be built, to the detriment of the economy's efficiency and the people's standard of living.

The economic damage caused by change in the price level would be reduced if, say, inflation occurred at a constant rate and was universally expected with certainty, and if laws and institutions permitted adjustment of contract terms and interest rates fully to allow for the expected inflation. If the inflation was occurring at 20 percent per year, it would then be understood by everyone that for a debt contract really to pay 5 percent interest, it should call for nominal interest (paid in the depreciating dollars) at 25 percent. But actual cases of inflation and deflation never fully satisfy the conditions required for such full compensation of their effect, in part because they do not occur at a constant and predictable rate.

What causes changes in the price level: The role of total demand

A change in the price of a single good we think of as reflecting excess supply or excess demand for the good. That is, the price of the good changes because it did not "clear the market" for the good and did not equate the quantity demanded to the quantity supplied. If at the original price buyers want to buy more of the good than sellers want to sell, the price will tend to be pushed up to the level at which the market is cleared. These familiar ideas carry over to explanation of the average of prices, or the price level. On balance, if excess demand exists in the various markets in the economy, the price level will be pushed up.

For the economy as a whole, the conditions of supply are more stable than those of demand. Historical episodes of inflation and deflation seem to have been caused mainly by variations in total demand. Supply conditions, especially upward pressure upon wages and prices, also are important in explaining present-day inflation, and we consider them in Chap. 15. The point to be emphasized here is that the changes in the price level that are a side effect of the existence of money seem to be largely caused by an inappropriate behavior of total demand.

Consider an idealized economy with a stable price level, producing goods and services worth $500 billion at the existing level of prices. This state of affairs can continue to exist only if the public continues to buy goods and services at exactly the rate of $500 billion per year. If the public begins to spend at the rate of $510 billion per year, the quantity demanded in markets for particular goods will exceed the quantity that would be supplied at the existing level of prices. On the other hand, if total demand falls below $500 billion, demand in various markets will be insufficient to sustain the existing level of prices and deflation will occur. Thus, at any particular point in time with given conditions of supply, there is only one amount of total demand that is consistent with price stability.

In the United States economy, the quantity of goods and services available to be bought does not remain constant from year to year but grows at a rather steady rate. The volume of goods and services the economy produces when fully employed depends upon the number of people available to work, or the "labor force," and on output per worker, which is often called "productivity." Thus, the rate at which the potential (or full-employment) output of the economy grows over time depends upon the rate of growth of the labor force and of productivity. If the labor force and productivity both grow at 2 percent per year, the potential output grows about 4 percent per year (more exactly, $1.02 \times 1.02 = 1.0404$, or 4.04 percent). Thus, in a simple and idealized example, avoiding some difficulties we shall consider later, what is consistent with price stability in such an economy is a growth of total demand of 4 percent per year. If total demand stayed constant while supply increased steadily, because of growth in population and productivity, there would not be enough demand to take the rising output of goods and services off the market at the existing prices. The deficiency of total demand would lead to price deflation. In the growing economies with which we shall be dealing, a necessary condition of price stability is growth of total demand along a time track that is defined in part by the rate of growth of the economy's labor force and productivity.

Why deflation causes unemployment

A change in total demand is not reflected entirely in change in prices, but in some combination of change in prices and change in the quantity of goods and services bought and produced. For example, if total demand in a nongrowing economy declined 10 percent, this could be reflected in a reduction of 10 percent in the quantity of goods and services bought and produced in the economy, with the prices remaining quite unchanged. At the other extreme, it could be reflected in a 10 percent reduction in prices with the quantity of output quite unchanged. Many intermediate combinations also are possible.

In practice, a decline in total demand is not immediately reflected entirely in prices. It leads also to a reduction in output and employment. When sales fall off, businesses do not immediately reduce their selling prices proportionately so as to maintain the physical volume of sales unchanged. Similarly, when hiring of labor by businesses declines, wage rates are not immediately reduced in such a way as to maintain the volume of employment unchanged. The dependence of this aspect of the economy's performance on institutions, laws, and behavior patterns we consider with some care in Chap. 15. For the present, we only note that changes in total demand in the short run cause changes not only in the price level but also in the volume of output and employment.

In particular, a decline in total demand will cause a reduction in output and employment. After a period of time for adjustment, however, it is conceivable that wages and prices will decline by enough to restore the volume of goods produced and sold, and the volume of employment, to the original level. Thus, the long-run response of the economy to a shortage or excess of total demand may be quite different from its short-run response.

The quantity of money as a determinant of total demand

In general, a change in the amount of money causes a change in total demand in the same direction. The process by which this effect occurs depends on the existing monetary system and the way the money supply is changed. The process is complex and is not fully understood or a matter of agreement among economists. Chapters 10 to 13 deal with it. For the present, we only assert that the money supply has such a positive causal influence on total demand.

This is not an implausible proposition. After all, total demand involves the spending of money for goods and services. Many individuals and businesses would like to spend more money for goods and services if they could get more money on satisfactory terms, by earning additional money income, by borrowing money, or by gaining it through sales of assets. Thus, if additional money is created and put into the hands of someone in the economy, this is likely to lead to additional expenditures for goods and services. Similarly, if a part of the existing stock of money is extinguished, some individuals and businesses will have to reduce their expenditures because they do not have enough money to continue spending at the old rate. For the present, we leave the argument at this rather vague and common-sense level.

The propositions that we have already worked out have a very important implication. If price stability requires total demand to grow along a defined path and the quantity of money exerts a causal influence upon total demand, this suggests that with the other factors given there is only one path for the money supply that is consistent with the path of total demand that is consistent with price stability, and consistent with an effective performance of the economy.

This introduces a new element into our subject. In pointing out that money is essential for an efficient, specialized economy, we considered money only as an institution. *A money* had to exist, but nothing was said about the *quantity* of this money. We now find that the quantity of money is important. If the amount of money grows too rapidly, this will cause total demand to grow too rapidly and lead to inflation, with adverse side effects on the performance of the economy. Too slow a growth of the money supply, or a decline in the money supply, will lead to deflation and unemployment, to recession or depression.

For money fully to realize its potential in permitting specialization and increasing the efficiency of the economy, it must be constant in value, since it serves as a unit of value. But it can be constant in value, even under the most favorable conditions, only if the quantity of money grows along a particular path dictated by growth of the labor force and productivity. Thus, the performance of the society depends not only on the efficiency of its money in making payments but also on the behavior of the quantity of this money.

The dependence of the quantity of money on the choice of the monetary system

The behavior over time of the quantity of money in any particular society, not suprisingly, depends on what that society has chosen to use as money. If the society is using gold as money, the quantity of money increases when new gold fields are discovered. If it is using tobacco as money, the quantity of money declines when the weather is unfavorable to tobacco growing. If it is using paper money, the quantity of money depends on the particular institutions and rules under which the paper money is created. As we show in Chap. 10, particular classes of monetary system characteristically produce certain patterns of behavior of the quantity of money. For the present, we want only to note that the way the quantity of money behaves over time depends on what particular thing a society has chosen to use as money.

Given that the performance of the economy depends on the behavior of total demand, which depends on the behavior of the money supply, societies that choose different kinds of monetary systems should be expected to show systematically different kinds of economic performance. If for any given society there is some ideal rate of growth of total demand, the achievement of which requires a corresponding ideal rate of growth of the money supply, monetary systems leading to some other behavior of the money supply will lead to some definable misperformance of the economy. Great importance, thus, may attach to the nation's choice of its monetary system.

Determinants of the choice of the monetary system

The origins of money go back beyond written history. We can imagine the development of a money occurring gradually as goods that are frequently traded and convenient for trading come to enjoy a preferred status as a trading item and the units in which "prices" are often quoted. Among the earliest goods to gain such status as a quasi money seem to have been cattle, cloth, cereals, metals, ornaments, and objects with a ceremonial or religious significance. Thus, the early moneys made up a variety of goods: from cattle to cowrie shells, from bronze to wampum.[2]

The development of coinage permitted the durability and high value in relation to size and weight of the scarce metals to be utilized in an efficient medium of exchange. This was accomplished by standardizing the weight and the fineness of the metal in coins. Coins from Lydia, in Asia Minor, probably go back to the ninth or eighth century B.C. Coins were made of silver, gold, copper, and combinations of metals. The governing considerations seem to have been the local availability of the metals and the choice of metals of such value as would yield coins of convenient size for making payments.

Although coinage probably began as a means of increasing the efficiency as money of the metals, it later gained an additional significance. When people became accustomed to coins, the effective monetary unit became not the weight of metal in the coin but *the coin itself*, that is, *a shilling, a penny, a dollar*. Thus, a coin would pass at its nominal value of a shilling even though it was worn or clipped and included metal worth less than a shilling. But this implied that the monetary unit continued to be pounds and shillings even though, say, the king modified the coins so that they contained metal of diminished value. If the king could do this, the quantity of money depended among other things upon actions of the king in debasing the currency. In England between 1540 and 1560 the price level about doubled, with great economic and social effects. This seems to have re-

[2]For a more detailed discussion of the historical development of money, see E. Victor Morgan, *A History of Money*, Penguin, Baltimore, 1965.

flected the increase in the quantity of money resulting from debasement of the coins by Henry VIII and Edward VI.

After coinage, the next major shift was to moneys of negligible cost of production, paper money in the form of circulating bank notes and checkbook money, or demand deposits. Accompanying this was an increase in the role of government as a determiner of what should serve as money and of the institutions determining the quantity of money. Modern economies use moneys created directly by governments or on authority delegated by the government. The quantity of such money depends on the laws defining the monetary system and, in some cases, on administrative decisions by central banks established by law.

Several points regarding the development and determination of monetary systems are important for our further work. We note, to begin with, that the choice of a money is not defined by any natural or economic law. That coal serves as fuel but granite does not is a matter over which government has no influence. But any of a great variety of things can serve as money. There is no room for dispute about this, since the record demonstrates it. The role of government in defining the nation's monetary system has increased until it now is dominant.

We recall, moreover, that the behavior of the quantity of money depends on what serves as money. The sixteenth-century English inflation following debasement of the coins would not have been possible if the money had been gold and silver circulating by weight, or some other commodity money. The extreme inflations caused by multiplication of the money supply under systems of paper money would not have occurred under a commodity money system. Thus, the choice of one kind of monetary system or another determines whether a society will experience great deflations or inflations, which can enormously influence all aspects of the society.

Finally, we observe that the historical adoption of monetary systems generally involved no mechanism to assure an appropriate behavior of the quantity of money. The early choice of moneys was governed largely by convenience in exchange. Later, the interest of kings and governments was paramount. The influence of producer groups in having their product used as money, as in the case of silver producers in the United States, had a bearing on the choice of a monetary system in some cases. Still later the interest of bankers, borrowers from banks, and those desiring inflation and a declining value of money played an important role in the United States in determining the government's choice of a monetary system.

The process of choice of a national monetary system is rich with accidental and political factors. It lacks any general mechanism to assure the choice of that monetary system which will produce that behavior of the money supply consistent with that growth rate of total demand consistent with price stability, full employment, and an effective performance from the economy.

Money and the Logic of the Economic System

A market economy—or noncentralized economy—appears to comprise a rational system of mutualistic dealings among individuals and organizations pursuing their purposes within a defined set of rules. The economic system, thus, has a logic, a coherency. It is a well-ordered game. Why should its performance depend importantly on the choice of a monetary system?

Although the argument has several links, it is straightforward. Efficiency in the economic game requires specialization. This requires efficient exchange. This requires a money in the sense of a medium of exchange and unit of value. But the money disrupts the economy if its value varies over time. If the value of money is not to vary, total demand must grow along a predetermined track. This requires that the quantity of money must grow along a given time track. The behavior of the quantity of money depends on the choice of a monetary system. This has depended largely on extraneous and accidental factors, and in the modern world is defined by government decisions. Thus, one nation may have chosen a monetary system that gives rise to explosive inflation; another, one leading to serious depression; another, one causing alternating periods of boom and depression. This is why money is an important factor in explaining differences in performance among economies. The nation's choice of a monetary system and monetary policy is not governed by the logic of the market economy, but is imposed from without by accidental or political factors. A poor choice is possible and can result in great mischief.

Thinking about money, it seems, can be confusing because it is a unique institution. We are accustomed to think by analogy, and analogies to money are hard to find. Money is like any good in that its long-run value depends on its quantity. But changes in the quantity of other things do not cause general inflation or deflation and unemployment, as is true of money.

Money is like a unit. It is a unit of value, as the yard is a unit of length. But preserving stability of the length of the yard involves no problem of controlling the number of yardsticks in existence, nothing analogous to the problem of controlling the quantity of money.

The difficulty seems to be that in combining the two functions of medium of exchange and unit of value, money is unlike anything else within our experience. It is this combination of functions that results in its peculiar role in the economy. As a unit of value, the dollar must be stabilized to avoid mischief to the economy, but as a medium of exchange its value can be stabilized only by a precise control over its quantity. These are the basic terms of reference of monetary theory and monetary policy.

Money and natural selection

The main way societies perfect their institutions is through trial and error, or natural selection. This works best when a wide variety of approaches can be tried and when the success of each is known without delay. Improvement in production methods occurs continuously through the experimentation of innumerable individuals and businesses, the approaches that work best being adopted and others rejected. Why has this process not resulted in steady improvement in monetary policy in the way that it has led to improvement in methods of growing corn and making steel?

There are several reasons why lessons regarding monetary systems are hard to learn. Since the efficiency of a monetary system depends on general use of the same thing as money, the nation cannot simultaneously experiment with a dozen different kinds of monetary system—as it can experiment with different ways of growing corn. Moreover, while some kinds of inefficiency of a monetary system are immediately apparent—such as the coins being too big to fit in one's pocket—others occur only sporadically or after a long lag and are difficult to diagnose. A monetary system that aggravates booms and depressions may not reveal itself as defective until after it has done a great deal of mischief. Even then, the diagnosis may not be successfully made. Since booms and depressions affect almost every aspect of life, it may be difficult to demonstrate that the performance of the monetary system is a *cause* of the economic instability rather than only an *effect* of it. Presumably, such considerations explain why the performance of monetary systems is not necessarily subject to continuous improvement, and why the meaning and importance of monetary policy continues to be a matter of disagreement even among economists.

These aspects combine to make money potentially the Achilles heel of a society. In making clear the function and importance of the monetary system, the subject of money and banking has a vital role to play.

Performance Standards for the Monetary System

To evaluate the monetary system and monetary policy and to define their role in determining United States economic developments requires performance standards against which to measure and interpret the way the actual monetary system has behaved. The ideas just reviewed provide the basis for a first approximation to such performance standards.

Desired average growth in total demand and in the money supply

The rate of growth of total demand consistent with price stability under ideal conditions depends on the rate of growth in the nation's labor force and in productivity. When the modern economy is operated near full employment, it may give rise not to price stability but to a certain rate of cost-push inflation. In such a case, to maintain full employment the growth rate of total demand must be large enough to buy the full-employment output of the economy at prices that are *rising* rather than stable. We extend this analysis also now to determination of the average rate of growth in the money supply consistent with the desired time path for total demand, using illustrative values that roughly depict the usual situation for the United States economy.

In the United States, the labor force from 1950 to 1970 increased at an average rate of about 1½ percent per year. This implies that if the proportion of the labor force employed—or the unemployment rate—is to be kept unchanged, total employment must also grow at 1½ percent per year. Efficiency in terms of real GNP per employed person rose during this period at an average rate of 2¼ percent per year. If real output per worker increases 2¼ percent and labor input increases by 1½ percent, total output must increase by about 3¾ percent per year (more precisely $1.015 \times 1.0225 = 1.0378375$, or about 3.785 percent).

The question that follows is, What rate of increase in total demand is necessary to take off the market an output growing at the rate of 3¾ percent per year? If the price level is stable, of course, the answer is that total demand also should grow at a 3¾ percent rate. This is the rate of growth of potential output at stable prices. In present-day economies, however, it is not usually possible to maintain unemployment at a low rate without getting some increase in the price level. So we take an illustrative rate of inflation about as low as has recently been achieved in the United States with acceptably full employment, an inflation rate of 2 percent per year. (The average increase from 1950 to 1970 in prices of output was about 3½ percent.)

Given this, the rate of growth of total demand required in our illustrative case is about 5¾ percent. This is the rate of growth of potential output at price levels rising at the relevant rate. Of this 5¾ percent growth in hypothetical total demand, 1½ percent reflects growth of the labor force, 2¼ percent reflects growth in economic efficiency, and 2 percent reflects increase in the average prices of goods and services. Starting from a point where the economy has acceptably full employment, what is required to maintain this condition while permitting only "unavoidable" inflation is that GNP should grow at the rate of 5¾ percent per year, no more and no less.

For total demand to grow by less than 5¾ percent would imply some combination of a slower rate of increase in prices and a slower rate of increase in real output and employment, which would imply a rising unemployment rate. For total demand to grow by more than 5¾ percent would imply a falling unemployment rate, but also would involve price increases of more than 2 percent per year. Such acceleration of inflation would adversely affect the later trade off between inflation and unemployment because of factors we consider in Chap. 15.

What rate of growth of the money supply was consistent with growth of GNP at 5¾ percent per year? The simplest framework within which this question can be approached is the equation of exchange: $M \times V = Y$. In this, velocity V reflects the whole set of institutional and behavioral factors determining the relation between the money supply M and total demand Y. The simplest case is that in which the net effect of all these factors is to bring about a constant value of velocity. In this case, the required rate of change in the money supply is the same as the desired rate of change in total demand.

In the United States in the 1950s and 1960s, velocity showed an upward trend, increasing on the average about 3 percent per year. This implies that a constant money supply is consistent with growth of total demand at 3 percent per year. The behavior of the money supply required to support a 5¾ percent growth rate for total demand then is about 2¾ percent, as indicated in the table.

This framework can be used to interpret the role of monetary policy in explaining deviation of the economy from its desired growth path. For example, in the United States during the inflationary period of 1967–1968 the money supply increased at a 7 percent rate, as compared with our hypothetical 2¾ percent. This was associated with an increase in total demand at the rapid rate of 9 percent, and an increase in the price level close to 5 percent, rather than the preferable 2 percent. For the money supply and total demand to grow a few percentage points too rapidly or too slowly causes serious economic problems.

We here use the term "monetary policy" to refer to the whole set of government actions that define the behavior of the money supply. In some cases, the monetary policy involves laws that define a set of monetary institutions, which then work automatically to produce a particular behavior of the money supply. Modern United States monetary policy involves one set of government decisions involving the establishment of the Federal Reserve System and the laws under which it operates; the decisions of Federal Reserve officials in issuing regulations and deciding their day-to-day actions make up another part of monetary policy. Since the behavior of the money supply reflects the joint action of this whole set of government actions, we think of them as jointly constituting monetary policy.

TABLE 2-1 Illustrative Growth of Total Demand and Money Supply Consistent with a Stable Unemployment Rate: 1950–1970

		Percent
	Change in labor force	+ 1½
+	Change in productivity	+ 2¼
=	Change in potential output at stable prices	+ 3¾
+	Relevant change in price level	+ 2
=	Change in potential output at relevant prices	+ 5¾
−	Relevant change in velocity	+ 3
=	Required change in the money supply	+ 2¾

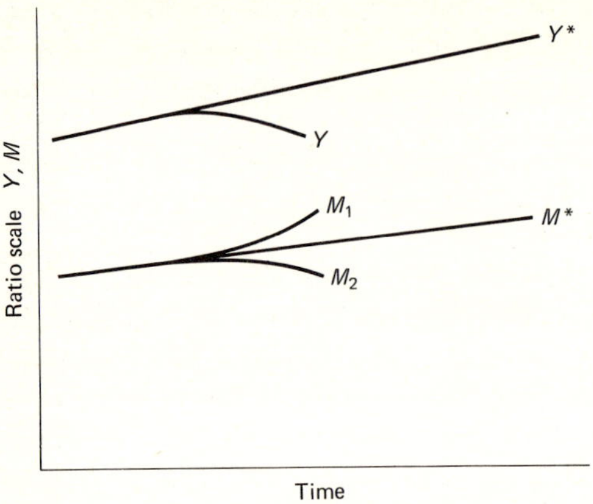

Fig. 2-2 Stabilizing and destabilizing monetary policies.

One performance standard for monetary policy is that it should produce an *average* rate of growth in the money supply that is suited to the needs of the economy, as these were defined above. If the average rate of growth of the money supply is too large, it will result in continuing inflation. If it is too small, it will result in a combination of rising, or large, unemployment and declining price level. That monetary policy shall avoid these twin faults is essential to a favorable performance of the economy.

Monetary policy and economic fluctuations

To meet acceptable performance standards, monetary policy not only should avoid causing protracted periods of excessive or deficient growth of total demand but also should not cause erratic variations in total demand or systematically aggravate fluctuations in total demand arising from other factors.

In Fig. 2-2, the desired growth path for total demand is Y^*. Deviations of actual total demand Y from this path on the upward side cause inflation and those on the downward side cause unemployment and deflation Defining the behavior of velocity that is consistent with time path Y^* permits definition of the time path of the money supply that is consistent with growth of total demand along its desired path M^*. In a certain sense, thus, deviations of the actual money supply M from this path are "errors" of monetary policy. The type of error discussed above is that the money supply on the average over a period of years grows too rapidly or too slowly. This is the case in which the slope of the average growth line of M is greater or smaller than that of M^*. We now are concerned with short-run variation of the money supply about its average growth path.

One possible kind of error is erratic short-run variations in the money supply. These would tend to cause erratic variation in the growth of total demand, leading to periods of inflation and of unemployment. Such erratic variation in the money supply might be combined with an average growth in the money supply that is about right or combined with error also on this score.

The final aspect of the behavior of the money supply considered is its tendency to amplify or to dampen fluctuations in total demand arising from other factors. For example, say Y is growing along Y^* but then adverse political developments cause it to decline and fall below Y^*. Under many kinds of monetary system and programs for monetary policy, the change in economic conditions would affect the behavior of the money supply. Under some monetary policies, such an economic recession would cause the money supply to grow unusually rapidly. In this case, illustrated by M_1 in Fig. 2-2, M would rise above M^*. Since a change in the money supply tends to cause a change in total demand in the same direction, such a monetary response would tend to cause total demand to grow more rapidly than usual. Thus, it would act to offset the initial disturbance and dampen the fluctuation in total demand.

This kind of monetary response is termed "negative monetary feedback." It involves *feedback* from the economy because the money supply responds systematically to economic developments. The feedback is *negative* because an economic disturbance causes a monetary response that tends to offset it, to drive the economy back toward its original path. This involves a deviation of the money supply from its initial path that is in the opposite direction from the deviation of total demand from its initial path. Negative monetary feedback is generally stabilizing, although it could be destabilizing if it occurred on too large a scale or with too long a lag. Negative monetary feedback corresponds to the common-sense idea of a *stabilizing* or *anticyclical* monetary policy.

Positive monetary feedback, the opposite case, involves a response of the money supply in the same direction as the change in total demand. Under systems of monetary policy involving positive monetary feedback, a recession causes the money supply to grow more slowly than usual or to decline, like M_2 in Fig. 2-2. In this case, the behavior of the money supply aggravates the disturbance of total demand. M deviates from M^* in such a way as to magnify, rather than to dampen, the deviation of Y from Y^*.

The other possible case is that of zero monetary feedback. Under this class of monetary policy, the money supply does not respond to the change in total demand in either direction. It simply continues unaffected along its steady, or erratic, growth path. This kind of monetary policy is neutral in the sense of acting neither to dampen or to aggravate economic fluctuations.

In terms of a causal diagram, in which the arrows represent causal relations, positive monetary feedback can be depicted as

$$Y \xrightarrow{(+)} M$$

and negative monetary feedback by

$$Y \xrightarrow{(-)} M$$

The sign indicates whether the money supply responds to changes in economic conditions in the same direction or in the opposite direction. We have assumed above that the money supply has a positive causal influence on total demand, or

$$M \xrightarrow{(+)} Y$$

The case of positive monetary feedback thus leads to a positive feedback loop, one in which a full circuit involves positive feedback

$$Y \underset{(+)}{\overset{(+)}{\rightleftarrows}} M$$

Positive feedback loops are generally destabilizing. In this case, a disturbance that increases Y will lead to an increase in M, which will lead to a further increase in Y, which will lead to a further increase in M, and so on.

The case of negative monetary feedback, however, leads to a negative feedback loop, one in which a full circuit works out to a net negative effect

$$Y \underset{(-)}{\overset{(+)}{\rightleftarrows}} M$$

In this case, a disturbance that increases Y leads to an induced *decline* in M, which tends to reduce Y (the plus sign means that a change in M causes a change in Y *in the same direction*, so a decline in M implies a decline in Y). The induced reduction in Y tends to offset the initial disturbance rather than to amplify it, so the negative feedback loop tends to exert a stabilizing rather than a destabilizing influence.

The performance standards for monetary policy thus include the provision that it should prevent erratic variations in the money supply and should avoid positive monetary feedback. If we knew enough about the behavior of the economy and the influence on it of the money supply, we might want to set up performance standards for monetary policy that are more exact. These probably would involve some specified formula for negative monetary feedback. However, the existing imperfections of knowledge make it difficult to be this exact. We can, however, characterize monetary policies involving positive monetary feedback as destabilizing and therefore objectionable.

The resulting criteria for monetary policy are these:

1. The average growth rate of the money supply should be consistent with the desired average growth rate of total demand.
2. The money supply should not vary erratically.
3. The money supply should not exhibit positive monetary feedback in response to changes in economic conditions.

SUMMARY

1. The economic efficiency of modern societies and their ability to support existing standards of living and existing populations depends on intensive specialization and division of labor. This, in turn, depends on the existence of efficient mechanisms of exchange.

2. A system of exchange of the required efficiency and complexity would be impossible in a barter economy because of the multiplicity of exchanges required and the multiplicity of barter prices generated.

3. The step required to overcome these problems is to settle on one thing to serve as a medium of exchange and a unit of value—that is, to develop a money. Use of money permits any exchange to be made with only two transactions, a sale of one good for money and a purchase of the other good for money. Such transactions using money generate a system of prices of other things defined in terms of money, one price for each good. This solves the problem of the multiplicity of barter prices.

4. The ability of money to perform these functions depends on its general acceptability and on general agreement to use a particular thing as money. This prevents a society from experimenting with a large number of moneys to see which one works best. Different societies have used many different things as money. The choice of the monetary system usually involves a large accidental element. In modern times, it is governed by political decisions.

5. The choice of a monetary system is very important because this governs the behavior of the amount of money, which affects the behavior of total demand, which determines whether the economy will experience inflation, on the one hand, or deflation and unemployment, on the other. Preservation of full employment and price stability requires a specific time path for total demand and, thus, a specific time path for the money supply.

6. Free systems of dealings or mutualistic exchange are not, in general, self-destructive or anomalous. But such systems can achieve only limited technical efficiency without the introduction of a medium of exchange and unit of value, a money. Introducing a money increases the technical efficiency of the exchange system, but it makes the performance of the economy contingent upon the behavior of the amount of money, which in turn depends upon what was chosen as money. The monetary economy thus pays for its efficiency by a fragility, a threat of failure because of misbehavior of the monetary system.

7. To minimize the side effects of money in inflation or in deflation and unemployment requires that the money supply grow along a particular time path. The required average rate of growth of the money supply is defined by the rate of growth of the labor force, plus the rate of growth in output per worker, plus any rate of inflation that is accepted as not practically avoidable, less the rate of increase in the velocity of circulation of money.

8. Performance criteria for monetary policy include average growth of the money supply at this required rate, avoidance of erratic variation in the money supply, and avoidance of positive monetary feedback (or response of the money supply that systematically amplifies economic fluctuations).

QUESTIONS FOR REVIEW AND DISCUSSION

1. Think of some cases in which the efficiency of the United States economy depends upon specialization, or division of labor. Show how the development and preservation of knowledge depends upon specialization. If the United States economy became less efficient, what effect would this have upon the population problem in this country? In other countries?

2. Think through some examples of the kinds of transactions that would be involved in trying to operate a complex economy with barter.

3. Explain how and by how much the use of money reduces the number of prices in the economy.

4. Distinguish between the exchange matrix of a money economy and a pure barter economy.

5. Review the effects of inflation. Discuss their influence upon the efficiency of the economy.

6. Explain why, under a given set of conditions, only a single behavior of the money supply could be consistent with price stability.

7. Give a hypothetical illustration of calculation of the average rate of growth of the money supply that is required for effective performance of a particular nation, taking into account all the factors determining this required growth rate of the money supply. Explain what would happen if the actual growth rate of the money supply were higher or lower than this one.

8. Explain the distinction between zero, positive, and negative monetary feedback. Explain the role of each in determining the way the economy responds to an international development that temporarily increases total demand.

9. State the criteria for evaluating monetary policy. Explain what kind of difficulties would result from a monetary policy that violated each criterion.

3

total demand, money, and the performance of the United States economy

The questions and problems dealt with in money and banking require quantitative analysis. Inflation, total demand, and business conditions; interest rates, unemployment, bank reserves, and bank credit—all of these can be measured and interpreted quantitatively. To do so requires first deciding how the relevant concepts are to be defined and measured. This chapter deals with the major concepts and measures used in our subject.

To understand the past performance of the banking and monetary system, past economic developments, and past monetary policy and its effects, requires familiarity with the facts of past experience. This chapter reviews the record of United States experience, which provides the factual terms of reference for our subject.

National Income and Product in Relation to Monetary Theory

Analysis of economic conditions and the effects of monetary and financial factors on the economy relies heavily on the data and framework provided by the national income and product accounts of the United States. These were constructed and are estimated by the U.S. Department of Commerce.

The focus of these accounts is the relation between the flow of money expenditures for the new output of the economy and the flow of money income derived from the production of this output. For monetary theory, the focal concept of the national income accounts is "gross national product" (GNP). This measures total expenditures for the current output of the economy. It provides a measure corresponding to the concept of "total demand." Changes in GNP (or total demand) are the main factor causing changes in the joint behavior of the economy's output and its price level.

The past growth rate of GNP in the United States and the way changes in the rate of growth of GNP have been reflected in changes in the growth rate of real output and in changes in the rate of inflation or deflation are shown in Fig. 3–1 and 3–2. In these charts, the vertical scale is a ratio scale or a logarithmic scale. This has the property that equal distances at any point on the scale involve the same relative or percentage change—rather than the same *absolute change* as in an arithmetic scale. Thus, a straight line represents growth at a constant relative rate, such as 5 percent per year, the steeper the line, the more rapid the growth rate.

Over the two decades from 1950 to 1970 (Fig. 3–1), GNP grew at an average rate of about 6 percent. This was reflected in an average growth of real output of about 3½ percent and an increase in the price level at a rate of 2½ percent. In the top panel of Fig. 3–1, the gap between the growth of GNP and the growth of output reflects the increase in the price level, which also is shown explicitly in the third line on the chart. The slow average growth of GNP after 1958 led to the deceleration of inflation, but also reduced growth of real output and employment, and thus led to rising unemployment. The more rapid growth of GNP after 1963 increased output and employment more rapidly, reducing unemployment again to a low level, but it also caused a marked acceleration of inflation. Fluctuations of total demand about its two-decade average path include the recessions of 1953–1954, 1957–1958, and 1960, the slow average growth of total demand in the early 1960s, the unusually rapid growth beginning in 1964, and the slowdown of 1970.

The central role of total demand as a causal factor in the economy is brought out by Fig. 3–1. Fluctuations in real output reflected mainly fluctuations in total demand, or GNP. Short-run changes in employment reflected mainly these changes in the growth rate of output, as can be seen by comparing the output and employment lines on the chart. Finally, the labor force grew rather steadily, so the short-run changes in employment were mirrored in changes in unemployment and the unemployment rate. Thus, during 1950–1970, variations in the rate of inflation and in the unemployment rate reflected mainly variations in the rate of growth of total demand. The record is consistent with the view that steady growth of total demand at the appropriate rate would have produced a performance much better than the actual one.

Taking a longer look backwards, the average performance of the economy over the four decades including the Great Depression and the Second World War is strikingly similar to the decades since 1950. Since 1929, GNP grew at a rate of over 5½ percent, output at just over 3 percent, and increase in the price level averaged 2½ percent. The outstanding thing about total demand in the Great Depression of the 1930s is its amazing decline—by nearly one half—from 1929 to 1933. Nearly one-half of the effect of the

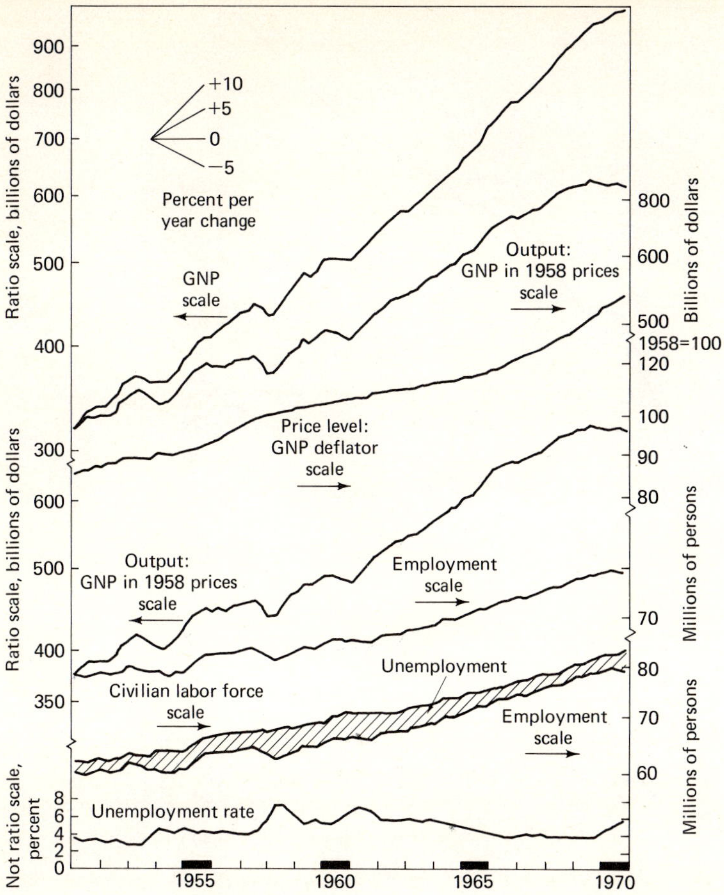

Fig. 3-1 GNP, output, prices, and unemployment, 1951-1970. (Data are seasonally adjusted. GNP and GNP in 1958 prices are at annual rates.) (U.S. Department of Commerce and U.S. Department of Labor.)

decline in GNP was reflected in falling prices rather than in decline in real output, as is shown in the top panel of Fig. 3–2. Despite this cushioning effect of adjustment of the price level, output declined by nearly one-third. Comparing the change in output with the change in employment, we note that output per worker declined during 1929–1933, in part because of reduction in the average number of hours worked per week, so that employment declined by less than one-fifth. Still, this involved a decline of nearly 10 million in the number of persons employed. Given the steady growth of the labor force, this reduction in employment raised unemployment to around 13 million persons, or one-fourth of the labor force. The cause of all this, once again, was the unparalleled decline in total demand.

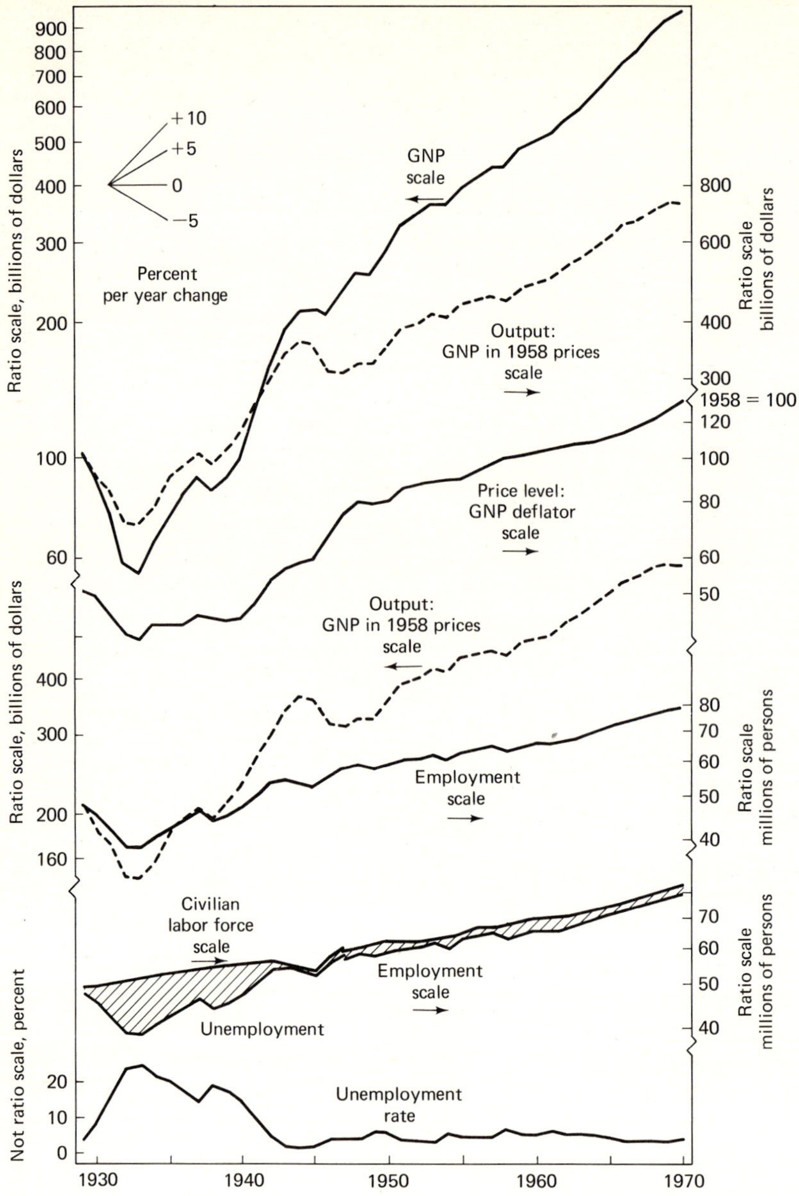

Fig. 3-2 GNP, output, prices, and unemployment, 1929–1970. (U.S. Department of Commerce and U.S. Department of Labor.)

After 1933, total demand increased rapidly—averaging a 12 percent growth rate until the recession of 1937. Curiously enough, in view of the extraordinary level of unemployment, the price level rose during this period at the rate of 3 percent per year. Thus, one-fourth of the increase in total demand was absorbed in inflation rather than being reflected in expansion of output and employment. The combination of the extraordinarily large decline in output in 1929–1933 and the fact that inflation ate up a part of subsequent increases in total demand implied that a long period of unusually large increases in total demand after 1933 was required to bring the economy back to full employment. It is important to note that the 1930s was not a period of "stagnation" in the literal sense of unusual stability of total demand, but was rather a period of remarkable instability, marked by a decline in total demand of unprecedented duration and depth, followed by a period of very rapid increase in total demand.

One kind of information relevant to explaining the behavior of total demand relates to expenditures for various kinds of goods and services (Fig. 3–3). The various components of expenditures are not equally involved in short-run fluctuations. Most systematically involved are investment expenditures, which account for much of short-run fluctuation in total demand. Changes in business expenditures for inventories characteristically play a leading role in economic fluctuations. Lagging somewhat behind these in time but also figuring importantly in economic fluctuations are changes in business expenditures for construction and equipment. On the other hand, consumer expenditures for services and for nondurable goods are but little involved in short-run economic fluctuations. Expenditures of state and local governments show a steady and inexorable upward

Fig. 3-3 Components of GNP. (U.S. Department of Commerce.)

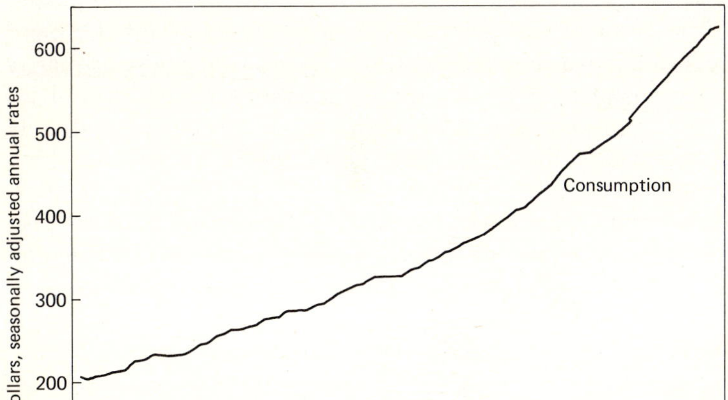

trend. Purchases of goods and services by the federal government show an erratic variation about their upward trend. This has reflected both fluctuations in government expenditures stemming from defense and war and the discontinuous nature of the process by which Congress changes other government expenditures programs.

The relation between total demand and income

Gross National Product, or total demand, measures the rate at which dollars are being exchanged for the goods and services that make up the final output of the economy, or the flow of expenditures for new output. The dollars that make up this flow of expenditures come mainly from current money income, or payments of dollars in exchange for contributions to production. The process of production and distribution of new output thus involves a continuing flow of money for expenditures, which become income payments, which finance expenditures, and so on. Letting Y stand for GNP, or total demand, and N stand for total income payments, this expenditures-income flow can be depicted in a causal diagram as

$$Y \underset{(+)}{\overset{(+)}{\rightleftarrows}} N$$

The allocation of GNP among the various classes of income in the United States is shown in Table 3–1. Of the GNP of $976.5 billion in 1970, about $300 billion, or an amount equal to nearly one-third of GNP, went to government in the form of taxes. This flow of money income to government is used to finance government expenditures.

The amount of income that flowed to corporations and was not passed on by them in the form of tax payments to governments and dividend payments to stockholders was about $14 billion. These funds flow primarily into purchases of investment goods by the corporations in the form of inventories, plant, and equipment. Insofar as the funds are not immediately invested in physical goods, they usually are invested in securities, which passes them on for someone else to use to buy goods and services. In addition, capital consumption allowances by corporate and noncorporate businesses reflect the costs of wear and obsolescence of plant and equipment. These funds are predominantly used for replacement investment expenditures. Logically, we should like to show the retained earnings of *unincorporated* businesses also in this category, but these are so difficult to distinguish from the personal income of the owner of the unincorporated business that this flow of money income is recorded below as disposable personal income.

To arrive at a measure of the flow of income to individuals (and unincorporated businesses and nonprofit institutions) requires some additions of flows of dollars that do not come from earnings derived from the production of GNP. A part of government tax receipts are channeled to individuals

TABLE 3-1 Relation of Gross National Product and Disposable Personal Income in the United States: 1970 (in billions of dollars)

Gross national product		$976.5
Less taxes		
Indirect business taxes	$ 92.1	
Contributions for social insurance	57.1	
Corporate profits taxes	37.5	
Personal income taxes	116.3	303.0
Less business retentions		
Corporate profits† after taxes and dividends	13.8	
Capital consumption allowances	84.3	98.1
Plus transfer payments and subsidies		
Government and consumer interest payments	31.8	
Government transfer payments	73.9	
Subsidies	1.8	107.5
Plus statistical discrepancy		1.8
Equals disposable personal income		684.8
Use of disposable personal income		
Personal consumption, expenditures	616.7	
Interest	17.0	
Personal transfer payments to foreigners	0.9	
Personal saving	50.2	

†Corporate profits after inventory valuation adjustment.
SOURCE: U.S. Department of Commerce.

as transfer payments and to businesses as subsidies. That is, this flow of money income from government is not used to buy goods and services or to pay its workers but rather is passed on to individuals and businesses in the form of payments that are not purchases but "gifts." Since in the national income accounts government and consumer interest payments are not treated as measuring an input of resources—a somewhat moot point—they are added in here as another transfer payment to individuals. In part as a check on their accuracy, gross national product and personal income are estimated independently from separate bodies of data. In 1970, the two independent estimates were inconsistent by nearly $2 billion.

This leaves about $685 billion of disposable personal income. This is used to finance the consumption expenditures of individuals and the investment expenditures of unincorporated businesses. In 1970, personal consumption expenditures amounted to $617 billion. Expenditures by consumers for interest amounted to $17 billion and for transfer payments to foreigners to about $1 billion. This left "personal saving" of $50 billion. A part of this reflected net investment by unincorporated business and expenditures by nonprofit institutions. The bulk of it was a flow of dollars that consumers invested in financial assets, mainly in debt. In this way, the flow of dollars was passed along by lenders to finance the expenditures of borrowers. The flow of expenditures and income through the United States

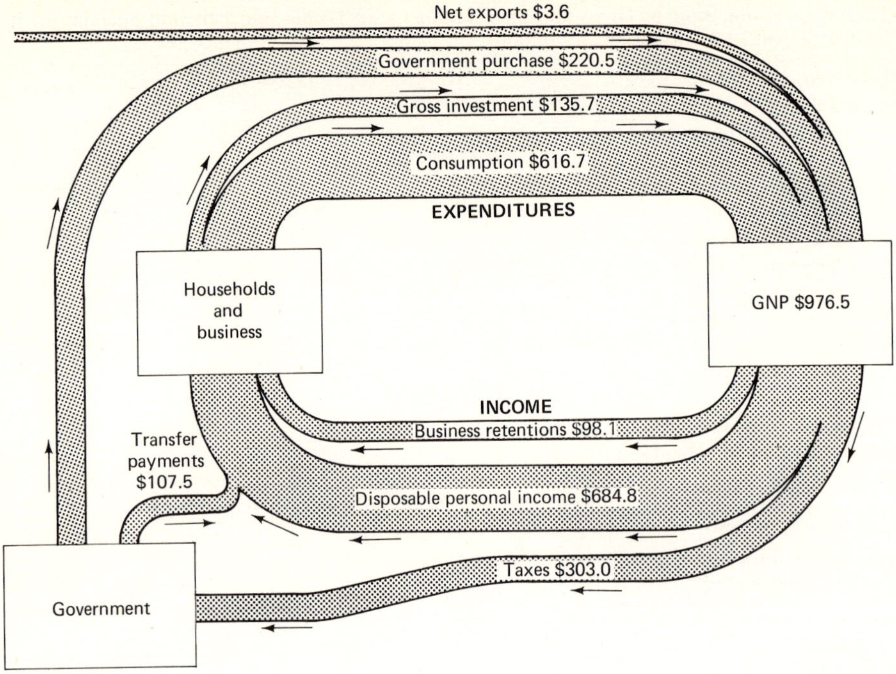

Fig. 3-4 Expenditures-income flow by components, 1970. (Amounts are in billions of dollars.) (U.S. Department of Commerce.)

economy, including the major components of total demand and income, are shown in Fig. 3-4. To be realistic, this diagram must be expanded to include the role of the financial system in providing funds for the financing of expenditures. This point is covered in Chap. 5.

Other systems of national accounts

The national income accounting system does not include information on the operation of the financial system. To remedy this shortcoming, the United States has had for about a decade a more inclusive system of national accounts called the "flow of funds" accounts, produced by the Board of Governors of the Federal Reserve System. These data have been constructed so as to be consistent with the national income accounts. By extending our knowledge of financial transactions, this system permits us to trace the flow of funds from savers into various credit markets. We can see what flow of savings is being used to finance what kind of expenditures. We can account for the sources of funds and the uses that are made of them in the markets for credit, where interest rates are determined. This provides a framework for explaining and predicting the behavior of interest rates.

The flow of funds accounts are used in Chap. 5 to develop an overall picture of the operation of the United States financial system.

For purposes of comparison, we refer to another system of national accounts that is oriented neither toward flows of expenditures and income nor toward financial flows. Rather, the "input-output" system characterizes the flows of materials and products between industries. For a given demand for final output, it shows, for example, the demand of the aircraft industry for the output of the aluminum industry, the resulting demand of the aluminum industry for electric power, the resulting demand of the power industry for coal, and so on. One use to which the input-output accounts have been put is in identifying bottlenecks or areas of shortages of goods that would result from a rapid increase in the production of military goods. This is quite a different problem from the one we deal with in monetary theory, and it requires its own set of national accounts.

Existing Measures of Total Demand, Output, and the Price Level

Gross national product is generally used as the measure of total demand and GNP in constant prices as the major measure of the real output of the United States economy. In the uses we shall make of these measures, it may be helpful to keep in mind the following points regarding them:

1. In its coverage, GNP measures the flow of output through the market. Thus, it does not include activities that are productive but do not result in a sale in a market, such as the work of housewives and noncommercial recreational activities. In this connection, it understates economic output and economic welfare. The understatement is greater for nations with less market oriented economies. The rate of growth of output in a nation such as the United States with a rising proportion of activities flowing through the market is overstated.
2. GNP does not allow for the negative welfare effects of pollution and crowding, except insofar as these are reflected in the prices of things sold through the market, such as air filters and the high prices of housing. This consideration limits its usefulness as a measure of economic welfare.
3. The product produced and sold by government is not independently measured, for obvious reasons, but is estimated on a cost basis by government expenditures for salaries of government employees and purchases from business.
4. The use of GNP to explain variations in employment and unemployment really calls for a different concept than the one related to economic welfare. The existing concept of GNP includes some types of "output" not related to employment, such as the estimated rental value of houses lived in by their owners. However, GNP serves adequately as an employment-related measure of total demand and real output.

Price indexes and the weighting problem

Since prices of individual goods and services ordinarily do not change in an identical manner, any price index is a measure of the *average* change in some set of prices. The simplest way to average the changes in prices of individual products would be simply to include each on an equal basis. Thus, if the price of steel increased by 5 percent and the price of artichokes by 1 percent, our price index would increase by 3 percent.

This approach runs into the difficulty that steel and artichokes are not equally important products in the output of the economy. It runs into the additional difficulty that with this approach the behavior of the price index depends upon what is defined as "a product." For example, if we distinguished 35 kinds of steel and included each of these as a product, then in our index the weight of steel would not be equal to that of artichokes but rather 35 times as great. We face a weighting problem that must be handled in some rational manner.

The problem can be handled by including the price change of each product in the index with a weight that measures its relative importance in the output of the economy. Then the behavior of the index no longer depends upon how many varieties of products are distinguished, since subdividing a product also subdivides its weight. Thus, each product is included in the index with a weight measuring its economic role as measured by the quantity purchased.

This then raises another issue, "Quantity purchased as of what point in time?" Comparing 1970 prices with 1900 prices, one price index could be produced using as weights the quantities of products produced in 1970, another could be based upon the relative importance of goods in 1900, and others could use various kinds of average weights.

A price index measuring current prices in relation to base-year weights can be represented as

$$P = \frac{\Sigma p_C q_B}{\Sigma p_B q_B}$$

where p is the prices of the set of commodities, q their quantities, and the subscripts B and C stand for the base year and the current year, respectively. An index based upon current-year weights is

$$P = \frac{\Sigma p_C q_C}{\Sigma p_B q_C}$$

A kind of average weight suggested by Irving Fisher is the geometric mean of these two indexes:

$$P = \sqrt{\frac{\Sigma p_C q_C}{\Sigma p_B q_C} \times \frac{p_C q_B}{p_B q_B}}$$

Unfortunately, extensive discussion of the relative merits of these approaches has turned up no definitive answer. The use of base-period weights understates the importance of new products, which may be declining in price and may be superior substitutes for older ones, making for an upward bias in the price index. On the other hand, the use of current-year weights is a computational burden, may lead to erratic variation in weights from year to year, and may lead to a downward bias by increasing the weights of goods whose purchases increased because of a temporarily low price. While price indexes computed in either of these ways can be thought of as measuring the change in price of a defined collection of goods and services—those bought in either the base year or the current year—it is somewhat difficult to say just what is measured by Irving Fisher's ideal index, which is also a computational burden. The most common practice is to use base-period weights, shifting the base period often to keep it from becoming too remote from the current period.

Existing price indexes

One prominent index of United States prices is the Consumer Price Index, constructed by the U.S. Bureau of Labor Statistics. This uses base-period weights, currently the average of 1957–1959. The products included and the weights are based specifically upon the purchases of wage earners and clerical workers in large cities. That is, the index shows the current cost relative to that of 1957–59 of the collection of goods and services typically bought by such consumers in the base period.

The Wholesale Price Index of the BLS also uses base-period weights but relates to the prices of goods sold at wholesale (thus omitting services) in proportion to the quantity of their wholesale sales. Some components of the Wholesale Price Index measure prices that are especially sensitive to changes in economic conditions and are more quickly responsive than the Comsumer Price Index. This index has the advantage of having been extrapolated backward to 1800, thus providing a rough measure of the long-run performance of prices.

Neither of these price indexes would provide even a rough approximation to the general price level in the sense of average prices of all goods produced in the economy. The most relevant price index for this purpose, and the one to which we shall mainly refer, is the GNP deflator. The expenditure figures for each component of GNP are deflated, or restated in 1958 prices, by being divided by whatever available price-index component most closely corresponds to the type of goods or services in question. The deflator for the GNP as a whole is then derived by dividing GNP by GNP in 1958 prices.

These measures of the price level and of real output probably overstate inflation and understate the growth of real output because of their reliance upon conventional units of output, or inadequate allowance for improvement in the usefulness of products. But on the other hand, they may overstate the increase in real output and, thus, implicitly understate the decline in the real value of the dollar because of the incompleteness with which they measure the human costs and benefits of changing patterns of economic activity and environmental deterioration. The net effect of these considerations is, for the present, a matter for conjecture. We here use these concepts and measures on the basis that they are the best now available.

Measurement of unemployment

The data on unemployment in the United States are derived from a monthly sample survey taken by the Bureau of Labor Statistics. Those people selected randomly for inclusion in the survey are asked whether they have been looking for work. If the answer is affirmative, they are included in the "labor force," which measures the number of people looking for employment. They then are asked whether they are employed and some more detailed questions. The estimate of unemployment is based upon the responses of people who say they are looking for a job but do not have one. To correct for growth in population and the scale of the economy, in comparisons involving different points in time we usually use the unemployment rate, which is unemployment divided by the labor force and is usually a figure like 4 or 5 percent.

The figure for the unemployment rate is commonly used as a measure of the success of the economy in providing jobs for individuals as well as the degree of utilization of other resources. Where it is used to compare the performance of different national economies or of a given economy during different periods of time, the unemployment rate may be misleading because of differences in the way unemployment is measured in different countries and because of differences in economic, legal, institutional, and social factors that affect the unemployment rate that is attainable in a given economy. Since these factors relate closely to the evaluation and understanding of cost-push inflation, we defer detailed discussion of them to a later point.

The United States Money Supply

The way the "money supply" or "money stock" should be defined is not entirely agreed upon among economists and financial analysts. The approach taken here, which is probably the majority view, associates the label "money" with the things that serve as a means of payment or generally used medium of exchange. Such money is defined in terms of the unit of value, which in the United States is the dollar, but many other financial assets also have this characteristic. In this approach, the money supply is defined to include currency and demand deposits (deposits against which checks can be written) held by the public. The reasoning underlying this approach is that spelled out in Chap. 2. The optionality and political determination of the monetary system and its side effects in influencing total demand in this view attach specifically to money in the sense of the medium of exchange.

Some financial assets that do not serve as a means of payment and that earn interest, termed "liquid assets," are an alternative to money in some uses. An increase in the volume of such liquid assets thus may reduce the quantity of money demanded, increase velocity, and increase the total demand consistent with a given money supply. But if the effects of changes in the quantity of such assets are not *the same as* those of changes in the quantity of money, it is preferable to treat them separately, rather than lumping them together with money. The alternative view—the one that is *not* taken here—is that some of what we term liquid assets should be lumped together with what we term money and the analysis based on this broader set of things.[1]

About three-quarters of the United States money supply in 1970 consisted of demand deposits held by the public at commercial banks (see Table 3-2). Of the one-quarter of the money supply consisting of currency and coin held by the public, nearly nine-tenths was paper money in the form of Federal Reserve notes. The contribution of the U.S. Treasury to the money supply is now a minor one, limited to provision of fractional coin.

The money supply is defined to exclude demand deposits and currency held by the United States government and by banks. It is assumed that for the purpose of interpreting the influence of money on total demand, it is only money held by the public (including state and local governments) that is relevant. The spending of the United States government is assumed to be but little affected by the size of its cash balance. Thus, Treasury balances at commercial banks and Federal Reserve banks, although they clearly are money in the general sense of means of payment, are excluded from the

TABLE 3-2 United States Money Supply, December 1970 (seasonally adjusted; in billions of dollars)

Demand deposits			$165.7
Currency and coin			48.9
Federal Reserve notes		$50.2	
Treasury currency		6.9	
Fractional coin	$5.8		
Standard silver dollars	0.5		
United States notes	0.3		
In process of retirement	0.3		
Less currency and coin held by banks and other adjustments		8.2	
Total money supply			$214.6

SOURCE: Fed. Reserve Bull.

[1]A major statement of this approach is found in Milton Friedman and Anna J. Schwartz, *Monetary Statistics of the United States*, pp. 89–197, Columbia University Press, New York, 1970.

money supply because of the particular purposes for which that concept is designed. Money held by the commercial banks themselves is viewed as inventories or goods in process that has not been placed in the hands of those whose spending it might affect.

Several deductions are required from the total value of demand deposits on the books of the commercial banks. Balances of other banks and of the United States government are excluded for the reasons mentioned above. In the case of checks that are in the process of collection, as we illustrate below, there is a stage when the check has been added to the deposit balance of the payee before it has been deducted from the balance of the payer, so this demand deposit is temporarily counted double on the books of the banks. To correct for this, the total checks in the process of collection—termed "cash items in process of collection" plus "Federal Reserve float"—are deducted from total demand deposits as recorded on the books of banks in estimating the money supply.

The money supply also is defined to include foreign demand balances at the Federal Reserve banks. Dollar balances held at United States commercial banks by foreigners are included in the United States money supply. On the other hand, balances at foreign banks even though denominated in dollars are not included in the United States money supply. No time deposits or obligations of savings institutions are included in the money supply as defined here, on the basis that these are best classified as liquid assets but not as means of payment. Demand deposits and currency held by financial institutions, of course, are counted as part of the money supply, as such institutions are treated as a part of the public.

The Record of the Money Supply and Velocity

The long-run relation between the money supply and total demand, measured in terms of annual data, is shown in Fig. 3-5. The money supply and total demand have usually varied inphase rather than out-of-phase with one another. Thus, the record is consistent with the interpretation that the monetary system caused or contributed to the fluctuations in total demand that largely explain variations in the rates of unemployment and inflation.

The sharp depression of 1921 reflected an abrupt decline in GNP—even more abrupt than that of 1929-1933. This was accompanied by a decline in the money supply that also was of record-breaking speed. Information on the chain of events makes it clear that monetary policy initiated the decline in this case and then amplified it with monetary contraction.

In the great contraction of 1929-1933, the decline in the money supply and in GNP was less rapid, but more prolonged. The main thing distin-

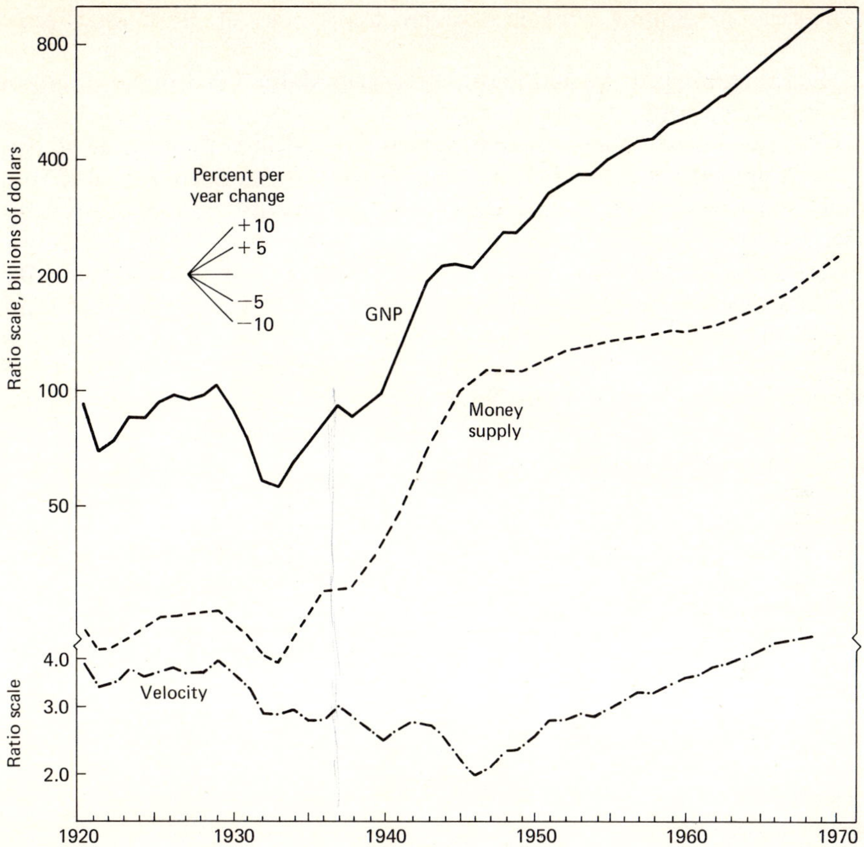

Fig. 3-5 Money supply, GNP, and velocity, 1920–1970. (U.S. Department of Commerce and Board of Governors of the Federal Reserve System.)

guishing this contraction from the earlier one was that the money supply and GNP did not turn up after a year or two, but continued to decline for more than 3 years.

The data argue that the monetary system was a cause also of the recession of 1938. The leveling off of the money supply in 1937 was not immediately reflected in GNP. Its momentum carried it further upward, this being reflected in an increase in velocity. However, continued increase in total demand in the face of lack of monetary growth did not continue long. Total demand and velocity came down in the recession of 1938. This was a modest recession compared to those of 1921 and 1929–1933, but more severe than any economic contraction of the postwar period. One way of noting the damage it did is to observe that the level that GNP might have otherwise reached in 1938 it now did not reach until 1940.

The postwar recessions were less severe than those of 1921 and 1929–1933.

Over the long pull, variation in GNP was explained mainly by variation in the money supply. Over the period as a whole, velocity increased only about one-third while the money supply increased about eight times. The decline in velocity in the 1930s and yet further in the Second World War reflected an unusual set of circumstances that made it attractive to hold money rather than to spend it or hold other assets. We review these in our discussion of the demand for money. The continued increase in velocity from 1946 through 1970 includes a long-run shift from this unusual kind of world to a quite different one, an optimistic, high-interest-rate, inflationary world in which the incentives to hold money are small and the attractions of other forms of wealth are great. The course of velocity in the 1970s will depend upon what kind of an economic world develops, which depends importantly upon policy choices.

Fig. 3-6 Money supply, GNP, and velocity, 1951–1970. (Data are seasonally adjusted. GNP data are at annual rates.) (U.S. Department of Commerce and Board of Governors of the Federal Reserve System.)

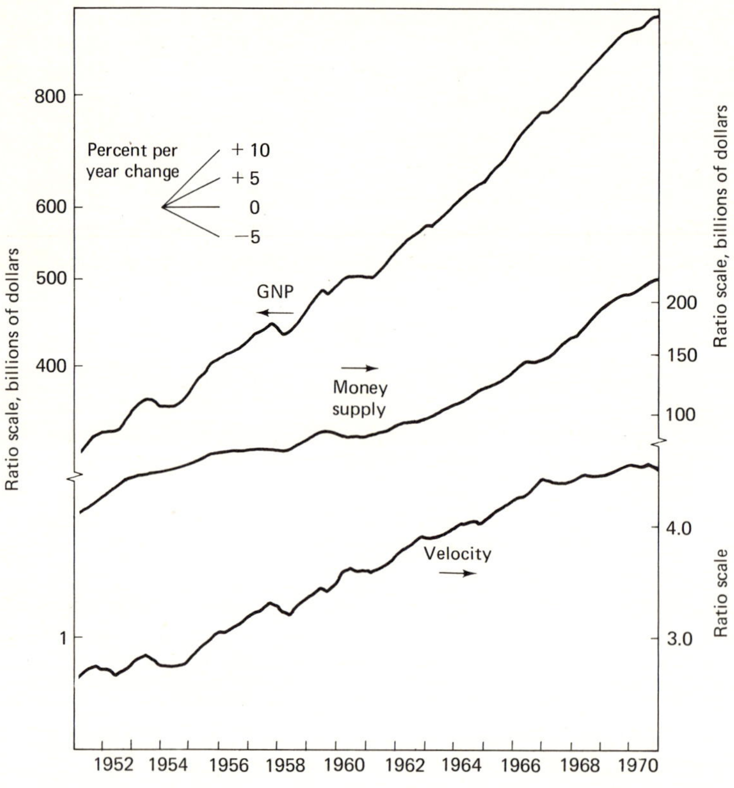

Total demand, money supply, and velocity since 1951

The past two decades have been within the period of long-run increase in velocity (Fig. 3–6). During this time, the increase in velocity in a direct sense accounted for a bit more of the increase in total demand than did the increase in the money supply. However, the money supply still seemed to play the same causal role in fluctuations in total demand. Each of the recessions was preceded by a decline or leveling off in the money supply (the small declines in GNP in 1952, 1959, and 1970 are not recessions but the effects of strikes). The decline in velocity thus can be interpreted as the result of the change in economic conditions arising in the recession, rather than the initial cause of the decline. The chart also shows the correspondence between the slow average growth in the money supply and in GNP from 1959 through 1965. Thus, the record is consistent with the interpretation that the monetary system and monetary policy explains the failure of GNP during this period to rise once again to a growth path consistent with a reduction in unemployment to the usual levels.

The more rapid growth of the money supply, beginning in 1963 and especially noticeable in 1965, potentially explains the accelerated growth of total demand that led to unusual inflationary pressures during that period. Details of the picture fit into this interpretation. The leveling off of the money supply in 1966 led to a slowdown in growth in total demand that—although scarcely visible on the chart in the first quarter of 1967—slowed the inflation and led to a "mini-recession."

The resumption of rapid growth of the money supply in 1967 led to resumption of rapid growth of GNP and 2 years of inflationary developments. The deceleration of growth of the money supply in 1969 was initially reflected in an increase in velocity, which then changed to a slowdown of growth of total demand beginning in late 1969. There are no substantial changes in the growth rate of GNP during this period that do not seem interpretable as reflecting mainly variations in the growth rate of the money supply.

The Behavior of Interest Rates

Another financial variable that figures importantly in money and banking is interest rates. Figure 3–7 shows that interest rates, in contrast to total demand and the money supply, show no clear trend. The level of interest rates now is not substantially different than 40 or 80 years ago. This is a significant factual observation. Some economists have expected that interest rates would decline as societies became wealthier and more "mature." This combination of circumstances, it was thought, would lead to an incapacity to generate sufficient growth in total demand, rising unemploy-

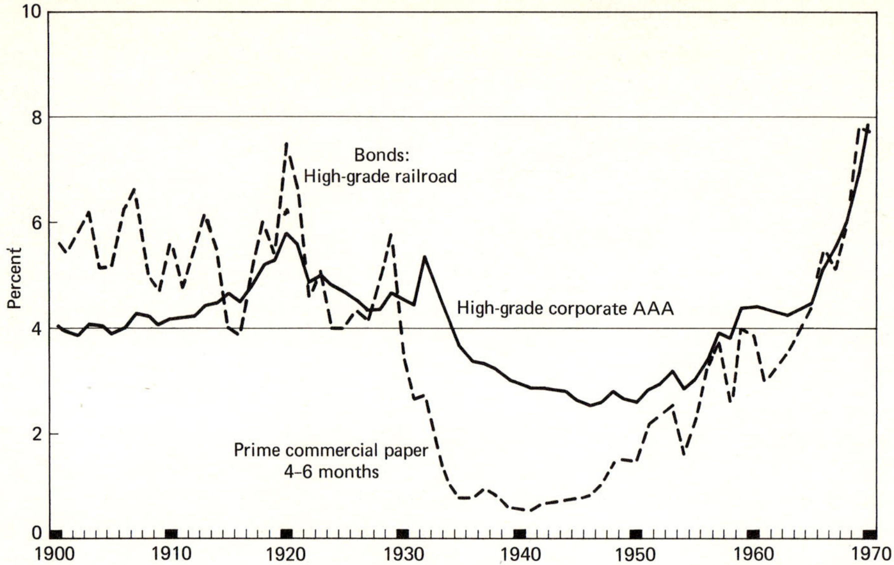

Fig. 3-7 Interest rates, 1900–1970. (Board of Governors of the Federal Reserve System and Standard and Poor's Corporation.)

ment, and economic stagnation. One interpretation of the Great Depression of the 1930's was that it reflected the arrival of such economic stagnation. Subsequent events have not borne out this theory.

The major movements in interest rates appear to have been associated with economic fluctuations. Interest rates have moved inphase with total demand and the money supply, rising during economic expansion and declining during economic contraction. The decline in interest rates in the Great Depression, thus, can be interpreted as reflecting the severe economic decline of the times.

Interest rates, atypically, did not rise during the economic expansion after 1933. Long-term interest rates (bond yields in Fig. 3–7) declined from 1933 until the Second World War, then moved sporadically upward. By the early 1960s, they had risen back to the levels of the mid-1920s. The very rapid increases in interest rates during the period of inflationary expansion of the economy in the late 1960s carried them to levels that are high in relation to past experience.

The movement of interest rates during the 1950s and 1960s was mainly a combination of this long-run upsweep with short-run variations inphase with swings in total demand and economic conditions. We noted above that short-run variations in the money supply also were inphase with swings in total demand, so the historical record is that the money supply and interest rates generally varied inphase with one another.

Another significant aspect of the behavior of interest rates is their relation to the rate of change in the price level. If inflation is expected, borrowers and lenders should adjust the terms of debt contracts to allow for the expected change in the value of money. In this connection a useful concept is "the real rate of interest," or the rate of interest after adjustment for change in the value of money. This is defined as $i_r = i - \Delta P/P$. If the stated or nominal interest rate i is 6 percent but the value of money is declining ($\Delta P/P$) at 4 percent a year, the real rate of interest i_r is only 2 percent. To keep the real rate of interest unchanged at 2 percent when the inflation rate rises to 8 percent would require an increase in the nominal interest rate to 10 percent.

Commonly, nominal interest rates seem to adjust in the expected direction in response to a change in the rate of inflation, but not by enough fully to compensate for it (Fig. 3-9). Under these conditions, an increase in the rate of inflation leads to an increase in nominal interest rates but to a reduction in real interest rates. Similarly, deflation—as in 1929-1933—leads to low nominal interest rates but high real interest rates. The real interest rate is, in many respects, a better indicator than the nominal interest rate of the true cost of credit to the borrower and of prevailing incentives to investment and other credit-financed expenditures.

As Fig. 3-9 shows, the extraordinarily sharp rise in nominal interest rates from 1965 to 1970 no more than offset the increase in the rate of

Fig. 3-8 Yields on U.S. Government securities, 1950-1970. (Board of Governors of the Federal Reserve System.)

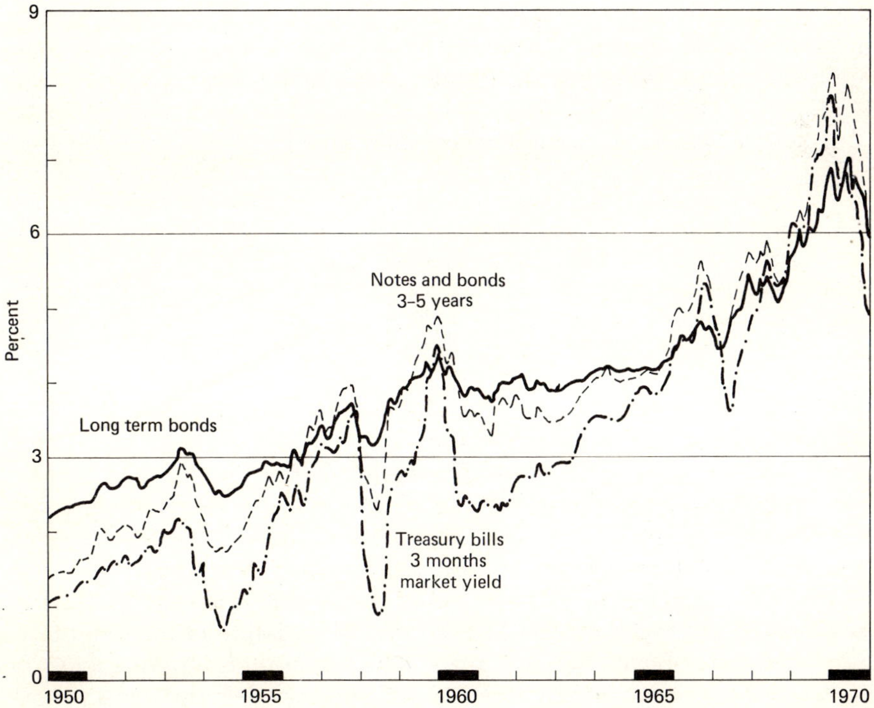

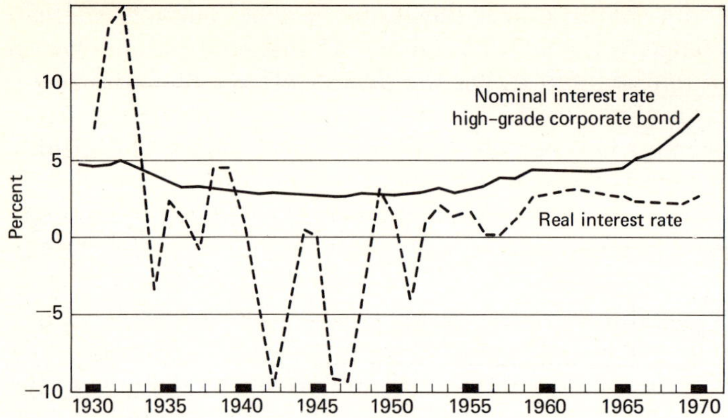

Fig. 3-9 Nominal and real interest rates. Nominal interest rate shown is the yield on high-grade corporate bonds (Moody's Aaa). The real interest rate shown is this yield less the rate of increase for the year in the GNP deflator. (Moody's Investors Service and U.S. Department of Commerce.)

inflation during that period. The real rate of interest as this is measured in Fig. 3-9 was actually a bit lower in 1970 than during the slack years 1961 and 1962. This is an important point to keep in mind for our later discussion of monetary policy. One approach to monetary policy interpreted it as being restrictive during this period on the basis that the high interest rates reflected "tight" credit conditions. We see that this may be true if the nominal interest rate is the relevant measure, but not if what matters is the real interest rate. Two further points are important for our later discussion:

1. Real interest rates during the economic contraction of 1929–1933 were extraordinarily high, as the declining price level implied that loans had to be paid back in dollars more valuable than those borrowed. In this sense, credit conditions during this period were not "easy," but were extremely unfavorable to the financing of expenditures.
2. In the past, wide variability of the real rate of interest has resulted from the changeable performance of the price level in conjunction with the restriction of the nominal interest rate to a narrow range of variation.

A final observation relates to the structure of interest rates, or the relation between interest rates on different kinds of debt. The complex story is fairly well summed up in these observations (see Fig. 3-8): (1) Movements in interest rates characteristically are inphase with one another. (2) Interest rates on short-term debt move over a wider range than those on long-term debt. (3) Short-term interest rates usually are lower than long-term interest rates, the exceptions being usually at times when interest rates generally are high and the greater range of variation of the short-term rates carries them above long-term rates. (4) Interest rates on less secure, or low-grade debt, rise more than others when business defaults rise and confidence in the future of the economy declines.

SUMMARY

1. Changes in the unemployment rate reflect mainly changes in output, as the labor force grows at a rather steady rate. Such changes in output reflect mainly changes in the rate of growth of total demand. The money supply is one of the major factors affecting total demand.

2. The best available measure of total demand is gross national product, which is designed to measure money expenditures for the final output of the economy.

3. Historical variation of unemployment and the price level in the United States, including that during the Great Depression, is explained by variation in the growth rate of total demand.

4. Past variation in the growth rate of total demand, in turn, is explainable in substantial part by variation in the growth rate of the money supply. The money supply in the past has commonly moved inphase with fluctuations in the economy.

5. Interest rates have shown no long-run trend, but fluctuate inphase with economic developments.

6. Variation in the rate of change of the price level tends to bring changes in nominal interest rates in the same direction. However, such changes in nominal interest rates often are smaller than the changes in the rate of price-level change, so the real rate of interest falls in inflation when nominal interest rates are rising and rises in deflation when nominal interest rates fall. Thus, interpretation of "credit tightness" or "credit ease" in terms of nominal interest rates may be misleading.

7. Short-term interest rates change over a wider range than long-term rates as both move in harmony with economic fluctuations.

8. Interest rates on low-grade debt rise in relation to those on high-grade debt during periods when economic prospects are adverse and defaults on debt unusually prevalent.

QUESTIONS FOR REVIEW AND DISCUSSION

1. Define the causal chain linking the money supply to unemployment.

2. "Since only about two-thirds of gross national product becomes disposable income, we must expect the expenditures-income stream to slow down as time goes on, causing rising unemployment." Comment critically.

3. Explain what is measured by the Consumer Price Index and by the GNP deflator.

4. "The Great Depression of the 1930s was caused by a slowing down in the growth rate of total demand because of the maturing of the American economy." Comment on this statement in relation to the behavior of total demand during this period.

5. "Short-run swings in the money supply usually run in the opposite direction from those in total demand, thus the money supply acts as an anticyclical force." Comment in relation to the facts of United States experience.

6. "As an economy becomes mature and accumulates wealth, its interest rate declines." Comment in relation to the facts of United States experience.

7. Characterize the usual relation between short-run swings in total demand and in interest rates.

8. Briefly describe the past relation between long-term and short-term interest rates; between rates on high-grade and low-grade debt.

4

theory of investment and intermediation

The kinds of physical wealth that are productive in a given economy depend upon its resources, the existing technology, and the preferences of consumers. These factors determine the usefulness to the society of oil wells, automobile factories, irrigation projects, and railroads. The amount and kind of assets people want to hold depend upon the time pattern of their expected income receipts and their desired expenditures. The financial system performs the function of dividing up wealth ownership in such a way as to best reconcile the requirements of production with the desires of savers.

This chapter covers basic concepts of investment theory, which will be used in considering the financial behavior of individuals, businesses, and financial institutions.

The Demand for and Supply of Financial Assets

The wealth of society is ultimately owned by individuals, either directly or indirectly through their ownership of businesses and other organizations. The starting point of an analysis of the financial system is behavior relating to wealth-holding choices.

The life cycle of holding wealth and financial assets

The holding of wealth and financial assets by individuals follows a life cycle. The person who inherits no wealth begins on the zero line as he enters working age, as indicated in the top panel in Fig. 4–1. Then he accumulates wealth gradually, the growth rate perhaps slowing during young adulthood when child-rearing expenses mount while income is still modest. When the expenses of children and their education are past and income is close to its peak, saving occurs more rapidly. After retirement, wealth is used up.

The usual pattern of living and consumption in the United States involves purchase of durable goods and, in many cases, home ownership during young adulthood. Thus, ownership of physical assets rises very rapidly during this phase of life, thereafter remaining fairly stable and finally declining.

The ownership of financial assets and the status of the individual as a net demander or supplier of credit reflects the joint operation of these two factors. The youthful home owner acquires a large mortgage along with his house, which may overbalance his other financial assets and make him a substantial net borrower in the credit market. As he pays off his mortgage, adds to his savings in pension systems, and builds up his wealth enough to have some free funds to invest in securities, he shifts from a net debtor position to the position of a creditor. Finally, the individual begins consuming his wealth and his financial assets.

The rationale of this life-cycle pattern is that it maximizes the individual's lifetime economic satisfactions, given the time pattern of his opportunities to earn income and given the nature of the consumption opportunities that confront him during the different phases of his life.[1] The individual's lifetime economic satisfactions would be greatly reduced if he had to consume each unit of his income when he earned it and could not make the intertemporal adjustments depicted in Fig. 4–1. Thus, an improvement in the ability of the consumer to make these intertemporal adjustments would increase his lifetime economic satisfactions just as would an increase in the lifetime income he was able to earn.

Adjustment of the time pattern of their consumption can be accomplished by individuals in ways other than varying their net holdings of financial assets. Insurance contracts provide a means of protection against many unfavorable contingencies against which protection otherwise would be sought by the holding of wealth. Examples are early death of the income earner, severe illness, and property damage.

Similarly, arrangements under which an individual or a business has assured access to credit provide a way of meeting unforeseen cash needs that otherwise would have had to be met by holding liquid assets. Thus,

[1]A major contribution to economic theory in this area was Franco Modigliani and Richard Brumberg, "Utility Analysis and the Consumption Function: An Interpretation of Cross-section Data," in K. K. Kurihara (ed.), *Post-Keynesian Economics*, pp. 388–436, George Allen and Unwin, Ltd., London, 1955. This formal analysis represents the consumer as attempting to maximize the value of his utility function, which defines his economic utility as depending upon consumption at different points of time and assets to be bequeathed, or

$$U = U\,(c_t, c_{t+1}, \ldots, c_L, a_{L+1})$$

To do this, he adjusts the timing of his consumption so that the additional utility conferred by the last dollar of consumption is the same in each time period, since this implies that utility cannot be increased by shifting any additional consumption to a different time period.

Another formulation of the theory of consumer behavior that is in some respects similar is Milton Friedman, *A Theory of the Consumption Function*, Princeton University Press, Princeton, N.J., 1957.

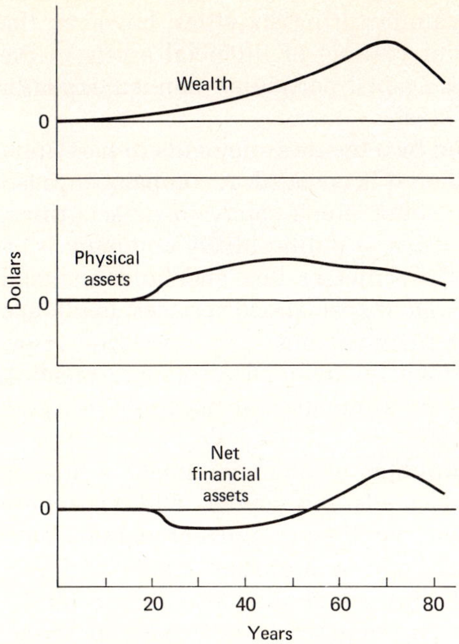

Fig. 4-1 Lifetime holdings of wealth and financial assets.

both of these kinds of institutional arrangement tend to reduce the amount of wealth that people must hold in order to meet given needs and uncertainties.

This depiction of wealth-holding behavior provides a basis for considering the forms in which the individual will want to hold his wealth, given the amount of it he holds during different periods of his life, his gross and net financial assets, and the timing of expected future changes in his financial position. His investment strategy arises from his lifetime financial plan, and it determines the kinds of financial assets that he prefers to hold and the kinds of debt that he wishes to create for others to hold.

Businesses and governments as suppliers and demanders of financial assets

A factual and quantitative picture of the contributions of various kinds of businesses as suppliers and demanders of financial assets is developed in Chap. 5. Businesses such as manufacturing corporations are major suppliers of financial assets, which they create as a means of financing the real investment assets they need to conduct their physical productive activities. The steel company creates shares of common stock and various kinds of debt securities as a way of raising money to buy its land, factories, and inventories. Incidentally to its manufacturing activities, however, the steel company also owns a substantial volume of financial assets in the form of contingency reserves, reserves against particular planned expenditures, and credit extended to buyers of steel.

The nature of the securities issued by a business depends in part upon the kind of productive activities in which it is engaged. A company engaged in a speculative search for oil cannot offer much safety in its securities, but can offer a chance of very large gains; a public utility company is in the opposite position. Some financial businesses buy and hold financial assets in conjunction with their provision of specialized services; insurance companies illustrate this case. Other financial businesses are true intermediaries or middlemen, holding primarily financial assets and creating in almost the same volume financial instruments that become the assets of others.

Governmental units are major suppliers of financial assets to finance the purchase of capital goods such as roads and schools and, especially in the case of the federal government, to finance current deficits and, because of the carry-over, deficits run in past wars that resulted in government debt that was not paid off. Governmental units also are substantial holders of financial assets, primarily in conjunction with special operations such as pension systems.

The logic of investment policy

To the various suppliers and demanders of financial assets who create the financial system, their activities in it are incidental to their production or consumption. This fact governs the basic logic of their financial activities. The manufacturing business is interested in raising the money it needs for plant, machinery, and working capital on the most favorable possible terms. It seeks to borrow at the lowest possible interest rate. The saver holding securities against his retirement wants to earn on the funds as high a rate of return as he can.

What makes financial decisions complex, however, is that both borrowers and lenders are operating under a number of side constraints. The length of time the borrower needs the funds, which affects the kinds of securities he can sell, depends upon the kind of physical assets in which he invests them. The riskiness of his securities depends on the kind of activities he engages in, and the riskiness of any one security depends on the terms of its contract in relation to those of his other securities.

Similarly, the holder of securities is concerned not only with what he expects to earn on them but also with the risk that they will not perform as expected, and with the question as to how much they will be worth if he has to sell them on short notice. These considerations make the investment game so complex that a special set of concepts and analytical tools is needed to deal with it rationally.

The Performance of Investments: Investment Yield

Investments usually involve a series of contractual or expected payments at different points of time. The investor makes a payment to buy an asset—a bond, a share of common stock, a rental property—at one point of time in the expectation of receiving a series of payments at future times. But how is he to go about comparing the attractiveness of alternative investments with different time patterns of expected future payments? Some kind of interpretative framework or conventional point of view is needed to make any sense out of the many kinds of existing investments involving different time patterns of payments.

It is clear from our earlier discussion that payments at different points in time are not regarded by people as equivalent. Paying out money now and receiving it back 10 years later is not the same thing as receiving money now and paying it back 10 years later. In financial transactions—as in many things in life—time is of the essence.

The present-value formula

In actual societies, money *now* commands a premium over money *in the future*. The balance between potential borrowers and potential lenders is such that financial markets are cleared when borrowers pay a fee to lenders, rather than the other way around. Rates of interest are positive rather than zero or negative. Society, and the market, values future payments lower than present payments.

This implies that money (or other forms of wealth, usually valued in terms of money) that is available in the future must be subjected to some rate of discount to determine its present value. If $105 a year hence is equivalent to $100 now, the rate at which future dollars are discounted is in this case $5 per hundred, or 5 percent. If we represent the present value by V (or present price by P) and a payment at the end of 1 year by Q_1, our simple illustration can be represented by

$$V \text{ (or } P) = \frac{Q_1}{1+i} \qquad \text{or } \$100 = \frac{\$105}{1.05}$$

in which i is the rate of discount, or the rate of return, 5 percent.

This expression can be used in three different ways, since by knowing the values of any two of its terms we can determine the value of the third. It can be used to determine the present value of an investment, given the payment expected at the end of the year and the rate of discount that is relevant. Because of its use in this way, it is called the "present-value formula." At a discount rate, or rate of return of 5 percent, the present value of $105 a year hence is $100.

By knowing the present value (or the price) of an asset and the relevant rate of discount or of return, we can solve for the amount of the required end-of-year payment. To earn 5 percent on \$100 requires an end-of-year payment of \$105.

Finally, knowing the present value or the price of an asset and the payment expected at the end of the year, we can solve for the rate of discount, the rate of return, or the "yield" of the investment. If \$100 invested now brings \$105 at the end of the year, the yield on the investment is 5 percent.

In order to extend this way of looking at investments to longer periods of time, we usually make the simplifying assumption that the same i applies to each year or subperiod. In this case, the extension is straightforward. What is the present value, at a discount rate of 5 percent, of a debt promising to pay \$5 interest at the end of 1 year and \$5 interest and \$100 principal at the end of 2 years? The present value of the amount becoming available a year hence is defined by

$$V = \frac{Q_1}{1+i}$$

Similarly, the value 1 year hence of the amount becoming available 2 years hence will be

$$\frac{Q_2}{1+i}$$

To determine the present value of this amount, it must be discounted again for the current year. Thus, its present value is

$$V = \frac{Q_2}{(1+i)(1+i)} = \frac{Q_2}{(1+i)^2}$$

By extension, the present value of an amount available at the end of n time periods is defined by

$$V = \frac{Q_n}{(1+i)^n}$$

The present value of an asset that promises payments at a number of different future times is the sum of the present values of each of these expected payments:

$$V = \frac{Q_1}{1+i} + \frac{Q_2}{(1+i)^2} + \frac{Q_3}{(1+i)^3} + \cdots + \frac{Q_n}{(1+i)^n}$$

Our simple example involves payments at only two future times, so its solution is

$$V = \frac{Q_1}{1+i} + \frac{Q_2}{(1+i)^2} = \frac{\$5}{1.05} + \frac{\$105}{(1.05)^2} = \$4.76 + \$95.24 = \$100$$

If the future payments were discounted at a lower rate such as 4 percent, the present value of each payment would be greater. Thus, the present value of this investment at 4 percent would be \$101.16. Turning the point around the other way, for this investment to yield 4 percent, it would have to have a present price of \$101.16. For investments involving fixed future payments, a decline in the yield rate implies an increase in the price of the asset, and the reverse.

The concept of investment yield

The concept of "investment yield," or the "rate of return," on an investment is a crucial one in investment analysis, for it reduces to a single measure the profitability or remunerativeness of investments.[2] Particular projects with very different time schedules can be compared in terms of their yields. In the case of debt securities, "yield" is used as a synonym for "interest rate." The promised yield on a bond is computed straightforwardly by application of the present-value formula. For a \$1,000 bond running for 20 years selling in the bond market at a price of \$985, whose contract specified annual interest payments of 4 percent, the calculation is

$$P = \frac{Q_1}{1+i} + \frac{Q_2}{(1+i)^2} + \cdots + \frac{Q_{20}}{(1+i)^{20}}$$

or

$$\$985 = \frac{\$40}{1+i} + \frac{\$40}{(1+i)^2} + \cdots + \frac{1{,}040}{(1+i)^{20}}$$

Solving for i in such problems cannot be done simply, and they are solved by referring to tables of bond prices and yields. In this case, the yield is higher than the nominal yield, or coupon yield, because the bond is bought at a price lower than par (par being the value against which the coupon rate of interest is figured). The yield in this illustration is 4.11 percent.

The term "long-term interest rate" ordinarily refers to the yield on long-term bonds. The way this interest rate actually changes, thus, is through changes in the market prices of bonds. An increase in the long-term interest rate really means a decline in bond prices that, given their fixed coupon interest payments, increases their yields.

An expected yield can be estimated for an investment that does not involve a contract specifying particular payments at particular future dates. The estimated yield on a rental property is based upon an estimate for each future period of the net earnings of the property, after maintenance and other operating costs, plus an estimate of its market value at the end of the period. This set of estimated earnings plus the terminal price of the property defines its estimated yield. The yield in such cases can be thought of as that rate of return for which the present value of expected future net earnings is equal to the price of the property.

The yield on common stock is estimated in the same way. Since a share

[2]For a more detailed treatment of the material of the following sections see William F. Sharpe, *Portfolio Theory and Capital Markets*, McGraw-Hill, New York, 1970; Basil J. Moore, *An Introduction to the Theory of Finance*, Free Press, New York, 1968; and Paul F. Smith, *Economics of Financial Institutions and Markets*, Irwin, Homewood, Ill., 1971.

of common stock does not promise to repay any particular sum at any particular future maturity date, as does a debt, an estimate of its yield over any period of time requires an estimate of what its market value will be at the end of the period. In order to avoid this issue, we also work with the "current yield" of common stocks, defined as the current dividend rate divided by the market price—thus leaving open the later value of the stock and the rate of return that actually will be earned by holding it for any particular period of time.

The yield actually realized on an investment depends upon the earnings that are made at each point in time, which need not equal the expected ones. In the case of bonds, the term yield usually refers to the promised yield, or the yield that will be realized if the payments promised in the bond contract all are made when promised. If any of these payments are not made when due, the "realized yield" on the bond may be less than its "promised yield." In general, realized yields on investments can be computed only in retrospect and may not be equal to promised yields or "expected yields."

We noted that the yield, or interest rate, on a debt is figured on the assumptions that the debt is held to its maturity, or repayment date, and that the debt contract is fulfilled. Many debts, including most bonds, are marketable and can be sold in the market before maturity. In this case, there is no presumption that the price at which the debt is sold will be equal to its par value or that the rate of return earned on the debt over the period of time it was held will be equal to its yield, which in this case means "yield to maturity."

In this connection, we can apply the concept of the "holding-period yield" of debts that are not held to maturity. This is computed in the same way as the yield of assets that do not have a maturity date, by inserting into the present-value formula the estimated market value of the debt (or, in retrospect, its actual sale value) at the end of the holding period for which the yield is being figured.

The concept of investment yield, or rate of return, is thus applied, with minor modifications, to a number of somewhat different cases. It is a very useful single-valued measure of the reward for investing. This measure is a simplification, or a convention. The assumption that the same i applies to each of the subperiods involved in the investment period, in some cases may be misleading. But for our purposes in this course, the concept of investment yield serves well enough.

The relation between changes in price and yield of marketable debt

As a background for thinking about changes over time in the prices and yields of bonds and other forms of debt, it is important to keep well in mind the effect of the term to maturity, or the duration, of a debt on the relation between the change in its price and the change in its yield. The longer the term of the debt, the greater the change in price required to bring about a given change in yield. The reason for this is easy enough to see. If the debt in question is a 1-day loan, the change in price required to change its yield by one percentage point—say, from 4 percent to 5 percent—is essentially 1 day's interest on the principle sum at 1 percent. But if the security in question is a 20-year bond, what is required is a change in price equivalent to 20 years' interest at 1 percent. The longer the term to maturity, thus, the greater the change in the price of a debt required to bring about a given change in its yield.

The extreme case of a long-term debt is the consols issued by the British government, which have no maturity debt and simply promise to pay interest forever—in effect, until the securities are repurchased in the market by the British government. The relation between price and yield for such perpetual bonds is

$$P = \frac{Q}{i} \quad \text{the limit of } P = \frac{\Sigma Qn}{(1+i)^n} \text{ as } n \rightarrow \infty$$

This implies that the relative changes in price and yield of the perpetual bond are proportional:

$$\frac{\Delta P}{P} = \frac{1}{\Delta i/i} \quad \text{or} \quad \frac{\Delta P}{P}\frac{\Delta i}{i} = 1$$

Thus, for the yield on such a bond to fall by one-half requires the price to double. The shorter the term to maturity, however, the smaller the relative change in price required to bring about a given relative change in yield.

This implies that if yields of marketable debts of all maturities fluctuated over the same range, fluctuations in debt prices would be smallest for debts of the shortest maturities. In fact, yields on short-term debt fluctuate over a wider range than yields on long-term debt, but it remains true, because of the price-yield relation discussed above, that fluctuations in prices are very much smaller for short-term debt. This stability of prices of short-term debt means that the holder of such debt can count on selling it without any substantial loss. This contributes to the superior liquidity of short-term debt, which affects the role that it plays in investor portfolios.

Investment Risk and Illiquidity

Investment analysis attempts to apply knowledge and judgment so as to define as closely as possible the outcome of each investment. Insofar as he can, the investor wants to take the guesswork out of his activities. In most cases, however, his knowledge is incomplete, and there remains an element of uncertainty as to how any given investment actually will turn out. We consider now the investor's strategy in dealing with this uncertainty or with the risk that an investment will not turn out as well as expected. The approach that we develop in this particular context provides a general model for the making of rational decisions based on incomplete information, which we shall later apply to some other decision problems.

Risk characteristics and probability distributions of yields

If we have perfect knowledge regarding an investment, there is no uncertainty and no risk. We *know* what is going to happen. In some cases, it is regarded as certain that the actual yield on a debt will be the promised yield and that the debtor will live up to his contract in every particular. Securities of the United States government usually are considered thus to be free of investment risk.

In considering investments whose outcome is uncertain, the concept of a probability distribution of possible outcomes is useful. Each outcome that is within the realm of possibility is listed. Then an estimate or judgment is made as to the relative likelihood or probability that each outcome will prove to be the actual one. These probability distributions are like odds on a bet. To say one thinks the true odds are 3 to 1 that Black Hat will beat Sleepy Boy is to say that the probability is .75 that Black Hat will win and .25 that Sleepy Boy will win. In recent years, weather forecasts have been given in terms of probability statements, such as in the forecast that the probability of rain today is 40 percent, or .4. These "subjective" probabilities may be interpreted as stating the proportion of times each outcome would occur in a very large number of cases just like the one in question.

The probabilities are stated in relative terms, adding up to 1.0. Thus, an equiprobable event such as a coin toss involves a probability of .5 of throwing a head and a probability of .5 of throwing a tail. A coin toss can be an investment, say, in which heads wins a dollar and tails loses a dollar. This involves the probability distribution of outcomes depicted in Fig. 4-2.

The term "expected value" of an investment is used not only in its everyday sense but also as a technical term to refer to the sum of each possible outcome times its probability of occurring. Letting $0_1, \ldots, 0_n$ stand for the n possible outcomes of a given investment and $\mathrm{Pr}_1, \ldots, \mathrm{Pr}_n$ for the probabilities associated with each of these, the expected value of an investment can be stated as

$$E = \mathrm{Pr}_1 0_1 + \mathrm{Pr}_2 0_2 + \cdots + \mathrm{Pr}_n 0_n$$

A more compact way of referring to such problems involving the addition of a set of terms is the use of the notation

$$E = \sum_{i=1}^{n} \mathrm{Pr}_i 0_i$$

In this notation, Σ (uppercase sigma) stands for "the sum of" and the "index" i successively takes on each of the values in the range indicated by the term below and above Σ, in this case each of the values from 1 to n.

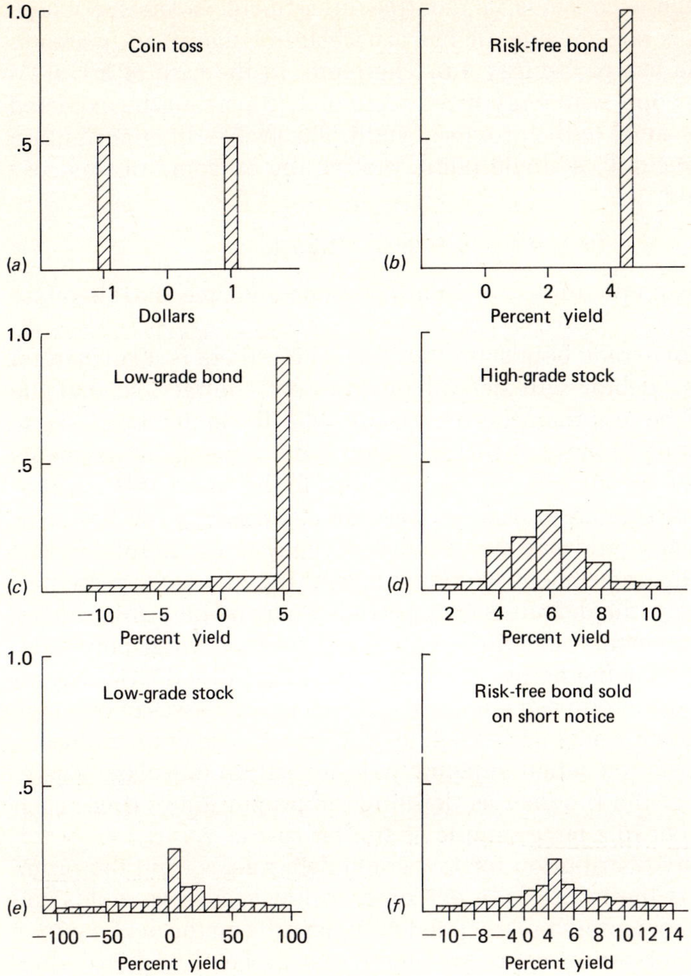

Fig. 4-2 Probability profiles of investments.

The coin-toss investment involves a .5 probability of losing a dollar and a .5 probability of winning a dollar. If one made a large number of such investments, the expectation is that he would break even. The expected value of the investment is

$$E = \sum_{i=1}^{2} \mathrm{Pr}_i 0_i = .5 \times \$1 + .5 \times - \$1 = \$0.50 + (\${-0.50}) = 0$$

In this case, the actual value of the investment in any particular instance cannot equal the expected value, zero, since in any particular toss one must either win or lose, but the presumption is that in a large sample of such investments the actual value would approximate the expected value thus figured.

In terms of these concepts, a risk-free investment is one for which only one outcome is conceivable, or has a probability significantly greater than zero, and this has probability 1.0. Therefore, in the case of a United States government bond with a promised yield of 4.25 percent the expected yield to maturity is equal to the promised yield. The probability distribution in this case involves only a single point. Stating the outcome in this case as an expected yield,

$$i = Pr_1 i_1 = 1.0 \times 4.25\% = 4.25\%$$

In this case, there is no possibility of an unfavorable outcome, and therefore no risk.

By contrast, low-grade bonds are those in which there is a substantial probability that the debtor will default on the debt contract, so that the realized yield will be less than the promised yield. If the debtor defaults, in the sense of failing to make at the promised time some of the payments prescribed by the debt contract, the loss involved to the investor is a matter of degree. In an extreme case, it could become clear during the first year that the debtor never would pay any interest or repay the principle. In this case, the yield on the investment would be something like −100 percent.

More commonly, the default is only partial. It may involve only a delay in some interest payments and thus reduce the realized yield below the promised yield by a small amount. To define the probability distribution of outcomes relating to such investments, we define a set of classes of outcome including all the possible ones and assign to each an estimate of the probability, or likelihood, that the actual outcome will fall within this class. Again, we also can think of the problem as defining the proportion of times each outcome would occur in a large sample of similar cases.

The probability distribution for low-grade debt ranges from the promised yield, which is the most likely outcome, to lower positive yields and to negative yields that would be associated with defaults on the debt contract of various degrees of seriousness. An illustrative probability distribution for a low-grade bond is shown in Fig. 4-2. Once again, the sum of the probabilities of each class of outcome is 1.0. Investment *risk* relates especially to the left-hand tail of this probability distribution, to the likelihood of an outcome that is unfavorable and might be damaging to the investor.

To find the expected yield on a low-grade bond we once again multiply each outcome (or class of outcome) by its probability and add up these probability-weighted outcomes. Since the low-grade bond has no probability of an outcome more favorable than the promised yield and has nonzero probabilities of outcomes less favorable than this, its expected yield must be lower than the promised yield.

Measurement of investment risk

The difference between the promised yield and the expected yield of a debt contract thus provides one measure of the risk of the debt. It is not an entirely satisfactory measure. Two low-grade bonds might have the same promised yield and expected yield but involve quite different likelihoods of *very large* losses. The degree of uncertainty attaching to an investment relates to the dispersion or spread of its probability distribution: the length of its tails.

The dispersion of a probability distribution is usually measured by its variance or its standard deviation. These are measures of the average difference between the center of the distribution, as measured by its expected value, and the individual outcomes that make it up. If the expected yield of the investment is denoted $\bar{i}$, the deviation from this of each of the possible yields making up the distribution is measured by $i_i - \bar{i}$. To compute the variance of the series, each of these deviations is squared and weighted by its probability; these values are then summed. That is, variance is defined as

$$\text{var} = \sum_{i=1}^{n} \Pr_i(i_i - \bar{i})^2$$

Squaring the deviations before summing them has the effect of giving extra weight to extreme values, since the square of the deviation increases more than proportionately with its value. If people are especially concerned with extreme values, with large deviations from the expected outcome of the investment, the variance may relate more closely to their perception of investment risk than a simple summing of deviations. The standard deviation of the series, usually denoted by a lowercase sigma, is simply the square root of the variance

$$\sigma = \sqrt{\text{var}}$$

These are not the only measures of the dispersion of a probability distribution. It may be that analysis of investment risk should be concerned only with the left tail of the distribution, since the investor is not disturbed by the chance of getting an extremely high rate of return on his investment—only by the chance of getting less than his expected rate of return. However, our discussion here is limited to the variance as a measure of the degree of uncertainty attaching to an investment, and in this sense to the degree of investment risk.

The definition and sources of illiquidity

The estimate of the probability distribution of outcomes of an investment will depend upon the circumstances under which the investment must be terminated. A 20-year government bond held to its maturity may be treated as involving no investment risk, having a probability of 1.0 of yielding its promised yield and .0 probability of any other yield. But what if this government bond were being held as a reserve for contingencies and when the funds were needed would have to be sold in the bond market at 1 week's notice? Then what is relevant is the probability distribution of holding-period yields on the bond, given liquidation on 1 week's notice. Since the price of long-term government bonds varies with economic conditions and general changes in interest rates over a range of roughly 15 percent, if the bond had to be sold at a time when bond prices were unusually low (interest rates were unusually high) the holding-period yield might be negative, as is indicated by Fig. 4-2.

When it is not to be held to maturity but may have to be sold on short notice, the government bond has a probability profile rather like that of a common stock. It involves a chance of a negative yield. Moreover, the probability distribution is two-tailed, since the investor may sell the bond at a time when bond prices are unusually high, make a capital gain on the bond, and thus earn a rate of return higher than the promised yield.

It is true of many other investments as well as government bonds that they involve more risk, more variance of expected outcome, if they may have to be turned into cash on short notice than if they are to be held to maturity or until some predetermined liquidation date in the future. But this is not true of all investments. Some others, such as a savings account, can be liquidated on short notice without any additional risk. To characterize the expected performance of financial assets, it is necessary to consider them in relation to the period of time they are to be held and the circumstances under which they may have to be liquidated.

One of the particular needs against which investors hold financial assets are situations that call for money on short notice. The money may be needed to meet unfavorable contingencies—medical emergencies for the family, an unexpected drop in a business' sales, or a slowdown in payments on accounts receivable. It may also reflect favorable contingencies—an unusual chance to take a vacation or a rare chance for a business to buy a desired piece of land. To meet such needs, investors want to hold financial assets that can be turned into cash on short notice without any substantial chance of a loss. What we mean by "loss" in this case is a yield much below the expected yield on the asset. Assets that meet this test are called "liquid assets" or "secondary reserve assets" (money being the "primary" reserve).

To pass this test and qualify as a liquid asset, a financial asset must have a probability distribution of yields involving no substantial tail to the left when the asset is liquidated on short notice. Long-term government bonds do not pass this test, as we have seen. They involve no investment risk, as this was defined above, but they do involve illiquidity. They are not liquid assets, because they must be sold in the market to be realized on short notice, and their market price varies over so wide a range that if sold on short notice they may have to be sold at a substantial loss.

An asset can achieve a high degree of liquidity in either of two ways:

1. A high-grade debt that matures very soon will automatically turn to cash at that time and is liquid on this account. Extreme cases are call loans, which can be "called" by the lender at any time, and 1-day loans such as

federal funds loans. In some cases, the investor is certain that he will not need the funds on quite such short notice as this and that, for example, a Treasury bill maturing in 1 month will provide the needed liquidity on the basis of its imminent maturity.

2. Any marketable asset can be liquidated at any time through sale. To qualify as a liquid asset, however, the asset would have to have a very stable market price, so the investor would know that no matter when he happened to have to sell his asset he would not take a substantial loss on it. The major markets involving prices sufficiently stable to meet this standard are certain markets for high-grade short-term debt. The most important assets deriving their liquidity from their salability at a stable price are short-term government securities, especially Treasury bills, marketable certificates of deposit of commercial banks, and commercial paper issued by well-known businesses.

To summarize, then, investment risk relates to the dispersion of the probability distribution of outcomes of an investment when it is not liquidated under forced conditions nor on short notice. The variance of the probability distribution of outcomes is the most widely used measure of investment risk. Liquidity refers to the dispersion of the probability distribution of outcomes under conditions of liquidation on short notice. In evaluating liquidity, special attention is paid to the left tail of the distribution, to the likelihood of a yield substantially below the expected one. Neither of these concepts is entirely precise, for there are a number of ways in which investment risk and illiquidity could be measured. They are, however, central ideas of investment theory and of practice in the investment planning of individuals and businesses.

Rational Investment Policy under Uncertainty

Rational behavior involves the attempt to achieve certain objectives under conditions that will or may prevent their full achievement. If there are no objectives, or no goals or wants, or if there are no constraints on our ability to achieve our objectives, there is no basis for rationality. Rational behavior, thus, can be cast into the form of an attempt to maximize utility—or the attainment of certain objectives—under constraints. The two parts of the problem are represented by a utility function, which defines the objectives, and some kind of a model that represents the constraints or the payoff matrix subject to which we are trying to achieve the objectives to the greatest possible degree.

Investor preferences toward risk

The preference function of the investor leads him to prefer a higher yield to a lower one. In defining how it is rational for him to behave when

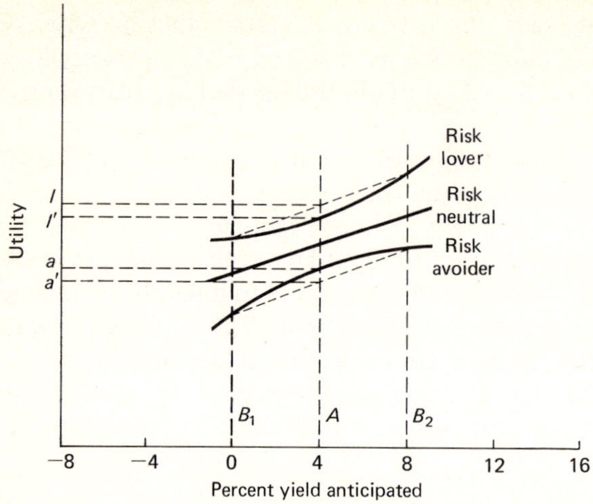

Fig. 4-3 Investor utility curves.

he has incomplete knowledge, however, it is necessary also to define how investment risk relates to his goals. The investor who wants to avoid risk will seek investment assets with narrow probability distributions, will prefer *high-grade* assets to *low-grade* assets. In particular, he will want to avoid investment projects with a long tail to the left, those that involve even a small possibility of a very large loss. On the other hand, some people do like to gamble, and seek out risky propositions. The most attractive kind of risky proposition seems to be not one with a long tail to the left but rather one with a long tail to the right, that is, one involving even a small chance of a very large gain.

A general representation of investor attitudes toward risk can be given by positing an explicit preference function, or utility function, for the investor.[3] Three illustrative utility functions are shown in Fig. 4-3. The slope of the curve at any point measures the marginal utility of yield at that point. We are not concerned with the total utility of the investor, how generally happy or unhappy he is, but only with the slope of the curve over the relevant range and the degree to which he prefers more or less risky investment packages.

This aspect of the investor's behavior can be illustrated by facing him with two investment projects that have the same expected value but involve different degrees of risk. Project *A* offers a 4 percent yield with a probability of 1.0, while project *B* offers a .5 probability of an 8 percent yield and a .5 probability of a 0 percent yield (.5 × 8 percent + .5 × 0 percent = 4 percent expected yield). Which one does the investor choose?

If his preference curve is concave downward, he is a risk avoider and

[3]An influential development of this approach is James Tobin, "The Theory of Portfolio Selection," in F. H. Hahn and F. P. R. Brechling (eds.), *The Theory of Interest Rates*, pp. 3–51 St. Martin's, New York, 1965.

chooses project *A*, the risk-free investment. We see graphically that if we average the utility that the investor would derive from the 8 and 0 percent yields (at *a*′), both of which are equally probable, this is less than the utility that he would derive from the 4 percent yield (at point *a*). Why is this? The fact that our utility curve is concave downward means that as we move to the left the loss of utility from any given decline in yield becomes progressively greater. The investor is extremely averse to unfavorable outcomes. Thus, in the case of an investment prospect such as *B*, the disutility to him of the unfavorable outcome more than overbalances the utility of the prospect of the favorable one. In his investment policy, this investor looks for ways to avoid risk.

On the other hand, the investor who is a risk lover has a preference curve that is concave upward. He derives greater utility from project *B* than from project *A* (utility *l*, compared with *l*′). The investor who is risk neutral has a preference function that is linear (a straight line) over the relevant range. He is indifferent to the degree of risk in various projects, responding only to their expected yield.

Rational Investor Policy

These concepts permit a rigorous definition of a rational investor policy. The investor confronted by a set of alternative investment projects should choose the one that maximizes his expected utility, not expected yield, but expected utility—which depends also on risk. In this way of formulating the decision, the investor behaves as if he first draws up a probability distribution of the outcomes of each investment project. Then he consults his utility function and defines the utility that would attach to each of these possible outcomes. Next he multiplies each of these utilities by the probability attaching to that outcome and sums these to define the expected utility of the project. He finally chooses that project, or that combination of projects, that maximizes his expected utility. That is, the rule is:

$$\text{Choose project to maximize } EU = \Pr_1 U(i_1) + \Pr_2 U(i_2) + \cdots + \Pr_n U(i_n) = \sum_{i=1}^{n} \Pr_i U(i_i)$$

This framework can be applied to any kind of decision under uncertainty. One of the contributions made by economists in recent years regarding the formation of monetary and fiscal policies has been to cast the decision problem into this framework. The Federal Reserve decision makers can be viewed as choosing among a set of policy strategies (analogous to alternative investments), defining as best they can a probability distribution of the outcomes of each (analogous to estimating the probability distribution of yields for each investment), and then making a choice that will maximize the expected utility for society.

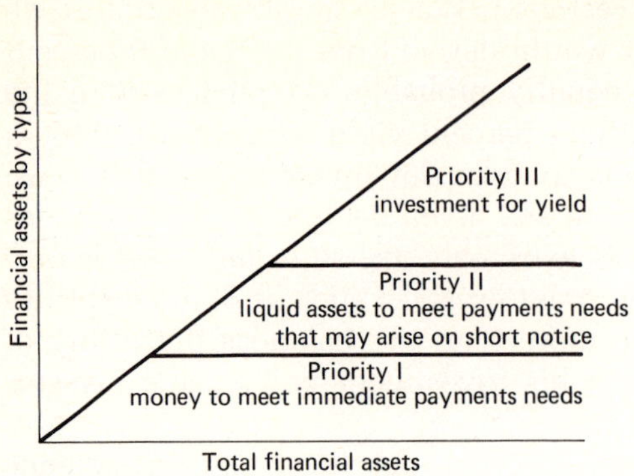

Fig. 4-4 Priorities among financial assets.

Whether or not we interpret their behavior within this framework, most investors seem to prefer to avoid risk in managing their investment portfolios. It is not difficult to understand in common-sense terms why this should be so. The business, the individual, and the financial institution attaches great weight to avoiding serious disruption of its activities and avoiding the hazard of bankruptcy. This creates a demand for high-grade assets and a basis for financial machinery that can reduce risk.

Priorities among asset categories

The desire of the business or individual to avoid costly, and for the business perhaps fatal, financial embarrassment leads to a basic strategy based on functional categories of assets. This strategy can be stated in terms of the priorities depicted in Fig. 4–4.[4] Number 1 priority goes to holding enough money to be able to meet immediate payments needs. Until this objective is met, no financial assets are held in other forms.

Possible payments needs that are not immediate can be met by holding liquid assets, or secondary reserve assets. Of course, this requirement also can be met by holding money. From the investor's viewpoint, however, liquid assets are generally a superior way of meeting this need, since they pay interest, and money does not. When dealing with the boundary line between money and liquid assets, the investor may vary the composition of his assets, depending upon the yields available on liquid assets and the transactions costs involved in keeping his temporarily available funds invested in liquid assets.

Once these two priorities are met, any further funds available for investment can be put into assets without regard for liquidity considerations. This ordinarily permits a higher yield to be earned on these funds.

[4]This approach derives from Roland I. Robinson, *The Management of Bank Funds*, 2d ed., pp. 11–18, McGraw-Hill, New York, 1962.

Reducing Risk through Diversification

Where the outcome of individual investment projects cannot be predicted with confidence but some information is available on the performance of classes of assets, diversification can permit the achievement of a given yield with a reduction in risk. The basic idea is this. While any one investment may turn out very badly, there is little chance that a diversified set of investments all will turn out badly. Thus, the worst conceivable outcome of the diversified portfolio is better than the worst conceivable outcome of any one of the investments that makes it up.

Theory of diversification

The term "investment portfolio" is used to refer to a set of investments, ordinarily in the form of securities. The rate of return on the portfolio is the average rate of return on the securities that make up the portfolio, each weighted by its importance in the portfolio. If q_1 stands for the proportion of the portfolio invested in security 1 and i_1 the yield on this security, the yield on a portfolio including n securities is

$$r = \sum_{i=1}^{n} q_i i_i$$

The potentialities of diversification in reducing risk are illustrated by Fig. 4-5.[5] Consider two investment projects A and B that involve different combinations of risk and expected yield. If the outcomes of these projects were perfectly correlated—if their success or failure depended on precisely the same factors—then the performance of portfolios involving various

Fig. 4-5 Risk reduction through diversification.

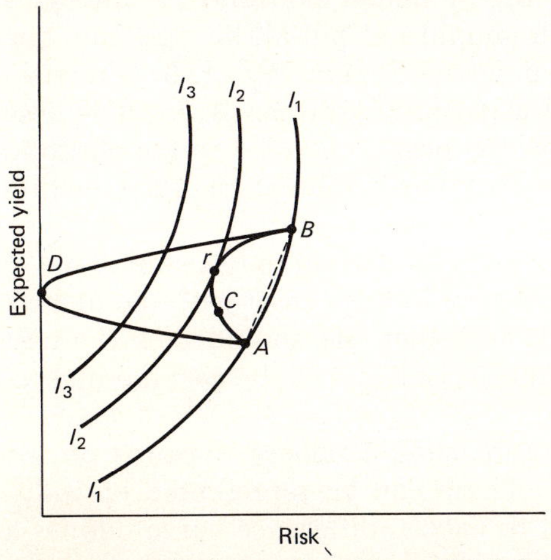

[5]This approach derives from Harry M. Markowitz, *Portfolio Selection: Efficient Diversification of Investments*, Wiley, New York, 1959.

combinations of them would lie along the dashed line *AB*. The position on the line of each portfolio would depend on the proportions of *A* and *B* in the portfolio. However, if we can choose an *A* and *B* so that under the conditions in which one of them does poorly the other does well, then a combination of the two will involve less risk than either one of the two. Then the performance of combinations of *A* and *B* will lie along a line such as *ACB*, offering the same yield at less risk because of the exclusion of extreme outcomes by the diversification

The degree of risk reduction that is possible through diversification depends upon the extent to which one can find investments involving hazards that are negatively correlated. That is, the goal is to find investments such that the circumstances that will cause one to do poorly will cause the other to do well. In the ideal case of perfectly offsetting variation among yields on the assets, the opportunity frontier is defined by a line such as *ADB*. Under these conditions, a portfolio can be defined that involves no risk at all.

In practice, such perfect negative correlation among asset yields cannot be found, but real opportunities do exist for "spreading one's risks," or "not putting all one's eggs into one basket." Much attention is given to the problem by investors. There are many possible bases of diversification, as there are many factors that may cause an investment to go sour. Geographical diversification avoids bad losses caused by the decline of a city or area. To diversify cyclically, one invests not only in cyclically sensitive industries but also in some that are cyclically insensitive or even, if they can be found, that will do relatively well during a business recession. Since prices of bonds commonly rise (interest rates decline) during recession, holding marketable bonds as well as common stock is one way of achieving some cyclical diversification of a portfolio.

For the risk-avoiding investor, the "efficient portfolio" is always a diversified portfolio. The risk avoider should *not* put all his eggs into one basket. This point can be clearly understood from Fig. 4-5. The risk-avoiding investor would never hold a portfolio between *A* and *C*—these are not efficient portfolios. To increase the proportion of *A* in the portfolio beyond that indicated at point *C* involves some combination of a reduction in expected yield and an increase in risk.

On the other hand, the investor who is indifferent to risk should never hold a diversified portfolio. He should pick out the asset with the highest expected yield and put all his funds into that. He should pick the best looking basket and put all his eggs into it. In Fig. 4-5, he gets the highest expected yield by entirely holding *B*.

The particular portfolio an investor should choose depends on his objectives relating to yield and risk. These can be represented by indifference curves such as those labeled II. Each indifference curve defines a set of combinations of expected yield and risk among which the investor is indifferent. One point on a curve is just as satisfactory to the investor as any other. The risk-avoiding investor has indifference curves that are concave upwards. To be willing to accept additional risk without feeling worse off, he requires a more than proportionate increase in yield. Indifference curves that are higher and further to the left in the diagram involve higher degrees of satisfaction to the investor, for they always involve higher yield or lower risk, or both. Thus, the investor chooses the portfolio that puts him on the highest attainable indifference curve. This is the one that is tangent to the best attainable opportunity frontier achievable through portfolio diversification. If the most favorable diversification his information permits the investor to achieve is that defined by the curve *ACB*, the best choice he can make is at point *r*. On the other hand, the investor who is indifferent to risk, who cares only about yield, has indifference curves that are horizontal and chooses a portfolio consisting entirely of *B*.

The efficiency of diversification derives from our possessing a particular kind of knowledge. If we could predict with certainty the outcome of each individual investment, we should simply choose the highest yielding investments and would have no use for diversification. If we knew nothing whatever about the outcomes of investments, we should have to make random choices. The situation favorable to diversification is that we have knowledge permitting us to predict the performance of defined categories of investment better than we can predict the outcome of individual investments in the category. This is a common situation. On the other hand, the investor who *does* have detailed information about particular investments may be better served by acting upon this information than by following a mechanical rule of diversification.

In relation to the efficiency of the economy as a whole, diversification is productive in reconciling the needs and desires of savers with the needs of the economy for particular kinds of physical capital. Such diversification, however, does not substitute for the providing of knowledge, analysis, and judgment that is a basic and crucial function of the investor. Within the framework of rational investor decisions, we assume that the information the investor uses in his decisions regarding diversified portfolios already reflects his collection and analysis of information to the full extent that these activities pay for themselves in improving the quality of choices.

Purchasing-power risk

So far we have dealt with investment risk in terms of probability distributions of yields, these being defined in terms of money. An additional and quite separate kind of risk relates to the hazard of change in the value of money. The United States government bond bought at a price involving a promised yield of 4 percent will surely yield its 4 percent. But the payments of interest and principal are made in dollars, and the value of the dollar is not constant over time. If, for, example, the value of the dollar declined by 3 percent per year over the period, the "real yield" (or the real rate of interest) earned by the investor would not be 4 percent but 1 percent. All investments promising a particular return in dollars are subject to the hazard that the value of the dollar will decline during the period the investment is held. In principle, this hazard is symmetrical, since the value of the dollar can increase as well as fall. But declining price levels have been rare in recent decades, and purchasing-power risk has come to mean almost entirely the risk of inflation.

The high-grade debts that minimize investment risk offer no protection against purchasing-power risk in the event of inflation, except where the inflation is anticipated and the promised yields are adjusted to compensate for it. To defend himself against inflation, the investor avoids assets promising sums defined in terms of dollars in favor of equities and the ownership of real property. Commonly, however, these assets involve more investment risk than high-grade debt. Diversification can be applied to this combination of risks by holding portfolios including high-grade debt that will rise in value in the event of deflation or depression, and equities and claims on real property that will rise in money value under inflationary conditions.

The Role of Financial Intermediaries

Financial intermediaries are institutions that take the funds of the ultimate wealth owners of the economy and pass them along to the ultimate users or borrowers. They are middlemen in credit. Since running such institutions involves operating costs, we ask what services or functions they perform that permit them to cover their costs and make them net contributers to the effectiveness of the economy.

Intermediaries and risk reduction through diversification

The investor with a large volume of wealth to invest can achieve diversification within his own portfolio. But this is not possible for the small investor. Moreover, economies of scale in financial transactions make it efficient for many investors to achieve their diversification through financial intermediaries. Reflecting the indirect nature of such investment, a distinction between the "direct debt" of those who borrow to spend the money and the "indirect debt" of financial intermediaries is drawn by Gurley and Shaw.[6] The investor who commits his funds to a savings and loan association can be viewed as buying, indirectly, a share in a diversified portfolio of residential mortgages. Investing in a mutual fund or investment company is equivalent to buying a claim on a diversified portfolio of common stocks, or of stocks and bonds. Offered the opportunity to achieve diversification

[6] J. G. Gurley and E. S. Shaw, "Financial Intermediaries and the Saving-Investment Process," J. Financ., **11**: 257–266 (1956).

in this way and to receive the net yield after the costs and earnings of the financial intermediaries have been deducted from the gross yield, the investor decides to what extent it is worth his while to make use of these services.

Liquidity creation by financial institutions

By a particular use of diversification, financial institutions can create liquidity in the sense of generating financial assets more liquid than the ones held in their own portfolios. This is done in part by diversification among the creditors of the financial institution. When the institution has a very large and diverse group of creditors, such as the savers of a mutual savings bank, it can count on their not all coming in for their money on the same day. Thus, it can offer to pay its obligations on demand, confident that the demands will be rather steady from day to day.

The other use of diversification to create liquidity is primarily a diversification over time to assure that the institution has a steady flow of funds from maturing securities sufficient to meet its possible cash needs. If in each year the institution knows it will only need cash equal to one-tenth of a portfolio, it can invest the funds in 10-year bonds so arranged that one-tenth of them come due each year. By in this way "rolling over" a portfolio of securities—a special case of diversification over time—the institution can enjoy the higher yields of long-term securities while assuring an adequate flow of cash to meet its needs.

Just as there is a limit to the amount of risk reduction that can be accomplished through diversification, and there are administrative costs of doing this, so the possible enhancement of liquidity in this way is limited. Thus, this liquidity creation is rather like physical production, with a limited output and some costs that must be incurred. For any given economy, there is in principle definable an optimal amount of such activity. Within an appropriate legal framework the price system leads to an approximation of this outcome.

Other services of financial institutions

Other services also are included in the packages offered by at least some of the financial institutions. The function of gathering and interpreting information associated with evaluation of investments, the function of investment analysis, is provided by all financial institutions. Many institutions also make kinds of loans involving administrative activities requiring organization and skill, which could not be conducted by individual investors. Examples are loans to businesses, consumer loans, and mortgage loans. These services, of course, not only contribute to the yield available to savers but also are enormously important to the borrowers who depend on these services in order to have access to credit.

Some financial institutions offer specialized services such as the various kinds of insurance, life insurance, fire insurance, and casuality insurance. The administration of pension systems is another complex financial service performed by such institutions. Closely related to this is the administration of annuities. The United States economy and the way of life of the ordinary individual is heavily dependent on the services performed by financial intermediaries.

Financial intermediaries such as savings institutions and mutual funds operate in this way. From the rate of return they can earn on their holdings of assets, they deduct the margin that is needed to cover their operating costs and the required rate of return on their own invested capital. This determines the yield they can offer on their obligations. They stand ready to offer the public as many of their obligations as it wishes to take at this yield—just as the producers of beer offer the public as much as it wishes to buy at a price that covers their costs. Thus, the financial institutions do not operate as a whimsical or erratic element in the economy, but exhibit systematic patterns of behavior just as do other businesses.

Supervision of financial institutions

In an ideal world in which perfect information was available at zero cost, it would be superfluous for the government to impose special regulations or supervision on financial institutions. Those who entrusted their funds to the institutions would make sure that the funds were properly managed and invested. Realistically, however, the individual with some funds in a savings bank cannot be expected to investigate and evaluate the investment policies or the administrative procedures of the organization. The free-market solution to regulating financial institutions is not fully effective because of this knowledge gap. Moreover, mismanagement of a financial institution that led it to fail with substantial losses to the public would impose serious damages upon individuals. Further, such failures could lead to chain reactions and adversely affect the stability of the whole economy. Thus, there are special reasons for government supervision of financial institutions.

The goal of this supervision is one not easily achieved. The institutions should be prevented from failing, but this should be done with minimum side effects and restriction of their activities. If the investment choices of the institutions are unnecessarily restricted, this damages their customers by offering them less attractive yields on their funds. It damages the whole economy by leading to a nonoptimal allocation of investment. Thus, we conceive of an ideal pattern of government supervision that achieves its objectives at minimum costs, but designing such a program is itself a difficult task.

The actual supervision of financial institutions may bear little relation to an idealized rationale for supervision. Regulations reflecting bad economic theory and misinterpretation of the lessons of past failures seem to persist almost indefinitely. Supervisory agencies, once established, often become responsive to the desires of the institutions they nominally regulate and issue regulations that have the effect of protecting the regulated institutions from competition. In the United States, competition among the regulatory agencies themselves has been a major influence in weakening supervision and, in some cases, leading to policies that are difficult to justify in terms of the public interest. Thus, the desirable scope of supervision of financial institutions, its particular form, and the kind of agencies through which it ought to be sought are all subjects of lively discussion in recent years.

Governmental supervision and protection of financial institutions takes five principal forms:

1. Limitations are imposed upon the kinds of assets the institutions can acquire. These are designed to protect against assets of excessive investment risk and insufficient liquidity and to guard against improper activities such as loans to the directors and officers of the institution.
2. Institutions are examined to determine that regulations are being followed and to provide a general scrutiny of the procedures of the institution and the adequacy of its management.
3. For the savings-type institutions, the government provides insurance systems protecting creditors from loss up to a certain maximum amount. For commercial banks and mutual savings banks, such insurance is provided by the Federal Deposit Insurance Corporation. For savings and loan associations, it is provided by the Federal Savings and Loan Insurance Corporation.
4. Again primarily for the savings institutions, the government provides some support in the form of assured access to credit by the institutions. Member banks of the Federal Reserve System have access to credit from Federal Reserve banks, and nonmember banks benefit indirectly from this in terms of their ability to borrow from their correspondent banks. The Federal Home Loan Bank System provides a similar service to savings and loan associations.
5. Limitations by regulatory agencies on the maximum interest rate that can be paid on their obligations apply to most of the savings institutions. Such regulation is said to protect the institutions from being forced by competition among themselves to pay such high interest rates that the weaker institutions fail or that institutions in general are forced into unduly risky assets in an effort to earn enough to cover these high interest rates.

Limitations imposed on the interest rates that savings institutions can offer have important side effects, however, and have been subjected to considerable criticism in recent years. Unless they are changed frequently to keep the maximum permitted interest rate in line with interest rates in the money markets, they promote large flows of funds into and out of the institutions, which are disruptive both to the institutions and to those borrowers who depend upon them for credit. During periods of economic expansion and high interest rates, yields on liquid assets in the money market rise rapidly. Savings institutions probably could not match this rise in any case, since their earnings depend in part upon longer term debt, the yields on which are less volatile, and on debt acquired earlier at lower levels of interest rates. However, government limitations on the interest rates that savings institutions can offer aggravate the outflow of funds from institutions that takes place under these circumstances and the starvation for credit of certain borrowers—especially housing and the mortgage market—to which this gives rise.

SUMMARY

1. The demand of individuals to hold financial assets and other wealth arises in part from their life cycle of financial positions. This stems from people's efforts to maximize the satisfactions derived from their lifetime pattern of opportunities for income earning and for consumption. The purposes for which they hold financial assets also affect the particular properties people desire in these assets.

2. The rate of return on investments is usually measured by investment yield. This is the discount rate that makes the expected future payments from the asset equal to its cost. The long-term interest rate is usually measured by the yield on long-term bonds.

3. The risk characteristics of investment assets can be represented by estimated probability distributions of their outcomes. Risky or low-grade assets have a wide probability distribution of outcomes. The most common measure of investment risk is the variance of the probability distribution of outcomes. The expected value of an investment is the sum of each possible outcome times its estimated probability. Illiquidity in an asset relates to its risk when liquidated on short notice.

4. A decision rule for the rational investor is, Choose the investment (or the investment portfolio) that maximizes your expected utility. Investors who are risk avoiders, which is the usual case, are willing to give up some expected yield in order to limit risk.

5. Investment risk can be reduced through diversification, where the risks of particular investments are random, or they can be assigned to classes, permitting the choice of assets with negatively correlated outcomes.

6. Financial intermediaries provide risk reduction, liquidity creation, and other financial services. Since their services have a limited demand

and involve costs, the activities of financial intermediaries are governed by the same kind of constraints as other productive activities.

QUESTIONS FOR REVIEW AND DISCUSSION

1. Define different life-cycle financial patterns that might apply to people in different circumstances. Consider the life pattern of changes in the types of assets the person would want to hold in each case.

2. A contract provides for the following payments: $50 in 1 year, $50 in 2 years, and $1,050 in 3 years. What is the promised yield of the contract if purchased at a price of $1,000? What is the present value of the contract at a discount rate of 2½ percent?

3. Explain the relation between the change in price required to bring about the same change in yield of a 1-year bond and a 20-year bond.

4. Draw illustrative probability distributions of the outcomes of the following investments: a horse-race bet, an oil-well speculation, a high-grade common stock, a low-grade bond, a risk-free bond, and a risk-free bond that is to be sold in the market on short notice.

5. What is the expected yield of an asset that has the following probabilities of alternative yields: 10 percent, Pr .20; 5 percent, Pr .60; 0 percent, Pr .10; and minus 10 percent, Pr .10? What is the variance of this probability distribution?

6. Define the possible sources of liquidity in an asset. Discuss some illustrations of very liquid and illiquid assets, pointing out the characteristics of each asset that determine its liquidity status.

7. Show with a diagram that the choice of an investor between two assets involving different yields and different degrees of risk depends on the shape of his utility curve.

8. Define the decision rule applied by the rational investor making a choice with incomplete knowledge. Illustrate how this same kind of decision rule could be applied to other problems of choice with incomplete knowledge.

9. Show with a diagram how diversification can reduce risk in an investment portfolio. Define the kind of knowledge that is needed for effective diversification. Think of some pairs of investments that would go well together in diversified portfolios.

10. Show how financial intermediaries are able to reduce risk and increase liquidity. If they can do this, why is it that risk and illiquidity are not entirely eliminated from the portfolios of investors?

11. List the principal forms of supervision of financial institutions. Indicate why supervision in practice may have undesirable side effects.

5
the United States financial system

This chapter discusses the functions of the financial system and gives a quantitative picture of the size and structure of the United States financial system and the flows of funds through it. It also reviews the major institutions of the United States financial system, the way each operates, its role in the economy, and the regulatory authorities that define the rules under which it operates.

Functions of the Financial System

Many of the institutions and activities of the advanced economy do not directly contribute to the production or the consumption of goods and services. Rather, they involve the creation and distribution of paper assets: stocks, bonds, mortgages, and other securities. Included are many types of financial institutions: savings banks, life insurance companies, mutual funds, and commercial banks. Also included are financial markets: the stock market, the bond market, the money market, and other over-the-counter securities markets. This sector of the economy we term "the financial system." Commercial banks belong to the financial system, playing a central and many-sided role. This section deals with the commercial banks as one element in the financial system. The special significance of the commercial banks as an element in the nation's monetary system is considered in Part 2 of this book.

To interpret the financial system and evaluate its performance requires an understanding of its functions in the economy. With reference to the allocation of resources and economic efficiency, the financial system performs three major functions: It facilitates the formation of productive capital. It contributes to an effective allocation of capital among competing uses. It provides to consumers services that increase the satisfaction they derive from their lifetime income.

The performance of the financial system also affects the stability of the economy.

The financial system and the formation of productive capital

A crucial difference between countries with high and low standards of living is that the economically effective countries have a large stock of productive capital: factories, roads, railroads, buildings, warehouses, and inventories of goods in process. One important reason for this difference is that the effective economy has a financial system that offers people the chance conveniently and safely to own a share in productive wealth, while in the less successful economy the institutions do not exist to give people this opportunity.

Just as is true of the physical aspects of production, the efficient formation of productive capital involves specialization, a complex differentiation of roles and functions among individuals and organizations. The potential ability of the society to accumulate productive capital can be fully tapped only through institutions that permit each person to make his maximum contribution.

The job of providing productive capital can be divided into five elements:

1. The provision of resources through saving, or through income earned and made available for the acquisition of capital goods.
2. Bearing the risk of loss if the investment does not work out as planned and the resources are lost.
3. Bearing illiquidity, in the sense of holding investment assets that cannot be changed into money on short notice without the risk of substantial loss.
4. Carrying out the administrative tasks involved in providing funds for the acquisition of real capital, collecting payments, supervising the carrying out of contractual agreements, and taking legal action where required.
5. Providing the knowledge, analysis, foresight, and imagination involved in effective choices as to what kinds of investment will be productive and what kinds will be sterile or wasteful.

The potentialities of division of labor are obvious. Some savers can provide funds to finance capital goods only if they are not called upon to perform any of the other functions—are offered the chance to invest in risk-free, liquid assets involving no administrative burdens and requiring no considerable knowledge or analysis. Other individuals can provide knowledge and foresight along with their funds and are able to take the risk of loss that must go along with the choice function. Organizations can be set up to handle administrative functions, so long as the institutional structure provides the means for them to cover their costs. Organizations also can gather information; can provide analysis and, to some extent, foresight; and, to a degree, can reduce the risk and illiquidity of securities.

The many kinds of securities created by the financial system perform the function of carving up the five elements in the task of providing productive capital into many different kinds of combination packages to suit the abilities of various kinds of investors. Securities, financial markets, and financial institutions constitute the machinery that permits specialization and efficiency in the economy's capital-formation function.[1]

The allocative function of the financial system

In the process of aiding in the formation of capital, the financial system also contributes to deciding just how the capital is to be used. Who does, and who does not, get a chance to go ahead with his business or consumption project? No veto will be exercised by sellers or builders of factories by sellers of raw materials, or by potential workers, so long as they believe they will be paid for what they sell. To judge whether the purpose for which their goods or services are being bought is wise or foolish is not their function.

The veto, rather, must come from the suppliers of funds, those who would buy stock in his undertaking or would lend funds for it. A reason for this is that the suppliers of funds assume a residual position, being the ones who will bear most of the loss if the venture is unsuccessful.

It is reasonable that the suppliers of funds should be cast in this role. The funds must be provided by those who can take a chance on losing them. For the risk of loss from failing investment projects and the choice as to which projects are to go forward to be taken by the providers of funds is an element in the system of purposive specialization or role differentiation that is the basic theme of the financial system.

If the financial system makes poor choices in deciding which economic projects are to be embarked upon, this leads to waste of resources. Economic progress implies increasing efficiency in economic activity, which requires successful innovation. This implies that investors must finance new activities that prove to be successes rather than failures. The process of economic advancement over time is one in which each successful step opens up opportunities for additional steps, a process of interacting learning and exploration over time. The better the quality of judgment exercised in innovatory investment, the smaller the proportion of failures and the more rapid economic progress will be.

Services of the financial system to individuals

The timing of his ability to buy goods and services is very important to the consumer. Acquiring a house at age sixty is in human terms not

[1]A formal analysis of this function of securities is given in Kenneth J. Arrow, "The Role of Securities in the Optimal Allocation of Risk-bearing," Rev. Econ. Stud., (1)**31**: 91–96 (1964).

at all the same thing as acquiring it at age twenty-five. Medical services are needed when they are needed and not when one has some spare income. An intangible part of the output that the economy provides to the consumer is his ability to control the timing of his expenditures, to get things when he wants or needs them.

To make expenditures before income to pay for them has been earned requires access to credit. Home ownership at a young age, such as prevails in the United States, depends on a system for the provision of mortgage credit that does not exist in most countries. Similarly, the prevalence of ownership of automobiles and other consumer durable goods is dependent upon elaborate institutions, in which the United States was the pioneering society, for the provision of consumer credit.

The other kind of transfer of wealth over time involves the holding of wealth after it is earned for later spending. This may include reserves for contingencies such as medical emergencies, funds acquired for special purposes such as the education of children, funds for living after working age or for retirement, and funds for bequests. In meeting these needs, the consumer's interests are served by being able to choose from among a variety of investment outlets those suited to his particular needs.

In an undeveloped financial system, the individual may have to hold his wealth in the form of gold or jewelry, running a chance that these will be stolen. In some countries the poor hold their limited wealth in the form of money that is depreciating in value, earning them a negative rate of return. The effective financial system offers the individual opportunities to hold wealth in forms that are secure and convenient, and that pay him a positive rate of return. Moreover, the holding of wealth in liquid forms confers upon the holder the ability to spend on short notice without incurring a loss. That is, it confers upon him a flexibility that is valuable in an uncertain world. The availability of these services of the financial system contributes importantly, if in an intangible way, to the satisfactions of consumers.

The financial system and the behavior of total demand

The role of the financial system as an influence on total demand can be represented in a diagram depicting the flow of expenditures and income through the economy, as in Fig. 5-1. Money income—mainly a flow of checkbook money—is paid from producing units to providers of labor and other inputs. Running in the other direction, but not shown in the diagram, is a flow of productive services for which the money income is the payment.

Recipients of income spend most of it themselves for goods and services. Some of what is not spent may be held in the form of money, to build up their cash balances. This results in a slowing down of the expenditures income stream. But people also can spend more money than they take in by reducing their cash balance, which tends to increase the expenditures-income flow. For people to reduce their cash balances tends to increase

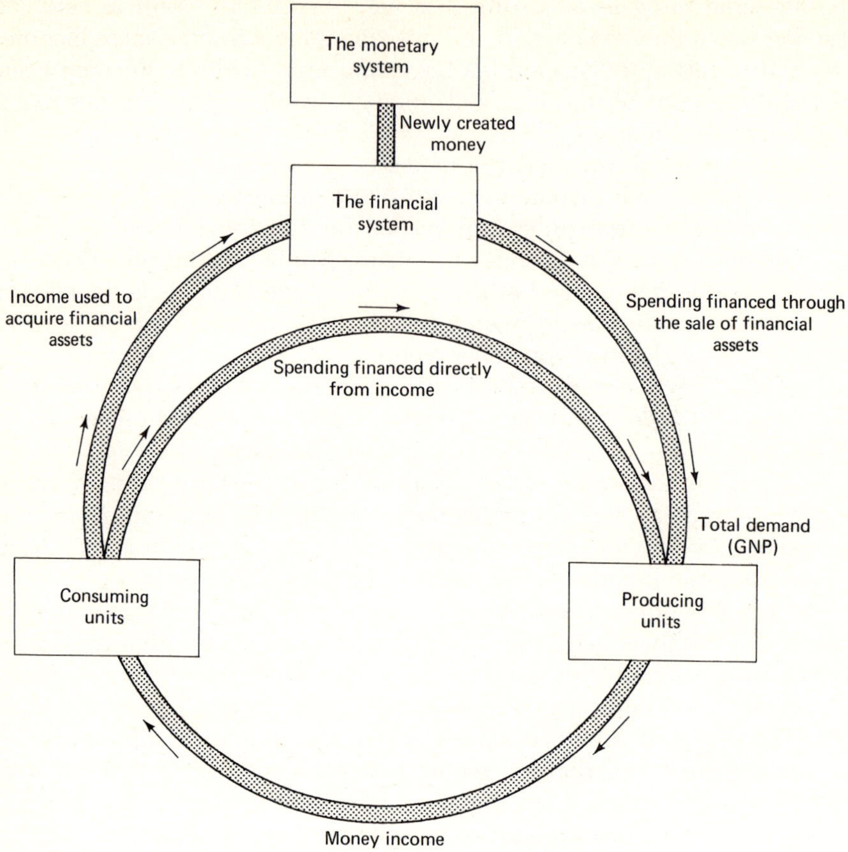

Fig. 5-1 The financial system in the expenditures-income flow.

the velocity of circulation of money, while for them to build up their cash balances reduces velocity of circulation.

Money income that is not spent for goods and services usually is not held as cash but is used to acquire a financial asset that earns income, such as a security or a savings account. By acquiring such financial assets the saver channels the flow of money into the financial system. His flow of dollars shows up not in the grocery store, but in the savings bank or the government securities market. In this case, the dollars are not lost to the expenditures-income flow but only channeled through an indirect loop. After flowing through whatever financial institutions or markets are involved, the money ordinarily is put into the hands of someone who borrows it to spend. Therefore, this flow of money finances the expenditures not of the person who earned the income but rather of the person to whom the money indirectly is made available through the financial system.

The rechanneling of funds does not involve any drain or loss from the expenditures-income flow. Thus, it does not pose any problem for the behavior of total demand, so long as the process goes on smoothly. If financial institutions engaged in erratic hoarding of money this would tend to cause erratic variation in total demand, but it is the same kind of effect that would result from erratic hoarding by anyone else in the economy. In fact, financial institutions are but little inclined to behave in this manner.

Rather than having a destabilizing or erratic influence upon total demand, a highly developed financial system may play a stabilizing role. Let us assume that some income-receiving units are erratic in their behavior, occasionally wanting to change their saving rate. If this leads them to change their holdings of money, the action will lead to changes in total demand and contribute to economic instability. The monetary system in principle could offset these variations in total demand by injecting an amount of newly created money just sufficient to offset the hoarding, if the monetary authority had the necessary information. Or the monetary system if it operated in a stabilizing manner could respond quickly to the change in total demand with an offsetting change in the money supply. But such monetary systems may be difficult to bring about and have not been common in the past.

But where the financial system provides attractive outlets for temporarily idle funds, the erratic saver is likely to channel his additional savings into liquid securities or a savings account. Then the funds will automatically be passed on through the financial pipeline and finance the spending of someone else, thus minimizing the disturbing effects of his variability in spending.

This stabilizing function is performed by the financial system of the United States on an important scale. During a recession, for example, businesses reduce their expenditures for inventories and for new plant and equipment. If the funds they diverted from these purposes sat idle, this would tend to aggravate the economic decline. In practice, however, businesses channel most of the funds thus freed into the financial system by acquiring liquid assets and by repaying their own debts. Thus the funds become available to finance other kinds of spending for final output.

The financial system and liquidity conditions

Another way the financial system affects the behavior of total demand is by affecting the quantity of liquid assets. Since liquid assets can be used to some extent to replace holdings of money, an increase in the supply of liquid assets may induce the public to reduce its holdings of money in relation to expenditures, thus increasing velocity. The time pattern with which the financial system creates and extinguishes liquid assets thus affects the behavior of total demand and the stability of the economy. The United States financial system commonly varies the quantity of liquid assets it creates in such a manner as to limit economic fluctuations, as we note in Chap. 23.

A final way in which the financial system affects total demand is by affecting expectations and financial practices. The wave of bullish speculation and unrealistically optimistic expectations associated with the stock market boom of the latter 1920s had an expansive effect on the economy. The abrupt reversal of this situation after 1929 contributed to the severity of the Great Depression. A financial system that contributed less enthusiastically to this swing in expectations and financial practices would have resulted in a better performance of the economy.

The United States Financial System

The total volume of credit market claims outstanding in the United States at the end of 1970 amounted to nearly $2½ trillion (Table 5-1) almost three times the size of the nation's gross national product in 1970. Looking first at the source of these securities, at the borrowing side of the market, the largest single item is outstanding corporate stock, worth $864 billion at current market value. This figure was less by $120 billion than it was 2 years earlier, reflecting the large-scale extinction of wealth (at market value) by the decline in the stock market. Adding debt claims against corporate and noncorporate business yields a figure of $1,350 billion for claims against business. Thus more than one-half of the total credit market claims outstanding originated in businesses that are mainly nonfinancial. The table shows, however, that households, governments, and financial institutions are also important creators of financial claims.

Turning to see who holds these securities, we find that the greatest single holder, accounting for about four-tenths of the total, is households. In addition to the funds supplied through thus holding securities directly, households are the ultimate source of most of the funds provided through

TABLE 5-1 United States Credit Market Claims Outstanding, December 31, 1970 (in billions of dollars)

Credit Market Debt Owed		Credit Market Claims Held as Assets	
Households	$ 461.6	Households	$ 967.9
Corporate nonfinancial business	363.4	Commercial banks	432.5
Federal government	301.4	Life insurance companies	188.5
State and local governments	148.2	Savings and loan associations	164.4
Noncorporate business	124.5	Private pension funds	101.4
Finance companies	55.9	Mutual savings banks	76.0
Foreign	50.8	Federal Reserve System	62.2
Investment companies	47.6	Open-end investment companies	46.9
Other debt	57.8	Federal government	56.9
Plus: corporate stock at market value	864.0	Corporate nonfinancial business	61.5
		Other	317.0
Total	$2,475.2	Total	$2,475.2

SOURCE: Board of Governors of the Federal Reserve System.

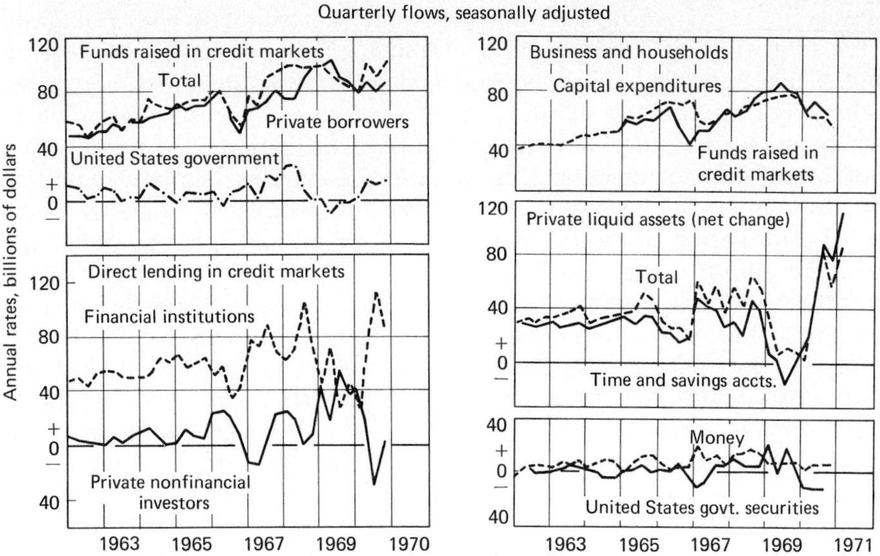

Fig. 5-2 Flow of funds through credit markets. (Board of Governors of the Federal Reserve System.)

financial institutions. The securities held by the federal government are largely related to social security and pension systems and thus involve funds held on behalf of individuals.

A rough picture of short-run changes in financial flows is provided by Fig. 5-2. This depicts not the *stock* of securities that are in existence at a point in time but the *flow* of funds through the credit markets during each period of time. The volume of funds raised in credit markets during a period of time is equal to the *increase* in the volume of securities outstanding. Accordingly, Fig. 5-2 shows the variation in the rate of growth of the economy's outstanding stock of certain kinds of securities.

One point made in Fig. 5-2 is that the rate of flow of funds through the credit markets varies considerably from year to year and is closely tied in with changes in business conditions. The chart shows the flow for each quarter, or 3-month period, stated at an annual rate. This shows what the rate would be if it continued unchanged for 1 year, and is derived by multiplying the seasonally adjusted quarterly figure by 4.

In late 1966, when an inflationary business situation was being checked by a restrictive monetary policy, the rate at which businesses were raising funds in credit markets dropped for a time by an annual rate of more than $20 billion. Then when monetary policy again became expansive and total demand again rose rapidly, funds raised by business went back up to new highs. In late 1969, the game was replayed, as a reduction in funds flowing through the credit markets accompanied a move to a restrictive monetary policy and a less expansive business situation.

The other point to be emphasized here is that variations in the flow of funds through financial institutions seem to occur inphase with variations in the total flow of funds through credit markets, but on an even larger scale. Thus, in 1969 lending by financial institutions declined more than total funds raised, being partially offset by a large increase in funds lent directly by private nonfinancial investors. This pattern of events arises in part from a factor discussed in Chap. 4, the existing regulations on the maximum interest rates permitted on the obligations of financial institutions. In a period of rapidly rising total demand and inflationary conditions, the strong demand of businesses and others for credit drives up interest rates in the credit markets. Since financial institutions are unable to increase the rates offered on their obligations to keep pace with the increase in interest rates in the credit markets, their obligations become relatively less attractive to the public. Therefore, the public pulls its funds out of savings institutions and invests them directly in securities. This illustrates the interconnectedness of the flows through credit markets and the way in which they are influenced by the regulations applying to financial institutions.

A final factual point to be drawn from Fig. 5-2 is the importance of the federal government as a factor contributing to variations in the funds available to private borrowers. We note within a year, in 1968, a shift at an annual rate of more than $20 billion in the funds being taken from the credit markets by the federal government, a change that looms large in relation to other shifts in flows through credit markets. This shift reflected the change in fiscal policy, or policy towards federal government receipts and expenditures, that was reflected in the imposition of the income tax surtax in 1968.

Another way to look at the financial system is in terms of the composition of the funds flowing through the system in a given year. In this case, we focus on the sources of the funds that are channeled into the financial system and the identity of those who take up these funds and use them. We have seen that these flows of funds vary a good deal from year to year, so the pattern that prevailed in 1970 is not necessarily typical of other years. Several groups appear on both sides of Table 5-2, both supplying and demanding funds. Business borrowing in 1970 comprised about half of the total funds raised. Households and governments also were large borrowers of funds.

Among direct sources of funds, we note the large contribution of funds invested directly by households and the large additional amount invested through savings institutions and insurance companies. The contribution of the Federal Reserve System and a part of that of commercial banks—that associated with demand deposits—constitute funds advanced to the credit markets from newly created money, as distinct from funds derived from savings. In the past, variation in the growth rate of the money supply has made this an unstable component of funds advanced. Indicating the instability of their role in the financial system, the commercial banks

TABLE 5-2 **Funds Raised and Advanced in United States Credit Markets: 1970 (in billions of dollars)**

Funds Raised		Funds Advanced	
United States government	$12.8	United States government and agencies	$ 4.4
Foreign	2.6	Federal Reserve System	5.0
State and local governments	12.2	Commercial banks, net	31.3
Households	21.1	Savings institutions	14.7
Corporate nonfinancial business	38.7	Insurance	24.9
Nonfarm noncorporate business	6.2	Other financial business	−0.3
Farm business	3.2	Foreign	10.9
Total	$96.9	Nonfinancial business	−1.0
		State and local governments	−3.8
		Households	9.5
		Less net security credit	−1.4
		Total	$96.9

SOURCE: Board of Governors of the Federal Reserve System.

advanced in credit markets about $31 billion in 1970 and $40 billion in 1968, but only $12 billion in 1969.

Financial Instruments, and Funds Raised, by Sector

While all credit involves the exchange of money *now* for money *later*, actual credit dealings can be classified in a number of ways. First, we are interested in mapping the flows among different classes of borrowers or sectors of the economy, in defining who finances whom. This we consider below.

We also are interested in classifying credit dealings according to a number of characteristics of the credit instrument. Thus, we may distinguish between debt instruments involving no specific security and those involving *collateral* in the form of securities, goods in inventory, goods in shipment, real estate, and so on. We also distinguish between debt contracts that can be sold by their holder and those that cannot, or marketable and nonmarketable securities. A subcategory of salable credit instruments is those that are negotiable instruments in the legal sense that the "holder in due course" possesses a perfect title to the instrument irrespective of the conditions under which it was obtained by prior holders. This provision facilitates multiple exchanges of such instruments by freeing such dealings of the investigations of titles that otherwise would be required.

Debt instruments also are classified by their term to maturity, this being relevant to liquidity considerations as discussed above. Finally, there are certain well-defined forms of credit instruments with which it is useful to be familiar: bonds, notes, bills, bills of exchange, and so on. A final distinction is between debts, which promise to pay a fixed sum of money, and equity instruments such as common stock that promise only a proportionate interest in a business. In actual practice, we find also a variety of intermediate instruments such as various kinds of preferred stocks that are like debts in promising a return limited to a stipulated dividend, but differ from them in that the prerogatives of the creditor in the event of nonpayment of dividends are more limited than in the case of nonpayment of interest or principal on debts.

Another hybrid instrument is the convertible bond. This provides the holder with an option to convert into common stock on stipulated terms. These bonds offer the holder the protections of a debt instrument but the opportunity of sharing in the success of the business if things go very well that attaches to common stock. Another hybrid instrument is income bonds that pay interest only when earnings permit this. Our present subject does not take us into a description of these instruments. We limit ourselves to mapping the structure of financial claims and characterizing major classes of credit instruments by which the various sectors of the economy are financed.

Business finance

The general picture of the financing transactions of corporate (nonfinancial) businesses is indicated in Table 5-3. Corporations as a whole, as well as individual corporations, both acquired additional financial assets during 1970 and borrowed additional funds from the credit markets. The accumulation of liquid assets by corporations in 1970 was modest, but note the large shift that occurred within this category. Corporate treasurers were shifting their liquid assets into time deposits, reversing an opposite swing in 1969, as yields on open market liquid assets fell below those on time deposits. Trade credit is mainly open-book credit extended by corporations to their customers. Since corporations also buy from one another, trade

TABLE 5-3 Financial Transactions of Nonfinancial Corporate Business: 1970 (in billions of dollars)

Net Acquisition of Financial Assets		
Cash		$ 0.2
Liquid assets		9.9
Time deposits	$12.8	
United States government securities	−3.2	
Open market paper	−1.1	
State and local obligations	1.4	
Consumer credit		1.4
Trade credit		6.2
Other financial assets		3.7
Total		$21.4

Net Increase in Liabilities	
Corporate bonds	$20.3
Corporate stock	6.8
Mortgages	5.2
Bank loans	1.2
Other loans	5.2
Profit tax liability	1.1
Trade debt	5.5
Other liabilities	3.1
Total	$48.3

Net financial investment $−27.0

SOURCE: Board of Governors of the Federal Reserve System.

TABLE 5-4 Financial Transactions of Households, Personal Trusts, and Nonprofit Organizations: 1970 (in billions of dollars)

Net Acquisition of Financial Assets		Net Increase in Liabilities	
Cash	$ 3.5	Home mortgages	$12.0
Savings accounts	32.2	Other mortgages	1.4
Life insurance reserves	4.9	Installment consumer credit	3.0
Pension fund reserves	18.6	Other consumer credit	1.3
United States government securities	−0.2	Bank loans	0.8
State and local obligations	−1.5	Other loans	2.6
Corporate and foreign bonds	12.0	Security credit	−1.9
Investment company shares	2.4	Trade debt	0.6
Other corporate shares	−5.2	Miscellaneous	0.4
Mortgages	2.0	Total	$20.2
Investment in noncorporate business	−2.4		
Security credit	−0.5		
Miscellaneous	2.5		
Total	$68.3		
Net financial investment $48.2			

SOURCE: Board of Governors of the Federal Reserve System.

debt shows up as a corresponding increase in liabilities during 1970.

If these were the forms in which corporations were putting funds into the credit markets in 1970, in what forms were they supplying debt or taking funds out of the credit market? Corporate bonds and stock and mortgage loans were the largest items. Corporate stock does not provide a large part of the funds raised by corporations, but it plays a crucial role in the system because of its relation to control of the business and its function in providing a preferred position to creditors.

Corporate businesses took more funds out of the credit markets than they put into them. With reference to this set of transactions, corporations were net borrowers to the extent of $27 billion in 1970. We should expect, of course, that households would be net savers and businesses net borrowers of funds.

Noncorporate nonfarm businesses also are net borrowers of funds, to the extent of $5.3 billion in 1970. These businesses do not issue bonds but borrow much more largely than corporations on the basis of mortgages. They rely also upon loans from banks and other financial institutions.

Financial transactions of households

Households (including personal trusts and nonprofit organizations) were net contributors of funds to financial markets to the extent of $48 billion in 1970 (See Table 5–4). The acquisitions of financial assets by households are diverse, including cash, savings accounts and other liquid assets (not shown separately here), and direct and indirect provision of funds to a number of types of borrower. We note the substantial amount of funds of households channeled through financial institutions, investment companies, life insurance companies, pension funds, and savings institutions. Acquisitions of savings accounts by households were much larger in 1970 than in 1969, $32 billion compared with $13 billion, reflecting the shift in the relative attractiveness of time deposits and other liquid assets. Individuals also are substantial direct investors in mortgages, corporate bonds, obligations of state and local governments, and United States government securities. In recent years, individuals have been shifting out of direct ownership of common stock, which has been taken up by financial institutions.

Households also are large borrowers of funds. By far the largest item is borrowing on home mortgages to finance home ownership. Borrowing on consumer installment credit is usually larger than it was in 1970. With reference to the financial transactions included in the table, households took about $20 billion out of the credit markets and put $68 billion into them, being net providers of funds to the amount of $48 billion in 1970, almost twice as much as in 1969.

Financial transactions of governmental units

The financial transactions of the federal government are highly variable from year to year because of the discontinuous nature of changes in governmental expenditures programs and in tax rates. The fiscal policy leading to this outcome is discussed below in Chap. 22. The kinds of securities sold by the government and the techniques by which they are sold are covered in Chap. 23.

State and local governments characteristically are net borrowers from the financial markets, primarily to finance construction projects and other capital outlays. The borrowing demands of state and local governments also are quite variable from year to year, their net financial investment in recent years has averaged around minus $5 billion. State and local governments borrow on their own securities in the debt markets, using both long-term and short-term securities. They also negotiate some loans directly with financial institutions.

Financial Institutions

A broad picture of the scale of operations of financial institutions in the United States economy is provided by Table 5-5. Although these financial institutions are in many ways diverse, their central role is to raise funds by offering to lenders financial obligations attractive to them and then to pass the funds on by lending them to borrowers to whom the financial institutions can provide financial services. In this role, the financial institutions are middlemen, or intermediaries, taking the savings of individuals, and to some extent of businesses, and passing them on to borrowers.

Because of this status as a financial middleman, we expect financial

TABLE 5-5 **Financial Transactions of Nonbank Financial Institutions: 1970 ($ billions)**

Net Acquisition of Financial Assets		Net Increase in Liabilities	
Cash	$ 1.3	Time and savings accounts	$17.2
Savings and loan shares	0.7	Insurance and pension reserves	21.0
United States government securities	3.7	Finance company bonds	2.5
State and local obligations	1.4	Investment company shares	2.4
Corporate and foreign bonds	10.6	Other loans	1.3
Corporate stocks	11.4	Security credit	1.2
Home mortgages	7.1	Taxes payable	0.2
Other mortgages	8.6	Miscellaneous liabilities	5.8
Consumer credit	0.6	Total	$51.6
Other loans	4.8		
Security credit	−1.4		
Trade credit	0.4		
Miscellaneous assets	2.6		
Total	$51.7		

SOURCE: Board of Governors of the Federal Reserve System. Includes savings and loan associations, mutual savings banks, credit unions, life insurance companies, private pension funds, state and local government employee retirement funds, other insurance companies, finance companies, security brokers and dealers, open-end investment companies, and agencies of foreign banks.

institutions to raise in credit markets about the same amount of money that they put back into them. In 1970, financial institutions thus served as middlemen on a flow of about $50 billion. The assets in which these funds are invested and the borrowers to whom they are channeled span a wide range, some institutions being quite specialized in their investing activities and others operating over a broad front. We note that financial institutions were large investors in corporate stocks, picking up these investments as individuals have been shifting out of them in recent years. Mortgages, bonds, consumer credit, and other loans all are numbered among the assets of financial institutions.

The operations by which financial institutions raise their funds and the kinds of financial obligations they create generally involve specialization. The savings institutions create savings accounts and other liquid assets; the life insurance companies and pension funds assume liabilities under life insurance policies and pension systems; investment companies sell a distinctive kind of share in their operations; and finance companies commonly borrow on loans and open market paper very similar to that used by nonfinancial businesses. In view of this diversity, we shall briefly review the characteristics of the leading financial institutions.

Savings institutions

Savings institutions are those that provide a form of liquid asset to individuals (and in some cases to other classes of economic unit) on the basis of their holdings of financial assets. Such institutions are characterized by the kinds of liabilities that they create—the liquid assets of their customers—and the principal classes of asset that they hold. The institutions included are mutual savings banks, the time-deposit activities of commercial banks, savings and loan associations, and credit unions.

Mutual savings banks are a typical savings institution. Their liabilities consist almost entirely of savings deposits. Although these have the same label as the "deposits" of commercial banks, they are not transferable by check and are not therefore a medium of exchange or a part of the money supply. Although mutual savings banks are under no legal obligation to redeem deposits in cash on demand, customarily this is done. These deposits, therefore, are a highly liquid asset.

Mutual savings banks pay interest on their deposits. The rate paid depends upon the size of the account and the conditions under which it can be withdrawn. Mutual savings banks insured by the Federal Deposit Insurance Corporation are subject to regulation by that agency on the maximum interest rates they can pay on their deposits. During 1969, this maximum rate was 5 percent, and the high levels of interest rates in the credit markets were causing funds to be withdrawn from mutual savings banks. In early 1970, the maximum rates permitted by the FDIC were increased to a range of from 5 to 7½ percent for various types of deposits. In 1969, the earnings of savings banks on their portfolios amounted to a rate of return of just over 6 percent in relation to deposits, and the interest they paid out amounted to just under 5 percent, leaving a spread of just over one percentage point to cover costs, additions to reserves, and income available to be paid out. Operating expenses amounted to about ¾ percent in relation to deposits.

Mutual savings banks have no owners but are run on behalf of the members rather than being operated in the manner of an ordinary business. Therefore, the liabilities side of their balance sheet does not show the usual capital stock and surplus but rather reserve accounts that in an ongoing institution have been built up from prior earnings. These play the usual role of owner equity in providing a cushion against losses.

The flow of money channeled to the mutual savings banks by individuals (and nonprofit institutions, their only other customers) are currently invested largely in mortgage loans. Second in importance are corporate and other bonds. Because of a favorable position under the federal income tax, mutual savings banks do not value so highly as some other investors the exemption from federal taxes that attaches to state and municipal securities and therefore hold practically none of these. Their holdings of United States government securities serve mutual savings banks largely in the role of liquid assets, or secondary-reserve assets.

In broad terms, the mutual savings banks take the savings of individuals and channel these primarily into mortgage loans, the borrowers predominantly being other individuals. The associations are liquidity-creating institutions, their deposits being to their holders assets much more liquid than the loans and securities held by the associations. This liquidity creation is accomplished by making use of the law of large numbers, through application of the principle of pooling and diversification. Other services of the associations are the development of information regarding loans and investments, the application of judgment and analysis in the selection of these, and paper work in connection with the making and servicing of loans as well as in connection with the administration of deposits. Deposits of mutual savings banks at the end of 1970 amounted to nearly $72 billion.

Mutual savings banks are chartered under state law, and are limited mainly to certain Eastern states, three-quarters of such banks being located in New York, Pennsylvania, and Connecticut. Savings banks can elect to become members of the Federal Reserve System and also may apply to have their deposits insured by the Federal Deposit Insurance Corporation. Most savings banks are insured by the FDIC or by other systems that exist in certain states. Savings banks are subject to supervision by the banking authorities of the state and by the Federal Reserve System and FDIC if they become members of these systems.

In principle, the activities of commercial banks as savings institutions are very similar to those of mutual savings banks. As savings institutions, the commercial banks offer several kinds of deposits. The "savings accounts" that are familiar to individuals are very similar to those of mutual savings banks. In addition, commercial banks offer time deposits, open account, and time certificates of deposit. The last are made available not only to individuals but also to businesses and governmental units. The CDs are issued in a number of maturities, all of them short, the interest rate paid being related to the term to maturity. In some cases, they are negotiable and can be sold in the market. Commercial banks in their savings activities offer a wider range of liquid assets and deal with a wider range of customers than other financial institutions. The scale of their activities is very great. Commercial bank time deposits at the end of 1970 amounted to about $230 billion.

In principle, certain of the assets of commercial banks could be associated with their time deposits and their activities as savings institutions, and others against their demand-deposit activities. In practice, commercial banks do not thus segregate their assets. Thus, there is no basis for defining the particular kinds of activities that are financed by the savings operations of commercial banks as distinct from their other activities. Chartering and supervision of commercial banks are discussed in Chap. 6.

Savings and loan associations are similar to mutual savings banks in their role in the financial system. Most such associations are organized on a mutual basis rather than being owned by a separate group of stockholders. The liabilities of the associations to their members go under a variety of labels, commonly being termed "savings accounts." These are not legally redeemable upon demand, but in practice are customarily so redeemed. The assets of savings and loan associations consist almost entirely of mortgages. Savings and loan associations are about twice as large as mutual savings banks, their liabilities on savings capital amounting to $147 billion at the end of 1970.

Savings and loan associations are organized under both federal and state charters. They are limited by their charters to home-mortgage loans. A federal agency exists specifically to insure the obligations of savings and loan associations, the Federal Savings and Loan Insurance Corporation. Federally chartered associations must be insured by this organization, and state chartered ones can apply for such insurance. The federal government also provides in the Federal Home Loan Bank System an organization paralleling the Federal Reserve System, which federally chartered associations must join and others may join.

The Federal Home Loan Bank Board, located in Washington, D.C., is the chartering and regulatory authority for the federal associations. The twelve regional Federal Home Loan banks make advances to member associations on the collateral of mortgages, raising the funds by selling in the capital markets (and thus acting as an intermediary for an intermediary) FHLB obligations. In 1969, the Federal Home Loan banks increased their advances to member associations by about $4 billion, from about $5 billion to $9 billion, raising the money in the capital markets. This reflected efforts to protect the mortgage market and the housing industry from the effects of the restrictive credit conditions that developed in that year.

Credit unions differ from other savings institutions in that the membership commonly is limited to the members of an organization or the employees of a business and in that the loans of the institution are largely made to its members in the form of mortgage loans and consumer loans.

Institutions for nonliquid investment by individuals

We should expect to find within the financial system a set of financial institutions that parallel the savings institutions but that offer nonliquid and, in some cases, lower grade obligations with a higher promised yield. The prototype of such an institution is the investment company. This holds some or all of its assets in the form of common stock. It offers an equity instrument that derives some safety and liquidity from the pooling and diversification practiced by the investment company as well as from the compilation of information and investment analysis by the professional staff of the company. Assets of investment companies amounted to nearly $50 billion at the end of 1970. They have grown rapidly, increasing nearly sixfold in the prior 12 years. Because of the decline in the stock market, however, assets of investment companies declined about $5 billion, or 10 percent, from the end of 1968 to the end of 1970.

Related services are provided by investment trusts and by the trust departments operated by many commercial banks. Through these and investment counseling firms, informational and analytical services in investing can be purchased, without the pooling aspect. The common (or nonsegregated) trust funds operated by commercial banks are very similar in function to open-end investment companies.

Insurance companies and pension systems

Yet another package of financial services is provided by various kinds of insurance companies and pension systems. A distinctive characteristic of these is that they apply the principle of pooling not only to their investment assets but also to their customers: their policy holders or members of pension systems. The pooling in this case serves the function of spreading the risks against which the insurance is taken—death, accident, sickness, fire, and so on. In the case of pension systems and annuities sold by life insurance companies, the principle of pooling also is applied to give predictability to the hazard of death.

Some kinds of insurance, casualty insurance and term insurance on life, do not involve the accumulation of large reserves. In this case, the service of the insurance company consists mainly of pooling the hazards insured against, rather than in serving as an investment medium. In the case of "ordinary" life insurance policies or limited-payment policies, annuities, and pension systems, the characteristic contract involves a prolonged period of in-payments followed by a later period of out-payments. Thus, the financial institution builds up large reserves that it invests, and the investment aspect of its activities is important. Since in many cases the individual can withdraw his interest in the contract or use it as collateral on a loan, we may think of the individual's equity in the contract as a peculiar kind of moderately liquid asset.

Life insurance companies and pension systems are quantitatively very important investors in the United States economy, investing largely in illiquid assets not of the highest grade. Thus, in connection with their investment activities, we can think of these institutions as providing the important services of provision of investment information and conduct of investment analysis. Through their application of pooling and diversification, they also make financing available to the classes of long-term private borrowers they serve, on terms more favorable than would otherwise be possible.

Institutions for business finance

A number of the financial institutions considered above provide services essential to the efficient channeling of funds for the financing of businesses. These services include the acquisition of detailed information on particular businesses, conduct of the paper work and administration involved in making loans, and supervision of the loans during the period that they are outstanding, including enforcement of conditions attached to the loan such as the safeguarding of collateral. Commercial banks traditionally have played a central role in providing businesses with short-term finance and providing the detailed services that are necessarily associated with this. Small businesses that do not have access to national capital markets, that cannot sell their own securities, particularly depend upon the services of commercial banks in providing them with financing. Some contribution to business finance is made by life insurance companies, pension funds, investment companies and trusts, and mutual savings banks—practically the whole range of financial institutions.

Some other financial institutions focus mainly on the channeling of funds to businesses, especially the smaller businesses and those in a somewhat precarious financial position that are limited in their access to funds through other channels. Factoring companies, or factors, are financial institutions specializing in the purchase of the accounts receivable of businesses, as well as in the provision of inventory and equipment financing, other loans, and advisory services. Closely related are commercial finance companies that provide accounts-receivable financing for businesses. The provision of open-book credit by the business may be an essential service, without which it cannot obtain customers. By using the services of a factoring company or a commercial finance company, the business is able to provide this service without it constituting a drain on its own limited funds. Thus, this is a channel of finance—a relatively high cost one in many cases—for businesses limited in access to funds from other sources or businesses that wish to pass on to a specialist the processing of accounts receivable.

Consumer finance institutions

The financing of consumers involves mortgage loans to finance homes and a number of short-term and intermediate-term loans for other purposes. The nonmortgage "consumer credit" dealings involve installment loans to finance consumer durable goods and for other purposes, single-payment loans, charge accounts, and loans against securities. We have mentioned above a number of institutions that provide finance to consumers. Mortgages are financed largely by savings and loan associations, mutual savings banks, credit unions, life insurance companies, and commercial banks. In addition, we should mention mortgage companies that perform the service of originating and servicing mortgages that then can be owned and financed by financial institutions in other localities.

Other forms of consumer credit also are extended by a number of these institutions, by the ubiquitous commercial banks and by credit unions. In addition to these we should mention sales finance companies, consumer finance companies, personal finance companies, and—perhaps at the bottom of the hierarchy—pawnbrokers. A number of these latter institutions are themselves financed in substantial part by commercial banks, their services consisting almost entirely of the making, administering, and collecting of consumer loans.

Commercial banks and the financial system

What is interesting about commercial banks is that they play virtually *all* of the roles we have just reviewed. Through their time-deposit activities, the commercial banks are the most important private provider of liquid assets to the economy. They provide services associated with the provision of nonliquid investment assets through their trust funds and trust services. The government securities departments of some commercial banks are among the leading brokers and dealers in this central market of the financial system. The commercial banks play a major and crucial role in business finance, especially in providing short-term and intermediate-term loans. In consumer finance, the commercial banks not only finance the finance companies but themselves are very important originators of, and servicers of, installment credit and mortgage loans. Some banks act as managers and administrators of private pension funds. The only financial service we have mentioned that the commercial banks in the United States are not in some manner connected with is the provision of insurance. We see that the term commonly applied to commercial banks in the United States, "department store banking," is well earned.

Financial Markets

Many of the securities to which we have referred are traded in active and well-developed markets. The marketability of securities performs a social function in permitting the investor flexibility in his holdings. Thus, he can withdraw or add funds in accordance with his personal needs and can give effect to his opinions of the merits and prospects of various kinds of investments, thus "voting" with his dollars. If investment markets were inefficient, the cost of trading would limit the capabilities of the financial system and thus the effectiveness of the economy. Where investment markets are excessively unstable—a fault from which they are not free—this may contribute to economic instability and adversely effect the quality of judgment reflected in the market. We review below some of the major financial markets.

The government securities market

The market for United States government securities is the key market of the United States financial system. It also is the preeminent financial market of the world in terms of the volume of its transactions, the importance of its effective performance, and the quality of the performance that it has displayed. The volume of transactions in this market recently has run in the neighborhood of half a trillion dollars per year, on a comparable basis, about five times as great as the volume of transactions on the New York Stock Exchange. In terms of volume of transactions, this is the largest market in the world.

The market for United States government securities is a dealer market. It is made up of about 20 major dealers, some of which are dealer departments of large commercial banks. Thus, this is an over-the-counter market, rather than an auction market like the major stock exchanges. More properly, it is an over-the-telephone market, since this is the principal method of dealing.

The principal transactors in this inner market are themselves financial institutions or large businesses: commercial banks, other financial institutions, large nonfinancial businesses, foreign holders of United States government securities, and agencies of the United States government. The Federal Reserve open market account, handled through the trading desk of the Federal Reserve Bank of New York, operates in this market.

The expeditious handling of such a large volume of transactions reflects the simplicity of the product being traded, the financial status of the transactors, and the large size of the typical transaction. The market for United States government securities does not involve a huge number of debt instruments, made by different borrowers and subject to financial risk, which must be analyzed, such as is characteristic of common stock. The number of issues of United States government securities is kept relatively small in order to facilitate the effectiveness of the secondary market in the securities. The unquestioned credit of major transactors in the market facilitates trading operations. The characteristic transaction in this inner market is a large one, running to millions of dollars.

From the social point of view, and especially because of its status as the basis for Federal Reserve open market operations, it is important that this market should not be erratic or subject to unreasonable price gyrations. From the viewpoint of the Federal Reserve, what is especially important is that the market should be able to absorb Federal Reserve transactions on the greatest scale that may be desired to effectuate monetary policy, without generating changes in the prices and yields of government securities such as would be economically or politically disturbing. In the terminology of a Federal Reserve report, it is desired that the market should posses "depth, breadth, and resiliency."

In general, the market has demonstrated these characteristics. Although the Federal Reserve often has been constrained in its open market operations by Treasury debt management operations, it does not appear that any substantial open market operations upon which it wished to embark were impossible because of the inability of the market to absorb the transactions.

In relation to the situation existing in other economies, this ability to use open market operations freely to maintain a precise control over bank reserves—to offset through debt-market dealings factors causing undesired changes in bank reserves—is a resource that is valuable and rare. No other economy seems to have a financial system that permits open market operations so little constrained by their side effects.

The money market

"The money market" is not "a market" in the usual sense of the term, which involves a single trading place or trading organization, but a network of markets that are grouped together because they deal in financial instruments that have a similar function in the economy and are to some degree substitutes from the point of view of holders. The instruments of the money market are liquid assets: interest-bearing debts that mature within a short period of time or are callable on demand. Some sectors of the money market, thus defined, have their separate dealer organizations or trading facilities, as does the market for United States government securities.

The central element in the money market in terms of volume of instruments, volume of transactions, and key role in the financial system of the economy is the part of the market for United States government securities involving short-term debt of the government. This we have referred to above. No other single instrument approaches in importance short-term government securities.

The money market includes a variety of short-term business obligations, a noteworthy component being the traditional commercial paper that is dealt with in its own dealer market. A hybrid financial obligation is the bankers' acceptance, paper originated by businesses, to which the name and credit rating of a bank is attached because of "acceptance," or guarantee, of the obligation by the bank through prior arrangement. Short-term securities of state and local governments are also included among money-market instruments. Call loans and other short-term loans of banks and nonfinancial businesses to finance the inventories of United States government securities dealers are a liquid asset to their holders, although these are not marketable and are not, in this sense, a money market instrument. Closely related to these are loans to brokers and dealers through which they finance their own and their customers' holdings of common stocks traded in the stock market.

An important money market instrument created by a financial institution that has developed within the past 10 years is the time certificate of deposit, or CD, created by commercial banks. This is an extension of the traditional time deposits of commercial banks into a marketable and negotiable issue. From the point of view of the holder, these instruments are similar to short-term government securities in being virtually risk free, short term, and traded in an active and effective market. The development of these instruments during the 1960s constitutes a substantial revision in the liquidity-creating machinery of the United States financial system. A final kind of short-term debt created by a different class of financial institution is the paper of finance companies, part of which is directly placed by the borrower with the lender, so that it, thus, has some of the characteristics of a loan. A very short term debt instrument of special importance to large banks is the federal funds loan. This is a 1-day loan of funds immediately available at Federal Reserve banks. Since this market is mainly used by commercial banks and is an important means of reserve adjustment by banks, it is discussed along with other banking operations in Chap. 7.

The capital market

Important as they are in other connections, the short-term financial instruments that we have been considering are not the major means of financing the credit-financed expenditures of households, businesses, and state and local governments. The principal instruments that finance these expenditures are long-term and intermediate-term debts: mortgages and consumer credit for households, bonds for corporations, and bonds and intermediate-term securities for state and local governments. Thus, it is mainly the market for these instruments that channels funds for the financing of these important expenditures, in the process applying judgment as to the relative terms on which different kinds of activities should be financed.

The market for long-term debt, like the money market, is really a group of related markets for financial instruments that are substitutes in the portfolios of some investors. While for some purposes it is useful to refer to "the bond market," in practice bonds differ from one another in a number of respects that concern investors: in their estimated default risk, in the size of the issue and the depth of the secondary market, in the scope of reputation of the borrower, and in many features of the bond contract. Of special importance is the exemption from federal income and profits taxes attaching to income from state and local securities. Since this privilege is most valuable to investors in high tax brackets, these securities naturally come to be held largely by high-income individuals and by financial institutions subject to the corporate profits tax, especially commercial banks.

Although the bonds of major corporations are listed on the stock exchanges, the bond market is mainly an over-the-counter market. The market, thus, does not correspond to a tidy structure with rigid lines between categories, since some dealers may specialize in certain kinds of bonds while others may deal in a wide range of securities. But because the overlapping among dealers and among potential investors ties the sectors of the market together sufficiently well, it is reasonable to talk of the bond market.

Residential mortgages are not so well suited as bonds for extensive trading in a secondary market. During the postwar period, however, the financial system has developed institutional arrangements that have importantly improved the secondary market for mortgages. Thus, it presently is realistic to speak of "the mortgage market" and to think of mortgages as possessing in some measure the salability that attaches to money-market instruments and bonds.

The stock market

The stock exchanges, and particularly the preeminent New York Stock Exchange, are the most conspicuous secondary markets for corporate equity securities. These are auction markets with complex institutionalized facilities for brokerage, for the execution of buy and sell orders from the public, for dealing, and for the operations of specialists who take a position in securities and thus contribute to the breadth of the market. But despite the focal position of the leading stock exchanges most United States corporations do not have their securities listed on such exchanges. The stock of small corporations and of some of the large ones, including some industries such as banking and insurance, are dealt with in an over-the-counter market, including many of the same dealers who do business in bonds.

New sales of common stock are not handled through the stock exchanges but through a special class of dealer termed, somewhat misleadingly, "investment bankers." In many cases, these institutions also perform as over-the-counter dealers, making a market, among others, in the securities of corporations whose new issues they market. When we are concerned with the terms on which corporations can raise new funds through the sale of common stock, it is especially the terms that are offered by investment bankers that are relevant. These are governed by the terms prevailing in "the stock market," the network of institutions which includes the stock exchanges and the activities of the over-the-counter market.

Given the open-ended yield on common stocks arising from their residual position in the financial structure of the corporation, it is only natural that their evaluation poses special problems—or that the uncertanties attached to estimating the investment qualities of a security are especially difficult in the case of a common stock. Therefore, it is not surprising that swings in prices of common stocks are wider than those of bonds. Neither is it surprising that in the case of the stock market there is more of a difficulty of self-feeding swings in prices. All the same, it is a mark of an effective stock market not to "run away with itself," not to "lose its head." It is widely agreed that the stock market in the United States was subject to this failing in the 1920s. There has since been no similar episode. From the point of view of effective performance of its economic function, it may be objected that even in the postwar period the stock market has been subject to excessive and ill-considered swings in stock prices. Considering the difficulty of its task, continuing attention to the institutions of the stock market and to opportunities to improve its contribution to the performance of the economy are appropriate.

SUMMARY

1. The financial system facilitates the formation of productive capital by permitting the necessary functions to be performed through specialization and division of "labor."

2. In allocating capital among competing uses, the financial system provides the judgment, imagination, and analysis that is a major determinant of the efficiency and progressiveness of an economy.

3. In facilitating the ability of the individual to shift his use of resources over time, the financial system makes an intangible but important contribution to the standard of living.

4. By steadily passing along the savings of individuals to finance the spending of others and by standing ready to provide liquid assets on relatively constant terms, the financial system can help to mitigate economic fluctuations. Unstable financial institutions, such as savings institutions that fail in depression, can aggravate economic fluctuations.

5. The United States credit markets are highly developed institutions through which in 1970 about $97 billion was raised, mainly by corporate businesses and households.

6. Corporate business on net raised about $27 billion in financial markets in 1970, most of it through bonds and loans, and noncorporate business about $5 billion.

7. Households in 1970 acquired financial assets to the amount of about $68 billion and increased their liabilities in financial transactions by $20 billion, on net providing about $48 billion through financial transactions to the credit markets.

8. Financial institutions in 1970 served as intermediaries in financial transactions amounting to about $52 billion. Except for the highly diversified commercial banks, the financial institutions are quite specialized in the kinds of liabilities they create and their services to customers, as well as in the type of earning assets they acquire.

9. Financial markets are primarily over-the-counter markets, the major exception being the stock market. The market for United States government securities plays a central role in the financial system not only because of its importance in financing the government but also because it is the central market of the financial system and the one in which Federal Reserve open market operations are conducted.

QUESTIONS FOR REVIEW AND DISCUSSION

1. Explain why the function of bearing investment risk and that of applying judgment and knowledge to the economy's investment choices naturally go together.

2. Give some examples of investment projects of a business or governmental unit that proved to be misguided and wasteful; of projects that proved to have a strategic importance in paving the way for other new developments.

3. List major factors that would cause a family to want to consume on a different time pattern than that of the lifetime income of the income earner. Review the kinds of financial arrangements that would be helpful in connection with each such factor.

4. "Since saving is income that is not spent, it necessarily reduces total spending and tends to cause economic slack." Comment critically.

5. Discuss ways in which the financial system could operate to aggravate the severity of economic fluctuations.

6. Identify the most important suppliers and demanders of funds in the United States credit markets.

7. Characterize the major classes of financial instrument.

8. Briefly describe the role of businesses in the credit markets; also describe the role of households.

9. Describe the functions of savings institutions. List and give the distinguishing characteristics of the major types of savings institution.

10. Explain what governs the amount of obligations savings institutions have outstanding at any time.

11. Describe the government securities market. Explain why it is of special importance to the financial system.

12. Define the money market. What are its principal instruments and institutions?

13. "The markets and institutions relating to long-term credit and common stock are the ones that play the central role in determining the progressiveness, and therefore the efficiency, of the economy." Develop this idea.

PART 2

banking and central banking

6
commercial banking

The term "commercial bank" is a carry-over from an institution and a theory of a century and more ago. The institution was the commercial bank that made short-term loans to business and in the process created paper money in the form of bank notes. The theory was that creation of paper money only for business loans assured that the amount of money would not be too great or too small.

Both the theory and this practice now are dead. Modern commercial banks still create money, but now in the form of checking accounts or demand deposits. These constitute the bulk of the United States money supply. But less than half of the credit created by commercial banks goes to business, and they engage in a wide variety of activities. The term commercial bank now is usually applied to institutions that do a checking-account business, whatever other activities they may also engage in.

Their central position in the financial system, their wide range of activities, and their involvement in many financial markets and kinds of transactions would in any case call for special attention to commercial banks in the study of the financial side of the economic system. A special basis for the attention given to banks (to save words, commercial banks will be referred to as banks, and other institutions, such as mutual savings banks and Federal Reserve banks, will be referred to by their full names) is that they are a major element in the nation's monetary system. Banking laws and banking practices affect the behavior of the nation's money supply, which in turn affects the behavior of total demand and the stability of the economy.

The Nature of Banking

The distinctive nature of banking is brought out by considering "the basic banking transaction," that in which the bank creates money and credit. The picture is most clear when the money is in the form of paper bank notes, as it largely was in the United States until 1913. The bank notes are injected into the economy when the bank uses them to acquire an "earning asset," to make a loan, or to buy a security.

The transaction is illustrated by a loan of bank A to Mr. Z. The bank accepts Mr. Z.'s $1,000 promissory note. In exchange, it issues him $1,000 in its hitherto unissued bank notes. In making the loan to Mr. Z., the bank is extending credit or "creating credit." Where did the funds come from? Are they the result of someone's saving? No, the bank got the notes not from a saver, but from the printer. In a very tangible and down-to-earth sense, the money and the credit extended when it was used to acquire Mr. Z.'s note were created by bank A.

This transaction increases the nation's money supply by $1,000. The new money initially is in the possession of Mr. Z. But he did not borrow the money to hold it idle, so he soon uses it to make payments. Then it is mixed in with all the other money making a continuing circuit through economy, or the expenditures-income stream.

What does this transaction look like on the books of the bank and of Mr. Z? The bank acquires an additional earning asset in the form of Mr. Z.'s note. This reflects the credit-creation aspect of the transaction, for the bank has extended to Mr. Z. credit that did not come from anyone's prior saving. The corresponding liability on the bank's books is the increase in its circulating bank notes outstanding, which represents the monetary side of the transaction. On Mr. Z.'s books, his note to the bank is a liability of $1,000. He has a corresponding increase in assets in the form of additional money, the $1,000 of bank notes. Since there are no offsetting transactions, Mr. Z.'s $1,000 in bank notes is a net addition to the nation's money supply. Neither the bank nor Mr. Z. is directly wealthier or poorer as a result of the transaction, as we should expect in a voluntary transaction. Both have offsetting increases in their assets and liabilities and no change in their wealth or net worth.

How does a bank reduce the money supply and extinguish credit? By this same type of transaction carried out in the reverse direction. The bank fails to renew a loan or sells a security, thus reducing its assets. The repayment of its loan or payment for its security is, in the simplest case, in the form of its circulating notes. It simply puts these back on the shelf.

Bank A		**Mr. Z**	
Assets	*Liabilities and Capital*	*Assets*	*Liabilities*
Mr. Z.'s promissory note +$1,000	Bank A bank notes (paper money) outstanding +$1,000	Money +$1,000	Note due to bank A +$1,000

The money has come back out of circulation and the money supply is reduced. The amount of credit the public is receiving from the bank is reduced correspondingly.

In both of these cases, the causation seems to run from the asset side of the bank's balance sheet to the liabilities side. The bank adds to its loans and investments, and because of this, the money supply increases. This is the most useful way to look at the matter.

The story would not be basically different if bank A instead of acquiring Mr. Z.'s promissory note had acquired a government security, a mortgage loan, or a corporate bond. In each of these cases, bank A increases its earning assets (loans and investments) and its outstanding notes, which add to the nation's money. The person with whom the bank dealt is richer by having the additional money but poorer for having sold a security, which in some cases is his own note.

Would it alter the story to specify that the bank's money is in the form not of circulating paper money but of checking accounts or demand deposits? In this case, the printer drops out of the story—or is put to printing checkbooks—for the bank's liabilities now are simply bookkeeping entries obligating it to accept checks drawn against the account of Mr. Z. Mr. Z. and others are willing to accept this checkbook money because they know they can make payments with it. That is what makes it money.

The dependence of banking on token money

Would it make any difference to the basic banking transaction if the only money in the economy were gold coin? Yes, this would put our bank right out of business. The bank can create checkbook money or bank notes and lend them out because the cost of the notes, and of the checks together with their bookkeeping entries, is nominal. But to lend out gold coin the bank first must acquire the gold coin. Where would it get the funds to do this? Gold coin is not created by banks but by gold mines plus mints. Even if the bank were given the power to mint coins, if the value of the gold in the coins had to be equal to the value of the coins as money, creating coins would not provide the bank with a source of funds to lend. Since the full value of the coin is required to pay for the gold from which it is made, there are no funds left over to lend. Thus, the bank could not create credit. It would be unable to engage in the basic banking transaction and, thus, would not really be a bank in the sense in which the term is used here. The institution of banking is associated only with token money, or with moneys made from things that are worth substantially less as a commodity than they are as money.

A similar situation exists when the bank creates a token money in the form of circulating paper notes or demand deposits, but is required to keep 100 percent reserves in the form of a kind of money that it cannot create. In this case of 100 percent reserve banking, to increase its demand deposits by $1,000 the bank would have to acquire from outside—since it cannot create it itself—$1,000 of reserve money. Creating the deposits, then, provides no source of funds to acquire earning assets. The bank, again, cannot create credit. The amount of its money that can be created also is defined entirely by the availability of reserve money. The distinctive functions and powers associated with banking, thus, exist only where banks create a token money on the basis of fractional reserves.

Banking distinguished from intermediation

Turning now to consider another kind of boundary line between banking and other activities, how are matters altered if our bank creates a financial instrument that does not serve as a medium of exchange? Our Mr. Z., we recall, wants to borrow *money*, which he can use to make the payments he needs to make. If it cannot create something that Mr. Z. can use as money, the bank cannot create credit to lend to him. Bereft of its ability to create credit and to affect the nation's money supply, our bank would no longer be a bank.

Losing its ability to create credit would not prevent the bank from being a middleman in credit, as are other intermediaries. It could create securities, such as negotiable certificates of deposit, sell these to someone else, and use the money thus raised to lend to Mr. Z. But, once again, it has not created this credit, which was created rather by some saver who became able to buy the bank's security by spending less than his income. These transactions may look quite similar, but in terms of their effect upon the flow of total demand, the difference between them is very important. The great inflations and deflations caused by variation in creation of money and credit by banks seem to have no counterpart in inflations or deflations caused by variations of financial intermediaries in the rate at which they pass credit along from ultimate savers to ultimate borrowers.

One indicator of the difference between banks and intermediaries is this: If the only money in the economy were gold coin, this would in no way affect the operations of the intermediaries. They would operate in quite the same manner as in a bank-note world. But the basic banking transaction would be impossible in this world, as we have noted, and commercial banks could not exist.

The need for a mechanism to limit bank creation of money

The activities of savings institutions and other intermediaries are limited by cost considerations, just as are those of other businesses. The savings institution deducts a margin to cover its operating costs from the yield it can earn on its assets and offers to borrow funds from the public at the interest rate that covers its costs and profit margin. The volume of obligations of the savings institutions is defined by the amount the public chooses to take on these terms.

How does the story differ in the case of the commercial bank? The bank's costs on its demand-deposit operations are only those of printing its paper notes or administering its checking operations and investing the funds. These ordinarily are small in relation to the interest the bank could earn on any given increase in its earning assets. Moreover, the bank does not have to wait for the public to bring funds in from its savings. Banks can take their self-created money and not only offer to lend it but go out and buy securities with it. So long as there are some securities in the economy that banks can buy that pay enough interest to cover the cost of creating the money, it is profitable for them to expand money and credit. If there were no more than this to the rules of the game, banks would create money in an explosive manner.

So another respect in which banks differ from financial institutions is that a mechanism is needed to prevent inflationary overissue of money and creation of credit by banks. This is the reserve mechanism, which is discussed in detail below. The reserve mechanism not only prevents explosive expansion of money and credit by banks but also serves to make the amount of bank-created money behave in a defined manner, or follow a defined rule, thereby affecting the nation's total money supply and the behavior of its total demand.

The Development of Banking

Banking, in the sense of the operation by which a token money is created and introduced into the economy through credit extension, was discovered in ancient times. Institutions holding the coins of others for safekeeping, such as Babylonian and Greek temples, found they could lend out some of the coin and still meet their obligations, since not all of their customers would demand their coin at the same time. In this way, they discovered fractional-reserve banking. If one added up the coin and claims of the public against these banks, they added up to more than the total amount of coin. Thus, these early banks were in effect creating money.

Banking naturally tends to be developed when an organization holds the funds of others and is not legally required to hold 100 percent reserves behind its obligations or forbidden to create claims that serve as means of payment. During the middle ages, banking was carried on by the religious orders and among individuals largely by the Jews and Levantines because of the Christian church's objections to the taking of interest. In England, banking developed from the keeping of gold for others by goldsmiths, leading to the issue by them of deposit receipts that had some of the prop-

TABLE 6-1 Combined Balance Sheet of All United States Commercial Banks, December 30, 1970 (in billions of dollars)

Assets		Liabilities and Capital Accounts	
Cash assets	$ 87.1	Interbank deposits	$ 29.5
Loans and investments	461.1	Government deposits	7.3
(earning assets)		Demand deposits of the public	203.4
Loans	314.3	Time deposits of the public	229.6
Investments (securities)	146.8	Borrowings (other debts)	22.1
Other assets	22.4	Other liabilities	36.2
Total	$570.6	Capital accounts	42.5
		Total	$570.6

SOURCE: *Fed. Reserve Bull.*

erties of paper money. Also developed were letters instructing the goldsmith to transfer gold to the account of another person, a precursor of the modern use of demand deposits.

Major public banks were established in Genoa in 1408, Venice in 1587, and Amsterdam in 1609, but these differed in some respects from modern banking institutions and did not survive, largely because of pressure to extend excessive credit to government. In a sense, modern banking history begins with the founding of a great note-issuing bank (creator of paper money) that remains one of the leading banking institutions of the world, the Bank of England, founded in 1694.

The development of banking was shaped by a number of major innovations. The transition from oral instructions to the bank to transfer funds to standard written instructions, the precursors of the modern bank check, greatly enlarged the possibilities of banking. The development of bank notes that circulated from hand to hand as circulating paper money was an important step. The great expansion of banking in Europe and the United States during the eighteenth century and the first half of the nineteenth century was based upon such circulating bank notes. After the Civil War in the United States, there was a sharp movement to checkbook money and demand deposits, leading to another major swing in the nature of commercial banking. In the 1960s, the principle of banking was applied to the creation of international monetary reserves in the form of International Monetary Fund Special Drawing Rights, which are discussed in Chap. 17.

The Bank Balance Sheet

A picture of the operation of the commercial bank is provided by the bank's balance sheet. This gives, at a moment of time, a listing of all the assets, or things of worth, belonging to the bank; a listing of the bank's liabilities or debts owed to others; and as a residual item, a statement of the capital accounts, the part of the value of the bank's assets that is not owed to others and, thus, measures the equity of the owners of the bank.

It is usual to divide both assets and liabilities into categories that are useful for analysis, such as the basic ones shown in the balance sheet of all commercial banks in the United States. Cash assets of $87 billion made up 15 percent of banks' total assets. The great bulk of bank assets are in the form of "loans and investments," or "earning assets," in the form of various kinds of interest-earning debt. These earning assets measure the volume of bank credit in existence, both the part created by the banks in conjunction with demand deposit activities and that arising from the intermediary function of banks in conjunction with their time deposits. The interest earned on these earning assets is the main source from which the bank pays its expenses and derives its net income. Other assets include bank buildings and equipment.

Looking at the asset side of the bank balance sheet from the viewpoint of the banker, the cash assets generally do not earn interest but are needed to meet legal requirements, to permit the making of transactions that are needed for operations, to provide the means of meeting net cash withdrawals by customers, and to remunerate correspondent banks for services provided by them. The banker's goal is to keep holdings of cash as low as is consistent with safety and to maximize holdings of earning assets.

Loans and investments can be categorized in a number of ways, by borrower, by duration of loan, by liquidity, and by type of debt instrument. The banker's goal is to maximize the rate of return on his earning assets within the constraints that apply to him, using the investment principles discussed in Chap. 4.

From the viewpoint of the public, the role of cash assets is to permit the bank to operate safely, but also as a part of the reserve mechanism that controls the total volume of bank assets and liabilities. From the public's point of view, the bank's earning assets represent a part of the total wealth of the society that the bank is allocating to particular uses. The public welfare requires that the choices made by the banker lead to productive use of credit and avoid inordinate risks of losses, which would threaten excessive bank failures. In this connection, we note that the capital accounts of all banks, at $42.5 billion, amounted to only 7 percent of total assets and liabilities. Accordingly, the amount of shrinkage in the value of their assets that banks could absorb without becoming insolvent, having liabilities greater than their assets, is rather limited. Because of this, banks follow a conservative policy in managing their loans and investments.

The liabilities of commercial banks consist largely of "deposits," a label that may be somewhat confusing. A deposit in this sense is the debt of the bank to its customer. It differs from the note, say, of a customer to the bank mainly in the terms on which payment is to be made. The note of the customer to the bank ordinarily specifies payment on a particular date. Some time deposits similarly specify the date on which the bank is

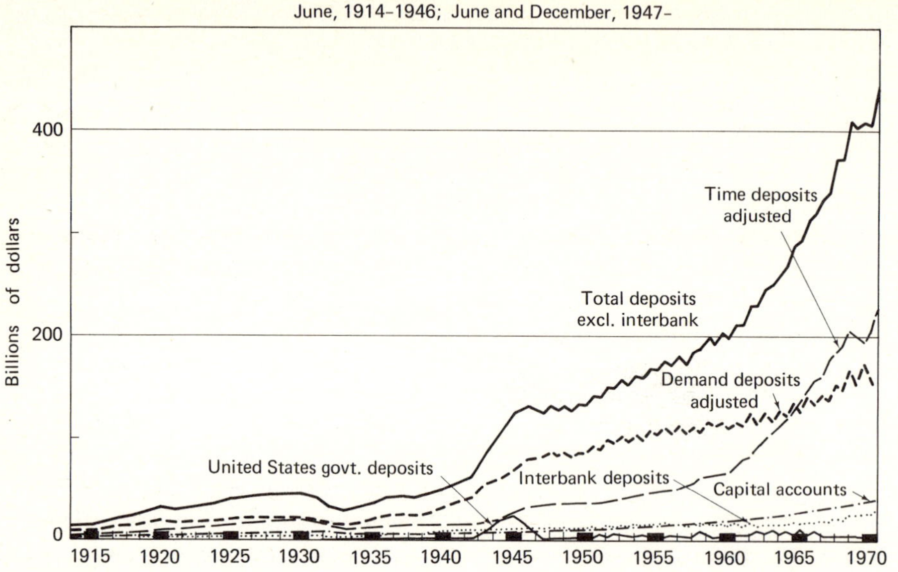

Fig. 6-1 Principal liabilities of United States commercial banks, 1914–1970. (Board of Governors of the Federal Reserve System.)

to make payment to the customer; others permit the customer to withdraw his funds only after 30 days' notice, a requirement that customarily is waived. Demand deposits are a unique kind of debt in providing that the bank not only will pay on demand but will pay to whomever presents a payment order from the customer in the form of a check drawn upon the bank. It is mainly in incorporating provision for payment on demand to others than the owner that demand deposits differ from some kinds of time deposits, and qualify as a medium of exchange and a part of the nation's money supply.

From the banker's viewpoint, inducing customers to hold funds with him in the form of deposits is the main way he gets funds to invest and is indirectly the source of his income. In the existing banking system with its reserve apparatus, the individual bank is not free to expand its demand deposits without limit as a means of acquiring loans and investments, but must compete against other banks for the favor of customers in an effort to gain for itself as large a share as possible of the limited total amount of demand deposits permitted to exist at any time.

From the point of view of the public, time deposits are liquid assets closely competitive with the other types, such as short-term government securities, listed above. The bank provides a service in making available such assets in forms that are attractive to the public. But the bank-created asset making the most distinctive contribution to the operation of the economy is the demand deposit, which makes up the bulk of the money supply of the United States.

Changes over time in bank balance sheets

The broad historical record of change in the assets and liabilities of United States commercial banks is laid out in Figs. 6–1 and 6–2. Some of the important points brought out by the charts are as follows:

1. Large declines in bank deposits and bank credit occurred in 1921 and—a unique case—in 1929–1933. Bank loans from 1933 until the early 1940s remained only about half as large as in the 1920s. The expansion of bank credit and money after 1933 stemmed from bank acquisitions of government securities.

2. Demand deposits and bank credit expanded very rapidly during 1942–1945 because of huge acquisitions by banks of government securities associated with the financing of the Second World War.

3. Demand deposits have grown since 1945 at a variable rate, showing some no-growth periods and increasing unusually rapidly in 1965–1969. Time deposits showed a marked acceleration of growth after 1960, then a sharp downturn in 1969, reflecting shifts in the relation between interest rates on time deposits and those available on competing liquid assets, as well as a banking innovation in the form of introduction of negotiable certificates of deposit.

4. On the asset side of bank balance sheets, the postwar period has seen rapid expansion of bank loans to something like the position they had in the 1920s, the relative importance of government securities showing a continuing decline since 1946.

Fig. 6–2 Principal assets of United States commercial banks, 1914–1970. (Board of Governors of the Federal Reserve System.)

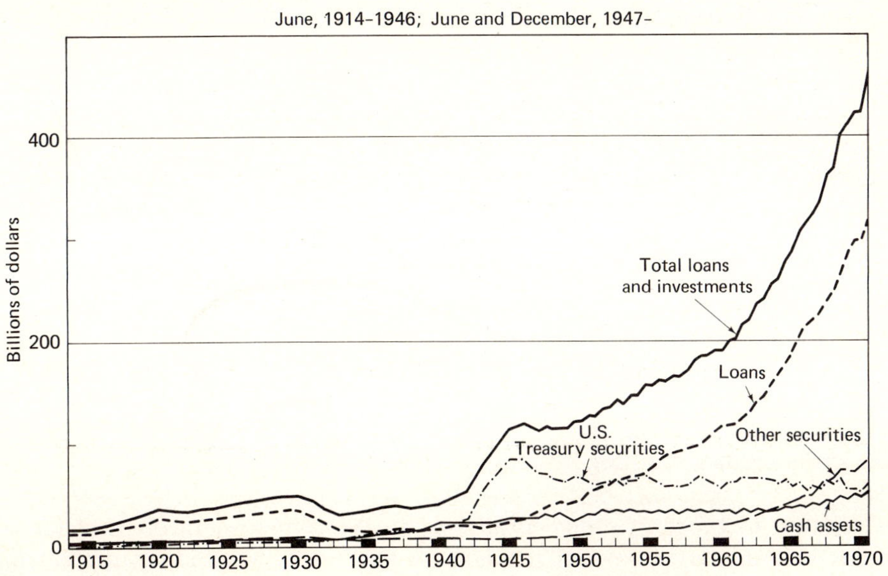

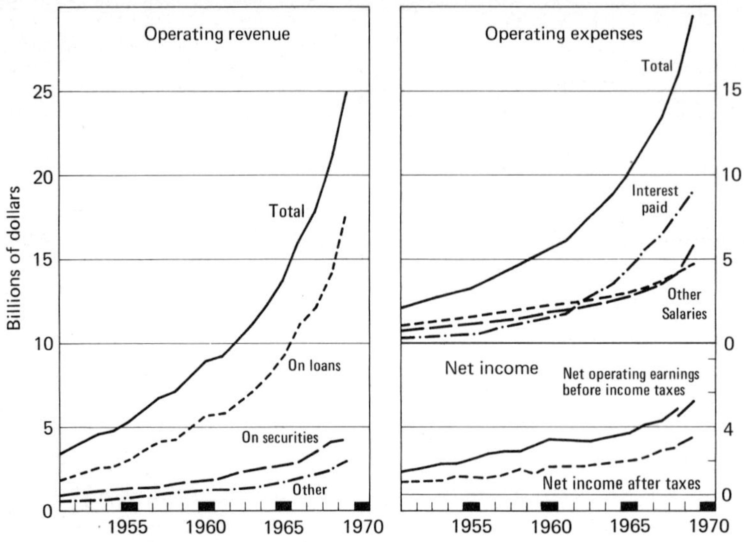

Fig. 6-3 Income and expenses of Federal Reserve Member Banks. (Board of Governors of the Federal Reserve System.)

Bank Income and Expenses

The factual pattern of commercial bank income and expenses is given in Fig. 6-3. As the proportion of loans among bank assets has grown, they have become by far the most important source of bank income. Growth of total bank income reflects both the continued rise in the volume of bank earning assets and the increase in interest rates from the unusually low level to which they fell during the Great Depression. Bank expenses also have increased continuously. The sharp rise in interest paid by banks on their time deposits after 1960 reflected the accelerated growth of time deposits that showed up in Fig. 6-1, along with the rise in time-deposit interest rates that was a cause of their accelerated growth.

Bank income increased sharply in 1969 as a result of the upsurge in interest rates. In 1970, the net income of Federal Reserve member banks increased further by more than 10 percent, as increases in income from higher average yield rates on earning assets and growth in their volume outpaced increases in operating costs. The profitability of member banks as measured by their net income as a percentage of total capital accounts hit a record high in 1970, measuring 11.5 percent compared with 11.1 percent in 1969 and the previous record of 10.9 percent in 1945.

The United States Banking System

In relation to those of other countries, the banking system of the United States is unusual in several respects. It includes a very large number of independent banks, while most countries have a few large banks with many branches. The United States system includes banks chartered both by the national and by the state governments, and supervised by agencies of the states as well as by three different federal agencies. Commercial banks in the United States have been more active than those in many countries in entering into new activities, gaining a diversified character that has led to the label "department store banking." The American banking system has a better reputation for enterprise than for stability. Only in recent decades have we not been, as Irving Fisher put it, "the land of runs and bank failures."

The makeup of the commercial banking system

In contrast to other nations, where a half-dozen banks with many branches dominate the banking scene, the United States has around 13,500 independent banks (Fig. 6–4). These operate over 20,000 branch offices, making the total number of banking offices in the country close to 35,000.

The structure of American banking has changed dramatically over time. Prior to the 1930s, there were severe restrictions on the establishment of branch banks, so in the 1920s the nation's banks consisted almost entirely of independent, one-office banks. However, there were a very large number of them, almost as many as the total number of banking offices existing today. The agricultural depression of the 1920s and then the Great Depression reduced the number of independent banks by one-half by the 1930s and increased the relative role of branch banking. Since then there has been little change in the number of independent banks, but the number of branch offices is more than five times what it was in the middle 1930s. There are now more branch offices in the United States banking system than head-office banks. While still vastly more decentralized than the

Fig. 6–4 Commercial Banking Offices in the United States. (Board of Governors of the Federal Reserve System.)

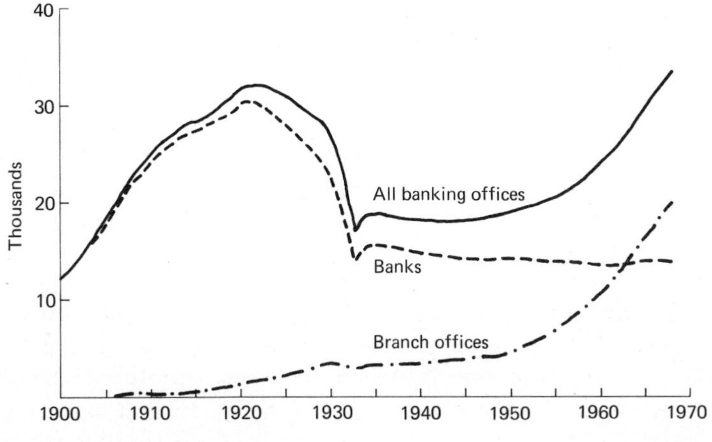

banking systems of other countries, the United States system has moved very rapidly in the past 15 years toward increased use of branch banks.

The United States has a "dual banking system" in that it includes both banks chartered under national legislation, called "national banks," and "state banks" chartered by state governments. Of the 13,671 commercial banks existing in the United States in June 1970, only about one-third were national banks, though these held nearly 60 percent of banking assets. National banks are required to be member banks of the Federal Reserve System. Of state banks, only about one in eight is a member bank of the Federal Reserve System, but these state member banks hold more than half the assets of all state banks. Member banks of the Federal Reserve System hold about 80 percent of the nation's banking assets. Member banks of the Federal Reserve System are required to be insured by the Federal Deposit Insurance Corporation, and most state nonmember banks also are insured. In 1970 less than 200 banks holding less than 1 percent of the nation's banking assets were not subject to deposit insurance.

Bank chartering and freedom of entry into banking

During the early history of United States banking, charters were granted to banks on an individual basis by state legislatures and, in two cases, by Congress. In response to charges of favoritism, corruption, and restriction of competition, the principle of "free banking" became prevalent. Adopted by New York in 1838 and by other states soon afterwards, it was applied to the chartering of national banks in the National Bank Act of 1863. The very large number of banks in the nation by the 1920s reflected the operation for almost a century of the principle of free access to the banking business. The principle of free banking involved the granting of a bank charter to any group that met certain explicit criteria, mainly involving a minimum amount of capital in relation to the size of the city in which the bank was operating.

The weak condition of many banks and the large number of bank failures in the 1920s were attributed in part to "overbanking," to the existence of such large numbers of banks that they could not earn sufficient income to stay in sound financial condition. Essentially, the diagnosis was one of excessive competition, or unhealthy competition. As a result of this diagnosis, the principle of free banking came to be applied in a much more limited way after 1933. To procure a charter for a new national bank during recent years, it has been necessary to demonstrate that an adequate potential for earnings existed for the proposed bank, that the needs and convenience of the community called for its establishment, that the proposed capital structure was adequate in relation to estimated bank size and competition, and that the proposed management merited confidence. Before granting a charter to a new bank, the Comptroller of the Currency receives recommendations from the Board of Governors of the Federal

Reserve System, from the Federal Deposit Insurance Corporation, and from his bank examiners in the district, and provides an opportunity for opposition to the chartering of the bank to be expressed.

How severely the chartering of new banks should be limited has been a matter for difference of opinion. When James J. Saxon became Comptroller of the Currency in 1961, he for a time greatly increased the rate at which new national banks were being chartered. The total number of new banks chartered ran to about 300 per year in 1963 and 1964, but dropped to about 100 per year in 1966–1968. Since terminations of independent banks—almost all from mergers, consolidations, and absorptions—were running around 120 per year, the number of independent commercial banks declined slightly in 1966–1967, after increasing for several years before this.[1]

Bank failures and deposit insurance

After bank failures were very large in the 1920s and decimated the nation's banking and monetary system in the early 1930s, Congress enacted legislation under which the Federal Deposit Insurance Corporation went into operation in 1934 and was placed on a permanent basis in the Banking Act of 1935. This system of deposit insurance is generally agreed to have been helpful in three respects: (1) It guarantees against loss all deposits up to a maximum size, presently $20,000, thereby assuring most depositors against loss. (2) It has removed the incentive for bank runs, which were a major source of United States bank failures and monetary instability. (3) It has given an agency of the federal government supervisory authority over state nonmember banks, consequently improving management standards in what had been the weakest part of the banking system.

The necessity for such a system of deposit insurance stems from the large number of units in the United States banking system, which, in turn, stems from legislation limiting branch banking. In nations with a few large banks each of which has innumerable branches, the functions assumed by the Federal Deposit Insurance Corporation are handled by the banks themselves. The management and procedures of small branch banks are supervised by the central organization of the bank. In the case of unfavorable developments that might jeopardize the solvency of an individual branch, taken by itself, the principle of pooling is applied and the gains of some banks are offset against the losses of others.

An objection to deposit insurance, which long prevented the adoption of such a program, was that it necessarily would substitute the judgment and standards of the insuring agency for that of the bank management, thus reducing the efficiency and innovative capacity of the banking system.

[1]For more information on this topic, see "Recent Changes in the Structure of Commercial Banking," *Fed. Reserve Bull.*, pp. 195–209, March 1970.

There is some force to this argument, and the question how far supervisory agencies should go in limiting bank discretion and innovation is one that will continue to be debated. However, students of banking now are widely agreed that a system of unit banking such as that in the United States requires some system of government insurance of deposits and that the existing system has worked very effectively.

The operation of the FDIC radically improved the performance of the United States banking and monetary system. The uncertainties and aggravated swings in the money supply earlier resulting from the runs and waves of bank failures that were a distinctive feature of the United States have been done away with and bank failures reduced to nominal proportions. Figures on bank failures are difficult to interpret in an exact way, because the policy of the FDIC has been to attempt to prevent banks from actually failing by implementing a plan of reorganization or merger for a potentially failing bank, thus avoiding the losses and inconveniences that would attach to actual liquidation of the bank.

Bank supervision

Banks are all subject to continuous supervision by a government agency. Four sets of supervisory agencies exist, and banks are potentially subject to the authority of as many as three supervisory agencies. The supervisory agencies are the U.S. Comptroller of the Currency, who has authority over all national banks; the Board of Governors of the Federal Reserve System, with authority over Federal Reserve member banks; the Federal Deposit Insurance Corporation, with authority over all insured banks; and the state banking departments of the various states, with authority over the state-chartered banks of the state. Since all national banks are required to be Federal Reserve member banks and to be insured by the FDIC, they are subject to regulations of these two agencies as well as the Comptroller of the Currency.

The supervisory authorities attempt to protect the public against the failure of and severe mismanagement of banks, by (1) imposing certain general standards and prohibitions against certain kinds of transactions and (2) periodic examinations of the bank and the application of more detailed and judgmental standards to bank management.

Banks generally are prohibited from acquiring certain classes of earning assets that are considered excessively risky for a commercial bank or that pose special problems. Such prohibited assets usually include common stock; real estate; low-grade debt; and loans to stockholders, officers, and employees of the bank.

Of particular importance is the "10 percent rule" under which a national bank is prohibited from holding the debt of any one maker to the amount of more than 10 percent of its capital and surplus. State banks are subject to a corresponding rule, but with the maximum figure running as high as 20 percent in some states. National banks also are limited in their holdings of conventional real estate mortgage loans to an amount equal to 100 percent of capital and surplus or 70 percent of time deposits, whichever is greater.

Federal Reserve member banks are subject to a ceiling on interest rates payable on their time deposits, which is specified under Federal Reserve Regulation Q. Insured nonmember banks are subject to a parallel regulation by the FDIC. One of the arguments in favor of this regulation is that it protects the safety of banks by preventing overcompetition from driving the interest rates paid on their time deposits too high, perhaps inducing banks to hold insecure assets in an effort to earn high enough yields to meet their interest obligations. However, the operation of regulation Q has had a significant effect on the direction of credit flows and the volume of bank deposits and is discussed below in that connection.

A central element in bank supervision is the examination of banks at least once a year by the supervisory authority. In the examination procedure, a team of examiners enter the bank without advance notice and evaluate its assets, financial position, and management procedures. The examiners look at individual assets, checking whether securities are of appropriate investment quality and checking that loans are properly administered, meet quality standards, and are not in default. A basic examination tool is to appraise assets at a conservative estimate of their value and to determine whether on this basis the banks assets exceed its liabilities and capital. If such is not the case, so that the bank's capital is impaired, corrective action is required. The supervisory authority attempts to deal with weak management or unsound investment practices before the bank gets into so severe a plight.

To avoid duplication in bank examinations, the three federal supervisory agencies have adopted a procedure by which national banks are ordinarily examined by only one federal agency, the other agencies receiving copies of the examination report. Under this system, national banks ordinarily are examined only by the Comptroller of the Currency, while the Federal Reserve Board limits its examinations to state member banks and the FDIC to state nonmember banks. The examinations of state banks by the Federal Reserve and the FDIC usually are done in conjunction with the examination by the state supervisory authority.

Correspondent banking

Another feature of United States banking stemming from the large number of independent banks is the important role of correspondent banking. This involves a smaller bank keeping a balance at a larger bank in exchange for a package of services. Of the nearly $28 billion of interbank deposits at the end of 1970, nearly all reflect such correspondent relationships. Some, however, are interest-earning time deposits or deposits of foreign banks that do not involve the correspondent relationship here under consideration.

One basis for the maintenance of a balance with a large bank is to use it as a clearing balance in connection with the check collection process. The small bank receiving as deposits by customers checks drawn on out-of-town banks faces the problem of collecting the funds from these banks (a problem treated in a later chapter). Member banks of the Federal Reserve System may do this through their Federal Reserve bank, but nonmember banks do it largely through correspondent banks, and member banks find it the more efficient procedure for some classes of checks. It is natural, then, for the smaller bank to keep in the larger one a balance to which the proceeds of such collected checks can be credited. This, however, is only the central element in a correspondent relationship that has many elements.

Keeping a balance with a correspondent bank is a way of reimbursing that bank for its services in check collection. Since the balance is a demand deposit, interest is not paid on it. To the bank holding the balance, it is a source of funds to be invested in earning assets, providing income to the extent of the interest earned on it. One side of the correspondent relation, thus, is that the small bank keeps a balance at the large bank as a way of paying for its services in check collection, and in some cases for a variety of other services. An alternative arrangement would be to pay for these services through explicit fees, but despite some pressure for such a change there has been little revision of practice in this direction.[2]

The other services provided in some cases in addition to check collection are numerous and diverse: If the small bank has an application for a loan larger than it can handle by itself, its correspondent bank may participate in the loan, or take a share of it. On the other hand, the small bank with a shortage of demand for loans may purchase loans or arrange loan participations through its correspondent. Other services from the large to the small bank are buying and selling securities and foreign exchange, investment advice, safekeeping of securities, reports on economic conditions and money markets, making a market in federal funds loans, credit information, counsel on management practices, advice on legal aspects of banking, audits, assistance in officer training and recruitment, and provision of data-processing services.

Where it works effectively, the correspondent banking relationship provides to small banks services and economies otherwise only available to large banks, and provides to banks in remote locations some of the ad-

[2]For a discussion of current practices in correspondent banking, see "Correspondent Banking: Part I, Balances and Services," *Fed. Reserve Bank Kansas City Mon. Rev.*, pp. 3–14, November 1970.

vantages of being in New York. Development of the correspondent banking system, at least in part, has overcome the inefficiences that otherwise would attach to the highly decentralized United States banking system.

Banking Structure and Competition

The state of competition in banking may have an important effect on competition in the rest of the economy. Since businesses in general depend on commercial banks for financing, for a bank to gain a monopoly position in an area would permit those who controlled it to gain control over other businesses or to gain a favored position for firms in which they had an interest. Thus, the degree of competition in banking has long been a matter of special interest and attention.

Branch, chain, and group banking

In discussing banking organization and structure, it is useful to make the following distinctions:

Unit bank	Independent, one-office bank
Branch bank	Bank operating one or more branch offices in addition to the head office
Group banking	Group of banks (two or more) controlled by a holding company
Chain banking	Group of banks owned by an individual or group

The organization and structure of banking in the United States varies widely among states, reflecting mainly differences in state law with regard to branch banking. In general, branch banking has spread and assumed a predominant position within whatever limits are permitted by state laws. In 1970, 19 states and the District of Columbia permitted statewide branch banking systems, 15 states prohibited any branch banking, while 16 states permitted branches only within a limited geographical area. The most conspicuous example of branch banking is California, where the nation's largest bank, The Bank of America National Trust and Savings Association, in 1968 had assets of more than $20 billion and about 1,000 branches.

The structure of the United States banking system was substantially altered by a "tidal wave of branching"[3] in the 1960s that in that decade

[3]"Recent Changes in the Structure of Banking," *Proceedings of a Conference on Bank Structure and Competition*, p. 36, Federal Reserve Bank of Chicago, Chicago, 1970.

more than doubled the number of branch offices in the country, adding 10,000 branch offices in 10 years. Nearly all of these branch offices were newly established, rather than reflecting the shifting of unit banks to branch status through mergers. The total number of independent banks changed little in the 1960s. The setting up of this large number of additional branch offices brought banking facilities to areas that had lacked them and reduced somewhat the average number of persons per banking office.

Almost as striking a development in banking structure was the abrupt expansion of one-bank holding companies between 1965 and 1970. Limited regulation by the Board of Governors of the Federal Reserve System of holding company affiliates of member banks had been provided by the Banking Act of 1933. The spread of bank holding companies in the 1950s led to concern over the effect of this development on competition in banking and the potential misuse of bank resources by holding companies. In response to this concern, Congress in the Bank Holding Company Act of 1956 gave the Board of Governors substantial new powers to limit the spread of holding companies with reference to both member and nonmember banks.

The Act required bank holding companies to register with the Board of Governors, thereby providing definite information on the number and importance of such organizations. At the end of 1957, such registered bank holding companies numbered 74, controlling 603 commercial banks with deposits of nearly $50 billion, about 13 percent of United States bank deposits. The Act required prior approval by the Board of Governors before any bank could be acquired by an existing or new holding company, in this way bringing under control the further spread of group banking. It also prohibited bank holding companies from engaging in nonbanking business, which limited the hazard of misuse of bank funds by controlling holding companies.

Unfortunately, the Bank Holding Company Act of 1956 contained an important loophole. It defined a bank holding company as a corporation that owns 25 percent or more of the voting shares of two or more banks, which meant it did not apply to holding companies that owned only one bank. After 1965, in part because of the effects of the 1966 amendments to the Bank Holding Company Act, an explosive expansion occurred in the number and importance of one-bank holding companies.[4] In 1965, banks subject to one-bank holding companies accounted for less than 5 percent of the nation's deposits, and the banks involved were all small. By 1970, such banks accounted for more than one-third of the nation's deposits and included 9 out of the 10 largest banks in the country and 43 out of the 100 largest banks. The effect of the spread of one-bank holding companies—

[4]A review of these developments and their implications is given in "The One-bank Holding Company—History, Issues, and Pending Legislation," *Business Conditions*, pp. 2–16, Federal Reserve Bank of Chicago, July 1970.

and the major impetus to their spread—was to free the banking companies involved to some extent from banking regulations to which they otherwise would be subject. One side effect of the incident was the abrupt rise in 1969 of the acquisition of funds by banking companies through the sale of commercial paper by bank affiliates under holding companies.

In response to wide agreement that the legislative loophole applying to one-bank holding companies had to be closed, Congress at the end of 1970 passed the Bank Holding Company Act of 1970. This extended the coverage of the Act of 1956 to include holding companies controlling only one bank and made some other changes in its provisions. The 1970 action of Congress did not provide for the dissolution of the holding companies formed before the earlier legislative oversight was corrected. The lasting effect of the episode on the United States banking structure and on competitive relations between banks with and without holding companies will require some time for evaluation.

Policy toward bank mergers

A wave of bank mergers in the 1950s led to some decline in the number of independent banks and to concern that continuation of this movement would significantly reduce banking competition. In response to this situation, Congress passed the Bank Merger Act of 1960. This stated that a proposed bank merger involving a federally regulated bank required the prior approval of the relevant regulatory authority. Where the acquiring bank was a national bank, this was the Comptroller of the Currency; for state member banks, it was the Board of Governors of the Federal Reserve System; and for insured state banks that were not member banks, it was the Federal Deposit Insurance Corporation. In deciding whether to approve a proposed merger, the agency was to consider the effect both on banking services and competition. The agency considering a particular case was to request advisory reports from the other two agencies and from the Justice Department on the effects of the merger on competition.

The situation, not surprisingly, led to differences of opinion among the government agencies as to the net effects on competition of particular proposed mergers and as to whether they should be approved. These differences of opinion became an acute public embarrassment when the Justice Department in 1965 contested in court the merger of two large New York banks (Manufacturers Trust Company and the Hanover Bank) that had been approved by the Board of Governors, and won its case.

In response to the resulting confusion, Congress passed the Bank Merger Act of 1966. This provided that the Justice Department was to cease prosecution of cases—including the one it had won—where prior approval of a merger had been given by the relevant agency. For the future, the Justice Department was to have only 30 days in which to challenge in the courts any merger approved by the other agencies, after which the merger was exempt from such action. Finally, the agencies were instructed to apply common standards in judging whether a proposed merger would on balance be beneficial—though this is an instruction easier to give than to follow.

With reference to bank mergers as with reference to bank holding companies, Congress, after its first attempt at legislation did not work out as planned, did come up with a procedure for controlling banking combinations that otherwise might seriously lessen banking competition. The laws on the books in 1971 provide that all bank mergers (of federally supervised banks) and all bank acquisitions by holding companies must be approved in advance by a federal agency. The hazard of a cumulative movement toward bank mergers or control of banks by holding companies seems to have been brought under control.

Issues Relating to Banking Structure and Supervision

A number of matters relating to banking structure and competition, the safety of banks and financial institutions, and the laws and administrative agencies through which the government should regulate the financial system are subject to continuing discussion among economists, representatives of banks and financial institutions, and governmental agencies. We give below a brief account of the pros and cons of some of these issues.

These concerns and others relating to the financial system have been extensively studied by policy-related bodies in recent years, with but little immediate effect upon legislation and policy. An extensive investigation including a large number of research studies by economists was carried out by The Commission on Money and Credit from 1957 to 1961. In 1962, a President's Committee on Financial Institutions established by President Kennedy also reviewed this area. In 1970 and 1971, it was under investigation by the Presidential Commission on Financial Structure and Regulation appointed by President Nixon, which planned to deliver its final report at the end of 1971.

The dual banking system

The situation in which banks (this also is true of savings and loan associations) can receive charters from either the federal government or the state government, and thus can choose the agency by which they will be chartered and regulated, has long been the subject of discussion and criticism. Substantial variation exists in the regulations imposed upon banks by the banking authorities of the various states and in the quality of the work done by the various state banking departments. The state banking law and the regulations of the state banking authorities generally are more lenient than those that the federal authorities would like to impose. But the federal authorities long have been restrained from taking actions they believe are called for because this would provide banks with an additional incentive to take state rather than federal charters and to give up membership in the Federal Reserve System. In this way, the laxity of state banking regulation has limited the effectiveness of federal regulation by leading to a "competition in laxity."

The main argument on the other side is that to bring all banks, or even all financial institutions, under a single regulatory authority would involve an excessive concentration of power in the regulatory agency, and permit the banking authorities to make their mistakes on too great a scale. It also is argued that the multiplicity of regulatory agencies permits experimentation and diversity within the overall national banking system. But perhaps the majority of independent observers, even those who are the greatest proponents of experimentation and diversity, believe that a system of regulation in which the regulated agency decides who is to regulate it is not a constructive form of experimentation and tends to produce ineffective regulation. It is too much like giving the criminal a choice of the judge by whom he is to be tried.

Proposals to require all banks to operate under federal charters have long been made, but have been vigorously opposed by the affected banks and state banking departments and have not come close to being enacted in recent years. Curiously enough, in the National Bank Act of 1863, Congress passed legislation that was expected to put state banks out of banking, in the strict sense, by taxing the notes of state banks, but this intention was thwarted by the development of banking based upon demand deposits, which was not subject to the tax. Probably, legislation to require federal charters and regulation for all commercial banks would be found constitutional, as the Constitution gives the power to regulate money to the federal government, but there seems to be no immediate prospect of passage of such legislation.

Compulsory membership of all banks in the Federal Reserve System

A proposal that is somewhat less far-reaching, and therefore may be less politically impractical, is to permit the continued existence of state-chartered banks but to require all of these banks to be member banks of the Federal Reserve System. This would make all banks subject to the same reserve requirements and would safeguard the control of the Federal Reserve System through the reserve mechanism over the volume of money and bank credit.[5] It would remove the pressure from the System to lower its

[5]The Chairman of the Board of Governors of the Federal Reserve System, Arthur F. Burns, testified in 1971 that "the main reason member banks are leaving the System now is that they believe reserve requirements are too costly." Statement before the Subcommittee on Financial Institutions of the Committee on Banking, Housing, and Urban Affairs, U.S. Senate, March 31, 1971, *Fed. Reserve Bull.*, April 1971, p. 305. The reserve requirements of Federal Reserve member banks are "too costly," of course, only by comparison with those of state nonmember banks.

reserve requirements, offer free services to member banks, and otherwise take actions that may not be justified by the public interest in order to prevent defections of banks from member-bank status. It also would give to a federal agency supervisory powers that could be used especially in states where state supervision is unsatisfactory to maintain the standards of the banking system. There is no doubt as to the constitutionality of such legislation, but the political pressures opposing it seem greater than those likely to be mustered in its favor.

Consolidation of federal supervisory agencies

In terms of orderly administrative arrangements, there is not much to be said for the existence of three federal agencies supervising commercial banks. A related problem is that the Federal Reserve System, in addition to its responsibilities for monetary policy, has a large number of administrative responsibilities involving bank supervision, antitrust policy relating to banking, and a number of other programs. This may seriously dilute the attention it can give to its monetary responsibilities. Moreover, it may be that these various tasks call for responsible officials of different abilities and backgrounds; that each of these diverse jobs could be better done if there were more specialization and division of labor. One proposal looking in this direction is to establish a new Federal Banking Commission to take over all of the other functions now shared by the Comptroller of the Currency, the Federal Deposit Insurance Corporation, and the Federal Reserve System, except those relating to monetary policy, which would remain with a Federal Reserve System that then could concentrate entirely upon these functions.[6] This very reasonable suggestion also appears unlikely to lead to action unless some political forces appear that will offset the resistances that always exist to terminating existing agencies.

Branch banking

We noted that the United States banking system differs from that of other countries in that in most states legislation prohibits or limits branch banking, so we have a much larger number of independent banks than in most nations and in a number of states have only unit or single-office banks. The pros and cons of branch banking have long been debated in this country. No radical change from the existing situation is likely. Federal legislation to impose branch banking in states where it is now prohibited by state law is most unlikely. The Commission on Money and Credit in 1961 did propose revision of the National Banking Act to permit national banks to establish

[6]Such a proposal was made by the Vice-chairman of the Board of Governors of the Federal Reserve System, J. L. Robertson. This and some other proposals for reform of bank supervisory arrangements are discussed in Paul M. Horvitz, *Monetary Policy and the Financial System*, 2d ed., chap. 30, Prentice-Hall, Englewood Cliffs, N.J., 1969.

branches within "trading areas" that might be defined to include more than one state, irrespective of the provisions of state laws, but this is one of the Commission's recommendations least likely to be enacted.

The debate over the merits of branch banking involves a number of dimensions. On the grounds of efficiency, branch banking has the advantages of permitting realization of the benefits of economies of large scale and intensive specialization and division of labor in those activities where it is efficient. The argument on the other side is that the bureaucratization and high management overhead of the large branch banking business can more than offset these potential advantages.[7]

Clearly, the branch bank can offer a wider range of services than the small unit bank could offer on its own resources. But the unit bank by working through a large correspondent bank may be able to offer such services without the disadvantages of being an element in a large branch-banking enterprise. Moreover, it is argued that the locally managed unit bank is more sympathetic to and more understanding of the borrowing needs of local business than the branch bank managed by officers who stay in one locality only temporarily and who operate under rules set by head-office management.

The branch-banking system has a greater capacity for moving funds geographically to areas of greatest demand, though the facilities for shifting funds through correspondent banks, federal funds transactions, and negotiable certificates of deposit also are increasingly efficient. The small cities and towns, where devotion to unit banking probably is strongest, however, may look on increased mobility of funds without enthusiasm. Rather than expecting funds to flow to them from the outside world they are fearful, with reason in some cases, that at least in times of monetary stringency, the funds generated in their community would flow out to the New York money market in pursuit of higher interest rates, leaving local borrowers more strapped than they are under unit banking or limited branch banking.

Perhaps the most influential argument against unlimited branch banking has been that it would limit competition in banking and thereby might limit competition in the businesses that depend upon banks for their financing. In this case, also, the case is not so clear as it might seem at first glance. A community that could support only a single unit bank could instead support two branch offices of outside banks, and might thereby have more banking competition. Moreover, in a small community, the local bank may be more likely to have ties leading to favoritism to certain businesses than is true of the branch of an outside bank. On the other hand, statewide branch banking—and this would be much more true

[7]These issues are discussed in Paul M. Horvitz, *Economies of Scale in Banking, Private Financial Institutions*, Commission on Money and Credit, Prentice-Hall, Englewood Cliffs, N.J., 1963; and in Fred Bell and Neil Murphy, *Returns to Scale in Commercial Banking*, Federal Reserve Bank of Boston, Boston, 1967.

of nationwide branch banking—does lead to banking businesses disposing of a very large bloc of wealth and, therefore, to a greater concentration of potential economic power than occurs when banking concentration is prevented.

If it really made a great deal of difference to the operation of the economy whether branch banking were permitted, doubtless we should have noticed more differences than we have in the economies of the states that permit statewide branch banking and those that do not permit branch banking. The likely course of events seems to be some further easing of limitations on branch banking, but no great departure from our past institutions.

Competition between banks and other financial institutions

Changes in economic conditions and in regulations have led to sweeping changes in the terms of competition among savings institutions, particularly between savings and loan associations and the time-deposit activities of commercial banks. After World War II, savings and loan associations grew very much more rapidly than the time-deposit activities of commercial banks. The commercial banks were subject to several disadvantages that then seemed likely to perpetuate this picture. They were subject to higher reserve requirements; had a less favorable tax situation because they were subject to the corporate income tax; were subject to limitations on their holding of mortgage loans, which then offered relatively favorable yields; and were subject to maximum interest rates payable on time deposits determined by the Federal Reserve (regulation Q) and by the FDIC for insured nonmember banks that in 1961 were still set at 3 percent. Moreover, the commercial banks had not been aggressive competitors for savings, in most cases seeming content to take whatever time deposits came their way at the low interest rates they offered.

A number of developments combined to bring about a marked acceleration of growth of commercial bank time deposits in the 1960s, and a deceleration of growth of savings and loan associations after 1965. Regulation Q ceilings were raised to 4 percent in 1962 and to 5½ percent on time deposits other than savings deposits in 1965, and were increased further in 1968 and 1970. The change in regulation Q in January 1970 permitted banks to pay 4½ percent on savings deposits and rates ranging up to 7½ percent on time deposits amounting to at least $100,000 and running for at least 1 year. These increases in ceiling rates were made in response to the continued rise in market interest rates, which was especially sharp in 1965–1969. In part in response to the new opportunities, banks became aggressive competitors for the short-term funds of the public and pioneered the negotiable certificate of deposit in 1961.

In the latter 1960s, consequently, the banks had several advantages over savings and loan associations and mutual savings banks in the competition for short-term funds. The savings and loan associations were limited by law largely to residential mortgages, while the banks could invest more widely; for example, they could make investments in short-term securities whose yields during periods of money stringency rise higher than the long-term rates applying to mortgages. Moreover, the average rate of return the savings and loan associations earned on their portfolios was heavily affected by the low-yield mortgages they had acquired before the sharp increase in the level of interest rates. Finally, with the negotiable certificate of deposit the banks could tap the short-term funds of businesses, which savings and loan associations could not do because they could not issue such securities and were in any case prohibited from accepting accounts of businesses.

However, while the savings and loan associations suffered from competition with the time-deposit activities of commercial banks, during periods of credit stringency both of these intermediaries suffered from the competition of open market liquid assets that offered higher yields than either of them. The latter difficulty applied most severely to the banks, for the large negotiable certificates of deposit they sold to businesses proved to be very responsive to interest rate differentials, leading in some periods to a rapid outflow of funds from such obligations with a resulting sharp reduction in total commercial bank time deposits.

The latter 1960s were an unusual period because of this combination of circumstances, especially because of the sharp rise in interest rates, which to a considerable extent seems to reflect inflationary conditions arising from monetary and fiscal policies. Thus, presumably, the same issues will not in the future ordinarily be raised in the same kind of context. Criticism and concern of supervisory agencies attached in particular to the marked deceleration of the inflow of funds to savings and loan associations at a time when the housing industry already was in unfavorable condition due to the severe competition for credit arising from the prevailing inflationary conditions and the large borrowing demands associated with government deficits. In an attempt to do something for the savings and loan associations, the Federal Reserve System, in September 1966, reduced the maximum interest rate banks could pay on certificates of deposit of under \$100,000 from 5½ to 5 percent, leaving the rates on other kinds of time deposits unchanged. This was criticized by the defenders of the savings and housing industries as inadequate and by others as unfair to the groups holding small certificates of deposit and as an unjustified meddling in the process of credit allocation.

If greater economic stability could be achieved through more carefully controlled use of monetary and fiscal policies, this would go far to correct the erratic flows of funds to savings institutions and the housing industry that accompanied recent swings in economic conditions. Many economists believe that efforts to protect savings institutions and the housing industry from the effects of economic fluctuations when these do occur may hurt the economy rather than help it.

The seemingly persistent shift in the terms of competition in favor of the time-deposit activities of commercial banks as against savings institutions presents several alternative courses of action:

1. Remove or reduce the limitations on the permitted activities of savings institutions, to permit them to become "competitively viable full-service family finance centers," and, thus, hold their own against commercial banks. Among the most far-reaching proposals to this effect is that mutual savings institutions be permitted to create demand deposits—to compete with banks by *becoming* banks.

2. Devise new kinds of protections or subsidies for the savings institutions to protect them against commercial bank competition.[8]

3. Permit the relative growth rates of various financial institutions to be governed by competition within the existing structure of laws and regulations.

The studies and recommendations of the Presidential Commission on Financial Structure and Regulation may provide a framework for convergence of opinion toward some rational program of regulation of financial institutions. The lack of rationality in the existing arrangements is widely conceded.

SUMMARY

1. Banking is the operation by which a token money is created on the basis of fractional reserves and introduced into the economy by being used by the bank to acquire debt or to extend credit. Banking in this sense involves the creation of both money and credit. In the United States the institutions performing such operations are called "commercial banks."

2. Banking developed out of situations in which those with whom money was left for safekeeping found that they could extend credit and earn interest income by keeping only fractional reserves and creating claims on themselves that were used as a medium of exchange, using the funds thus freed to invest at interest. Modern forms of banking go back only about three centuries, a landmark being the establishment of the Bank of England in 1694.

3. The bank balance sheet reflects bank credit extension on its asset side in loans and investments, and on the liabilities side reflects the bank's operations as an intermediary in time deposits and its role as an element in the nation's monetary system in demand deposits.

4. Among respects in which the banking system of the United States

[8]These two alternatives are posed in *Mutual Savings Banking, Annual Report*, National Association of Mutual Savings Banks, New York, 1971, with a preference expressed for the first alternative.

differs from those of most other countries are the following: (1) Severe limitations on branch banking have led to the existence of a very large number of independent banks, in contrast to the small number of multibranch banks in most countries. (2) Banks are chartered and regulated both by the national government and by state governments, giving rise to a "dual banking system." State-chartered banks can choose whether to join the Federal Deposit Insurance System and the Federal Reserve System (although doing the latter requires the former). (3) United States banks have gone into many types of activities in addition to "commercial banking" proper, becoming "department-store banks."

5. Relaxation of state legislation limiting branch banking has led to a rapid rise of branch banking, the number of branch offices about tripling in the past 15 years.

6. A wave of bank mergers in the 1950s led to passage of the Bank Merger Act of 1960. This led to jurisdictional conflicts among government agencies that were resolved by the Bank Merger Act of 1966. This act requires prior approval of a proposed bank merger by the Comptroller of the Currency, the Board of Governors of the Federal Reserve System, or the Federal Deposit Insurance Corporation, where the acquiring bank is, respectively, a national bank, a state member bank, or a nonmember insured bank. A favorable decision by the relevant agency on a proposed merger can be contested in the courts by the Justice Department within 30 days but not thereafter.

7. Control over the increasing role of bank holding companies was sought in the Bank Holding Company Act of 1956, which required prior approval by the Board of Governors of the Federal Reserve System of any acquisition of a bank by a holding company. This act did not apply to holding companies controlling only one bank, and an explosive increase in the number and importance of one-bank holding companies occurred during 1966–1970. This loophole was closed by the Bank Holding Company Act Amendments of 1970, which extended the provisions of the 1956 act to one-bank holding companies.

8. Among major issues relating to banking structure and supervision are the relative powers of federal and state banking authorities, possible consolidation of federal banking authorities, continuation of limitations on branch banking, restrictions to be placed upon bank mergers, establishment of new banks, and operations of bank holding companies.

QUESTIONS FOR REVIEW AND DISCUSSION

1. Define the basic banking transaction. Depict an illustrative case on the balance sheet of a bank.

2. Characterize the basic differences between banking and financial intermediation.

3. Describe the process by which banking developed from non-banking arrangements.

4. Define the elements on the bank balance sheet associated with (*a*) bank credit, (*b*) intermediation, and (*c*) the bank contribution to the money supply.

5. Review major changes in the number and structure of United States banks since the 1920s.

6. Review developments of the past decade in bank mergers and the extension of bank holding companies and discuss the policy response in each area.

7. Define what you think would be an ideal bank supervisory system and indicate how it would differ from the existing arrangements.

8. Discuss the pros and cons of branch banking. What policies toward branch banking do you think would on balance be most beneficial?

7
commercial banking operations

The operations of the commercial bank are two-sided. One side involves attracting and holding the funds of customers. The other side involves investing the funds in such a way as to maximize the bank's income. The bank as an investor applies investment theory, seeking to choose a portfolio of earning assets that maximize expected yield subject to the set of constraints applying to banks. This chapter deals with banking operations and the strategy of bank management.

Establishment of a Commercial Bank

Once the founding group has obtained a national or state charter for a new bank, it raises the bank's initial capital by the sale of the capital stock of the bank. Let us say $360,000 is thus raised by the sale of 3,000 shares of common stock of par value $100, sold at $120 per share. Of these funds, $100,000 is spent for a bank building and equipment and $10,800 is subscribed to the capital stock of the Federal Reserve bank of the district. Such a paid-in subscription of 3 percent of the bank's capital and surplus is required for membership in the Federal Reserve System. At this point, the balance sheet of the bank looks like this:

Assets		*Liabilities and Capital Accounts*	
Cash	$249,200		
Stock of Federal Reserve bank	10,800		
Bank building and equipment	100,000	Capital stock	$300,000
		Surplus: paid in	60,000
Total	$360,000	Total	$360,000

From this point, the bank attempts to grow and prosper by carrying out two kinds of operations: (1) attract additional funds from the public, mainly in the form of deposits; and (2) invest these funds to get the highest attainable yield. The operation of the commercial bank is more complex than that of savings institutions because it offers a wider range of obligations to the public as a way of attracting funds and because of the fact that one of its obligations, demand deposits, serves as a medium of exchange, giving banks in the aggregate some ability to create money and credit.

Bank operations are analyzed by the use of the "T account." This is an abbreviated balance sheet of the bank that shows only those items in which changes occur. Since balance sheets always balance, these T account entries when correctly carried out involve (1) equal changes in the asset side and the liabilities (and capital accounts, the reference usually omitted for brevity) side of the balance sheet or (2) offsetting entries on either the asset side or the liabilities side of the balance sheet, which leave the totals unchanged.

Acquisition of Time Deposits

One aspect of the operations of the commercial bank is to offer to the public its interest-bearing obligations, which serve holders as liquid assets. With reference to these operations, the management problems of the bank are these:

1. To design obligations, varieties of time deposits, that are attractive to customers.

2. To offer good service to hold the loyalty of the customer, while minimizing operating costs so as to be able to offer him favorable terms on his money.

3. In connection with the other side of bank operations, to earn the highest possible rate of return on the bank's earning assets, so as to be able to offer the public attractive yields on time deposits, thus attracting their funds from competing banks, savings institutions, and money-market instruments such as short-term government securities.

There is little reason to believe that the individual bank by offering to the public its time deposits has any appreciable effect upon the amount the public saves and holds in the form of financial assets. The individual bank is competing for a share of the savings of the public, just as a grocery store competes for a share of the public's purchases of food.[1]

[1]A recent study finds close substitutability among commercial bank and mutual savings bank time deposits, shares at savings and loan associations, and open market liquid assets. George K. Kardouche, *The Competition for Savings*, The National Industrial Conference Board, New York, 1969.

The T account entries in this case are:

Bank Q

Assets	*Liabilities*
Cash + 100	Time deposits + 100

The customer pays for his time deposits with, or he "deposits," money in the form of currency and coin or a check drawn on his checking account, let us say a checking account in another bank. In the first case, the bank has an addition to its cash, or primary reserves, in the form of currency. In the second case, it has a demand claim against another bank, which it immediately collects through processes described below, gaining cash in the form of an addition to its own checking account in another bank, commonly its district Federal Reserve bank. Since this transaction adds as much to the bank's cash reserves as it adds to deposits and banks characteristically keep only fractional reserves behind deposits, this transaction tends to put the bank into an excess-reserve position.

The kinds of time deposits

The kinds of obligations offered by banks under the general label of "time deposits" differ from one another in important respects. The three main categories are these:

1. "Savings deposits" are limited by regulation to individuals and nonprofit organizations, and compete closely with the savings obligations of mutual savings banks and savings and loan associations. They have no maturity date but are withdrawable usually on 30 days' notice, the requirement that notice be given almost never being enforced. Savings accounts are evidenced by a passbook or the equivalent, rather than by any form of security.

2. "Time deposits, open account," can be held by businesses and in some cases have defined maturity dates, but are otherwise similar to savings deposits.

3. "Certificates of deposit" differ from savings deposits in being a form of security rather than a debt on the books of the bank and in having a defined maturity date. CDs are essentially short-term securities sold by banks to the public. Most CDs are negotiable and can be sold by the holder in the market just as can a short-term government security.

Negotiable certificates of deposit, first issued in 1961, are an important innovation in banking. In the competitive relations between banks and other financial institutions, the ability to offer a negotiable money-market instrument gives commercial banks an important new advantage over other institutions, extending their earlier advantage of being the only savings-type institution that could offer its obligations to businesses. In terms of the operation of the economic system, the introduction of negotiable CDs is a modification of the set of institutions through which the economy can create liquid assets. The conditions under which the volume of CDs increases and decreases affect the liquidity system of the economy and potentially influence the stability of the economy.

In terms of the strategy of bank management, negotiable CDs offer the bank an opportunity not only to attempt to lure local customers into depositing their funds but to actually go to the national money market and "buy funds," to borrow from the market just as would a nonfinancial business or governmental unit. One effect of this is to alter the bank's need for and management of liquidity. Having available to it the option of buying short-term money in the market, the bank is not so dependent upon meeting cash needs by using its liquid assets or borrowing from its Federal Reserve bank. On the other hand, if banks in general should get into an illiquid condition and then find themselves in need of raising funds by selling a large volume of CDs, this could cause a liquidity crisis, somewhat like the ones that characterized the United States banking system in the decades before the Second World War, unless the Federal Reserve System were willing and able to bail out banks and businesses that had put themselves into a precarious liquidity position. Such implications of negotiable CDs are still being considered by economists and the regulatory authorities.

Since negotiable CDs are held mainly by businesses, governmental units, and large individual investors, who treat them as competitive with other open market liquid assets, the volume of such obligations demanded by the public is closely responsive to the interest rates offered on CDs by the banks in relation to yields available on other money-market instruments. Since rates on CDs commonly vary less widely than other money-market rates during economic fluctuations, they are generally most attractive to the public during periods of economic slack, when interest rates generally decline and rates on CDs decline less than other money-market rates. The counterpart of this is that CDs are relatively unattractive to the public during periods of tight credit, since their rates do not rise as high as do others. One reason for this is that interest rates paid on CDs, as well as on other time deposits, are subject to maximum levels under Federal Reserve Regulation Q. Since these maximum permitted rates are changed only infrequently, a period of generally rising interest rates that brings banks up against their interest rate ceiling can cause a large outflow of funds from banks, as the public cashes in its CDs and puts the funds into other liquid instruments.

The general tendency for the volume of CDs to rise during recession and decline during boom periods might be justified as promoting economic stability, since the creation of additional liquid assets presumably helps to buoy up total demand. Erratic variation in CDs or large and abrupt outflows from banks because of the operation of maximum interest rates on time deposits is more difficult to justify and has called into question the desirability of existing regulations on time-deposit interest rates.

Borrowing from foreign branches: Eurodollars

An important financial innovation of the latter part of the 1960s made borrowing from abroad through foreign branches of United States banks a significant source of funds to commercial banks with foreign branches (Fig. 7-1).[2] When an owner of dollars, usually in the form of a demand deposit in a United States bank, makes a dollar deposit in a foreign bank, this gives rise to Eurodollars, dollar balances held abroad—usually in Europe. Ordinarily, residents of other countries who want balances in dollars hold them in United States banks, while funds held abroad are held in the local currency. Thus, a resident of France who gets funds in

Fig. 7-1 Eurodollar borrowings of United States banks. (Federal Reserve Bank of St. Louis.)

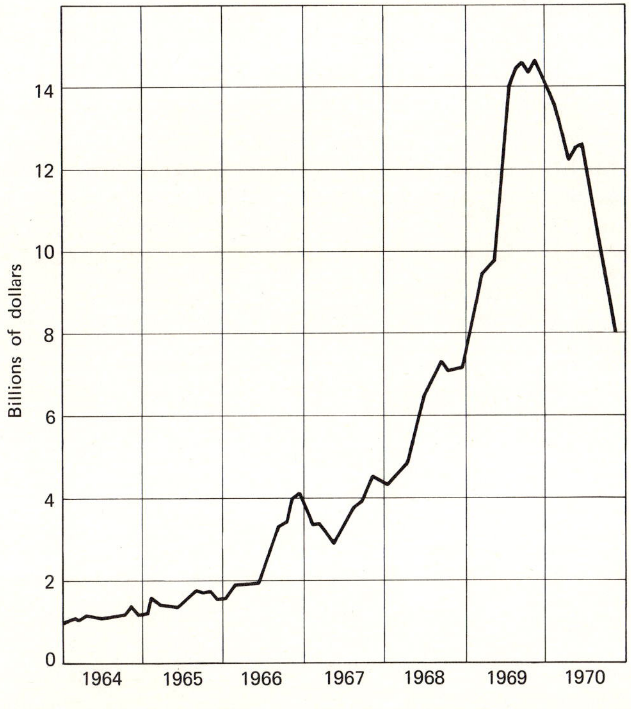

[2]For more information on this subject, see "Euro-dollars: A Changing Market," *Fed. Reserve Bull.*, pp. 765-784, October 1969; Vincent G. Massaro, "Eurodollars and U.S. Banks," *The Conf. Board Rec.*, October 1970; and Fred H. Klopstock, "Euro-Dollars in the Liquidity and Reserve Management of United States Banks," *Fed. Reserve Bank N. Y. Mon. Rev.*, July 1968.

the form of a check drawn on a dollar account in a New York bank would arrange for a deposit in francs in his French bank, the bank selling the dollars for francs in the foreign exchange market.

A combination of factors, however, created a demand for Eurodollars, which put banks in Europe in a position to pay favorable interest rates on Eurodollar deposits, which gave rise in 1969 to a sharp increase in the volume of such deposits. A major factor in the demand for Eurodollars was borrowing by United States banks. Confronted with very strong demands for credit in the United States and rising interest rates, coupled with a huge decline in CDs from late 1968 to the end of 1969 (largely because interest rates on CDs hit the ceiling permitted under regulation Q and could not rise further to stay competitive with money-market rates), United States banks were seizing every opportunity to get funds to lend and invest at the high prevailing interest rates.

The usual mechanism by which the funds were loaned to United States banks was through their foreign branches. In the simplest case, the Eurodollar deposit is taken by the foreign branch of a United States bank. The funds are then loaned to the head office in the United States, ordinarily in the form of an interest-bearing deposit, but with some loans made for periods of over 1 year.

Such Eurodollar transactions have several kinds of interesting implications, and we meet them again later on. From the viewpoint of the United States bank, to borrow Eurodollars from its foreign branch is just another way for it to borrow short-term funds, like raising funds by selling negotiable certificates of deposit. Borrowing Eurodollars has some advantages from the bank's point of view. Such borrowings are not subject to the interest-

	Foreign branch of United States bank B		**United States bank B**	
	Assets	*Liabilities*	*Assets*	*Liabilities*
1. Eurodollar deposit taken	$Demand deposit at United States bank A + 100	$(Eurodollar) deposit +100		
2. Funds loaned to head office	$Demand deposit at United States bank A − 100 $Due from head office + 100		Cash (Demand deposit at bank A) +100	Due to foreign branch + 100
Net effect	$Due from head office + 100	$(Eurodollar) deposit + 100	Cash + 100	$Due to foreign branch + 100

rate ceilings of regulation Q and are not subject to ordinary reserve requirements. Because of these circumstances, the volume of liabilities of United States banks to their foreign branches rose from less than $2 billion in early 1966 to $6 billion at the end of 1968 and then—a great upsurge—to $14.5 billion by July 1969. Thereafter, the Eurodollar borrowings of United States banks declined slightly through mid-1970 and then more rapidly, falling to $4.5 billion by March 1971.

The Federal Reserve System sought to moderate Eurodollar borrowings during the period of their sharp increase. Effective September 1969, it imposed reserve requirements equal to 10 percent of the *increase* in banks' liabilities to foreign branches above their average level of the 4 weeks ending May 28, 1969. Requiring banks to keep an amount equal to 10 percent of additional Eurodollar borrowings in cash, which does not earn interest, made such borrowing less attractive to banks. This tended to reduce the volume of Eurodollar borrowings, unless it was offset by other factors. The role of Eurodollar transactions in international capital movements of funds and the effects upon national balances of payments are discussed in Chap. 16. The future role of such transactions as a means of raising funds by United States banks will depend on whether credit stringencies such as that of 1969 develop again, on the relation between United States and foreign interest rates, and on any further restrictions placed upon such transactions by United States and foreign banking authorities.

In December 1970, the Federal Reserve Board increased the reserve requirement applying to new borrowings of Eurodollars from 10 to 20 percent. The reported intention of this, however, was the opposite of what one would offhand infer. It was meant to limit *reductions* in Eurodollar borrowings, which would have an adverse effect upon the already weak United States balance of payments. A reduction in a bank's Eurodollar borrowings was deducted from the base amount (based upon the May 1969 average) that is free of the reserve requirement. Thus, it increased the susceptibility of the bank to reserve requirements if it wished to increase its Eurodollar borrowings in the future. The higher the reserve requirement expected to apply to such future borrowings, the more worthwhile it was for the bank to avoid present reductions in its borrowings, thereby preserving its full quota of borrowings exempt from reserve requirements. The effort of the Federal Reserve, in this roundabout way, to discourage reductions in Eurodollar borrowings of United States banks was of limited effectiveness.

Sales of commercial paper by bank holding companies and nonbank affiliates

Another innovation in bank acquisition of funds in 1969 was a sharp increase in borrowing on the basis of commercial paper by bank holding companies and nonbank affiliates of bank holding companies. This development reflected the same factors that gave rise to the sharp increase in borrowing of Eurodollars: the great pressure on banks to acquire funds to lend and invest, in conjunction with the abrupt rise in the late 1960s in one-bank holding companies. Borrowing on commercial paper by bank affiliates was not subject to regulation Q, and the avoidance of this regulation in 1969 was an important incentive for exploiting this means of raising funds. In comparison with borrowing Eurodollars, commercial paper offered funds at lower interest rates during much of 1969. This avenue also was available to banks that had holding companies but did not have foreign branches through which to acquire Eurodollars. As a result of these considerations, such borrowing increased from less than $1 billion in mid-1969 to nearly $8 billion a year later.

The banks themselves could not raise funds by selling commercial paper, but when funds were raised in this way by bank affiliates that used the funds to buy some of the earning assets of the bank this provided the bank with additional funds to make customer loans. For the consolidated operation of the banking organization, including the affiliate, borrowing on commercial paper operated in much the same way as borrowing on CDs or Eurodollar loans.[3]

In August 1970, The Board of Governors of the Federal Reserve System imposed, effective in October, a reserve requirement of 5 percent on funds raised by the sale of bank-related commercial paper with a maturity of 30 days or more and the regular regulation D reserve requirements on demand deposits on bank-related paper of less than 30 days' maturity. At the same time, the Board of Governors reduced the reserve requirement on large CDs from 6 to 5 percent. Since CDs were not at this time severely limited by the regulation Q ceiling, these changes in regulations made borrowing on commercial paper no longer more attractive than borrowing on CDs. They led to a sharp reduction in outstanding bank-related commercial paper, while the rapid increase in the volume of outstanding CDs continued.

Acquisition of Demand Deposits

The commercial banks as a group may have some effect upon the total volume of demand deposits and the money supply in the economy by varying their reserve ratio, or their ratio of cash to demand deposits, so long as the Federal Reserve System does not offset this by a proportionate variation in the volume of bank reserves. From the viewpoint of the individual bank, however, the important determinant of the volume of its demand deposits is its success in competing against other banks for the favor of customers. This determines the share of the total demand deposits

[3] *Fed. Reserve Bank N. Y. Mon. Rev.*, pp 249–250, November 1970.

existing in the economy that are held in this bank, thereby affecting the volume of funds that the bank has to lend and invest.

In the case of time deposits, the service the bank performs for the customer is basically that of a financial intermediary, or agent in the investment of his funds. With reference to demand deposits, the bank again plays the role of investment agent, for under fractional-reserve banking, the major asset item corresponding to the demand deposit liabilities of the bank is its earning assets. But the distinctive function of the bank in connection with demand deposits is serving as the customer's agent in making payments. The great bulk of the money payments in the United States economy are made by the transfer of funds by commercial banks on the orders of their customers who write checks against their demand deposits. To satisfy the customer and attract customers, the bank must offer efficient service in this payments function. A highly institutionalized and elaborate system has been developed for the payment and collection of checks among banks.

The procedure for collecting checks is so well standardized that competition among banks for demand deposits depends largely upon other services that go along with the check collection function. One such service is making credit available to customers when they want a loan. This is especially important to business customers, some of whom are heavily dependent on credit from their bank to finance their activities. Thus, the bank tries to cultivate a continuing relationship with the smaller business customer, developing a familiarity with his business operations that permits it to make and service his loans expeditiously, as well as offering financial counsel and other services. This implies a constraint upon the way the bank manages the other side of its activities, the investment of its funds. To meet the loan demands of its business customers, it must keep itself in a sufficiently liquid position to have funds to lend them even during peak periods of business activity and financial stringency.

An institutional factor affecting the amount of demand deposits held by business customers is the practice of banks to require of businesses making loans that they keep a certain minimum amount of funds in the bank as a demand deposit. The amount of such "compensating balances" required varies among banks and is to some extent a matter of negotiation with the customer. It commonly runs from 10 to 20 percent of the amount of a loan. If the amount the business is thus required to keep with the bank is more than he otherwise would need, this practice has the effect of making the effective cost to it of the loan higher than the stated cost. To the bank, it is a way of holding more deposits than it otherwise could and thereby having a larger volume of funds available on which to earn interest.

In some cases, compensating balances are kept by businesses with banks that perform services for them other than the making of loans. An agreement to keep a certain minimum balance may be used by a business in place of service charges as a way of compensating the bank for accounts that involve a large number of transactions. Some large businesses keep deposits in banks in localities in which they have facilities as a way of compensating the local banker for financial advice and goodwill in relation to the company's local activities.

In addition to these variegated services, banks within the past decade have moved into the use of credit cards as a way of providing credit, and into arrangements to offer to individual customers a guaranteed line of credit that they can use when they wish. Banks also offer bookkeeping and other financial services, using computerized records. Banks will transfer salary payments directly to the accounts of individuals for the employer, and are offering billing services to businesses. The larger banks also usually will buy and sell certain foreign currencies and United States government securities. The large banks in large cities that serve as correspondent banks for smaller banks endeavor to attract and hold such balances by providing the complex packages of services described in Chap. 6.

The Management of Bank Funds

Commercial bank investment policy emerges from a straightforward application of the theory of portfolio management to the particular circumstances of commercial banks. The commercial bank is a risk avoider. It has a relatively thin cushion of owner equity, commonly less than 10 percent of liabilities, and is not in a position to absorb large losses. It only accepts limited investment risk in its earning assets. This risk is largely concentrated in customer loans, where banks have a special function to perform, and bank loans to businesses and bank mortgage loans are among the high-grade loans of these types, other lenders providing funds to the high-risk borrowers.

The commercial bank also needs a high degree of liquidity in its assets. Its liabilities are, again, large in relation to its assets because of its small capital cushion. It relies on the law of large numbers to assure that its depositors will not all want their funds at the same time, but the liabilities are, in practice, largely payable on demand. Actual fluctuations in deposits of banks, with the losses of funds this may entail, are substantial and not entirely predictable. Accordingly, the bank must hold a substantial proportion of its assets in the form of cash and of liquid assets or, as these are termed in connection with banks, primary reserves and secondary reserves.

Priorities in the allocation of bank funds

One way of approaching the allocation of bank funds among types of use is in terms of a set of priorities:[4]

[4]This approach comes from Roland I. Robinson, *The Management of Bank Funds*, 2d. ed., chap. 1, McGraw-Hill, New York, 1962.

1. The first priority is cash, or primary reserves. The minimum amount of cash needed is defined by legal minimum reserve requirements, plus cash that is needed in forms that do not meet these requirements. Reserve requirements for Federal Reserve member banks are determined by the Board of Governors of the Federal Reserve System, as described below. Those of state banks are defined by state legislation or the state banking authorities.

2. The second priority is "protective investment" or secondary reserves. These are liquid assets that can be turned into cash on short notice without hazard of substantial loss. While a part of secondary reserves are held against generalized uncertainties, certain amounts of liquid assets may be held against particular anticipated future cash drains. Many banks are subject to certain seasonal patterns in their demand deposits, which depend upon seasonal factors in the receipts and expenditures of cash by their customers. Anticipated losses of these funds may be met by holding debt that matures at just about the right time. Banks also must anticipate possible losses of funds that could be associated with a change in economic conditions, and hold assets of such liquidity and term to maturity that they will not be caught short of cash.

Recent studies of bank operations support the view that even after banks have allowed for changes in deposits that can be anticipated because of seasonal and secular factors, they are subject to large day-to-day variations that require adjustment of their cash position. The behavior of banks under these conditions seems explainable in terms of an investment model of attempted maximization of bank profits under uncertainty, subject to avoidance of excessive risks.[5]

Member banks of the Federal Reserve System can meet short-term cash needs by borrowing from their district Federal Reserve banks. The availability of this credit is a way of meeting short-term cash drains as an alternative to selling liquid assets or letting short-term debts run off. The ability of the bank to borrow in this way is limited, however, and the bank may prefer to keep at least a part of this resource in reserve. Individual banks differ widely in the extent to which they are willing to be in debt to their Federal Reserve banks.

Another means of meeting short-term cash needs—and even longer term needs—is short-term borrowing from other banks or the public. This can be done on 1-day loans in funds immediately available at Federal Reserve banks, loans termed "federal funds." Cash also can be raised, especially by large banks, by selling negotiable certificates of deposit at whatever interest rate is required to raise the needed funds (so long as

[5]William G. Dewald and G. Richard Dreese, "Bank Behavior with respect to Deposit Variability," *J. Financ.*, **25:** 869–879, (1970); William Poole, "Commercial Bank Reserve Management in a Stochastic Model: Implications for Monetary Policy," *J. Financ.*, **23:** 769–791 (1968); Leonall C. Andersen and Albert E. Burger, "Asset Management and Commercial Bank Portfolio Behavior: Theory and Practice," *J. Financ.*, **24:** 207–222 (1969).

this is not precluded by interest rate ceilings under regulation Q), although such adjustments cannot be made on a day-to-day basis. Eurodollar loans and commercial paper sales by bank affiliates are further means of raising cash that were developed by banks in the late 1960s. The extent to which banks are willing to depend upon such ways of meeting cash drains, and the extent to which they should be permitted to do so by law and the banking supervisors, is still being explored, as these financial instruments and the practices associated with them developed largely in the 1960s.

3. The third priority in allocating bank funds is meeting customer demands for loans. This is a function for which commercial banks have a unique capability. It is especially profitable to banks because interest rates on loans usually are higher than on securities and because maintaining a good relationship with customers encourages them to continue as bank borrowers and as depositors. On these bases, it is reasonable to give customer loans priority over the purchase of securities.

4. The fourth and final priority is open market investment for income. The funds available after the other priorities are met are invested in securities, maximizing expected yield subject to constraints of liquidity and investment risk.

The approach to problems of business management in terms of operations research and the use of formal models to explore alternative courses of action is being applied to banking, and may lead to different ways of thinking about the allocation of bank funds among various types of assets.[6] The system of priorities for bank funds is intended to promote maximum bank income in the long run by maximizing yields subject to safety-related constraints, but quantitative strategies or models are a more effective way of achieving such a goal than are general rules of thumb, and the movement of management towards more exacting decision-making techniques probably will lead to more elaborate decision rules for the allocation of the funds of commercial banks.

In the 1960s there was considerable discussion as to whether banks, in the allocation of funds, were departing from the principles they had followed in the past and were becoming much more willing to take risks, perhaps meriting concern that they might put themselves into an excessively weak position and invite another banking collapse. By conventional measures of bank liquidity, the loan-deposit ratio and the liquid-asset ratio, bank liquidity declined sharply in 1969, but then recovered to some degree in 1970. It appeared that banks were being managed more closely and were perhaps increasingly quick to respond to opportunities to take actions that would increase their earnings, but this did not appear to be a revolutionary change from the practices of the past.

[6]For references on this and other aspects of recent thinking and research about banking, see Paul F. Jessup (ed.), *Innovations in Bank Management*, Holt, New York, 1969.

Bank Cash: Primary Reserves

The decisions of commercial banks regarding cash management involve the amount of cash of various kinds to be held. Primary reserves, or cash, is held in several different forms: (1) currency and coin, (2) deposits with the district Federal Reserve bank, and (3) balances with other commercial banks. These are by no means perfect substitutes for one another. If customers want to withdraw currency, say, because the Fourth-of-July weekend is coming up and they are going away on trips, the bank must have the currency and coin to give them; it cannot give them checks on its balances at correspondent banks. Similarly, if the bank wants to buy some government securities, it may find it most convenient to pay with a check drawn on its Federal Reserve bank or a correspondent bank; it cannot conveniently pay with currency from the till. While the bank can exchange one form of primary reserve for another, this takes some time and may involve a modest expense. Thus, the management of cash involves the management of several imperfectly substitutable assets.

Like other assets, the various types of cash are held to meet certain functional needs. The bank estimates the amount of each kind of cash it needs to have on hand to meet the particular need it fills. The function for which currency and coin is held is to meet withdrawals in this form by customers. This shows a seasonal variation—it *does* increase before holiday weekends. The bank keeps daily records over the years, estimates as closely as it can how much currency and coin of each type it will need on a particular day, and leaves some allowance for safety. Currency and coin meet the legal reserve requirements of banks, but these requirements can be met by holding balances at other banks, which are useful for some additional purposes also, so the efficient bank limits its holdings of currency and coin to the amount needed to meet withdrawals.

Balances at Federal Reserve banks are limited to member banks (although nonmember banks hold some such balances in order to participate in the Federal Reserve System check-clearing services). They serve more than one function. They count against reserve requirements for member banks. In addition, these funds can be transferred by wire immediately to a bank in any other part of the country, checks can be written by the bank against this balance to make payments to other banks or to others, and unneeded funds in this form can be loaned each day as federal funds. Thus, the working balances with which settlements are made by member banks are largely their balances at their Federal Reserve banks, which serve also as legal reserves.

This function is also performed by balances at other commercial banks. Such correspondent balances are counted as legal reserves for nonmember banks under state laws, so for the nonmember bank such balances at other banks play a role similar to the one balances at Federal Reserve banks play for member banks. Such correspondent balances also serve, however, as a means by which small banks remunerate their large correspondent banks for the various services they receive from them. The amount of balances the bank holds for this purpose depends upon the volume of services it buys from its correspondent bank. Correspondent balances, therefore, serve at least three functions: legal reserves, working balances for making settlements, and as a means of remunerating the correspondent bank for services received.

To some extent, a given balance can simultaneously perform all three functions. Legal reserves ordinarily are defined in terms of average balances over a period of time, so the balance counted as legal reserves can also be used, within limits, as a working balance. Arrangements with the big city correspondent may define the balance required as compensation for services as a minimum rather than an average balance, however, which constrains the manner in which it can be used as a working balance. But in some cases, the balance required to compensate a correspondent bank for services may be larger than would be required for either legal reserves or working balances.

We now see that cash of the various types meets a number of specific functions that are related to one another in a complex way. Optimal management of bank cash is not a simple matter. The logic of this functional management of cash is illustrated by Table 7-1. Member banks in New York City include giant money-market banks to whom currency withdrawals are not so important as to banks dealing with small customers. Moreover, these banks can quickly get more currency from the Federal Reserve Bank of New York, which for many of them is just down the street. Therefore, only a small proportion of their cash is held in the form of currency and coin. Similarly, these banks function as the big-city corre-

TABLE 7-1 Cash Held by Commercial Banks, December 31, 1969 (in billions of dollars)

	Reserves with Federal Reserve Banks	Currency and Coin	Balances with Domestic Banks	Total
All commercial banks	21.4 (44%)	7.3 (15%)	20.3 (41%)	49.1
All member banks	21.4 (55%)	5.7 (15%)	11.9 (30%)	39.1
New York City member banks	4.4 (82%)	0.5 (9%)	0.5 (9%)	5.3
Reserve city member banks other than New York and Chicago	9.0 (63%)	1.8 (13%)	3.5 (24%)	14.3
Country member banks	7.2 (39%)	3.3 (18%)	7.9 (43%)	18.4
Nonmember banks	......	1.6 (16%)	8.4 (84%)	10.0

SOURCE: *Fed. Reserve Bull.*

TABLE 7-2 Reserve Requirements of Member Banks, March 31, 1971 (percent of deposits)

	Net Demand Deposits				Time Deposits (all classes of bank)		
	RESERVE CITY BANKS		COUNTRY BANKS		SAVINGS DEPOSITS	OTHER TIME DEPOSITS	
	Under $5 million	*Over $5 million*	*Under $5 million*	*Over $5 million*		*Under $5 million*	*Over $5 million*
Requirements in effect Oct. 31, 1971	17	17½	12½	13	3	3	5
Legal range of requirements	10 to 22		7 to 14			3 to 10	

SOURCE: Fed. Reserve Bull.

†In addition, a reserve requirement of up to 20 percent applied to balances due to and certain assets purchased by foreign branches that are in excess of certain base amounts. A reserve requirement of 5 percent applied to funds raised through the sale of bank-related commercial paper with a maturity of 30 days or longer, and a requirement equal to that for demand deposits applied in the case of such paper having a maturity of less than 30 days.

spondents of other banks; they themselves hold few balances in other commercial banks. Practically all of their primary reserves are held in the form of balances at the Federal Reserve Bank of New York.

At the other extreme are the member banks that are not in large cities, termed "country banks." They hold twice as high a proportion of their cash in the form of currency and coin as do the New York banks. Reflecting increasing reliance on correspondent banking, the proportion of cash held as balances in other commercial banks rises as we move from New York banks to country member banks and to nonmember banks.

Required reserves of member banks

The reserves that Federal Reserve member banks are required to hold are defined as including only balances at Federal Reserve banks and currency and coin. Before November 1959, only balances at Federal Reserve banks were counted as legal reserves. The amount of reserves, thus defined, that member banks are required to keep depends upon the volume of their deposits. Different reserve requirements are assessed against demand deposits and time deposits. Since 1966 the Federal Reserve has assessed higher reserve requirements against banks with total deposits of over $5 million than against small banks. Reserve requirements also differ between reserve city banks and country banks. The reserve requirements in effect on October 31, 1971 are shown in Table 7-2. The present law permits reserve requirements to be changed by the Board of Governors of the Federal Reserve System over the range shown.

Reserve requirements other than those against deposits were first levied in 1969. The imposition of reserve requirements against deposits of foreign branches and other loans from foreign branches in October 1969 and against funds raised by commercial paper sold by bank affiliates in October 1970 involved departures from the conception of the reserve mechanism as a means for controlling the money supply and associated bank credit.

For purposes of defining reserve requirements, banks are divided into two categories: reserve city banks and country banks. Reserve city banks are those located in a designated list of over 50 of the larger cities in the country, the "reserve cities." All other banks are designated as country banks. Banks in the outlying parts of reserve cities may be classified as country banks at their request if their business justifies this designation.

Classifying banks in this manner and assessing higher reserve requirements against city banks is a carry-over from the provisions of the National Bank Act of 1863. The logic of this approach related to the pyramiding of reserves resulting from the way correspondent relations among banks operated at that time. Correspondent balances then were counted as bank reserves. Thus, the banks in the larger cities included among their liabilities deposits that were the reserves of the smaller banks. In time of financial crisis, it had to be presumed that these reserves might be needed in the form of currency and, therefore, would be withdrawn from the banks that had been their custodians. To provide against this contingency, it seemed appropriate that those banks holding the reserve balances of other banks should themselves keep larger reserves in order to be able to meet such demands.

Since 1914, only a small part of the legal reserves of commercial banks—only those of some state banks—are held in the form of correspondent balances at other commercial banks. Moreover, in a period of credit stringency or bank runs it is presumed that the Federal Reserve System will make available whatever additional currency and reserves are needed to offset an increase in the demand of the public for currency and prevent widespread bank failures. So it is not certain that the earlier rationale for assessing higher reserve requirements against city banks is relevant to present-day circumstances.

Another possible basis for assessing reserve requirements by size of city is that it gives an advantage to small banks as compared to large banks and thereby acts to prevent banking concentration and preserve unit banking. In effect, the system of graduated reserves acts as a tax on banks related to their size or as a subsidy to country banks, thus limiting the acquisition of small banks by large banks. To suit this rationale, however, reserve requirements should be levied according to the size of the bank rather than the size of the city in which it is located. The existing set of requirements must be viewed as a compromise among various viewpoints and political factors, plus a dash of historical accident. One proposed reform of the framework of Federal Reserve policy involves setting uniform reserve requirements on demand deposits at all banks and not changing these requirements over time.

Required reserves are computed in relation to net demand deposits, the bank's total demand deposits less cash items in the process of collection and demand balances due from domestic banks. The purpose of this complex formula is to avoid implicitly double counting deposits for purposes of computing required reserves.

For the purposes of computing required reserves of Federal Reserve member banks, deposits are averaged over one a week ending with the close of business each Wednesday. The reserves to be matched against these deposits include the currency and coin held in the same week as the deposits and the deposits at Federal Reserve banks held during the corresponding period 2 weeks later. Therefore, the bank can know before the beginning of the statement week what average balance at its Federal Reserve bank it must keep in order just to meet its reserve requirement. This lag in meeting reserve requirements, which was first provided for in late 1968, makes it easy for the bank to avoid a reserve deficiency. Moreover, an excess or deficiency of reserves up to 2 percent of required reserves can be carried forward to the next reserve week.

A bank recording a reserve deficiency beyond this limit is subject to a penalty on the amount of such deficiency. This has commonly involved interest at 2 percentage points above the Federal Reserve discount rate on such deficiency. Reserve banks can levy more severe penalties, and frequent or continuous failure to meet reserve requirements could be a basis for withdrawing a bank's membership in the Federal Reserve System and perhaps for withdrawing its charter in the case of a national bank.

"Excess reserves" of member banks are defined as legal reserves, defined as above, minus required reserves. These excess reserves are not necessarily excess in the sense that banks do not want to hold them or are not holding them for some well defined purposes. In recent years, however, excess reserves of member banks have been trivial in amount. In 1969 and 1970, they were very steady, apart from a week-to-week variation at about $200 million, compared with total reserves of close to $30 billion.

Secondary Reserves: Managing the Money Position

The investment strategy of the commercial bank requires a certain volume of funds to be kept in cash plus liquid assets to assure the ability of the bank to meet any cash drain that might occur within the near future. Liquid assets, we recall, are earning assets that can be turned into cash on short notice without the hazard of substantial loss.

The volume of cash plus liquid assets that the bank needs to hold depends in part on factors that apply to all banks and that operate in about the same manner from year to year, such as the hazard of a general business deterioration or of a regional decline in business activity and deposits. The required volume of liquid assets also depends on the degree of unpredictable variation from week to week and from month to month in the deposits of the particular bank. This varies among banks, depending on the nature of the customers and the businesses to which the customers are related. Finally, liquidity needs depend also on seasonal variations in the bank's deposits and in the demand of its customers for loans. The bank attempts to predict these seasonal patterns, varying the volume of its liquid assets to offset them and choosing assets suited to the time when additional funds are expected to be needed.

Since liquid assets earn interest while cash does not, the basic management strategy of banks, as well as of other businesses, is to keep cash as small as it can, meeting liquidity needs as far as possible through the holding of interest-earning liquid assets. Management of the bank's "money position" consists of the detailed operations involved in retaining just as much cash as is needed and making sure that every dollar not needed in cash is invested in liquid assets and earning interest. However, close management of the money position also involves some expenses. The more closely cash is managed, the larger the staff required for the job; the more phone calls made, the more brokerage fees incurred. Thus, there is a trade off between the expenses incurred in money management and the interest earned on the additional funds kept invested. The higher the level of interest rates on liquid assets, the further it is worthwhile to incur costs in order to economize holdings of cash.

If interest rates on liquid assets fell very low, close to zero, the rewards for keeping funds invested would not cover the additional costs, and banks would rationally hold an unusually large part of their total liquidity reserves in cash. This, of course, would involve an unusually high level of excess reserves—which would not be undesired by banks, but would be held in lieu of liquid assets as secondary reserves. The outstanding example of such a situation is the 1930s, when yields on liquid assets were near zero, and banks did hold very large excess reserves. At the very high levels of short-term interest rates in the latter part of the 1960s, it was profitable for banks and businesses to manage their money positions very closely.

In managing the money position of a commercial bank, the goal is to average zero excess reserves over the reserve period, making short-run adjustments in a way that maximizes the average rate of return to the bank's funds. As checks flow into and out of the bank, it continually gains and loses both demand deposits and cash. The net outcome of these transactions is watched closely to determine whether the bank in any given day needs to acquire some additional cash or whether it has some extra cash it can invest in earning assets. The three main means of day-to-day adjustment of the cash position are (1) purchases and sales of short-term

Bank A		Bank B		Government Securities Dealer	
Assets	*Liabilities*	*Assets*	*Liabilities*	*Assets*	*Liabilities*
Government securities −100		Cash −100	Demand deposit −100	Government securities +100	
Cash +100				Demand deposit −100	

United States government securities, (2) operations in federal funds, and (3) borrowings from the Federal Reserve Bank.[7]

One course open to a bank needing some cash is to sell government securities from its holdings. The bank receives payment in the form of the check of the government securities dealer who is the buyer. This reduces his balance in his bank, gives this bank an unfavorable clearing balance, and shifts reserves from it to the bank selling the securities. In the case shown above, bank A shifts reserves to itself from bank B by selling the government securities. When the dealer sells these securities or some others and rebuilds his cash balance, bank B will regain its cash and deposits, but at the expense of some other bank and some other buyer of securities. Operations in government securities are a way of shifting reserves among banks, but do not add to total reserves. The bank with unneeded reserves can operate in the other direction, using excess cash to buy short-term government securities.

A method of adjustment generally more favorable for very temporary adjustments—and one that may sometimes offer a better yield even over longer periods of time—is to buy or sell federal funds. This involves 1-day loans of funds payable on the same day at a Federal Reserve bank. Transactions in government securities are conducted either in federal funds or in clearinghouse funds, which do not become available until the next day, as specified by the trading parties. The bank that borrows federal funds gains reserves the same day and leaves its government securities portfolio undisturbed, which may be desirable if the funds are needed only for a day or two.

In the case shown below, the entries on the books of the borrowing bank (bank A) are the increase in cash and an increase in a liability, the amount payable to the lending bank in federal funds. On the books of bank B, we find the reduction in cash and an increase in an asset item, the amount due from bank A in federal funds. The next day these trans-

[7]For more information, see "Reserve Adjustment Behavior of Tenth District Banks," *Fed. Reserve Bank Kansas City Mon. Rev.*, pp. 3–9, May 1970.

Bank A		Bank B	
Assets	*Liabilities*	*Assets*	*Liabilities*
Cash (balance at Federal Reserve bank) +100	Due to bank B (federal funds) +100	Cash (balance at Federal Reserve bank) −100 due from bank B (federal funds) +100	

actions are all reversed and both balance sheets turn to their original position. If bank A needs funds continually, however, it can simply borrow again each day.

The bank with excess reserves can put them to work—as an alternative to buying securities or investing them elsewhere in the money market—by selling federal funds. That is what bank B did in the example. Since funds immediately available at the Federal Reserve bank are the reserves of member banks, operations in federal funds are sometimes thought of as involving the lending of reserves.[8]

The usual trading unit in federal funds loans is $1 million, which implies that the market is most useful to very large banks. The great bulk of trading in federal funds is done by 100 large banks. Some large banks will to some extent make a market in federal funds for their correspondent banks. The most common way of transferring the funds is through phone calls to the Federal Reserve bank or instructions over the Federal Reserve bank leased wire. Confirming letters are then sent. Interest usually is settled by check or through a correspondent bank.

Federal funds loans provide a means of shifting funds and lending capacity from one bank to another and from one section of the country to another. By being a continuous borrower of federal funds, a bank essentially borrows reserves. A bank in an area of strong demand for credit can thus extend more credit than would be possible on the basis of the deposits it is able to hold. In 1970, federal funds transactions were large in relation to bank reserve balances, and dwarfed borrowings from Federal Reserve banks, as well as excess reserves. In the fall of 1970, various samples of banks were net borrowers of federal funds in amounts running from 33 1/3 to more than 100 percent of their required reserves.[9] The development of the federal funds market is one of several major innovations in banking practices, which took place in the 1950s and 1960s, that require rethinking about the logic of banking regulation.

For the limited number of banks that engage in it, an alternative to the federal funds loan as a way of investing excess reserves is a 1-day (or slightly longer) loan to a government securities dealer. To finance

[8]For further information, see Dorothy M. Nichols, *Trading in Federal Funds,* Board of Governors of the Federal Reserve System, Washington, D.C., 1965.

[9]*Fed. Reserve Bull.*, p. A8, November 1970.

their inventories of government securities, the dealers are continuously in the market for funds. They borrow both from bank and nonbank sources, using federal funds and clearing house funds, and 1-day and longer loans.

The extension of credit by a bank to a government securities dealer usually is handled not through a loan but through a repurchase agreement (also called RP, or buy-back). This transaction takes the form of a purchase of government securities by the bank from the dealer today, with payment usually in federal funds today, coupled with an agreement by the dealer to repurchase the securities tomorrow, with payment tomorrow in federal funds. Interest is charged at the rate on federal funds loans and has no relation to the coupon interest rate on the securities involved. This transaction accomplishes the same thing as a 1-day loan secured by government securities, but the arrangement as a repurchase agreement has some legal advantages.

Repurchase agreements with government securities dealers in some cases run for more than 1 day, and in some cases are left open in duration, running until one party wishes to terminate the arrangement, with interest charged at each day's federal funds rate. In terms of management of the money position of the bank, such loans to government securities dealers for the banks having associations with the dealers serve as an outlet for short-term funds as do federal funds loans.

A third way for a member bank to get funds to correct a temporary reserve deficiency is by borrowing from its Federal Reserve bank. This approach has some advantages: it can be done later in the day than the other methods and still gain reserves by the close of the day; access to funds is assured at a cost that is known in advance; and the Federal Reserve discount rate often is lower than the cost of borrowing federal funds or the interest foregone on the government securities that might be sold. However, some member banks are reluctant to borrow, which involves subjecting themselves to the scrutiny and possible criticism of the Federal Reserve lending officer, or they may want to save their goodwill at the Federal Reserve bank for a time of special need. Some banks as a matter of policy do not borrow from their Federal Reserve banks at any time.

In the case of borrowing from a Federal Reserve bank, the offset to the addition to cash on the books of the borrowing bank A is its debt to the Federal Reserve bank, On the books of the Federal Reserve bank (see below), we find the asset item "discounts and advances" (bank A) and

Bank A		Federal Reserve Bank	
Assets	*Liabilities*	*Assets*	*Liabilities*
Cash (balance at Federal Reserve bank) +100	Due to Federal Reserve bank +100	Discounts and advances (bank A) +100	Member bank reserve deposits (bank A) +100

the liabilities item "deposits of member banks" (bank A). This transaction differs from those considered above in that bank A in this case has not borrowed the reserves of other banks but has caused the Federal Reserve bank to create some additional reserves. Total reserves and the monetary base are increased because of this action.

Until late 1970, the member bank borrowing from its district Federal Reserve bank did so on the basis of its promissory note, accompanied as collateral by government securities or, less frequently, notes of the bank's customers. In late 1970, the Federal Reserve Board announced a simplification of this procedure to permit member bank borrowing essentially on an open-book basis. Certain side conditions are attached to member bank borrowing from the Federal Reserve System. Since these relate to monetary policy, they are discussed in Chap. 21.

In addition to these means of making day-to-day adjustments in its cash position, the bank in recent years may have considerable control over longer periods of time in the inflow of funds it attracts through sales of negotiable CDs, and in Eurodollar borrowings and sales of bank-related commercial paper for those banks that engage in these activities. These activities are alternatives to adjustments in holdings of government securities as a means of making adjustments over periods of weeks and months. In addition, Eurodollar borrowings have been used for some daily adjustments, especially in raising funds for the weekend.

Bank Loans

Most loans of banks are made directly to the borrower, usually on the basis of his promissory note. The making of a loan entails an evaluation of the creditworthiness of the borrower and, in some cases, designing the terms of the note to meet his particular situation and ability to repay the loan. Some loans are secured by collateral, property available to the lender should the borrower default on his contractual payments. In the case of business loans, the arrangements for administering provisions regarding collateral require an organization specializing in such activities and familiarity with the business involved. This kind of activity is a distinctive speciality of the commercial banks.

Business loans

Loans to business are the most important and in the 1960s were the most rapidly growing category of bank loans. Commercial and industrial loans of commercial banks in June 1970 amounted to $108 billion, nearly 40 percent of bank loans and about 25 percent of total loans and investments. Other large and growing components of bank loans are loans to individuals and real estate loans.

Most business loans of banks are made for short periods to meet the working capital needs of business, largely the financing of business inventories. In many cases, such loans involve a large seasonal variation. Rather than arranging for such loans on a one-by-one basis, the business and the bank often negotiate a "line of credit" indicating an amount of credit the bank will extend to the business upon request.

A substantial proportion of business loans are "term loans," involving a maturity ordinarily from 1 to 5 years. Since these loans cannot be sold by the bank, they are an illiquid asset. Moreover, making loans for longer periods requires additional precautions against credit risk, since there is more time for unexpected adversities to affect the borrower's ability to repay. However, so long as their quantity is held within limits, term loans have proved remunerative to the banks and meet an important credit need of small and medium-sized businesses.

Mortgage loans

The second largest category of bank loans is mortgage loans on residential properties. As a supplier of mortgage credit, the commercial banks compete with mutual savings banks, savings and loan associations, and life insurance companies. In June 1970, commercial banks held $71 billion in real estate loans, amounting to about one-fourth of their total loans. As holders of mortgages, the commercial banks are a bit more important than mutual savings banks and slightly less important than life insurance companies, but they hold only about one-half as many mortgage loans as savings and loan associations.

Consumer loans

Loans of banks to individuals, other than loans for purchasing or carrying securities, amounted to $64 billion in June 1970, just over one-fifth of total loans. About $41 billion of these loans were in the form of installment credit, loans repayable by regular monthly payments. This makes the banks the largest single source of installment credit in the economy, sales finance companies being only about half as important and credit unions, the next contender, holding just over one-fourth as much installment credit as the banks. It may be interesting to note that installment loans to purchase automobiles in the United States at the end of 1970 amounted to the striking sum of over $35 billion, about $20 billion of this debt being held by commercial banks.

Bank Investments

Commercial banks became holders of a substantial volume of government securities during the First World War and during the 1920s held about an equal volume of corporate securities and a small but rising volume of state and local government securities. When the demand for credit from business dried up during the Great Depression, banks shifted on a large scale into government securities, which were being created by the government deficits of the 1930s. During the Second World War, their holdings of government securities increased more than fourfold.

Since 1945, bank holdings of government securities have declined somewhat, while their total assets and their loans have grown enormously. The relative importance of government securities in bank portfolios is now back to something like the position of the 1920s. These securities serve almost entirely as secondary reserves. Bank holdings of government securities with more than 5 years to maturity declined markedly in 1969 and were very small in late 1970.

A component of bank holdings of securities that grew at an accelerated rate in the 1960s was state and local government securities. The special appeal of these securities to banks lies in the exemption of their interest from federal taxes. As corporations, banks are subject to the corporate income tax and so are a relatively heavily taxed investor. Many of the other major institutions that invest in debt are mutual organizations, rather than corporations, or for other reasons are subject to a somewhat more favorable tax treatment. Since the tax exemption of the state and local securities is worth more to banks than to potential investors in lower tax brackets, it is natural—though perhaps not economically rational—that high tax rates should cause these securities to shift to bank investors.

SUMMARY

1. Time deposits are of three major classes; savings deposits, time deposits, open account, and certificates of deposit, or CDs, the last of which may be either negotiable or nonnegotiable.

2. In attracting time deposits, commercial banks attempt to provide liquid assets at attractive yields. They compete most closely with mutual savings banks and savings and loan associations for savings deposits, and with short-term government securities and other open market liquid assets in the case of negotiable CDs.

3. The use of negotiable CDs was an important banking innovation of the 1960s in that it permits a bank to bid actively for funds in the national money market. Paralleling this development was the rapid expansion in 1969 in borrowing Eurodollars by United States banks through their foreign branches. Another source of funds other than deposits is bank-related commercial paper issued by bank holding companies or nonbank affiliates. Reserve requirements imposed by the Federal Reserve on Eurodollar borrowing and funds raised through bank-related commercial paper in 1969 and 1970 reduced the attractiveness of these sources of bank funds.

4. In competing for demand deposits, banks attempt to offer efficient service relating to the making of payments by check. They also compete for correspondent balances, require compensating balances, and offer a variety of services to attract and hold the demand deposits of customers.

5. The management of bank funds can be characterized in terms of four priorities: (1) cash or primary reserves, (2) protective investment, secondary reserves, or liquid assets, (3) meeting loan demands of customers, and (4) investment in securities for income.

6. The cash held by member banks is virtually limited to their required reserves plus correspondent balances held by the smaller banks. Excess reserves in recent years have been trivial in amount.

7. A focal activity of the commercial bank is managing the money position to avoid excessive or deficient reserves, so keeping the bank's funds invested in earning assets to the maximum possible extent. The principal means of making day-to-day adjustments in the money position of the bank are through federal funds loans, dealings in short-term government securities, and borrowing from the Federal Reserve bank.

8. Banks have a special role in the making of business loans, especially to small and local businesses. They also are the nation's major lender to consumers and a major holder of residential mortgage loans.

9. Bank investments consist largely of government securities, which are held as secondary-reserve assets, and a rapidly growing volume of state and local securities that are held because the exemption of their interest from federal taxes makes them attractive to banks, which are subject to the corporation income tax.

QUESTIONS FOR REVIEW AND DISCUSSION

1. Show the T account entries for a bank gaining time deposits. How do the main categories of time deposits differ from the viewpoint of bank management?

2. Describe the process by which a bank would raise funds through Eurodollar transactions, showing relevant T accounts. What factors affect the attractiveness to the bank of raising funds through Eurodollars as against CDs? What special factors caused the large increase in Eurodollar borrowing by United States banks in 1969?

3. Explain the ways in which a bank might seek to gain demand deposits.

4. Explain how the priorities for bank funds can be an approximate method of maximizing expected bank income under uncertainty.

5. Indicate the particular functions performed by each type of bank cash and the amount and composition of cash that would presumably be held by different types of banks.

6. Describe how required reserves of member banks are computed.

7. Discuss the options open to the manager of a bank's money position who finds himself near the end of the reserve week with an expected reserve deficiency.

8. "Any bank that wants to increase its deposits can buy the necessary reserves in the federal funds market. Thus, the reserve mechanism does not limit the volume of deposits." Comment.

9. Explain why since World War II the relative importance of government securities in bank portfolios has declined and that of state and local securities has increased.

8 the federal reserve system

The Federal Reserve System serves as the central bank of the United States. By "central bank" we mean a bank that acts on behalf of the government. Early in the nineteenth century, the United States was in the forefront of central banking. The Second Bank of the United States was assuming the functions of a central bank, along with or perhaps even ahead of the Bank of England. But for complex political reasons the government declined to renew the charter of the Second Bank of the United States. While central banking was being developed by the Bank of England and was spreading throughout the world, the United States had no such institution.

It was not until 1914, reflecting the Federal Reserve Act of 1913, that the Federal Reserve System began operations. The way this institution grew out of the thinking and the events of its time we consider in Chap. 19 in dealing with the background of United States monetary policy. At this point, we consider the structure and operations of the Federal Reserve System as it exists today, its relation to the commercial banks, its role in the operation of the reserve mechanism, and its influence upon the amount of money and commercial bank credit.

The Organization and Structure of the Federal Reserve System

The principal operating agencies of the Federal Reserve System are the 12 regional Federal Reserve banks.[1] These have substantial powers, exercised primarily by the presidents of the banks. The major source of power and decisions, however, is the Board of Governors of the Federal Reserve System, which is located in Washing-

[1]A more detailed, but now somewhat dated, discussion of the Federal Reserve System is given in, *The Federal Reserve System: Purposes and Functions*, Board of Governors of the Federal Reserve System, Washington, D.C., 1963.

ton, D.C. The other important decision-making agency is the Federal Open Market Committee, which is made up of the members of the Board of Governors and has minority representation of presidents of Federal Reserve banks. We now review these organizations and their powers and functions.

The Federal Reserve banks

To see the Federal Reserve System as a central *bank*, we must look at the Federal Reserve banks, for these are the agencies that operate as banks for bankers and for the government. The Federal Reserve Act provided for not less than eight nor more than twelve Federal Reserve districts, each to have its own Federal Reserve bank (Fig. 8–1). We have had 12 Federal Reserve banks since 1914, the territory of the Federal Reserve Bank of San Francisco being enlarged to incorporate Alaska and Hawaii when these became part of the nation. Most of the Federal Reserve banks have one or more branches in addition to the head office. There now are 24 of these branches of Federal Reserve banks.

The Federal Reserve banks differ widely in size and in importance. The Federal Reserve Bank of New York is the largest and most important, followed by the Federal Reserve Banks of Chicago and San Francisco. These three Federal Reserve banks (consolidated with their branches) in August, 1971 had assets of over $49 billion, more than all of the other Federal Reserve banks combined. The Federal Reserve Bank of New York

Fig. 8–1 Federal Reserve Districts. (The Twelfth Federal Reserve District includes also Hawaii and Alaska.) (Board of Governors of the Federal Reserve System.)

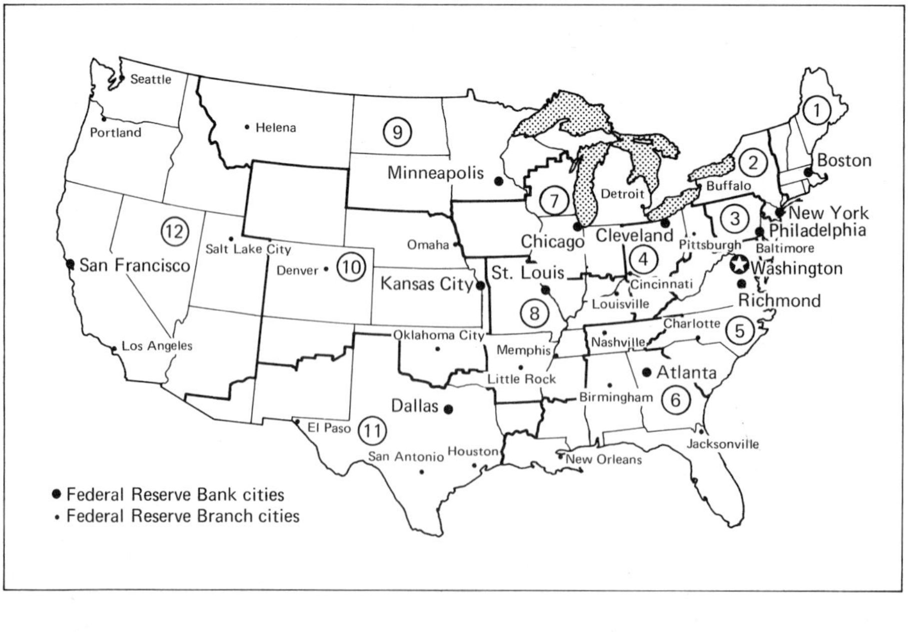

has a place of special importance in the System not only because of its size but because of its location in the leading money market of the nation and the world and in a major market for foreign exchange. All of the actual operations of the Federal Reserve System in buying and selling government securities and foreign exchange and the bulk of activities as fiscal agent for the Treasury are carried out by the Federal Reserve Bank of New York, acting as the agent of the whole Federal Reserve System.

In conformity with the goal of its founders to decentralize power within the Federal Reserve System and maximize private participation, the Federal Reserve banks were set up as federally chartered corporations owned by the member banks in each district. Each member bank is required to subscribe to the capital of the Federal Reserve bank an amount equal to 6 percent of its own capital and surplus. The amount of this capital subscription is adjusted when the member bank's capital and surplus change. Only one-half of this 6 percent subscription has been paid up, the other half remaining subject to call upon need. But while the member banks nominally own the Federal Reserve bank, payment of dividends on their capital stock of the Reserve bank is limited to 6 percent. The income of the Federal Reserve banks is used to defray their expenses and those of the Board of Governors of the Federal Reserve System. Earnings not needed for these purposes, after some increase in the surplus of the Federal Reserve banks, are paid to the U.S. Department of the Treasury. In 1970 this payment to the Treasury amounted to $3.5 billion.

The arrangements for control of Federal Reserve banks are as unusual as those for their ownership and income distribution. Each Reserve bank has a Board of Directors consisting of nine members. Six of these are elected by the member banks and three by the Board of Governors, for 3-year terms. Of the six directors elected by the member banks, three (the Class A directors) are to be bankers and the other three (Class B directors) must be engaged in commerce, agriculture, or industry. The remaining three (the Class C directors), who are appointed by the Board of Governors, are not restricted as to occupation and are to represent the general public. One of the Class C directors is designated by the Board of Governors as Chairman of the Board and as Federal Reserve Agent.

The chief executive officer of the Federal Reserve bank is the president of the bank. He is chosen by the Board of Directors for a 5-year term, subject to the approval of the Board of Governors. Ordinarily, the management of the bank and its policy decisions are made by the president, the Board of Directors exercising only nominal authority. The men appointed to be presidents of the Federal Reserve banks usually have had many years experience within the Federal Reserve System.

The Board of Governors of the Federal Reserve System

The central governing body and main source of power in the Federal Reserve System is the Board of Governors, which is located in Washington,

D.C. The Board consists of seven members, appointed by the President of the United States for a term of 14 years subject to confirmation by the Senate. The President chooses one of the members to be Chairman and another to be Vice-chairman, each for a period of 4 years. The Federal Reserve Act provides that not more than one member of the Board may be chosen from any Federal Reserve district. A member who has served a full term is not eligible for reappointment. The Board of Governors is a decision-making and coordinating body rather than an operating agency. The specific allocation of powers and functions among agencies of the Federal Reserve System we shall consider below.

The Federal Open Market Committee

When the Federal Reserve System was established in 1913, it was not expected to engage actively in purchases and sales of United States government securities, which we term "open market operations." During the 1920s, it was discovered that such operations were a means of achieving the goals of the System, and, indeed, were essential to its effective operation. To have the individual Federal Reserve banks buying and selling government securities in an uncoordinated manner would obviously be unsatisfactory. Thus, following earlier informal arrangements to coordinate such activities, legislation in 1933 and 1935 officially established the Federal Open Market Committee in almost its present form.

This Committee consists of all seven members of the Board of Governors, plus the presidents of five of the Federal Reserve banks. The Federal Reserve Bank of New York, as the operating agency of the Open Market Committee, is always represented on the Committee. The other four positions are rotated among the presidents of four geographic groups of Federal Reserve banks. Ordinarily, the presidents of all of the Federal Reserve banks attend meetings of the Federal Open Market Committee and participate in the discussion, although only the designated five of them have a vote at any time.

The Federal Open Market Committee has been accustomed to meet every 3 weeks in the offices of the Board in Washington. Its main function is to direct the policy of the System in its open market operations, its purchases and sales of United States government securities. However the meetings, which bring together all of the major policy-making officials of the System, have provided a framework for general discussion of policy issues and coordination of actions within the System.

The open market operations directed by the Federal Open Market Committee are carried out by the Federal Reserve Bank of New York. A vice-president of the Federal Reserve Bank of New York is designated as Manager of the System Open Market Account and oversees the hour-to-hour activities of the traders who actually buy and sell in the government securities market. The Manager of the System Open Market Account is responsible to the Open Market Committee. He reports to the Committee at each meeting and receives from it some general directive to guide his activities until the next meeting. To guard against misunderstanding or error in the carrying out of the Open Market Committee's directive, a telephone conference is held each day between the Manager of the System Account and an Executive Committee of the Open Market Committee. If circumstances require it, modern communications facilities permit a telephone conference of the full Open Market Committee to be convened within a matter of hours, or even of minutes.

The Federal Advisory Council

The Federal Advisory Council consists of 12 members, one chosen by the Board of Directors of each Federal Reserve bank. The Council has no power and operates only as an advisory body. It meets at least four times a year, usually in Washington. It does not seem to have an important influence upon Federal Reserve policy, but it is a means of formally making available to the System the views of a group of men who are prominent in financial affairs and who represent different sections of the country.

Member banks of the Federal Reserve System

The Federal Reserve Act required all national banks to become member banks of the Federal Reserve System, thereby subjecting themselves to the requirements and the benefits discussed below. State-chartered banks are permitted to become member banks. Membership is available to mutual savings banks and Morris Plan banks, but private (noncorporate) bankers are not permitted to join the System.

Membership of a bank in the Federal Reserve System involves several kinds of obligations and requirements that deter state banks from joining the System. The reserve requirements imposed upon member banks are higher than those to which most state nonmember banks are subject under regulations by their state banking authorities. Moreover, the Federal Reserve defines reserves more narrowly, since state banking authorities include correspondent balances and even short-term United States government securities as reserves. The additional cost of the higher reserve requirements probably is the main factor discouraging membership in the Federal Reserve System by large state banks.

In addition, to become a member bank a state bank must meet standards of the Federal Reserve System as to management and capital stock and surplus in relation to deposits, and must be accepted by the Federal Deposit Insurance Corporation for the granting of insurance. The restrictions of the Federal Reserve System as to the kinds of assets banks can hold and the activities in which they can engage are more rigorous than those of some state banking authorities.

Finally, membership in the Federal Reserve System requires a bank when presented for payment with a check drawn upon it to pay at par rather than levying a service charge on the one presenting the check for payment. Such failure of banks to remit at par seriously limits the efficiency of the payments system and the Federal Reserve from its inception has attempted to remedy the defect. However, there were at the end of 1969 still nearly 800 banks in the country that did not remit at par and were thereby debarred from membership in the Federal Reserve System.

On the other hand, membership in the Federal Reserve System also gains a bank certain privileges. Member banks can borrow from their Federal Reserve banks on the conditions considered below. They can use the services of the Federal Reserve banks in collecting checks, transferring funds, obtaining information, and obtaining advice on management problems. However, a nonmember bank that maintains a correspondent relation with a member bank is able indirectly to receive most of these benefits through its corespondent. Also available is a limited type of association with the Federal Reserve System whereby checks can be cleared directly through the Federal Reserve System by meeting certain requirements without full membership in the System.

The Federal Reserve System has never succeeded in enticing as many as one-half of the nation's commercial banks to become member banks. Since the largest banks are nearly all national banks, which are required to be member banks, and state member banks, the great bulk of the nation's deposits are held by the minority of banks that are member banks. Since the Second World War, however, the proportion of banks maintaining membership in the Federal Reserve System and the proportion of the nation's deposits held in member banks have declined.

Federal Reserve Activities Related to Economic Stabilization

We shall now review the various activities engaged in by the Federal Reserve System, their purposes, and the procedures by which they are controlled. The operation of the Reserve mechanism and the quantitative aspects of Federal Reserve influence on the money supply and bank credit are considered in the next chapter.

Open market operations

Open market operations are the most important instrument through which the Federal Reserve affects the money supply and the amount of bank credit. The activities are controlled, as we noted above, by the Federal Open Market Committee, acting through its agent the Manager of the System Open Market Account at the Federal Reserve Bank of New York. Most open market operations involve United States government securities. They are called open market operations because the government securities are bought from dealers in the private market rather than through direct dealings with the U.S. Treasury. Framers of central banking legislation have feared that if the central bank dealt directly with the Treasury it might be pressured into buying securities to suit the convenience of the Treasury rather than tending strictly to its function of regulating bank reserves and the money supply.

The open market operations are conducted just as would be the purchases and sales of any large participant in the government securities market.[2] Around the trading desk in the Federal Reserve Bank of New York sit a team of traders who phone the government securities dealers to buy or sell whatever suits the System's purposes. In this market, purchases or sales running into tens of millions of dollars can be conducted in a matter of minutes.

If open market operations occurred only when it was necessary to implement a change in monetary policy, they would be rather infrequent. Actually, most open market operations do not bear any easily defined relation to changes in monetary policy. They are made to offset some of the many factors that affect bank reserves or in response to day-to-day changes in conditions in the money market. Acting for these reasons, the Federal Reserve participates in open market operations on many if not most days. Not only can open market operations be conducted that do not reflect any change in monetary policy but changes in monetary policy can be made without any open market operations—simply by failing to offset some factor affecting bank reserves that is pushing them in the desired direction. Thus, it is not possible to find any simple relation between open market operations and changes in monetary policy.

Most Federal Reserve open market operations are conducted in short-term securities, primarily those with less than 1 year to maturity. Ordinarily, the preferred instrument for open market operations is Treasury bills. There are several reasons for this preference:

1. The market for short-term Treasury securities, and especially Treasury bills, is the most stable and largest volume element in the debt markets. Consequently, the Federal Reserve can buy and sell the large amounts in which it deals in this market without delay or disruption of the market.

2. On some past occasions, especially during the Second World War and through 1950, the Federal Reserve has been charged with responsibility for stabilizing the prices and yields of United States government securities. This thwarts its effort to bring about any desired pattern of bank reserves. If the Federal Reserve is to buy government securities whenever their price falls below some defined price, evidently its purchases and sales are governed by the behavior of the market rather than

[2]A detailed discussion of these arrangements is given in Alan R. Holmes, "A Day at the Trading Desk," *Fed. Reserve Bank N. Y. Mon. Rev.*, October 1970.

by the volume of reserves that the banking system ought to have. To be completely free to govern its open market operations with reference to bank reserves, the Federal Reserve must be able to ignore changes in prices and yields of government securities. Such an approach ordinarily is feasible if the Federal Reserve limits itself to the short-term end of the market. However, an effort of the Federal Reserve to buy or sell large amounts in the thinner and more sensitive long-term market would be likely so to disrupt that market as to bring about a hazard that the Federal Reserve would be diverted into open market operations focused on stabilizing prices of government bonds.

3. The Federal Reserve authorities realize that their ability to conduct large-scale open market operations depends on the quality of the government securities market. In many other nations, the central bank cannot effectuate policy through open market operations because the government securities market is so unstable and sensitive that large-scale purchases or sales by the central bank would plunge it into disorder. Therefore, the Federal Reserve wishes to maintain and even to improve the "depth, breadth, and resiliency" of the government securities market.

Some officers of the Federal Reserve System have argued that this goal is best sought by limiting Federal Reserve activities to the more stable short-term end of the market in the hope that this will facilitate stabilizing speculation in the long-term end of the market by government securities dealers. It is argued that such activities by dealers would be hampered by Federal Reserve activities in the long-term market, which the dealers would be unable to predict, and that if the dealers were thereby deterred from performing a stabilizing role in the long-term market and the Federal Reserve had to take over this function, its ability to carry out its primary function of controlling bank reserves would be impeded.

4. Another aspect of the argument is that if the Federal Reserve is operating simultaneously in all sectors of the government securities market and shifting its purchases and sales back and forth in that market, it is doing essentially what the Treasury does in its "debt management" activities. This creates a potential conflict between the Federal Reserve and the Treasury that could lead the Federal Reserve to be forced into accommodating the Treasury.

While some observers have found these arguments persuasive, those who have thought of monetary policy as measured by the interest rate rather than by bank reserves and the money supply have argued that the Federal Reserve would have more effect upon the long-term interest rate by operating directly in the bond market. This difference of opinion relates to other aspects of a divergence of views about monetary policy, which we shall discuss in later chapters. In response to criticism of what was interpreted to be a rigid "bills-only policy," the Federal Reserve has shifted to a less well defined position and has conducted a substantial volume of operations in intermediate-term and some operations in long-term government securities. Most of its operations, however, continue to be in short-term securities.

The Federal Reserve also conducts some open market operations in a private money-market instrument, "bankers' acceptances." These are short-term commercial obligations that have been accepted and guaranteed by a banker. During the early years of the Federal Reserve System, it was believed that the development of this market would serve the public interest by creating a debt instrument similar to the private bills that dominated the London money market and through which the Bank of England traditionally operated. Actually, the instrument never became very important and its intended role as the central instrument of the money market was assumed after the 1930s by the Treasury bill. Early Federal Reserve operations in acceptances were sometimes mischievous, since the System was preoccupied with maintaining the prices and yields of the acceptances and this sometimes led to the same kind of perverse open market operations as result from Federal Reserve operations to peg prices of government securities. Acceptances still appear as an asset of the Federal Reserve banks, but they are not now important.

When the Federal Reserve wishes to buy some government securities for no more than a few days, to offset a factor temporarily depressing bank reserves or a money-market stringency believed to be temporary, it often will do this not through outright purchase of the securities but rather by "repurchase agreements," or RPs. In this case, the Federal Reserve purchase is combined with an agreement that the dealer will buy back the securities after a specified number of days, interest being charged at a specified rate, ordinarily the prevailing Federal Reserve discount rate. This may simplify the task of the Federal Reserve, and it also signals to the market that the purchase is only a temporary one. However, a repurchase agreement has almost exactly the same effect as if the Federal Reserve had made a loan to the government securities dealer on the collateral of the securities. Therefore, RPs can be used also, in effect, to provide financing to government securities dealers when they are unable to find it elsewhere and would otherwise have to lighten their inventories at a time when the Federal Reserve may not want the market burdened with additional securities. Commonly, this situation arises when the money market is temporarily very tight, which is a time when the Federal Reserve may wish to provide some additional bank reserves in any case.

Reserve requirements

The operation of the reserve mechanism as a control instrument over bank credit and the money supply requires that member banks have some minimum ratio of reserves to the deposits that they hold through law or custom. Reserve requirements of member banks are defined by the

Board of Governors of the Federal Reserve System within a range specified by legislation. The requirements applying at the end of 1970 and the range over which the law at that time permitted the Federal Reserve to change reserve requirements are shown in Table 7–2.

A change in reserve requirements alters the required reserves of banks for any given volume of deposits and thus, since it does not affect their actual (legal) reserves, changes their excess reserves. Consider a bank with only demand deposits of $1 million and a 20 percent reserve requirement, whose reserves are just equal to required reserves at $200,000. If now the reserve requirement is increased to 22 percent, required reserves are $220,000 and the bank must find another $20,000 in reserves to avoid a deficiency. If the reserve requirement had been reduced to 18 percent, the bank would have found itself with excess reserves of $20,000. Such changes in reserve requirements can be used to bring about large and abrupt changes in the reserve position of banks.

A change in reserve requirements not only changes the excess reserves of member banks and thereby provides an inducement for them to expand or contract their loans and investments and their deposits, but it also has two important side effects. The first is that an increase in reserve requirements reduces the base-money multiplier, the change in the money supply that results from any given absolute change in bank reserves and the monetary base. This is a significant effect, to which there attach some pros and some cons. The second side effect is on the profit position of the member banks. Increasing reserve requirements means that for any volume of deposits and total assets banks must keep more reserves, on which they do not earn interest, and a smaller volume of earning assets. These side effects must be weighed by the Federal Reserve in considering a proposed change in reserve requirements.

Changes in Federal Reserve discount rates

The ability to borrow from one's Federal Reserve bank is one of the privileges of membership in the Federal Reserve System. The interest rate charged on such loans is called the Federal Reserve discount rate. Other things being equal, the lower the Federal Reserve discount rate, the greater the incentive for member banks to meet reserve needs by borrowing from the Reserve bank, so the greater such borrowings, and the greater the member bank reserves. However, in practice the Federal Reserve discount rate must be interpreted in relation to other interest rates and surrounding circumstances, making up a more complex story.

The process by which Federal Reserve discount rates are set is a somewhat intricate one. The discount rate of each Federal Reserve bank is set by its Board of Directors, which meets at least every 2 weeks to consider this matter. However, the decision of the bank's Board of Directors is subject to review *and determination* by the Board of Governors. This means that the Board of Governors can, if it wishes, overrule the directors of any Federal Reserve bank and set its discount rate.

One way the Federal Reserve might control the amount member banks borrow from it is simply to set the discount rate at the level that brings about the desired amount of borrowing by member banks. Rationing of Federal Reserve credit to member banks then would be accomplished by the price mechanism. The Federal Reserve has not taken this approach. The Federal Reserve discount rate often has been lower than the interest rate banks earn on their earning assets, so if there were no side restrictions on their borrowing from Reserve banks they would increase it greatly.

The approach taken by the Federal Reserve is to discourage member banks from borrowing, except to meet purely temporary shortages of reserves such as those associated with a sudden withdrawal of deposits or unexpectedly large seasonal increases in demand for credit from a bank. The Federal Reserve takes the position that a member bank applying for a loan from its Federal Reserve bank should be subjected to general scrutiny to assure that it is not borrowing "primarily for the purpose of obtaining a tax advantage or profiting from interest differentials and whether the bank is extending an undue amount of credit for the speculative carrying of or trading in securities, real estate, or commodities, . . . " The prospect of having the Federal Reserve bank tell them it does not like the way they are running their business is enough to deter many bankers from ever borrowing from Federal Reserve banks. The maintenance of a "reluctance to borrow" on the part of member banks is a considered part of the Federal Reserve administration of loans to member banks.

This approach to administering loans to member banks introduces an element of uncertainty into the banking and monetary system. If, over time, the Federal Reserve became tougher in defining the conditions under which member banks could borrow—or even if the member banks thought it was being tougher though it was not—this would change the interpretation that should be put upon any given amount of member bank borrowing. Since the amount of such borrowing has been taken by the Federal Reserve as a measure of the degree of "credit ease" or "credit restraint," this possible error in interpreting the amount of member bank borrowing has been a problem in the system of administering monetary policy.

Regulation Q

The Banking Act of 1933 prohibited the payment of interest on demand deposits and gave the Board of Governors of the Federal Reserve System the power to specify the maximum rate of interest member banks can pay on various categories of time deposits. The Federal Deposit Insurance Corporation exercises the same powers for insured nonmember banks and has, in practice, issued regulations identical with those of the Federal Reserve. The Interest Rate Control Act passed in 1966 and subsequently

TABLE 8-1 Maximum Interest Rates Payable on Time and Savings Deposits

	Effective Date		
TYPE OF DEPOSIT	SEPT. 26, 1966	APRIL 19, 1968	JAN. 21, 1970
Savings deposits	4	4	4½
Other time deposits			
Multiple maturity†			
30–89 days	4	4	4½
90 days–1 year	5	5	5
1 to 2 years			5½
2 years and over			5¾
Single-maturity			
Less than $100,000			
30 days to 1 year	5	5	5
1 year to 2 years			5½
2 years and over			5¾
$100,000 and over			
30–59 days	5½	5½	‡
60–89 days		5¾	‡
90–179 days		6	6¾
180 days to 1 year		6¼	7
1 year or more			7½

†Multiple-maturity time deposits include those automatically renewable at maturity without action by the depositor and those that are payable after written notice of withdrawal.

‡Ceilings on these categories were suspended June 24, 1970 until further notice. From Jan. 21 through June 23, 1970, the ceilings were 6¼ percent on maturities of 30 to 59 days and 6½ percent on maturities of 60 to 89 days.

SOURCE: Board of Governors of the Federal Reserve System.

renewed several times granted some additional powers to these agencies, as well as giving parallel powers to the Federal Home Loan Bank to apply interest rate ceilings to savings and loan associations. The Federal Reserve in March 1971 recommended that these powers be made permanent.

The Federal Reserve has changed the interest rates permitted under regulation Q periodically in response to changes in market interest rates and economic conditions. It has increasingly drawn distinctions among different classes of time deposits, in 1970 distinguishing among time deposits by class of contract, term to maturity, and size of deposit, as shown in Table 8-1.

The adoption of ceilings on bank interest rates during the Great Depression reflected the idea that excessive competition among banks led them to pay unrealistically high interest rates, which in turn forced them to buy risky assets in an effort to earn a high enough yield to meet their interest obligations. The regulations meant little until the 1950s, when they were made effective by increases in market interest rates and the rates banks could earn on their assets. Although adjusted upward a number of times, the regulation Q ceilings on a number of occasions, especially in 1966 and 1968–1969, prevented banks from paying on time deposits interest rates competitive with those on open market liquid assets. This led to reductions in the volume of time deposits and to major rechannelings of credit flows through the economy.

The use by the Federal Reserve of regulation Q during the 1950s and 1960s did not reflect the ideas that led to the initiation of this regulation in 1933. Rather, it stemmed from the Federal Reserve's view that the interest rate ceilings were a way of affecting economic conditions by affecting the volume of bank credit. When banks were prevented by the interest rate ceilings from paying competitive interest rates on time deposits, the volume of time deposits declined, which tended to reduce the volume of bank credit. This view was criticized by economists who saw the Federal Reserve's function as regulation of the money supply, rather than the amount of bank credit. As they saw it, regulation Q caused costly side effects in disruption of credit flows, with but little effect on economic conditions.[3] The role of regulation Q as a way of controlling total demand, thus, depends heavily on the theoretical framework within which it is interpreted, and we consider it further below.

Regulation Q seems to have been viewed by the Federal Reserve also as a way of affecting the allocation of credit among different classes of users as well as of influencing competitive relations between commercial banks and savings institutions. The desirability and the effects of using interest rate ceilings for these purposes also are matters on which opinion is divided.

Changes in margin requirements

Since 1934, the Board of Governors of the Federal Reserve System has had the authority to define the maximum extent to which purchases of certain securities can be financed on credit. This power was given to the Federal Reserve by the Securities Exchange Act of 1934 because it was believed that the stock market boom of the latter 1920s contributed to the Great Depression and that the boom, in turn, derived from excessive purchases of common stock on credit. When securities are purchased on credit, the security is used as collateral for the loan. The term "margin requirement" refers to the proportion of the purchase price that the buyer must put up in cash. It is like the downpayment requirement applied to a house or durable good. Thus, a margin requirement of 80 percent means that the buyer must put up 80 percent of the purchase price in cash and can borrow only the remaining 20 percent on the collateral of the securities. Therefore, the higher the margin requirement, the smaller the extent to which securities can be purchased on credit. The Board of Governors regulation T governs the extension of credit by brokers and dealers on listed

[3]A major statement of this approach is in Milton Friedman, "Controls on Interest Rates Paid by Banks," *J. Money, Credit, Banking,* **2:** 15–32 (1970). A general discussion is in Lawrence S. Ritter, *Regulation Q: Issues and Alternatives,* Association of Reserve City Bankers, Chicago, 1965.

securities, while its regulation U applies to bank loans on common stock, and regulation G applies to other lenders. In the past 20 years, margin requirements have varied only within the range of 50 to 90 percent. They were 80 percent from June 1968 to May 5, 1970, at which time they were reduced to 65 percent (a lower rate being applied to convertible bonds).

If there again developed a great speculative boom in the stock market, the existence of these margin requirements would be very helpful, and there would be wide agreement as to how the Federal Reserve should use its power. By raising margin requirements to high levels, even to 100 percent, and cutting off the flow of credit into the purchase of securities, an important limitation could be placed upon an incipient speculative boom.

Just what the Federal Reserve should do with margin requirements when there is not a stock market boom is not so certain. Margin requirements might be raised when stock prices increased and lowered when they decreased; raised when the amount of credit going to the stock market increased; raised when developments in the stock market were adjudged to be unsound; or made responsive to yet other criteria. Federal Reserve statements characterize the policy as designed "to curb the excessive use of credit for purchasing or carrying securities," but the criteria by which it is determined when the use of credit is excessive are, perhaps necessarily, somewhat vague.

Other selective credit controls

Margin requirements are representative of a class of policy instrument commonly termed "selective credit controls." Such controls have two important characteristics: (1) They operate not by limiting the supply of credit, as does the reserve apparatus, but rather by prohibiting certain kinds of borrowing and thus limiting the demand for credit. The additional limitation of credit through the general credit control implemented through the reserve apparatus has the direct effect of reducing the supply of credit and increasing the interest rate, while additional policy restrictions implemented through selective credit controls reduce the demand for credit and tend to reduce the rate of interest. (2) The selective credit control applies only to a particular type of borrower or credit, while the general credit control instruments leave the allocation of credit to market forces.

Margin requirements are the only permanent selective credit control implemented by the Federal Reserve System. However, such controls have in the past been applied to consumer credit and residential mortgage credit. These credit controls operated by defining minimum downpayments and maximum maturities on loans to buy houses and consumer durable goods. By increasing the required downpayment, the control excludes from borrowing, and from buying, that set of potential buyers who do not have enough cash to meet the higher downpayment requirements. Similarly, shortening the allowable maturity of the loan increases the required monthly payments and rules out of the market those potential buyers whose income is not great enough to meet the larger monthly payments. The selective credit controls operate as a rationing system, excluding from the market those with limited cash and those with smaller incomes.

Informal and extralegal controls

A final way in which officers of the Federal Reserve System can attempt to influence the behavior of banks and others is by making statements as to the kind of behavior they think is appropriate and by persuasion attempting to bring about results that cannot be achieved through existing policy instruments. This approach is sometimes called moral suasion or—less piously—the jawbone approach. If the suggestions of the authority imply some kind of retaliation against those who do not comply, then compliance ceases to be truly voluntary and what is in question is a kind of mandatory control that is not sanctioned by legislation. As an example of this approach, in September 1966 the Board of Governors sent a letter to all member banks requesting "restraint" in granting business loans, especially loans for "nonproductive" purposes. It was indicated that such loans would be viewed less favorably than other assets when considering the requests of member banks to borrow from their Federal Reserve bank. Since the conditions under which the Federal Reserve banks will lend to member banks are not explicitly defined, the threat of denial of such credit, explicit or only implied, can be used as a way of putting pressure on member banks to take actions desired by the Federal Reserve authorities. Some observers view such Federal Reserve actions as a desirable addition to the power and flexibility of control, while others see such extralegal exercise of power as unfair to those subjected to it and as violating sound principles of governing regulation by explicit legislation.

Service Activities of the Federal Reserve System

In addition to the activities related to monetary policy and bank supervisory functions described in Chap. 6, the Federal Reserve System also engages in a set of service activities on behalf of the nation's payments system and of the government, in particular the U.S. Department of the Treasury.

Check clearing and collection

The making of payments by checks in a banking system involving many banks requires some means for the bank in which a check is deposited to collect the funds from the bank on which it is drawn. When the two banks are in the same city, this is accomplished through the local clearinghouse. Each day every bank will find that its customers have deposited with it a great many checks drawn on other banks in the city. At the same time, checks that its customers have written have been deposited in other banks in the city. It would be wasteful to transfer funds from one bank to another in payment of each of these checks, for in any given day the flows of checks in the two directions will largely cancel out.

Instead, each bank each day sorts out all the checks it has received that are drawn on other banks. Then agents of all the banks meet together, present their checks on one another, and make payments to settle the net balances. This is accomplished by the local clearinghouse. The net claims of the banks against one another are settled on the books of the clearinghouse itself, a local bank, a correspondent bank outside the city, or the Federal Reserve bank. This portion of the check clearing and collection system does not require the assistance of the Federal Reserve System.

In the case of out-of-town checks, the Federal Reserve System provides a similar mechanism for check collection. In the case of two member banks within the same Federal Reserve district, the bank receiving the check sends it to the Federal Reserve bank for collection. The Federal Reserve bank forwards it to the bank on which it is drawn. The transfer of funds is made directly on the books of the Federal Reserve bank, since both member banks have accounts there. The Federal Reserve bank simply transfers the necessary funds from the account of the payer's bank to that of the payee.

When the two member banks are in different Federal Reserve districts, there is an additional step in the process. The bank receiving the check again forwards it to its Federal Reserve bank for collection. In this case, the Federal Reserve bank cannot collect the check directly but sends it for collection to the Federal Reserve bank in the appropriate district, which then presents it for collection. Once again the payment is made on the books of the Federal Reserve banks, but in this case a mechanism is needed to transfer funds from the one Federal Reserve bank to the other. The mechanism in this case is the Interdistrict Settlement Fund.

Let us say that a check drawn on a Chicago bank is deposited in a bank in San Francisco. The San Francisco bank sends it for collection to the Federal Reserve Bank of San Francisco. After a certain delay to allow time for collection, the Reserve bank at San Francisco increases the balance of the commercial bank by the amount of the check. The Reserve bank at San Francisco sends the check to the Reserve bank at Chicago to collect from the Chicago bank. When the check is presented for payment, the Reserve bank at Chicago reduces the balance of the Chicago bank by the amount of the check. The remaining step is to transfer funds in the amount of the check from the Reserve bank at Chicago to the Reserve bank at San Francisco.

The Interdistrict Settlement Fund is a clearing mechanism for the Federal Reserve banks conducted by the Board of Governors in Washington. At the end of each day, each Federal Reserve bank transmits the amount of its claims on each other bank. These claims are netted out, just as were those of commercial banks in the local clearinghouse. The transfer of funds is made on the books of the Interdistrict Settlement Fund. Each of the Federal Reserve banks maintains in the Interdistrict Settlement Fund, physically in the vaults of the Treasury in Washington, a substantial part of its assets in the form of gold certificates. It is claims against these gold certificates that are passed back and forth between Federal Reserve banks as required by the net flow of checks from one district to another.

Wire transfer of funds

The Federal Reserve System maintains a service permitting almost immediate transfer of funds among Federal Reserve districts by wire. A member bank may ask that funds be transferred from its account to that of a member bank in another district. The funds are available almost immediately, the necessary entries being made on the books of the two Federal Reserve banks, which then include this transaction in their daily report to the Interdistrict Settlement Fund. In their capacity as a fiscal agent, the Federal Reserve banks also make wire transfers of United States government securities. The security to be transmitted is invalidated and the Reserve bank on the other end of the transfer issues the required new security.

The Federal Reserve banks as fiscal agents

The Federal Reserve System acts as the banker for the government. The finances of the government are handled by the U. S. Treasury, and the actual banking operations are carried out by the Federal Reserve banks. The accounts on which the Treasury, as paymaster for the government, writes its checks are almost all kept in the Federal Reserve banks.

The Treasury administers its cash balance, through agreement with the Federal Reserve System, in such a way as to minimize disturbing effects on the volume of bank reserves. An increase in Treasury balances at Federal Reserve banks, other things being equal, implies a reduction in the balances of member banks and in the volume of bank reserves. In order to avoid causing undesired variations in bank reserves, the Treasury attempts to keep its balance at the Federal Reserve banks about constant.

The *total* cash balance of the Treasury cannot be kept constant, since it depends on irregular factors such as the timing of tax payments and of sales of securities by the Treasury. In addition to its working balances at the Federal Reserve banks, the Treasury keeps balances at commercial banks, which are called tax and loan accounts. Since changes in the tax and loan accounts do not affect bank reserves (although they do affect the required reserves of the banks holding them), by permitting variations in these the Treasury can keep its balances at the Federal Reserve banks almost constant and avoid playing a disturbing role in monetary policy.

Elaborate procedures are required to stabilize Treasury balances at Federal Reserve banks. Commercial banks desiring to hold tax and loan accounts must qualify by pledging government securities to assure the safety of the deposits and by meeting other requirements. When the Treasury receives, as in payment of taxes, a check drawn on such a bank, it redeposits the check in the commercial bank on which it is drawn. The funds then are transferred to a Federal Reserve bank on a precisely calculated timetable that is geared to the Treasury's expected payments from these accounts. Thus, despite the enormous flow of payments made through the Treasury accounts at Federal Reserve banks, this careful control mechanism permits the amount in these balances each day to be kept very close to constant.

The Federal Reserve also acts as agent for the Treasury in issuing and retiring government securities and in buying and selling securities for trust funds and other government accounts. All of the mechanical work in publicizing new security issues, receiving bids, determining which bids to accept, and collecting payments is carried out by the Federal Reserve banks. Maturing United States government securities are redeemed by the Federal Reserve banks. The Federal Reserve banks also do the administrative work of introducing new currency and coin into circulation and withdrawing from circulation currency and coin that needs to be replaced.

The Federal Reserve Bank of New York also acts as the agent of the Treasury in foreign exchange transactions. Further, it is the depository of the International Monetary Fund and the International Bank for Reconstruction and Development, besides conducting operations for foreign central banks. Finally, the Federal Reserve System, operating in this connection under the direction of the Federal Open Market Committee, acts on behalf of the government and the Treasury in assuring that the market for United States government securities does not become disorderly, standing ready to support prices of government securities in such a case.

Activities Related to International Monetary Affairs

Along with its activities as agent for the U.S. Department of the Treasury, the Federal Reserve Bank of New York, acting for the U.S. Treasury's Exchange Stabilization Fund, buys and sells foreign currencies with the goal of stabilizing exchange rates and preventing destabilizing speculative swings in the foreign exchange markets. Since 1962, the Federal Reserve System has operated in the foreign exchange market on its own account, in addition to serving as agent for the Treasury. These operations also are carried out by the Federal Reserve Bank of New York, but in this case they involve the funds of the Federal Reserve banks and are under the direction of the Federal Open Market Committee. These operations in foreign currencies are conducted with the close cooperation of the U.S. Treasury, the Federal Reserve System, foreign central banks, and the International Monetary Fund.

Acting in this case as agent for the executive branch of the government and the President, the Federal Reserve since 1965 has administered the portion of the voluntary foreign credit restraint program applying to banks and nonbank financial institutions. This program is designed to limit the flow of capital from the United States to other countries in view of the burden that this imposes upon the United States balance of payments position and the international strength of the dollar. Under this program, the Board of Governors of the Federal Reserve System has issued and revised guidelines that banks and other financial institutions have been asked to follow in order to limit increases in loans and investments abroad.

The Federal Reserve System in Comparison with Foreign Central Banks

How does the Federal Reserve System compare with the central banks of other nations? Most foreign central banks, including the preeminent Bank of England, are controlled directly by the government, rather than having a high degree of independence as does the Federal Reserve. In internal control and structure, the Federal Reserve is unique among major central banks in its decentralized structure and diffusion of decision-making power.

The activities and powers of many foreign central banks are much more limited by considerations of foreign exchange and the balance of payments than the Federal Reserve has been in the past, as their international transactions are much more important in relation to their domestic ones than in the United States. Foreign central banks are generally more involved in influencing the allocation of credit among competing uses than the Federal Reserve has been, entering into a wider range of activities for a wider list of objectives.

Only a few of the world's central banks deal with government securities markets sufficiently large and stable to permit open market operations to be used as a major instrument of monetary policy, perhaps only the Bank of England and the Deutsche Bundesbank of West Germany, along with the Federal Reserve. None uses open market operations as extensively as the Federal Reserve. Most central banks rely on instruments of monetary control that are much less exact and flexible than open market operations; these controls consist mainly of changes in discount rates and in reserve requirements.[4]

[4]For further information, see "Commentary on Central Bank Activities," *Business Conditions*, Federal Reserve Bank of Chicago, April 1971.

SUMMARY

1. The Federal Reserve System operates through 12 regional Federal Reserve banks. Its central authority is the Board of Governors of the Federal Reserve System, located in Washington, D.C. The Board consists of seven members appointed for 14-year terms. The Chairman of the Board is appointed as Chairman for a 4-year term. The other main decision-making body in the System is the Federal Open Market Committee, consisting of the seven members of the Board of Governors and the presidents of five of the Federal Reserve banks.

2. Membership of commercial banks in the Federal Reserve System is compulsory for national banks and is optional for state-chartered banks that meet certain requirements. The fact that state banks at their option can resign from membership in the Federal Reserve System limits the effective power of the System in its regulatory policies.

3. The principal actions of the Federal Reserve System relating to economic stabilization and control of the money supply are (1) open market operations, (2) changes in reserve requirements, and (3) changes in the Federal Reserve discount rate. Open market operations are the most important of these.

4. The Federal Reserve System also performs service activities, the most important of which are acting as fiscal agent for the federal government, clearing and collecting checks, and providing for wire transfer of funds.

5. The Federal Reserve System, on its own authority, and the Federal Reserve Bank of New York, acting as agent for the U.S. Treasury, carry out activities relating to the stabilization of the value of the dollar in the foreign exchange markets and the support of the international monetary system.

QUESTIONS FOR REVIEW AND DISCUSSION

1. Enumerate the policy-making bodies of the Federal Reserve System and the powers that each exercises.

2. Describe the decision-making process by which open market operations are controlled. Describe what actions by whom are involved in an actual open market operation.

3. Discuss the factors pro and con that you would weigh in deciding whether to join the Federal Reserve System if you controlled a state-chartered bank. Why does it matter if state banks desist from joining, or decide to withdraw from the Federal Reserve System?

4. Review each of the policy actions of the Federal Reserve System that directly affects economic stability. In each case, review the way the decisions are made, the particular kinds of actions that are taken, and the mechanisms through which each is thought to affect total demand and economic developments.

5. Review the service functions of the Federal Reserve, in each case indicating how the decision is made, what actions are taken, and what the significance is for the operation of the economy.

9 the federal reserve, bank reserves, and the money supply

The behavior of the money supply and bank credit in the United States depends importantly on actions of the Federal Reserve System. But the linkages through which the Federal Reserve System operates are complex. The meaning of Federal Reserve actions can be understood only through knowledge of these linkages and of the factors the Federal Reserve must offset if the money supply is to behave in a manner consistent with a satisfactory performance of the economy. This chapter deals with the relation between Federal Reserve actions and the behavior of the money supply.

The Federal Reserve Balance Sheet

The operation of the Federal Reserve banks is to be interpreted in terms of the same principles as apply to commercial banks. The monetary obligations of commercial banks are their demand deposits; those of the Federal Reserve banks are their deposits (which are all demand deposits) and their circulating banknotes, the Federal Reserve notes. These constitute a superior or high-powered money, which the commercial banks must hold as reserves and which they cannot themselves create. The total of member bank reserve balances at Federal Reserve banks plus currency in circulation is termed "high-powered money," or "the monetary base." This is a central concept in the analysis of the behavior of the United States monetary system and the role in it of the Federal Reserve System. The monetary base consists almost entirely of money created by the Federal Reserve banks.

The major earning asset of the Federal Reserve banks is United States government securities. The Reserve banks alter their assets and liabilities mainly by buying and selling government securities, or engaging in open market operations. Just as is true of commercial banks, the causation runs from the asset side to the liabilities side of the Federal Reserve balance sheet. Open market operations cause changes in Federal Reserve notes and deposits, not the other way around. Since the Federal Reserve banks, acting as a consolidated unit, are a monopoly bank, they need not be concerned with cash drains as must the individual commercial bank in a multibank system. Over a wide range, the Federal Reserve banks can change their earning assets, and the amount of high-powered money, as they choose.

The major reserve asset of the Federal Reserve banks has been gold certificates, representing the monetary gold reserves of the United States. But beginning in January 1970, a new international monetary reserve asset was created through the International Monetary Fund, the special drawing rights, or SDRs. Certificates representing the Treasury's holdings of SDRs, beginning in 1970, show up as an asset of Federal Reserve banks, playing essentially the same role as gold certificates. The way SDRs are acquired and monetized is discussed below.

Federal Reserve notes and deposits

About two-thirds of the monetary liabilities of the Federal Reserve banks consist of Federal Reserve notes, which make up most of the nation's currency (see Table 9-1). Federal Reserve notes are like the circulating bank notes that used to be issued by private commercial banks before the practice was abolished by the Federal Reserve Act of 1913. The other liabilities of the Federal Reserve banks that directly affect the United States money supply are the demand deposits of the member banks. These are included as a part of the reserves of member banks. The Federal Reserve contribution to the

TABLE 9-1 Consolidated Balance Sheet of All Federal Reserve Banks December 31, 1970 (in billions of dollars)

Assets		Liabilities and Capital Accounts	
Gold certificate account	$10.5	Federal Reserve notes	$51.4
Special drawing rights		Member bank deposits	24.1
certificate account	0.4	U.S. Treasury deposit	1.2
Cash	1.3	Foreign deposits	0.1
Member bank borrowings	0.3	Other deposits	1.2
Banker's acceptances	0.1	Deferred availability	
		cash items	10.1
United States government securities	62.1	Other liabilities and	
		accrued dividends	0.6
Cash items in process of collection	14.3	Capital accounts	1.4
Assets denominated in foreign		Total liabilities and	
currencies	0.3	capital accounts	$90.1
Other assets	0.8		
Total assets	$90.1		

SOURCE: Fed. Reserve Bull.

nation's monetary base, thus, consists of Federal Reserve notes outstanding and deposits of member banks.

The Federal Reserve banks stand ready to convert their notes to deposits and their deposits to notes at no charge. A member bank finding itself short of currency to pay out to its customers asks the Federal Reserve bank to deduct something from its deposit and give it the funds in Federal Reserve notes. The Federal Reserve banks can shift their monetary liabilities between notes and deposits without disturbing the asset side of their balance sheets. From the viewpoint of the Federal Reserve bank, the two kinds of liability are essentially equivalent.

Since the Federal Reserve banks hold other deposits that do not enter into the monetary base, a change in total Federal Reserve assets and liabilities does not necessarily imply a change in the monetary base. For example, a Federal Reserve open market purchase that increased Reserve bank holdings of United States government securities by $100 million conceivably could be associated with an increase of $100 million in foreign deposits at Federal Reserve banks. In this way, the monetary base would be unchanged despite the open market purchase. In defining the relation between open market operations and the monetary base, changes in these other deposits at Federal Reserve banks must be taken into account. A framework for doing this is provided below.

Assets of Federal Reserve banks

Looking at the asset side of the Federal Reserve balance sheet, the most important earning asset of the Federal Reserve banks as measured both in absolute amount and in significant variation is United States government securities. Loans to member banks are not large in amount, but short-run changes in their amount are sometimes important. Loans to member banks differ from other earning assets in that the initiative is not with the Federal Reserve banks. Rather, the Federal Reserve banks are obligated to make loans to member banks at their request under a complex set of conditions. Potentially, therefore, loans to member banks may change in a way that does not suit Federal Reserve purposes. In its effect upon total Federal Reserve assets and monetary liabilities, this could be offset by Federal Reserve open market operations, which are taken at the initiative of the System and are usually entirely within the control of the System. Another earning asset, banker's acceptances, is now not important in amount.

Gold certificates and SDR certificates are essentially warehouse certificates issued by the U.S. Treasury against its holdings of SDRs and the monetary gold reserves of the United States. Changes in Federal Reserve holdings of such certificates reflect mainly changes in the balance of payments position of the United States. Details of the way such transactions are conducted are considered later in this chapter, and the economic and political factors underlying the balance of payments position are reviewed in Chap. 16. If an outflow of gold from the United States led to reductions in Federal Reserve holdings of gold certificates of, say, \$200 million, and the Federal Reserve did not wish to permit this to reduce the monetary base, it would offset it by an open market purchase of \$200 million of government securities.

A category of Federal Reserve asset that has become important only within the past decade is "assets denominated in foreign currencies." These assets have the characteristic that they are not stated, or denominated, in dollars but rather in terms of francs, pounds, marks, or some other foreign currency. These assets arise out of Federal Reserve operations in foreign currencies. The assets may take the form of deposits in a foreign central bank or commercial bank, which may or may not pay interest. They could also represent balances in a United States bank that are stated not in terms of dollars but in a foreign currency. Also included may be short-term securities such as those of foreign governments, which are stated in terms of their currencies rather than in dollars.

The generic label for such short-term claims against foreign currencies is "foreign exchange." An increase, for example, in the holdings of foreign exchange by Federal Reserve banks increases its total assets and liabilities in just the same way as an increase in gold certificates or in earning assets. Consequently, changes in holdings of foreign exchange might have to be offset by open market operations in United States government securities to prevent their having an undesired effect upon the monetary base.

Federal Reserve float

We consider jointly the asset item "cash items in process of collection" and the liability item "deferred availability cash items." These items arise from the Federal Reserve check-collection activities described in Chap. 8. The checks that have been received by a Federal Reserve bank and sent forward for collection but are not yet collected are an asset item to the Federal Reserve bank, since it will receive funds when it does collect them. These checks are aptly described as "cash items in process of collection." We noted that credit for these checks is given to the bank presenting them not when they are actually collected but according to a time schedule related to the average time it takes to collect checks. This gives rise to a liability of the Federal Reserve banks, "deferred availability cash items," since at stated future dates it is obligated to increase the deposits of the member banks for which it is collecting checks.

The schedule of deferred availability is so set up that credit on checks being collected on the average is given before they are actually collected. Commonly, the liability item will be changed from deferred availability cash items to "member bank deposits" before the corresponding adjustment is made in cash items in process of collection. Subtracting deferred availability cash items from cash items in process of collection, measures what is termed "Federal Reserve float." This is a particular kind of credit extended by Federal Reserve banks to member banks by giving them cash for checks that have not yet been collected. Changes in the amount of Federal Reserve float, unless offset by other changes on the Federal Reserve balance sheet, affect the monetary base.

If Federal Reserve banks had only one kind of asset and one kind of liability, say, government securities for the asset and member bank reserves for the liability, there would be a nice one-for-one correspondence between the two. Then we should know that a Federal Reserve purchase of $100 million in government securities implied a $100 million increase in bank reserves. Unfortunately, the existing institutions are not that simple. The Federal Reserve banks hold a diversity of assets and a number of other kinds of liabilities in addition to the liabilities that enter into the monetary base. The effect of Federal Reserve operations on the monetary base must be interpreted as the joint outcome of changes in all these factors. However, insofar as the Federal Reserve can, through open market operations, offset factors having an undesired influence on the monetary base, it can cause the monetary base to behave as it wishes.

The Reserve Mechanism, Bank Deposits, and the Money Supply

We indicated earlier that unless commercial banks were subject to some restraining mechanism they would increase the money supply without limit, since the interest they could earn on additional loans and investments is greater than the additional cost of creating additional demand deposits.[1] The restraining mechanism is a requirement that the banks maintain their money convertible into another kind of money, a superior money, or that they maintain reserves of this superior money in some minimum relation to their own money. In earlier times, the superior money commonly was gold and silver coin. In the modern world, it usually is a money created by the national government or the government-controlled central bank. We shall consider in general terms the relation between the amount of bank money (and associated bank credit) and the amount of superior or high-powered money where this reserve mechanism operates. For present purposes, it makes no difference whether the bank money is in the form of circulating banknotes or demand deposits.

The reserve-deposit multiplier—Reserves not circulating

In the simplest case, the high-powered money, or base money, is used only as reserves behind the inferior money, none of it circulating from hand

[1]Some economists prefer a different interpretation on this point. The issues raised are considered in Chap. 11.

to hand. Consider a case in which money consists only of demand deposits of commercial banks ($M = D$) and base money is used only as bank reserves ($B = R$). Banks are required to hold as reserves a base money created by the central bank, the minimum reserve requirement being defined by $B = r_1 D$. Since this is a fractional-reserve banking system, $r_1 < 1$.

These conditions define the maximum amount of deposits that can exist with a given amount of base money. Dividing both sides of the equation by r_1 gives us $D = B\ (1/r_1)$. Since $r_1 < 1$ (read, r_1 is less than 1), $1/r_1 > 1$; the reserve-deposit multiplier is greater than 1.

The maximum amount of deposits that can exist is thus determined by two factors. The first of these is the monetary base B, which is determined by the central bank. The second is a multiplier that defines how many dollars of deposits can exist for each dollar of base money (since, dividing by B, $D/B = 1/r_1$). This is determined by the central bank or the government in defining the legal minimum reserve requirement.

If the actual reserve ratio always stayed precisely at r_1, the multiplier would always be constant. Then changes in D would be caused only by changes in B, and any change in B would cause an immediate and proportionate change in D. By controlling B, the money supply could be perfectly controlled in rather a simple manner. For example, if $r_1 = 0.20$, or 1/5, then $1/r_1 = 5$, and the amount of money in existence at all times is just 5 times the amount of base money. This implies that any change in the monetary base brings a change in the money supply 5 times as large, $\Delta M = \Delta B \times 5$. In general, the change in deposits will be equal to the change in high-powered money times the relevant multiplier.[2]

In practice, the government does not specify a *mandatory* reserve ratio, but only a *minimum* reserve requirement. This defines only a maximum reserve-deposit multiplier and a maximum money supply that can exist for any given monetary base. If the actual reserve ratio varied over some range, this would produce a corresponding variation in the money supply even though the amount of high-powered money were constant. Since we are concerned with variation in the money supply and its possible contribution to economic instability, we consider how this might happen in the simple monetary system now before us.

Since banks are not paid interest on reserves and can earn interest by using unneeded reserves to acquire earning assets, they will not add to their reserves without limit. However, we can visualize the actual reserve ratio ($r = R/D$) of a bank as varying over some range, for example, because of changes in bank confidence and expectations. When bankers are optimistic, they let the reserve ratio fall to the minimum legal ratio r_i. When they are pessimistic, they increase their ratio of reserves to deposits to r_a. With a given monetary base, the money supply then can fluctuate between a maximum value of $M_a = D_a = B(1/r_i)$, when bankers are optimistic, and a mini-

[2]This can be demonstrated as follows: $M_1 = B_1(1/r_1)$, $M_2 = B_2(1/r_1)$; thus, $\Delta M = M_2 - M_1 = B_2(1/r_1) - B_1(1/r_1) = (B_2 - B_1)(1/r_1) = \Delta B(1/r_1)$.

mum value of $M_i = D_i = B(1/r_a)$, when bankers are pessimistic. For a given monetary base, the range of fluctuation in the money supply depends on the range of fluctuation of the actual reserve ratio of the banking system; $r_a - r_i$.

This kind of monetary system can generate a pattern of interaction between the economic situation (represented by total demand Y), banker confidence, the reserve ratio, the volume of deposits and the money supply, and the economic situation, as follows:

$$Y \xrightarrow{(-)} r \xrightarrow{(-)} \frac{1}{r} \xrightarrow{(+)} M \quad (M \xrightarrow{(+)} Y)$$

An increase, for example, in total demand improves business conditions, makes bankers more optimistic, and leads them to reduce their reserve ratio. Since an increase in Y leads to a decrease in r, a change in the opposite direction, we indicate by (−) that the causal relation is negative. But a reduction in r causes an increase in $1/r$, the reserve-deposit multiplier, another negative causal relation. This implies that an increase in Y causes an increase in $1/r$. In causal chains, two minuses make a plus. To proceed along the causal chain, an increase in the multiplier—for any given behavior of high-powered money—will increase deposits and the money supply.

We know, however, that an increase in the money supply will tend to increase total demand. This will increase confidence and reduce the reserve ratio further, increasing the money supply further, and so on. This is a positive-feedback loop. A change in either direction tends to be self-feeding, self-aggravating, and to continue in the same direction until it hits something that turns it around. This interpretation can be quite symmetrical. A reduction in total demand increases pessimism, and leads to an increase in the reserve ratio and a reduction in the multiplier and in the amount of money with any given monetary base, which reduces total demand and leads to more pessimism.

What is interesting about this class of monetary system is that it can contribute to explaining why economic upswings and downswings are self-feeding (Fig. 9–1). It also provides a possible explanation of their turning points: the boundary mechanisms that ordinarily turn them around so that neither upswings nor downswings run on without limit. The relevant element in the monetary system is the limit to the range of variation in r, the actual reserve ratio. If r hits a minimum at r_i, this sets a ceiling on $1/r$ at $1/r_i$, and thereby defines a ceiling of M for any given B. At the point defined, the monetary system no longer contributes to the positive-feedback loop discussed above. If the economy cannot continue expanding without such positive monetary feedback, this monetary ceiling will suffice to explain a ceiling for the economy, to explain why, under this kind of monetary system, upswings do not usually continue without limit but hit an upper turning point.

This interpretation applies also to the lower turning point. The maximum reserve ratio banks are willing to hold (r_a) defines a minimum multi-

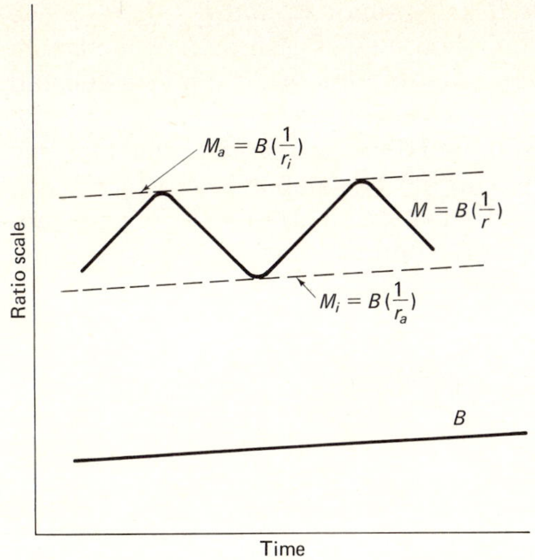

Fig. 9-1 Monetary fluctuations in a simple monetary system.

plier $(1/r_a)$ and a minimum money supply for any given monetary base. If the economy cannot continue on a downswing without continued reductions in the money supply, the boundary in the monetary system will define a boundary on the economic downswing. The kind of time path that the money supply would trace out in such a system is illustrated in Fig. 9-1. As r varies between r_i and r_a, the money supply fluctuates over the range defined above. The time path of the money supply is then defined by the time path of B plus the pattern and range of variation in r.

The base-money multiplier—Base money circulating

In the kind of monetary system now prevalent, the base money that serves as reserves of the banks also circulates among the public and is used directly as money in the form of currency. The commercial banks maintain their money convertible at par into the base money, so the public may choose whatever currency-deposit ratio it chooses. For any given monetary base, then, the money supply depends not only on the reserve ratio of the banks but also on the proportion of its money that the public chooses to hold in the form of base money or currency.

Each dollar of base money would support the creation of many dollars of bank money, as defined by the reserve-deposit multiplier just discussed. But when used as currency, of course, it supports only $1 of money. Therefore, if the public chooses to shift from using deposits toward using currency, this will drain reserves from the banks and require a reduction in the money supply.

Base money held by the public is currency C. Then base money is either in the form of bank reserves R or currency C, and $B = R + C$. The banks' behavior with reference to their holdings of cash defines the actual reserve ratio $r = R/D$. In a parallel way, we can think of the public's demand for currency as against deposits as defining the currency ratio $c = C/D$. Therefore, (multiplying this expression by D) we can think of the currency in circulation as equaling the currency ratio times deposits, or $C = cD$.

These definitions and behavioral relations permit defining the dependence of the volume of bank deposits upon the amount of base money, the currency ratio, and the reserve ratio:

Since $B = R + C$, $R = rD$, and $C = cD$,

$$B = rD + cD = D(c + r)$$

Dividing by $(c + r)$ yields

$$D = B \times \frac{1}{c + r}$$

To define the behavior of the money supply requires an additional step, since in this monetary system the money supply includes currency in circulation as well as bank-created money in the form of demand deposits. Thus, the money supply is $M = D + C$. Since $C = cD$, this can be expressed as

$$M = D + cD = D(1 + c)$$

But for D we can substitute from above

$$D = B \times \frac{1}{c + r}$$

Yielding

$$M = B\frac{1}{c + r}(1 + c) = B\frac{1 + c}{c + r}$$

Analogous to the reserve-deposit multiplier of the simpler monetary system is the monetary-base, money, or base-money multiplier of this monetary system, defined by $(1 + c)/(c + r)$. The value of this multiplier is increased by a reduction in the value of either c or r.[3] Accordingly, factors that increase the money supply are (1) an increase in the monetary base, and (2) an increase in the base-money multiplier resulting from reduction of the currency ratio or the reserve ratio.

Since all these variables are measurable and each can be given a meaningful interpretation in terms of economic behavior and government policy actions, this approach is used as a framework for theory and empirical studies of the determinants of the behavior of the money supply and the role of the monetary system in economic instability. Although this may seem an obvious and straightforward way to explore the performance of the monetary

[3] As $c \to 0$, $(1 + c)/(c + r) \to 1/r$, the multiplier of the earlier system. At the other extreme, if money were held only in the form of currency, M would equal B and the multiplier would be 1.

system, practically no studies of this type were done before the 1960s. As a result, despite the long history of monetary theory, our factual knowledge of the performance of the United States monetary system is limited and in an exploratory state of development.

This somewhat more complex monetary system can produce the same pattern of behavior as the simpler one discussed above and depicted in Fig. 9–1. Even though the monetary base were to grow along a steady path, this system would produce procyclical or destabilizing behavior of the money supply if the currency ratio and the reserve ratio characteristically declined during economic upswings and rose during economic downswings. This would tend to happen if the money created by banks were not entirely secure, if there was a chance that commercial banks would fail and their demand deposits lose all or a part of their value. Then when confidence in the economy and the banks declined, people would want to hold more currency and fewer deposits, so that the currency ratio would rise. This would reduce the base-money multiplier and tend to reduce the money supply, thus reducing total demand and further weakening confidence.

If the currency ratio and the reserve ratio generally decline during economic upswings and increase during economic downswings, this class of monetary system can generate a systematic variation in the base-money multiplier that contributes to explaining the instability of the economy in its upswings and downswings and the turning points that end those self-feeding movements. The range of the base-money multiplier runs from a maximum, when the currency ratio and the reserve ratio are at low values, to a minimum, when they are at high values.

The reserve mechanism and the behavior of the money supply

The reserve mechanism does something more than set a ceiling on the money supply. Bounded oscillation in the currency ratio and the reserve ratio can produce bounded fluctuations in the money supply, even when the monetary base grows at a steady rate. Since such bounded fluctuations in the money supply may be a major factor in explaining the bounded fluctuations of total demand that have characterized most economies, it may be that the existence of monetary systems of this particular class will prove to be a conspicuous explanatory factor in the theory of business fluctuations. Recent studies have indicated that procyclical variation in the money supply in the United States has to an important extent reflected such variation in the currency ratio and the reserve ratio.

The Reserve Mechanism in a Multibank System

The reserve ratio relevant to determining the money supply in a system including a large number of banks is the weighted average reserve ratio of all the banks in the system. The legal required reserve ratio varies between classes of Federal Reserve member banks. Nonmember banks have still different reserve requirements, which are met in part by holding deposits at commercial banks, that is, with ordinary money rather than high-powered money. The relation between total demand deposits and the amount of base money required to be held against them is subject to variation as deposits shift among banks. In practice, such variation appears to be so small as not significantly to affect the operation of the reserve mechanism as a system for controlling the money supply.

Check collection and cash flows among banks

When a person writes a check on his demand deposit to make a payment, ordinarily the payee is the customer of a different bank, and he deposits the check in his bank. In order to credit the sum to his account, his bank must collect it from the bank of the payer. If Mr. A. makes a payment to Mr. B., the resulting entries on the books of the two banks are as shown below. Mr. B.'s bank credits the amount of the check to his account and then sends the check for collection from Mr. A.'s bank, the settlement being made in cash or reserves. Thus, Mr. B.'s bank gains equal amounts of demand deposits and of cash—or reserves. The entries on the books of the two banks fully net out. The effect is only to shift some deposits and some reserves from Mr. A.'s bank to Mr. B.'s bank.

The change of 100 in reserves and deposits does not involve an equal change in excess reserves, since the change in deposits implies a change in required reserves. Assuming an illustrative 10 percent reserve requirement, the change of 100 in deposits involves a change of 10 in required reserves. Thus, the bank losing 100 in deposits and reserves loses 90 in excess reserves—or shifts to a reserve deficiency of 90 if it had no excess reserves at the outset—and the bank gaining 100 in deposits and reserves gains 90 in excess reserves.

A.'s Bank

Assets	*Liabilities*	*Reserves*	*Required Reserves*	*Excess Reserves*
Reserves −100 (cash)	Demand deposits −100	−100	−10	−90

B.'s Bank

Assets	*Liabilities*	*Reserves*	*Required Reserves*	*Excess Reserves*
Reserves +100 (cash)	Demand deposits +100	+100	+10	+90

Response to changes in the monetary base

The next question is how this multibank system responds to a change in the monetary base. A change in aggregate bank reserves is not an observable fact of experience to which the individual banks respond. Rather, each bank reacts to its own inflows and outflows of funds. In any particular day, each bank has a net inflow or a net outflow of funds. Unless it takes offsetting action it will record either an increase or a decrease in its excess reserves. The response of each bank to its daily flows of funds is what determines the response of the banking system as a whole to the total flow of funds and to any change in aggregate bank reserves that is implicit in it.

The total gross movement of funds through banks in any given day is very large in relation to the net change in total bank reserves. Checks drawn against private demand deposit accounts, at about $10 trillion a year in 1970, run to something like $40 billion on an average day. The average turnover rate for such accounts in 1970 was about 70 times a year. This implies that on the average working day the average bank experienced withdrawals of something like three-tenths of its total demand deposits, with inpayments on a similar scale. For banks in New York, the turnover rate in 1970 was around 150 times a year, or the flow of payments on the average day ran to more than one-half of total demand deposits.

Many of these payments, including those collected through the Federal Reserve check clearing system, involve "federal funds" in that they flow through accounts in Federal Reserve banks. In addition, transactions of the United States government ran to something close to $1 billion on the average day, and gross transactions in federal funds loans among banks to something like $10 billion a day.

The individual bank, of course, does not separately confront any particular transactions that uniquely lead to changes in total bank reserves. The net change in reserves is simply the net outcome of all these transactions. It is trivial in relative amount, running ordinarily to a few hundred million dollars in a day compared to gross flows of something like $50 billion.

No mechanism exists to equate the daily inpayments of an individual bank to its outpayments. The flow of payments through checking accounts and among banks causes the individual bank to gain deposits and reserves one day and lose them another day. It is to these erratic gains and losses of funds by the bank, arising from the inequality of its inflow and outflow of funds, that the manager of the bank's money position responds in doing his job of keeping the bank's reserve position on target. What is remarkable is that with these enormous flows of funds through demand deposit accounts banks are able, through close management of their money positions, to hold variations in excess reserves on a weekly basis to the order of a few hundred million dollars. In 1970 the variation in average excess reserves over a period of 2 or 3 weeks ordinarily ran to less than $100 million.

Under these conditions, a change in the monetary base does not cause any substantial change in excess reserves and in the base-money multiplier. Therefore, it is fully reflected in the money supply without any appreciable lag. This is accomplished by the adjustments by which banks keep their money positions under close control. Banks that would otherwise have excess reserves and are at the margin of buying some earning assets use the potential excess reserves to do so. If the addition to earning assets is expected to be relatively temporary, it will take the form of short-term government securities or loans to government securities dealers, but at any particular time some banks always will be at the margin of adding assets other than liquid ones. Banks that do not wish to commit themselves to an increase in their earning assets, lend their potential excess reserves in the federal funds market, where they are borrowed by banks that do wish to do so.

Factors Affecting the Base-money Multiplier

Changes in the base-money multiplier have not contributed importantly to explaining the long-run growth of the money supply, which stems rather from growth in the monetary base. However, variation in the multiplier was sometimes important in explaining short-run swings in the money supply. We shall review here the factors relevant to explaining variation in the currency ratio and the reserve ratio.

Variation in the currency ratio

The currency ratio depends upon the relative attractiveness to the public of currency as against demand deposits as an asset to use for making payments. It may also reflect shifts of deposits among various types of holders and changes in the relative importance of different types of transactions. Present knowledge on this matter is far from complete. We list below a set of relevant factors, stating the direction of change in each that would tend to reduce the currency ratio and increase the base-money multiplier.[4]

1. A rise in the practice of making payments with checks, which is related to urbanization and to an increase in the standard of living.

2. Improvement in the relative safety of demand deposits, such as occurred when they were made subject to government insurance in 1933.

[4]The major source is Phillip Cagan, *Determinants and Effects of Changes in the Stock of Money, 1875–1960*, National Bureau of Economic Research, New York, 1965.

3. Reduction in short-run fears of bank failures. The currency ratio rose sharply during periods of bank runs and loss of confidence in the banking system. This tended to reduce the money supply, worsening financial conditions and further weakening the banks. Thus, such variations in the currency ratio contributed to economic instability.

4. Increase in the geographical availability of banking services and reduction in the service charges on checking accounts.

5. Reduction in the demand for currency associated with tax evasion, black marketing, and other illegal activities. The increase in the currency ratio during the Second World War is interpreted as in part reflecting efforts to evade taxes.

6. Before 1934 when interest was paid on some large demand deposits, an increase in such interest on demand deposits would tend to reduce the currency ratio.

7. Shifts in income and cash balances from consumers and small holders to large holders and businesses that are accustomed to use deposits would reduce the currency ratio. The contribution of changes in the currency ratio to cyclical variation in the money supply may derive in part from such shifts.

Variation in the reserve ratio

The other factor causing variation in the base-money multiplier is variation in the average reserve ratio of the commercial banks. The determinants of the average reserve ratio can be separated into two groups: those affecting the required-reserve ratio and those affecting the excess-reserve ratio. The reserves of member banks can be divided into required reserves, or those that must be held to meet legal requirements, and excess reserves, or actual reserves in excess of required reserves: $R = R_r + R_e$. To interpret the behavior of banks in terms of reserve ratios, we define the actual reserve ratio as $r = R/D$, the required-reserve ratio as $r_r = R_r/D$, and the excess-reserve ratio as $r_e = R_e/D$. By dividing $R = R_r + R_e$ by D, we see that $r = r_r + r_e$. The actual reserve ratio is the sum of the required-reserve ratio and the excess-reserve ratio.

Changes in the required-reserve ratio r_r reflect mainly two kinds of factors:

1. Changes in reserve requirements by the Federal Reserve. A reduction in reserve requirements, of course, reduces the required-reserve ratio.

2. Shifts in the distribution of deposits between categories of banks that have different required-reserve ratios. Among member banks, reserve requirements for reserve city banks are slightly higher than for country banks. A shift of deposits from one category of bank to another affects the value of the weighted-average required-reserve ratio.

What of changes in the excess-reserve ratio? Over the long run in the United States this ratio has declined. This seems to reflect the more stable environment of banks, the reduction in their fears of runs after the institution of deposit insurance, the existence of the Federal Reserve System, and, recently, a prolonged period of experience without banking panics and widespread bank failures. Also relevant are a set of institutional changes that increase the feasibility and attractiveness of holding the sum of primary and secondary reserves more largely in the form of secondary reserves: liquid earning assets. Such changes include improvements in communications that permit remote banks to operate effectively in the money market, development of money-market instruments such as federal funds loans and repurchase agreements, and an improvement in the efficiency of the money market.

Another factor operating to reduce excess reserves was the change in the definition of required reserves (and excess reserves) in 1968. The system operating earlier involved only a 1-day lag between the period of time over which required reserves were calculated and the period during which reserves were averaged to meet this requirement. Average deposits over a period of 1 week ending each Wednesday morning (effectively, Tuesday night) determined required reserves to be held over a period of 1 week ending at the close of business each Wednesday. The period of time during which the manager of the money position knew exactly what reserves he had to hold to come out with zero excess reserves for the week was 1 day, Wednesday. This gave rise to great money-market activities on Wednesday as each bank made the final adjustments needed to come out with its desired reserve position for the week.

Under the new regulations applied by the Board of Governors of the Federal Reserve System since 1968, the bank's deposits of a given week are matched against its reserves in the form of currency held in the same week but its reserves in the form of balances at its Federal Reserve bank in the week 2 weeks later. Thus, the money manager knows before the statement week begins just what average balance for the week he must hold at his Federal Reserve Bank to balance the amounts. This means that coming out very close to zero excess reserves does not require such precise management as under the earlier arrangements.

Short-run changes in the excess-reserve ratio of banks have in the past contributed along with changes in the currency ratio to procyclical behavior of the money supply. That is, the reserve ratio sometimes declined during economic upswings, contributing to expansion of the money supply, and increased on downswings. Where banking panics and bank runs existed, including those of the early 1930s, these events contributed to the sharp rise in the excess-reserve ratio that aggravated the economic downswing. In the panic, banks became fearful of failing and wanted to hold extra cash for self-protection. Banks hoarded reserves, or cash, for the same reason that the public did. Again, however, this behavior reflected the peculiarity of the United States banking system: the large number of failure-prone individual banks. In recent decades, banking panic has not entered the picture and procyclical variation in the excess-reserve ratio has been smaller and less consistent than in earlier periods.

Determinants of the Monetary Base

The factors determining the amount of high-powered money, or the monetary base, can be defined in terms of a set of sources of such funds for the monetary base less a set of competing uses of these funds, as defined in Table 9-2. The monetary base is defined here as only those assets available for currency holdings by the public plus reserves of commercial banks available for their demand deposits held by the public. Since the money supply is defined as including only currency and demand deposits held by the public, this is the relevant definition of the monetary base.

The sources of funds for the monetary base are four. The earning

TABLE 9-2 Determinants of the monetary base, December, 1970 (in billions of dollars)

Monetary base		
Member bank reserves available for private demand deposits		$21.2
+		
Currency held by the public		51.7
Equals *sources*		
Reserve Bank credit		66.7
United States government securities	$61.7	
Loans to member banks	0.3	
Federal Reserve float	3.6	
Other Federal Reserve assets	1.0	
+		
Gold Stock		11.1
+		
SDR certificates		0.4
+		
Treasury currency outstanding		7.1
Minus *competing uses*		
Treasury deposits with Federal Reserve banks		0.8
+		
Other deposits with Federal Reserve banks		0.9
+		
Other Federal Reserve liabilities and capital		2.3
+		
Treasury cash holdings		0.4
+		
Member bank reserves not available for private demand deposits		8.1
Reserves for government deposits	.9	
Reserves for time deposits	7.0	
Reserves for Eurodollar borrowings	.0	
Reserves for bank-related commercial paper	.2	

SOURCE: *Fed. Reserve Bull.* Allocations of member bank reserves estimated by the author.

assets of the Federal Reserve banks are the main asset item that gives rise to Federal Reserve notes and deposits. Thus, Reserve Bank credit is a source of funds for the monetary base.

The gold certificates held by Federal Reserve banks, reflecting the nation's monetary gold stock held by the Treasury, are another asset item of Federal Reserve banks that gives rise to Federal Reserve notes and deposits. This is another source of the monetary base. The Special Drawing Rights certificates first created in 1970 operate in much the same manner as gold as an element in the nation's monetary system.

Currency created by the U.S. Department of the Treasury, in the form mainly of coin, is another source of the assets that make up bank reserves and currency in circulation.

Some of the funds made available from these sources are reflected not in currency held by the public and bank reserves related to private demand deposits but in other liabilities of the monetary system: Treasury deposits with Federal Reserve banks, other deposits with Federal Reserve banks, and other Federal Reserve liabilities and capital. An increase in these items while total sources remain unchanged implies a reduction in the monetary base. The same status attaches to Treasury cash holdings. This is currency held by the Treasury rather than by the public.

Finally, not all reserves held by member banks are relevant to the public's demand deposits and, therefore, to the money supply. Some of these reserves are held as required reserves against government deposits. Since government deposits are not included in the money supply, these reserves do not belong among the determinants of the money supply. The same reasoning applies to required reserves held against time deposits of commercial banks, as well as those held against Eurodollar borrowings and against bank-related commercial paper.[5]

The magnitudes of these determinants of the monetary base in late 1970 are given in Table 9-2. The main use of this framework is in analyzing the factors accounting for the behavior of the money supply over time, to determine which particular elements in the monetary mechanism account for changes in the money supply that are erratic, stabilizing, or destabilizing to the economy.

[5]An alternative formulation defines the monetary base as including all bank reserves. The fact that some reserves are required for other uses and are not related to demand deposits and currency is dealt with in this approach by incorporating into the base-money multiplier (along with the currency ratio and the reserve ratio) ratios of time deposits and government deposits to demand deposits. To update this approach to 1970 conditions would require incorporating also ratios of Eurodollar borrowings and bank-related commercial paper to demand deposits. The reason for preferring to treat these uses of reserves as adjustments to the monetary base rather than to the base-money multiplier is that the amount of reserves needed for these uses, in actuality, depends on factors that are not systematically related to the amount of demand deposits. For alternative approaches and a more detailed discussion, see Leonall C. Andersen and Jerry L. Jordan, "The Monetary Base—Explanation and Analytical Use," *Fed. Reserve Bank St. Louis Rev.*, pp. 7-14, August 1968; and Leonall C. Andersen, "Three Approaches to Money Stock Determination," *Fed. Reserve Bank St. Louis Rev.*, pp. 6-13, October 1967.

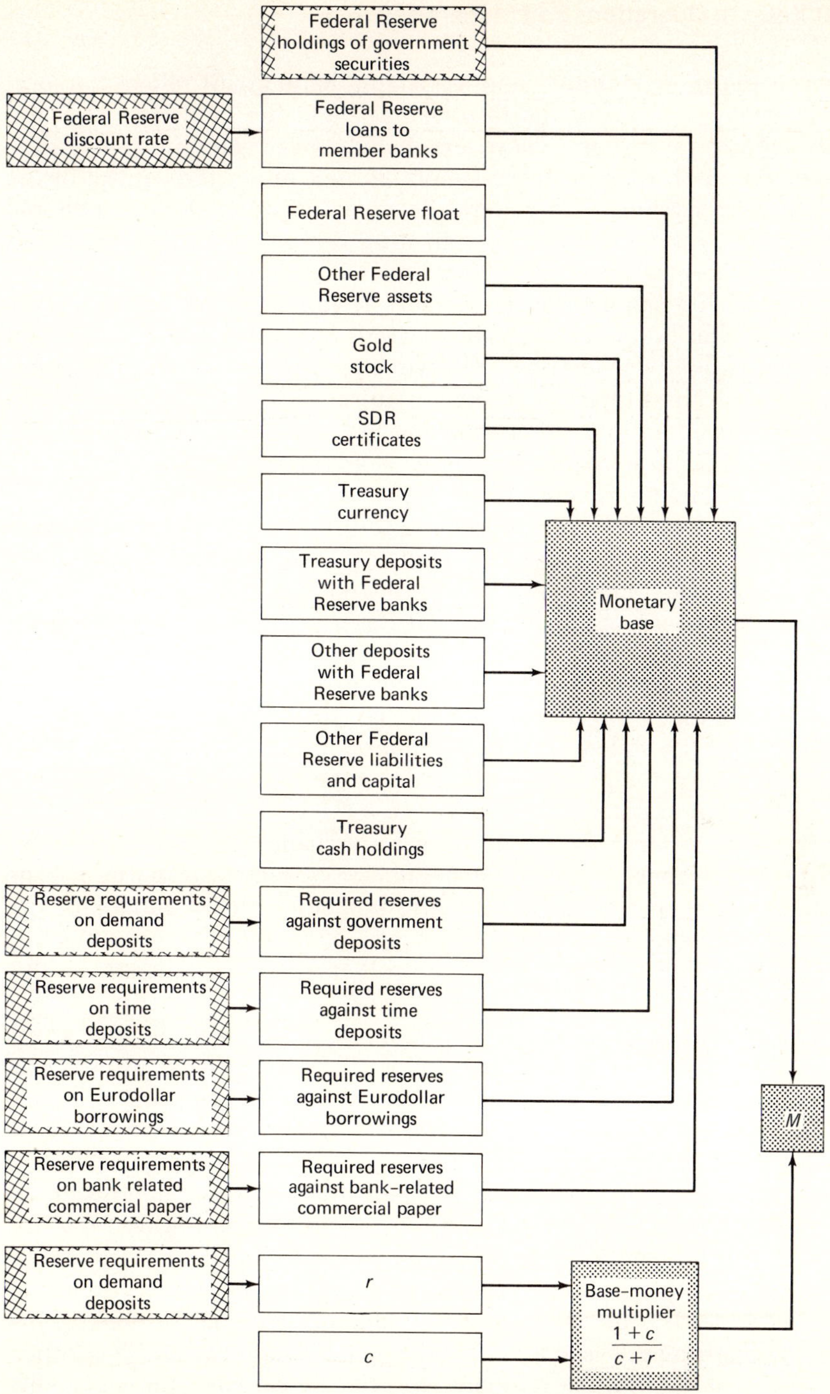

Fig. 9-2 Controlled and uncontrolled factors affecting the money supply.

Federal Reserve Operations and Monetary Policy

Changes in the money supply and associated bank credit reflect the joint effects of changes in all of the factors that affect the monetary base and the base-money multiplier. These are listed once again in the middle column of Fig. 9–2. Most of these factors are not under the control of the Federal Reserve System. The Federal Reserve can bring about occasional changes in the reserve ratio r by adjusting reserve requirements, but it has no direct control over the excess-reserve ratio of banks (although usually this is too small to be important). It can affect required reserves against Eurodollar borrowings and borrowings on bank-related commercial paper by occasionally changing its reserve requirements on these liabilities, but changes in these special reserve requirements have been made in response to considerations other than the behavior of the money supply. Thus, variation in these required reserves is not an instrument of monetary control, but is another uncontrolled factor affecting the money supply. Although the Federal Reserve has nominal control over all the cross-hatched items, the only item among those immediately affecting the monetary base and the base-money multiplier that is available for continuous use in controlling the money supply is Federal Reserve holdings of government securities.

It may seem that if the Federal Reserve Board has effective control over only one out of seventeen factors that affect the money supply, it must have very little ability to make the money supply behave as it wishes—one-seventeenth of total control over the money supply, if we may put it so. Such an interpretation, however, would be quite erroneous. It is possible to achieve very close control over a variable even though we have control over only one among a large number of factors affecting it. The way this is done, of course, is by using our controlled variable—or our "instrument variable"—to "offset" changes in all other factors affecting the "target variable." Virtually all controlled processes operate in this manner.

Such offsetting of undesired influences is an example of "error-controlled negative feedback." Any factor that would tend to cause an error in the target variable we respond to (which is "feedback") in such a way as to offset it (which implies that the feedback is "negative"). The manager of the bank's money position applies error-controlled negative feedback. Of a great many factors affecting the bank's cash position he controls only a few. He uses these to offset anything and everything that tends to make the bank's excess reserves deviate from their target value.

Using this kind of control system to offset factors that otherwise would cause an undesired value of the target variable has the effect of making the value of the instrument variable responsive to the values of the uncontrolled factors. If a customer makes a large cash withdrawal from the bank, this

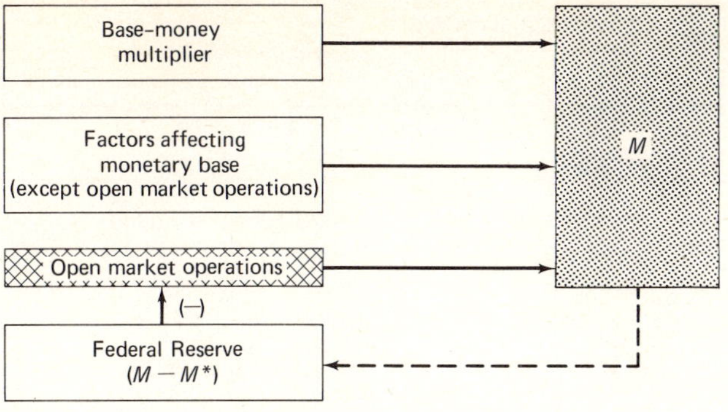

Fig. 9-3 Open market operations as a feedback control system.

sends the manager of the money position into the federal funds market as a borrower.

In order to control the money supply with the limited powers it possesses, the Federal Reserve behaves in this same manner. It uses open market operations to offset anything and everything that would cause an undesired change in the monetary base, and it varies the monetary base in such a way as to offset any changes that occur in the base-money multiplier. That is, the basic control system would be that depicted in Fig. 9-3. When changes in the base-money multiplier or in other factors affecting the monetary base cause M to deviate from its target value M^*, the Federal Reserve responds by making open market operations to drive M back toward M^*, implicitly offsetting the disturbing factors.

Application of this approach to Federal Reserve policy does not require that the target value of the money supply M^* should be a fixed quantity. On the contrary, M^* can be defined as any time path for the money supply, including one defined by an explicit decision rule or strategy. By applying error-controlled negative feedback, Federal Reserve policy then offsets factors tending to cause any deviation of M from this path.

These same principles would apply if the target for Federal Reserve policy were taken to be something else rather than control of the money supply. If, as was the case during the Second World War, the Federal Reserve takes its goal to be keeping interest rates unchanged, it responds to $i - i^*$ just as it responded in our example to $M - M^*$. When the interest rate tends to decline below the target value, it sells government securities; when $i > i^*$, it buys.

If the Federal Reserve is coherently pursuing almost any defined target, the basic pattern of its operations will be to use its powers in a pattern of error-controlled negative feedback, offsetting factors that tend to cause a target variable to depart from its desired value. In reviewing the mechanics of various actions by the Federal Reserve and the Treasury, the broad pic-

Commercial Bank A

	Assets	Liabilities	Reserves	Required Reserves	Excess Reserves	Money Supply
	Cash $200,000	Demand deposits $1,000,000	$200,000	$200,000	$0	
1. Change in reserve requirements				+20,000	−20,000	
2. Bank sells government securities	Government securities −$20,000 Cash +$20,000		+20,000	....	+20,000	
Net change	Government securities −$20,000 Cash +$20,000		+20,000	+20,000		

ture we have in the back of our minds is one in which these actions will either be useful to the Federal Reserve in offsetting undesired influences upon the monetary base, or else they will be factors that the Federal Reserve will have to offset in order to make its target variable behave in the desired way.

Changes in Member Bank Reserve Requirements

Taking a closer look at Federal Reserve policy actions and their effects on the money supply, let us consider first the effects of a change in Federal Reserve reserve requirements on demand deposits. Commercial bank A initially has no excess reserves. It holds demand deposits of $1 million and cash (currency plus the balance at its Federal Reserve bank) of $200,000. We ignore other items on the balance sheet but in our example assume the bank has no time deposits or other claims on its cash. The initial reserve requirement is 20 percent. Thus, the required reserves of the bank are $200,000, just equal to its actual reserves, and excess reserves are zero.

Now the Federal Reserve increases the reserve requirement for this class of bank to 22 percent. From here on, in using the T accounts we note only the changes in balance sheet items. The change in reserve requirements does not alter the bank's balance sheet or its actual reserves, which remain at $200,000. However, it does increase the required reserves of the bank by $20,000. Since actual reserves are unchanged, this increase in required reserves means a corresponding decrease in excess reserves and in this case makes them negative.

How does the bank respond to this reserve deficiency? As indicated in our earlier discussion of management of the bank's money position, several alternative courses of action are available. In this case, we assume it meets the deficiency by selling some of its United States government securities. To raise just the needed amount of cash, it sells $20,000 of government securities. It is paid by a check drawn on another bank. It collects the check, having the amount added to its balance at the Reserve bank. Thus increasing reserves by $20,000 increases excess reserves by the same amount, since deposits are unchanged.

The action of bank A solves its reserve problem, but what contribution does it make to solving the reserve problem of banks in the aggregate? Assuming a given monetary base and no change in currency in circulation, total bank reserves are unchanged. Banks in the aggregate can only respond to the increase in reserve requirements by a reduction in their demand deposits.

Although it gained its additional reserves only at the expense of another bank, bank A contributed to the reduction in the earning assets and the deposits of the banking system by selling government securities. The incremental effect of this on the bank of the buyer of the government securities is this:

Commercial Bank B

	Assets	Liabilities	Reserves	Required Reserves	Excess Reserves	Money Supply
Customer purchase of government securities	Cash −$20,000	Demand deposits −$20,000	−$20,000	−$4,400	−$15,600	−$20,000

The reduction in bank deposits, the money supply, and required reserves (at any given level of reserve requirements) initiated by bank A shows up on the books of bank B.

If banks in general confront a reserve deficiency because of the increase in reserve requirements, the resulting preponderance of seekers of additional funds tends to increase the federal funds rate to the point at which banks in general make their cash adjustments through reductions in other earning assets. The reduction in bank assets and in demand deposits can occur quickly through the same interaction process that permits banks to adapt immediately to cash flows and maintain excess reserves at a closely controlled level.

In practice, when the Board of Governors increases reserve requirements, it gives enough advance notice before the effective date of the change for banks to be able to adjust their positions gradually, avoiding the abrupt increase in federal funds rates and the unsettlement of the money market that would occur if such a change were made without notice. In some cases, the Federal Reserve also has cushioned the effect of an increase in reserve requirements by engaging in open market purchases of government securities as required to limit any increase in the federal funds rate and other money-market interest rates. Another potential cushioning device is an increase in member bank borrowing from Reserve banks. If the federal funds rate is high and prices of government securities depressed, this increases the attractiveness to banks of getting needed reserves by borrowing from Reserve banks. Federal Reserve open market purchases or an increase in member bank borrowing temporarily increases the monetary base and the total volume of bank reserves available, thus cushioning the adjustment of banks in the aggregate to the higher reserve requirements.

Usually such a change in reserve requirements would be imposed on all banks at the same time. Therefore, in our example, bank A, bank B, and all other banks would simultaneously be attempting to reduce their earning assets. As a result, an increase in reserve requirements can cause an abrupt decline in availability of credit and reductions in securities prices. This problem is illustrated by the response to the large increase in reserve requirements administered by the Federal Reserve System in 1936–1937. Increases in reserve requirements are unpopular with banks since they place on the banks the burden of making adjustments of a kind that they do not face in the normal course of business.

Federal Reserve Open Market Operations

The next theoretical case is a $1 million Federal Reserve open market purchase of government securities. The Federal Reserve Bank of New York buys the government securities from a government securities dealer, paying him with a check drawn on itself. He deposits the check in his bank, which presents it for payment and has the amount added to its balance at the Federal Reserve bank. At this point, the effect of the changes is as depicted in Table 9–3.

On the books of the Federal Reserve bank (and on the consolidated books of all of the Federal Reserve banks), there is an increase in assets in the form of the additional government securities. The increase in liability is the deposit account of the commercial bank in which the check was deposited. The books of the commercial bank show the increase in the bank's deposit at the Federal Reserve bank, listing this as cash (or reserves). The commercial bank's liability is the deposit account of the customer who sold the government securities.

Matters will not remain for long as we depict them in Table 9–3. The government securities dealer will not hoard the funds from the sale of the securities, but ordinarily will use them within minutes or hours to pay off the loans with which he finances his inventory or to buy other securities. Thus, the $1 million directly added to the money supply by the

TABLE 9-3 Federal Reserve and Treasury Operations

Federal Reserve Open Market Operations

	Federal Reserve Banks		Commercial Banks		Reserves	Required Reserves	Excess Reserves	M
	Assets	*Liabilities*	*Assets*	*Liabilities*				
a. Federal Reserve buys government securities	Government securities +$1,000,000	Deposits of member banks +$1,000,000	Cash (deposits at Federal Reserve bank) +$1,000,000	Demand deposits +$1,000,000	+$1,000,000	+$200,000	+$800,000	+$1,000,000
a. Federal Reserve buys foreign exchange	Assets den. in foreign currency +$100	Deposits of member banks +$100	Deposits at Federal Reserve bank +$100	Demand deposits +$100	+$100	+$20	+$80	+$100

Member Bank Borrowing from Federal Reserve bank

	Federal Reserve Banks Assets	Federal Reserve Banks Liabilities	Commercial Banks Assets	Commercial Banks Liabilities	Reserves	Required Reserves	Excess Reserves	M
a. Member bank borrows from its Federal Reserve bank	Discounts and advances +$100	Deposits of member banks +$100	Deposits at Federal Reserve bank +$100	Due to Federal Reserve bank +$100	+$100		+$100	

Withdrawal of Currency by the Public

	Mr. A		Bank A		Reserves	Required Reserves	Excess Reserves	M
	Assets	*Liabilities*	*Assets*	*Liabilities*				
a. Mr. A. withdraws currency from his deposits at bank A	Demand deposits at bank A −$1,000 Currency +$1,000		Currency −$1,000	Demand deposits −$1,000	−$1,000	−$200	−$800	

TABLE 9–3 (continued)

Check Collection through Federal Reserve

	Federal Reserve Banks		Bank C		Bank P					
	Assets	*Liabilities*	*Assets*	*Liabilities*	*Assets*	*Liabilities*	**Reserves**	**Required Reserves**	**Excess Reserves**	**M**
a. Check drawn on bank P deposited in bank C			Cash items . . . +$100	Demand deposits +$100						
b. Check forwarded to Federal Reserve bank for collection	Cash items . . . +$100	Deferred availability cash items +$100								
c. Federal Reserve bank credits deposit of bank C		Deferred availability cash items −$100 Member bank deposits +$100	Cash items . . . −$100 Deposits at Federal Reserve bank +$100				+$100		+$100	
d. Federal Reserve bank collects check from bank P	Cash items . . . −$100	Member bank deposits −$100			Deposits at Federal Reserve bank −$100	Demand deposits −$100	−$100		−$100	
Net change			Deposits at Federal Reserve bank +$100	Demand deposits +$100	Deposits at Federal Reserve bank −$100	Demand deposits −$100				

TABLE 9-3 (continued)

Transfers of Treasury Balances

	U.S. Treasury		Federal Reserve Banks		Commercial Banks					
	Assets	*Liabilities*	*Assets*	*Liabilities*	*Assets*	*Liabilities*	Reserves	Required Reserves	Excess Reserves	M
a. Increase in Treasury deposit at commercial banks	Taxes receivable −$100 Deposits at commercial bank +$100					Demand deposits of public −$100 Demand deposits of Treasury +$100				−$100
b. Treasury transfers funds to Federal Reserve banks	Deposits at commercial banks −$100 Deposit at Federal Reserve bank +$100			Deposits of Treasury +$100 Deposits of commercial banks −$100	Deposits at Federal Reserve bank −$100	Demand deposits of Treasury −$100	−$100	−$20	−$80	
c. Treasury spends funds	Deposits at Federal Reserve bank −$100	Accounts payable −$100		Deposits of Treasury −$100 Deposits of commercial banks +$100	Deposits at Federal Reserve bank +$100	Demand deposits of public +$100	+$100	+$20	+$80	+$100
Net change	Taxes receivable −$100	Accounts payable −$100								

TABLE 9-3 (continued)

Treasury Purchase of Gold

	U.S. Treasury *Assets*	U.S. Treasury *Liabilities*	Federal Reserve Banks *Assets*	Federal Reserve Banks *Liabilities*	Commercial Banks *Assets*	Commercial Banks *Liabilities*	Reserves	Required Reserves	Excess Reserves	M
a. Treasury buys gold from Bank of England	Gold stock +$100 Deposits at Federal Reserve bank −$100			Deposits of Treasury −$100 Deposits of Bank of England +$100						+$100
b. Treasury issues gold certificates	Deposits at Federal Reserve bank +$100	Gold certificates +$100	Gold Certificates +$100	Deposits of Treasury +$100						
c. Bank of England invests funds				Deposits of Bank of England −$100 Deposits of member banks +$100	Deposits at Federal Reserve bank +$100	Demand deposits +$100	+$100	+$20	+$80	
Net change	Gold Stock +$100	Gold certificates +$100	Gold Certificates +$100	Deposits of member banks +$100	Deposits at Federal Reserve bank +$100	Demand deposits +$100	+$100	+$20	+$80	+$100

(Gold Purchase Sterilized)

	U.S. Treasury *Assets*	U.S. Treasury *Liabilities*	Federal Reserve Banks *Assets*	Federal Reserve Banks *Liabilities*	Commercial Banks *Assets*	Commercial Banks *Liabilities*	Reserves	Required Reserves	Excess Reserves	M
b′. Treasury borrows to replenish balance	Deposits at Federal Reserve bank +$100	Government securities +$100		Deposits of Treasury +$100 Deposits of member banks −$100	Deposits at Federal Reserve bank −$100	Demand deposits −$100	−$100	−$20	−$80	−$100
c′. Bank of England invests funds				Deposits of Bank of England −$100 Deposits of member banks +$100	Deposits at Federal Reserve bank +$100	Demand deposits +$100	+$100	+$20	+$80	
Net change	Gold stock +$100	Government securities +$100								

Federal Reserve open market operation is set in motion as a part of the money supply being used by the public.

The immediate effect of the open market operation is to give commercial bank A excess reserves. Assuming a 20 percent reserve requirement, the increase in deposits of $1 million implies an increase in required reserves of $200,000. However, actual reserves are up by $1 million and, therefore, excess reserves are increased by this transaction by $800,000. There are no offsets to this elsewhere in the banking system, so if we consolidated all commercial banks we should find that for the banks as a whole the open market operation has increased deposits by $1 million, reserves by $1 million, and excess reserves by $800,000.

To commercial bank A, however, this cash inflow of $1 million is just like all of the other inflows and outflows to which the manager of the money position is responding. Through the same process by which he offsets the other transactions to maintain approximately zero excess reserves, he will offset this one also. As a consequence, the excess reserves that bank A otherwise would derive from the open market operation ordinarily find their way immediately into the federal funds market, other earning assets, or repayment of borrowing from the Federal Reserve bank.

The effect on bank reserves, the monetary base, and the money supply of Federal Reserve purchases and sales is quite the same regardless of what asset is involved. In such connections, Federal Reserve operations in the foreign exchange market on behalf of the Federal Open Market Committee have quite the same effects upon these variables as open market operations in government securities, as is indicated in Table 9–3.

Member Bank Borrowing

Member bank borrowing is initiated by individual commercial banks that face a reserve deficiency. On the books of the Federal Reserve banks (here treated on a consolidated basis) the asset item is discounts and advances, or loans to member banks. The liability item is the deposit of the bank that borrows. This liability of the Federal Reserve bank is the asset of the commercial bank, namely, its cash or reserves. The liability of the commercial bank is its obligation to repay the Federal Reserve bank.

Changes in member bank borrowings have no direct effect on deposits or the money supply. In a direct sense, the change in reserves is reflected entirely in a change in excess reserves of the commercial banks. Changes in bank reserves brought about through the borrowing of individual member banks add to the total monetary base.

Because the commercial banks respond very quickly to changes in the reserves available to them through the negative feedback operations of the manager of the money position, indirect effects of a change in reserves may occur at virtually the same time as the direct ones. So long as an addition to member bank borrowing does not increase average excess reserves for the commercial banks in the aggregate, it will be reflected immediately in a change in deposits and in required reserves, rather than having only the direct effects shown in Table 9–3.

Currency Flows

We have noted that the proportion of its total money holdings that the public chooses to hold in currency rather than demand deposits affects the size of the money supply. We consider now a particular transaction involving an outflow of base money from bank reserves to currency. Mr. A., a depositor in bank A, decides to shift $1,000 of his money from deposits to currency. He goes to bank A and withdraws the cash. The entries on the books of Mr. A. and bank A are as shown in Table 9–3. The money supply is not directly changed by the transaction. Its restrictive effects result from the altered reserve position of bank A. Because bank A's reserves are down $1,000 but (assuming 20 percent reserve requirement) its required reserves are down only $200, its excess reserves are reduced by $800. If the bank was initially in a balanced position, it now has a reserve deficit. The loss of reserves is immediately felt by the banking system in general as a result of actions of bank A to adjust its money position.

So long as the additional currency remains in circulation, the loss of reserves of $1,000 by bank A is a loss to the banking system as a whole. In the absence of some offsetting changes, the commercial banks in the aggregate would have to respond by reducing their required reserves by $800. This requires a reduction in earning assets and deposits of $4,000. But since the public's demand for currency depends on the deposit volume, a decline in deposits would reduce the amount of currency the public wants to have. To deal with this interaction among variables, we analyze the *total* effect on the money supply, including indirect effects, by using the money supply formula $M = B\ (1 + c)/(c + r)$. The present case involves an increase in the currency ratio, leading to a decline in the base-money multiplier and in the M consistent with any given B.

Federal Reserve Float

Federal Reserve float is the credit extended by Federal Reserve banks in conjunction with their check-collection activities. It is useful now to see how this involuntary or automatic kind of loan to member banks looks on the books of the Federal Reserve banks and the commercial banks. We consider the entries on the books of the collecting bank, bank C; the paying bank, bank P; and the consolidated Federal Reserve banks. The check drawn on bank P is deposited in bank C, giving rise to an increase in its deposits. The corresponding asset item is "cash items in process of collection." At this time, the deposit is being double-counted on the books of the banks. Bank C records a deposit for the recipient of the check while bank P has not yet made any deduction from the account of the writer of the check. To derive from the books of the banks a figure for total demand deposits that does not involve double counting it is necessary to deduct cash items in process of collection from the gross total.

The check is now sent by bank C to its Federal Reserve bank. The entries on the books of the Federal Reserve bank are the asset item "cash items in process of collection" and the liabilities item "deferred availability cash items." The Federal Reserve bank operates under a deferred availability schedule that defines for checks to be collected in various localities how many days must lapse before the collecting bank is given credit for the check being collected. This is 1 or 2 days. When this date arrives, the entry on the books of the Federal Reserve bank is changed from deferred availability cash items to "deposits," specifically the deposit of bank C. The corresponding adjustment on the books of bank C involves a reduction in cash items in process of collection and an increase in cash in the form of a deposit at the Federal Reserve bank. At this point, bank C has an increase in its reserves.

We now run into a problem of the double-counting of reserves. The Federal Reserve bank has added the amount of the check to the balance of bank C as if the check had been collected. But the check has not been collected and therefore no deduction has yet been made from the reserve balance of bank P. It is this stage of the process that gives rise to the Federal Reserve float, which is a source of funds for bank reserves and the monetary base.

This source of Federal Reserve credit disappears when the check is collected by the Federal Reserve bank from bank P. After this is done, the items on the balance sheet of the Federal Reserve banks net out to zero. There is no longer any extension of Federal Reserve credit and no Federal Reserve float. The Federal Reserve credit existed only during the period in which the deferred availability cash item had been changed into a deposit, while the cash items in process of collection entry remained on the books because the check had not yet been collected. Thus, Federal Reserve float is measured by the difference between these two items, or cash items in process of collection less deferred availability cash items. The end result of the process is the same as for a local check collection: a shift of deposits and reserves from the paying bank to the collecting bank.

When the deferred-availability schedule is unchanged, the amount of Federal Reserve float varies with the volume of checks being processed and is responsive to any transportation tie-ups that delay the collection of checks. Accordingly, float increases regularly in the middle of the month when check payments are highest and is larger in seasonally large months than in small months. Somewhat anomolously, float is quite responsive to the weather. A winter storm or a pervasive fog that keeps the airplanes on the ground prevents the collection of checks on schedule and leads to an unusual increase in float. Other things being equal, a widespread fog increases bank reserves, increases the money supply, and reduces interest rates in the money market.

Treasury Operations

An increase in Treasury balances at commercial banks, such as that associated with tax receipts, does not affect bank reserves, but does reduce the money supply and bank reserves available for private demand deposits. Such Treasury balances are subject to seasonal and erratic variation associated with variations in tax receipts, government expenditures, and flotations and retirements of government securities.

An increase in Treasury balances at Federal Reserve banks does reduce bank reserves and the monetary base, since such balances compete with member bank reserves for a fixed total set of sources of funds, as indicated in Table 9-3. In order to prevent variation in its balance at Federal Reserve banks from being an important erratic influence on the monetary base, the U.S. Treasury, in cooperation with the Federal Reserve, follows an elaborate procedure of transferring funds from its balances at commercial banks to the Federal Reserve banks at just the rate that—given estimated Treasury expenditures—will keep the Federal Reserve balance stable at $1 billion. In most weeks, the average Treasury balance at the Federal Reserve banks comes within $100 million of this target.

Treasury operations in gold and SDRs

We consider next a Treasury purchase of gold from a foreign central bank. If the foreign central bank has a working balance at the Federal Reserve Bank of New York, payment is made by transferring funds on the books of that bank from the Treasury to the foreign central bank. This increases the money supply, which is defined to include foreign deposits at Federal Reserve banks but not U.S. government deposits. The Treasury's books at this stage show a decline in one asset item, the Treasury balance at the Federal Reserve Bank of New York, and an increase in another asset item, the Treasury's holdings of gold, or the gold stock.

To replenish its cash balance, the Treasury "monetizes" the gold by issuing against it "gold certificates," which it "sells" to the Federal Reserve in exchange for an increase in its deposit. The Treasury's cash balance is now back to its initial position.

An increase in Federal Reserve holdings of gold certificates, other things being equal, increases bank reserves and the monetary base. In Table 9-3, other things are not yet equal, for the balance of the Bank of England is still 100 larger than at the outset. However, foreign central banks keep only working balances at the Federal Reserve Bank of New York, so the extra funds will shortly be shifted to a commercial bank, to the purchase of an earning asset such as a Treasury bill, or perhaps to a purchase of foreign exchange. In any case, the Bank of England's check drawn on the Federal Reserve Bank of New York is deposited in a commercial bank by the recipient. This leads to an increase in reserves (and the monetary base) that is equal to the amount of the Treasury gold purchase. The acquisition of assets in the form of gold certificates by the Federal Reserve banks has the same effect as an acquisition of government securities or foreign exchange.

In some cases, a government may find itself forced to acquire gold (or foreign exchange) at a time when an increase in its monetary base and money supply would be inflationary and undesirable. It can "sterilize" the gold inflow—prevent it from affecting the monetary base—by financing the acquisition of gold by some other means and desisting from monetizing the gold. This can be done by selling government securities to the public or by running a current surplus and replenishing its cash balance out of its net receipts. Step *b*′ shows the Treasury replenishing its balance by the sale of securities to the public.

Summing transactions *a*, *b*′, and *c*′, the only net result is a Treasury purchase of gold financed by the sale of securities. In this case, there is no implicit Federal Reserve open market operation. Federal Reserve assets are unchanged, and so are Federal Reserve liabilities, bank reserves, demand deposits, and the money supply. It is thus possible for the Treasury to sterilize a gold inflow, if it is willing and able to finance the transactions on its own resources, without resort to the central bank.

If a gold inflow (or outflow) were not sterilized by the Treasury, it could be offset by the Federal Reserve through a sale of government securities equal to the acquisition of gold certificates. This would alter the position of the public in the same way as would the sterilization operation of the Treasury. If the Federal Reserve were acting to keep the money supply on a defined target path, it would automatically sterilize gold transactions along with all other factors that would cause the money supply to deviate from its desired path.

Operations in Special Drawing Rights of the International Monetary Fund, which began in January 1970, closely parallel those in gold. The SDRs are acquired by the Treasury, on behalf of the United States government, through allocation of a part of a new issue of SDRs by the IMF or by acquisition from other nations. The initial allocation of SDRs to the United States on January 1, 1970 amounted to $866.9 million, its share of total allocations to all participating nations of $3.5 billion.

The SDRs, like gold, are monetized by the sale to the Federal Reserve banks by the Treasury of SDR certificates. These are bookkeeping entries rather then physical certificates, as is true of gold certificates. The initial allocation of SDRs and some subsequent purchases by the Treasury have only been partially monetized by the Treasury, SDR certificates issued by August, 1971 amounting to only $400 million.

SUMMARY

1. The monetary base (or high-powered money) is defined to include currency in circulation and the reserves held by commercial banks against the demand deposits of the public. The monetary base consists almost entirely of the circulating notes and the demand deposits of the Federal Reserve banks. The most important Federal Reserve asset is government securities. Although small in absolute amount, member bank borrowings from Federal Reserve banks may importantly affect short-run variation in the monetary base.

2. The factors determining the behavior of the money supply are usefully divided into two sets: those determining the monetary base and those setting the value of the base-money multiplier. The dependence of the money supply on these two sets of factors in the present United States monetary system is defined by $M = B(1 + c)/(c + r)$. If the currency ratio and the reserve ratio decline over some limited range during economic upswings and rise during economic downswings, this tends to produce a procyclical variation of the money supply that contributes to economic fluctuations.

3. In a commercial banking system including a large number of individual banks, the making of a payment by check usually involves a shift of the deposit and an equal amount of reserves between two banks, from the payer's bank to the payee's bank. Such flows among banks each day amount to a substantial proportion of all outstanding demand deposits. As each bank each day adjusts its holdings of cash and earning assets, this maintains the excess reserves of the banking system as a whole close to zero and maintains the reserve ratio of the banking system virtually unchanged from day to day and week to week. This implies that changes in the monetary base ordinarily almost immediately cause a proportionate change in the money supply.

4. Analysis of changes in the monetary base is carried out in terms of a set of sources of funds for the monetary base minus a set of competing uses of these funds that make them unavailable for use as currency and reserves for private demand deposits.

5. Although a large number of factors affect the monetary base, the Federal Reserve can keep its value close to any desired time path by using its powers—mainly open market operations—to offset changes in any factors that tend to move the monetary base away from the desired value. Such use of offsetting operations, or error-controlled negative feedback, is also the process by which the manager of the money position of a commercial bank keeps the money position on target despite the very large gross flows of funds to which the bank is subject.

6. Federal Reserve open market operations in government securities have an equal effect on the monetary base and an equal *direct* effect on the money supply. Open market operations are the only Federal Reserve tool permitting day-to-day and hour-to-hour actions to adjust the money supply, and are the major, and perhaps the only essential, instrument of Federal Reserve monetary policy.

7. Changes in reserve requirements of member banks by the Board of Governors of the Federal Reserve System alter the required reserve ratio and tend to produce a corresponding change in the actual reserve ratio. Thus, they alter the base-money multiplier and the money supply that is consistent with any given monetary base.

8. Member bank borrowing from Federal Reserve banks affects the monetary base. Such borrowing occurs at the initiative of the borrowing member bank, so is not subject to close Federal Reserve control.

QUESTIONS FOR REVIEW AND DISCUSSION

1. Identify and explain the significance of the following items on the balance sheet of the Federal Reserve banks: SDR certificates, United States government securities, deferred availability cash items, deposits of member banks, Federal Reserve notes.

2. Give the formula defining the dependence of the money supply on the monetary base, the currency ratio, and the reserve ratio, in a monetary system in which base money circulates. Explain how a monetary system of this class can give rise to bounded oscillations in the money supply. Explain the effect on the money supply of a change in member bank reserve requirements.

3. Explain the process by which the excess-reserve ratio of the banking system is kept near zero, thereby stabilizing the actual reserve ratio. Indicate the relevance of the management of the money position of the individual commercial bank.

4. Indicate the effect on the money supply, other things being equal, of an increase in Federal Reserve float, a decline in Federal Reserve holdings of SDR certificates, a Federal Reserve RP with a government securities dealer, a decline in Treasury cash holdings, and an increase in commercial bank required reserves against Eurodollars. Review the list of factors affecting the monetary base.

5. Explain how the Federal Reserve can control the monetary base even though it fully controls only one of a large number of factors affecting it. Show the parallelism between this task and that of the manager of the money position of the commercial bank. Give some other examples of analagous control problems. Illustrate how the Federal Reserve could use this control over the monetary base to offset variations in the reserve ratio or currency ratio.

6. Using T accounts, show the following operations, indicating also their effects upon reserves, required reserves, excess reserves, and the money supply: a reduction in commercial bank reserve requirements, a sale of government securities by the Federal Reserve, a reduction in borrowings of member banks, a reduction in currency held by the public, an increase in Federal Reserve float, an increase in Treasury balances at commercial banks that is then transferred to a Federal Reserve bank and spent, and a Federal Reserve acquisition of SDR certificates.

PART 3

monetary theory

10
monetary systems and money supply functions

A basic idea of money and banking is that the behavior of the money supply of a nation has a peculiar indeterminacy or optionality. It is not governed by any economic law, but rather depends upon the legal and institutional factors that define the monetary system operating in a particular nation during a particular period. Because it is optional and has varied from case to case and from period to period, the monetary system plays an important role in explaining differences in performance among economies. This chapter reviews the major types of monetary system and the characteristic performance of each. It provides the background needed to interpret and evaluate the past and present monetary systems of the United States.

Kinds of Monetary System

The two main classes of monetary system involve "commodity money" and "token money." A commodity money (also called full-bodied money) involves a commodity whose value as a commodity is approximately equal to its value as money. A $5 gold piece that when melted down yields gold that can be sold in the gold bullion market for $5 illustrates commodity money. The amount of a commodity money is limited by the cost of its production. When money is gold coins, what causes rapid increase in the money supply (other than through international transactions) is the discovery of new gold mines or improved efficiency in the gold-mining industry.

A token money, by contrast, is of less than full value as a commodity. The most common token moneys are of negligible value as commodities and of negligible cost of production in relation to their value. This is true of paper money and the bookkeeping entries that comprise demand deposits. To increase the amount of money of this type requires only printing larger numbers on the circulating paper notes or making larger entries in demand deposit accounts. The cost of doing this is negligible. The amount of such moneys is not defined or limited by their cost of production, but must be restricted by legal and institutional factors. To explain the behavior of the money supply in such cases, we look to these legal and institutional factors. Coins whose value as metal is appreciably less than their value as money we treat as token money, since their amount is governed by considerations other than production cost.

As indicated in Fig. 10–1, several variants of each of these classes of monetary system can be distinguished. In the simplest form of commodity money, the commodity actually circulates from hand to hand, as in the case of full-weight coins of gold or silver. This was a major monetary system in the nineteenth century. Subclasses can be distinguisehed. In the "monometallic" systems, the coins are all of one metal. The "bimetallic" system defines the monetary unit (e.g., the dollar) as *either* a gold coin or a silver coin. In the "symmetallic" system each coin consists of a combination of gold and silver. Curiously enough, these monetary systems differ from one another significantly in their expected performance. Bimetallic monetary systems were prominent in the nineteenth century, but disappeared late in the century because of performance failings reviewed below. They were temporarily replaced, until World War I, by a monometallic system using gold coin, plus the kinds of token money discussed below.

A number of advantages of efficiency and flexibility are gained if the money commodity does not actually circulate from hand to hand. The commodity then is stored and warehouse certificates representing the commodity circulate as money. This is a system of paper money with 100 percent commodity reserves. It retains the characteristic that the amount of money depends upon the supply function of the commodity. If the reserves were fractional rather than 100 percent, this would no longer be true, for then the moncy in circulation would be worth more than the commodity held in reserve. Creation of such money would not be strictly limited by its production cost, and the amount of money would depend not only on the avail-

Fig. 10–1 Kinds of monetary system.

Commodity moneys	Commodity circulates	Monometallism Bimetallism Symmetalism
	Warehouse certificates circulate (100 percent reserve)	One commodity Two commodities More than two commodities
Token moneys	Bank-created money	Circulating banknotes Demand deposits
	Government paper money	Circulating government paper money

able amount of the commodity but also on the reserve ratio. Money based upon fractional reserves falls into the category of token money.

The warehousing approach with 100 percent reserves, or "representative commodity money," permits the use as money of commodities that could not conveniently pass from hand to hand because of their physical properties or because of a weight-to-value ratio that would yield coins of an inconvenient size. It also permits the use as money of a defined combination package of a large number of commodities. Under such a system, a $100 bill could be defined, for example, as a warehouse certificate representing 20 lb of steel, 1 ton of hay, a bu of oats, 10 lb of crude rubber, and ½ oz of gold. This particular type of monetary system has never been used on an important scale, but it has often been recommended as offering some important performance advantages. The warehouse approach was applied to a single money commodity, however, in the gold certificates and silver certificates that circulated in the United States in the past.

Among token-money systems, we distinguish those based upon banking from government paper money. Since the token money has a cost of production substantially smaller than its value, the creator of such money can use it to finance expenditures—rather than using it to pay for its own production costs. In the case of bank-created moneys, the new money is injected into the economy through credit extension by the banks. It finances the acquisition of debt by banks, which then collect the interest on the debt. Government paper money is introduced into the economy by being used to cover a government deficit. The difference in performance between the two becomes very small where banks are obligated to buy government securities, since then the government deficit is financed through the creation of new money by the banks to buy government securities. An important example of government paper money was the United States notes, or greenbacks, issued to help finance the Civil War. Subsequent wars were financed by token money indirectly through purchases of government securities by the Federal Reserve banks and commercial banks. Dissimilar though they seem, circulating paper money and deposits subject to transfer by check (demand deposits) operate in essentially the same way as alternative varieties of token money.

Another distinction among moneys is between those that serve only within a nation and those serving on an international scale. The latter can be used for payments across national boundaries. A special class of international money is that used only in making settlements among national governments and central banks, such as the new Special Drawing Rights of the International Monetary Fund.

To make the story more complicated, national monetary systems in recent centuries have included more than one kind of money. A common system involves an inferior, or common, money and a superior money, base money, or high-powered money. The latter serves as reserves for, or "backs up," the inferior money, whose acceptability and value depends on its convertibility into the superior money. When this class of system evolved in the nineteenth century, the superior money was a commodity money that served also as an international money, mainly gold. The inferior money was mainly token money created by commercial banks in the form of circulating bank notes or demand deposits. Present-day monetary systems are a slightly more complex adaptation of this one. An important performance characteristic of such two-level, or multilevel, monetary systems is their tendency to generate bounded oscillations in the money supply that contribute to explaining the familiar short-run fluctuations of economies such as ours.

Money Supply Functions

The behavior of the money supply generated by any particular monetary system can be characterized by a "money supply function" that states the way the money supply changes over time, showing how it responds to whatever factors determine it. The simplest possible monetary system is one in which the money supply never changes, has the same value in each time period. This can be represented by the money supply function.

$$M_t = M_1 \qquad (10-1)$$

This says that the money supply in any time period t (M_t) is equal to the fixed quantity M_1.

Another simple class of monetary system is that in which the money supply grows at a fixed rate, and depends only on its initial value M_0 and time. This is represented by the money supply function

$$M_t = M_0 \, (1 + g)^t \qquad (10-2)$$

To illustrate the derivation and meaning of this class of money supply function, let us assume the money supply is M_0 in the year 0 and that it grows steadily at the rate of 5 percent a year thereafter. The value of the money supply at the end of any subsequent year will be $M_0 \times 1.05$ multiplied together the appropriate number of times, or raised to the relevant power. As we see from the right-hand column, this is simply an illustrative case of our money supply function, that in which $g = 0.05$, or 5 percent. With the appropriate value of g, this money supply function depicts a steady growth of the money supply at any defined rate.

Period	*Money Supply*	
0	M_0	M_0
1	$M_0 \times 1.05$	$= M_0(1 + g)$
2	$(M_0 \times 1.05)1.05 = M_0(1.05)^2$	$= M_0(1 + g)^2$
3	$M_0(1.05)^2\ 1.05 = M_0(1.05)^3$	$= M_0(1 + g)^3$
⋮	⋮	⋮
t	$M_0(1.05)^t$	$= M_0(1 + g)^t$

Actual monetary systems may also be subject to certain erratic influences that cause the money supply to vary randomly, i.e., in a manner that is not systematically dependent upon any other economic variables. A trend-governed money supply such as that of Eq. (10–2), which is subject also to random variation, can be represented by adding a random term to the money supply function as in

$$M_t = M_0(1 + g)^t + u_t \tag{10–3}$$

in which u takes on a set of values that vary randomly over time and average to zero.

Monetary systems involving feedback

Most monetary systems cause the money supply to respond systematically to other economic variables. In one class of monetary system, economic expansion leads to an increase in the money supply. Since the monetary response is in the same direction as the change in economic conditions, we term this "positive monetary feedback." In the case of "negative monetary feedback," the money supply responds in the opposite direction to a change in economic conditions. As was indicated in Chap. 2, monetary systems involving positive monetary feedback tend to amplify economic fluctuations. Monetary systems involving negative monetary feedback can be stabilizing, acting to dampen fluctuations.

One simple way to represent monetary systems involving feedback is by a money supply function in which deviation of total demand from its average path Y^* causes the money supply to deviate from its average path M^*:

$$M_t - M_t^* = h(Y_t - Y_t^*) \qquad \text{or} \qquad M_t = M_t^* + h(Y_t - Y_t^*) \tag{10–4}$$

This money supply function involves positive monetary feedback when $h > 0$, and negative monetary feedback when $h < 0$. The scale or potency of the feedback depends on the absolute size of the feedback coefficient h. The case of $h = 0$ is that of zero monetary feedback, of a money supply that does not respond in either direction to variations in total demand and economic conditions.

Such money supply functions provide a means of specifying performance standards for the monetary system such as were discussed in Chap. 2. We refer to a money supply function including a time trend, or average growth rate, a feedback component, and a component of random variation in the money supply as

$$M_t = M_0(1 + g)^t + h(Y_t - Y_t^*) + u_t \tag{10–5}$$

We recall that for any particular economy there will be a best-available growth rate of total demand, which depends on the growth rates of the labor force and of output per worker as well as the best-available behavior of the price level. One performance specification is that the average rate of growth of the money supply, defined by the value of g, should be consistent with this desired growth rate of total demand. If g is too small, the result will be too slow a rate of growth of total demand, and a continuing problem of unemployment and perhaps of price-level decline; too large a value of g leads to excessive growth of Y and to inflation.

With reference to the feedback properties of the monetary system, positive monetary feedback ($h > 0$) is to be avoided because it aggravates short-run economic fluctuations. Zero feedback is better than positive monetary feedback. Some value of negative monetary feedback ($h < 0$), constitutes the best possible monetary system, one that is actively stabilizing to the economy; but negative monetary feedback that is too large or operates with too long a lag would be worse than zero feedback. So what is desired is a money supply function in which $h = 0$ or $h < 0$, with a particular value that can be justified as positively stabilizing to the economy. Finally, erratic variation in the money supply is not desired and is to be minimized.

Commodity-money Systems

Commodity-money systems involve negative monetary feedback. Consider a society in which tobacco is used as money. The money supply is increased by expanding the production of tobacco. The amount of tobacco produced depends positively on its market value. The higher the price of tobacco, the more tobacco will be produced.

But if prices of other things are quoted in terms of tobacco, because it is used as money, an increase in the value of tobacco takes the form of a decline in these prices. The purchasing power or value of tobacco is increased by a decline in the general price level. This leads to an increase in tobacco production.

Under commodity-money systems, the amount of money, thus, responds negatively to changes in the general price level. The main monetary feedback is

$$P \xrightarrow{(-)} M.$$

An increase in the general price level means that the unit of the money commodity buys less of other things, its value is smaller, and less of it will be produced.

Strengths and weaknesses of commodity-money systems

What is the effect of a commodity-money system upon the stability of the economy? We have noted that an increase in total demand tends to cause an increase in the price level. Under a commodity-money system, however, the increase in the price level has a negative effect upon the amount of money. The feedback system is

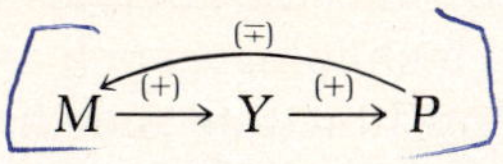

This is a negative-feedback loop, since the signs net to a negative. In terms of our discussion above, it should have a stabilizing effect, opposing self-feeding movements in the economy.

If a disturbance caused an increase in total demand, this would cause an increase in the general price level. But this would cause a *decrease* in the money supply, which would tend to reduce total demand, thus acting to offset the initial disturbance.

This implies that a commodity-money system could not contribute to cumulative inflation or deflation. As the price level rose and the value of money declined, production of the money commodity would be slowed and even halted. Without continued increases in the money supply, the inflation could not continue. Similarly, a cumulative deflation such as that of the Great Depression could not occur under a commodity-money system. The reduction in the price level would *increase* the money supply, which would halt the reductions in total demand and the price level. The historical cases of extreme inflation and deflation were not caused by commodity-money systems.

This is an important favorable characteristic of commodity-money systems. It provides a useful reference point in evaluating other classes of monetary system. Why do we not then consider adopting a commodity-money system for the modern world? This class of monetary system also has some unfavorable performance characteristics, which can be summarized in this way:

1. If the money commodity is actually to circulate from hand to hand, this narrowly limits the choice of the commodities that could be used without intolerable inconvenience and inefficiency. Some are too bulky, some indivisible, some too fragile, and some not valuable enough to make large payments feasible. If the money commodity is actually to circulate from hand to hand, the choice is limited to a few metals, the values of which are such that their coins are a convenient size for making payments. Even so, any metal of a value such as to make its coins convenient for small payments would be inefficient for large payments because of the volume and weight of the coins required.

2. If by these practical considerations our choice is effectively limited to, say, gold or silver, then the behavior of the money supply is closely tied to the conditions of production of these particular metals. This limits the possibility of tailoring the monetary system to the performance needs of the society.

3. The cost of production of gold and silver historically has been fairly steady from one year to the next but has shown large erratic variations over longer periods of time. Discoveries of new gold fields and improvements in gold-refining technology, such as occurred in the 1850s and 1890s, shifted the production function and the supply function for gold. By reducing the production cost of gold and increasing the amount of it, they naturally led to a period of inflation, of increase in the general price level measured in terms of gold.

4. Apart from these erratic increases in the supply of gold, the expectation is that in the long run gold as a money commodity would lead to a modest but steady deflation. The reason for this is that growth in population and productivity implies continued increases in the amount of gold needed as money in order to keep the price level constant. However, gold mining is an extractive industry, subject in the long run to rising costs. Thus, to continue to get expansion of the stock of monetary gold would require increases in the value of gold. This, of course, implies reductions in the level of prices measured in terms of gold. That is to say, it implies continued deflation.

5. A final unfavorable characteristic of commodity moneys is the real cost involved in production of the money commodity. Digging gold out of the ground, refining it, and coining it require labor and capital that otherwise could be used to produce goods for consumption. If other monetary systems could be found, leading to as desirable a performance of the amount of money, that do not involve such use of real resources for the production of money, this would be a point in their favor. Where the commodity actually circulates from hand to hand, as in the case of coins, there is the additional cost of continually replacing the coins as they wear out from abrasion in use.

Representative commodity money

Several of the shortcomings of commodity moneys could be overcome if the commodity did not have to circulate from hand to hand. The choice of the money commodity would no longer be effectively limited to gold or silver. If the money commodity were not a mineral, this would reduce the hazard of long-run deflation associated with the depletion of mineral resources. The warehousing approach would not eliminate the cost of producing the money commodities. It would eliminate the cost from the wearing out of the money material in circulation, but would replace this with the cost of operating the warehouses and printing the warehouse certificates and replacing them as they wore out.

The use of warehouse certificates permits the use of a monetary unit defined as a package of fixed proportions of a number of commodities. The advantage of this is that the money supply function then would no longer be dependent upon the conditions of supply of a single commodity.

Erratic variations in a behavior of the money supply, such as those associated with past discoveries of gold fields, would be reduced if the money were based upon a number of commodities. Then a change in the conditions of production of any one commodity would have a smaller effect, and in some cases these changes for individual commodities would partially offset one another. By diversification in the set of commodities serving as money, the expected erratic variation in the money supply would be reduced.

Just how would this system operate? The government, let us say, would define $100 as equivalent to a package consisting of 1 ton of steel, 5 bu of wheat, 8 bu of corn, and 20 lb of aluminum. The government would establish a monetary authority, instructing it to operate in this manner. Whenever $100 will buy the package of goods just defined, the authority is to buy the goods and store them, issuing the $100 warehouse certificate as a means of paying for them. It is to buy as much as it can buy at prices that cover its costs. If prices of the goods defined as backing the $100 bill rise to more than $100, it will be profitable for the public to use the warehouse certificates to buy the package of commodities from the monetary authority and sell the goods. This will reduce the money supply. But it will occur, of course, only when the prices of the commodities are rising, which is to say under conditions of inflation. Then it will constitute negative monetary feedback.

What this system does is to tie the value of a $100 warehouse certificate to the value of the specified package of commodities. When the value of the certificates rises above the market value of the package of commodities, the monetary authority issues the certificates without limit until the prices of the commodities are driven up. This prevents price deflation, or increase in the value of money. When the value of the certificates falls below the market value of the package of commodites, the public buys the commodities from the monetary authority, which reduces the money supply. This prevents inflation.

Consequently, this system preserves the negative response of the amount of money to the price level that we characterized above. In this case, the amount of money responds specifically to prices of the package of goods defined as backing—or constituting—the dollar. If these prices could be chosen to constitute a representative sample of prices in general, the negative feedback of the monetary system would operate in such a manner as to tend to stabilize the price level. Evidently, this type of monetary system is not without its advantages, and it is a useful point of comparison with actual monetary systems.

Bimetallic monetary systems

A class of monetary system that may look similar but behaves quite differently is the bimetallic monetary system. In this class of monetary system, the monetary unit is defined not as X units of A *plus* Y units of B, but as X units of A *or* Y units of B. In an important historical example, dollars consisted of gold coins *or* silver coins.

Historically, it was, for some reason, expected that under such a system both gold and silver coins would circulate from hand to hand as money. One important reason for adopting the system was to ensure the availability of silver coins for making small transactions and the dearer gold coins for large payments. It was found, however, that characteristically only one kind of coin would circulate.

The principle that produced this outcome is best illustrated by another historically significant case. Suppose the monetary unit is defined as *a cow*. Can one say anything about the quality of the cows that will be used as a medium of exchange? If in making payments any cow has the same value as any other cow, the person wishing to make a payment will use his poorest cow, keeping the best ones for uses in which quality matters. Indeed, in this case, if all cows have the same value as money it will be worthwhile to raise very poor quality cows, which might be of little use for anything else, since as money they have the same value as high-grade cattle. If the monetary unit is defined as either a good cow or a poor cow, obviously one pays in poor cows. As money, poor cows drive good cows out of circulation. This is a graphic illustration of the principle that has become known as Gresham's law, cheap money drives out dear, or bad money drives out good.

How does the principle apply in the case of gold or silver coins? The dollar was defined as either X oz of gold or Y oz of silver. Gold and silver had some nonmonetary demand and demand from foreign monetary systems, and were traded like commodities in bullion markets. In the normal course of events, we should not expect X oz of silver and Y oz of gold to have precisely the same market value. Whichever is cheaper evidently is the one that would be used to make payments. De facto, the dollar was whichever of the two metals in the specified quantities had the smaller value. The increase in gold output in the middle of the nineteenth century and reduction in the relative value of gold implied that gold drove silver from circulation. The great expansion in silver production in the 1890s would have meant that silver drove gold from circulation had not the major nations—their disenchantment with bimetallism by this time complete—abandoned this curiously faulty monetary system.

Conclusions

Commodity-money systems have the desirable performance characteristic of negative feedback from the general price level. Thus, they tend to dampen fluctuations in total demand associated with changes in the price level. However, commodity-money systems tied to a single commodity may produce erratic variation of the money supply in response to changes in production conditions for that commodity. The version of this class of monetary system that is most interesting as a reference point for the modern world is that in which the monetary unit is tied to a specified group of commodities, the circulating money consisting of warehouse certificates issued against these commodities. This monetary system would produce negative monetary feedback in response to changes in the prices of this group of commodities. It would tend to cause variation in the money supply and, thus, in total demand such as to dampen changes in the general price level.

Token Money Systems

The behavior of the money supply under a token money system depends upon details of the institutions and rules governing the system, which must be considered on a case-by-case basis. The indeterminacy of behavior of the amount of token money opens some new possibilities. If we can write an ideal formula defining the way we wish the money supply to behave, it should be possible to design institutions under which this formula can be carried out. We later consider such ideal monetary systems, which are made possible by the use of token money. First, we consider the performance of token-money systems such as have existed.

Government token money

Government token money is most straightforwardly illustrated by circulating paper notes—ordinary paper money—created by the government. The amount of such money depends upon political factors and the operating procedures of government. An important historical case involves creation of paper money by governments that are unable to raise in taxes the amount that they wish to spend. The government deficit is covered by printing paper money and using it, along with tax receipts, to finance government expenditures. In such a case, the increase in the money supply depends on the government deficit. Political pressures for a government deficit are in some cases very strong. Government expenditures are popular; taxes are unpopular, and in some societies difficult to collect.

Under this monetary system, a government deficit leads to expansion of the money supply, which leads to inflation. The higher prices, then, require the government to print money more rapidly to meet its rising expenditures, which accelerates the inflation, and so on. Most historical cases of runaway inflation have been of this type. The case involves the positive-feedback loop:

$$M \xrightarrow[(+)]{} Y \xrightarrow[(+)]{} P \xrightarrow[(+)]{} D \xrightarrow{(+)} M$$

The potential explosive force of this destabilizing positive-feedback loop has been illustrated persuasively by history. The characteristic cases are governments in wartime and under conditions of postwar stress, and low-income countries with ambitious governmental programs.

The destabilizing potential of government token money is an asymmetrical story. It produces inflation, but not deflation. Governments have difficulties in controlling expenditures and in raising taxes, but no problem in increasing expenditures or reducing taxes.

Banking, credit-related monetary systems

Among the many possible kinds of money supply function that might arise from a token money created by banking, special interest attaches to one in which the money supply responds positively to the interest rate. This may happen because the commercial banks are willing to reduce their reserve ratio within some limits when interest rates rise and acquisitions of earning assets become more attractive. This increases the base-money multiplier and so increases the money supply. An important case in the modern world is that in which the government and the central bank vary high-powered money in an effort to combat variations in interest rates, or to meet the "needs of trade" at "reasonable" interest rates. Given this approach, during a period of economic expansion when rising demand for credit pushes up interest rates, the central bank buys government securities and increases the monetary base in an effort to keep money from becoming "too tight." Either of these mechanisms contributes to the positive-feedback loop:

$$M \xrightarrow{(+)} Y \xrightarrow{(+)} i \quad (i \xrightarrow{(+)} M)$$

This class of monetary system aggravates short-run swings in the economy. It has been very important in United States monetary history.

Two-level Monetary Systems

In Chap. 9, we discussed a type of monetary system leading to positive monetary feedback only with certain boundaries. This class of monetary system is interesting because it can contribute to explaining not only why the economy is subject to self-feeding short-run swings, but also why these movements ordinarily are bounded, i.e., go only a certain distance and then are reversed. The relevant class of money supply function is one in which positive monetary feedback prevails under some conditions or within a certain corridor—but negative or zero monetary feedback prevails under other conditions. That is, with reference to the basic money supply function

[Eq. (10–5)] the feedback coefficient h has different values under different sets of conditions:

$$h = \begin{cases} h_i(> 0) & \text{when } |M_t - M_0(1+g)^t| \leq c[M_0(1+g)^t] \\ h_o(\leq 0) & \text{when } |M_t - M_0(1+g)^t| > c[M_0(1+g)^t] \end{cases}$$

The feedback coefficient now shifts in value when the money supply gets a certain distance away from its average track, which is defined by $M_0(1 + g)^t$. This happens when the absolute value of the deviation of M from its trend path (deviation in either direction) reaches the factor c times that trend value. The feedback coefficient prevailing within the corridor, h_i, is positive, indicating positive monetary feedback, so that the monetary system contributes to economic fluctuations. When the boundary of the corridor is passed, however, the feedback coefficient shifts to a new value h_o, which is zero or negative, no longer supporting and perhaps opposing the short-run movement of the economy. If this nonsupportive money behavior suffices, given the many other factors affecting the behavior of total demand, to turn the economy around, the boundary in the money supply function may be the major factor explaining turning points in economic activity. The time path generated by a money supply function of this type is depicted in Fig. 10–2.

The range over which the monetary system supports economic fluctuations, with width of its corridor of positive monetary feedback, is measured by the factor c. The width of the corridor is $2c[M_0(1 + g)^t]$. The value of c is defined by those institutional and legal factors that determine how far

Fig. 10–2 Positive monetary feedback within boundaries.

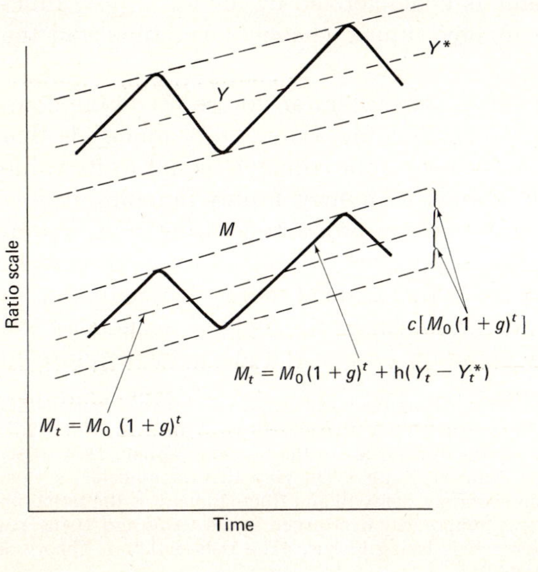

money creation is permitted to run during economic upswings before it is cut off.

Under monetary institutions that were common during the nineteenth century, the average growth rate of M (the factor g) was defined by the nation's gold reserves, which depended on world production of monetary gold. The width of the corridor of fluctuation of the national money supply about this value (the factor c) depended mainly on the range of variation in the base-money multiplier, which in turn depended on the range of variation in the reserve ratio and the currency ratio. This variation in the reserve and currency ratios depended on banking legislation, the way banks operated, and swings in public confidence in the value of bank-created money.

Finally, the degree of positive monetary feedback within the economy's corridor of fluctuation (the factor h_i) depends on a set of legal and institutional factors that determine the responses to changes in economic conditions and interest rates of the currency ratio, the reserve ratio, and the monetary base. Explaining the behavior of the money supply and the role of the monetary system and monetary policy in determining economic growth and fluctuations involves investigating the legal and institutional factors determining these aspects of the performance of the monetary system.[1]

SUMMARY

1. A basic idea of money and banking is that the performance of an economy depends importantly on the behavior of its money supply, which depends on the particular monetary system existing in the nation. The performance of monetary systems is characterized by money supply functions that define the way the money supply changes over time and the factors determining its behavior.

2. Two major classes of monetary system are those involving commodity money and those using token money. Commodity money is that which has a value in nonmonetary uses approximately equal to its value as money. The amount of such money, its money supply function, is governed by supply conditions and the cost of production of the money commodity. An increase in the money supply tends to result from an increase in the value of money. An increase in the value of money is a reduction in the general price level. Thus, such monetary systems tend to increase the money supply in response to deflation and to reduce it in response to

[1]The major studies of these topics are Milton Friedman and Anna J. Schwartz, *A Monetary History of the United States, 1867–1960*, Princeton University Press, Princeton, N.J., 1963; and Phillip Cagan, *Determinants and Effects of Changes in the Stock of Money, 1875–1960*, National Bureau of Economic Research, New York, 1965. The view that the monetary system played a central role in determining an economy's growth and fluctuations was the predominant view among economists until it was temporarily overturned in the 1930s and 1940s. An important statement of the earlier approach is Irving Fisher, "The Debt-deflation Theory of Great Depressions," *Econometrica*, **1** (1933).

inflation. This is negative monetary feedback. Its operation tends to limit swings in total demand and prices.

3. Token money has a value in other uses and a cost of production that is less than its value as money. The creation of such money must be limited by legal and institutional factors, otherwise its amount would be increased rapidly and cause severe inflation. The money supply function applying to token money is governed by the institutional and legal factors defining the conditions on which it is created.

4. This indeterminacy of behavior of token money permits the design of monetary systems to meet optimal performance standards. The historical systems of token money that have evolved, commonly, have involved positive monetary feedback and contributed to economic fluctuations. Especially important have been the two-level monetary systems including bank-created token money combined with high-powered money consisting of commodity money in the form of gold or gold and silver coin. This usually has produced positive monetary feedback within boundaries, which contributed to causing economic fluctuations.

5. The behavior of the money supply can be represented in terms of a basic money supply function

$$M_t = M_0(1 + g)^t + h(Y_t - Y_t^*) + u_t$$

in which g defines the trend factor, *h* the feedback properties of the monetary system, and *u* erratic variation in the money supply. A desirable monetary system would have a value of g attuned to the economy's growth needs, a zero or negative value of *h*, and a minimal variation in *u*.

6. Bimetallic monetary systems define the monetary unit as either *A* or *B*. This is an unstable system in the sense that, in conformity with Gresham's law, the money that is less valuable in other connections will be used to make payments and will drive the other one from circulation.

7. A representative commodity money based upon 100 percent reserves in a defined package of commodities would produce negative monetary feedback of such a form as to tend to stabilize an index of prices of the group of commodities. Critics of historical monetary systems have argued that this is a better performance than has been produced by actual monetary systems.

8. Analysis of past and present economic conditions depends on definition of the prevailing money supply function and the legal and institutional factors that determine it.

QUESTIONS FOR REVIEW AND DISCUSSION

1. What is the difference between commodity money and token money? What generalization can be made about the money supply functions of monetary systems of the two types?

2. Discuss the strong and weak points of a monetary system using only gold coins. What additional options would be opened and what advantages gained by using representative commodity money?

3. Write out a basic money supply function including a trend term, feedback term, and random term. What characteristics would a desirable money supply function have? What are the usual defects of the money supply function associated with gold coin, of money created by commercial banks that reflects changes in interest rates and the demand for credit, and of money determined by the government deficit?

4. Define positive and negative monetary feedback. Describe a monetary system that illustrates each. Illustrate how each monetary system would act in response to a disturbance in total demand.

5. Distinguish a bimetallic monetary system from a symmetallic one. Explain in terms of an illustration why in a bimetallic system both moneys do not ordinarily circulate.

6. Explain, using a relevant money supply function and a diagram, the operation of a two-level monetary system producing bounded fluctuations in the money supply.

11

the equation of exchange and the demand for money

Since the behavior of its money supply seems to have a major influence on the performance of an economy, it is important to define the causal linkages by which the money supply affects total demand and economic conditions. If a nation adopts a monetary system leading to an unusually unstable money supply, through what linkages and in what quantitative way does this cause instability of total demand?

A common-sense picture of the process is easy to formulate. Total demand measures the spending of money for goods and services. It is limited at any time by the ability of potential spenders to get money from income, borrowing, or sale of assets. Injection of additional money into the credit markets provides money to finance additional expenditures, thus increasing the expenditures-income stream. Moreover, as the new money is spent those who subsequently receive it as income will use it to buy goods and services or investment assets. The new money, which looks like the old, circulates with it in the expenditures-income flow, causing total demand to stay at the higher level. Similarly, reduction in the money supply requires people to spend less than their incomes and thus is a drain from the expenditures-income stream. To develop this picture in greater detail, we review the factors determining how much money people want to hold in relation to their expenditures, or the demand for money. This determines the relation that exists at any time between the amount of money in existence and the rate of flow of total demand.

To formulate a theory of total demand requires a framework within which the various factors affecting the supply of, and the demand for, money can be pulled together in a quantitative way. There are a number of different models of, or theoretical frameworks for, the theory of total demand. Discussion and research relating to the relative merits of different approaches and the development of new approaches continues. We begin in this chapter with the simplest monetary model of total demand, the equation of exchange.

The Equation of Exchange and the Theory of Total Demand

In the theory of total demand, the dependent variable, or the effect, is total demand Y. The simplest framework emphasizing the causal role of money sets it up as the only factor determining the behavior of total demand. The theory, then, is of the form:

$$M \xrightarrow{(+)} Y$$

The independent variable, the causal variable, is the money supply M. The dependent variable, the effect, is total demand Y. A change in M causes a change in Y in the same direction.

To make this theory quantitative requires only the provision of a variable to measure the quantitative relation between the independent and dependent variables. This gives us $M \times ? = Y$, or

$$M \times V = Y \qquad or \qquad Y = MV \tag{11-1}$$

It is customary to call V the "velocity of circulation of money" or simply "velocity." This may be a misleading name. It does not imply that money moves physically through the economy at a fixed rate, like an automobile traveling down the road at 40 mph. Think of velocity, rather, as the coefficient defining the response of Y to M, and, thus, defining the effects on Y of changes in M.[1] This expression is termed the "income equation of exchange" because its dependent variable is total demand, or gross income.

The usefulness of this equation of exchange depends on our ability to give a meaningful interpretation to V, since it defines the relation between the independent variable M and the dependent variable Y. To aid in interpreting V, let us restate the equation as $V = Y/M$ (by dividing both sides of it by M). This shows that velocity over any period is defined by the average number of times that each dollar is used to make an expenditure for final output. For example, if total demand is $500 billion per year and the money supply is $125 billion, velocity is 4.

If velocity were constant and M were indeed the causal variable, this simple model would be fully satisfactory. We would say that any change in total demand was caused by a simultaneous and proportionate change in the money supply. If velocity is constant and equal to 4, what is needed to increase total demand by $1 billion is simply to increase the money supply by $250 million. If this were the truth of the matter, income theory would be a simple subject and control of total demand would pose no difficult intellectual problems. But we have noted, and these are questions of fact, that velocity is not universally constant and that the money supply may *respond to* economic developments as well as *cause* them. The equation

[1]That is, from $Y = MV$, $dY/dM = V$.

of exchange can still be a useful framework for the theory of total demand, however, if (1) V is *approximately* constant or (2) the variation in V can be explained and predicted.

Instead of thinking about the relation between the money supply and total demand in terms of a concept of velocity defined as $V = Y/M$, we could think about it in terms of a concept of the *"cash-balance ratio,"* or *"cash ratio,"* defined as $k = M/Y$. Since by definition $k = 1/V$, it is clear that anything that can be said in terms of one of these expressions can be said in terms of the other. If on the average each dollar is spent to buy final output four times a year, then the average amount of money held by people must be equal to one-quarter of their expenditures for final output. By definition, if the velocity is 4, the cash ratio is 1/4. If the amount of money that people hold in relation to their expenditures declines to one-fifth, the dollars on the average must be used to buy output more frequently and velocity rises to 5.

Nevertheless, in some connections one version may be more convenient or suggestive than the other. Therefore, we keep them both at hand. The equation of exchange can be stated either as

$$Y = MV \tag{11-2}$$

or as

$$Y = M\frac{1}{k}$$

given that

$$k = \frac{1}{V}$$

The second approach is commonly termed the cash-balance version of the equation of exchange, since it focuses attention on the amount of peoples' average cash balances in relation to their expenditures.

A basic monetary model of income determination

The rationale underlying the equation of exchange can be clarified by specifying explicitly a basic model of income determination (the determination of gross income, or total demand) that emphasizes the money supply as the crucial causal variable. This involves three equations. The money supply function defines the behavior of the money supply, the only explicit causal variable of the model. The money supply function, expressed as Eq. (11-5), is the simplest conceivable one. It says that the money supply is equal to some given amount M_1, which is determined outside of the model. Thus, the money supply is in this version of the model an exogenous or autonomous variable; it affects other variables of the model but is not influenced by them.

The money demand function [Eq. (11–4)] defines the amount of money that people hold in relation to their expenditures. This simple version of a money demand function says that the amount of money demanded is proportional to expenditures for final output. This implies that when people hold the amount of money they want to hold, velocity is constant. The other equation of the model says that the equilibrium position toward which the system tends is one in which the amount of money people hold is the amount they want to hold.

$$M = M_d \quad \text{defining condition of equilibrium} \quad (11-3)$$

$$M_d = kY \quad \text{or} \quad M_d = \frac{1}{V} Y \quad \text{money demand function} \quad (11-4)$$

$$M = M_1 \quad \text{money supply function} \quad (11-5)$$

In using and interpreting such macroeconomic models, we usually "solve" the model for the dependent variable, or put the model into "reduced form." By substituting Eqs. (11–4) and (11–5) into Eq. (11–3), we derive the model's solution equation:

$$Y = M_1 \frac{1}{k} \quad \text{or} \quad Y = M_1 V \quad (11-6)$$

This is the equation of exchange, which can be interpreted as the solution equation of a simple monetary model of total demand. The coefficient that defines the dependence of total demand on the money supply, V or k, derives from the money demand function. In further justifying or developing the model, the central focus is upon explaining the demand for money.

A common tool in macroeconomics is the multiplier. This defines the effect on a dependent variable of a unit change in an independent or causal variable. In this case, the multiplier would define the change in total demand for each dollar of change in the money supply, or $\Delta Y/\Delta M$. The value of the multiplier is readily derived from the equation of exchange [(Eq. 11–6)]:

$$Y_1 = M_1 V \quad \text{and} \quad Y_2 = M_2 V$$

Thus,

$$Y_2 - Y_1 = (M_2 - M_1)V \quad \text{or} \quad \Delta Y = \Delta M V$$

and

$$\frac{\Delta Y}{\Delta M} = V \left(= \frac{1}{k}\right)$$

So long as velocity is constant, the money multiplier is equal to velocity, or the reciprocal of the cash ratio.

Total demand, output, and the price level in the equation of exchange

In the 1920s and earlier, the dependent variable of the equation of exchange was more commonly defined not as total demand but as total output times the price level of output. The income equation of exchange can be expressed as

$$Y = OP = MV \tag{11-7}$$

The additional information now included is this: Any change in total demand can be regarded as consisting of a change in the volume of real output purchased (O), and a change in the average prices of this output (P). This point is familiar from Chap. 2.

Historically, the equation of exchange was used mainly as a framework for the theory of the price level rather than for a theory of total demand. The increase in availability of data and the development of more complex economic models in recent decades has led to the breaking down of the analysis into two stages: (1) the determination of total demand, which we are now considering, and (2) the determination of change in the price level for a given behavior of total demand, which is dealt with in Chap. 15.

The major contributor to the modern equation of exchange, the great American economist Irving Fisher, used it in this way.[2] He presented an extended argument to show that changes in the money supply could be interpreted as a cause of changes in economic conditions. Then he treated the behavior of velocity as a factual question. If, in fact, velocity showed large and unexplainable variations, this would imply that factors other than the monetary system were major determinants of total demand and that the equation of exchange was of little use in explaining changes in economic conditions and prices.

The behavior of velocity turned up in his exploratory investigation continues to be borne out by the intensive recent empirical studies. He found that velocity is not constant, although over long periods of time changes in velocity are small relative to changes in the money supply. Variations in velocity did not offset the effects upon Y of changes in M. Indeed, in the short-run swings in which changes in velocity played the most important role, they amplified the effects of changes in the money supply rather than offsetting them. This turns our attention to versions of the equation of exchange, and of the money demand function, that provide an explanation of such changes in velocity. In the short-run, velocity, as well as the money supply, varied inphase with economic fluctuations.

The equation of exchange with nonconstant velocity

Even under circumstances in which velocity is not constant, the equation of exchange can be used as a framework for the theory of total demand

[2]Irving Fisher, *The Purchasing Power of Money*, Augustus M. Kelley, New York, 1963 (first published in 1911).

by providing an explanation of the variation in velocity. For example, if we could specify that velocity varies in a definable way in response to changes in the level of interest rates i and in expected changes in price level ΔP_{ex}, we could write an equation of exchange in this form:

$$Y = M \times V_1(i, \Delta P_{ex}) \tag{11-8}$$

This represents velocity not as constant but as depending upon i and ΔP_{ex} in a manner defined by the function V_1, which is not here specified. Rather than the fixed velocity V, we now have the velocity function V_1, which defines a value of velocity for each value of the interest rate and of price expectations. In this more complex theory, explaining history and making predictions regarding the effects of changes in the money supply depends upon knowing the way velocity varies in response to i and ΔP_{ex}.

The Demand for Money and the Theory of Velocity

The velocity, or the cash ratio, for the economy as a whole is the average of those of individual spending units. Therefore, it reflects the behavior of each family, business, and governmental unit in deciding its cash holdings in relation to its expenditures. In explaining the behavior of velocity, we can think in terms of the way representative spending units would behave under various circumstances.

The starting point of the theory of demand for money is the fact that all of the in-payments of economic units, including those defining its income, come to it in the form of money. Moreover, its expenditures of all kinds, including its purchases of investment assets, are made with money. In the process of receiving these in-payments and of making out-payments, the economic unit necessarily has some positive cash balance on the average.

Any individual economic unit can keep its average cash balance low by careful management of its in-payments and out-payments, and by getting rid of any money not immediately needed to make payments of other types by investing it in liquid assets. However, keeping invested in liquid assets involves some operating costs and, for individuals, some inconvenience, and there is a limit beyond which it is not pushed. Furthermore, with a given payments interval—such as a custom of paying salaries and bills at the end of each month—for any particular economic unit to reduce its average cash holdings by careful management of its money position may only mean that someone else must hold a larger average balance, so having little effect upon the average cash ratio (and velocity) of the economy.

Keeping an average cash balance of any given size involves an "opportunity cost." Money can be directly spent to buy goods and services or investment assets. Consequently, by holding any given amount of money an economic unit foregoes the opportunity to spend the money. This is the opportunity cost of holding the money, the spending opportunity that must be foregone. For each economic unit, the opportunity cost is measured by the opportunity thus foregone that is to it most attractive.

For an individual to use his money for consumption expenditures or a business to use it to pay dividends would reduce their net worth, and may be ruled out because of this, since economic units generally have some desired wealth position defined by their basic strategy of operations. But any economic unit can always reduce its average cash balance without altering its net worth by keeping any money not immediately needed to make payments invested in liquid assets or using it to repay debt. An important opportunity cost of holding any given amount of money is foregoing investment of the funds in liquid assets. The advantage of keeping funds in liquid assets, of course, is that they pay interest, which money does not. The major disadvantages are that keeping funds not immediately needed invested in liquid assets involves operating costs and perhaps inconvenience.

Determinants of short-run variation in velocity

The observed tendency for velocity to vary inphase with economic fluctuations may be explained in terms of an interrelated set of factors. The relative importance of these factors and the way they interact with one another are difficult to define and remain to be clarified by further research. The observed data for velocity under such conditions do not represent full equilibrium positions, but may reflect in part lags of the public in responding to changes in the factors impinging upon it. All of the factors listed below presumably operate symmetrically, and for simplicity we illustrate the role of each in contributing to *increase* in velocity during an economic upswing. Explaining an increase in velocity, of course, involves explaining a decline in the cash ratio (M/Y) or in the amount of money demanded at any given Y.

To understand the causes of cyclical variation in velocity requires some knowledge of *what happens* during economic fluctuations. Relevant aspects of the cyclical story can be sketched in this way. In an economic upswing, incomes and business sales rise more rapidly than usual. Businesses feel that they must prepare for further increases in sales, so they spend for increased investment in plant and equipment and order enough goods to enlarge their inventories. This increases the orders and sales of other businesses and tends to make the economic swing self-feeding.

To make these investment expenditures, businesses borrow more than usual from banks and other lenders. This increase in demand for credit leads to increases in interest rates. Interest rates characteristically move inphase with economic fluctuations.

The increases in sales and incomes of businesses, incomes of individuals, and tax receipts of state and local governmental units make them optimistic over their future incomes. They not only increase their spending in line with the increase in income, but in some cases want to increase their spending by a larger amount. We referred to the large investment expenditures made by businesses under these conditions. Similarly, state and local governments may be led by their seemingly favorable prospective tax receipts to embark upon programs of new construction. In the same spirit, individuals may be more willing to buy houses, automobiles, and other durable goods. Such behavior need not involve a naive extrapolation into the future of current economic trends. It also can result from economic units playing a cyclical strategy in which they make their optional expenditures during good times with the understanding that they will retrench and follow an austerity program during bad times or uncertain times.

In an economic upswing, the desire to increase spending by more than income has increased leads to an effort to finance a part of the additional spending by borrowing the money, by selling holdings of liquid assets or other financial assets, or by making do with smaller holdings of money. The last of these, of course, directly increases the velocity of circulation, since it involves a deliberate reduction in the cash ratio. The increased demand for credit tends to increase interest rates. The sale of liquid assets and other financial assets involves a decline in the supply of credit. This reduction in the supply of credit joins the increase in the demand in making for an increase in interest rates.

The factors explaining short-run changes in velocity can be organized into two groups: (1) those affecting the opportunity cost of holding money, and (2) those affecting the financial conservatism of the public or its willingness to take an extended financial position. A listing of factors in these categories is given in Table 11-1.

The opportunity cost of holding money increases in an economic upswing because many of the things that could be done with money are—

TABLE 11-1 Factors Explaining Short-run Increase in Velocity

Factors affecting the opportunity cost of holding money
- Increase in interest rates on liquid assets
- Increase in interest rates on other investment assets
- Increase in interest rates on loans to finance expenditures
- Expectations of increases in prices
- Expectations of shortages of goods or increased delivery delays
- Expectations of continued increases in business sales
- Shortage of productive capacity because of increased sales
- Shortage of inventories because of increased sales

Factors affecting willingness to take an extended financial position
- Expectations of continued increases in sales and profits by business
- Expectations of continued increases in incomes by individuals
- Expectations of continued increases in tax receipts by governmental units
- Pursuit of a cyclical financial strategy, involving reductions in cash and liquidity during economic upswings

or seem—more attractive. Interest rates are higher, so by putting a part of one's money to work in a savings account, a short-term government security, or another kind of debt, one can earn at a higher rate. If what one can earn on his temporarily idle money increases from 2 to 6 percent, there is an incentive to make do with a smaller average cash balance and put a part of one's funds to work.

Even more important in causing some people to make do with less money is the increase in their desire to buy more than they can finance from income and from readily available credit. Businesses want to expand their inventories, governmental units want to start investment projects, consumers want to buy houses. They face not only high interest rates but also other limitations on the amount they can borrow. Thus, they scrape the bottom of the barrel and use as much of their own money as they can to finance these desired expenditures.

Another important part of this story is the role of changes in prices and of expected future changes in prices. In the upswing, prices characteristically are rising because of the increase in the demand for goods. At least early in the game, the price increases lead to expectations of further price increases. When prices are expected to rise, anything that one is expecting to buy—new plant, government buildings, a new house—is better bought now than later. The seeming attractiveness of buying, therefore, is further increased by the expectation that things in general will cost more in the future. So one is tempted to pull down his cash balance and buy them now. A different way of making this same point is to say that the purchasing power of money is expected to decline, so it is better to shift from holding money to holding goods as soon as possible.

Closely related to expectations of future price increases, commonly, are expectations of future shortages of goods, or of lengthening lead times on items that must be ordered in advance. This also provides an incentive to buy now while the items are available and in this way increases the seeming opportunity cost of holding money.

The other set of factors involve not a change in the desire of people to spend a part of their cash holdings but a shift in their standards as to how much money they insist on holding for safety reasons. These factors involve a change in attitudes as to how far down in the barrel people are willing to scrape. To be short on cash—and even more so to be short on cash plus liquid assets—evidently involves some hazard of financial embarrassment—a bill that cannot be met on time, an attractive opportunity that has to be passed up for lack of funds. The extent to which people are willing to take a chance of such financial embarrassment depends upon their degree of optimism over the future. When the future looks bright, as most people see it during an upswing, they are willing to scrape low in the barrel, to pull their cash ratio down low. When storm clouds appear, they will want to adjust back in the other direction. Moreover, within the framework of a coherent cyclical expenditures strategy, it is reasonable in the economic upswing when spending opportunities are bright and financing costs high to pull one's cash position and liquidity position down to a bare minimum, with the expectation of replenishing cash and liquidity by cutting expenditures sharply or by borrowing long-term funds during an economic pause or economic recession.

This whole interpretation is symmetrical. In a full-fledged downswing, everything that we just discussed is operating in the other direction. Incomes and sales are falling; capacity and inventories are excessive and businesses have no desire to expand them; interest rates are declining; the price level is expected to fall and the availability of goods to be ample. There may be very little one wants to do with his surplus money, and the rewards for investing it may be small. The opportunity cost of holding money may fall drastically.

At the same time, a bad decline leads to business failures, families in dire straits from loss of jobs, and governmental units unable to meet their obligations. If one earlier had been scraping the bottom of the barrel of his financial security, he may now want to fill it up generously, to build defenses against an uncertain and even frightening future.

We see that there is no difficulty in finding reasons why velocity varies procyclically: rises in upswings and declines in downswings. Indeed, our explanation is so impressive that we must keep in mind the limited quantitative scale of the variation that is to be explained. One might infer from the story we have just told that velocity in a recession would decline by three-quarters or more. In truth, we recall, velocity declined by about one-quarter in the early 1930s in one of history's greatest economic contractions. In ordinary-scale economic fluctuations in recent decades, cyclical variation in velocity is on the order of 5 percent.

A final point to be noted is this: The factors identified as causing variation in velocity during short-run economic fluctuations all were contingent upon, or derived from, the fluctuation itself. If an economic upswing is started by something else, this will increase the opportunity cost of holding money and lead to an increase in velocity, which will feed the upswing. But if nothing else starts an upswing, no basis will exist for the increase in velocity. Thus, short-run changes in velocity appear to play the role of amplifying factors rather than initiating factors in economic fluctuations. In a final accounting of causal factors, the contribution that in a direct sense is made to the economic fluctuation by changes in velocity must be attributed to the other factors that initiate the fluctuations and that, in conjunction with change in velocity, keep them going.

The relative importance of factors causing short-run changes in velocity

The relative importance of the various factors causing short-run changes in velocity is a matter of some interest because it affects estimates of the direct influence on total demand of changes in the money supply. Insofar as short-run variation in velocity reflects changes in interest rates, this implies that the direct effects of changes in the money supply on total demand are partially offset by the changes in interest rates they cause. For example, an increase in the money supply will increase the supply of credit and reduce interest rates, which will reduce velocity, which will tend to offset the effects on Y of the increase in M. But insofar as short-run changes in velocity reflect other factors, such as changes in expected sales, incomes, or prices, this mechanism does not operate. Indeed, insofar as changes in monetary policy have expectational effects, an increase in the money supply will make expectations more favorable, leading to an *increase* in velocity, which will amplify the effects upon Y of the change in M.

To define the relative importance of various factors in determining short-run changes in velocity (or in the demand for money) is difficult because these factors commonly all change more or less together in economic fluctuations, and so are very difficult or perhaps even impossible to disentangle. Empirical studies have not yet achieved such disentanglement. Usually, the interest rate is the only factor among the ones listed in Table 11–1 that is included in statistical studies of the demand for money, mainly because of the difficulty of measuring the other factors. This implies, however, that such studies overstate the responsiveness of velocity and of demand for money to the interest rate by attributing to this factor the joint influence that actually is exercised by the whole set of factors.

Determinants of long-run variation in velocity

Changes in velocity in the long run also can be interpreted, in part, in terms of factors affecting the opportunity cost of holding money and those affecting the willingness of people to adopt an extended financial position. In this case, the relevant developments are not those involved in cyclical swings of the economy, but those that operate over longer periods independent of economic fluctuations. Two additional sets of factors are relevant that could be excluded above because they would not ordinarily change enough during an economic fluctuation to have a significant effect upon velocity. These are (1) developments altering the technical efficiency of money or the amount of money that must be held on the average to make a given volume of payments, and (2) changes in the extent to which people are willing and able to afford the convenience of holding cash balances. We briefly consider some of the specific factors in these sets, which are listed in Table 11–2.

While the cyclical behavior of velocity shows a systematic pattern from one case to the next, its long-run behavior shows no such well-defined pattern. This does not imply that average velocity is necessarily stable

TABLE 11-2 Factors Explaining Long-run Increase in Velocity

Factors affecting the opportunity cost of holding money
Increase in interest rates
Increase in the quality and variety of liquid assets available
Actual and expected rate of increase in price level
Factors affecting willingness to take an extended financial position
Long-run increase in optimism
Structural changes increasing the stability of the economy
Factors affecting the efficiency of money
Increase in rapidity of transfer of money
Reduction in payments interval
Improvement in overlapping of payments
Increase in availability of credit, credit cards
Reduction in use of compensating balances
Operation of economies of scale in the use of cash
Factors affecting willingness to hold money as a consumption good
Decrease in real income

over long periods of time, but rather that its behavior depends upon a diverse set of factors the effects of which may or may not balance out, but that have about balanced out in the past.

Changes in the opportunity cost of holding money because of changes in the level of interest rates and yields on investment assets, historically, have been small, for the level of interest rates has shown no clear trend. Historical variation in interest rates has been associated mainly with economic fluctuations and wars, and therefore has been temporary and episodic. Substantial improvements in the quality and variety of available liquid assets have occurred through continued innovation of financial institutions. The spread of savings and loan associations during the 1920s and the development of negotiable certificates of deposits during the 1960s are only two examples of such financial innovation. This factor, taken by itself, has operated in the direction of making for a long-run increase in the velocity of circulation.

A factor that can affect velocity over both short and long periods of time is the rate of actual and expected change in the price level. Some economies experience continued inflation decade after decade, and mild inflation has become endemic in the modern world. We should expect that the more rapid the inflation, other variables kept constant, the higher the velocity, for inflation means that there is always a gain from spending money now rather than later or—another way of saying the same thing—means that the value of money is declining and there is a loss from holding it. The increase in inflationary expectations during the past 20 years, accordingly, has been another factor making for increase in velocity of circulation.

Changes in the willingness of people to maintain an extended financial position are mainly short-run and cyclical. However, in some cases there seem to have been significant changes associated with more basic and lasting revisions of the public's view of the stability of the economy. The new-era thinking of the 1920s may well have been a significant factor in making velocity higher than it otherwise would have been. The loss of this optimism in the 1930s and then its gradual resurrection from the late 1940s to the 1960s figured in movements of velocity over a period of time much longer than a business cycle.

A number of changes in government policy and business practices since the 1920s, presumably, have operated to reduce the instability of the United States economy, especially its susceptability to a severe downswing: insurance of bank deposits and accounts in savings and loan associations, controls over speculation, regulation of business practices in security sales and in release of information, and the assumption by the government of responsibility for economic developments in the Employment Act of 1946. These structural changes, apart from any purely psychological factors, presumably operate in the direction of reducing the amount of cash that businesses and individuals need to hold, thereby increasing velocity.

We next consider factors affecting the efficiency of money and thus the amount of it that is required to make any given volume of payments. Increase over time in the speed with which money can be transported for the making of payments at a distance evidently increases the efficiency of money. The improvements in transportation and in arrangements for the wire transfer of funds that have occurred in the past century have made for an increase in velocity.

Another factor potentially affecting the efficiency of money is change in the customary payments interval, the frequency with which wages are paid and bills are paid. In an illustrative case in which income is paid periodically, spending goes on at a steady rate, and the minimum money holdings are approximately zero, the average cash balance held is equal to one-half of the income of the period, as Fig. 11-1 shows. If we assume a $12,000 per year income, this implies that the average cash balance would

Fig. 11-1 The payments interval and average money holdings.

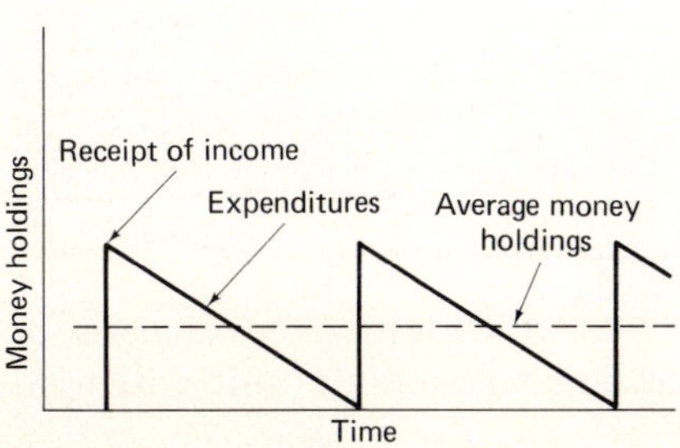

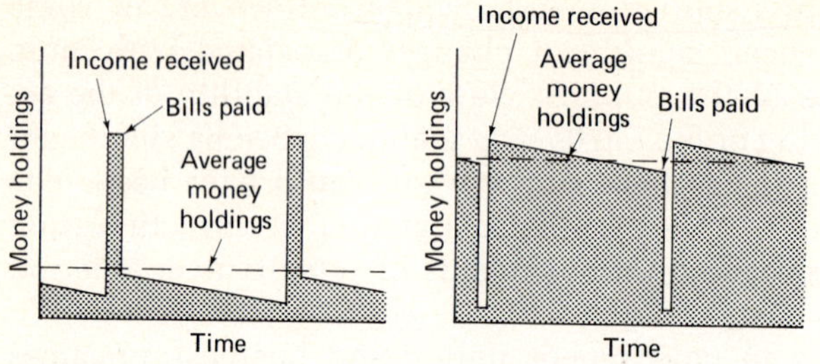

Fig. 11–2 Income-expenditure coordination and average money holdings.

be $6,000 if income were paid annually, $500 if income were paid monthly, or $250 if income were paid twice a month. In general, a shorter payments interval makes for a more efficient use of money and a smaller average cash ratio. There is no clear evidence which way this factor has operated in the United States in recent decades, and the presumption is that it has not had significant effect.

Another factor affecting the efficiency of money is the degree of overlapping or coordination in payments. Again, the point is made by a simple illustration. In Fig. 11–2, good coordination is the case in which one pays his bills shortly after receiving, say, his monthly income, so that for most of the month he is holding but little money and his average money holdings for the month are small.

As Fig. 11–2 suggests, if bills generally are paid early in the month, for one person to achieve good coordination simply involves passing the money along to someone else at a time when he will have to hold it until the beginning of the next month. Unless there are some special subcircuits that money can make within the month, it is not possible for everyone to achieve good coordination.

Acceleration of velocity, thus, requires a general shortening of the payments interval. As a matter of experience, during severe inflations when the value of money was falling sharply and the opportunity cost of holding money was very high, it was through extreme shortening of the payments period that people kept their average cash balance very low and caused velocity to skyrocket. At the height of the German inflation in 1923, wages in some cases were paid twice a day. But the economic cost of such shortening of the payments interval is itself very high. As a consequence, this will be done only when it is made worthwhile by an extremely high opportunity cost of holding money. Under normal conditions, therefore, the traditional monthly payment period seems to be an important constraint on increase in velocity.

Recent studies have demonstrated that if certain fixed charges or minimum sizes exist for transactions, the larger economic unit will tend to keep smaller cash balances in relation to expenditures, there will be economies of scale with reference to cash balances. If growth of the economy over time implies growth in the scale of economic units (and the fixed charges or minimum transactions size are not equivalently escalated), this implies an increase over time in the velocity of circulation.[3] On the other hand, there also may be some diseconomies of scale in administering cash balances, especially when increase in the size of the firm is associated with decentralization of operations. Whether net economies of scale in administering cash balances are a significant factor making for long-run increase in velocity is somewhat uncertain.[4]

The thesis has been advanced by Milton Friedman that money is a luxury good in the sense that long-run increases in income lead to more than proportionate increases in desired cash balances. This tends to make for a decrease in velocity in a nation with rising living standards. The luxury-good argument applies only to individuals, and not to the businesses, institutions, and governmental units that hold most of the nation's money. Moreover, it might apply only to individuals over a certain range of incomes. Accordingly, even if the point were true, it might have little significance for the behavior of average velocity. An empirical study by Friedman supports his thesis, but other studies have reached the opposite conclusion, and the role of this relation remains uncertain.[5]

Implications for monetary theory of technological change in the payments system

The developments of the 1950s and 1960s in data transmission and computation may lead to replacement of the making of payments by writing checks with some kind of system for the instantaneous making of payments. Some observers have assumed that this would make monetary policy obsolete,[6] but further investigation has indicated the need for a careful analysis of the implications of alternative payments institutions.[7] The making

[3]William J. Baumol, "The Transactions Demand for Cash: An Inventory Theoretic Approach," *Q. J. Econ.*, **78** (1963); James Tobin, "The Interest Elasticity of the Transactions Demand for Money," *Rev. Econ. Stat.*, **38** (1956).

[4]This point is made and limitations of the assumptions underlying the argument for economies of scale pointed out in Karl Brunner and Allan H. Meltzer, "Economies of Scale in Cash Balances Reconsidered," *Q. J. Econ.*, **81:** 422–436 (1967).

[5]Milton Friedman, "The Demand for Money: Some Theoretical and Empirical Results," *J. Polit. Econ.*, **67:** 327–351 (1959); Allan H. Meltzer, "The Demand for Money: The Evidence from the Time Series," *J. Polit. Econ.*, **71** (1963). Friedman's support of his thesis depends, among other things, on his defining the money supply to include time deposits at commercial banks, which grew more rapidly than demand deposits and currency during the period investigated. Thus, velocity defined with relation to Friedman's concept of money declines when velocity as defined here does not.

[6]George Garvy and Martin R. Blyn, *The Velocity of Money*, pp. 92–94, Federal Reserve Bank of New York, New York, 1969.

[7]Lawrence S. Ritter and Thomas R. Atkinson, "Monetary Theory and Policy in the Payments System of the Future," *J. Money, Credit, Banking*, **2:** 493–503 (1970).

of payments electronically on the basis of coded cards, say, would not seem to require any substantial modification of monetary theory. For demand deposits to be transferred in this way rather than by written checks would in no way alter the status of demand deposits as money and probably would not greatly affect the demand for money.

If the lower cost of the new system led to shortening of the payments period, this would increase velocity. A large increase in velocity might require the achievement of closer control over the quantity of money to avoid an increase in instability in the economy. But shortening the payments period and increasing the number of discrete transactions—as by paying wages every day—not only increases the payments costs but also imposes a burden on the record keeping of the payer and the payee, and the realities of the future may be but little changed from present practices.

The development of payments facilities by institutions other than the commercial banks would raise problems for monetary policy. Presumably, any new institution offering payments services that substituted for the making of payments with currency or demand deposits ought to be considered as "creating money" and subjected to the reserve mechanism that is applied to commercial banks.

A final point sometimes raised is that the new institutions might offer overdraft facilities, which would cause some problems for the conventional calculation of the money supply. Overdrafts involve the automatic granting of credit up to some limit as checks are written. This can be viewed as permitting the making of payments with a negative demand deposit balance. But such overdraft arrangements are technically quite feasible under the present commercial banking institutions and are used in England. It appears that overdrafts also can be accomodated by monetary theory. On the basis of present conjectures, therefore, it does not appear that technological changes in the payments system are likely to make monetary theory obsolete.

Interpreting Economic Events with the Equation of Exchange

The equation of exchange can be used to interpret and forecast economic developments. In the great economic collapse of 1929–1933, about half of the decline in total demand reflects decline in the money supply and the other half reduction in velocity. The reduction in velocity, however, seems explainable in terms of factors listed in Table 11–1. Once the contraction was under way, it brought into play all the factors making for reduction in velocity, for example very low interest rates, unattractive investment opportunities, and a rapid drop in prices, the whole list of factors. Under these extreme conditions velocity declined by about one-quarter.

The unusual factor, and within this framework the cause of the contraction, is the decline in the money supply by one-quarter. This is an extraordinary, unparalleled, event. The reasons why it happened we shall consider later. But given that the money supply declined by one-quarter over 3 years, the outcome is much what could roughly have been predicted by applying the equation of exchange.

From 1933 until the Second World War, it seems possible to interpret GNP as dancing to money's tune, for velocity changed but little in relation to the rapid increase in the money supply and GNP. Total demand rose rapidly, though not rapidly enough to restore prosperity. Total demand had fallen so long and so far that it had a great distance to grow before again reaching the prosperity level. The fact that prices had stopped declining and were rising after 1933 tended to make for an increase in velocity. However, many other factors favored continued low velocity: low interest rates, generally low profit rates and unfavorable investment prospects, and continued pessimism as to the long-run future of the economy.

The further reduction of velocity during the Second World War can be interpreted as reflecting special wartime factors affecting the opportunity cost of holding money. The unavailability of consumer goods and producers' goods, coupled with rationing and other direct controls, along with very low interest rates on liquid assets explain why individuals and businesses built up their holdings of money during the war, with the expectation of spending them after the war.

If the great decline in velocity was explained by conditions brought about by the Depression and then by the war, we should expect that the restoration of prosperity and the gradual return of confidence after the war would lead to a rise in velocity to something like its pre-Depression level. We find that this is what did happen. Why did it happen so slowly and gradually? Contributing factors were the slowness of the return of confidence in the future of the economy, the lag in the increase in interest rates to pre-Depression levels, and the slowness of businesses and individuals to change their ways of managing money as its opportunity cost rose. In the 1950s and 1960s, growing price increase and inflationary expectations added to the opportunity cost of holding money and contributed to further increases in velocity.

The equation of exchange, thus, appears to work. An interpretation in terms of the equation of exchange also fits the more modest variations in total demand during the 1950s and 1960s. The economic forecaster who kept a close eye on the money supply could have predicted the recessions of 1954, 1958, and 1960, the economic slack of 1960–1963, the accelerated growth of total demand after 1963, the lull of 1966, the inflationary developments of 1967–1969, and the softening of economic conditions in late 1969. That is pretty much the whole story. The equation of exchange approach works in a very practical sense. Some more elaborate theories do not pass this test.

The Development of Monetary Theory

Although monetary theory goes back much earlier, a useful point from which to pick up its development is with the sixteenth century statement by Jean Bodin of the "quantity theory of money." Large increases in prices and wages in sixteenth century Europe led to a search for an explanation. One interpretation, based upon the "commodity theory of money," was that since the value of money was declining the amount of metal in the coins must be declining from debasement of the coins, shrinkage of their physical size in various ways. The basis of the theory is that the value of the metals making up the coins is inherently stable.

Bodin argued that the main cause of the inflation was "the abundance of gold and silver," or the increase in the quantity of money, reflecting the large influx of the precious metals from the New World. This increase in the quantity of money, he argued, sufficed to raise the price level (reduce the value of money) even though there was no reduction in the amount of metal in each coin. This interpretation is consistent with a monetary theory using the equation of exchange. Within this framework, a large increase in the quantity of money would increase total demand so much as to lead to increases in prices. This general approach was accepted by Adam Smith and most of the major economists during the era of "classical economics," roughly the century beginning with the publication of "The Wealth of Nations" in 1776.

Neoclassical monetary theory

The "neoclassical economics" that predominated until "the Keynesian revolution" of the 1930s and 1940s, was a further development of the quantity theory of money using various versions of the equation of exchange. One major contribution, that of the Swedish economist Knut Wicksell, involved mainly a defense of the quantity theory against the credit approach to banking and is discussed later in connection with the credit approach. The major versions of the equation of exchange were those developed at Cambridge University under the leadership of Alfred Marshall and by Irving Fisher of Yale University (Table 11-3). The Cambridge approach characterized the demand for money in terms of the cash ratio (k) rather than velocity, and is termed a cash-balance version of the equation

TABLE 11-3 Versions of the Equation of Exchange

	Velocity		Cash-balance	
Income	$MV = Y$ modern		$M = kRp$	Cambridge, Marshall
Transactions	$MV_t = PT$ $MV_t + M'V_t' = PT$	Irving Fisher		

of exchange. It also defined as its dependent variable not total demand but output (R, for real output) and the price level of output (p).

The versions of the equation of exchange used by Irving Fisher treated the demand for money in terms of the velocity approach but differed from other approaches in that they related not to expenditures for final output but to all transactions in the economy made with money. His are transactions equations of exchange, using the velocity approach.

Fisher's major reason for relating the equation to transactions rather than income is that since money is used for all transactions rather than only for purchases of final output one might best explain velocity by relating the equation to total transactions. Another special feature of Fisher's work is that he in some cases divided the money supply into currency M and demand deposits M', each with its own velocity, V and V'. A feature of Fisher's approach that has more largely carried over to modern work is that he did not limit his use of the equation of exchange to the long-run or to equilibrium situations but also considered how the equation could be applied, and how velocity would behave, in transition or disequilibrium situations.

Although the term velocity is applied in both the income version and the transactions version of the equation of exchange, velocity does not have the same value in the two cases. Since total transactions, or Fisher's PT, have a larger value than expenditures for final output, Y (or Rp or OP) and both equations have the same M, Fisher's transactions velocity V_t must have a larger value than income velocity V. In our subsequent work, we do not use the transactions version of the equation, so velocity always will refer to income velocity.

Fisher's reasons for using transactions velocity rather than income velocity are not without merit. The difference in magnitude between the two is substantial; transactions velocity in recent years running about eight times as large as income velocity.[8] The relation between the two has shown practically no net change in the past 50 years, but has changed considerably during some short periods of time. During the stock-market boom of the late 1920s, transactions velocity rose in relation to income velocity because of the rise in stock-market transactions, a movement that was reversed in the early 1930s.

The main reason for emphasizing the income version of the equation of exchange in modern work is that total demand, rather than transactions, is the variable whose behavior we wish to explain, and that we hope to control. But because of the erratic role of financial transactions, it is also arguable that income velocity is analytically the more tractable.

The best-developed version of monetary theory before the tide of thought was turned by the Keynesian revolution was that of Irving Fisher.[9] Apart from differences in terminology and institutions, his approach was

[8]Data and some discussion of this approach are given in Garvy and Blyn, *op. cit.*, chaps. 4 and 5.
[9]Expressed in *op. cit.*; and "The Debt-deflation Theory of Great Depressions," *Econometrica*, **1**: 337–357 (1933).

similar to the one taken earlier in this chapter. Fisher investigated the behavior of the money supply and velocity. He recognized that velocity varied inphase with economic fluctuations, and he viewed both the long-run and the short-run behavior of velocity as reflecting the net outcome of a number of factors. He interpreted economic fluctuations as reflecting the complex interaction of a number of factors (he listed nine in The Debt-deflation Theory of Great Depressions). He depicted short-run changes in velocity as contributing to economic fluctuations. The behavior of the money supply under the monetary system then existing in the United States he saw as contributing both to upswings and downswings and being the major determinant of turning points. In his theory, variations in velocity were not of such a nature as to offset changes in the money supply. Consequently, given all the other factors consistently affecting the way the economy responded, variation in the nation's monetary system was a major factor explaining variations over time in the stability and performance of the economy.

Beginning in the 1930s the stronghold of monetary theory was the Chicago School, at the University of Chicago, including Frank Knight, Jacob Viner, Henry C. Simons, and Lloyd W. Mints. Their approach was based upon that of Fisher, but placed more emphasis on large and potentially erratic variations in velocity. These were interpreted, however, not as reducing the effectiveness of monetary policy so much as increasing the need for monetary policy. This approach emphasized that with a token money system the money supply could be changed by policy by very large amounts if this was needed, by enough to offset whatever changes occurred in velocity.[10]

The leading American monetary economists active during the early 1930s interpreted the catastrophic decline in total demand of 1929–1933 not as refuting their approach to monetary theory but as confirming it. They were extremely critical of the Federal Reserve for not taking effective action to prevent the great decline in the money supply that occurred. They thought the failure of the United States monetary system and Federal Reserve policy was so severe as to call for radical reform. In 1934 both Irving Fisher and Henry Simons published proposals to put an end to the creation of money by commercial banks by establishing 100 percent reserves behind demand deposits.[11] Their interpretation of this experience was not that a desirable monetary policy had been applied and been found ineffective, but that an extremely inappropriate policy had been applied and

[10]A recent characterization of the Chicago School is given in Don Patinkin, "The Chicago Tradition, The Quantity of Theory, and Friedman," *J. Money, Credit, Banking*, **1:** 46–70 (1969).

[11]Henry C. Simons, "A Positive Program for Laissez Faire: Some Proposals for a Liberal Economic Policy," in his *Economic Policy for a Free Society*, The University of Chicago Press, Chicago, 1948; and Irving Fisher, *100% Money*, The Adelphi Company, New York, 1935. Another important contribution that spelled out the factors causing the monetary contraction and the role of Federal Reserve policy was Lauchlin Currie, *The Supply and Control of Money in the United States*, Harvard University Press, Cambridge, Mass., 1934.

had proved all too effective in producing the result that should have been expected.

The Credit Approach to Banking and Central Banking

In monetary theory, the effect of commercial banks on the behavior of total demand is interpreted in terms of the role of banks as a determinant of the economy's money supply function. Similarly, the place of the central bank (the Federal Reserve System) in this picture is as a potential controller of the money supply function. By offsetting any factors operating in an undesired manner the central bank can bring about that money supply function that is consistent with the desired behavior of total demand.

A competing approach to interpreting the economic role of banks and the central bank, "the credit approach," leads to a very different interpretation and evaluation of the historical record. This approach predominates among bankers and has been espoused by a minority of economists. This approach interprets banks not in relation to the money supply function but as credit institutions affecting interest rates and credit conditions. The key idea of the credit approach is that if commercial banks are operated according to proper banking principles, they cannot be charged with contributing to economic instability or misperformance of the economy. An extreme version of this theory holds that commercial banks are inherently self-regulating and cannot possibly contribute to inflation or deflation. This view is quite at variance with monetary theory. On some important points, it leads to conclusions that are quite the opposite of those of monetary theory.

Although it has never been supported by a large proportion of economists, the credit approach, because of its predominance among bankers, has been much more important than monetary theory as a basis for government policy. The establishment of the Federal Reserve System and its policy actions for more than a half century have reflected the ideas of the credit approach to banking.

The early credit approach: The bullionist controversy and the banking school

A profound controversy over monetary policy, raising issues that have been debated ever since, was provoked in England by inflationary developments associated with the Napoleonic Wars. After the Bank of England stopped buying and selling gold at a fixed price in 1797, bank notes, or "the paper pound," declined in value in terms of gold and silver, and an increase in the price level seemed to occur (there were no official price indexes in those days). The "bullionists" applied orthodox monetary theory, attributing the decline in the external and internal value of the pound to an increase in the quantity of money in the form of the circulating notes of commercial banks. The antibullionists replied that this was impossible. Bank notes could not be issued to excess or cause inflation so long as bank credit was extended only to meet the needs of trade. Therefore, the inflation and the depreciation of the pound must be due to something else. The antibullionists applied a credit approach to the problem in emphasizing the *quality of credit* rather than the *quantity of money.*

In a continuation of this controversy, about 50 years later, between the "currency school," the successors to the bullionists, and the "banking school," following the approach of the antibullionists, the principle that bank notes could not be excessive or disturbing if issued only in conjunction with sound business loans was termed "the banking principle." To this argument Thomas Tooke, the leader of the banking school, added the "law of reflux." This asserted that any excessive notes issued by banks would automatically return to the banks in liquidation of loans. Thus, banks could not issue an excessive amount of notes. Banking, if properly conducted, was inherently and automatically self-regulating, and incapable of causing inflation or deflation.[12]

The currency school rejected all of these contentions. Members of this school pointed out that bank notes being created by making loans at interest surely did not prevent their being inflationary, for great inflations such as that engineered by John Law in France had been based upon bank loans made at interest. They argued that the "needs of trade" did not precisely define any correct amount of bank credit, for the amount that the banks would be able to lend depended upon the rate of interest they were asking. If they offered to lend at too low a rate of interest, presumably, they would make too many loans and cause inflation. This raises the question as to what rate of interest would be just high enough that the banks would not make too many loans and just low enough that they would not make too few loans and cause a deficiency of bank notes and money.

Moreover, it was stated that an error in applying the credit approach could be cumulative or self-aggravating. Suppose the banks did offer to lend at too low an interest rate, created too many bank notes, and, thus, unduly increased the money supply and caused inflation. The resulting economic expansion would make people more willing to borrow and thereby increase the rate of interest the public is willing to pay. Furthermore, the inflation would mean that the real rate of interest was lower than the nominal interest rate. Apart from other effects, the nominal interest rate would have to rise by as much as the rate of price increase just to prevent a *decline* in the real rate of interest. That is, if the banks loaned at too low an interest rate and, as a consequence, created too much bank credit and money, causing inflation at 4 percent per year, the nominal interest

[12]Accounts of this literature are given in Jacob Viner, *Studies in the Theory of International Trade*, A. M. Kelley, Publisher, New York, 1965; Lloyd W. Mints, *A History of Banking Theory*, The University of Chicago Press, Chicago, 1945; and Joseph A. Schumpeter, *History of Economic Analysis*, Oxford University Press, New York, 1954.

rate would have to increase, say, from 5 to 9 percent just to offset the effects of the inflation. If the banks kept lending at 5 percent, this would lead to an accelerating overissue of bank credit and money and an accelerating inflation.

This difficulty with the credit approach was clarified at the turn of the century by the Swedish economist Knut Wicksell, the state of knowledge not having advanced appreciably in the meantime.[13] To illustrate that bank credit could be self-regulating only if its quantity was limited by the extension of bank credit at just the appropriate rate of interest, he labeled this concept "the natural rate of interest."

Anything that made the public more willing to borrow money—improved profits expectations, inflationary expectations, or more favorable consumption opportunities—would require an increase in the interest rate to limit their borrowing to the amount consistent with economic stability. Thus, it would raise the natural rate of interest. But if the natural rate of interest varies in the short run and responds to all the factors affecting the demand for credit—as well as the supply—it may be impossible accurately to tell what the natural rate of interest is at any particular time. Wicksell did not offer a satisfactory way of estimating the natural rate of interest, and the problem has not been solved to this day.

Wicksell's concept of the natural rate of interest poses a crucial challenge to the credit approach to banking. Unless its proponents can demonstrate that the same amount of bank credit and money would be created by banks no matter what the interest rate at which they offer to extend credit—which seems an untenable position—there will be only some particular interest rate at which banks must offer to extend credit if they are not to promote inflation or deflation. This can be termed the natural rate of interest. To justify the credit approach, it would be necessary to show that the banks (or, later, the central bank) have some way of defining the natural rate of interest and that they always offer tc extend credit at only that rate. No serious attempt has been made to demonstrate this, or even to demonstrate that the natural rate of interest at various times can be accurately estimated.

The commercial loan theory of banking

The version of the credit approach to banking and central banking that was influential around the turn of the century and that underlay the Federal Reserve Act of 1913 has been termed the "commercial loan theory of banking," or the "real bills doctrine."[14] This retained the flaws of the earlier credit theories of banking.

[13]Knut Wicksell, *Interest and Prices*, A. M. Kelley, Publishers, New York, 1965 (first published in 1898).

[14]On this, see Mints, *op. cit.*; and Currie, *op. cit.*

A basic idea of this approach was that if bank credit were extended only to meet the working-capital needs of business, the amount of bank credit would automatically adjust to the needs of trade. Accordingly, quantitative control over the activities of commercial banks would not be needed, or appropriate. As interpreted in terms of monetary theory, this idea is basically fallacious. In an economic upswing, the demands of businesses for inventory credit increase more rapidly than total income or output, and in an economic contraction, they decline more than proportionately with most economic series. As a result, to tie changes in the money supply to business demands for inventory financing would produce a monetary system with positive monetary feedback on a large scale, one that would systematically aggravate economic upswings and downswings.

The other major idea of the theory was that limiting bank credit to short-term loans to business would protect the safety of banks and guard against bank failures in cumulative banking contractions. Inventory loans were said to be "self-liquidating," since the funds to repay the loan automatically became available when the goods were sold from inventory. This idea would be acceptable if what had to be liquidated were only an isolated loan, but how does the idea hold up when the banking system is under pressure for general contraction—as in the case of bank runs and a currency outflow? If businesses in general try to reduce their inventories to repay their bank loans, this causes economic contraction, declines in sales and income, and business losses and failures. The adverse effects of a general contraction of bank credit, therefore, are not prevented by the fact that the credit is tied to inventory loans. The only way to avoid the damage caused by an abrupt banking contraction is to set up a stable banking system that will never be subject to abrupt contraction.

The major intellectual underpinning of the Federal Reserve System was the model of a banking system that automatically expands and contracts bank credit in conformity with the needs of trade, based on the commercial loan theory. The outcome bore out the diagnosis of monetary theory that this was a formula for a destabilizing monetary system.

The credit approach and the Federal Reserve System

The passage of the Federal Reserve Act in 1913 establishing the Federal Reserve System reflected a curious lack of agreement as to the functions and operating goals of the System. When the officials of the new institution set out to organize their activities, they suffered from the absence of any clear agreement as to what it was they were supposed to be doing: "Discussions at official meetings revealed several ideas but no consensus as to the System's aims and responsibilities."[15]

[15]Clay J. Anderson, *A Half-century of Federal Reserve Policymaking, 1914–1964*, p. 4, Federal Reserve Bank of Philadelphia, Philadelphia, 1965. The intellectual background of the Federal Reserve Act is reviewed in Mints, *op. cit.*, chap. 11.

It is quite clear, however, the the Federal Reserve System was not based on monetary theory. Among the suggestions as to what the Federal Reserve ought to do, no serious attention was given to controlling the behavior of the money supply. The discussions viewed the Federal Reserve as a banking institution, its problem as the regulation of *credit*. The gap between the monetary theory of the economists (Fisher's "The Purchasing Power of Money" was published in 1911) and the ideas underlying the establishment and operation of the Federal Reserve System is remarkable. Twenty years later, Currie wrote: "For the banking authorities to hold to one theory of banking while the great majority of monetary writers have adhered to an entirely different theory is obviously an undesirable state of affairs."[16]

The only specific statement about policy objectives in the 1913 act was that discount rates should be established, "with a view of accommodating commerce and business." Officials followed a narrow interpretation of accomodating commerce and business. They believed a major aim of policy should be making credit available for "legitimate" business purposes at reasonable rates.[17]

The fact that the Federal Reserve interpreted its goals in terms of the credit approach rather than the monetary approach and that it took this particular view of the credit targets at which it should aim had far-reaching implications. They are most easily seen in terms of Wicksell's analysis (which was published 15 years before the establishment of the Federal Reserve System, though not published in English translation until 1936).

The operating procedure following from this credit target is for the Federal Reserve to create additional bank reserves in an attempt to prevent interest rates from rising "unreasonably" high, and to extinguish bank reserves as needed to prevent interest rates from falling "unreasonably" low. This implies that during an economic contraction such as that of 1929–1933, when deflation and reduction in demand for credit reduced nominal interest rates, Federal Reserve officials would permit or cause reductions in bank reserves and the money supply because they did not want credit to become excessively easy or redundant. Such monetary contraction would lead to further economic deterioration and deflation, which would further reduce interest rates, which—given Federal Reserve actions and ideas—would lead to further reductions in the money supply. A major point of Wicksell was that an effort by the central bank to keep the market rate of interest at a level higher or lower than the natural rate of interest would lead to such a cumulative process.

The reduction in the money supply by one-quarter from 1929 to 1933 would not conceivably have been permitted by the Federal Reserve had it been applying monetary theory. But its policy program was quite natural in terms of the credit approach to central banking by which it was governed.

[16]*Op. cit.*, p. 35.

[17]Anderson, *op. cit.*, *p*. 5.

In the crucial years 1929–1933, therefore, the two theories led to two quite different interpretations of the causes of the catastrophic economic decline. A straightforward application of monetary theory led to the interpretation that the unparalleled shrinkage of the money supply was the major cause of the severity of the decline. Irving Fisher thought the economic contraction could have been reversed at any time or, even more easily, prevented almost altogether by an appropriate Federal Reserve monetary policy.[18] The prevailing monetary system and monetary policy was severely contractive, and caused the depression.

A straightforward application of the Federal Reserve's credit approach to central banking led to quite the opposite story. Monetary policy was "easy" because (nominal) interest rates had declined.[19] Thus, if economic contraction continued, it must be due to something else. Federal Reserve powers were limited, in this interpretation, since it could do nothing more than make credit available. As an easy monetary policy was being followed but was not preventing further economic contraction, this demonstrated that Federal Reserve powers were inadequate to prevent depression; monetary policy was ineffective.

These two competing views of the Great Depression set the terms of reference for the debate over monetary theory for decades to come.

SUMMARY

1. The equation of exchange, $Y = MV$, is a simple framework for a monetary theory of total demand in which M is the primary causal variable.

2. The equation of exchange may be useful as a framework for the theory of total demand if M is an independent or causal variable and V is approximately constant or varies in a definable way.

3. Velocity characteristically varies inphase with economic fluctuations, rising during upswings and declining during downswings. This variation is interpretable as reflecting changes in a number of factors affecting the incentives to economize holdings of money.

4. Velocity in the past 50 years has shown no clear long-run trend, but has responded to broad changes in the incentives to hold money arising from the Great Depression, the Second World War, the gradual return to more normal conditions and expectations, and the high interest rates and inflationary expectations of the latter part of the 1960s.

[18] "The Debt-deflation Theory of Great Depressions," p. 347.

[19] Real interest rates had not declined, but had increased, as price-level declines on the order of 10 percent per year implied that a nominal interest rate of 4 percent was a real interest rate of 14 percent. Moreover, presumably the decline in the natural rate of interest must have been larger than the decline in the market interest rates—and a monetary policy involving actual interest rates higher than the natural rate of interest is contractionist. But the Federal Reserve version of the credit approach never recognized the distinction between nominal, real, and natural rates of interest; it was formulated entirely in terms of nominal interest rates.

5. Economic developments in the United States seem meaningfully interpreted, and potentially forecast, in terms of a major causal role for change in the money supply, with velocity responding to the economic conditions that emerge.

6. Monetary theory evolved from the quantity theory of money into theories expressed in equations of exchange. Major versions of neoclassical monetary theory were those of Irving Fisher, the Cambridge approach, and the Chicago School. The leading monetary theorists of the 1930s interpreted the Great Depression in the United States as caused by the unstable United States monetary system and unfavorable Federal Reserve actions, and as quite consistent with their theories.

7. Most bankers and central bankers and some economists have not accepted monetary theory, but have applied the credit approach to banking. This holds that banks will play a constructive economic role if they extend credit in such a way as to meet the legitimate needs of business for credit. Wicksell pointed out that banks could extend just the right amount of credit only if they offered their credit at just the right interest rate, which he termed the natural rate of interest. The natural rate of interest may change continually, and no procedure exists for estimating it accurately. Wicksell showed that if the banks and the central bank extend credit at an interest rate lower than the natural rate of interest, this will lead to a cumulative inflation. Proponents of the credit approach never effectively dealt with Wicksell's point.

8. The Federal Reserve Act of 1913 and subsequent Federal Reserve actions were based on the credit approach. The Federal Reserve interpretation of events of 1929–1933 was that credit was available to meet the needs of trade, and, thus, the depression was caused by something else, against which monetary policy was ineffective.

QUESTIONS FOR REVIEW AND DISCUSSION

1. What conditions are required to make the equation of exchange a useful tool for the theory of total demand?

2. "Since velocity is not constant, an increase in the money supply is likely to be offset by a reduction in velocity, thus having no effect upon total demand." Comment critically.

3. "During a severe economic contraction, a number of factors would be operating jointly to reduce velocity of circulation." List the relevant factors, showing how each would operate in an economic contraction.

4. "The lack of substantial net change in velocity over the past half-century, presumably, reflects the offsetting effects of factors that have operated to increase velocity and others that have operated to reduce it." Discuss factors that have operated in each direction during this period of time.

5. Distinguish the quantity theory of money and the commodity theory of money as explanations of an increase in the price level.

6. Explain how the economic contraction of 1929–1933 was interpreted by monetary theorists such as Irving Fisher.

7. Give a summary of the way banks and central banks should behave as defined by the credit approach.

8. "Bank credit cannot become excessive if credit is granted only to meet the legitimate needs of trade." How would this proposition be criticized in terms of the approach of Wicksell?

9. Explain how central bank actions based on the credit approach can lead to a cumulative process of expansion or contraction in the money supply, total demand, and prices.

10. Briefly characterize and evaluate Federal Reserve monetary policy in 1929–1933 as it appeared in terms of the credit approach as applied by the Federal Reserve, and in terms of monetary theory.

12

the Keynesian theory: monetary theory in the 1940s and 1950s

The Great Depression led to a drastic change in the theory of total demand that predominated among economists and governed economic policy. Neoclassical monetary theory was upheld by only a minority of economists, most prominantly by the Chicago School. The predominant theory, based upon the work of the English economist John Maynard Keynes (pronounced Kanes), was a major departure from earlier economic throught.

The immediate cause of the Great Depression, it was widely understood, was the decline in total demand, which reflected mainly a decline in expenditures for business investment. Monetary theory interpreted the decline in investment as an *effect* of the economic contraction, an element in Fisher's complex process of interaction among the money supply, deflation, total demand, interest rates, and investment. But monetary policy was the *cause* of the Depression in the sense that (1) what was unusual about 1929–1933 was the economy's money supply function rather than potential investment opportunities or people's economic behavior, and (2) the economic contraction could be halted at any time by changing monetary policy and—as we now term it—the money supply function.

An interpretation of the Depression in terms of the credit approach as this was applied by the Federal Reserve (not a Wicksellian credit approach) led to a radically different picture. Since credit was easy—the nominal rate of interest on high-grade debt had declined—monetary factors could not be causing economic contraction. Therefore it must be caused by something else. The problem was to find this something else. A host of possible nonmonetary causes of the depression were suggested: the postwar depression in agriculture, the collapse of the stock-market boom, reaction against excessive investment during the 1920s, and excessive business profits. Opposition within the Federal Reserve System to actions to combat the economic decline were

> based largely on the theory that the depression was the result mainly of nonmonetary causes such as overproduction and excess capacity in a number of industries. Therefore, cheaper and more abundant credit would not stimulate business recovery. Instead, more ease might encourage increases in productive capacity, defer essential readjustments, and retard recovery.[1]

In one version of this general approach, the cause of the Depression was earlier excesses and maladjustments in the economy, for which the Depression was itself the natural and inescapable cure. A memorandum submitted by the president of a Reserve bank in 1930 to the precursor of the Federal Open Market Committee put it in this way: "We believe that the correction must come about through reduced production, reduced inventories, the gradual reduction of consumer credit, the liquidation of security loans, and the accumulation of savings through the exercise of thrift."[2] This theory was by no means unanimous within the Federal Reserve System, and was vigorously opposed by some officials. But it was an important influence on Federal Reserve actions.

In this theory, the Depression was caused by a decline in investment that, in turn, was caused by earlier excesses and maladjustments. Once the unsound elements in the economy were corrected by the Depression, investment, presumably, would return to its regular level, and prosperity would automatically return.

Keynes also interpreted the Depression as caused by lack of investment spending. However, he did not see the lack of investment opportunities as reflecting maladjustments that would be corrected within a few years. Rather he saw them as based on an inherent anomaly of the nonsocialist economy that probably would grow more severe with each passing decade. The basic defect was that when an economy grew mature and incomes reached a certain level, it no longer generated enough investment opportunities to provide a use for the savings that people insisted on making. The shortage of investment opportunities, thus, was not temporary, but permanent. The problem was not an unusually severe economic contraction; it was the onset of secular stagnation.

We can identify a number of the influences that led Keynes to formulate "the stagnation thesis":

1. England experienced economic slack and large unemployment during most of the 1920s, before these afflicted other countries, and, therefore, its problem was not so conspicuously cyclical as in the United States. England's economic slack can be interpreted in other ways, emphasizing its balance of payments problem and restrictive monetary policy, but it also could then be interpreted to fit the stagnation model.

[1]Clay J. Anderson, *A Half-century of Federal Reserve Policymaking, 1914–1964*, p. 63, Federal Reserve Bank of Philadelphia, Philadelphia, 1965.

[2]Quoted in *ibid.*, p. 64.

2. Prolonged periods of depression in the past had given rise to stagnation theories, so the general idea was not new.

3. A prominent idea in the socialist thinking of the times, and in the Fabian Society of which Keynes was a member, was that the capitalist system would in time destroy itself by its internal inconsistencies and be followed by socialism as a higher stage of societal evolution. This political theory offered an obvious basis for a hypothesis regarding the Depression.

4. In an essential part of this theory, the ineffectiveness of monetary policy, Keynes seems to have been importantly influenced by Federal Reserve ideas based on the credit approach.

We shall consider later the evidence that was brought to bear in support of the theory and in opposition to it, and the subsequent trends in the contest of ideas. But first we shall review the theory that resulted from Keynes's work, the model that wrought "The Keynesian Revolution."[3]

The Nonfinancial Model

We work with two versions of the Keynesian theory, a simple one that does not include the financial variables (money supply and interest rates) and a standard version of the model that does include financial variables. The nonfinancial model is the counterpart of the simple financial model discussed in Chap. 11. A financial variable whose value was determined outside of the economy plays the main causal role in monetary theory, which we can diagram simply as $M \rightarrow Y$. The theory we now consider asserts that a nonfinancial variable whose value is determined outside of the economy, investment expenditures, plays the main causal role. This theory we can diagram as $I \rightarrow Y$.

The model expressing this theory also closely parallels the model for our simple monetary theory. It contains three equations: one defining the equilibrium condition, one defining a behavioral function, and one specifying an independently determined or *exogenous* causal variable.

In this case, the causal variable is investment expenditures, and the investment function only asserts that these have the independently determined value I_1. The single behavioral equation in this model is the consumption function. This asserts that the amount people want to spend for consumption (C) depends on income and responds systematically to no other variable. Finally, the equilibrium condition is that total expenditures for the economy's output must be such that the independently given investment expenditures plus the internally determined consumption expenditures just equal income and, therefore, keep it unchanged. The

[3]John Maynard Keynes, *The General Theory of Employment, Interest, and Money*, Harcourt, Brace, New York, 1936.

model[4] thus is:

$$Y = C + I \qquad \text{equilibrium condition} \qquad (12\text{-}1)$$

$$C = f_c Y = C_0 + bY \qquad \text{consumption function} \qquad (12\text{-}2)$$

$$I = I_1 \qquad \text{investment function} \qquad (12\text{-}3)$$

We consider below the logic and evidence lying behind the consumption function, the one behavioral relation of this model. The simple linear version of the consumption function says that consumption expenditures consist of two components, one of which is exogenous, or determined outside of the model (C_0) and the other of which reflects a systematic response of consumers to their income (bY). The response of consumption to a change in income, $\Delta C/\Delta Y$ or the "marginal propensity to consume," is defined by b, the coefficient of income in the consumption function, as well as by the slope of the consumption function in Fig. 12–1. Keynes saw it as a "fundamental psychological law" that the marginal propensity to consume would be positive but less than 1, or $0 < b < 1$. That is, if a person's income changes, he will change his consumption in the same direction, but by less. The value of C_0, the intercept of the consumption function in Fig. 12–1, ordinarily is taken as positive.

We also use the concept of the "average propensity to consume,"

[4]This model commonly has been stated in real terms rather than in terms of money values of consumption, investment, and gross national product, or total demand. That is, the assertion of the consumption function is that real or price-adjusted consumption depends on real income, or $C/P = f_r\,(Y/P)$. When prices are not changing appreciably, the two forms of the model are substantially identical. When prices are changing appreciably, presumably, neither version of the model is satisfactory, for then price expectations would affect consumption, and the consumption function—whether stated in real terms or money terms—would have to be enlarged to incorporate this factor. Consequently, to relate the theory to the problem to which it is really addressed, control of total demand, we state the model in money terms, recognizing that it is inadequate to describe behavior under conditions of changing prices.

Fig. 12–1 The consumption function.

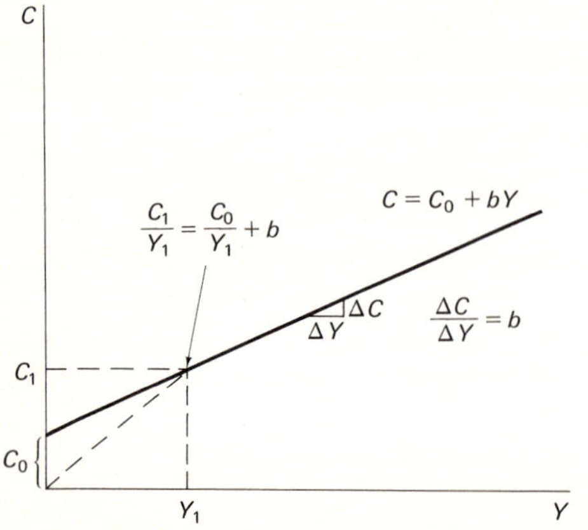

the absolute amount of consumption divided by absolute income, or C/Y. By dividing Eq. (12–2) by Y, we define the average propensity to consume as $C/Y = C_0/Y + b$. Since the value of the term C_0/Y differs for each value of Y, the average propensity to consume is not constant but different for each level of income. Since C_0 is positive, C/Y will become smaller as Y increases. Graphically, in Fig. 12–1, the value of C/Y for any point on the consumption function is defined by the slope of a ray from the origin. If we draw a set of such rays, their slope becomes smaller as we move further out of the consumption function to larger values of Y. The value of the marginal propensity to consume, by contrast, is the same for all values of Y.

Solving the model

This model is used mainly to define the value of the dependent variable Y in terms of the independent variable I and the behavioral coefficient, the marginal propensity to consume (b). The model is solved for Y by substituting Eqs. (12–2) and (12–3) into Eq. (12–1) in this manner:

$$Y = C + I$$
$$Y = C_0 + bY + I_1$$
$$Y - bY = C_0 + I_1$$
$$Y(1 - b) = C_0 + I_1$$
$$Y = (C_0 + I_1)\frac{1}{1-b} \qquad \text{solution equation} \qquad (12\text{–}4)$$

The solution equation of the model [Eq. (12–4)] provides an explanation of total demand in terms of two classes of factors: (1) Autonomous (or exogenous) expenditures, including all investment expenditures (I_1) and that part of consumption expenditures that do not depend on income (C_0). (2) An expression in the form of a multiplier, which shows how much total demand results from each dollar of exogenous expenditures. This depends upon the model's only behavioral coefficient b, its specific form being $1/(1-b)$.

This model is as readily solved numerically as is the equation of exchange, which it closely parallels. The multiplier depends only on the marginal propensity to consume (just as velocity depended only on the cash ratio). When $b = 3/4$, $1/(1-b) = 1/(1/4) = 4$; when $b = 7/8$, $1/(1-b) = 8$, and so on. Given values for autonomous expenditures and the marginal propensity to consume, the equilibrium value of Y is easily determined by substitution in the solution equation of the model. For example, if $I_1 = 20$, $C_0 = 10$, and $b = 3/4$,

$$Y = (I_1 + C_0)\frac{1}{1-b} = (20 + 10)\frac{1}{1-3/4} = 30 \times 4 = 120$$

The problem to which the model is most commonly applied is to determine the change in Y that will result from a given change in I. This problem can be dealt with simply by solving the model for the new value of Y. For example, if I changed from 20 to 30, we could solve the model for $I_2 = 30$. Substituting these values in the solution equation yields $160 = 40 \times 4$. An increase in investment by 10 led to an increase in equilibrium income by 40, from 120 to 160. The change in income was defined by the change in investment times the multiplier. The investment multiplier derived from this model is

$$\Delta Y = \Delta I \frac{1}{1-b} \qquad \text{or} \qquad \frac{\Delta Y}{\Delta I} = \frac{1^{\dagger}}{1-b}$$

The multiplier applicable to C_0, by the same reasoning, is also $1/(1 - b)$.

The model thus provides a statement of the amount of increase in investment that is required to bring about a given increase in GNP. For simplicity, we have discussed this model in relation to an economy involving only consumption and investment expenditures, with no governmental or international transactions. So long as financial variables are not introduced, the model can be readily extended to government expenditures and receipts, and to exports and imports, defining also multipliers applying to these. If government expenditures are treated as autonomous, they play the same role in the model as investment expenditures and, thus, can be interpreted in terms of the multiplier. During the 1940s, analysis of the effects of fiscal policy often was carried out in terms of this model. Such further developments and applications of the model are discussed in Appendix A to this chapter.

The process of income change as depicted by the nonfinancial model

The nonfinancial model is a *static* model in that it defines only equilibrium values of Y. The use of the multiplier is "comparative-statics" analysis. This involves defining the change in the equilibrium position that results from a defined change in a causal variable. In a formal sense, the model defines only the two equilibrium positions. It does not say anything about the path by which the economy moves from one position to the other, nor how long it will take to get there. Indeed, as we recall from our charts on

† Working from Eq. (12-4),

$$Y_1 = (I_1 + C_0) \frac{1}{1-b} \qquad Y_2 = (I_2 + C_0) \frac{1}{1-b}$$

Thus,

$$\Delta Y = Y_2 - Y_1 = [(I_2 + C_0) - (I_1 - C_0)] \frac{1}{1-b} = (I_2 - I_1) \frac{1}{1-b}$$

$$\Delta Y = \Delta I \frac{1}{1-b} \qquad \text{and} \qquad \frac{\Delta Y}{\Delta I} = \frac{1}{1-b}$$

GNP, the very concept of an "equilibrium position" is something of a fiction, since GNP never really stands still but is always moving up or down.

The very first step from static theory towards "dynamic theory"—which is not limited to equilibrium positions and does define how GNP changes over time—is to accept for a bit longer the fiction of the equilibrium position and adapt the model so it can portray a time path from one equilibrium position to another. In a dynamic model, thc variables may have different values at different points in time. To describe these, it is necessary to attach dates to the variables. This is usually done by assuming discrete time intervals, commonly quarter-years, and numbering the periods from some initial point, as in Y_t, Y_{t+1}, Y_{t+2}, . . .

The dynamic version of the nonfinancial model must somewhere include a time lag. Otherwise, it would represent changes in income as occurring instantaneously, which is not the way actual economies behave. The usual way to incorporate a lag into this simple model is to specify that consumption responds to income with a lag, or that C_t depends not on Y_t but rather on Y_{t-1}. This yields the model:

$$Y_t = C_t + I_t \qquad (12-5)$$

$$C_t = C_0 + bY_{t-1} \qquad (12-6)$$

$$I_t = I_1 \qquad (12-7)$$

Substituting Eqs. (12-6) and (12-7) into Eq. (12-5), yields the solution equation:

$$Y_t = C_0 + I_1 + bY_{t-1} \qquad (12-8)$$

This solution equation takes a different form from that of the static model. We no longer can solve for Y, for the model relates not to a single-valued equilibrium Y but to a set of Y's at different points in time. What we derive is not a formula for an equilibrium position but rather a formula that defines the value of Y_t in terms of autonomous expenditures and Y_{t-1}. Such expressions involving values of variables for different discrete time periods are called "difference equations." Given values of the exogenous variables (here I_1 and C_0) and of the response coefficients (in this case, only b) such a difference equation will generate a time path of values of the dependent variables.

Let us see how this model works by assuming illustrative values for the variables, defining an equilibrium position, then changing investment and looking at the resulting time path. Such an exercise is illustrated in Table 12-1. Investment is initially taken as 20 and C_0 as 10, with the economy in the relevant equilibrium position. Then we change investment to 30 and see what happens.

How do we find the initial equilibrium value of Y? This is the position in which the value of income and the other variables of the system are not changing. Therefore, $Y_{t-2} = Y_{t-1} = Y_t$. If Y can be substituted for all of the

TABLE 12-1 Dynamic Version of the Nonfinancial Model

Period	Y_t	=	C_0 (10)	+	bY_{t-1} (4/5)	+	I_t (20,30)	ΔY
0	150		10		120		20	0
1	160		10		120		30	$+10 = \Delta I$
2	168		10		128		30	$+\ 8 = b\ \Delta I$
3	174.4		10		134.4		30	$+6.4 = b(b\ \Delta I) = b^2\ \Delta I$
.	.		.		.		.	.
.	.		.		.		.	.
.	.		.		.		.	.
n	200		10		160		30	$\Sigma\Delta Y = 50 = \Delta I \frac{1}{1-b}$

dated Y's, the model can be solved in the usual way for the solution equation defining its static equilibrium position. This gives an equilibrium income of 150, autonomous expenditures of 30, times a multiplier of 5. When we fill in these numbers for period 0, we find that they fit. If income were 150, this would generate consumption of 120, which plus the autonomous expenditures equals 150, so the system would have no tendency to move and is, indeed, in equilibrium.

We now assume that investment increases from 20 to 30, and explore the consequences as these are defined by the model. In period 1, income is defined by adding up the components of expenditures and is 160. The change in income is equal to the change in autonomous expenditures. Since consumption responds only with a lag, in period 1 it is defined by the income of period 0.

In subsequent periods, autonomous expenditures are assumed to be unchanged. Subsequent developments reflect entirely interaction between changes in income and changes in consumption. In period 2, the earlier increase in income of 10 is reflected in an increase of consumption of 8, which implies an increase in income of 8. So the process continues with a succession of smaller increases in income and consumption as the variables approach new equilibrium values.

The new equilibrium value of Y can be defined by applying the multiplier value of 5 to the revised value of exogenous expenditures of 40, yielding $Y = 200$. Alternatively, the investment multiplier can be applied to the change in investment of 10, $\Delta Y = \Delta I\,[1/(1-b)] = 10 \times 5 = 50$, which is consistent. The total change in Y is the sum of the set of increases that occurred period by period.[5]

The main causal system depicted by the model is, thus,

$$I \xrightarrow{(+)} Y \underset{(+)}{\overset{(+)}{\rightleftarrows}} C$$

[5]The multiplier formula $\Delta Y = \Delta I\,[1/(1-b)]$ can be interpreted as the summation of the series $\Delta I + b\Delta I + b^2\Delta I + \cdots + b^n\Delta I$, the value of which approaches $\Delta I\,[1/(1-b)]$.

A change in investment causes an equal change in income, which leads after a lag to an increase in consumption, which increases income, and so on. The positive-feedback loop involving income and consumption continues to operate after the precipitating change in *I*, leading to a total change in *Y* that is a multiple of the one directly caused by the change in *I*.

Why does the system approach a new equilibrium position rather than showing interacting changes in *Y* and *C* that continue without any limit? Because in every income-consumption circuit there is a drain into savings. Not all of income is consumed; some of it is saved. As a consequence, the increments of income and consumption become smaller in each circuit, and the economy approaches a new equilibrium position. If the marginal propensity to consume equaled 1, there would be no savings drain, the increment of consumption and income would not become smaller in successive circuits, and the system would not approach a new equilibrium position. In the sense of not generating convergence to an equilibrium position, the model would then be unstable.

There is no general problem in interpreting the economy in terms of an unstable dynamic model. Indeed, since the economy does not experience equilibrium positions, but shows a pattern of fluctuating growth, a static model systematically misrepresents its behavior. However, its limitation to static models is a distinctive characteristic of the Keynesian theory.

Significance of the nonfinancial model

The nonfinancial model depicts an economy that is highly stable, converging when disturbed to an equilibrium position, and in which the financial variables, the money supply and interest rates, have no appreciable effect upon total demand. The model, thus, fits Keynes's view of the Great Depression. Economists who accepted Keynes's interpretation applied the model to explaining actual economic developments and prescribing policy actions. As experience indicated that economic systems after the Second World War had returned to their earlier patterns of fluctuations and growth —the stagnation problem did not appear—and as the evidence mounted that economies remained heavily responsive to monetary and financial variables, belief in the realism of the nonfinancial model waned. It does not have a significant place in modern economic theory. The issues raised by Keynes that continue to be considered and debated are better dealt with in terms of the standard Keynesian model, which includes financial variables.

The Standard Keynesian Model

The standard Keynesian model expands the nonfinancial model to introduce financial variables by these steps: (1) It introduces a financial variable as a direct determinant of total demand by asserting that investment expenditures depend on the interest rate. (2) To provide a way of determining the interest rate, it adds a financial submodel similar to the monetary model considered in Chap. 11.

The investment function

The change in the investment function replaces $I = I_1$ by

$$I = f_i(i) = I_o - ci \tag{12-9}$$

Investment expenditures, we now assert, do not depend systematically upon anything except the interest rate i. The higher the interest rate, the smaller are investment expenditures.

In the linear investment function, the absolute change in investment caused by a change in the rate of interest (dI/di) is measured by c. We indicate that this is a negative dependency explicitly by putting a minus sign before c, so that its value, then, is positive. If investment declines with higher rates of interest but still is positive at positive rates of interest, I_0 must have a positive value. It defines the intercept of the investment function with the horizontal axis in Fig. 12-3. The downward slope of the investment curve is defined by the value of c ($di/dI = -1/c$). The greater the value of c, the greater the quantitative dependence of investment upon the rate of interest and the flatter the investment function.

Why is it that investment depends negatively upon the rate of interest? The basic idea is that the interest rate measures one of the costs of investing. Other variables maintained constant, the higher the costs of investing, the smaller the volume of investment projects that will be undertaken. To illustrate the point, assume that at a particular time potential investors make an inventory of all of the investment projects on which they might embark.

Fig. 12-2 Inventory of investment projects, by expected yield.

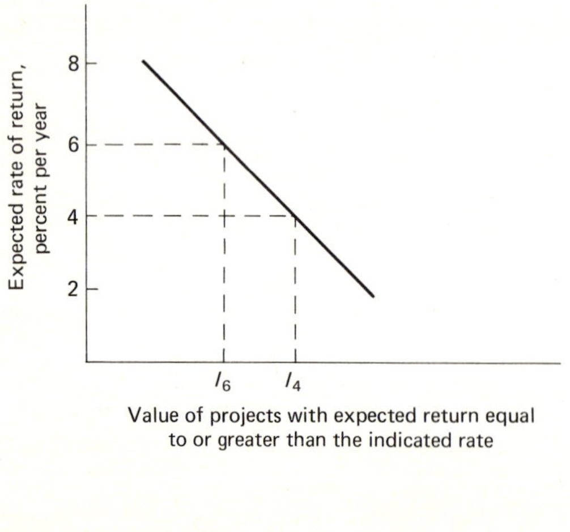

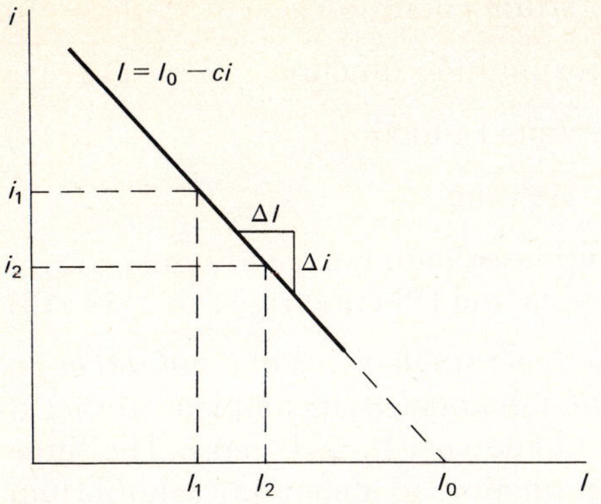

Fig. 12-3 The investment function.

They state for each of these projects the rate of return they expect: 8 percent for one project, 6 percent for another, and −2 percent for yet another.

Ranking the projects in order of expected yield from the highest to the lowest, we can plot the cumulative value of potential investment projects as in Fig. 12-2. The curve must be downward sloping so long as the potential investment projects do not all have the same yield. The total value of investment projects that would yield 4 percent or more is greater than the value of investment projects that would yield 6 percent or more, since the first class includes the second one plus some other projects that yield more then 4 percent but less than 6 percent. We should expect a large and diverse economy to generate a wide variety of potential investment projects of different expected yields and, thus, not to give rise to a vertical curve in a figure such as Fig. 12-2.

The reasoning behind the investment function, then, is this: The rate of interest determines how deep it is profitable to dip, as it were, into this barrel of potential investment projects. At an interest rate of 6 percent, it is worthwhile to undertake all potential investment projects expected to yield a rate of return (after allowance for risk) greater than 6 percent. If the rate of interest declined to 4 percent, some investment projects that would not have been feasible at a 6 percent interest rate now become worthwhile, specifically, those with expected yields of between 6 and 4 percent.

The slope of the investment function (and the value of c, or dI/di) depends upon the slope of the curve traced out by the inventory of potential investment projects. A steep slope depicts the situation in which a decline in the rate of interest adds but few investment projects to the set of profitable ones.

The expenditures submodel and its solution

Substituting the new investment function into the nonfinancial model considered above yields

$$Y = C + I \qquad \text{equilibrium condition} \qquad (12\text{-}10)$$

$$C = C_0 + bY \qquad \text{consumption function} \qquad (12\text{-}11)$$

$$I = I_0 - ci \qquad \text{investment function} \qquad (12\text{-}12)$$

The system is solved in this case for i, yielding

$$i = \frac{C_0 + I_0 - (1 - b)Y\dagger}{c} \qquad \text{solution equation, expenditures submodel (IS curve)} \qquad (12\text{-}13)$$

The solution equation does not define a single value of i, but rather an equilibrium value of i for each Y. The submodel is incomplete in that it involves only three equations in four unknowns, Y, C, I, and i. The three equations do not include enough information to determine equilibrium values of the four unknowns. To define equilibrium total demand, this partial model, or submodel, is joined to another submodel dealing with the financial side of the economy and providing a value for i. The two submodels together make up a model with as many equations as unknowns and define equilibrium values for both Y and i.

The solution equation of the expenditures submodel [Eq. (12-13)] can be plotted as *IS* in Fig. 12-4. It is called the *IS* curve, since it defines the combinations of Y and i for which intended investment I equals intended saving ($S = Y - C$). From Eq. (12-13), the curve is downward-sloping. A larger Y implies a smaller i. The change in i associated with a unit change in Y, the slope of the curve, is $\Delta i/\Delta Y \, (di/dY) = -(1 - b)/c$. A steep downward slope of the *IS* curve implies that a large change in i is required to bring

†The solution equation in Y is similar to that of the nonfinancial model:

$$Y = (C_0 + I_0 - ci)\frac{1}{1 - b}$$

This expression indicates that with reference to the expenditures submodel a reduction in i increases I (by an amount governed by c), which increases Y by an amount determined by the multiplier.

Fig. 12-4 Graphical solution of the standard Keynesian model.

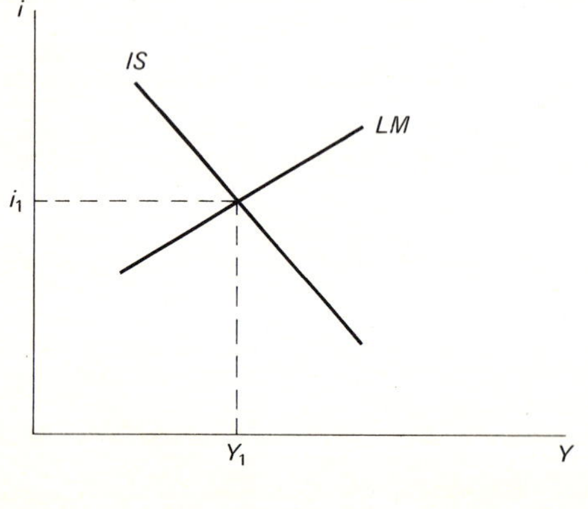

about a given change in Y. This may be troublesome, since large changes in i may be difficult to bring about. Thus, a relatively flat IS curve would be preferable to a steeply downward-sloping one.

A relatively flat IS curve results from a large value of b. As $b \to 1$, the numerator of the fraction $(1 - b) \to 0$, and the curve approaches the horizontal. A large value of c also contributes to a flat IS curve. How can all of this be interpreted in common-sense terms? In terms of the expenditures submodel, Y can increase only by reductions in i, which increase I, which increases Y directly and also indirectly through the investment multiplier. For a given reduction in i, the resulting increase in Y will be greater if I is highly responsive to i (large value of c, measuring dI/di) and if the multiplier is large (b is large, making $1/(1 - b)$ large).

The monetary submodel

The monetary submodel of the standard Keynesian model is identical with the equation of exchange stated in model form, except for additional elements in its money-demand function. We now specify that the demand for money depends not only on total demand but also on the rate of interest (and also add a constant term $M_0{}^D$ to the money demand function). The monetary submodel then is

$$M = M^D \qquad \text{equilibrium condition} \qquad (12\text{-}14)$$

$$M^D = M_0{}^D + m_1 Y - m_2 i \qquad \text{money-demand function} \qquad (12\text{-}15)$$

$$M = M_1 \qquad \text{money-supply function} \qquad (12\text{-}16)$$

The discussion in Chap. 11 of the demand for money emphasized that the amount of money businesses and individuals want to hold depends upon the opportunity cost of holding money. The rate of interest is one factor affecting the opportunity cost of holding money. The higher the rate of interest, the greater the interest reward that could be earned by making do with less money and putting the funds thus freed into a savings institution or a security. Therefore, introducing the interest rate into the money-demand function quite fits in with our earlier discussion. In terms of that discussion, however, this still does not give anything like a complete description of the way people behave with respect to their money holdings.

In this money demand function, the coefficient m_2 measures the quantitative responsiveness of the demand for money to the interest rate ($\partial M^D/\partial i$). A change in i leads to a change in the amount of money demanded equal to $-m_2\,\Delta i$.

Solution of the monetary submodel

Solving the monetary submodel for i yields

$$i = \frac{M_0{}^D + m_1 Y - M_1}{m_2} \qquad \text{solution equation of monetary submodel (}LM\text{ curve)} \qquad (12\text{-}17)$$

The solution equation of the monetary submodel parallels that of the expenditures submodel in providing not a definition of equilibrium income but rather a set of equilibrium pairs of income and interest rate. This submodel defines the combinations of interest rate and income for which the amount of money demanded is equal to the independently given money supply.

Such a set of combinations of income and interest rate consistent with monetary equilibrium is shown in Fig. 12–4. This is called the *LM* curve, since it has to do with the amount of money M and the demand for money M^D, or "liquidity preference." Equation (12–17) indicates that the association of Y and i is a positive one. A higher i means a larger value of Y. Thus, the *LM* curve is upward-sloping.

Why is this the case? We recall that the *LM* curve depicts a set of values of Y all of which must be consistent in equilibrium with the fixed money supply M_1. Thus, the higher Y requires a higher velocity of circulation, or a lower demand for money. A higher i achieves this by increasing the opportunity cost of holding money, by squeezing more expenditures out of a given money supply.

The slope of the *LM* curve measures the change in i required for monetary equilibrium in conjunction with a unit change in Y. From Eq. (12–17), $\Delta i/\ \Delta Y\ (di/dY) = m_1/m_2$. The slope is relatively flat if m_2 is large (velocity of circulation is highly responsive to i) and m_1 is small (a change in income has little effect upon the amount of money demanded).

Solution of the model

The model is usually solved graphically.[6] A mathematical solution of the linear version of the model may be more satisfying to students who are at home with basic mathematics and is given in Appendix B to this chapter.

The two submodels define sets of combinations of income and interest rates that are consistent with equilibrium in connection with the two sides of the economy, the income-expenditures side and the monetary and financial side. Neither submodel suffices to define equilibrium income because each involves four unknown variables and only three equations. However, the submodels include two overlapping equations. Income and the interest rate appear in both of them. Therefore, combining the two submodels yields a model involving six equations in six unknowns, Y, C, I, i, M, and M^D. Thus, the full model suffices to define equilibrium positions for both income and the rate of interest.

The values of Y and i that are the solution values of the model are those that are consistent with both of the two submodels. Graphically,

[6]This approach to solving the model and some points relating to its interpretation stem originally from J. R. Hicks, "Mr. Keynes and the Classics: A Suggested Interpretation," *Econometrica*, 147–159 (1937).

these are given by the point of intersection of the *IS* and *LM* curves. Thus, in Fig. 12-4, the equilibrium values of the system are given at Y_1 and i_1. This is the only combination of values of these two variables that is consistent with equilibrium for both the expenditures submodel and the monetary submodel.

The usual exercise conducted with the model is to shift the value of one autonomous variable and define the resulting change in the equilibrium values of *Y* and *i*. We do this first for factors affecting the consumption and investment functions. What is the effect of an increase in the desire to invest, interpreted as an increase in the autonomous component of the investment function I_0? This can only affect the *IS* curve. The investment function enters into the determination of the *IS* curve but has nothing to do with defining the *LM* curve. Which way, then must the *IS* curve shift? An increase in the desire to invest must mean more expenditures at any given interest rate, thus, it must shift the *IS* curve to the right. Shifting the *IS* curve to the right, as in Fig. 12-5, causes an increase in both *Y* and *i*.

An increase in the autonomous component of consumption (C_0) has exactly the same effect. Decreases in either of these components of autonomous expenditures shift the *IS* curve to the left. This results in decreases in both *Y* and *i*. These are the basic problems relating to changes in the desire to spend to which the model is applied.

Figure 12-5 draws attention to an important difference between the nonfinancial model and the model with which we are now working. In the latter, an increase in expenditures resulting from an increase in desire to spend leads to an increase in interest rates. We recall the reason for this. The money supply is assumed constant. Thus, increase in *Y* requires increase in velocity of circulation. Within the model, this can be brought about only by an increase in *i*, which induces people to reduce their cash ratio. However, this increase in *i* also tends to cut off some investment

Fig. 12-5 Effects of an increase in the desire to spend.

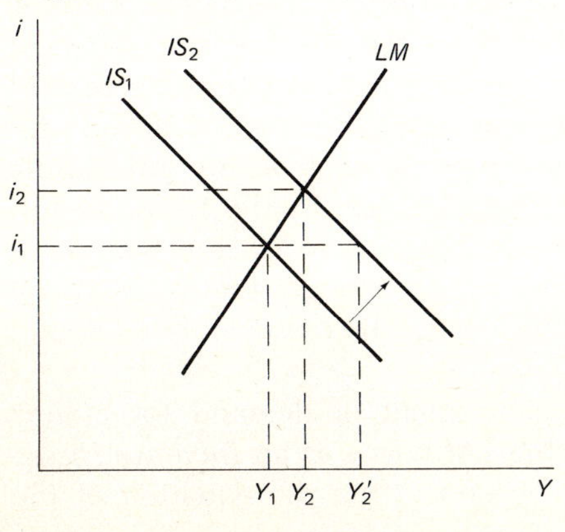

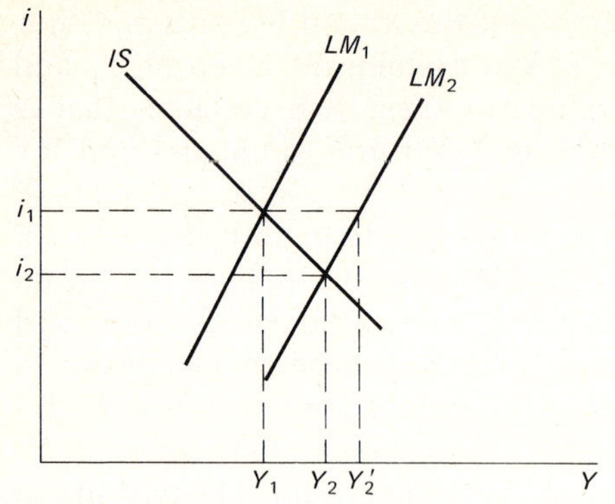

Fig. 12-6 Effects of an increase in the money supply.

spending that would otherwise occur, which makes the increase in income less than it otherwise would be.

With the shift in the *IS* curve in Fig. 12-5, Y would have increased to Y_2' had there been no increase in i. This is the answer that we would have received had we posed this problem in terms of the nonfinancial model. But the standard Keynesian model shows income as increasing only to Y_2. The difference between Y_2 and Y_2' reflects the effect on Y of the investment expenditures that are cut off because of the increase in the interest rate. In general, the changes in total demand resulting from changes in autonomous expenditures in the standard Keynesian model are smaller than those defined by the multiplier of the nonfinancial model.

Changes in monetary factors affect only the monetary submodel and, therefore, only the *LM* curve. An increase in the money supply shifts *LM* curve to the right. It has the effect of producing a larger Y for any given i. This results in an increase in Y and a reduction in i, as shown in Fig. 12-6. The story can be interpreted in this way. We now have a case in which the desire of the public to spend is unchanged. The increase in the money supply, as a result, can bring about additional spending only by reducing the rate of interest and thereby motivating additional investment spending. But the reduction in the rate of interest also has the effect of increasing the public's demand for money and reducing velocity of circulation. Because of this, the increase in Y is smaller than it would have been if i were unchanged, which is the result that would have been given by our simple monetary model with its fixed velocity of circulation. In Fig. 12-6, the full effect of the money multiplier would have increased Y to Y_2'. However, within this model the effect of the reduction of the interest rate in reducing velocity of circulation accounts for the fact that Y increases only to Y_2 and not to Y_2'.

A *reduction* in the autonomous component of demand for money $M_0{}^D$ has exactly the same effect upon the *LM* curve as an *increase* in the money supply. You can confirm this by consulting the equation of the

LM curve, Eq. (12–17). On the other hand, either a reduction in the money supply or an increase in the autonomous component of the demand for money would shift the *LM* curve in the opposite direction, to the left, and result in an increase in *i* and a reduction in *Y*.

These are the usual problems posed for solution with the standard Keynesian model. As you see, there are only four classes of things that can happen, involving movement in one or the other direction in either the *IS* or the *LM* curve. If you have a clear picture of the meaning of the *IS* and *LM* curves and their relation to the two submodels, you will have no difficulty in solving such problems with the model.

The Stagnation Thesis

The stagnation thesis is that the mature nonsocialist economy will be increasingly unable to generate the growth of total demand required to prevent rising unemployment and that monetary policy will be ineffective against this problem. The result will be economic stagnation, rising unemployment, and permanent depression.

If the Keynesian model is applied to long-run growth in the economy, a diagnosis of stagnation is implicit in the downward-sloping *IS* curve. Consider an economy in which population and productivity are growing, so that to preserve full employment and price stability total demand must continually grow. This implies that the economy must continually move to the right along the horizontal axis in the left panel of Fig. 12–7. But what the *IS* curve tells us is that total demand can grow only if there is a reduction in the rate of interest.

This seems to put a limit on the economy's possible growth. Even

Fig. 12–7 Stagnationist and nonstagnationist versions of the Keynesian model.

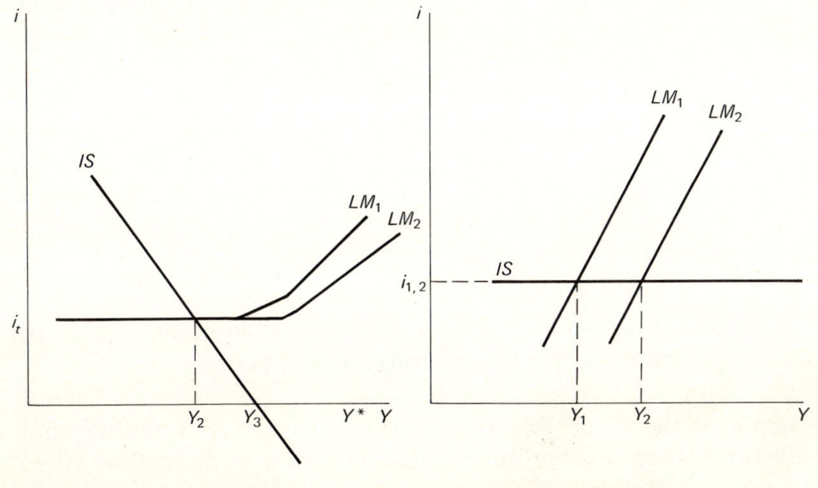

if the interest rate could be reduced to zero, total demand could not grow beyond Y_3. Thus, when the total demand required for prosperity reached Y^*, the economy surely would have encountered economic stagnation. As growth of population and productivity shifted Y^* to the right, the problem would become ever more severe.

How, in terms of the model, can a stagnation problem be permanently avoided? Evidently, the long-run *IS* curve would have to be horizontal, so that total demand could grow without requiring reductions in the rate of interest. Such a case is shown in the right panel of Fig. 12–7. In this case, the problems we have been discussing do not arise. Increases in the money supply, reflected in the diagram by shifts in the *LM* curve to the right, could increase Y without any limit. This would occur with no long-run change in the interest rate and, thus, no change in velocity of circulation.

Where does the truth lie? The interest rate in the United States declined in the 1930s, but since the Second World War it has moved irregularly upward, and interest rates in the late 1960s were at record highs. Such credibility as the downward-sloping long-run *IS* curve might have had in the 1930s has been undercut by subsequent experience. The worldwide problem of the 1960s was not stagnation, but inflation.

But how in terms of the Keynesian model can we rationalize a horizontal long-run *IS* curve? The model's investment function seems seriously deficient in making no provision for response of investment to total demand or to increase in the scale of the economy. To argue that at a given interest rate investment would be the same in the \$1 trillion economy of 1971 as in the \$100 billion economy of 1929 clearly does not make any sense. One way of correcting this omission is to stipulate that investment depends not only upon i but also upon Y, yielding the expanded investment function

$$I = I_0 - ci + dY \qquad \text{expanded investment function} \qquad (12\text{–}18)$$

Such a revision of the investment function requires reinterpretation of the model. It now includes a marginal propensity to invest out of income ($\partial I/\partial Y = d$) as well as to consume. The marginal propensity to spend out of income now includes not only the marginal propensity to consume but also the marginal propensity to invest. In the nonfinancial model this leads to a "supermultiplier" that is larger than the conventional multiplier $1/[1 - (b + d)]$ rather than $1/(1 - b)$. In the standard Keynesian model, the expanded investment function leads to a revised solution equation of the expenditures submodel, which defines the *IS* curve:

$$i = \frac{C_0 + I_0 - [1 - (b + d)]Y}{c} \qquad \text{solution equation, expanded expenditures submodel (IS curve)} \qquad (12\text{–}19)$$

The slope of the *IS* curve (and the response of i to Y within equilibrium positions of the expenditures submodel) now is defined by $\Delta i/\Delta Y$ $(di/dY) = [1 - (b + d)]/c$. The *IS* curve is horizontal, of zero slope, if $b + d =$

1. This is the case in which additional income is all spent either for consumption or investment. When velocity of circulation is not changing, this implies that income is not being used to finance increases in cash ratio and also that expenditures greater than income are not being financed by reductions in cash ratio. In this case, expenditures for consumption plus investment are equal to income. All income is spent, some of it indirectly through financial transactions, and the marginal propensity to spend is equal to 1.

This expanded version of the Keynesian model yields the outcome depicted by the right-hand panel of Fig. 12–7. There is no problem of economic stagnation; the interest rate shows no long-run change; and velocity shows no long-run change. Monetary policy is entirely effective in the sense that an increase in the money supply produces a proportionate increase in total demand. Modifying the Keynesian model to incorporate the dependence of investment upon total demand is thus a way of reconciling the Keynesian model with the neoclassical theory of total demand and with the record of recent experience.

Extending this line of thought, the downward-sloping *IS* curve of the Keynesian theory is inconsistent both with neoclassical theory and with the observed fact that in short-run swings in the economy higher values of Y are associated with *higher* values of i. To interpret this situation in terms of the *IS* curve requires that the curve be upward-sloping. In terms of the model, this is the case in which the marginal propensity to consume plus the marginal propensity to invest is greater than 1 ($b + d > 1$). During an economic upswing, for example, an increase in income leads to an increase in consumption plus investment greater than itself. We have noted that velocity characteristically is rising under these conditions. This is consistent with a marginal propensity to consume plus invest of greater than 1, the rising expenditures being financed not only out of income but also from the pulling down of the cash ratio. Accordingly, the special case of the Keynesian model with upward-sloping *IS* curve corresponds to the case of the short-run swings in Y and V discussed earlier. If the Keynesian model were to be applied to the analysis of short-run economic developments, this would be the relevant version of the model.

During the 1960s, theory has swung to treatment of such short-run economic developments in terms of dynamic models, but these are models that put a heavy emphasis upon the response of investment to changes in economic conditions. As a consequence, the version of the static Keynesian model that is most similar to them is the one just discussed, with the upward-sloping *IS* curve.

The liquidity trap

An additional bit of pessimism in the Keynesian model of the 1940s and 1950s was the doctrine of the liquidity trap. This posits that at some low interest rate the public stands ready unanimously to shift from holding debt to holding money. This will prevent the interest rate from going below this level. Once i reaches this low level, increasing M will not reduce it further and so (in terms of the Keynesian model) will be entirely reflected in reductions in velocity. As a result, monetary policy in this situation will be totally ineffective.

This situation is depicted in terms of the model by stipulating that at the liquidity-trap interest rate (i_1) the coefficient of response of the demand for money to the interest rate (m_2) approaches infinity. This extreme case of a large value of m_2 leads to a horizontal *LM* curve [since from Eq. (12–17) the slope of the *LM* curve is m_1/m_2]. In this case, an increase in the money supply will continue to shift to the right the portion of the *LM* curve that is not horizontal (Fig. 12–7 left-hand panel) but will have no effect upon the horizontal portion of the curve. Thus, if an economy were in the liquidity trap situation—if the *IS* curve cut the *LM* curve in the horizontal zone—a change in the money supply would have no effect on either i or Y. But in this case, any policy action that shifted the *IS* curve to the right would have the full multiplier effect, since no increase in i would occur. The liquidity trap therefore provides a rationale for asserting that monetary policy is ineffective and fiscal policy or policy towards investment is highly effective.

The doctrine of the liquidity trap, however, depicts a situation in which the interest rate is quite frozen at a low level and velocity varies in such a manner as fully to offset the effects of changes in the money supply. Although the liquidity trap doctrine has sometimes been applied to the Great Depression, the facts do not fit this pattern. We recall from our earlier discussion of United States experience that the interest rate was not constant at a low level. Neither did velocity vary in such manner as to offset changes in the money supply. In 1929–1933 when the money supply was declining, velocity also declined, augmenting the effects of the monetary contraction. After 1933 when the money supply was increasing, velocity changed little, the increases in the money supply being fully reflected in total demand.

The liquidity trap is neither a necessary nor a sufficient condition for economic stagnation. If the long-run *IS* curve is downward-sloping, stagnation must come in any case before the interest rate reaches zero. The effect of the liquidity trap is only to make it come a bit earlier and at an interest rate above zero, in Fig. 12–7 at Y_2 rather than Y_3. On the other hand, if the long-run *IS* curve is horizontal, the interest rate will not be subject to long-run decline. In this case, even though a potential liquidity trap existed at some low rate of interest, it would not be relevant to actual events.

Implications of the Keynesian theory

The implications for interpretation of economic events and prescription of economic policy commonly drawn from the Keynesian theory (not mainly by Keynes, who unfortunately died in 1946) were as follows:

1. The Great Depression was interpreted as reflecting the onset of secular stagnation caused by a basic deficiency of investment opportunities.

This contrasts with the interpretation of monetary theory that it was an aggravated short-run contraction caused by monetary factors, the decline in investment reflecting economic events rather than being an independent cause of them.

2. Monetary policy was interpreted as being ineffective against this situation. The cure was rather fiscal policy, primarily increases in government expenditures. If, or when, this became inadequate to cope with economic stagnation, the answer lay in a basic reformulation of the economic system through redistribution of income, in an effort to reduce saving, and through socialization of investment. This contrasts with the interpretation, based upon monetary theory, that a different monetary policy could have halted the Depression at any time, or have prevented it almost entirely.[7]

3. Monetary policy was interpreted in terms of the interest rate rather than the money supply. The stagnationist view of the future called for keeping interest rates as low as possible. Permitting interest rates to rise in response to a temporary inflationary situation, or to fluctuate, was interpreted as weakening the position of the economy for its basic problem of combating stagnation.

Monetary Theory in the 1940s and 1950s: The Surviving Heretics

The victory of the Keynesian interpretation over monetary theory in the 1940s in the economics literature and regarding its influence upon government policy was virtually complete. Indeed, the extremity of this swing in opinion—in view of the evidence on which it was based and its substantial reversal in the 1960s—makes it an interesting case for the student of thought. Many economists continued to express reservations about aspects of the Keynesian revolution, but only a few voices were heard—although there may have been a substantial silent minority on the point—pointing out that conventional monetary theory really provided a better explanation of the Great Depression and subsequent events than the Keynesian theory.[8]

The leader and figurehead among the "monetarists" came to be Milton Friedman, who succeeded to the leadership position in a later generation of the Chicago School. The theoretical contributions and research studies of Friedman and his students provided a major basis of the resurgence of monetary theory in the 1960s.

[7] An important statement of this interpretation is found in Irving Fisher, "The Debt-deflation Theory of Great Depressions," *Econometrica*, **1**:346–347 (1933).

[8] A lonely voice for many years was that of Clark Warburton, among whose relevant articles is "Quantity and Frequency of Use of Money in the United States, 1919–45." *J. Polit. Econ.*, **54**:442–450 (October 1946). Among prominent economists who early took exception to the Keynesian theory and the Keynesian view of the Great Depression were Milton Friedman, D. H. Robertson, J. R. Hicks, Jacob Viner, A. C. Pigou, and Gottfried Haberler.

APPENDIX A: THE NONFINANCIAL KEYNESIAN MODEL

The basic nonfinancial Keynesian model [Eqs. (12–1) to (12–3)] can be solved graphically by drawing the curve for each of the three equations of the model and finding the point that satisfies the three equations. Figure 12–8 shows the conventional consumption function, $C = C_0 + bY$. The investment function simply asserts that $I = I_1$ whatever the value of Y, so it is a horizontal line. The equation defining the equilibrium condition asserts that Y, on the horizontal axis, is equal to $C + I$, on the vertical axis. If these are specified in the same units, the set of points meeting this condition is defined by a straight line of unitary slope, or a 45° line. The model now is laid out in graphical form.

To find the point satisfying the condition $C_0 + bY + I_1 = Y$, we make $C + I$ visually meaningful by adding the fixed amount I_1 to C at each Y, yielding the curve $C + I = C_0 + bY + I_1$. This shows for each Y the amount of consumption plus investment expenditures generated. The equilibrium point is that at which these expenditures are equal to the gross income that gives rise to them. That is, the intersection of the $C + I$ line with the $Y = C + I$ line. At equilibrium income Y_1, the consumption function indicates that consumption would be C_1.

The usual problem of a change in investment is illustrated in Fig. 12–9. An increase in investment from I_1 to I_2 leads to a larger total demand and consumption. The amount of the change in income for any given change in investment, that is to say, the multiplier, depends only upon the slope of the consumption function and, thus, of the $C + I$ line, which is defined by the marginal propensity to consume.

Fiscal Policy in the Nonfinancial Model

Incorporation of government into the nonfinancial model is a convenient, though perhaps misleading, way of treating fiscal policy. We introduce

Fig. 12–8 Graphical solution of the nonfinancial Keynesian model.

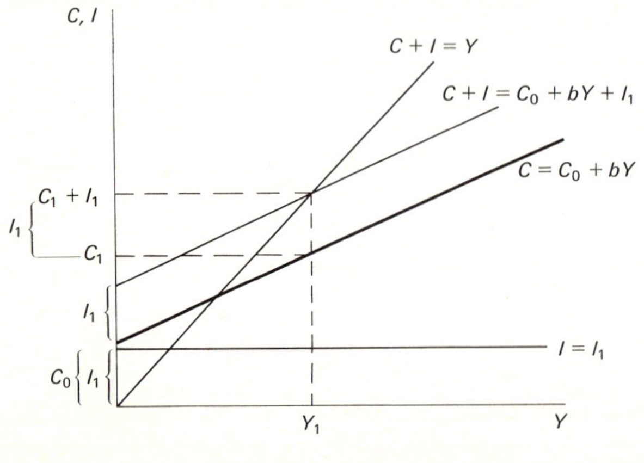

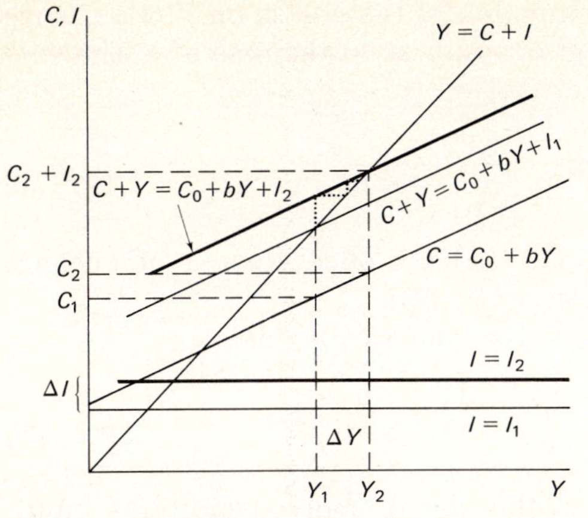

Fig. 12-9 Graphical representation of change in investment and total demand.

government purchases of goods and services as a component of GNP, initially taking these to be exogenous, or determined outside of the model [Eqs. (12-20) and (12-23)]. We also take the amount of tax receipts as determined outside of the model [Eq. (12-24)]. We enter this into the model as a determinant of consumption expenditures, now revising the consumption function to provide that consumption depends upon income after tax $(Y - T)$ [Eq. (12-21)]. The expanded model then is

$$Y = C + I + G \qquad (12\text{-}20)$$
$$C = C_0 + b(Y - T) \qquad (12\text{-}21)$$
$$I = I_1 \qquad (12\text{-}22)$$
$$G = G_1 \qquad (12\text{-}23)$$
$$T = T_1 \qquad (12\text{-}24)$$

Solving the model by substituting into Eq. (12-20) yields the solution equation or reduced form of the model:

$$Y = (C_0 + I_1 + G_1 - bT_1)\frac{1}{1-b} \qquad (12\text{-}25)$$

This is the same kind of expression that resulted from the simpler model. There are now two additional terms in the group of components of autonomous expenditures. The first is government purchases, which plays exactly the same role as investment. The second, tax receipts, has a negative sign and is governed by the marginal propensity to consume $(-bT_1)$. It is essentially the consumption that is prevented by the loss to disposable income resulting from tax payments to the government. An increase in T reduces disposable income by an equal amount. It reduces consumption by a smaller amount, $b\,\Delta T$, since not all income is consumed in any case.

Applying the model to the estimation of the effects on Y of a change in G leads to exactly the same kind of result as in the case of I. The government expenditures multiplier is

$$\Delta Y = \Delta G \frac{1}{1-b} \quad \text{or} \quad \frac{\Delta Y}{\Delta G} = \frac{1}{1-b} \tag{12-26}$$

This defines, with reference to Eq. (12–25), the effect upon Y of a change in G, with other variables unchanged (or $\partial Y/\partial G$).

Approaching the tax multiplier in the same way yields

$$\Delta Y = -b\,\Delta T \frac{1}{1-b} \quad \text{or} \quad \frac{\Delta Y}{\Delta T} = \frac{-b}{1-b} \tag{12-27}$$

The tax multiplier is smaller than the government-expenditures multiplier, we recall, because a change in taxes does not fall dollar-for-dollar upon expenditures. Rather, it falls partially on saving, the proportion falling upon expenditures being defined by the marginal propensity to consume. The tax multiplier has a negative sign, since an increase in taxes reduces disposable income, which reduces consumption, which reduces total demand.

A further question that can be raised in terms of this model is the balanced-budget multiplier, that is, the effect on Y of an equal change in both government expenditures and tax receipts. Letting ΔB stand for the change in the budget, or $\Delta B \equiv \Delta G = \Delta T$, these are defined, from Eqs. (12–26) and (12–27),

$$\Delta Y = \Delta G \frac{1}{1-b} - b\,\Delta T \frac{1}{1-b} \quad \text{or} \quad \Delta B \frac{1}{1-b} - b\,\Delta B \frac{1}{1-b}$$

or (12–28)

$$\Delta Y = \Delta B \frac{1-b}{1-b} = \Delta B \quad \text{and} \quad \frac{\Delta Y}{\Delta B} = 1$$

This tidy, and somewhat surprising, result is that the balanced-budget multiplier is 1. When both taxes and government expenditures are changed by the same amount, this results in an equal change in GNP. This implies that increasing the scale of government operations increases total demand, even though there is no increase in the government deficit.

In the past, some significance was attributed to this definition of the balanced-budget multiplier. However, it seems more realistically viewed as an implication deriving from shortcomings of the model than as a finding about the real world. Because the model does not incorporate any dependence of investment on income and stipulates that the marginal propensity to consume is less than 1, it is inherently a stagnationist model, representing private income as always partially unspent—and, implicitly, hoarded.

The balanced-budget illustration implies that additional income going to the government in the form of taxes is all spent; it is not hoarded. It is the specification that private income is subject to a nonspending drain while that of the government is not that leads to the positive balanced-budget multiplier. A specification that private income is characteristically spent for either consumption or investment leads to a balanced-budget multiplier of zero.

A further expansion of this class of model depicts tax receipts as no longer exogenous, but as depending systematically upon income, as they would with a given set of tax rates. This can be done by substituting for Eq. (12–24) a new tax function

$$T = T_0 + tY \tag{12–29}$$

This divides taxes into two components. The autonomous component T_0 will show up on the solution equation of the expanded model just as did the earlier tax term, which also represented autonomous tax receipts. The second term in the new tax function tY represents a component of taxes that is dependent upon income. Therefore, the tax coefficient t must show up not among the autonomous expenditures but among the determinants of the multiplier. Solving the model in the same way through substitution into Eq. (12–20) now leads to the new solution equation:

$$Y = (C_0 + I_1 + G_1 - bT_0) \frac{1}{1 - b + bt}$$

or (12–30)

$$Y = (C_0 + I_1 + G_1 - bT_0) \frac{1}{1 - b(1 - t)}$$

We should expect the tax rate to enter into the multiplier expression with the opposite sign of the marginal propensity to consume, since it measures income lost to the financing of consumption and diverted to government. For the same reason, the new term in the multiplier is not t but bt, since the diversion of income to government is not reflected dollar-for-dollar in expenditures but rather only partially so reflected in a manner governed by the marginal propensity to consume.

The incorporation of endogenous taxes into the model reduces its multiplier, makes it more stable, and aggravates its stagnation problem. To the savings leakage of the system now is added a tax leakage of income that goes unspent. Since government characteristically spends its tax receipts, the model can be expanded further to incorporate endogenous government expenditures. How about replacing Eq. (12–23) by

$$G = G_0 + gY \tag{12–31}$$

The marginal propensity of the government to spend from income (g) now plays the same role in the model as the marginal propensity to consume.

Solving the expanded model now leads to the solution equation

$$Y = (C_0 + I_1 + G_0 - bT_0)\frac{1}{1 - (b + g) + bt} \tag{12-32}$$

Incorporating government expenditures into the model increases the multiplier, makes the system less stable, and reduces any stagnation problem. With reference to the expanded model, we now have a new set of multipliers for all the components of autonomous expenditures:

$$\frac{\Delta Y}{\Delta I}, \frac{\Delta Y}{\Delta G_0}, \text{ etc.} = \frac{1}{1 - (b + g) + bt} \tag{12-33}$$

These more elaborate versions of the nonfinancial model remain fully subject to the deficiencies applying to the basic version: the depiction of the economy as unrealistically stable and as totally unresponsive to monetary and financial variables. Thus, they are not now viewed as a realistic representation of the economy.

APPENDIX B: MATHEMATICAL INTERPRETATION OF THE STANDARD KEYNESIAN MODEL

Solving and interpreting the standard Keynesian model analytically permits some applications of the model that are too cumbersome to be carried out in terms of the graphical approach. The solution equation of the whole model is derived by solving Eqs. (12–13) and (12–17) for Y. This leads to

$$Y = [C_0 + I_0 + \frac{c}{m_2}(M_1 - M_0)] \frac{1}{1 - b + cm_1/m_2} \tag{12-34}$$

This permits the following definition of full-system multipliers, with the indicated values for extreme values of certain behavioral coefficients:

	Multiplier	Value as: $m_2 \to 0$	Value as: $m_2 \to \infty$
$\frac{\Delta Y}{\Delta I}, \frac{\Delta Y}{\Delta C_0}$	$\frac{1}{1 - b + cm_1/m_2}$	0	$\frac{1}{1-b}$
$\frac{\Delta Y}{\Delta M}$	$\frac{1}{(1-b)m_2/c + m_1}$	$\frac{1}{m_1}$	0

Within the framework of this model, the special case in which the demand for money is not responsive to the interest rate ($m_2 \to 0$) produces the case of constant velocity of circulation and zero investment multiplier. This is a case in which total demand is dominated by monetary factors.

The opposite extreme is the liquidity-trap situation in which the response of the demand for money to the interest rate approaches infinity ($m_2 \to \infty$). This leads to a zero money multiplier and to the full investment multiplier of the nonfinancial model. If the model were expanded to include government receipts and expenditures and to interpretation of fiscal policy, the government-expenditures multiplier would be the same as the investment multiplier.

Expansion of the model to provide for response of investment to income, where $\partial I/\partial Y = d$, leads to:

	Multiplier	Value as: $(b+d) \to 1$	Value as: $(b+d) > 1$
$\frac{\Delta Y}{\Delta I}, \frac{\Delta Y}{\Delta C_0}$	$\frac{1}{1-(b+d) + cm_1/m_2}$	$\frac{1}{cm_1/m_2}$	Finite when denominator > 0
$\frac{\Delta Y}{\Delta M}$	$\frac{1}{1-(b+d)m_2/c + m_1}$	$\frac{1}{m_1}$	Finite when denominator > 0

In the case in which the marginal propensities to consume plus invest equal 1—no income is hoarded—the model again generates the ideal money multiplier. This case does not require that demand for money be unresponsive to the interest rate, and seems a more interesting "optimistic" version of the model than the one that makes velocity invariably constant. In this case, the investment multiplier is not zero. Its size depends upon behavioral factors in the financial side of the economy.

The situation in which an increase in income leads to a further increase in a self-feeding manner can be roughly represented within this model by the case in which the marginal propensity to consume plus the marginal propensity to invest is greater than 1 ($b + d > 1$). The model still produces a finite multiplier, and a new equilibrium position, in cases in which the financial side of the economy has enough influence to prevent a runaway movement of a potentially unstable nonfinancial sector. In this case, a large interest responsiveness of the demand for money to interest rates (m_2) makes the economy *unstable* by weakening the operation of its financial constraints.

A more interesting case that we do not explicitly formulate here is that in which positive monetary feedback weakens the financial constraint and makes the system unstable. If the money supply function is modified to incorporate a response of the money supply to the interest rate—a behavior often produced by monetary systems based upon commercial banks—the coefficient of monetary feedback plays the same role in the model as m_2, making the economy unstable. Expansion of the model along these lines is a way of adapting it to convey some of the ideas of monetary theory considered below.

SUMMARY

1. The Keynesian theory grew out of Keynes's interpretation of England's depression of the 1920s and the Great Depression as reflecting a chronic deficiency of investment opportunities in mature economies. He saw monetary policy as ineffective because it could not reduce the interest rate low enough to bring forth the level of investment required for full employment. This approach contrasts with the interpretation in terms of monetary theory in which the decline in total demand in the Great Depression reflected monetary contraction, the decline in investment being a part of the interaction process of economic contraction rather than its ultimate cause. In this approach, monetary policy was never ineffective, and could have halted the Depression earlier or even largely have prevented it. The Keynesian theory dominated economic thought in the 1940s and 1950s, but the inconsistency of events with the theory's predictions led to a swing to the monetary or neoclassical approach in the 1960s.

2. The simplest version of the Keynesian theory is expressed in the nonfinancial model. This includes no financial variables and includes only one behavioral relation, the consumption function. The investment multiplier and analysis of fiscal policy in terms of the multiplier is based upon this model. Growing evidence of the importance of financial factors argues that this model does not accurately represent the determination of total demand.

3. The standard Keynesian model involves an expenditures submodel and a financial submodel, and is usually applied using the *IS-LM* diagram. It depicts the response of the economy to changes in spending incentives and to changes in the money supply as depending upon the values of a set of behavioral factors, which are reflected in the slopes of the *IS* and LM curves.

4. In terms of this model, an increase in people's desire to consume or invest shifts the *IS* curve to the right, increasing income and the interest rate; a reduction in their desire to consume or invest shifts the *IS* curve to the left, reducing income and the interest rate. An increase in the money supply shifts the *LM* curve to the right, increasing income and lowering the interest rate; a reduction in the money supply shifts the *LM* curve to the left, reducing income and increasing the interest rate.

5. The stagnation problem is implicit in the downward-sloping *IS* curve of the conventional Keynesian model, which implies that growth of total demand can be achieved through monetary policy only by reductions in the interest rate. Since the interest rate cannot be reduced below zero, and in practice doubtless cannot be reduced that low, at some point the further reductions in the interest rate required to generate the growth of total demand required to prevent deflation and unemployment will become impossible.

6. This implication of the model, which has not been borne out by experience, can be modified by expanding the model to provide for a dependence of investment on income. The model then can express the nonstagnationist long-run case in which total demand grows without significant change in i or V, which fits with experience and with the neoclassical theory. This is the case in which the marginal propensities to consume plus invest equal 1, which means that additional income is spent either for consumption or investment rather than hoarded. The short-run case in which Y and i move in the same direction can be represented in terms of the model as the case in which the marginal propensities to consume plus invest are greater than 1, the case in which change in total demand causes change in velocity in the same direction. This involves an upward-sloping *IS* curve. These cases have not been emphasized in work with the Keynesian model, but they provide a bridge to the monetary theory of the 1960s, as well as to earlier neoclassical theory.

QUESTIONS FOR REVIEW AND DISCUSSION

1. Explain and contrast the interpretations of the Great Depression of Keynes, the Federal Reserve majority, and Irving Fisher. Indicate the role of the decline in investment in each of these approaches. What differences in the theories cause them to have different implications for the effectiveness of monetary policy?

2. Write out the nonfinancial Keynesian model. Find equilibrium

Y for the case: $C_0 = 10$, $I_1 = 30$, $b = 3/4$. What is the investment multiplier in this case? Show in two ways the effect on income if investment changes to $I_2 = 40$.

3. Define "marginal propensity to consume," and "average propensity to consume." Explain how their values differ at different levels of income.

4. Write out the standard Keynesian model and the solution equations of the two submodels, and draw the *IS-LM* diagram, indicating equilibrium Y and i. In terms of the diagram, show the effects on Y and i of an increase in M, M_0^D, C_0, and I_0. Explain in each case what happens, and why the resulting changes are finite.

5. Use the model as the framework for characterizing the unfavorable case in which economic stagnation exists and monetary policy is ineffective. Show which behavioral factors in the model account for this outcome. Show what modification of the model and of the *IS-LM* diagram is necessary to represent a case in which long-run growth of Y occurs without change in i and monetary policy is effective.

13

dynamic monetary theory: monetary theory since 1960

The rapid development of monetary theory during the 1960s involved a synthesis of elements derived from the Keynesian theory, neoclassical theory, and some other lines of study. The new theory resembled the Keynesian theory in being formulated in explicit models, but these models resembled the earlier neoclassical theory in being dynamic rather than static, emphasizing interaction processes involving investment, and depicting the monetary system as an important causal factor. The recent work has relied heavily on empirical studies using statistical techniques. These ingredients are combined in the econometric model, an explicit dynamic model that is quantified by the use of statistical estimates of behavioral relations. The pioneering econometric models of Jan Tinbergen[1] were contemporary with the work of Keynes. The revolutionary change in economics wrought by statistical studies has depended also on the proliferation of economic data, of which few were available before the 1930s.

The outcome of all of this activity and change is a matter on which the judgments of economists sill differ. On substantive issues, however, the 1960s saw a great swing away from the Keynesian view of the economy and toward ideas much like those of Irving Fisher and other neoclassical economists. We shall here review empirical studies relating to monetary theory and recent formulations of monetary theory, and characterize the current state of thought in the area.

Empirical Studies Relating to Monetary Theory

The shift of opinion toward a greater emphasis upon the causal influence of monetary factors during the 1960s derived largely from judgmental interpretation of the lessons of experience, the fact that

[1]*An Econometric Approach to Business Cycle Problems*, Hermann & Cie, Paris, 1937; *Statistical Testing of Business-cycle Theories*, League of Nations, Geneva, 1939.

what met the eye was a world more Fisherian than Keynesian. But the changing ideas of economists have both reflected and been reflected in the empirical studies that have multiplied since the 1940s. Initially, these studies were based on the Keynesian theory and seemed strongly to support that theory. Further studies, however, raised difficulties for this interpretation. Still later studies based on monetary theory showed that the data could be made to support that theory, perhaps even more strongly than the Keynesian theory. The proliferation of studies producing seemingly conflicting findings raised methodological issues of interpreting the meaning of such studies and pointed up the difficulties of deriving decisive results from statistical studies of economic time series.

The consumption function

Empirical work for many years seemed strongly to support the Keynesian consumption function. Annual data for consumption and income over a period of years approximated very closely the kind of relation depicted in Fig. 12–1. Data from budget studies comparing at one point in time the consumption of families with different levels of income also fell into this pattern. But then studies with time-series data covering a longer period of time, published in the early 1950s,[2] showed a different relation, one that can be expressed as $C = b'Y$. In this (linear homogeneous) consumption function, the marginal propensity to consume is equal to the average propensity to consume; and the latter, of course, does not decline as income rises (since $C/Y = b'$, which is constant).

The idea that the fraction C/Y would continue to decline with the long-run growth of Y was one factor contributing to the pessimism of the Keynesian view of the world. For if the fraction of output taken as consumption continually declined, this implied that the fraction taken as investment goods or by government would have to rise. Such a continued rise in investment in relation to output raises the problem of a shortage of investment opportunities, or of inability to bring about interest rate reductions great enough to motivate such increases in investment. Continued increases in the role of government in the economy would have important political implications. The new factual information disposed of these troublesome prospects.

The new information posed a puzzle for theorists. It appeared that the income-consumption relation defined by Keynes could be interpreted as applying in the short run while the new relation applied in the long run. A number of theoretical contributions were made during the 1950s aimed at reconciling these long-run and short-run consumption func-

[2]Simon Kuznets, "Proportion of Capital Formation to National Product," *Am. Econ. Rev. Pap. Proc.*, **42**:507–526 (1952).

tions.[3] The approaches that have proved to have the greatest continuing influence depict the consumer as adjusting his average consumption expenditures proportionately to his expected lifetime income, or to his "permanent income," thus accounting for the long-run income-consumption relation.[4]

This interpretation leaves the short-run relation between income and consumption—to which less attention has been given—somewhat open. The Keynesian consumption function, now interpreted as a short-run relation, can be explained on the basis that short-run changes in income lead to a less-than-proportional change in consumption because they are expected to be temporary, and the consumer is thinking of his longer-run needs. This view still permits the Keynesian consumption function to be used to estimate short-run multipliers related to fiscal and monetary policy, although it rules out its use in relation to long-run developments and possible economic stagnation.

Another line of study published in the early 1960s raises serious questions as to the validity of the Keynesian consumption function in short-run analysis.[5] The use of the consumption function in a short-run analysis of total demand requires it to measure the causal influence of income on consumption, or the relation $Y \rightarrow C$. Suits discovered that the relation between Y and C measured in studies of the Keynesian consumption function reflected not only such short-run response of consumption to income but also (1) that both Y and C were growing because of the long-run factors and (2) the influences of C on Y, or $C \rightarrow Y$, reflecting the fact that consumption makes up about two-thirds of GNP. He found that a study set up so as to exclude these sources of spurious correlation disclosed no close causal influence of short-run changes in income on consumption: "On a true quarterly basis a useful Keynesian-type consumption function does not exist at all!"[6]

When we think of the way consumers behave, we may not find this surprising. Many consumption expenditures are optional in timing. The consumer buys at the time he thinks best, rather than responding mechanically to month-to-month variations in his income, and makes corresponding adjustments in his cash balance, his holdings of liquid assets, and his use of credit.

[3]These are reviewed in Milton Friedman, *A Theory of the Consumption Function*, chap. 1, Princeton University Press, Princeton, 1957.

[4]*Ibid.*, chap. 9; Albert Ando and Franco Modigliani, "The 'Life Cycle' Hypothesis of Saving: Aggregate Implications and Tests," *Am. Econ. Rev.*, **53** (1963). Alternative approaches are characterized in M. J. Farrell, "The New Theories of the Consumption Function," *Econ. J.*, **69** (1959).

[5]Daniel B. Suits, "The Determinants of Consumer Expenditure: A Review of Present Knowledge," in *Impacts of Monetary Policy*, pp. 1–57, Commission on Money and Credit, Prentice-Hall, Englewood Cliffs, N.J., 1963.

[6]*Ibid.*, p. 39.

But the short-run Keynesian consumption function was the foundation of the whole Keynesian theory—everything was built on the marginal propensity to consume. Suits's findings, which are still being digested and evaluated by other economists, provide one basis for an almost complete rejection of the Keynesian theory of short-run income determination.

The investment function

A major basis of the difference between neoclassical monetary theory and the Keynesian theory, as we pointed out earlier, is that the Keynesian theory depicts investment as determined autonomously rather than determined by economic developments. Modifying the Keynesian model to provide for a response of I to Y, we illustrated, can produce horizontal or upward-sloping IS curves that lead to the usual conclusions of monetary theory: that monetary policy is highly effective in changing total demand, that the interest rate need not decline in the long run, and that short-run swings in the economy can be accompanied by swings in the interest rate in the same direction. Thus, the findings of the research of recent decades on the investment function bear on some basic issues of monetary theory.

While investment behavior has been found to be complex and difficult to characterize in a precise way, modern research does find it responsive to economic conditions as well as financial variables.[7] The dynamic models that have been the major framework for the theory of total demand in the 1960s, which are discussed later, invariably represent investment as responding to changes in economic conditions, most commonly in the form of an accelerator relation. Therefore, this body of modern research also produces findings inconsistent with the Keynesian model.

Explaining experience with monetary theory

The contention of earlier monetary theorists that the Great Depression as well as other United States experience was quite consistent with neoclassical monetary theory was supported in detail by a monumental study by Milton Friedman and Anna J. Schwartz published in 1963.[8] Major conclusions of this study were:

1. Changes in the behavior of the money stock have been closely associated with changes in economic activity, money income, and prices.
2. The interrelation between monetary and economic change has been highly stable.

[7]Robert Eisner and Robert H. Strotz, "Determinants of Business Investment," in *Impacts of Monetary Policy*, pp. 59–337, Commission on Money and Credit, Prentice-Hall, Englewood Cliffs, N.J., 1963.

[8]*A Monetary History of the United States, 1867–1960*, Princeton University Press, Princeton, 1963.

3. Monetary changes have often had an independent origin; they have not been simply a reflection of changes in economic activity.[9]

The view that money had played a very important causal role in United States economic developments also was strongly supported by a somewhat more quantitative study by Cagan that placed special emphasis upon the determinants of the money supply function of the United States.[10] Cagan's demonstration that the behavior of the money supply, which seems to have been a major factor in explaining the behavior of total demand, could be explained in terms of the particular machinery of the United States monetary system was a valuable contribution to monetary theory and stimulated further study of the United States money supply function.

The demand for money: The behavior of velocity

Critics of monetary theory argued that velocity of money was erratic and that it varied in such a way as to offset changes in the money supply. Empirical studies of velocity and of the demand for money provide a means of reducing difference of opinion on this question. The studies of velocity and the demand for money made during the 1960s leave a number of important points unresolved and disclose the inherent difficulties of measuring the behavior in question, but they give impressive support to monetary theory.

In studies of the demand for money based on the neoclassical theory emphasizing money as the means of payment, it has been found that variations in velocity can largely be explained in statistical studies as reflecting changes in interest rates.[11] As indicated in our earlier discussion, this probably is not a fully satisfactory specification of the demand for money, for other factors affecting the opportunity cost of holding money that are less readily measured than interest rates are left out of the explanation. However, such studies have not seemed to support the view that velocity is highly erratic or that it varies in such manner as to offset changes in the money supply.

A major strand in recent work has emphasized wealth or "permanent income" as a factor governing the demand for money over long periods of time. In Friedman's interpretation of the demand for money as based upon permanent income, he uses a concept of "money supply" including time deposits at commercial banks, thereby including an asset—though

[9] *Ibid.*, p. 676.

[10] Phillip Cagan, *Determinants and Effects of Changes in the Stock of Money, 1875–1960*, Columbia University Press, New York, 1965.

[11] Ronald L. Teigen, "Demand and Supply Functions for Money in the United States: Some Structural Estimates," *Econometrica*, 476–509 (1964); Stephen M. Goldfeld, *Commercial Bank Behavior and Economic Activity*, North-Holland Publishing Company, Amsterdam, 1966; Frank de Leeuw and Edward Gramlich, "The Federal Reserve-MIT Econometric Model," *Fed. Reserve Bull.*, pp. 11–40, January 1968.

not all assets—that earns interest but serves as a liquidity reserve.[12] Other studies of the demand for money based upon wealth have used the medium-of-exchange definition of the money supply.[13] The fact that economists testing quite different theories by statistical means have found that the data can be interpreted as supporting their position has pointed up the need for caution in interpreting such tests and the need for methods of making a competitive evaluation of the support for alternative theories.

The money supply function

On the side of the supply of money, a major contention of proponents of the credit approach to banking is that the money supply is not a significant causal variable because it plays a passive role in the economy, adjusting to changes in economic conditions rather than causing them. The extreme version of this approach—essentially Thomas Tooke's "law of reflux" of more than a century ago—that the amount of bank-created money in circulation cannot exceed the amount demanded by the public, was put forth by Tobin.[14] The view embodied in neoclassical monetary theory, on the other hand, was that while within any given set of monetary institutions and policies the money supply would respond to economic developments in a defined way, changes in monetary institutions and policies would alter the response function of the monetary system and, thus, the behavior of the economy. A finding that the behavior of the money supply depends upon details of the monetary mechanism and in recent decades that it depends upon Federal Reserve open market operations lends support to this theory.

As a consequence, the illustrations of Friedman and Schwartz that the behavior of the United States money supply in important cases reflected political factors and changes in the monetary mechanism and monetary policy, plus Cagan's demonstration of the dependence of the behavior of the money supply on the monetary mechanism, lent significant support to monetary theory. Further research has shown how the behavior of the money supply depends on particular features of the United States monetary mechanism.[15] Especially important in relation to the role of the money supply as a causal factor in recent decades has been the demonstration that the major factor underlying variation in its behavior was changes

[12]Milton Friedman, "The Demand for Money: Some Theoretical and Empirical Results," *J. Polit. Econ.*, **67** (1959).

[13]Karl Brunner and Allan H. Meltzer, "Predicting Velocity: Implications for Theory and Policy," *J. Financ.*, **18**:319–354 (1963); Allan H. Meltzer, "The Demand for Money: The Evidence from the Time Series," *J. Polit. Econ.*, **71**:219–246 (1963).

[14]James Tobin, "Commercial Banks as Creators of 'Money,'" in Deane Carson (ed.), *Banking and Monetary Studies*, p. 414, Irwin, Homewood, Ill., 1963.

[15]Following the much earlier contribution of Lauchlin Currie and the work of Friedman and Schwartz and of Cagan were such contributions as Karl Brunner and Allan H. Meltzer, "Liquidity Traps for Money, Bank Credit, and Interest Rates," *J. Polit. Econ.*, **76** (1968); and Jerry L. Jordan, "Elements of Money Stock Determination," *Fed. Reserve Bank St. Louis Rev.*, October 1969.

in Federal Reserve open market operations, which follow no predetermined rule but depend on the theory and objectives that guide the Federal Reserve.[16]

Competitive tests of monetary theory and Keynesian theory

We have noted that early empirical tests of the Keynesian theory seemed to support that approach, but that subsequent studies have raised the possibility that the rules of evidence being applied were not sufficiently tight, so that, within limits, whatever theory was being the most tested would seem to be the most supported. One way to deal with this difficulty was to run a competitive test of alternative theories under the same set of ground rules, to see whether in this way one theory could be clearly preferred to the other. An important study by Friedman and Meiselman published in 1963 was the pathbreaker in this line of research.[17]

A competitive test was set up to see whether a better explanation of historical data could be produced by a Keynesian theory explaining changes in total demand by changes in autonomous expenditures or by a monetary theory explaining them in terms of changes in the money supply. As Friedman and Meiselman ran the test, the monetary approach won hands down. Although the initial response of many economists to the Friedman-Meiselman test was one of skepticism, critics of the study were not able to show that it violated accepted methodological rules or was demonstrably less valid than the studies that had been interpreted as supporting the Keynesian theory. It no longer could be taken that existing empirical studies persuasively supported the Keynesian theory. On the contrary, the Keynesian theory was put on the defensive to show that under a fair competitive race it could muster support more impressive than that of the monetary approach.

A series of competitive tests of Keynesian versus monetary theories by economists at the Federal Reserve Bank of St. Louis seemed strongly to support the superior explanatory power of monetary theory. These were cast specifically in the form of a comparison of monetary policy and of fiscal policy in explaining the behavior of total demand. In a series of tests of recent United States experience, of long-run United States experience, and of the experience of other nations, it was found that the influence of monetary policy on total demand was larger, more reliable, and more prompt than that of fiscal policy.[18] Initial efforts to overturn these findings by showing

[16]This is persuasively shown in William G. Dewald, "Money Supply versus Interest Rates as Proximate Objectives of Monetary Policy," *The Natl. Banking Rev.*, **3** (1966).

[17]Milton Friedman and David Meiselman, "The Relative Stability of Monetary Velocity and the Investment Multiplier in the United States, 1897–1958," in *Stabilization Policies*, pp. 165–268, Commission on Money and Credit, Prentice-Hall, Englewood Cliffs, N.J., 1963.

[18]Leonall C. Andersen and Jerry L. Jordan, "Monetary and Fiscal Actions: A Test of Their Relative Importance in Economic Stabilization," *Fed. Reserve Bank St. Louis Rev.* pp. 11–24, November 1968; Michael W. Keran, "Monetary and Fiscal Influences on Economic Activity—The Historical Evidence," *Fed. Reserve Bank St. Louis Rev.*, pp. 5–24, November 1969; Keran, "Monetary and Fiscal Influences on Economic Activity: The Foreign Experience," *Fed. Reserve Bank St. Louis Rev.*, pp. 16–28, February 1970.

that by modifying the test procedure one could produce the opposite conclusions had produced an outcome only moderately more favorable to fiscal policy. As a result, in 1971, in marked contrast to the situation a decade earlier, the proponents of monetary theory were pressing forward with the empirical testing of theory and the Keynesian theory was on the defensive. These tests, however, were by no means decisive. They raised but did not answer some basic questions as to the rules that ought to apply in formulating and interpreting empirical tests of economic theories.

Monetary theory and econometric models

An econometric model is a representation of the economic system in the form of a system of equations, the values of whose behavioral factors are estimated statistically. The basic rationale of the econometric model is that the equations are specified on the basis of economic theory, so if with estimated values of behavioral factors the model produces a good statistical fit to the data—explains a large part of past variation in the data—this creates a presumption that the model is a useful representation of the behavior of the economy. This would imply that the model can be used to test the effects of alternative policies by making the necessary adjustments in the policy-related equations of the model and seeing what performance arises from the various policies. Consequently, one way to answer such questions as the relative effectiveness of monetary and fiscal policy is through inserting alternative policy equations into a sufficiently accurate econometric model of the United States economy. But if existing knowledge does not offer the econometrician a single economic theory but a set of competing theories and if a good statistical fit has been demonstrated not to be a sufficient basis for accepting a theory, difficulties are raised for the immediate use of econometric models to settle disputed issues and provide guidance to monetary policy.

Monetary variables did not play an important role in the performance of earlier econometric models, but this was recognized as possibly reflecting limitations in the specification of the models. Adequately incorporating monetary and financial variables into an econometric model is very difficult, because of the complexity with which financial flows are interconnected and the existence of a large number of alternative ways of achieving a given financing objective. Serious efforts in the late 1960s to build econometric models that more adequately represent the monetary and financial side of the economy produced a model that seemed to achieve considerable success. An econometric model produced by economists at the Board of Governors of the Federal Reserve System in cooperation with economists from the Massachusetts Institute of Technology gave particular attention to monetary and financial variables. It represented monetary factors as a more important determinant of total demand than had earlier models.[19] The gap between

[19]de Leeuw and Gramlich, *op. cit.*

existing models and the ones required for accurate evaluation of the effects of alternative policies still seemed to be large.

Contributions to Monetary Theory

While the tenor of experience and the broad findings of empirical studies in the 1960s produced a convergence of opinion that monetary policy was important and monetary theory a valid approach to explaining total demand, contributions to monetary theory generated some new dimensions of disagreement among monetary theorists, which call for further study and research before any detailed synthesis of monetary theory can be achieved.

The real balance effect

The long-run branch of neoclassical theory held that under certain necessary conditions the market economy in the long run produced an outcome of full employment. Given that the money supply did not decline, total demand would not continue to decline, though it might show limited short-run swings. Given a determinate level of money demand for output, there was some level of wages and prices at which this total demand would suffice to buy the full-employment output of the economy. The issue, then, was one of flexibility of wages and prices, or openness of markets to unrequited sellers. If unemployed workers would and could offer to work for a wage rate lower than the existing one, wage rates would decline so long as there was unemployment. This would bring parallel reductions in prices. This would mean that the given total demand would buy a larger real output and support a larger volume of employment. Since wages and prices would decline so long as unemployment existed, the only possible long-run outcome—given a stable money supply and flexibility of wages and prices—was full employment.

The Great Depression could be explained without questioning this basic logic, by interpreting it as a short-run phenomenon, by noting that the money supply (at least in the United States) was not stable but declining rapidly, and by noting that institutional changes in the 1920s and 1930s perhaps implied that downward wage flexibility operated only with a lag. But Keynes and his followers at first went further than raising these factual points and claimed to have found a basic flaw in the logic of earlier economic theory. Given a chronic deficiency of investment opportunities, they argued, and given a liquidity trap so the interest rate could not be reduced through monetary policy, no tendency would exist for the economy to move toward a full employment position.

The reply was that this might be true if wage and price flexibility did not exist—but then no tendency towards full employment existed in any case. If wages and prices were flexible, but investment outlets were inadequate and the liquidity trap prevailed, it seemed that wages and prices would decline without any limit. The liquidity trap would prevent the reduction in the price level from causing a decline in the interest rate and, given the fixed interest rate, output could not be increased to the full employment level. All the same, the diagnosis of forever-falling wages and prices did not seem either realistic or intellectually satisfying, and an effort was made to find a better answer to the issue posed by Keynes.

In the light of subsequent experience and thought, probably the best answer is to deny the meaningfulness of the problem, deriving as it does from the stipulation that investment is not responsive to total demand and that the long-run *IS* curve is downward-sloping. This is the answer that fits the events of recent decades. A different answer offered by Pigou in 1943 is important because it started a line of thought that forms one strand in recent monetary theory.[20] Pigou's answer was that in the unfavorable circumstances hypothesized, the outcome would not be unlimited deflation with permanent unemployment for this reason: The reductions in prices would increase the purchasing power or real value of the public's holdings of money (the money supply being assumed constant), thus adding to the public's wealth. Since people were wealthier, Pigou reasoned, they would not want to save as much from their current income. Accordingly, the deflation would not continue indefinitely, but only until the increase in the real value of the money supply added sufficiently to people's wealth to shift the consumption function to increase output enough to remove the unemployment. The economy would reach full employment despite the shortage of investment opportunities and the existence of the liquidity trap by increasing the public's wealth to the point where it increased its consumption enough to get full employment. The increase in the public's wealth caused by the increase in the real value of its cash balances caused by deflation is termed "the real balance effect."

A thoroughgoing restatement of monetary theory based on the real balance effect was later carried through by Don Patinkin.[21] This was essentially a restatement of the long-run branch of neoclassical monetary theory which represented the money supply as affecting total demand through adjustments in the wealth of the public. Patinkin argued that earlier monetary theory had been in error in not defining any particular long-run level of prices and that the real-balance effect was required to rescue the theory from this omission. Subsequent critics have replied that the error is not in neoclassical monetary theory but in Patinkin's representation of it. The neoclassical theory produced a defined price level because it posited a limited demand of the public for money for transactions purposes, leading to a defined velocity of circulation. But the model Patinkin constructed to consider the subject was essentially a barter

[20] A. C. Pigou, "The Classical Stationary State," *Econ. J.*, 343–351 (1943).
[21] *Money, Interest, and Prices*, 2d ed., Harper & Row, New York, 1965.

model that provided no basis for a transactions demand for money, and this is the source of subsequent confusion.[22]

A number of economists, however, followed Patinkin into an approach to monetary theory focused on the long-run demand for money, which was interpreted as related not to transactions requirements but to a desire of the public to hold a certain proportion of its wealth in the form of money. One side effect of this approach is that it removes the rationale for defining "money" in the medium-of-exchange sense, since it is not held to make transactions, leaving somewhat open what ought to be defined as money and even whether the concept is a useful one. The approach to monetary theory put forward in this book is the neoclassical approach, emphasizing the role of money as a medium of exchange. Further research and exchange of ideas will be required to determine which approach to monetary economics will prevail in the future.

Friedman and "the new quantity theory"

A very influential contribution to recent monetary theory is Friedman's 1956 version of "the quantity theory of money," which he represented as a restatement of the ideas of the Chicago School.[23] The approach of Friedman has been a focal point of "the new quantity theory" of the 1960s. But Patinkin later pointed out that Friedman's theory is not really a restatement of neoclassical monetary theory as formulated by the Chicago School: "Milton Friedman provided us in 1956 with a most elegant and sophisticated statement of modern Keynesian monetary theory—misleading entitled 'The Quantity Theory of Money—A Restatement.' "[24]

While the monetary theory of the Chicago School had focused to a great extent on short-run adjustments, dealt with the concept of money and the demand for money in terms of money as a medium of exchange, and interpreted short-run variation in velocity as reflecting primarily other factors with little emphasis upon the rate of interest, Friedman's theory was oriented toward long-run demand for money, did not define money in the medium-of-exchange sense and interpreted the demand for money as an element in wealth holding, and emphasized relative yields on money and other assets as the basis of demand for money. Other recent versions of monetary theory, thus, have been closer to the neoclassical tradition than that of Friedman, which as Patinkin points out is Keynesian in its wealth-

[22]Robert Clower, "A Reconsideration of the Microfoundations of Monetary Theory," *West. Econ. J.*, **6**:1–8 (1967).

[23]Milton Friedman, "The Quantity Theory of Money—A Restatement," in Friedman (ed.), *Studies in the Quantity Theory of Money*, The University of Chicago Press, Chicago, 1956. A more recent restatement and further development of these ideas is Friedman, "A Theoretical Framework for Monetary Analysis," *J. Polit. Econ.*, **78**:193–238 (1970).

[24]Don Patinkin, "The Chicago Tradition, The Quantity Theory," and Friedman, *J. Money, Credit Banking*, **1**:61 (1969).

holding rationale for the demand for money. Among Friedman's numerous and important contributions to monetary theory is an interpretation of the demand for money as based upon permanent income—which is closely related to wealth.[25]

Extensions of neoclassical monetary theory

Many monetary economists have continued to accept an approach to monetary theory emphasizing the medium-of-exchange function of money and the making of transactions as the purpose for which money is held. A contribution to the foundations of this approach is Clower's spelling out of the difference between a barter economy and a money economy: "In the latter goods cannot be exchanged for one another; if one wants to buy, he must have money, and this is a basis for the demand of money.[26] A number of empirical studies have been based explicitly on the transactions rationale for the demand for money.[27] Most empirical studies, even when based on a wealth rationale, have used the medium-of-exchange definition of money and find that formulations on this basis are consistent with the data. The important studies by Brunner and Meltzer have been based on the medium-of-exchange definition of money, finding it yields the best fit to the data, but have been based on a wealth rationale for the demand for money and have emphasized long-run analysis.[28]

Monetary Theory in Dynamic Models

The availability of economic data and the expression of the Keynesian static theory in the form of an explicit model, plus Tinbergen's pioneering work with dynamic econometric models, led to the development of dynamic theoretical models of total demand. The early versions of these were Keynesian in spirit in focusing on real variables rather than monetary factors, but the work of the 1960s put increasing emphasis on the incorporation of monetary factors into dynamic models of total demand. The major dynamic model used for the exploration of economic fluctuations and growth has been the multiplier-accelerator model, which we now consider.

[25] "The Demand for Money: Some Theoretical and Empirical Results," *J. Polit. Econ.*, **67**:327–351 (1959).

[26] *Op. cit.*

[27] Teigen, *op. cit.*; Goldfeld, *op. cit.*

[28] Karl Brunner and Allan H. Meltzer, "Predicting Velocity: Implications for Theory and Policy," *J. Financ.*, **18**:319–354 (1963); "Some Further Investigations of Demand and Supply Functions for Money," *J. Financ.*, **19**:240–283 (1964); "Liquidity Traps for Money, Bank Credit, and Interest Rates," *J. Polit. Econ.*, **76**:1–37 (1968).

The accelerator relation

The discussion of the investment function in Chap. 12 depicted investment as depending on the rate of interest and in the expanded version of the investment function, on total expenditures. Thinking of investment goods and total output in terms of physical quantities, a relation can be posited between the level of output and the total amount of capital goods needed to produce the output. For capital equipment of given efficiency that is fully employed, such a relation can be defined as

$$\left(\frac{K}{P}\right)_t = \beta_1\left(\frac{Y}{P}\right)_t \qquad (13-1)$$

in which K/P is the real amount of capital goods used in producing real output Y/P. We posit a fixed relation between the stock of capital goods and the output it produces, defined by the capital-output ratio $(\beta_1 = (K/P_t \,/\, Y/P_t)$.

Since net investment of the economy is the change in the size of the capital stock, we can make the following derivation:

$$\left(\frac{I}{P}\right)_t = \left(\frac{K}{P}\right)_t - \left(\frac{K}{P}\right)_{t-1}$$

but since

$$\left(\frac{K}{P}\right)_t = \beta_1\left(\frac{Y}{P}\right)_t$$

$$\left(\frac{I}{P}\right)_t = \beta_1\left(\frac{Y}{P}\right)_t - \beta_1\left(\frac{Y}{P}\right)_{t-1} = \beta_1\left[\left(\frac{Y}{P}\right)_t - \left(\frac{Y}{P}\right)_{t-1}\right] = \beta_1\, \Delta\left(\frac{Y}{P}\right)_t$$

This relation says that real investment in "equilibrium" depends on the rate of change of real output. This relation is called "the accelerator." As thus applied to investment, it derives from the assumption of a fixed capital-output ratio.

The accelerator relation also can be used as a way of representing other kinds of behavior that tends to make a movement in the economy self-feeding, such as the formation of expectations in such a way that when total demand rises people expect it to rise further, so they increase their spending. If when business is getting better people expect it to get still better and when it is getting worse people expect it to get still worse, incorporation of accelerator terms into equations representing expenditures will roughly represent this aspect of their behavior. In this case, the size of the accelerator coefficient β depends upon the way people form their expectations.

Interpreted literally as a relation between physical output and physical plant and equipment, the accelerator relation applies only to explaining net investment, or investment that changes the size of the stock of capital goods. The implication is that replacement investment goes on steadily. In practice, the line between investment to replace existing facilities and investment to increase output is a hazy one, and the timing of all investment expenditures depends on business expectations and judgments as to whether the present is a good or a bad time to invest. Thus, if we interpret the accelerator relation in a broad way as depicting behavior and expectations, we can think of it as explaining gross investment rather than only net investment.

The multiplier-accelerator model

The multiplier-accelerator model involves three terms:

1. A component of autonomous expenditures (A_t). These are expenditures that are determined outside of the model and do not depend upon other variables of the model. The autonomous component of the consumption function (C_0) and of the investment function (I_0) would here be grouped into A_t.
2. A term defining the dependence of expenditures on the expenditures of the prior period (αY_{t-1}). This is the multiplier term. The relation depicted is like the multiplier relation of the nonfinancial Keynesian model. In that case, the relation was defined by the marginal propensity to consume. In this case, the value of α (alpha) can be interpreted as reflecting only the marginal propensity to consume, or it can be given a broader interpretation.
3. The accelerator term defines a dependence of expenditures on the prior rate of change of expenditures, $Y_t = \ldots \beta(Y_{t-1} - Y_{t-2})$. This is the relation just discussed. If it is interpreted narrowly, the value of β_1 depends on the economy's capital-output ratio. However, the model may be given a broader interpretation in which the value of β (beta) depends also on expectational factors and the influence of expectations on expenditures. The model thus is:

$$Y_t = A_t + \alpha Y_{t-1} + \beta(Y_{t-1} - Y_{t-2}) \tag{13-2}$$

This is a dynamic model. Its variables are dated and it will trace out a time path for total demand. A change in autonomous expenditures will act as a disturbance to the system, pushing it off its original position or time path. Various combinations of values of α and β will produce various kinds of time paths for the model. The association of classes of time path, illustrated in Fig. 13-1, with sets of values of α and β is depicted in Fig. 13-2.

Most past applications of the model have assumed a value of α of less than 1. This makes it consistent with the Keynesian model, in which the marginal propensity to consume is less than 1. If the value of β is zero, or sufficiently small, this gives the same kind of time path as the multiplier model discussed in Chap. 12 (case A). When disturbed, the system moves without fluctuation to a new equilibrium position.

Larger values of α and β make the system more unstable, the zones of increasing instability being (case B) damped oscillations that tend to die

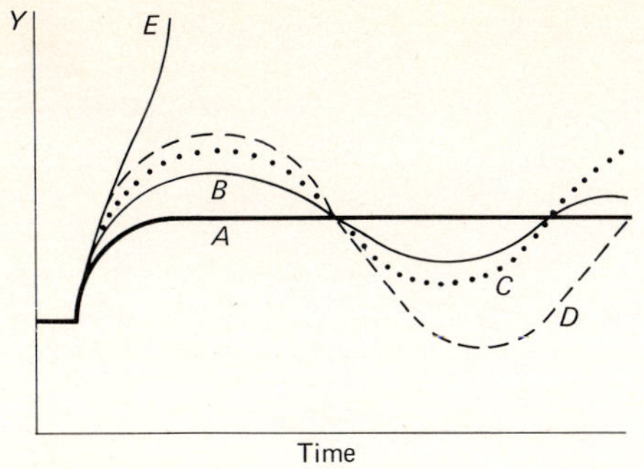

Fig. 13-1 Classes of performance of multiplier-accelerator model.

away unless the system is again disturbed, (case C) fluctuations of constant amplitude that thus can continue indefinitely, (case D) fluctuations of increasing amplitude, and (case E) an explosive response in which the system neither fluctuates nor moves to a new equilibrium position but simply keeps moving in the same direction without any limit. Several of these classes of behavior can be used as the framework for theories of economic fluctuations.

The theory of economic fluctuations should provide answers to three questions (Fig. 13-3): (1) What determines the degree of short-run instability of the economy, the steepness of its self-feeding upswings and downswings? (2) What causes turning points and determines the location of these boundaries or limits on short-run swings in the economy? (3) What determines the average rate of growth over a period of time?

Money in economic fluctuations and growth

Early interpretations of economic fluctuations and growth in terms of the multiplier-accelerator model, in line with the thinking of the times, did not emphasize monetary or financial factors. The influential theory of J. R. Hicks, published in 1950, was in this pattern:[29] It assumed that the relevant case of the multiplier-accelerator model based on the consumption function and an accelerator investment function was an explosive one. That implied that cyclical turning points were explained not by any internal tendency of short-run swings in the economy to be self-limiting but by some external constraint.

Hicks explained the upper turning point as reflecting the inability of real output to keep growing without diminution when labor became fully utilized. Since investment depends on the rate of change of output, such slowing down of growth of output leads to a decline in investment

[29] *A Contribution to the Theory of the Trade Cycle*, Oxford University Press, London, 1950.

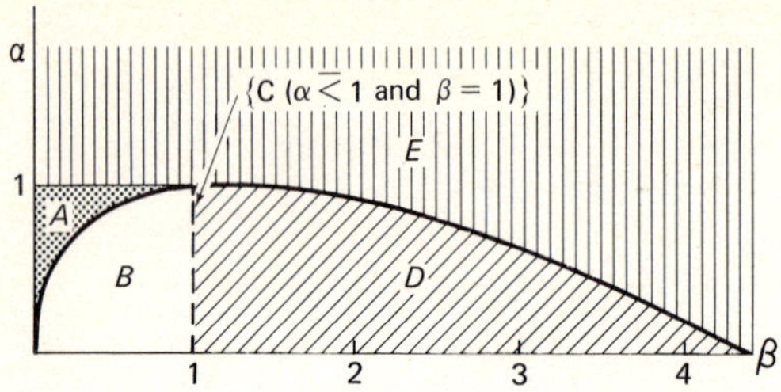

Fig. 13–2 Performance of multiplier-accelerator model in relation to values of α and β.

and causes a downturn. The reductions in output aggravate the problem of excess capacity, and the downswing also continues until it hits an external constraint. The lower boundary was defined by a component of investment not dependent upon current output, which increased steadily because of growth in population and technological change. When investment hit this floor and began increasing because of the floor's upward trend, this brought the accelerator into play again in an upward direction, setting the economy on another self-feeding upswing.

Among unrealistic aspects of this theory was its lack of emphasis of monetary and financial factors. Hicks actually did lay considerable stress on monetary factors and gave an essentially neoclassical interpretation of the Great Depression, but he did not integrate them into his basic model, which was what influenced later writers.

In one of the leading recent statements on this point Haberler expressed the view that monetary factors played a crucial role—operating in conjunction with nonmonetary factors—in determining the severity and duration of short-run swings in the economy and that experience in this connection supported the general view of the economy of neoclassical economics.[30] Subsequent experience has confirmed this interpretation. The usual cause of a cyclical downturn in postwar experience seems to have been financial stringency arising out of the halting of expansion of the money supply.

Reflecting the growing acceptance of this view, in the 1960s many versions were offered of dynamic models that incorporate monetary as well as nonmonetary feedbacks but that are consistent with the important role seemingly played by monetary factors in governing the short-run swings of actual economies.[31] There is not yet a consensus as to how best

[30] Gottfried Haberler, "Monetary and Real Factors Affecting Economic Stability: A Critique of Certain Tendencies in Modern Economic Theory," *Banca Naz. Lav. Q. Rev.*, **9** (1956); reprinted in Robert A. Gordon and Lawrence R. Klein (eds.), *Readings in Business Cycles*, Irwin, Homewood, Ill., 1965.

[31] Among recent contributions are Hugh Rose, "Real and Monetary Factors in the Business Cycle," *J. Money, Credit Banking*, **1**:138–152 (1969); Jerome L. Stein, "'Neoclassical' and 'Keynes-Wicksell' Monetary Growth Models," *J. Money, Credit Banking*, **1**:153–171 (1969).

to represent monetary factors in either econometric models or the simpler models used as a framework for thinking about how the economy operates. We can, however, indicate in general terms how a simple dynamic model such as the multiplier-accelerator model can depict the kind of complex interaction of monetary and nonmonetary factors that now is widely accepted as underlying fluctuations and growth of total demand.

A short-run swing of the economy in either direction reflects values of the multiplier and accelerator coefficients that make the movement self-feeding without any necessary limit. Prominent among the factors combining to generate this behavior are the following:

1. An increase in total demand leads to an increase in real output and, thus, in the utilization of plant capacity. Therefore, an upswing creates a shortage of capacity and business inventories; a downswing leads to the existence of excess capacity. This causes investment to respond strongly to changes in total demand and output. This, of course, is the investment accelerator.

2. The second factor is positive monetary feedback. This comes from a monetary system or a system of monetary policy in which increases in total demand and interest rates lead to an increase in the money supply, and vice versa. Put in other terms, it comes from a monetary system that holds the market interest rate below the natural rate of interest in economic upswings and keeps the market interest rate above the natural rate of interest in economic downswings. This factor applies only in cases that have monetary systems leading to positive monetary feedback. These have been quite prevalent.

3. Swings in total demand characteristically lead to swings in prices. But an upswing in prices leads people to expect further price increases and so causes them to buy goods and services before prices rise further, thereby feeding the upswing. Similarly, in an economic contraction when prices are falling price expectations are an incentive to defer spending, which contributes to the downswing.

4. A change in the price level especially affects the position of those who are in debt. This includes most businesses. In an upswing when prices are rising, it is relatively easy to repay debts. In effect, the debtor is repaying in dollars that are worth less than the ones he borrowed. In a downswing, especially if prices are falling substantially, repaying debt may be difficult or impossible. This factor was emphasized by Irving Fisher as applying particularly in the case of very severe downswings.[32]

5. Increase in the price level causes the real rate of interest to be lower than the nominal interest rate ($i_r = i - \Delta P/P$) and the reverse. Institutional impediments to sufficient adjustment in nominal interest rates

[32]"The Debt-deflation Theory of Great Depressions," *Econometrica*, **1**:337–357 (1933).

thus lead to declines in real interest rate during upswings, and vice versa, which tend to make such swings self-feeding. The natural tendency for nominal interest rates to adjust to offset expected changes in price level (and to prevent such procyclical variations in the real rate of interest) will, in a monetary system or monetary policy oriented towards stabilizing nominal interest rates, lead to positive monetary feedback. This seems to have been a major source of destabilizing monetary policy.

6. In many cases, an upswing in sales leads businesses to expect further increases in sales. They expect a continuation of what has been happening in the past. As a result, an economic upswing causes general optimism and favorable expectations, which tends to stimulate expenditures, which feeds the upswing. Again, a downswing leads to pessimism and unfavorable expectations, which feeds the downswing.

In setting limits on such self-feeding movements and defining turning points, monetary factors seem to play an especially prominent role. The many examples of long-continued and rapid inflationary expansion of total demand indicate that if the monetary system continues to provide sufficient expansion in the money supply an upswing can continue until the economic and political system is destroyed by inflation. Similarly, long-continued reduction in the money supply in the Great Depression led to continued self-feeding economic contraction. But upswings do not seem able to continue without the continued collaboration of the monetary system, and the cessation of economic contraction in the Great Depression and in more modest recessions seems to have been related to the turnaround in the money supply.

As a consequence, the monetary system and monetary policy seem to play a crucial role as the boundary-setter of short-run swings in the economy. In the multiplier-accelerator model, one way of representing this is by specifying that at some point determined by the monetary system or monetary policy positive monetary feedback is halted or reversed, so that increases in interest rates and total demand no longer lead to increases in the money supply. This leads to a shift in the value of the accelerator coefficient (or both coefficients) and—interacting with all of the other factors affecting the economy's dynamic properties—suffices to turn the economy around.

The long-run rate of growth of total demand, in this approach, is defined by the mechanisms that determine the turning points of economic fluctuations. For example, we can think of the slope of the top of the corridor in Fig. 13–3 as being defined by the mechanism that sets the upper turning points and calls a halt to economic upswings. If each upswing were permitted to run longer, we should have a more steeply upward-sloping corridor and a more rapid average rate of growth of total demand. On the other hand, if each upswing were cut off at the same absolute level

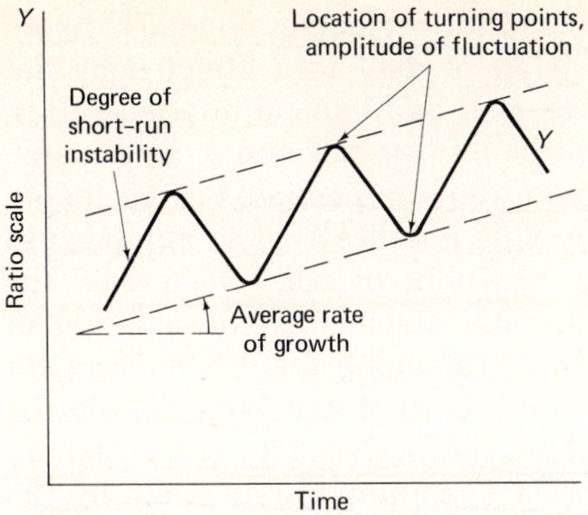

Fig. 13–3 Components of economic fluctuations.

the corridor would be horizontal and there would be no average growth at all in total demand.

Accordingly, if the monetary system is the major factor determining the location of turning points, it also determines the average rate of growth of total demand. The Great Depression in the United States reflected not unusual short-run behavior of total demand but rather an unusual location of turning points. The economic contraction of 1929–1933 was not unusually rapid, but it ran unusually long before it hit its turning point. Similarly, variations in the average rate of growth of total demand during more recent periods, including the 1960s, largely reflect variation in the location of turning points and in the duration of upswings and downswings. Therefore, this dynamic theory of total demand provides an interpretation of the Great Depression and of the possibility of persistent deficiency of total demand that is quite different from the stagnation thesis.

The Credit Approach: Federal Reserve Monetary Theory

The credit approach to banking and central banking continued to be influential during the 1960s, providing the framework of ideas within which Federal Reserve policy was formulated. A complex formulation of monetary theory by Gurley and Shaw relates to some strands from the credit approach and others from wealth-related approaches to the demand for money.[33] In relation to basic issues of monetary theory, it supported the idea of the credit approach that the amount of bank-created money is

[33]John G. Gurley and E. S. Shaw, "Financial Intermediaries and the Saving-Investment Process," *J. Financ.*, **11** (1956); *Money in a Theory of Finance*, The Brookings Institution, Washington, D.C., 1960.

regulated by the demand for it and argued for replacing monetary theory by an approach structured into a division of debt into direct debt and indirect debt. The latter includes debt created by financial intermediaries, of which, in this approach, commercial banks are just one among many. Thus, monetary theory would be replaced by an intermediated-assets theory with a quite different rationale and implying a radically new approach to stabilization policy. A later statement by Tobin of what he termed the "new view" of banks and money especially argued that the amount of bank-created money was determined by the demand for it.[34] Subsequent empirical studies reaffirming earlier findings that the behavior of the money supply was mainly determined by the behavior of the monetary base and by Federal Reserve open market operations (rather than by the demand of the public for money) seemed damaging to this approach.

Despite the growing support among economists for monetary theory and the empirical studies supporting it, Federal Reserve policy, until 1969, continued to be determined within the framework of the credit approach.[35] While the Federal Reserve unquestionably was oriented towards controlling credit conditions rather than controlling the nation's money supply function, its credit objectives could not be closely defined. It was a part of the Federal Reserve approach to argue that no single indicator sufficiently measured credit conditions and that what credit conditions were appropriate could not be explicitly stated. Among the credit indicators by which Federal Reserve actions seem mainly to have been governed were free reserves (excess reserves of member banks minus their borrowings from Federal Reserve banks), short-term interest rates and conditions in the New York money market, and total commercial bank credit (not distinguishing that arising from money creation from that associated with time deposits). The way Federal Reserve actions and the behavior of the money supply stemmed from this approach is discussed in Chap. 21.

The State of Knowledge

The events and the empirical studies of the 1960s produced an important shift in economic thought. Gaining support were the ideas that monetary policy is an important determinant of total demand, that it is best measured by the behavior of the money supply (or, at any rate, not by the nominal rate of interest), and that stagnationist predictions regarding the future of market economies were basically erroneous.

At the same time, while monetary theory—or dynamic theories involving a monetary-Keynesian synthesis—gained in influence, proponents

[34] *Op. cit.*

[35] The Federal Reserve Bank of St. Louis, whose economists made important studies that proved to support the monetary approach, was a conspicuous but seemingly isolated voice within the System for the monetary approach.

of this general approach created new issues to be settled by further work: how "money" is to be defined and what rationale justifies this approach, whether the demand for money is governed by transactions or wealth-holding considerations, and the relative importance of interest rates against other factors affecting the demand for money. The experience of this very active period of monetary thought and research also emphasized the ease of finding empirical tests that would seem to support one or another theory—and, thus, the difficulty of interpreting the meaning of empirical tests and of separating truth from error.

SUMMARY

1. While early empirical studies seemed to support the Keynesian consumption function, later studies indicated that the long-run consumption function did not involve an average propensity to consume that declined as income rose. Still later work indicated that the measured short-run relation between income and consumption largely reflected factors other than the causal influence of income on consumption, leaving the status of the short-run consumption function in doubt.

2. Empirical studies of the investment function have indicated that investment is responsive to changes in economic conditions and total demand.

3. Studies of the demand for money and the behavior of velocity, although leaving many issues unresolved, do not support the view that velocity behaves erratically or that it varies in such a manner as to offset the effects of changes in the money supply.

4. Studies of the money supply in the United States show it to be closely responsive to changes in the monetary base, which can be controlled by Federal Reserve open market operations.

5. Recent interpretation of United States economic developments finds that monetary factors seem to have played an important causal role, in the Great Depression as well as at other times, and, thus, supports neoclassical monetary theory.

6. While some recent contributions to monetary theory have developed the neoclassical approach, others have emphasized a long-run monetary theory in which the demand for money is based on wealth rather than on transactions and have raised questions as to the basis of the concept of money.

7. The major framework for recent monetary theory is not the equation of exchange approach but dynamic theoretical models and econometric models depicting the interaction of monetary and nonmonetary factors. The neoclassical monetary theory can be set into this framework.

8. The credit approach to banking and central banking has continued to be influential. Federal Reserve policies, until, 1969, were governed by credit criteria defined in terms of free reserves, bank credit, and interest rates and conditions in the money market.

QUESTIONS FOR REVIEW AND DISCUSSION

1. Show the relevance to the stagnation thesis of the finding that the average propensity to consume does not decline in the long run as income rises. Show the implications for the Keynesian approach to short-run analysis of total demand of studies casting doubt on the Keynesian conception of the marginal propensity to consume.

2. Does the finding that investment responds to changes in economic conditions and total demand support the Keynesian model? What modification of the Keynesian model would make it consistent in this respect with the multiplier-accelerator model and with neoclassical theories of business cycles?

3. Write out the multiplier-accelerator model. Explain what behavior the model generates with different values of the multiplier and accelerator coefficients.

4. Describe the set of interacting developments that are involved in short-run self-feeding movements of the economy. What seems to be the major factor determining whether and when such movements hit a boundary and are reversed? In an economy characterized by such bounded fluctuations, explain what determines the average rate of growth over longer periods of time.

5. Describe the ideas underlying Federal Reserve monetary policy until 1969. As interpreted in terms of monetary theory, what hazard does this approach involve?

14

the theory of interest rates

Interest rates are prices, set like other prices in markets by voluntary dealings between buyers and sellers. The good exchanged in this case is credit, or the use of money for a period of time. Interest rates are intimately involved with the role of time in economic activities and in the lives of the actors in the economic game. To the consumer, business, and government, money *now* is not the same thing as money next year. Interest rates arise out of, and in a sense measure, this preference for the present over the future.

In adjusting to changes in the public's desire for present spending, interest rates can play a stabilizing role in the economy. In an economic upswing when spending incentives seem especially attractive and individuals and businesses want to spend more money than they are receiving in income, the resulting increase in the demand for credit pushes up interest rates, and the increase in interest rates requires some potential spenders to postpone their proposed spending. In a recession when many economic units view spending incentives less favorably and want to postpone their spending, the resulting declines in interest rates provide an inducement to spend now to those who are at the margin of doing so. Such adjustments in interest rates are a part of the mechanism by which fluctuations in total demand are dampened by the monetary and financial system—so long as the monetary system does not nullify the mechanism by permitting spending to be financed by newly created money during upswings and using savings to extinguish money during downswings.

While the money that is borrowed is a standardized good, the contracts under which it is borrowed differ in a number of ways, in duration or term to maturity, in hazard of default, and in particulars of repayment terms and security offered. The interest rates applying to different kinds of debt contract differ systematically from one another, leading to a multidimensional structure of interest rates. The most prominent features of the interest rate structure are the term structure of rates, relating to the term to maturity of the debt; and the risk structure of yields, relating to the quality or default risk of the debt.

In addition to differing among broad categories of debt, interest rates and accompanying nonprice terms on which credit is extended differ among individual cases. The terms on which credit is made available to a particular borrower and a particular project reflect the probable outcome as estimated by lenders. In voting with their dollars and taking the risk of loss when they are wrong, lenders play a central role in allocating resources in the market economy. The quality of the imagination and judgment they exercise in determining the terms on which credit is to be made available to potential borrowers is an important determinant of the rate of increase in efficiency of an economy, and so of the degree of efficiency and the standard of living prevailing at any particular time.

In thinking about interest rates, it is important to keep in mind that a given absolute interest rate does not have the same meaning at one time as at another, 4 percent in 1970 is not necessarily the same as 4 percent in 1963. One reason for this is that the meaning of the stated or "nominal interest rate" is affected by changes in the price level. Since they involve exchanging money at one point in time for money at another point, credit dealings or debt contracts are very sensitive to changes in the value of money itself.

A useful concept in this connection is the "real rate of interest," or the rate of interest after adjustment for change in the value of money. This is defined as $i_r = i - \Delta P/P$. When the price level is not stable, nominal interest rates may give a quite misleading picture of the true rate of return earned by the lender and the true cost to the borrower. Analysis in terms of the real rate of interest is one way of clarifying the matter.

Another reason why a given nominal interest rate may not have the same meaning at different times is that people's ideas as to the attractiveness of lending and borrowing change with economic conditions, for other reasons as well as because of expected changes in the value of money. Thus, if a 4 percent interest rate were consistent with economic stability and the public became more sanguine about economic prospects and increased its demands for credit, the interest rate consistent with economic stability would then be a higher one. The interest rate that is consistent with economic stability we term, after Wicksell, the "natural rate of interest." Having refreshed our acquaintance with these concepts we now ask what determines the level and structure of interest rates.

The Level of Interest Rates in the Long Run

We consider first what determines average levels of interest rates, or long-run movements, as distinguished from the changes in interest rates associated with economic fluctuations and other temporary factors. Unlike population, GNP, and even prices, interest rates have not been subject to any long-run trend. It appears that interest rates in ancient Greece were as low as 6 percent and in Rome, during favored periods, as low as 4 percent, about as low as they have been for any considerable period of time since.[1]

Changes in average interest rates over prolonged periods of time have occurred. Homer found in ancient times a saucer-shaped pattern in which interest rates declined as a society prospered and reached maturity, and then rose again as it became disorganized and deteriorated. European interest rates declined from around 10 percent in the twelfth century to 4 to 5 percent in the fifteenth century, followed by a rise in the sixteenth century and a sharp fall in the seventeenth.[2] Long-term interest rates in the United States declined in the last three decades of the nineteenth century, rose until 1920, declined modestly during the 1920s and sharply during the 1930s, and increased in the 1950s and 1960s. What explains such movements of interest rates?

The basic framework applied is that of supply and demand; the interest rate will be at an average level that equates the quantity of credit demanded with the quantity supplied under the conditions that prevail.[3] Since short-run changes in expectations and in the money supply do not affect the average level of the interest rate, attention is limited to more basic or lasting determinants of the supply of and demand for credit. The supply of and demand for credit can be simply characterized, as in Fig. 14-1, although the set of factors lying behind these schedules is very complex and difficult to define. Stated in flow terms, as is usual in supply and demand analysis, the determination of the interest rate is defined by the supply of credit and the demand for it, as in the left panel of Fig. 14-1. In such long-run

Fig. 14-1 Determination of interest rates.

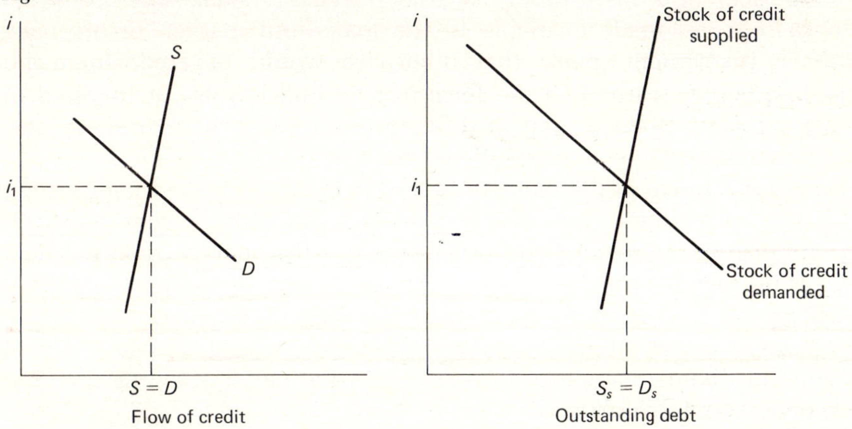

[1]An interesting discussion of historical trends in interest rates is given in Sidney Homer, *A History of Interest Rates*, Rutgers University Press, New Brunswick, N.J., 1963.

[2]*Ibid.*, p. 140.

[3]Basic sources on this subject are Friedrich A. Lutz, *The Theory of Interest*, Aldine, Chicago, 1968; J. W. Conard, *An Introduction to the Theory of Interest*, University of California Press, Berkeley, 1959.

analysis, however, the total amount of claims on wealth and the stock of physical assets of the society will mainly be carried over from earlier periods rather than created by current saving and investment. Thus, it may be more useful to think of schedules (right panel) defining the total stock of debt the public under any particular set of conditions is willing to hold at various interest rates, and the total demand for outstanding credit (or supply of debt). The substance of the analysis then turns on characterization of the factors lying behind these schedules, and the way in which long-run changes in interest rates can be interpreted in terms of them.

In discussing fundamental determinants of interest rates, Irving Fisher emphasized time preference (or "impatience") as a factor limiting the supply of credit, and investment opportunity as underlying the demand for credit. If people did not care about time, they would save and lend more of their incomes so long as the rate of interest were positive, so clearly the existence of time preference is necessary to explain the existence of interest. Similarly, if opportunities to produce more effectively by using factories and machines did not exist, if capital goods were not productive, much of the basis would be removed for the demand for credit. Thus, Fisher's time preference and investment opportunity are basic factors underlying the long-run supply of and demand for credit.

To explain actual long-run movements in interest rates, however, we must recognize a number of other factors as potentially important influences on the supply of and demand for credit. The effective time preference of a society depends importantly upon its distribution of income and wealth, and upon the political and legal framework that influence these. Political and institutional factors decisively affect the extent to which savings are made available in the loan fund market (or are used to finance investment goods that otherwise would be credit-financed) rather than being hoarded in the form of gold and jewelry or invested in a foreign country. A major part of differences in the level of interest rates among countries may be explainable by such factors.

Moreover, much of the demand for credit arises from the financing not of business investment but of consumption and government expenditures. The use of credit for these purposes depends heavily upon political and institutional factors. The large increase in the amount of outstanding debt of these types in recent decades has tended to make interest rates in the United States higher than they otherwise would be. Government borrowing to finance wars has been an important factor affecting the total supply of outstanding debt.

Finally, average interest rates are affected by movements in the price level. The decline in United States interest rates during the late nineteenth century and their subsequent rise seem explainable in part by the deflation of the earlier period and the inflation of the later one. The increase in United States interest rates in the latter part of the 1960s also appears partly a response to inflation and inflationary expectations. The relative importance of the various relevant factors in explaining long-run movements in interest rates, however, is a matter on which our knowledge is limited.

Short-run Interest Theory

In explaining changes in interest rates from year to year and over shorter periods, it is necessary to bring into the picture some factors that could be neglected in the case of average interest rates over long periods. Changes in the money supply now may be a significant influence upon the supply of credit, as may changes in the desire of the public to hold money. Moreover, in this case, changes in economic conditions and short-run swings in expectations are among the variables potentially affecting interest rates.

The adaptation to the short run of the framework of supply and demand for credit is termed the "loanable funds approach" to interest theory. The explicit development of this approach did not occur until the 1930s. A group of Swedish economists and the English economist D. H. Robertson were the major contributors. We consider first a conventional formulation of this approach and then make some adjustments to suit it to an actual interpretation of changes in interest rates.

As a first approximation, the total supply of credit (or loan funds) can be represented as arising from two sources: saving (S_a) and increase in the money supply (ΔM). You recall that under present-day monetary systems, an increase in the money supply is accompanied (on the asset side of the books of the commercial banks and the Federal Reserve banks) by an increase in bank credit. Therefore, a change in the money supply involves an approximately equal flow of funds into the credit market. This analysis is entirely in terms of flows of funds; we do not formulate it in terms of the stock of outstanding debt.

Aggregate saving rarely takes on a negative value, although, of course, individuals can dissave. The money supply, however, often shows periods of decrease. In this case, the decline in the money supply enters as a source of loan funds with a negative sign. In effect, some savings are used to retire debt in connection with extinction of money and are not available for other purposes.

On the side of demand for credit, the major factor in this formulation is taken to be the financing of investment I. The other factor, a less obvious one, is termed "hoarding" H. If people decide to build up their holdings of idle cash, or to increase their cash ratio, this uses money that otherwise would be put into the credit market. With any given total sources of funds, the more people are adding to their cash balances, the less investment can be financed. Hoarding can take on a negative value, when it is called dishoarding. In this case, people are reducing their holdings of idle balances, or reducing their cash ratio, and using the money made available as an additional source of funds to finance investment. The statement of supply of and demand for credit, or sources and uses of loan funds, then is

$$S_a + \Delta M = H + I \tag{14-1}$$

A representation of this approach in a supply and demand diagram is given in Fig. 14-2. What is depicted is the quantity of credit that would be supplied and demanded at various rates of interest for a *given total demand* Y_1 and given expectations. The implications of changes in these we shall consider in a moment.

The H curve is downward-sloping because the interest rate affects the opportunity cost for holding money and, so, the quantity of money demanded. The I curve also is downward-sloping for reasons discussed earlier. The lower the interest rate, the larger the amount of investment that will be undertaken and the greater the amount of money borrowed to finance it. The curve for total demand for credit D, thus, is downward-sloping.

The slope of the ΔM curve depends upon the money supply function and the monetary policy in the society. A system of monetary policy in which the money supply responds positively to the rate of interest involves an upward-sloping ΔM curve. This is a monetary system involving positive monetary feedback. But under other systems of monetary policy, the money supply would be quite unaffected by the rate of interest and would be represented by a vertical ΔM curve such as is shown. The response of saving S_a to the interest rate, presumably, is positive, although perhaps not great (in which case the curve is steep). In any case, we derive a curve representing the total supply of credit S that is upward-sloping.

The rate of interest is defined by the intersection of the *D* and *S* curves, this being the interest rate that equates the quantity of credit demanded to the quantity supplied, or that clears the market for credit. On the horizontal axis, we have defined the total flow of funds through the credit market and the amount of this that comes from saving, from creation of new money, and from dishoarding.[4]

This approach is useful for thinking about the direct effect on the interest rate of a change in a causal factor. If the rate of growth of the money supply increased, this would shift the ΔM curve and the total supply of credit curve to the right and reduce the rate of interest. You can see how

[4]Since in the case illustrated by Fig. 14-2 the creation of new money is adding more to the supply of loan funds than hoarding is adding to the demand for them, some funds are being supplied on net to the loan fund market by monetary factors. This implies that investment is greater than saving. But as they usually are defined S and I should be equal ($S = Y - C$, and since $Y = C + I$, $I = Y - C$). Proponents of the loanable funds approach try to get around this difficulty by characterizing their formulation as referring to planned or ex ante saving and investment, which need not be equal. But they are then left with the difficulty of explaining how the interest rate is determined in part by plans for savings or investment that are not realized. Correcting the unrealistic identification of demand for credit with investment, as done below, is one way of solving this problem.

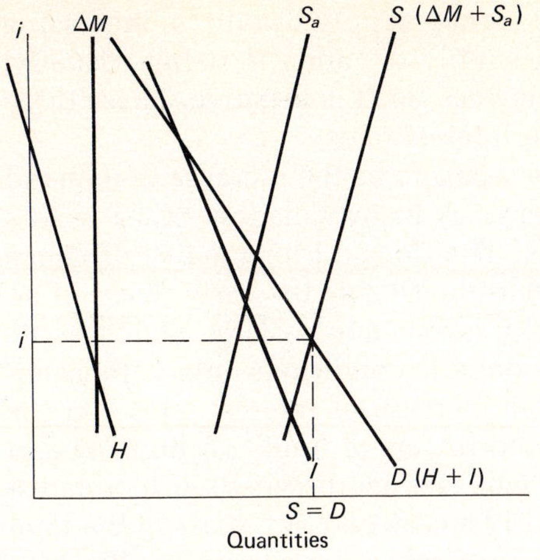

Fig. 14-2 Loanable funds interest theory.

this kind of interpretation can be given to either an increase or a decrease in any of the factors dealt with in our discussion. Some practice at this type of exercise is helpful.

A shortcoming of this analysis is that it assumes a given total demand and expectations. Yet the very developments whose impact on the interest rate we are discussing would cause total demand to change. If the rate of growth of the money supply increased, indeed, this would increase the supply of credit and reduce the interest rate, but it also would increase Y and so indirectly affect both S and I.

The loanable funds approach provides no means of dealing with such factors. It is not a *general theory* of the whole economy, but only a *partial theory* limited to the credit market. However, if one can provide from some other source an interpretation of changes in economic developments, he can use the loanable funds framework to interpret their implications for the credit market and interest rates.

To make the loanable funds approach realistic, we must again note that a large part of the demand for credit is not to finance investment goods but rather consumption and government borrowing. The latter is especially volatile and irregular and, thus, an important determinant of variations in interest rates. Moreover, a large part of investment borrowing is not for business but reflects residential mortgages. To give effect to this point, let us restate the loanable funds equation to recognize borrowing by government B_g, by consumers B_c, by business B_b, for housing B_h, and to finance speculation B_s:

$$S_a + \Delta M = H + B_g + B_c + B_b + B_h + B_s \qquad (14\text{-}2)$$

Within this framework, how would we interpret the cause of the usual increase in interest rates during an economic upswing? Ordinarily, saving is increasing in this situation, and the money supply usually is increasing more rapidly than usual. So the total supply of funds is rising. Usually, velocity of circulation is declining somewhat, so *H* is negative. These three factors all tend to make for a decline in interest rates.

The major factor on the other side seems to be the increase in demand for credit by business, which is so large as to overshadow other factors and cause an increase in interest rates. The demand for credit to finance securities speculation also may be increasing. During the early phase of an upswing, the federal government usually is financing a large deficit as its fiscal position responds to change in economic conditions only with a substantial lag. These factors also make for increase of interest rates. On the other hand, as interest rates rise, some borrowers of funds for housing and state and local government projects, who are more sensitive to interest rates than other kinds of borrowers, will be crowded out, making the total amount of credit demanded smaller than it otherwise would be. We now have a complex pattern of interacting developments, with the change in demand for credit by business seemingly playing the dominating role.

The Keynesian Theory of Interest Rates

The standard Keynesian model, we recall, provides a joint explanation of total demand and the interest rate. It has the advantage, as compared to the loanable funds framework, of tying its explanation of the interest rate into a general model of the economy and an explanation of total demand. On the other hand, it has the disadvantage of applying only to equilibrium positions—which are not conspicuously present in our economy—while the loanable funds framework can be applied to the interpretation of changing interest rates. Moreover, the loanable funds approach seems to represent the realities of the financial system in tying the demand for credit to the need of economic units to finance their expenditures. It can be interpreted as relating meaningfully to what goes on in credit markets.

One of the elements of simplification in the Keynesian model is that it does not incorporate credit markets or the need to finance expenditures before they can be made. The only financial variables in the Keynesian model are the interest rate and the supply of and demand for money. In thus interpreting the interest rate as equating, in equilibrium, the demand for money to the money supply rather than interpreting the interest rate as determined in credit markets by the supply of and demand for credit, the Keynesian theory appears to achieve its simplification at the expense of a loss of realism.

The two major ideas about the interest rate associated with the Keynesian theory have not been supported by recent research. The first is the idea, an aspect of the stagnation thesis, that continued declines in interest

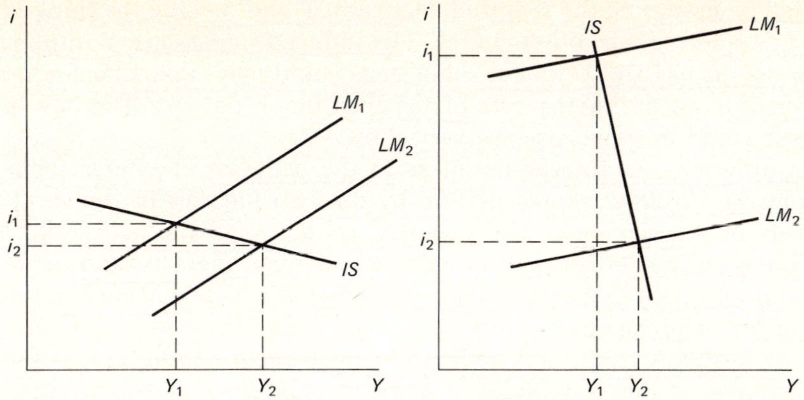

Fig. 14-3 Problems posed by the Keynesian interest theory.

rates would be necessary to permit long-run growth of total demand as the economy moved to the right along the downward-sloping *IS* curve of the left panel of Fig. 14-3. The increase in interest rates in the 1950s and 1960s, and Homer's documentation that interest rates in ancient Rome were lower than they are now, have weakened the plausibility of this idea, which now seems to reflect a misinterpretation of the implications of the Great Depression.

The other major idea, illustrated by the right-hand panel of Fig. 14-3, is that in the short run to bring about any substantial change in total demand through the use of monetary policy would require a large and permanent change in the interest rate. This raises both the question as to whether such a policy is workable, since impediments may exist to the required adjustment in interest rates, and the question as to whether it is in any case desirable, since the required changes in interest rates may have substantial adverse side effects.

A rather different picture of the effect upon interest rates of a change in the money supply is presented by the neoclassical theory. In this view, an increase in the money supply may cause some temporary decline in interest rates, but its indirect effects—which may not lag significantly behind its direct effects—will be to increase interest rates, by increasing total demand and the demand for credit. In this case, total demand can be affected by monetary policy without very large changes in interest rates. Indeed, perhaps the most significant effect upon interest rates of a change in the money supply runs in the opposite direction from the one depicted by the Keynesian theory—increasing the money supply will increase interest rates.

How is this chain of events represented within the loanable funds interest theory? Shifting the ΔM curve to right in Fig. 14-2 depicts the direct effects in lowering the interest rate. The indirect effects must be represented by assuming the required change in Y and making the implied shifts in I, S, and perhaps other curves. The induced increase in Y implies a rightward shift in I and D that at some stage could more than offset other factors, resulting in an interest rate higher than the initial one. The lags in this process could in some cases be very short.

This difference in interpretation as to the behavior of interest rates arises from the different representation by the two theories of the short-run stability of the economy. The potential instability of the neoclassical model implies indirect effects upon total demand, investment expenditures, and demand for credit that overbalance the direct effects of a change in the money supply. The Keynesian model is more stable because it does not provide for feedback from total demand to investment. Additionally, the neoclassical interest rate is depicted as more unstable since it is determined by the supply of and demand for credit to finance expenditures, while the Keynesian interest rate is determined by the money supply of and demand for money.

On this factual point as to the way the economy operates, the generally inphase movements in M, Y, and i support the neoclassical interpretation if the view is accepted that the changes in M are to an important extent independent and causal. Some empirical studies of the late 1960s seemed also to support this view. Gibson found that the indirect effects of an increase in the money supply in increasing interest rates fully offset its direct effects in lowering it within a few months.[5] But disentanglement of the causal links among these interconnected variables poses methodological problems that are far from fully solved, and our present knowledge on the matter is at best tentative.

Recent Development of Interest Theory

The major framework for the recent development of interest theory is within the dynamic models being applied to the theory of total demand. This approach can be viewed as a synthesis that weds the Keynesian theory's advantage of a general and explicit model to the neoclassical theory's dynamic nature and emphasis upon interaction processes. What has proved especially difficult to do, and largely remains for the future, is to incorporate into such dynamic models a representation of the determination of interest rates through financing flows in credit markets.

The econometric model with the best-developed financial side, the Federal Reserve-MIT model, seems to come closer than its predecessors to replicating the way interest rates respond to changes in economic developments and to changes in policy.

[5]William E. Gibson, "Interest Rates and Monetary Policy," *J. Polit. Econ.* **78**: 431–455 (1970).

The Structure of Interest Rates

The interest rates on various kinds of debts differ substantially, and the relations among these various interest rates change over time. Moreover, these interest rates, and the kinds of debt to which they apply, do not play the same role in the economy. As a result, changes in the structure of interest rates may affect total demand. Therefore, we must supplement our discussion of the general level of interest rates with a consideration of the structure of rates. Although many different categories of interest rates could be considered, the major emphasis is upon the maturity structure or term structure of rates and the risk structure.

The term structure of interest rates

The term structure of interest rates can be depicted in a yield curve such as those of Fig. 14–4. The interest rates for debts very near to maturity, short-term debts, are on the left-hand end of the curve, and on the right end the interest rates at the same date for long-term debts. The figure shows three rather common patterns. When interest rates in general are low, the yield curve sweeps upward; short-term interest rates are lower than long-term rates. At times of money stringency when interest rates are unusually high, however, short-term rates show greater volatility and move above long-term rates. Sometimes the yield curve has a hump, intermediate-term securities a few years from maturity having the highest yield.

The past behavior of the term structure of interest rates on United States government securities is shown in Fig. 3–8. We see depicted the characteristic pattern that Irving Fisher described thus:

Fig. 14–4 Interest rate yield curves.

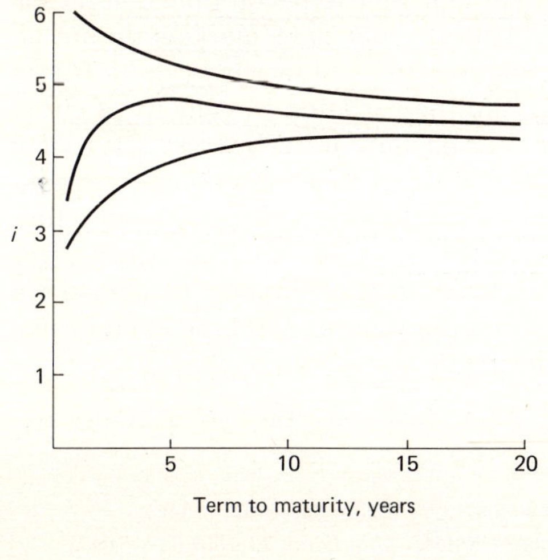

> There is a see-saw between the rates on short term and long term loans. That is, if the short term rate is greatly above the long term, it is likely to fall, or if greatly below, to rise. The long term rates thus set a rough norm for the short term rates, which are much more variable.[6]

Fisher thought short-term rates averaged lower than long-term rates because of the attractiveness to lenders of their superior liquidity.[7]

The greater volatility of the short-term yields can be explained mainly in terms of two factors: (1) Demand for short-term funds may vary more widely with changes in economic conditions, in response to changes in business inventories and in speculation. (2) A given change in yields (or "interest rates") involves a change in debt price that is nearly proportional to the duration of the debt. Thus, for long-term *yields* to be as volatile as short-term yields would imply that prices of such debt would be many times as volatile. Speculation that limits variation in debt prices probably contributes to limiting yields on long-term debt to swings narrower than those applying to short-term debt.

The economic literature relating to the term structure of interest rates in recent decades has centered about a relation that Fisher pointed out but did not represent as practically important. If people had perfect foresight, they would so behave as to bring yields from holding various equivalent investment assets to equality over any period of time. Thus, if they formulated expectations regarding future short-term rates of interest, long-term rates would be adjusted to bring the same yield as would be obtained from holding a succession of short-term debts over the same period. As was pointed out in the influential statement of this theory by Lutz,[8] if long-term interest rates are determined by the short-term rates expected over the same time period (say, 20 years and more), they would tend to be difficult to change and but little responsive to changes in monetary policy that are believed to be temporary.

Critics of this approach pointed out that such expectational determination of long-term interest rates would imply that debt markets do not effectively perform the stabilizing function they otherwise could fill in channeling savings to borrowers and limiting variation in velocity of circulation. It also was pointed out that in fact long term interest rates were not highly sticky or insensitive to temporary changes in economic conditions and policy. Moreover the effect of expectations on the rate structure depends sensitively upon the time period over which the expectations are formed, whether they are formulated with reference to short-term yields or the prices of long-term debt, and the process and kinds of information on the basis of which they are formed.[9]

[6]*The Theory of Interest*, pp. 209–210, A. M. Kelley, Publishers, New York, 1965 (first published in 1930).

[7]*Ibid.*

[8]Friedrich A. Lutz, "The Structure of Interest Rates," *Q. J. Econ.* **55**:36–63 (1940).

[9]J. M. Culbertson, "The Term Structure of Interest Rates," *Q. J. Econ.* **71**:485–517 (1957).

Ushering in an era of formal statistical studies of the interest rate structure, Meiselman demonstrated that the past behavior of the rate structure was consistent with the expectational theory as formulated by Lutz, if one assumed that expectations were formed in a certain manner.[10] A subsequent study by Malkiel demonstrated the consistency of the data with a more complex model, providing for imperfect substitutability among debts of different maturity and for formation of expectations with reference to future bond prices as well as short-term yields.[11]

On the major substantive issue, experience continues to support the view that long-term interest rates do fluctuate over a range sufficiently large to be important to lenders and borrowers and that they can respond promptly to changes in economic conditions and policy. The great increase in long-term interest rates in 1966–1969 and their declines in response to weakening in total demand in 1966–1967 and in 1970 illustrate the point. The relative importance of various patterns of economic behavior in producing this outcome and the quantitative response of the debt markets to changes in policy and economic conditions are matters that have proved difficult to pin down.

The risk structure of interest rates

The risk structure of interest rates defines the relation among yields of debts that as rated by investment analysts appear to involve different degrees of default risk. The principal measure of the risk structure of interest rates available is provided by yields on bonds that have been assigned by rating agencies to different risk categories.

Since interest rates are measured by the promised yield—the one that will be realized if there is no default on the contract—in cases where any defaults do occur, the yield actually realized on the average will be lower than this "interest rate." Such data on interest rates, therefore, must be interpreted with care, since they do not measure the yield actually received by debt holders. They do measure, however, the interest rate that has to be paid by new borrowers of this class who do not default. Consequently, they indicate the terms on which credit is available to various classes of borrowers, and aid in interpreting the restraint imposed by credit terms on the credit-financed expenditures of such borrowers.

The differential in yields between the interest rate on a low-grade debt and risk-free debt can be thought of as involving two components: (1) an allowance or reserve to compensate for the rate of default expected by lenders to occur on the average in debt of this class, and (2) a premium required to induce lenders to accept the greater risk involved in the low-

[10]David Meiselman, *The Term Structure of Interest Rates*, Prentice-Hall, Englewood Cliffs, N.J., 1962.

[11]Burton G. Malkiel, *The Term Structure of Interest Rates*, Princeton University Press, Princeton, 1966.

grade debt. The reserve for defaults required by lenders is responsive to a wide range of political and economic factors. It increases when economic conditions deteriorate or the public becomes fearful regarding the future. The premium required by lenders to hold risky debt depends on the proportion of risk lovers as against risk avoiders among lenders and on the extent to which institutions exist to reduce investment risk through pooling. An increase in the amount of risk perceived by investors to attach to debt may increase risk premiums more than proportionately by requiring risk premiums to rise high enough to induce the holding of such debt by reluctant investors who really prefer safe debt.

For both of these reasons, the differential between yields on low-grade and high-grade debt tend to widen out when economic conditions deteriorate and the default rate rises or is expected to rise. Under such conditions, changes in the interest rate on government securities are a misleading indicator of the terms on which credit is available to finance private expenditures. Some interpretations seem to have understated the influence of interest rates on investment by not looking at the relevant interest rates or noting the wide range of variation that has occurred in the terms on which credit is available to potential borrowers whose credit rating is not the highest.

Forecasting Interest Rates

Forecasting interest rates involves applying interest theory to diagnosis and prediction. In attempting to form a judgment as to the direction interest rates will move over some decades into the future one attempts to predict the factors discussed above as affecting the average level of interest rates. Changes in institutions affecting the total supply and demand for credit, tax changes, the size of the average government deficit, the average flow of capital into and out of the country—these are considerations to be weighed.

A very important consideration may be the degree of inflation and expectations regarding future inflation. In this connection, it is useful to keep in mind the concept of the real rate of interest. Sustained changes in the average rate of increase in price level probably will in the long run be at least partially reflected in the nominal level of interest rates.

Short-run swings in interest rates derive mainly from economic fluctuations. As a consequence, the interest rate forecast must be made jointly with an economic forecast. The usual framework for forecasting changes in interest rates is a set of estimates of the sources and uses of loan funds much like the one applied conceptually in the loanable funds theory of interest. In realistic analysis, the sources of funds are broken down by type of lender, as was done in the flow of funds accounts reviewed in Chap. 5. If it appears that under the assumed economic conditions the demand for funds will outrun the supply, this indicates an upward movement in interest rates.

Important factors causing short-run change in the supply-demand balance in the credit markets are changes in the rate at which funds are provided from money creation by the commercial banks and Federal Reserve banks and changes in the net borrowing demands of the federal government.

This kind of approach can be applied not only to the total prospective flow of credit but also to particular markets: the market for long-term funds in general, the mortgage market that is a sector of this, and the money market. This permits judgments to be formed not only as to whether interest rates will move upward or downward but also as to the relations among developments in various submarkets. Insofar as efforts to incorporate financial markets into dynamic economic models prove to be successful, increasing use probably will be made in the future of more formal systems of forecasting interest rates and financial conditions with such models.

SUMMARY

1. Major economic functions of interest rates are (1) guiding investment decisions and performing a rationing function to permit simultaneous full employment of capital and labor, (2) guiding the choice among particular projects and, thus, affecting the efficiency and progressiveness of the economy, and (3) rationing spending power over time and, thus, contributing to limiting fluctations of total demand.

2. For some purposes the real rate of interest, the rate of interest after adjustment for changes in the value of money, is more significant than the stated or nominal rate of interest.

3. To be consistent with economic stability, the nominal rate of interest should change to reflect changes in the attractiveness of investment opportunities and the willingness of the public to borrow. The interest rate that at any time would be consistent with economic stability was termed by Wicksell the natural rate of interest.

4. The average level of interest rates can be interpreted as reflecting the sets of factors determining the total demand by the public and the government to be in debt and by the willingness of the public to save and to hold wealth in the form of debt.

5. The loanable funds interest theory applies the usual supply and demand approach to interpretation of factors governing the supply of credit and the demand for credit.

6. Short-term interest rates fluctuate over a wider range than long-term rates (though they show less fluctuation in *prices* of the debts), both moving roughly together in response to economic fluctuations, and are lower except when interest rates in general are unusually high.

7. Interest rates on low-grade debt rise when there is an increase in the expected rate of defaults on debts, and so are an index of confidence in future economic developments.

8. Forecasting of interest rates is done through an integrated economic-financial forecast in which a major role is played by expected economic developments and by monetary and fiscal policies.

QUESTIONS FOR REVIEW AND DISCUSSION

1. "Since the interest rate is an important determinant of economic activity, a good way for the central bank to stabilize economic activity is to stabilize the interest rate, picking a reasonable interest rate such as 4 percent and then preventing disruptive fluctuations in the interest rates." Comment critically.

2. Invent hypothetical situations that would lead to a long-run decline in the interest rate. Try to illustrate all the major economic and political factors that are relevant.

3. Show diagrammatically the long-run effect upon the interest rate of an invention that makes factory production of furniture more efficient than hand production; of an invention that permits the same volume of steel to be produced with a plant only half as costly.

4. Explain with its equation and diagram the loanable funds interest theory. Show the direct effects upon the interest rate of an increase in saving; of a reduction in the rate of increase of the money supply.

5. Use the loanable funds approach to explain the direct and indirect effects upon the interest rate of an increase in the rate of growth of the money supply.

6. "The Keynesian theory demonstrates conclusively that an increase in the money supply can increase total demand only by reducing the interest rate." Indicate the objections that could be raised to this statement and the way the Keynesian theory could be modified to produce a different outcome.

7. Discuss in terms of ideas covered earlier in the course factors limiting the substitutability between long-term and short-term debt.

8. Describe the usual behavior of the term structure of interest rates.

9. "The pure rate of interest, or the rate applying to risk-free debt, is the only fundamental measure of the influence of credit factors in the economy." Comment critically.

10. Explain in detail why the spread in yields between low-grade and high-grade debt widened during the early 1930s and why it gradually narrowed after the Second World War.

11. Make and explain a forecast of changes in long-term and short-term interest rates over the coming year.

15 total demand, inflation, and unemployment

The price of any particular good we expect to adjust so as to clear the market; to equate the quantity demanded to the quantity supplied. Existence of excess demand, or shortages, indicates that the price should rise to the point where it rations the available goods and eliminates the shortage. Similarly, excess supply implies that the price should decline to the point at which all who want to sell are able to do so. If shortages or excess supply do not exist in individual markets, they will not exist in markets in general. They are prevented by changes in the general level of prices, which is nothing more than the average of the prices that adjust as required to clear their particular markets.

This picture seems to fit the way the world actually works when confronted by excess demand. An excessive growth of total demand does not lead to generalized and persistent shortages. Rather, prices and wage rates adjust upward to clear markets, the general price level rises, and we have inflation. Given the excessive total demand, inflation probably is preferable to persistent shortages. Serious economic costs might attach to a situation in which a favored ingroup of buyers is able to buy at low prices while an unfortunate outgroup is unable to buy at all.

When total demand declines or becomes insufficient to support the existing price level, however, we are not in the modern world accustomed to expect the price level to decline. We expect surpluses or excess supply that businesses would like to sell at the existing prices but cannot. More strikingly, we expect surpluses of labor, or unemployment, large numbers of people who would like to have jobs at the existing level of wages and salaries but cannot get them.

If the price level can rise but not fall, the long-run expectation is for inflation on the average. Moreover, the inability of the price level to adjust downward implies that individual markets are not operating as they are depicted in our rational version of an economic system. Questions are raised as to what lies behind this kind of economic performance, what its implications are, and what can be done about it.

This inability of the price level to decline is for the United States a recent thing. Before the 1930s, the usual peacetime performance of the United States economy involved declining prices. The price level declined by more than one-half over a period of decades after the War of 1812, the Civil War, and the First World War. Despite the great inflations caused by these major wars, the Wholesale Price Index in the United States was lower in the early 1930s than it was in 1800. As late as 1920, United States consumer prices declined by about 15 percent in a single year. But an example of a case in which prices did not adjust downward in response to excess supply was the United States after 1933. With around 10 million men out of work and an unemployment rate of around 20 percent, the price level after 1933 was *rising* rapidly. This was perhaps a unique combination of great unemployment with inflation.

The prevalent behavior of present-day economies seems to involve not only resistances to reductions in wages and prices but even—as in the 1930s—increases in wages and prices in the face of substantial unemployment of labor and industrial capacity. This implies that perfect control of total demand would not assure full employment and price stability. If the growth rate of total demand were set to produce price stability, it might generate large unemployment; if it were chosen to bring full employment, this might involve rapid inflation. The makers of monetary and fiscal policy, thus, would face a dilemma, a choice among second bests. We ask, then, how can this aspect of economic performance be characterized? what factors determine it? and what policies are relevant to changing it?

The Short-run Unemployment-Inflation Trade-off: The Phillips Curve

The usual way of depicting the performance of an economy at any particular time with reference to unemployment and the rate of change in price level is "the Phillips curve" (Fig. 15–1).[1] This depicts for each hypothetical unemployment rate the associated rate of change in the price level (or in wage rates, as in Phillips' original study). The slope of the curve over any range defines the short-run trade-off between unemployment and inflation, the change in the inflation rate that would accompany a given change in the unemployment rate. The height of the curve in the full-employment zone indicates whether full employment is consistent with price stability. If we sketch in a "target zone" involving, say, not more than 4 percent unemployment and not more than 1 percent per year change in price level, we see that curve P_1P_1 passes above the zone. This indicates that when the economy is operated at the desired unemployment rates, it generates in-

[1] Although the idea goes back earlier, the label derives from an empirical study by A. W. Phillips, "The Relation between Unemployment and the Rate of Change of Money Wages in the United Kingdom, 1861–1957," *Economica, New Series*, **25**:283–299 (1958).

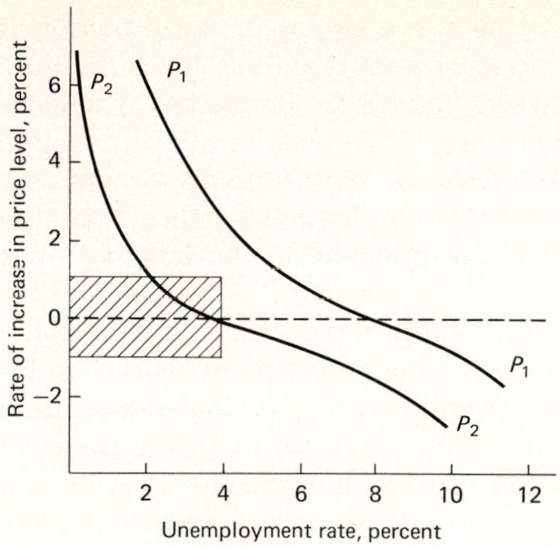

Fig. 15-1 Phillips curves.

flation. Or, picking points further to the right on the curve, if the economy is operated in such a manner as to generate price stability, it has a high unemployment rate.

Through control over the growth rate of total demand, the government can shift the economy along the relevant Phillips curve or can pick whatever point it wishes and keep the economy there. To move to the left, or to stay at a point further to the left, requires a more rapid rate of growth of total demand. To stabilize the economy at any point on the curve involves providing the rate of growth of total demand that will just buy total output with stable unemployment (an output that is rising because of growth of the labor force and of productivity) with the average prices of output changing as indicated by the Phillips curve. To stay at a point further to the left on the curve requires more rapid growth of total demand because of the more rapid rate increase in the prices at which goods and services are to be bought.

Control over total demand, if it is sufficiently accurate, thus permits the government to put the economy where it wants on the relevant Phillips curve, but of course does not permit it to choose a point that is not on the curve. The Phillips curve is a useful way of representing the dilemma faced by many governments in that nothing they do with total demand through monetary and fiscal policies will, at least in the short run, bring price stability and full employment. Such a Phillips curve confronts the authorities with a range of second-best choices. It requires them to decide how much price stability they want to buy by having unemployment, or how much reduction in unemployment they want to buy by having more inflation. The decision is complicated by the fact, as we see later, that today's choice will affect the possibilities among which the government can choose in later periods.

The basic reasons why the Phillips curve slopes in the direction it does are the ones that explain the slope of supply curves for individual markets. Excess demand leads to wage and price increases. A greater quantity will be supplied only at higher prices.[2] Indeed, the Phillips curve would look like an aggregate supply curve for the economy, except that since the horizontal axis is assigned to unemployment rather than the employment rate (and larger quantities supplied lie to the left) it slopes in the opposite direction.

While Phillip's key study seemed to support the existence of a stable relation that applied over long periods of time, subsequent work has indicated the contrary. The view now most widely accepted is that a Phillips curve may be drawn to indicate the unemployment-inflation trade-off prevailing in any particular short period of time, but that this curve shifts in response to experience. In fact, the center of discussion in recent years is the question as to what causes the short-run Phillips curve to shift, how effective alternative policies would be in shifting it downward (or to the left) into a position that would make full employment compatable with price stability (as would P_2P_2 in Fig. 15–1), and the nature of the long-run relation between unemployment and inflation.

Determinants of the Position of the Phillips Curve

In relation both to economic theory and to desired economic performance, what is anomalous about the kind of Phillips curves that seem to predominate in recent decades is that they sit so high in the diagram and pass above the target zone. It would not be surprising for wage rates and prices to rise when demand exceeded supply at the existing price,[3] but the Phillips curves in question imply that the price level rises *when there is excess supply*, when there are unrequited sellers at the existing price. This leads to a contrast between the position of an ingroup of workers and other sellers who can sell at rising prices and an outgroup who cannot sell at all, the unemployed. The focal question is why prices rise when there is unemployment, and what institutional changes or policy actions would prevent this and make full employment consistent with price stability.

[2]Bent Hansen, "Excess Demand, Unemployment, Vacancies, and Wages," *Q. J. Econ.*, **84**: 1–23 (1970); Edmund S. Phelps, "Money-Wage Dynamics and Labor-Market Equilibrium," *J. Polit. Econ.*, **76**:678–711 (1968); and Frank Brechling, "The Trade-off between Inflation and Unemployment," *J. Polit. Econ.*, **76**:712–735 (1968).

[3]In an economy of rising efficiency, price stability implies a certain rate of increase in wage rates. If output per man-hour were increasing 2 percent per year, then wage increases of 2 percent would stabilize labor cost per unit of output and be consistent with price stability. The discussion here is put mainly in terms of the rate of price level change. For the United States economy, any given rate of increase in the price level generally implies an increase in wage rates (including fringe benefits) at least two percentage points higher.

Immobility and market imperfections

The labor market is far from being a perfect market for a standardized product. It is not *a* market at all, but a conglomerate of innumerable markets for various kinds of services in various localities. Because of the inevitable imperfection of the market, it is not surprising that there are unfilled vacancies, which push up wage rates, in some localities or some occupations even though there is unemployment in others. This is true because it is not practically possible to achieve a perfect matching of unemployed workers and unfilled vacancies. One reason for this is that it takes some time for workers to move from one job to another. Such "frictional" unemployment may amount to several percent of the labor force.

This aspect of the labor market—and it applies to some extent in other markets as well—is illuminated by the presentation of Bent Hansen[4] shown in Fig. 15-2. The *DD* and *SS* curves show the amounts of labor that are offered and demanded at various wage rates in a local labor market. In practice, however, it is not possible to achieve a position on the demand curve, which would imply the absence of unfilled vacancies. There are always some employers who have vacancies at the going wage rate that they have not yet filled. Similarly, a point on the supply curve cannot be achieved, for there are always some workers who are between jobs. The simultaneous existence of unemployment and unfilled vacancies, therefore, is a normal state of affairs in the case of a nonhomogeneous product like labor services in an economy in which change is always occurring.

[4]*Op. cit.*, p. 7.

Fig. 15-2 Unemployment and vacancies.

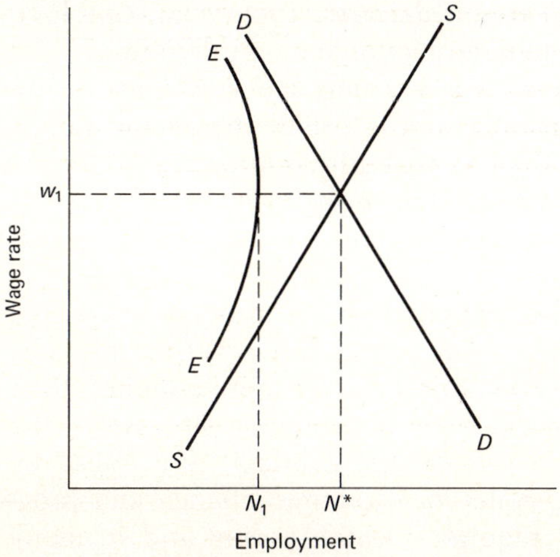

In Fig. 15–2, the *EE* curve depicts the set of positions that are attainable in a given economy with a given set of institutions. The number of vacancies that would exist at any wage rate is depicted by the distance between the relevant points on *EE* and *DD*, while unemployment is measured by the distance between *EE* and *SS*. Wage rate W_1 would involve no vacancies and no unemployment if this were a perfect market, with employment at N^*. Because of market imperfections and immobilities, however, this wage rate involves both unemployment and vacancies, which in this case are equal at $N^* - N_1$. Lower wage rates would involve less unemployment and more vacancies, the latter exceeding the former; higher wage rates would have the opposite effect. The Phillips curve does not provide information on vacancies, but only unemployment.

The aspect of the relation between unemployment and inflation that is illuminated by this diagram is the role of immobilities and market imperfections. Improving markets and reducing immobilities would shift the *EE* curve to the right, making it possible to get more of the unemployed workers into the vacant slots, thereby reducing the level of unemployment consistent with any given behavior of wage rates. Consequently, shifting the *EE* curve to the right would shift the Phillips curve to the left. Attention, therefore, is called to that heterogeneous set of factors that impede the matching of unemployed workers with job vacancies.

The inability of the unemployed to fill existing vacancies and prevent upward wage push stems in part from imperfections of the labor market. Mechanisms for providing the information required for speedy job transfers may be inadequate. Information and arrangements to facilitate geographical shifts of workers may be lacking. There may be an imbalance between the kinds of vacancies available and the training, skills, and abilities of the unemployed. This would be especially severe during periods of rapid change in labor demands and labor migrations such as the movement from the South to Northern cities in recent decades. Factors causing high labor turnover also would contribute to large frictional unemployment.

Perfect matching of unemployed workers and job vacancies is not possible. Therefore, zero unemployment is not a feasible target for policy. The reasonable unemployment target is one that allows for some minimum amount of frictional unemployment associated with the shifts of workers among jobs and the search period of new entrants into the labor market before they find jobs suited to them.

The amount of such frictional unemployment must be expected to vary between nations and within a given nation between time periods. In the United States, shifts of workers among jobs are more common than in other economies. This has commonly been viewed as a strength of the United States economy, insofar as it reflects the availability of jobs, the adaptability of workers, and the existence of economic change and progress. But if such shifts among jobs require a search period and in many cases a geographical move, they will involve temporary unemployment. Thus, as among countries and time periods, the more mobile the labor force, the higher the amount of frictional unemployment that must be expected.[5]

The amount of frictional unemployment also depends upon the age structure of workers. Young people first entering the labor force take longer to find jobs and change jobs more frequently than older workers who are more firmly settled in a particular job and have earned seniority. This implies that an increase in the proportion of young people in the labor force should be expected to push the Phillips curve to the right (and to push the *EE* curve in Fig. 15–2 to the left) and perhaps require acceptance of a larger figure for unemployment as par for the course. One study estimated that from the mid-1950s to 1970 such shift in the composition of the United States labor force accounted for an upward shift in the Phillips curve of 1.7 percentage points in the area of 4 percent unemployment. This study estimated that in the mid-1950s the inflation rate consistent with 4 percent unemployment was 2.8 percent, but that shifts in labor-force composition had raised it in 1970 to 4.5 percent.[6]

So far as poor matching of unemployed workers and vacancies stems from these factors, the policies relevant to shifting the Phillips curve to the left are those relating to improvement of employment information, facilitation of mobility, and training of workers.[7] Policies aimed at such improvements have been adopted in the United States in recent years.

Institutional, legal, and political factors

To minimize unemployment of labor is a formidable organizational task. It involves getting every potential worker to a job that he can do at a wage that he can earn and will accept. If substantial changes in the structure of jobs are required, these may necessitate a process of bumping that involves many moves. For example, when untrained workers from the South moved to Northern cities, they might have been expected to bump other workers upward into more demanding jobs, taking over those requiring the least skill until their experience suited them for other types of work. Such a process of bumping, however, may require many moves before everyone settles down in his appropriate niche. For it to occur, the structure of wages and other employment inducements must be able to bring about the needed job shifts.

Modern labor-market institutions are not suited to performing this

[5]The turnover rate is higher in the United States than in most other countries. Within the United States, it appears to differ among types of workers, for a rather different set of reasons. Voluntary quit rates, layoff rates, and, as a consequence, turnover rates have been higher for Negroes and women than for white males, thus explaining the higher average unemployment rates for these groups. Robert E. Hall, "Why is the Unemployment Rate So High at Full Employment?" *Brookings Pap. Econ. Act.*, **3**:393–396 (1970).

[6]George L. Perry, "Changing Labor Markets and Inflation," *ibid.*, p. 433.

[7]An interpretation emphasizing these factors is Charles C. Holt, C. Duncan MacRae, Stuart O. Schweitzer, and Ralph E. Smith, *The Unemployment-Inflation Dilemma: A Manpower Solution*, The Urban Institute, Washington, D.C., 1971.

task. The structure of wages is heavily influenced by the relative power of labor unions and similar trade and professional organizations. Seniority provisions, pension rights, and other institutions limit the willingness of workers to shift jobs. In many occupations and professions, the wage rate is not related to the demands of the job but to impediments that have been erected by insiders to limit competition.

In this situation, a new group of unskilled workers may find that the jobs for which they can potentially compete are occupied by well-protected, high-wage workers that they cannot displace by wage competition. If the competition of the new workers in the limited number of occupations open to them drives the wage in this area very low, the workers may be prohibited from employment by minimum wage legislation.

The institutions of the labor market were designed mainly with an eye to the direct benefits conferred on workers receiving certain protections and privileges. They were designed to protect the "job security" and to raise the incomes of the employed, with little attention to their implications for the opportunities open to others. These institutions contribute to explaining the high Phillips curve and the wage-push problem.

Policies aimed at these causes of wage push may go in more than one direction. One class of policy attempts to move toward more competitive markets, reducing the power of labor unions, trade associations, and professional associations to protect their members at the expense of outsiders. Another course, from a political point of view an opposite one, is to impose wage and price controls and override private power in this way by government power. Intermediate courses also are possible.

Markup inflation and excessive income claims

A closely related aspect of the price-push problem is highlighted by Ackley's concept of *markup inflation*.[8] Many prices and wages are in an immediate sense set by businesses and labor and professional organizations essentially on the basis of a markup over costs or of some conception of the relative income that the seller ought to get. That is, the plumber's union has an idea of what plumber's incomes ought to be in relation to those of others, General Motors has an idea of what its profit rate ought to be, the local medical association has an idea what kinds of income physicians ought to receive. The difficulty is that when these various claims against society's total income are added up, they sum to more than there is to divide up, to more than 100 percent of total real output.

As a consequence, an equilibrium position where everyone is satisfied with his income is not possible—unless some groups' demands are adjusted downward. But the way the economy performs depends on the game to which these excessive claims give rise. The game is that each seller group raises its selling price in an effort to get its desired income. This contributes

[8] Gardner Ackley, *Macroeconomic Theory*, pp. 453–459, Macmillan, New York, 1961.

to inflation that reduces the real income of others and leads them to push up their selling prices. Since the income claims being asserted by increases in selling prices add up to more than 100 percent, the game never ends.

The playing of this game, of course, implies that the price setters have some way of preventing or limiting the undercutting of their prices by outsiders. The reason why economic slack and enlarged unemployment reduce the rate of inflation is that they increase the ranks of outsiders who are potential price cutters. Some groups are thus deterred from pushing up their selling prices; otherwise, the Phillips curve (so far as it is governed by this factor) would be horizontal. But groups that have built strong impediments against any invasion of their domain by outsiders may be quite undeterred by economic slack from pushing up their income claims. Policy actions and institutional changes that will reduce this cause of an adverse Phillips curve are those that will reduce the income claims of price-setting groups or will reduce their power to exclude outsiders—including the unemployed—from access to markets.

Factors causing wage-push: Excessive demands

The wage rates and employment conditions that the economy can offer are limited by its productivity. Workers will not be hired at wage rates that add more to their employers' costs than they do to receipts. Growth of the idea that service and laboring employment is menial and unsatisfactory, along with improvement in welfare payments, reportedly have had some effect in increasing unemployment resulting from workers declining to accept the kinds of jobs open to them.

Economic instability as a cause of wage-price push

Since wage rates probably are in the short run more flexible upward than downward, economic fluctuations tend to add to wage push. If wage rates rise more rapidly during prosperity than they decline during recession, this leads to an upward wage ratchet over time. Shifts in demand among industries caused by economic fluctuations have a similar effect if wage rates rise more rapidly in industries with strong demand than they decline in industries with weak demand. This effect is especially strong if wage rates in other parts of the economy tend to follow those in the industries where they are increasing most rapidly. Insofar as an unfavorable Phillips curve arises from this factor, it could be improved by reducing economic fluctuations by more effective control over the growth rate of total demand.

Inflationary expectations: Lagging effects of prior inflation

Another reason for an unfavorable Phillips curve is because of the lagging effects of inflation in an earlier period. The earlier inflation could have been caused by excessive total demand, as was true of that of the mid-

1960s. One recent study interprets the lagging effects of prior inflation as operating through two channels:

1. Increases in prices and wages in response to excess demand occur with a lag, reflecting in part the fact that those who set prices want to see that the increase in demand is not purely temporary before raising prices and lags in adjustment of labor contracts and other contracts.

2. Prices are pushed up by increases in prices of inputs—raw materials, parts, utilities—this process operating only with a lag. A model explaining the rate of increase in the price level as reflecting the lagging effects of earlier demand pressure was successful in closely predicting variation in the rate of change in prices during 1956–1970.[9]

Another approach to explaining an unfavorable Phillips curve as reflecting prior inflation emphasizes the role of expected future price increases as determining demands for wage increases and anticipatory increases in product prices. One version of such a theory also proved to do a good job as a statistical explanation of changes in the inflation rate,[10] but the two theories have such similar implications as to be difficult to distinguish in statistical studies.[11] For if expectations of future price increases derive from past experience with actual price increases, price increases reflecting such expectations would occur in much the same way as increases involving other types of lagging response to inflation.

It seems clear that the Phillips curve must reflect the earlier rate of inflation because of both lagging price and wage adjustments and expectational factors. This implies that if a nation permits a gradual acceleration of inflation, say, from 2 percent per year to 10 to 20 percent, its short-run Phillips curve will shift upward. In fact, countries that have very high inflation rates sustained over a long period of time do not seem to have lower unemployment rates than others. Moreover, when a country accustomed to 30 percent per year inflation tries to slow down the inflation rate, say, to 20 percent by slowing the growth rate of total demand, it experiences the same kind of increase in unemployment as does a country trying to slow inflation from 3 to 2 percent. That is, its experience seems interpretable in terms of a Phillips curve of the usual shape but sitting very high in the diagram, normal unemployment rates being associated not with 3 percent inflation but rather with 30 percent inflation.

The long-run equilibrium unemployment rate

If the Phillips curve thus shifts in response to the actual rate of inflation, this raises questions as to the kinds of time patterns of changes

[9]Ray C. Fair, "Aggregate Price Changes and Price Expectations," *Fed. Reserve Bank St. Louis Rev.*, p. 19, November 1970.

[10]Leonall C. Andersen and Keith M. Carlson, "A Monetarist Model for Economic Stabilization," *Fed. Reserve Bank St. Louis Rev.*, pp. 7–25, April 1970.

[11]This is pointed out in Fair, *op. cit.*, pp. 26–28.

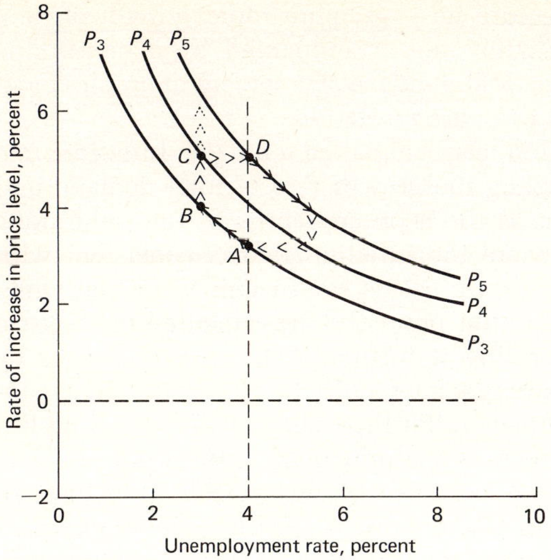

Fig. 15–3 Shifts in the Phillips curve.

in unemployment and inflation that may occur. On any given Phillips curve, there will be only one point that can be sustained over a period of time. This is the point at which the actual inflation rate is equal to the one underlying the existing Phillips curve, so the curve itself does not shift. In Fig. 15–3, Phillips curve P_3 will persist only so long as actual inflation is 3 percent per year, since only this experience produces the expectations and the lagging responses consistent with the economic performance represented in the curve. Accordingly, if total demand grows at just the rate consistent with 3 percent inflation and 4 percent unemployment, the situation can continue unchanged indefinitely.

What would happen if the government decided to reduce the unemployment rate by increasing the growth rate of total demand? This would shift the economy to the left along Phillips curve P_3, say, to point B, involving 3 percent unemployment and 4 percent inflation. The existence of 4 percent inflation leads, after some lag, to replacement of Phillips curve P_3 by P_4, which reflects the behavior that arises from 4 percent inflation.[12]

One pattern of developments from this point involves a further acceleration of growth of total demand in order to maintain the 3 percent unemployment. This now involves a 5 percent inflation rate. But this experience undermines Phillips curve P_4 and leads to its replacement by P_5, which then requires further acceleration of growth of total demand and 6 percent inflation to stay at 3 percent unemployment. In this model, an effort to keep the economy at 3 percent unemployment by accelerating

[12]The study by George L. Perry (*op. cit.*, pp. 428–431) does not find support for "the accelerationist theory" in the recent behavior of wage rates through 1970, but this could reflect only the existence of a substantial lag in the early stages of the process.

growth of total demand will require an ever more rapid growth of total demand and an ever-rising inflation rate accompanied by a continuing upward shift in the Phillips curve. Maintenance of 3 percent unemployment requires not *rapid* inflation but *accelerating* inflation.

The acceleration of inflation can be halted and the inflation rate stabilized at any time by stabilizing the growth rate of total demand and permitting rising unemployment as the economy shifts to the right along a Phillips curve to the point where the inflation rate is consistent with the expectations underlying the curve. Let us say in Fig. 15–3 that when the inflation rate reached 5 percent at point *C* it was decided to stabilize the inflation rather than accelerating it further. This could be done by permitting the increase in unemployment required to hold the actual inflation rate at 5 percent, as defined by Phillips curve P_5. In the simplest case, this requires again 4 percent unemployment, and point *D*, once reached, is a sustainable position. Because of this historical pattern of developments, the sustainable point is now 4 percent unemployment with 5 percent—rather than the initial 3 percent—inflation. The temporary period of low unemployment left a potentially permanent increase in the inflation rate.

What would be required to get back again to the original position? To bring Phillips curve P_3 back to reality requires reducing the actual inflation rate to 3 percent. This can be done, in terms of this simple model, by reducing the growth rate of total demand and permitting an increase in unemployment above 4 percent. As illustrated, letting the unemployment rate rise above 4 percent would shift the economy back to P_4 and then to P_3, permitting finally a return to the initial position *A*, with its 4 percent unemployment and 3 percent inflation. How long a period of high unemployment would this require? It depends on the length of the lags in adjustment of the Phillips curve to price experience. This is a point of some importance for policy, but one on which knowledge is limited.

At each rate of inflation there is some unemployment rate that leads to just enough increase in wage rates to perpetuate the inflation rate, thus leading to no change in expectations. It is conceivable, although not inevitable, that this unemployment rate is the same for all rates of inflation. In Fig. 15–3 this "long-run equilibrium unemployment rate" is depicted as 4 percent for all rates of inflation, shown as a vertical line in the diagram. In this case, the rate of inflation or deflation can always be stabilized by bringing about a behavior of total demand that will keep the unemployment rate at 4 percent, as was done in the illustration in shifting from point *C* to point *D*, and later to point *A*. Thus, the economy could continue indefinitely with 4 percent unemployment and 30 percent per year inflation or 4 percent per year unemployment and 2 percent per year inflation, or even 4 percent unemployment and 5 percent per year deflation or reduction in the price level. But to maintain permanently any unemployment rate smaller than 4 percent would require a continued acceleration of inflation.

Even if the view is accepted that the long-run relation between inflation and unemployment is described by a vertical long-run Phillips curve, it may be that the relation thus depicted applies in some cases only after a very long period of time for adjustment. If for periods of time measured even in decades this relation does not hold, this slowness of adjustment must be kept in mind. Some economists have argued that even in the long run the relevant relation is not a vertical line and that the long-run Phillips curve also sweeps upward to the left.[13]

Accepting for the sake of discussion the proposition that under a state of full adjustment the vertical Phillips curve is relevant, what is it that determines for a particular society whether its equilibrium unemployment rate is 2 percent or 5 percent.[14] All the factors discussed earlier would be relevant. Policy actions and institutional changes that would improve the effectiveness of the labor market and other markets, shifting the *EE* curve in Fig. 15–2 to the right and permitting unemployed workers to be fitted into vacancies, would shift both the long-run equilibrium unemployment rate and the Phillips curve to the left, permitting long-run operation with a lower unemployment rate. The relative effectiveness of such policy actions in shifting the equilibrium unemployment rate, however, depends upon the initial situation of the particular economy and is a matter on which present knowledge is limited.

Inflation and policy: Dance today, pay later

This interpretation indicates why policy actions leading to inflation may be attractive in the short run but costly in the long run. The immediate effect of acceleration of growth of total demand is to reduce unemployment, cause general prosperity, and make everyone happy. This is especially so if there is some lag before the inflation begins to show up, as generally is the case. In the longer run, the economy is left with a higher rate of inflation, but unless it is willing to accelerate the inflation rate—which is not feasible for very long—it does not have the reduced unemployment and the unusual prosperity. After a time, the economy is worse off than at the start, having no less unemployment but more inflation.

An interpretation such as this underlies the long-held view that there is a political temptation toward inflation. That is, unless the general public is very wise and self-disciplined, a government can always make

[13]See Holt and others, *op. cit.* In this interpretation, the long-run Phillips curve can be either more or less steeply sloping than the short-run curve.

[14]An expository article on this approach is Roger W. Spencer, "The Relation between Prices and Employment: Two Views," *Fed. Reserve Bank St. Louis Rev.*, pp. 15–21, March 1969. Major contributions to this approach were Edmund S. Phelps, "Phillips Curves, Expectations of Inflation and Optimal Unemployment over Time," *Economica*, **34**:254–281 (1967); and Milton Friedman, "The Role of Monetary Policy," *Am. Econ. Rev.*, **58**:10 (1968). An empirical study supporting the approach is Robert E. Lucas, Jr. and Leonard A. Rapping, "Price Expectations and the Phillips Curve," *Am. Econ. Rev.*, **59**:342–350 (1969).

itself temporarily popular by initiating an inflationary policy. When the costs of the policy come along later, they may fall upon another political party, or it may be possible politically to blame them on something else. It was this kind of thinking that led to the practice of making the central bank independent of the government and organizing it in a way that was expected to free it from political pressures and make its behavior responsive to the long-run needs of the economy.

Wage-price experience in 1970 and 1971

The behavior of prices in 1970 and 1971 was worse than seemed consistent with the ideas summed up in the Phillips curve. Unemployment rose during 1970 close to 6 percent, but inflation did not decelerate. Prices kept rising by about 5 percent per year. As one observer put it: "Economists of all persuasions, monetarists and fiscalists alike, have been surprised by the stubborn refusal of the U. S. rate of inflation to decelerate during 1970. . . . The significant rise in unemployment in 1970, accompanied by a virtually unchanged rate of inflation, contrasts with the inverse relation between inflation and unemployment—known as the Phillips curve—that is usually assumed by economists, including the administration game-plan strategists."[15] The situation had improved little by August 1971.

The ideas reviewed above provide the basis for a number of different interpretations of the unfavorable 1970–1971 case, which have rather different policy implications. One kind of interpretation is that the Phillips curve shifted upward as a result of earlier inflation and would shift back down again as a result of higher unemployment, but that this happened only with a lag and would occur in 1971. Or the adverse 1970 experience might be explained in terms of deceleration of growth of productivity, which would later be reversed with favorable effects in 1971. A more pessimistic interpretation is that the Phillips curve had shifted upward because of changes in the structure of the labor force or lasting behavioral shifts and would not shift back down, continuing to face policy makers in coming years with an extremely unfavorable trade-off between inflation and unemployment. Another type of interpretation rejects the whole idea of the Phillips curve and its implication that there is a consistent trade-off between inflation and unemployment. The experiment was ended in August 1971 when President Nixon imposed a 90-day freeze on wages and prices.

Policy toward Wage-Price Push

The situation represented by an adverse short-run Phillips curve is a legitimate target of policy actions because it precludes a satisfactory per-

[15]Robert J. Gordon, "Prices in 1970: The Horizontal Phillips Curve?" *ibid.*, p. 449. A factor contributing to the adverse outcome pointed out in this paper is an unusually low rate of increase in productivity from mid-1968 to 1970.

formance by the economy, since it makes full employment inconsistent with price stability. The relative effectiveness of various policy actions and institutional changes in correcting this situation depends upon the causal system that underlies it. Insofar as the high Phillips curve reflects the lagging effects of prior inflation or the exercise of power by economic interest groups, for example, programs to retrain the unemployed may have practically no beneficial effect. An accurate assessment of the usefulness of the various policy actions that might be taken depends on an accurate characterization of the causes of the wage-price push situation.

To take a dose of each kind of policy medicine that has been proposed is not a satisfactory course, for some of them may have side effects worse than the problem they purport to cure. On the other hand, it seems reasonable to believe that the wage-price push situation arises from a complex interaction process involving a number of factors, and some of the proposed action process involving a number of factors, and some of the proposed corrective actions may be mutually supportive rather than being properly regarded as mutually exclusive.

Different economic theories and political philosophies lead to distinguishable strategies of approach to inflation. An approach oriented toward improvement of the performance of markets and minimization of direct governmental controls emphasizes a strict control over the growth rate of total demand to prevent episodes of politically motivated inflation that then have lagging effects, along with limitation of the power of interest groups to protect their privileges and push up their selling prices at the expense of outsiders. The logic of this approach is that within a framework of proper behavior of total demand and appropriate rules of the game for economic dealings with inflation problem would be brought under control. Proponents of this approach believe that detailed governmental programs designed to correct various symptoms of inflation may in the end damage the economy more than inflation.

An opposite strategy places more emphasis on direct government programs relating to inflation. Relevant policies are "incomes policies," which may mean informational programs such as wage-price guideposts or systems of wage and price controls; retraining and education programs for unemployed workers; and more governmental responsibility for labor market information, for bringing about geographical movement of workers, and for providing guaranteed jobs.

Incomes policies

The prevalence of inflation seemingly associated with wage-price push led in the 1960s to increased interest in incomes policies, policies to limit the upward pressure of incomes, wages, and costs. The goal of incomes policies has been more clear than the means that would suffice to accomplish it, but the term commonly is used to include three classes of policies involving different degrees of government intervention in the determination of wages and prices: moral suasion, wage-price guideposts, and wage and price controls.

Moral suasion, or the "jawbone approach," attempts to use public opinion and the sense of responsibility of setters of wages and prices to induce them to moderate their demand and lessen wage-price push problems. This approach is most relevant to a problem that arises from excessive income claims, such as the type discussed earlier under the label of markup inflation.

A shortcoming of moral suasion is that it does not define principles that even the conscientious price setter can apply to determine how in his own case to distinguish a justified from an unjustified increase in the wage or price. The Council of Economic Advisers in 1962 undertook to provide such wage-price guideposts. The general rule was that the average increase in wage rates (including fringe benefits) should equal the increase in productivity for the economy as a whole. This implies that product prices should decline in industries with an above-average increase in productivity and should rise in industries with a below-average rise of productivity. Supplementary rules provided that wages and prices could rise by more than the standard amount where shortages existed but should rise by less where there were surpluses.[16]

The effect of these rules would be to make wages and prices behave as they would if set in competitive markets, rather than by seller groups exercising substantial power on their own behalf. The Council's idea was that the public through discussion and application of the guideposts would decide whether a particular wage or price increase was in the public interest and apply pressure to violators of the public interest. In 1964, the Council of Economic Advisers became more specific and set at 3.2 percent the average rate of growth in the economy's productivity that should guide wage increases.

Some of the difficulties in this approach probably are obvious: In any particular case there are usually some special arguments to be advanced to the effect that the increase in wage or price should be larger than in the standard case, and evaluating the merits of these arguments is very difficult. A common argument is that the wage or price was unduly low when the game started and needs to be adjusted upward before the guidepost rule can be applied. The public is in no position to evaluate such arguments, nor to apply effective pressure to most groups that might violate the rules. The economy includes so many wages and prices that evaluating all changes is practically impossible, and surely cannot be done by the public. Accordingly, with or without some rationalization for their action, seller groups must be expected to use their power to push up their prices. If a few businesses or unions that are prominently in the public eye or are subjected to special government pressure are deterred from doing what others are doing,

[16] *Annu. Rep. Counc. Econ. Advis.*, pp. 185–190, January 1962.

this may do more harm than good by getting wages and prices out of balance and by confronting the groups involved with an incentive to achieve through devious means what they cannot do openly.

In any case, the position of the wage-price guideposts was made virtually untenable after 1965 by the accelerating inflation arising from the excessive growth of total demand. Workers who asked for only a 3.2 percent increase in wage rates when prices were rising more rapidly than this would suffer a decline in the purchasing power of their income. On the other hand, for the Council of Economic Advisers to add to the productivity increase an allowance for past inflation would have yielded an embarrassingly high "guidepost" figure. Efforts of the Council of Economic Advisers to pursue the guideposts approach in this unpromising environment met with little success in 1967 and 1968, and the Nixon administration that took office in 1969 abandoned the approach.

For the government to push the guideposts approach further, to define just how each wage and price should behave, and to set mandatory ceilings for each wage and price leads to a system of wage and price controls. These avoid the ambiguity of the guideposts, their reliance upon implementation by the affected groups, and the lack of rigorous enforcement. But they bring into play a new set of difficulties and social costs. Past systems of wage and price controls have not developed any arrangement for adjusting wages and prices in such a way as to permit them to perform their economic functions. The administrative task of assembling and evaluating all of the relevant information is extremely complex.

Moreover, political factors commonly have intruded, leading to a bias in favor of wage and price increases of groups with more political influence. Efforts to hold prices below the level that clears the market leads to shortages, to black markets and under-the-counter sales in violation of price ceilings, and to a growing disenchantment and disrespect for the system. Setting low price ceilings on important or essential products leads to the diversion of resources into the production of unessential goods whose prices are not so rigorously restricted. Probably, most economists would agree that moderate inflation is a lesser evil than suppressed inflation under wage and price controls.

Wage-price policy in the first half of 1971

The Nixon administration in formulating its program of stabilization policy in early 1971 had to decide (1) what actions to take with regard to wage-price push, (2) what resulting inflation-unemployment trade-off to anticipate during 1971 and 1972, (3) what compromise between inflation and unemployment (given the expected trade-off) best served the country, and (4) what time path for GNP was consistent with the stabilization program's target outcome.

The administration based its policies on the view that the unemployment-inflation trade-off would improve during 1971. It defined as a goal the achievement of about a 4½ percent unemployment rate accompanied by about a 3 percent rate of price increase by mid-1972—compared to the 6 percent unemployment and 5 percent inflation of late 1970. The belief that the Phillips curve would shift favorably was based in part on the view that it responded to economic conditions with a lag: "There is a lag between the emergence of slack in the economy and its effect on the inflation rate so that the full effects on prices of the sluggish economy in 1970 have yet to be felt. . . . If, as expected, employment rises at a moderate rate during 1971, sufficient slack will still remain in the economy to exert downward pressure on the rate of inflation."[17] Another basis of the expectation of a favorable shift in the Phillips curve was the prediction of a high rate of increase in productivity in 1971.

A government action intended to improve the inflation-unemployment trade-off was periodic "Inflation Alerts" to bring to bear on important wage and price decisions a more informed and sharply focused public attention."[18] Other planned policies included a review of government purchasing policies, possible actions on import restrictions relating to wages and prices, and possible exceptional actions to limit inflation in the construction industry.

The new economic policy

By the summer of 1971, it became clear that the Nixon administration's conservative policy program was not working rapidly enough to deal with the situation. With unemployment still over 6 percent and little abatement of inflation, the administration came under growing pressure to take some stronger actions that would promise prompt results. Moreover, declining confidence abroad in the value of the dollar led to an international monetary crisis requiring huge purchases of the dollar by central banks to support its exchange rate. The international monetary crisis forced the administration to take some action. Since continued United States inflation was a source of the dollar's weakness, the action had to include policies to slow the increases in wages and prices.

Forced by circumstances to abandon his earlier "game plan," President Nixon announced on August 15 a drastically changed policy program. This involved three branches (the first two of which are discussed in later chapters):

1. A set of actions intended to improve the United States balance of payments and strengthen the international position of the dollar.
2. A set of actions intended to increase the growth rate of total demand.
3. A 90-day freeze on wages and prices which was to be followed by a new

[17] *Annu. Rep. Counc. Econ. Advis.*, p. 77, February 1971.
[18] *Ibid.*, p. 80.

program to limit wage-price push and permit reductions in unemployment to occur along with a decline in the rate of inflation.

The phase-two policies toward wages and prices that were to go into effect at the expiration of the wage-price freeze on November 14 were announced by President Nixon in October. In a move that was unprecedented in peacetime United States economic policy and that had few parallels elsewhere, the President instituted a system of wage and price controls. Permitted increases in wages and prices were to be defined by a set of boards. The highest authority was the Cost of Living Council, consisting only of high government officials and initially presided over by Secretary of the Treasury John Connally. Wage increases were supervised by a Wage Board consisting of five members representing labor, five members representing business, and five members representing the public. A Price Commission consisting of seven public members was also established to set standards for permissible increases in prices and rents. Finally, an Interest and Dividend Committee consisting of six government officials was formed, headed by Arthur Burns, the Chairman of the Board of Governors of the Federal Reserve System. It was hoped that compliance with the rules and policies of these agencies would be voluntary, but arrangements were made for investigation and compliance administration by the Internal Revenue Service.

The initial guidelines issued by these agencies in November 1971 were aimed at holding price increases generally to 2½ percent a year and wage increases to 5½ percent. The two figures are consistent with one another if output per man-hour increases 3 percent a year. In connection with these early decisions, attention focused on the uncertain role of labor union leaders on the Wage Board, and the degree of support or opposition the system would receive from organized labor.

The new activist policy was greeted enthusiastically in August; interest rates fell abruptly and the stock market skyrocketed. By November the public had come to a more realistic picture of what the program entailed, enthusiasm had waned, and the stock market was down to a new low for the year. The inevitable uncertainties as to how wage and price controls would work in peacetime were compounded by uncertainties as to how the system of boards and commissions would operate and as to the degree of cooperation the system would receive.

The general considerations that have led economists to shrink from peacetime wage and price controls have led other nations with inflation problems to avoid them, and had led the Nixon administration earlier to oppose them vigorously—these seemed to apply fully to the new program. That it would have a long and successful life seemed improbable. But how rapidly its difficulties would mount, how long it would survive, and whether in retrospect the program would appear to have been a wise response to the unusual economic difficulties of the summer of 1971 remain to be shown by experience.

SUMMARY

1. A market to which all buyers and sellers have open access adjusts price to clear the market, avoiding shortages or surpluses. When markets in general behave in this way, the price level adjusts to excess or deficiency of total demand in such a way as to avoid shortages or surpluses and unemployment. In the past, the United States economy has experienced both increases and decreases in the price level.

2. Modern economies are subject to a wage-price push leading to surpluses and unemployment accompanied by increases in prices. This condition is represented by a Phillips curve that associates price stability with large unemployment and full employment with inflation.

3. The factors that may contribute to explaining this condition are numerous, their relative importance in any particular case being difficult to define. Among these are (*a*) the lagging effects of past inflation, which may operate at least in part through causing expectations of further inflation; (*b*) imperfections in labor markets that prevent fitting unemployed workers into existing vacancies; (*c*) impediments to the movement of workers and other resources among types of work and locations; (*d*) institutional, legal, and political factors that prevent unemployed workers from gaining jobs or from limiting the demands for wage increases by employed workers; (*e*) competition among economic groups to increase their incomes by pushing up their selling prices; (*f*) demands of unemployed workers for wages greater than they are capable of earning; and (g) economic fluctuations in conjunction with a greater tendency for prices to rise in areas of short supply than to decline in areas of surplus.

4. The Phillips curve appears to adjust over time to the actual inflation rate, being pushed up by an acceleration of inflation. Thus, unemployment may not be permanently reduced by increasing total demand and moving to the left along the Phillips curve, since the resulting more rapid increase in prices will shift the Phillips curve upward. In the very long view, there may be only one unemployment rate that is consistent with a constant rate of inflation. In the simplest case, this long-run equilibrium unemployment rate is the same for all rates of inflation. It is determined by the laws and institutions of the society. Most of the factors listed under (3) are relevant to shifting the long-run equilibrium unemployment rate, as well as to shifting the Phillips curve.

5. The fact that the costly effects of an increase in total demand in the form of inflation and lagging tendencies towards wage-price push lag behind its pleasant effects in reducing unemployment and increasing output poses a political problem.

6. Incomes policies in the form of moral suasion and wage-price guidelines seem to have had a limited effect in reducing wage-price push, but some economists believe their favorable effects merit their use. Wage and price controls would be more effective in limiting overt inflation, but involve heavy costs in promoting economic inefficiency, shortages, and concealed inflation.

7. Continued high unemployment and inflation, along with international weakness of the dollar, caused the Nixon administration to impose a wage-price freeze in August 1971, followed in November by a system of wage and price controls.

QUESTIONS FOR REVIEW AND DISCUSSION

1. Explain how a market normally adjusts to prevent excess supply. How would this apply to a market for labor? Explain some factors that might operate to prevent the operation of this mechanism in the case of a market for labor; for products.

2. Explain how reductions in wages and prices can reduce unemployment if total demand is independently determined.

3. Draw a Phillips curve and explain what it represents. Draw the kind of Phillips curve we should want if we had our choice. Contrast with this the kind of Phillips curve now prevalent, and define the implications of the latter.

4. List factors that could contribute to explaining the existence of an unsatisfactory Phillips curve, explaining the relevance of each.

5. Show how the existence of a labor market in which vacancies coexist with unemployment contributes to an unfavorable Phillips curve.

6. Explain how concept of the Phillips curve can be reconciled with the idea of a long-run equilibrium unemployment rate. What evidence can you cite for the existence of such a long-run equilibrium unemployment rate? On the basis of this concept, explain the options that would be open to an economy that had recently increased its rate of growth of total demand and reduced its unemployment from 4 to 2 percent while increasing its rate of inflation from 3 to 7 percent.

7. Explain why lags in the inflation process add to the political difficulty of preventing and of halting inflation.

8. Draw up the program that you personally think would be the best way of dealing with the present inflation problem of the United States.

PART 4

international aspects of money and banking

16

international finance

Our discussion so far has related to a single nation, treated as if it were alone in the world. The real world involves economic dealings among individuals and businesses belonging to different nations, and among national governments. These international dealings are not random or haphazard but fall into a system. They can be interpreted as involving an international economic and financial system. One way in which this differs from the national economy is that there is here no central authority, no rule maker. The rule makers of the national economies, the national governments, are here participants in the game. Thus, international economic policy is worked out through evolution, negotiation, or international conflict rather than imposed by any central authority.

At any given time, however, the international economic system does involve rules that limit the actions of private individuals and governments. These rules importantly affect monetary policy, among other things. Restrictive monetary policies often are imposed by national governments because the rules of the international economic system call for such an action in response to a deficit in the nation's balance of payments. Therefore, the environment in which national stabilization policy is carried out depends heavily on the prevailing international economic system and the rules of behavior of national governments that this defines. Yet more basically, the success of any group of nations depends in part on whether the rules of its international economic system work well or poorly. To the national economic game, the international economic system is a metagame, the game behind the game. Its influence on the future course of the civilized world may be great.

The Mechanisms of International Financial Dealings

An important characteristic of the modern world that we take for granted is the existence of national monetary systems and national monetary units: the franc, mark, pound, peso, and bolivar. The relations among national currencies and some implications of the existence of national monetary systems concern us in this chapter.

Mechanisms of international trade and payments

From the viewpoint of the private individuals and businesses engaged in them, what distinguishes international dealings from economic exchanges within the boundaries of a nation is that they involve an additional step. They require the exchange of one national currency for another. Consider a United States business buying some woolen cloth. If it buys from another United States business, payment is made in dollars through the payments machinery we have described. If the purchase is from a British business, the seller must be paid in British pounds, since United States dollars do not serve as a medium of exchange in the United Kingdom. To make payment, thus, the importer must in effect use his dollars to buy some pounds and pay the British exporter in pounds. Alternatively, the exporter may be willing to quote a price and accept payment in United States dollars, in which case he exchanges the dollars for pounds in order to use the money for his ordinary purposes.

Such an exchange of one national currency for another, or dealings in the "foreign exchange market," involve a small trading cost. However, if the cost of British pounds in terms of United States dollars changes between the time the contract for an international purchase is signed and the time the deal is consummated, the exchange will not work out as contemplated. If the British pound depreciates on the foreign exchange market during this period and the contract is denominated in (defined in units of) pounds, the American importer can buy his required pounds for fewer dollars. As a consequence, he pays a smaller number of dollars than he expected. If the contract is denominated in dollars, on the other hand, the importer will pay the expected number of dollars—losing any advantage from the depreciation of the pound—and the importer will gain the expected number of dollars but more than the expected number of pounds. The prospect of such a shift in exchange rates while a business deal is in progress—a stage that in some cases may last a long period of time—involves an "exchange risk."

As viewed by the private transactors, an international capital movement may not look very different from a trade deal. An American may wish to buy not woolen cloth but British government bonds. This also involves buying British pounds with United States dollars in the foreign exchange market. So also do funds sent to relatives abroad, as well as to United States government transactions involving the purchase of British goods.

In practice, payments in private international dealings commonly are made through banks, which are the major retailers of "foreign exchange," or claims on foreign currencies. An importer of goods might make payment in any of several ways. The foreign exporter might require payment in pounds in advance or might require payment on delivery. He might extend credit, selling on open-book account and permitting payment weeks or months later, the payment commonly denominated in his currency.

If the English exporter will accept payment in dollars, the American importer can simply mail his check (denominated in dollars) to the British exporter, who then sells this to his bank for pounds, his bank completing the transaction in the foreign exchange market. Alternatively, the exporter may maintain an account in an American bank to which the importer can send his check, this bank then making the necessary foreign exchange transaction and transferring the funds to the exporter's British bank in pounds.

If the British exporter requires payment directly in pounds, the importer can accomplish this by buying from his bank a "bank draft" in pounds. This will be drawn upon an English bank by prior arrangement with the American bank. This payment in pounds, then, can be deposited directly by the importer in his British bank. Alternatively, the same effect is accomplished by a mail transfer or telegraphic or cable transfer of funds by the importer's bank. In this case, the bank entrusts its foreign branch or correspondent with making payment to the foreign payee, the importer receiving simply a receipt for his payment rather than a draft that he mails to the exporter. Whatever the particular arrangement, the transactions commonly are made through banks, which handle the mechanical aspects of the transaction and which accomplish the actual exchange of national currencies that constitutes the foreign exchange market.

The foreign exchange market

In the United States, the foreign exchange market is an over-the-counter type of market rather than a geographically centralized auction-type market like the stock exchange. Commercial banks serve the function of retailer in foreign exchange dealings, standing ready to sell or buy foreign exchange from customers. The wholesale function or inner market in foreign exchange also consists largely of commercial banks, the foreign exchange departments of these constituting a separate aspect of their activities. The inner market also includes nonbank dealers and some brokers performing a specialized informational and trading function. The function of this market, as of others, is to bring together suppliers and demanders of any

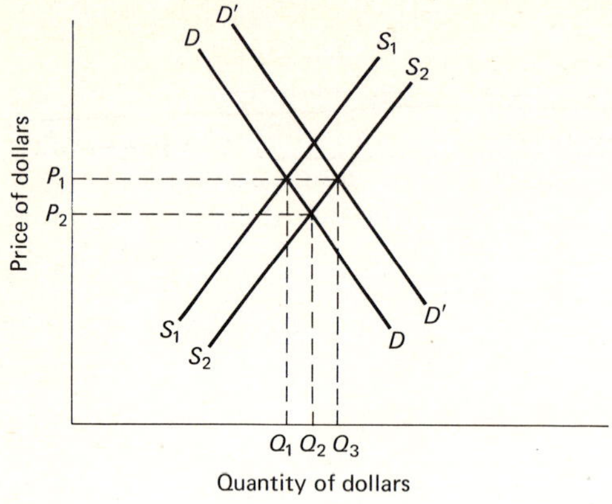

Fig. 16-1 Foreign exchange market.

national currency in foreign exchange dealings, offsetting these against one another and clearing the market.[1]

The external value of a national currency, or its exchange rate, can be interpreted with the supply and demand analysis that we apply to price determination in markets generally. The quantities of dollars demanded and supplied in the foreign exchange market at alternative prices are depicted in Fig. 16-1. These are prices of the dollar in terms of foreign currencies. Given demand curve *DD* and supply curve *SS*, price P_1 is the one that clears the market. At this price, the quantity demanded equals the quantity supplied, both amounting to Q_1.

What specific kinds of transactions add to the supply of or demand for dollars? The various categories of international transactions involving the dollar are reviewed below, in connection with the nation's balance of payments. But any international transaction involving the dollar entails either selling dollars for a foreign currency or buying dollars with a foreign currency. In connection with the export of goods from the United States, the foreign buyers have to acquire dollars with which to pay for the goods. This increases the demand for dollars and strengthens the price of the dollar on the foreign exchange market. For Americans to buy German securities requires them to buy marks, and thus to sell dollars, so it weakens the dollar on the foreign exchange market. By looking at the currency side of the transaction, you can see whether it involves a sale or a purchase of dollars, and whether it weakens or strengthens the dollar on the foreign exchange market.

[1]For more detailed information, see Alan R. Holmes and Francis H. Schott, *The New York Foreign Exchange Market*, Federal Reserve Bank of New York, New York, 1965. The topics of this chapter and the next are covered more fully in Leland B. Yeager, *International Monetary Relations*, Harper & Row, New York, 1966.

National governments usually maintain a fixed exchange rate for their currencies, fixed values in terms of foreign currencies on the foreign exchange market. Then they must stand ready to buy or sell whatever amounts are required to stabilize the price. With reference to Fig. 16–1, if the supply of dollars on the foreign exchange market increased from S_1S_1 to S_2S_2 because Americans increased their purchase of foreign securities, this would depress the price of the dollar to P_2. If the United States government wants the external value of the dollar to stay at P_1, it must buy up the excess supply of dollars that otherwise would exist at P_1. That is, it must provide enough additional demand for dollars to shift the total demand schedule to $D'D'$, and must buy dollars equal to $Q_3 - Q_1$. This is the kind of operation that the Federal Reserve Bank of New York, acting as agent for the U.S. Treasury or the Federal Open Market Committee, conducts.

However, the illustration raises the question as to what the Federal Reserve bank uses as "money" with which to buy the dollars. Consideration of the means by which central banks can support their currencies in the foreign exchange markets raises the question of a supermoney, an international money, or international monetary reserves.

The foreign-exchange market involves not only exchanges for immediate delivery but also a "forward market," involving contracts for exchange 30, 60, or 90 days hence, as well as forward contracts tailored to the needs of particular demanders. These contracts play the same role as futures contracts in the commodities markets. Among demanders of forward pounds, for example, would be foreigners committed to future payments in pounds who wish to protect themselves against the hazard of an increase in the value of the pound during the interim. Among suppliers of forward pounds are British businesses committed to future payments in a foreign currency. The various sectors of the forward market, thus, are separate submarkets with supply and demand schedules. Each sets a price of the forward currency that will clear the market.

The forward markets are also a potential vehicle for speculation. The speculator expecting an increase in the price of the pound in relation to the dollar can buy pounds for delivery at a date after the expected change in exchange rates. If he proves to be right, he can then sell his pounds in the "spot market" at the higher price and realize a profit. A speculator who expected the pound to depreciate could assume a short position in the pound by selling pounds forward, later liquidating his contract at a profit if his expectations proved to be correct by buying the depreciated pound in the spot market (for current delivery) to meet his commitment. Thus, if people expect the value of the pound to rise, their demand for forward pounds will drive the forward price above the spot price. Similarly, if people expect the pound to be worth less in a month, they will be willing to sell forward pounds at a price below the spot price, and this will drive the forward price below the spot price.

Foreign-exchange speculation and arbitrage

In terms of the goals and operating procedures of participants, activities in the foreign exchange market can be put into four categories: (1) individuals, businesses, and governments desirous of making an international payment; (2) governments desirous of affecting the exchange rate or the external value of the national currency; (3) foreign exchange speculators; and (4) arbitragers. Individuals and businesses buy foreign currencies because they desire to make payments in a foreign currency. The national government may buy foreign currencies, or sell the national currency, in order to prevent the external value of the national currency from deviating excessively from its official value.

Foreign exchange speculators buy or sell a foreign currency in the hope of profiting from a change in exchange rates. This involves the same principles as any other kind of speculation. The inducement to speculation is an expected change in a price. The objective is before the change in prices to move out of assets that will depreciate and into an asset that will appreciate. In the case of currency speculation, one need not hold money, but can hold any asset denominated in a national currency—or any asset that when sold realizes the national currency in question. For example, to benefit from an increase in the external value of the German mark one need not hold the marks in the form of currency or a bank deposit but can hold any investment asset that will be sold for marks.

One expecting the German mark to appreciate, could buy marks and invest in liquid assets in Germany. After the mark appreciates, he could liquidate the transaction at a profit by buying back the currency he held at the outset. An expectation of appreciation of the mark, thus, would cause a speculative inflow of funds, a flow of "hot money," to Germany to benefit from the appreciation.

"Exchange-rate arbitrage" differs from the speculation in seeking to profit not from expected future changes in exchange rates but rather from inconsistencies in the existing pattern of exchange rates. Given the complexity of a system of exchange rates involving a large number of currencies, a situation may arise in which one can make a profit, say, by buying pounds with dollars, francs with the pounds, and dollars again with the francs. Profiting by this situation would involve an arbitrage transaction. It requires no expectations regarding future exchange rates, so involves no risk that the expectations will prove to be incorrect. Commonly, it involves a small margin of profit and requires large funds and low operating costs in making transactions. Exchange-rate arbitrage, thus, is an insider's game.

"Interest arbitrage" responds to differences in interest rates in different economies. For example, a United States investor may find that short-term interest rates in London are higher than those in New York by enough to make it profitable for him to shift his liquid funds to London. This involves an exchange risk, a hazard that depreciation of the pound in terms of the dollar would involve losses greater than the gains arising from the difference in interest rates. However, protection against the exchange risk can be achieved by buying forward dollars. The investor then can enjoy his higher interest rate secure in the knowledge that his funds can be returned to dollars on defined terms. This "covered interest arbitrage" is profitable when the foreign interest rate is higher than the domestic one by enough to more than cover transactions costs plus any premium of the forward rate over the spot rate for the home currency. Interest arbitrage involves international movement of funds not because of expected revisions of exchange rates but because of differences in national levels of interest rates.

The National Balance of Payments

The United States balance of payments shows the transactions of United States residents with foreigners. By grouping items in a meaningful way, it permits analysis of improvement or deterioration in the international liquidity position of the United States and the probable future strength of the dollar.

In the United States balance of payments (Table 16–1), items involving payments to United States residents by foreigners are shown as plus items and are termed "credits." They lead to purchases of dollars by foreigners with their local currencies and add to the demand for dollars on the foreign exchange market, thus tending to increase the price of the dollar in terms of foreign currencies. Items involving out-payments from the dollar, sales of dollars and purchases of foreign currencies, termed "debits" in the United States balance of payments, are shown with a minus sign. Any transaction, of course, has two sides: If one person is buying dollars, someone else must be selling them. The total volume of dollars bought in the foreign exchange market must be equal to the total volume sold, and the total balance of payments adds up to zero.

Different patterns of transactions, however, have different implications for the international liquidity position of the United States. If United States residents are earning the foreign currencies they are spending mainly with exports of goods and services that can continue year after year, no sustainability problem is posed. But if these foreign currencies are acquired by short-term borrowing from foreigners or by sales of gold by the U.S. Treasury, a sustainability problem does exist, and the position of the dollar is weakened.

The presentation of the balance of payments groups items roughly in terms of their sustainability or stability. At the top of the statement is the merchandise trade balance, or the excess of merchandise exports over imports. The United States in 1970 did have an excess of exports of $2.1 billion so we show a plus item of this amount. These net exports, taken by themselves, give rise to a net demand of foreigners for $2.1 billion,

TABLE 16-1 United States Balance of Payments: 1970 (in billions of dollars)

Merchandise trade balance	$ 2.1
Military transactions, net	−3.4
Travel and transportation, net	−2.0
Investment income, net	6.2
Other services, net	0.6
Balance on goods and services	**3.6**
Remittances, pensions and other transfers	−1.4
Balance on goods, services and remittances	**2.2**
United States government grants (excluding military)	−1.7
Balance on current account	**0.4**
Long-term private capital flows, net	−1.5
Long-term United States government capital flows, net	−2.0
Balance on current account and long-term capital	**−3.0**
Nonliquid short-term private capital flows, net	−0.5
Allocations of special drawing rights (SDRs)	0.9
Errors and omissions, net	−1.1
Net liquidity balance	**−3.8**
Liquid private capital flows, net	−6.0
Official reserve transactions balance	**−9.8**
Financed by changes in:	
Liabilities to foreign official agencies	7.3
United States official reserve assets	
Gold	0.8
SDRs	−0.9
Convertible currencies (foreign exchange)	2.2
Gold tranche position in International Monetary Fund	0.4

SOURCE: Surv. Curr. Bus., Sept. 1971.

in dollars to pay for the excess of what they bought from us over what they sold to us.

After recording several other types of dealings in goods and services, we strike our first subtotal, or "balance," the "balance on goods and services." Each of these balances can be interpreted in two ways. First, it is the sum of the items that are "above the line" to this point, or with reference to this balance. The balance on goods and services shows us whether transactions in goods and services, taken by themselves, would lead to net out-payments or in-payments in relation to the dollar. In 1970, they implied net in-payments of $3.6 billion.

But we know that total in-payments to the dollar must equal total out-payments. So if the items that are above the line to this point sum to +$3.6 billion, those below the line must sum to −$3.6 billion. That is, we can think of all the items that are below the line with reference to the balance on goods and services as explaining, in this case, where foreigners got the dollars that permitted them to spend $3.6 billion more than they earned in transactions in goods and services. Another way of putting it is that below-the-line items explain how the balance is financed.

The new presentation of the United States balance of payments first used by the U.S. Department of Commerce in 1971 strikes six different subtotals or balances, or draws six different lines with reference to which we distinguish above-the-line and below-the-line items. Since gifts and pensions in 1970 contributed –$1.4 billion, the "balance on goods and services and remittances" amounted to $2.2 billion. Next adding government grants we draw the line at the "balance on current account," which in 1970 was $0.4 billion. The above-the-line items now include everything except capital movements and official reserve transactions. We see that in 1970 nearly all the United States surplus on goods and services was offset by deficits on government and private remittances and grants.

The net liquidity balance is perhaps the most important single measure of the change in the international liquidity position of the United States. The below-the-line items that finance the net liquidity balance are private flows of liquid funds and official reserve transactions. Thus a deficit on the net liquidity balance implies that the nation is spending down its cash and liquid assets and borrowing internationally at short term, a situation that raises a warning flag.

To get to the net liquidity balance from the balance on current account we add net long-term and nonliquid short-term capital flows. These were all minus items in the 1970 balance of payments. This reflects a net outflow of capital, a net shift of funds from United States securities and investment assets to foreign ones giving rise to a net demand for foreign currencies and a net supply of dollars on the foreign exchange market. To get to the net liquidity balance we also add the United States allocation of new SDRs. This is a free gift, the United States share in the newly created international monetary reserve asset created by the International Monetary Fund, which is discussed in Chap. 17. Finally, we add "errors and omissions." These are flows that cannot be specifically identified but are presumably mainly short-term capital movements.

The net liquidity balance of the United States in 1970 of –$3.8 billion indicated that we were running down our international liquidity position at a rapid rate. The indicated weakening of the international position of the dollar contributed to explaining the speculative attack on the dollar in the summer of 1971.

There also was in 1970 a large outflow of private short-term capital from the United States. The reasons for this we have discussed earlier. In 1969 when interest rates in the United States were higher than in Europe and United States banks, pinched by regulation Q, were borrowing heavily in the Eurodollar market, short-term capital flowed into the United States in large volume. In 1970, United States interest rates declined, and it flowed back out no less rapidly.

Official reserve transactions act as a residual or balancing item in international transactions. These reflect the operations of the Federal Reserve Bank of New York in foreign exchange and borrowings and currency swaps with foreign central banks, as well as Treasury dealings in gold and

SDRs. A large deficit on the official reserve transactions balance—and that of 1970 was very large—means that United States official agencies have to borrow abroad and use their reserves to buy dollars in order to support the dollar in the foreign exchange market.

The below-the-line items with reference to the balance on official reserve transactions show just how the official agencies covered in 1970 the deficit of $9.8 billion. They did so mainly by borrowing from foreign central banks. They also drew heavily on their holdings of convertible foreign currencies. These operations show up as plus items in the balance of payments because they give rise to a demand for dollars on the foreign exchange market. But they are a sign of weakness rather than of strength. They show how the nation covered or financed the deficit that it ran on its more sustainable types of transactions.

Nations in different economic positions characteristically have different patterns in the balance of payments. A developing country may be importing long-term capital and using the foreign exchange thus gained to run a deficit on trade account while it builds up its stock of capital goods. A country that has made large foreign investments in the past can run a trade deficit continuously, offsetting this by investment income from abroad.

A special case is that in which foreigners and foreign central banks want to hold a prominent currency such as the United States dollar or the British pound as an international reserve asset or as working balances for international dealings. For foreigners to build up their holdings of dollars (including liquid assets in the United States) ordinarily requires a deficit in the United States net liquidity balance. If foreigners wanted to increase their holdings of dollars on this account year after year because of growth in world trade and income, continued deficits in the United States balance of payments would be called for to permit the foreigners to acquire the dollars they wanted. But this would justify United States deficits of only a certain size. If the deficits became too large and provided foreigners with more dollars than they wanted, the dollar would tend to depreciate on the foreign exchange market and would require support from official reserve transactions.

The United States balance of payments position

For more than a decade after the Second World War, United States balance-of-payments deficits were not large enough to permit foreigners to acquire as many dollars as they wanted; there was a "dollar shortage." About 1958 we shifted to the opposite problem, entering the era of the "dollar glut." The United States inflation after 1965 was accompanied by rapid deterioration in the international position of the dollar. The United States trade balance weakened gradually after 1964 and drastically after 1967 (Fig. 16-2). In 1968 the basic weakness of the dollar was partially masked by a temporary inflow of capital, some of it reflecting foreign invest-

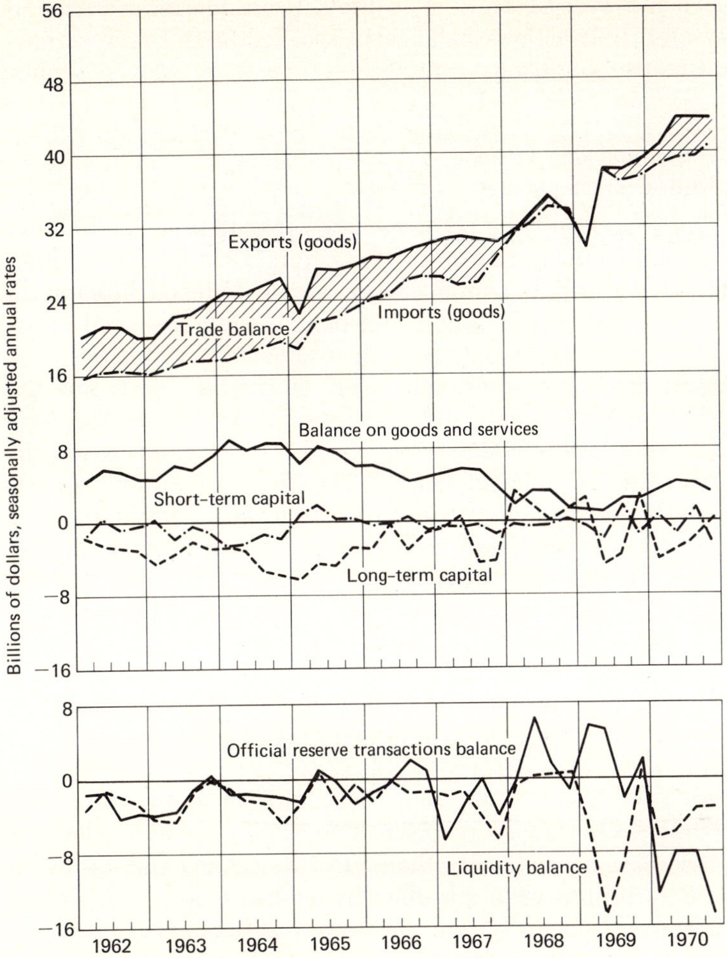

Fig. 16-2 United States balance of payment (U.S. Department of Commerce and Federal Reserve Bank of St. Louis.)

ment in our booming stock market. An inflow of short-term capital in response to high United States interest rates and borrowing abroad by United States banks to avoid regulation Q ceilings in 1968 and especially in 1969 kept the official reserve transactions balance favorable despite deterioration in 1969 in the net liquidity balance.

The United States trade balance improved somewhat in 1970, as did the net liquidity balance, but a reversal of the earlier temporary capital in-flow dropped the official reserve transactions balance to a record deficit. In the first half of 1971, matters went from bad to worse. The trade balance deteriorated and the out-flow of capital accelerated. The net liquidity balance was in deficit by an annual rate of about $10 billion in the first quarter of the year and over $20 billion in the second quarter. The deficit in the official reserve transactions balance was at an annual rate of more than $20 billion in both quarters.

The 1971 international monetary crises and the changed United States policies

Beginning in March 1971, exchange-rate speculation became an increasingly important factor in the short-term capital flow from the dollar. As fears mounted that the dollar might be devalued (reduced in value in relation to other currencies), individuals and businesses transferred funds from the dollar into currencies thought to be in an especially strong position, notably the German mark. An additional incentive to shift funds into the mark was provided by high German interest rates. The flow of short-term capital out of the dollar and into the mark caused the mark to rise and the dollar to fall on the foreign exchange market. The German central bank was forced to buy dollars and sell marks in an effort to keep the mark at its official exchange rate, or par value. As the speculative crisis mounted, the Bundesbank had to buy more than $1 billion on May 3 and 4 and a further $1 billion in the first forty minutes of trading in the foreign exchange market on May 5. At this point, it gave up its efforts to maintain its exchange rate, and it let the foreign value of the mark float upward somewhat. Within a few days, the Dutch guilder also was allowed to find its own exchange rate while the Swiss and Austrian governments revalued their currencies upward.

These modest adjustments of exchange rates did not stem the speculative run on the dollar. On August 6, the U.S. Treasury reported a loss of gold and other reserve assets of more than $1 billion. Over the following week, more than $3.7 billion were absorbed by central banks. The United States had to take some strong action. On Sunday, August 15, President Nixon announced a package of drastic policies to deal with the crisis. The international economic actions included a temporary cessation of United States sales of gold to other central banks, a 10-percent surtax on most imports, and a request to nations with balance-of-payments surpluses to revalue their currencies upward in relation to the dollar. The United States position was that if other nations would sufficiently revalue their currencies upward and would reduce their restrictions on imports and capital in-flows from the United States, the United States balance-of-payments deficit and the weakness of the dollar would be cured. Then the United States would remove the surtax on imports and resume gold sales, and the international economic system could function as before. In late 1971, other nations remained unwilling to adjust their exchange rates as much as the United States wished and the future of the international economic system was uncertain.

Alternative International Economic Systems

When a nation is confronted by a lasting balance of payments deficit, there are a number of kinds of action it conceivably can take. It can simply prevent all residents of the nation from buying foreign goods or services, thus halting such demand for foreign currencies. It can use its political power to force weak foreign governments to buy things from its nationals. Or it can just let its currency fall to whatever price clears the foreign exchange market.

While all of these and other actions are conceivable, the actions taken by a government will depend upon a set of rules of the game to which it and other governments are adhering. Even though not all are written down or explicitly formulated, such rules do exist. Because of them, international economic dealings are not random or anarchic, but constitute a coherent system.

Before discussing the specific kinds of actions taken in our existing system to correct persistent imbalance in international payments, it is useful to see where the existing arrangements fit into the broader picture of conceivable systems.

Some respects in which the performance of the international economic system is important are as follows:

1. The terms on which individuals and businesses are permitted to engage in dealings across national boundaries significantly affect the scope of individual action and—the other side of the same coin—the scope of government action or the power of the state. By imposing restrictions on international dealings, the government increases its power at the expense of the prerogatives of individuals.

2. International dealings permit specialization of production among nations and regions. They also permit sharing of resources and production possibilities that are regionally specialized. This specialization of production can increase real output and living standards in the participating nations generally. It is especially important to small nations and nations lacking the natural resources for diversified production, since they would suffer most if forced to produce for themselves everything that they use. Therefore, the system of international dealings affects not only the average economic welfare of nations but also the distribution of benefits among them.

3. Economic efficiency is favored by terms of international dealings that are stable over time and that offer a guarantee against violent and unexpected revision. The small nation that built its economy around a particular export industry would be grievously damaged if foreign governments abruptly closed their borders to its products. Moreover, the terms of international dealings involve considerations of fairness. Nations that are more powerful or that are less dependent upon international dealings may be able to use their power position to gain advantageous terms.

4. International dealings commonly involve two or more national moneys. Instability of exchange rates hampers international trade and capital movements. On the other hand, restrictions on the convertibility of currencies (exchange controls) as well as restrictions on international trade and capital movements also have adverse economic side effects. Working out a set of rules that will produce a favorable performance with relation to these considerations is difficult.

5. The stability of the international economic system, which is its defense against a cumulative deterioration that would destroy it, is an important consideration. The danger is illustrated by the experience of the 1930s, when the existing set of rules for international dealings collapsed, leading to a dog-eat-dog situation that was economically and politically destructive. In relation to these considerations or rough criteria, we shall consider several general classes of systems of international economic dealings.

Free trade and capital movements

One model of an international economic system against which others can be compared is the one that minimizes the role of national governments and maximizes the scope of individual and business transactions across national boundaries. National governments impose on international dealings no special restraints whatever. Foreigners can sell goods or sell securities in United States markets on quite the same terms as United States residents. Similarly, United States residents can buy foreign goods or securities without being subject to government restraints, taxes, or subsidies.

It may take a moment's thought to see how this model limits the economic powers of the national government. In the United States, the powers of state governments for economic regulation are severely limited by competition among the states. The state government that imposes on businesses regulations that they do not like tends to lose businesses to other states, so long as they are sure they can ship their product back into the state without government restrictions.

With perfectly free international trade, national governments in dealing with regulation of business, with provisions of their tax systems affecting businesses or businessmen, and with procedures for government planning would have to take into account the effect in driving business abroad. Thus, this system is not consistent with the powers that national governments are accustomed to exercise.

Free private international economic dealings contribute to maximum international division of labor. Economic activities would seek their most efficient location across national boundaries unhampered by government regulations in the same manner that they presently do within the nation. But if economic activities are located by efficiency criteria, the most advanced and rewarding economic activities may come to be concentrated within the boundaries of a few nations rather than distributed uniformly about the world on a geographical basis. We find great concentration of economic activity within a single nation such as the United States, and it is to be expected that if economic criteria rule there would be no more tendency towards an equal distribution of economic activity among nations than there presently is among states in the United States. This also may be inconsistent with a nationalistic orientation of economic and political life.

Under the free international movement of trade and capital, the terms of trade—the rates of remuneration to various factors of production and kinds of economic activity—would be governed by economic factors. This also may pose conflicts with prevailing political standards of income distribution and of distribution of power among regions and groups.

How would this class of international economic system maintain a balance in international payments? This would be accomplished by changes in relative prices, just as it is within a national economy. If all nations had the same money, the parallel to the role of prices within a national economy would be complete. If national currencies existed, the adjustments could be made in either of two ways. The national currencies could be maintained in a fixed relation to one another and particular prices and the general level of prices in each nation would adjust in such a way as to correct imbalance in international payments. The nation with a balance of payments deficit would have to reduce its price level, to make its exports more attractive to foreigners. The other approach is simply to let the exchange rate vary in such a way as to accomplish the needed adjustment. Instead of the deficit nation reducing the prices of individual goods and services—which would not be easy with prevailing Phillips curves—it makes the adjustment by changing its exchange rate. This avoids some problems, but it leads to others.

What can be said about the hazard of instability of this system? The hazard of violent instability is that national governments will abruptly change the rules under which they are playing the international economic game. In the system we are now considering, the governments have little role in the game. They would be a source of instability only if they kicked over the traces and began exercising powers that were not permitted under the rules here under discussion.

International dealings limited to governments

The opposite extreme case is an international economic system in which individuals and businesses are entirely prevented from economic dealings across national boundaries, such dealings being limited entirely to national governments. In its political content, this system is not consistent with an individualistic political philosophy, but with a highly centralized or totalitarian government. The principal illustrations of this approach are the bilateral trade agreements among Communist governments and those entered into during its existence by the Nazi government of Germany.

With reference to the scope permitted for international specialization and division of labor, this system is very restrictive. Since relations among governments are heavily influenced by political considerations, this class of system subjects potential exchanges to a political criterion in addition to economic criteria, thereby excluding many that otherwise would be possible. Moreover, limitations on the complexity of the international dealings that can be negotiated directly among governments are an important constraint upon the extent to which the economic potential for international specialization can be utilized.

Government-negotiated trade agreements usually are bilateral, involving exchanges between two countries, while free trade is multilateral, involving very complex networks of dealings. For example, in a pattern of free trade we should not expect to find that the exports of the United States to Canada just balance the exports of Canada to the United States, or that trade between New York and New Mexico is in balance. Rather, the trade between each of these pairs is only one aspect of a very complex pattern involving many other trading partners as well. Thus, if government-negotiated trade is limited to the dealings that can be handled through bilateral agreements, a large part of the potential for international trade and specialization must be lost.

The equity of trade negotiated between governments depends on the political relations among governments. Past experience illustrates that in this kind of dealing the politically and economically powerful trading partner commonly exploits the weaker one. This is illustrated by the dealings of Nazi Germany and the Soviet Union with weaker trading partners.

One respect in which this system is tractable is that, at least on the surface, it involves no balance of payments problem. The bilateral negotiations between governments determine what is to be shipped in each direction, and no further governing mechanism is required. In practice, however, a nation can, in effect, run a balance of payments deficit by delaying its shipments to its trading partner beyond the contract date, by falling behind in meeting its obligations, this being "financed" by an involuntary loan by the trading partner. In some cases, this seemingly has been done as a matter of policy, being one means by which the powerful trading partner exploits the weaker one.

Finally, potential instability of this system would arise from changes in governments or government policies in the trading partners, which might seriously disrupt the pattern of trade. A general and cumulative deterioration of such a system, however, would be associated only with a general political deterioration in a political and economic bloc.

Systems intermediate between free trade and government dealings

The political conditions in the leading nations of the West call for a system intermediate between the two extreme bench-mark cases we have reviewed. The economic role of national governments is congenial neither to their assuming a monopoly on international dealings nor to their accepting the loss of power that would result from completely free trade and capital movements.

Defining on this basis a framework for an orderly, stable, and equitable system of international dealings poses a difficult challenge. It requires defining what constraints on international dealings—international trade and capital movements—can properly be imposed by national governments under various conditions. It involves spelling out a set of rules of the game for national governments that is equitable and stable, and does not unduly impede international specialization and economic efficiency.

Means of Correcting Imbalance in International Payments

With the existing class of international economic system, a contribution to correction of payments imbalance can be made by several different kinds of mechanism. Their operation is discussed in relation to the adjustments to be made by the country with the balance of payments deficit:

1. In terms of trade policy, the nation with a payments deficit could impose additional restrictions on imports, thus limiting its outpayments and improving its balance of payments.

2. In relation to policy toward international capital movements, the deficit nation could impose additional restrictions upon lending and investing abroad by its nationals (or against the importation of foreign securities), thereby reducing its outpayments.

3. In relation to its domestic total demand and price level, the deficit nation could limit total demand and attempt to reduce its price level (or cause it to increase less rapidly than those of other nations, if these are increasing). This makes its goods and services more attractive to foreigners, and makes foreign goods and services less attractive to its residents.

4. In relation to its exchange rate, the deficit nation could permit the value of its currency to decline in relation to other national currencies; permit its currency to depreciate or devalue it. This has effects similar to those of (3).

The problem is from these relevant mechanisms to define some set of rules for behavior of national governments that will constitute an orderly and efficient system for correcting payments imbalance and that will be politically acceptable to the governments participating in the system.

Policy toward international trade

Restrictions on international trade should be symmetrical or equitable, limit international trade no more than is justified by considerations of economic nationalism, not be changed capriciously, and constitute a system that is not likely to collapse under stress. It also may be desirable that changes in trade restrictions should make some contribution to maintaining balance in international payments, at least when this poses a special difficulty. To use trade restrictions in this way, however, requires a set of rules.

Commonly, governments seek to impose restrictions on imports more severe than those imposed by other countries. These restrictions usually are in the form of tariffs (special taxes on imported goods) or quotas (fixed quantitative limitations on the amount of particular kinds of goods that can be imported).

National governments may seek such asymmetrical trade restrictions because they seek an excess of exports over imports and an excess of inpayments in order to increase their share in the supply of international monetary reserves. When the total amount of international monetary reserves is deficient, national governments generally will try to get more than they have. This will incline them to seek additional trade restrictions. Thus, during the early 1930s when collapse of the international monetary system led to a seriously deficient supply of international monetary reserves, it is understandable that nations, in general, tried to export more than they imported in order to limit domestic unemployment. Of course, this is a zero-sum game, a dog-eat-dog or beggar-my-neighbor—to use terms applied at the time—affair, since it does not cure the general misery but only affects the allocation of relative miseries among nations.

A second major reason why governments may seek asymmetrical trade restrictions against imports is that the political pressure from domestic business and workers for "protection" from competition by imports characteristically seems stronger than the pressure exerted by interests running in the opposite direction.

Since the Second World War, government policy toward international trade has focused on an effort to correct the widespread trade restrictions that developed during the 1930s. Goals were reduction in the level of trade barriers and elimination of policies that discriminated among nations.

The basic framework of trade policy among Western nations since the Second World War has been the General Agreement on Tariffs and Trade (GATT) negotiated among major trading countries in 1947. This roughly defines an approved system of policies toward international trade. An important provision is the "most favored nation" clause providing that a nation reducing a tariff in negotiations with one nation will apply the reduction to all others as well. The defined code rules out discrimination among nations in trade policy and prohibits the use of quantitative trade restrictions or quotas except by countries that have a balance of payments problem or that impose similar quantitative controls domestically.

The GATT code has two "escape clauses." It allows a country to raise tariffs if a domestic industry is injured by imports and provides that a nation may be freed of its GATT obligations under special conditions (though not necessarily without penalty) if this is agreed to by other GATT members. The code sanctions retaliatory actions by nations injured by increases in trade restrictions by another nation. Within this framework, a major focus in the postwar period has been generalized bilateral negotiations for reciprocal reductions in restrictions on international trade.

By the latter part of the 1960s, the movement for further lowering of impediments to international trade had at least for the time being come to a halt. A growing problem was the imposition of restrictions on imports through devices other than tariffs and quotas, various kinds of covert and hidden restrictions on international trade. Pressures within each nation for protection of particular industries will continue to challenge the maintenance of rules of governmental behavior consistent with wide freedom of trade.

GATT permits temporary quantitative restrictions, as well as tariff increases, to deal with a balance of payments problem, but no systematic program has been worked out to use such changes in trade restrictions as a way of correcting payments imbalance. These restrictions have costly side effects in disrupting patterns of trade and particular industries in the countries involved. For trade restrictions to be successful in improving the balance of payments of a nation, they must not lead to retaliation. If other nations react by imposing similar restrictions, nothing has been done for the payments imbalance and all nations are worse off. Flexible and carefully calculated adjustments in trade policy are difficult for national governments to make because of their selective effects upon various domestic interests. In August 1971 the United States, in response to a ballooning balance-of-payments deficit and a speculative attack on the dollar imposed a special 10-percent surtax on most imports. The surtax was to be removed when other nations sufficiently reduced their trade restrictions and increased the values of their currencies in relation to the dollar. After prolonged negotiations, the ten leading trading nations on December 18, 1971 announced an important agreement whereby the United States would remove the import surtax in exchange for a general realignment of exchange rates. Discussion aimed at reducing trade restrictions of other nations were to continue in 1972.

International capital movements and balance in international payments

International capital movements are purchases of investment assets, including securities, that go across national boundaries. Long-term movements of international capital are potentially productive for reasons similar to those applying to international trade. They permit international specialization and permit the more advanced countries to finance the development of the less advanced—as the United States development was advanced by large investment from Europe. Such capital movements have been thought of as especially helpful to low-income nations that lack the means to finance large-scale investment. Another point is that freedom of the individual to move his wealth across national boundaries may be regarded as an important kind of freedom.

In the international political climate that has developed in recent decades, it may be that these ideas all must be reconsidered. If international capital flows are regarded in the recipient country as a source of exploitation rather than as economically helpful, this may impose political costs that prevent their potentially helpful economic role from being realized.

It has long been recognized that short-term movements of international capital may not be economically productive but may simply be destabilizing all around. The charter of rules for the international financial system, the Bretton Woods agreements, approved restrictions on short-term capital movements to protect a nation's balance of payments. The impediment to doing so is not a matter of principle but the practical consideration that the system of controls necessary to prevent such capital movements has serious side effects.

Let us see what is involved in such controls on dealings in foreign exchange, or "exchange controls." If the French government wished to prevent French nationals from shifting their funds from the country and thereby weakening the international position of the franc, it would have to prevent people who want to shift funds from gaining access to foreign currencies. To do this, the government must gain control over all claims to foreign currencies that come into the possession of Frenchmen and could be sold to exporters of capital. Since a great many Frenchmen gain command over foreign currencies through a great variety of kinds of transactions, an extensive and onorous network of controls is necessary.

Even the most ambitious system of controls may be evaded to a considerable extent. People will smuggle goods from the country and sell them abroad or engage in black-market currency dealings with visiting foreigners. Businesses dealing with foreigners may arrange for their billings to be padded, the collaborator investing the excess funds abroad on behalf of the French firm. To attempt to track down each technique of evasion and impose an additional control to deal with it has been found to lead to a network of restrictions that is very costly and unsatisfactory. Accordingly, restrictions on short-term capital movements are widely approved in principle but agreed not to be feasible for very long in practice. When a nation's balance of payments position is jeopardized by a large and presumably temporary outflow of capital, however, restrictions to limit the outflow commonly are imposed.

The United States government since 1963 has maintained some limited restrictions on capital outflow. These are aimed not primarily at a short-run speculative outflow but at limiting a persistent flow of funds from the United States to other countries. This program involved an "interest equalization tax" designed to reduce the incentive to foreign investment at a time when interest rates are higher abroad, a program to restrict direct investment abroad, and a set of guidelines for banks and financial institutions designed to discourage them from increasing their foreign lending. The announced goal of the Nixon administration was to move away from such controls on capital movements and some steps to reduce the controls were taken in 1969.

How can the present state of affairs regarding restrictions on international capital movements as a way of correcting payments imbalance be characterized? Where a severe problem for a nation's balance of payments traces to a large outflow of funds, commonly restrictions against the export of capital are applied, even though they are only partially successful in preventing the outflow of funds. The problems of controlling capital movements are so difficult that variations in international capital flows are likely to continue to be a source of disturbance in the international payments picture. The major defense against international flows of hot money has been loan agreements among central banks that provide them with foreign exchange to offset temporary capital flows. The improvement in the 1960s in mechanisms for international capital movements—most notably development of the Eurodollar market—seemed to aggravate difficulties arising from international capital movements associated with interest arbitrage and currency speculation.

The growth in technical efficiency and quantitative importance during the 1960s of the Eurodollar market, or Eurocurrency market, increased the international mobility of liquid funds and posed a new challenge to the international economic system. Eurocurrency deposits in eight European nations were estimated at $57 billion at the end of 1970, an increase of about 30 percent during that year. Of these balances, about 80 percent were denominated in dollars, or were Eurodollar deposits in the literal sense; the remainder were mainly in German marks and the British pound sterling. Beginning in 1968, a similar Asian dollar market developed in Singapore. Its size in 1970 was estimated to be still less than $500 million.

In June 1971, European central bankers agreed to withdraw the funds they had placed in the Eurocurrency market, which were estimated at $3 billion. The central bankers, acting through the Bank for International Settlements in Basel, were studying curbs that might be imposed on the market, such as the imposition of cash reserves against Eurocurrency loans and the imposition of exchange controls on the international flows of funds associated with them.

National stabilization policy and the balance of payments

Another way a nation can combat a deficit in its international payments is through limiting growth in domestic total demand and permitting a rise in its unemployment rate. This works through several channels. If businesses have excess capacity, they will make greater efforts to sell abroad and will be able to offer prompt deliveries to foreign buyers, tending to increase exports. Slackening of output will mean reduction in incomes, which will tend to reduce expenditures of individuals and businesses—including their expenditures for imports.

In accordance with the relation depicted in the Phillips curve, greater unemployment will ordinarily lead to smaller increases in wages and prices. If prices in the country in question rise less rapidly than in other countries, this also will make its goods more attractive to foreign buyers. It also will encourage domestic buyers to buy at home rather than abroad. Consequently, both the income effects and the price effects of a slowing of growth of total demand improve the nation's trade position and its balance of payments.

There is another line of effects running in the opposite direction. Causing economic slack in a country, as we have seen, ordinarily leads to a reduction in its interest rates. This will tend to cause both domestic and foreign investors to shift their funds from that country to others where interest rates are higher. In some cases, this capital outflow might at least temporarily more than offset the favorable effects upon the nation's trade balance of a restrictive stabilization policy.

Under the international economic system associated with the gold standard as it existed before the First World War, changes in national stabilization policy were considered the major means of correcting payments imbalance. Moreover, the corrective mechamism worked almost automatically. If a nation experienced a continued balance of payments deficit, this would lead to reduction in the value of its currency on the foreign exchange market. When the value of the currency declined to the "gold export point," it became profitable to exchange, say, dollars for gold and export the gold as a means of acquiring foreign currencies. While this export of gold financed the deficit and maintained the exchange rate within a stable corridor, it reduced the money supply in the country exporting gold. We recall that unless offset or sterilized, an export of gold reduces the monetary base and the money supply. This reduction in the money supply is an automatic restrictive response of stabilization policy to the balance of payments deficit.

While this mechanism was thought at the time to work satisfactorily before the First World War,[2] experience with it in the 1920s and 1930s was less favorable. The crucial difficulty was the inability of Great Britain—in contrast to the performance of the United States—to reduce its price level by enough to successfully carry out its plan of returning to the gold standard after the First World War at the old gold value of the pound, a case that we shall consider later. Given its adverse Phillips curve of that period, England suffered large unemployment and depressed economic conditions during most of the 1920s. The British view came to take for granted its adverse Phillips curve and—given this—its unwise decision to return to gold at the old parity, blaming Britain's plight on the inadequate adjustability of exchange rates in the gold-standard system. Thus when the time came to try to put together the pieces of the international economic system after the Second World War, the British adamantly opposed a return to fixed exchange rates. The compromise result of the Bretton Woods Conference of 1944 was the adjustable-peg system.

Correction of payments imbalance under the adjustable-peg system

The effort to preserve as much as possible of the advantages of fixed exchange rates while meeting the British objection that national prosperity should not be sacrificed to stability of exchange rates led to an approach by which exchanges rates would be adjusted only occasionally, as required to correct "fundamental" imbalance in international payments. The logic of the system is that it preserves fixity of exchange rates as far as possible but permits adjustment where this is necessary. The rules to be followed by national governments are defined by the Articles of Agreement of the International Monetary Fund. They provide that each national currency shall be maintained within 1 percent of a stated par value, which is to be changed only with the concurrence of the IMF.

In practice, this approach has proved to have a number of shortcomings:

1. Adjustment of exchange rates is delayed for a long period of time until it is certain that the balance of payments problem is fundamental. Thus, international payments may be out of balance in one direction or the

[2] Just how the system worked, and why it worked as well as it did, are reconsidered in recent research. For a summary, see Robert Triffin, *Our International Monetary System*, chap. 1, Random House, New York, 1968; Arthur I. Bloomfield, *Monetary Policy under the International Gold Standard: 1880–1914*, Federal Reserve Bank of New York, New York, 1959.

other most of the time. Responding to these inappropriate exchange rates may lead to misallocation of resources.

2. By the time an adjustment of exchange rates is made, it is clear to everyone including speculators which way the adjustment must go. This leads to a speculative outflow of capital from the nation whose currency is to be devalued. This creates an awkward situation in international payments, the more so since government officials until the very moment the devaluation occurs must officially deny that it is going to occur in order to avoid encouraging the adverse speculation.

3. When a nation's balance of payments has been out of balance for some time and the required adjustment is rather large, there may be no way of knowing just how much of a change in exchange rates is needed. Ideally, the nation would like to run a payments surplus for a time to build up its depleted monetary reserves and then shift to a balanced position. But occasional adjustments of exchange rates cannot achieve all of this.

4. In view of the uncertainty as to how they will work out and their political and economic costs, national governments are reluctant to make adjustments in exchange rates.[3] This leads them into trade restrictions and other actions that although undesirable at least are not so conspicuous and so uncertain in their outcome as adjustments in exchange rates.

The adjustable-peg system is perhaps a logical one if, indeed, changes in exchange rates will be needed only rarely. This would be true if nations ordinarily accepted "the discipline of the balance of payments" and in almost all cases prevented a lasting imbalance in international payments through adjustments in their domestic price levels. This would be possible despite the prevalence of inflation if nations with deficits in international payments could run less-than-average inflation while those with surpluses did the opposite.

But in recent decades, national governments have only temporarily when confronted with crisis situations in their balance of payments been able to exert much influence on their average rate of inflation. France, for example, characteristically has experienced a more rapid increase in price level than Germany. If various nations are inflating at different rates and are reluctant even temporarily to slow their inflation rate and permit increased unemployment to mitigate a deficit in international payments, then what is needed is not occasional adjustments in exchange rates but frequent, if not continuous, adjustments.

[3]As one observer puts it: "It has been realized that under the present system, a devaluation has become a symbol of political defeat by, and a revaluation (appreciation) a symbol of political surrender to, other countries, both of which the government in power will resist to the last ditch; and that this political symbolism prevents adjustments of exchange rates that otherwise would or should be accepted as necessary to the proper functioning of the international monetary system." Harry G. Johnson, "The Case for Flexible Exchange Rates, 1969," *Fed. Reserve Bank St. Louis Rev.*, p. 22, June 1969.

The international monetary crises of the summer of 1971 led to a period of partial departure from the adjustable-peg system, as several major currencies were not assigned par values by their governments but permitted to float, with some management by the central banks. The agreement of the ten major trading nations in December provided for a return to the adjustable peg, but with the corridor of permitted fluctuation widened from 1 percent to 2¼ percent on either side of par value.

Efforts of the United States to keep the tie of the dollar to gold unchanged but induce other nations to increase the values of their currencies in relation to the dollar were not successful. The December agreement provided for an increase in the dollar price of gold from $35 to $38, along with increases in the value of many other currencies in relation to the dollar. Loosening the link of the dollar to gold may lead to important changes in the operation of the system.

Proposals for Increasing the Flexibility of Exchange Rates

An approach that has been widely supported among economists is to depart entirely from the pegging of exchange rates, letting them adjust continuously as required to equate supply and demand in the foreign exchange markets.[4] Surely this approach responds to the need for a mechanism for correcting payments imbalance that operates continuously—rather than only occasionally as in the case of the adjustable-peg system. Proponents of the approach characterize it as one relying on market adjustments, in the foreign exchange markets, rather than on governmental price fixing of currencies.

Another way to think about the question is in terms of international monetary integration. Fixed exchange rates can be thought of as tieing together the monetary policies of the included nations, and therefore as being inappropriate when the various nations do not accept such monetary integration as a policy goal and pursue separate national monetary policies—which are partially determined by the wage-price push situation in the various nations.

Among objections raised by critics of flexible exchange rates are that the resulting shifts in exchange rates would impede international trade and long-term capital movements. This would be the more true if, as is feared, flexible exchange rates proved responsive to political factors and destabilizing speculation and—like the stock market—fluctuated widely with little evident relation to relevant economic factors. Critics point out that,

[4]A readable statement of the case for this approach is Johnson, *op. cit.* The basic statement of the approach is Milton Friedman, "The Case for Flexible Exchange Rates," in his *Essays in Positive Economics*, The University of Chicago Press, Chicago, 1953.

far from being painless, correction of payments imbalance by adjustments in exchange rates disrupts patterns of international trade, causes real economic waste, and leads to unstable employment in industries related to international trade.

For example, an increase in the value of the dollar caused by a speculative inflow of hot money would mean that United States exporters would lose their regular customers abroad because of the increase in the foreign cost of United States goods. To the point that national governments could and, presumably, would limit variations in their exchange rates even though not required to do so, the rejoinder is made that unless some rules are defined for manipulations of their exchange rates by national governments, their politically motivated actions may be an additional basis for uneconomic and potentially unstable behavior of exchange rates.

Bankers, central bankers, and others actually involved in international financial operations have mainly favored retention of the adjustable-peg system. Most economists, recognizing that it is uncertain how a system of completely flexible rates would work out and that such a system in any case is unlikely to be adopted, have been interested in proposals that increase the flexibility of rates but maintain some limitations on the behavior of exchange rates.

One such proposal involves a widening of the range of permitted fluctuation in exchange rates about their par values. Changing the maximum deviation of currencies from their par values from 1 percent to 2¼ percent widens the corridor of their permitted fluctuation from 2 percent to 4½ percent. Clearly, this permits greater flexibility of exchange rates. So long as the exchange rate is not at a boundary of its permitted corridor of fluctuation, this deprives exchange speculators of the "free ride" they otherwise would have in betting on a change in the par value of a currency. The wider range of variation of forward rates might help governments limit unwanted interest rate arbitrage by manipulation of forward rates.

But on the other hand, if the basic problem is the need for one-directional adjustments of exchange rates because of differences in increases in prices and in productivity in the various nations, this proposal would be of little benefit. The countries experiencing the greatest inflation would soon sink to the floor of their permitted corridor of fluctuation and those with the most stable prices would rise to the top, whereupon all of the difficulties of the existing system would be relevant. Accordingly, the skeptic may argue that this approach does not solve the major problem, but increases short-run fluctuations in exchange rates to little avail.

So far as what is wanted is a capacity for continuous adjustment of exchange rates in either direction but with limitations on the scale of short-run fluctuation, a relevant proposal is the "crawling peg" or "creeping peg." This again provides for a par value of each currency and a maximum deviation of day-to-day prices from that value (the present 1 percent, or 5 percent, or some intermediate value). Its distinctive feature is that the par value is adjusted not occasionally and by large amounts as in the adjustable-peg system but continuously and slowly. This could be done by permitting weekly, monthly, or quarterly adjustments of exchange rates but only up to some maximum rate of change, such as an annual rate of 2 or 3 percent. Alternatively, the par value could be set automatically as a moving average of actual past exchange rates, the maximum rate of change being then determined by details of the provisions for averaging actual rates and the adjustment period.

Advantages of this approach are that it would limit short-run fluctuations of exchange rates—and their disruption of international trade—while permitting continuous adjustment and thus preventing rates from ever getting far out of line. It would suit the case in which countries are continuously subject to modestly different rates of inflation or growth of productivity. On the other hand, it provides no new capabilities for dealing with hot-money movements or interest arbitrage. Moreover, if the permitted rate of change in exchange rates were small enough not to discourage trade or encourage speculation it would not provide enough flexibility of rates to maintain adjustment between nations with quite different inflation rates.

That each proposal seems to have shortcomings to offset its strengths is discouraging, but not really surprising. We face the basic dilemma that both international economic integration and economic nationalism have their attractive points, but there is no way to go down both roads at the same time.

Opinion in recent years has shifted toward favoring greater flexibility of exchange rates, perhaps toward a creeping-peg system for at least those countries that wish to try it. Modification of the IMF Articles of Agreement to permit such experimentation may come in the 1970s. Since it is difficult to get agreement as to the one *best* way of getting more flexibility of exchange rates and the particular problems of various countries may be best served by different arrangements, one suggested approach to policy is to permit various kinds of experimentation with the concurrence and advice of the IMF.[5]

Let us now restate the major features of the existing international economic system and some of the directions of change that have been discussed in recent years. In relation to government policies with reference to restrictions on international trade, there seems to be a continuing problem of preventing political pressures from adding new restrictions on trade, especially concealed or indirect restrictions. Many economists and political leaders would like to see further reductions in the general level of trade restrictions.

[5]Wolfgang Schmitz, "More Flexibility in Exchange Rates—And in Methods," *Fed. Reserve Bank of St. Louis Rev.*, pp. 11–14, March 1970. Dr. Schmitz' proposal has special interest because of his position as President of the Austrian National Bank and Governor of the International Monetary Fund for Austria.

A development with both good and bad features is the regional trading area such as the European Common Market. This had been encouraged by the United States as a means of reducing trade barriers within Europe and increasing the efficiency of the economies of the European nations. It does seem to be having this effect. This is its good side. But it has resulted in increases in restrictions on importing into Europe some products, such as farm products, that are American exports. Such increases in trade restrictions are widely viewed as unfortunate. Continued goodwill and cooperative action among national governments is necessary to prevent a cumulative build up of trade restrictions.

With reference to international capital movements, no proposals for important changes in the system are under discussion. It is widely recognized that many short-term movements of capital among nations may be more disruptive than helpful, but no way of preventing these that does not bring even greater problems has been discovered. Major reliance will continue to be placed on cooperative action among national monetary authorities and central banks to offset so far as possible the disruptive effects of short-term capital movements. The way this is done is discussed in the next chapter.

A decade or two ago most economists and political leaders would have objected to the suggestion that the stabilization policy of a nation should be governed to any significant extent by balance of payments considerations. Since then, there has been some shifting of opinion away from this view. The view has been increasingly accepted that national policy must deal with the inflation problem, in any case, and that restraint on growth of total demand is an essential program of inflation control. Thus, there is more sympathy recently than there would have been earlier toward the view that the balance of payments may serve as a politically useful discipline in aiding national governments to pursue policies that limit inflation. The fact that restrictive stabilization policies in recent experiments have proved successful in both limiting inflation and improving the nation's balance of payments—contrary to what some economists predicted—lends some reinforcement to this change of view.

The debate about introducing greater flexibility into exchange rates doubtless will continue. There are advantages and disadvantages in both fixity and flexibility of exchange rates, and it is natural that judgments should differ as to how these balance off. No drastic revision of the international economic system is likely. However, individual nations may experiment with greater adjustability of exchange rates, and some modification of the general rules of the game as defined by the International Monetary Fund to permit such experimentation and to foster greater adjustability of exchange rates is possible.

The international monetary crises of 1971 and the important agreement of December 1971 pointed the way to major changes in the international economic system. The multilateral agreement among the leading nations for a general realignment of exchange rates, a devaluation of the dollar in relation to gold, a widening of the band of permitted fluctuation in exchange rates, and for continuing negotiation over reductions in certain trade restrictions was another great decision point for the international economic system.

SUMMARY

1. An exchange rate is the price of one national currency in terms of another. It is determined, like other prices, by supply and demand. However, national governments commonly buy and sell their national currencies as necessary to stabilize their exchange rates.

2. The value of a currency on the foreign exchange market (or its exchange rate) tends to be increased by transactions involving a demand for the currency, such as exports of goods and services and the export of securities (or inflow of capital).

3. The net liquidity balance measures changes in the sum of private and official positions with reference to international liquidity. The balance on official reserve transactions measures the change in the resources available to the authorities to support the national currencies.

4. The problem of the United States balance of payments in the 1960s was one of excessive deficit, which called into question the continued value and free convertibility of the dollar.

5. There are four classes of action a nation can take to correct a deficit in its international payments: (*a*) restrict its imports of goods and services by additional trade restrictions; (*b*) limit the outflow of capital; (*c*) limit growth of total demand, thereby affecting domestic prices and incomes; and (*d*) permit a reduction in the external value of its currency, or devalue the currency.

6. The existing international economic system involves infrequent adjustments of exchange rates for major currencies (the adjustable-peg system) to deal only with "fundamental disequilibrium" in international payments. Restrictions on international capital flows are reserved largely for temporary speculative movements of capital. In effect, some adjustments of trade restrictions are made to combat payments imbalance. Limiting inflation is essential to avoidance of payments deficits; the use of monetary and fiscal policies to deal with payments imbalance has been viewed with diminishing disfavor in recent years.

7. Shortcomings of the adjustable-peg system led to increasing discussion of ways of making greater use of exchange-rate adjustments to correct imbalance in international payments, through free-floating exchange rates or the creeping peg. The crises of 1971 highlighted the need for more effective ways of correcting imbalance in international payments.

QUESTIONS FOR REVIEW AND DISCUSSION

1. Explain how a United States importer of French goods might pay for them. What effects would this transaction tend to have on the value of the dollar in the foreign exchange market? on the franc? How would it affect the United States balance of payments? If the importer planned to pay for the goods 90 days after ordering, how could he use the forward market to avoid exchange risk?

2. How might a Frenchman engage in speculative transactions if he believed the franc was likely to be devalued? How might a German attempt to benefit from an expected devaluation of the franc? What effect would each of these transactions have on the foreign exchange markets?

3. How might interest arbitrage lead an Englishman to buy dollars? Explain the role of exchange risk in this transaction and the conditions under which covered interest arbitrage is profitable.

4. Indicate the effect on the United States balance of payments deficit or surplus of (*a*) an increase in United States imports, (*b*) foreign aid expenditures of the United States governments, (*c*) receipts of interest on foreign investments of private United States investors, (*d*) an inflow of short-term capital into the United States, and (*e*) the sale of gold by the U.S. Treasury to a foreign central bank.

5. Distinguish the balance of payments deficit on the official reserve transactions basis from the deficit in the net liquidity balance.

6. "A balance of payments deficit is always a sign of weakness, which every country should try to avoid." Comment critically. Are there any particular circumstances in which a balance of payments deficit is normal or desirable?

7. Explain the political implications of alternative international economic systems.

8. Assume Italy is facing an undesired balance of payments deficit. Review the various steps the Italian government might take to deal with the situation, commenting on the pros and cons of each. In what ways, if any, would the response differ if the country with the payments deficit was the United States?

9. What are exchange controls? Why would a nation want to use them? What problems do they raise?

10. What is the automatic mechanism for correction of imbalance in international payments that operated under the gold-standard system?

How could this mechanism be instituted in the modern world? Do you think it would be a good idea? How would the feasibility of the mechanism relate to the Phillips curves prevailing in the various nations?

11. Describe the adjustable-peg system. What are its major shortcomings? Discuss and evaluate the major proposals for increasing the flexibility of exchange rates.

12. Describe the role of the United States dollar and the German mark in the international monetary crises of 1971. Discuss the shortcomings of the prevailing international economic system that led to this outcome.

17

the international monetary system

Under the adjustable-peg system of exchange rates, national monetary authorities and central banks must buy and sell their national currencies in the foreign exchange market to keep exchange rates within a certain range from par value. Such operations in gold and foreign exchange carried on by the Federal Reserve Bank of New York as agent for the Federal Open Market Committee and the U.S. Treasury were discussed in Chap. 8. These operations affect the monetary base and the supply.

In their activities as residual buyers of their national currencies in the foreign exchange markets, the central banks must have some agreed means of settlement that they will accept from one another. This central-banker money is termed "international monetary reserves" (also sometimes called "international liquidity"). The amount of international monetary reserves (IMRs) and changes in their amount over time depend upon what it is that central bankers agree to define as IMRs. We can think of this as defined by an international monetary system (i.e., a system for generating IMRs) that they establish and maintain.

The International Monetary System and Its Implications

In international transactions, no single money serves as a universally acceptable medium of exchange as the dollar is the medium of exchange in the United States. Private transactions ordinarily involve the exchange of currencies in the foreign exchange market. Businesses engaged in large foreign operations may hold balances in some of the national currencies that are most widely acceptable, using these as a kind of "international money." In the modern world, the dollar is the currency most widely used in this way. The subject of this chapter is not the international money, in this limited sense, used by individuals and businesses, but rather the reserve assets held by central banks and national monetary authorities. (To save words, we refer only to central banks below, recognizing that some of their foreign operations are conducted on behalf of or jointly with Treasury departments or national monetary authorities.) It is international monetary reserves in the specific sense of the assets held by central banks as reserves that affect monetary policy in the various nations.

Under the gold standard, such international monetary reserves consisted of the holdings of gold by central banks. After the First World War, the definition of international monetary reserves was broadened to include not only gold but also holdings of balances in certain key currencies, mainly the British pound. After the Second World War, the dollar and certain freely available balances at the International Monetary Fund were added.

The United States is not in a typical position in this system, since the dollar is the leading key currency. While other nations can hold dollars to sell as needed to support their currencies, obviously the United States cannot sell dollars to support the dollar. Its international monetary reserves must be held in other forms. As is indicated by Fig. 17–1, the monetary reserves of the United States consist primarily of gold, but the nation's gold reserves declined nearly one-half from 1957 to 1970. Our reserve position in the International Monetary Fund was the second largest component of our IMRs in 1970, but was not much larger than a decade earlier. Holdings of foreign exchange, or convertible foreign currencies, played a growing role in the 1960s as an active or variable component of our IMRs. The new Special Drawing Rights entered the picture in 1970.

International monetary reserves and monetary theory

Monetary theory tells us that money is an important causal variable in the economy, in part because the choice of a monetary system is optional, because it is politically based, and because the amount of money affects the performance of the economy. Thus, a possible explanation of why Brazil has inflation while Germany does not is that Germany chose to adopt a different set of monetary institutions. Does this logic carry over to international monetary reserves?

International monetary reserves differ from ordinary money in several ways. They are used only by central banks, which are limited in number. Moreover, central banks do not use international monetary reserves for hour-to-hour transactions as a national money is used, but only as a means of settling net claims in one direction or the other. However, despite these differences, the points emphasized above do apply to international monetary reserves. The definition of what is to serve as international monetary reserves is optional; it is not governed by any strict economic logic but is a matter of political choice. The central banks and governments of the world

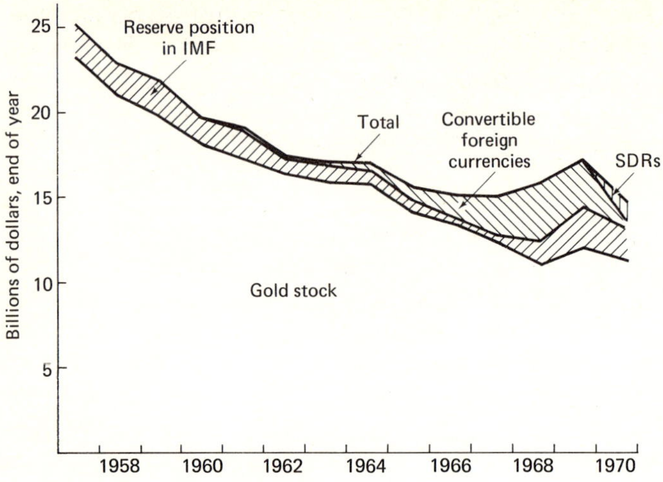

Fig. 17-1 International monetary reserves of the United States. (U.S. Department of the Treasury.)

in recent years, after long negotiation, have agreed to establish a new kind of asset as international monetary reserves: the Special Drawing Rights of the International Monetary Fund. This surely illustrates the point.

It must be granted, also, that the amount of international reserve assets depends upon what are defined as international reserve assets. The desire to define Special Drawing Rights as an international reserve asset stemmed from the belief that the amount of international monetary reserves otherwise would not grow as rapidly as was needed.

The final step in the logic also must be accepted. The behavior of central banks and national money supplies is affected by the amount of IMRs held by the central banks. Therefore, monetary theory applies to international monetary reserves in the sense that the amount of these stems from a political choice and that this affects the performance of the economies of the various nations.

The desired behavior of international monetary reserves

The desired performance of the national money supply is that it should provide the public with the amount of money it wants to use when total demand grows along the optimal path and when interest rates, expectations, and other factors are consistent with this pattern of events. This implies in a growing economy that the money supply should grow rather steadily from year to year. Definition of the desired behavior of international monetary reserves involves the same logic. There is some best-attainable average rate of growth of money incomes for the nations as a whole, some best-attainable rate of growth of world trade consistent with this, and paths of other variables consistent with this package. In most if not all nations in the present-day world, the best-attainable course of events will involve some inflation, since prevailing institutions make price stability inconsistent with full employment. Therefore, for the world as a whole, the best-attainable set of developments will include some inflation and will require a rate of growth of international monetary reserves that will permit this.

Since money incomes in the various nations are rising and international trade in money terms is increasing, it is to be expected that the desired behavior of international monetary reserves will involve a rather steady rate of growth. A precise formula for the optimal growth rate of international monetary reserves cannot be defined, since this depends in part upon the behavior of central banks in deciding their desired ratios of reserves to their liabilities.[1] The desired reserve ratio of central banks, in turn, depends on the responsibilities they assume to support their exchange rates and on the desire of national governments to hold reserves of international purchasing power for other purposes.

In an extreme system of floating exchange rates, the central banks would not intervene in foreign exchange markets at all, but would let exchange rates be set entirely by market forces. Within such a system, no international monetary reserves would be needed. If the existing international economic system were revised so as to correct imbalance in international payments largely through continuous adjustments of exchange rates—perhaps by adopting the crawling peg—this would reduce the responsibilities of central banks to combat movements in exchange rates and could be expected to reduce the amount of reserves they want to hold. In the absence of such changes in the international economic system, it is reasonable to expect the required growth of international monetary reserves to be roughly proportional to the growth of world money incomes and the money value of international trade. Judgments as to whether IMRs are excessive or deficient can be based, in part, on certain symptoms we can define.

Even if the amount of international monetary reserves began at precisely the right level and grew at just the right rate, this would not mean that *each central bank* would hold just the amount of reserves that it desired. The distribution of reserves among nations depends on the balance of payments positions of the various nations. Thus, even though the total amount of IMRs may be exactly right, nations with unwanted surpluses in their balance of payments will have acquired more reserves that they wish, while nations with unwanted deficits will hold less reserves than they desire. Correction of the distribution of reserves must be approached through improving mechanisms for correcting imbalance in international payments, along the lines discussed in Chap. 16.

But if the total amount of international monetary reserves is right, this implies that if some central banks have less reserves than they wish

[1] A recent discussion of the question is Julio H. G. Olivera, "A Note on the Optimal Rate of Growth of International Reserves," *J. Polit. Econ.*, **77**:245–248 (1969).

other central banks must have more than they wish. The unfulfilled desires of the central banks will be symmetrical. If almost all central bankers want more international monetary reserves than they have when world income and trade are on the appropriate path, then the amount of IMRs is deficient. There simply are not enough to go around, to meet the demand.

Results of too much or too little IMRs

The effects of a general deficiency of international monetary reserves can be defined on the basis of the discussion in Chap. 16 of policies toward the national balance of payments. If most central bankers think their international monetary reserves are too small, then most nations will be trying to run balance of payments surpluses in order to increase their reserves. A nation in this position imposes additional restrictions on imports and on outflow of capital, restricts growth of total demand and thereby causes greater unemployment than would otherwise be deemed desirable, and devalues the national currency or permits its international value to decline.

For these actions to be effective in improving the balance of payments of a nation, they must not be retaliated upon by others. Once again, the balance-of-payments game is a zero-sum game. Deficits must offset surpluses. Everyone cannot run a surplus. Therefore efforts by most nations to run balance-of-payments surpluses will be self-defeating, leading to a combination of increasing restrictions on trade and capital movements, deflation and excessive unemployment in the various nations, and competitive devaluations of the national currencies. This is exactly what happened in the early 1930s when the collapse of the international monetary system resulted in a general deficiency of international monetary reserves. The tearing apart of the international economic system in that period was caused in substantial part by the failure of the international monetary system and the efforts of most nations to run balance-of-payments surpluses.

An excessive growth rate of international monetary reserves would lead to undesired inflationary developments in the various nations and to widespread efforts by central banks to sterilize inflows of reserves and to reduce their balance-of-payments surpluses.

International monetary reserves and the national money supply

The behavior of the national money supply was interpreted above in terms of three determinants: The amount of high-powered money, or the monetary base, the currency ratio, and the reserve ratio of commercial banks. Their holdings of international monetary reserves are to the central banks rather like what holdings of reserves are to the commercial banks. In some cases, central banks may wish to hold an amount of international monetary reserves that bears a fairly steady relation to their monetary liabilities. In the United States, until recently the Federal Reserve System was obliged by law to hold gold certificates equal to a minimum proportion of its notes and deposits. Thus, one framework for interpreting the influence of international monetary reserves is in terms of a reserve ratio that central banks maintain between their IMRs and their monetary liabilities.

Assume a central bank desires to hold IMRs equal to some proportion z of the nation's monetary base B, or IMRs $= zB$. So long as the bank maintains this relation, the monetary base is determined by its holdings of IMRs and an IMRs–monetary base multiplier defined by $1/z$, or $B =$ IMRs$(1/z)$. Thus, changes in the monetary base can be interpreted in terms of changes in the central bank's holdings of international monetary reserves and changes in its reserve ratio.

Central banks commonly do not insist upon a completely fixed reserve ratio; however, they may have some minimum reserve ratio below which they are unwilling to go (z_{min}). They may also have a maximum reserve ratio (z_{max}) beyond which they become quite uncomfortable. These circumstances define a corridor for the monetary base as depicted in Fig. 17–2. The slope of this corridor depends upon the rate of increase in the central bank's holdings of international monetary reserves. Its width depends upon the range over which the central bank is willing to let its reserve ratio vary.

This way of interpreting the behavior of the monetary base can be incorporated into the basic formula for the money supply:

$$M = B\frac{1 + c}{c + r}$$

Substituting for B the expression just derived yields an expression that explains the behavior of the national money supply in terms of the nation's holdings of international monetary reserves and three behavioral ratios: the reserve ratio of the central bank (z) the reserve ratio of the commercial banks (r), and the currency ratio of the public (c):

$$M = \text{IMRs}\frac{1 + c}{z(c + r)}$$

Fig. 17–2 Dependence of monetary base on international monetary reserves.

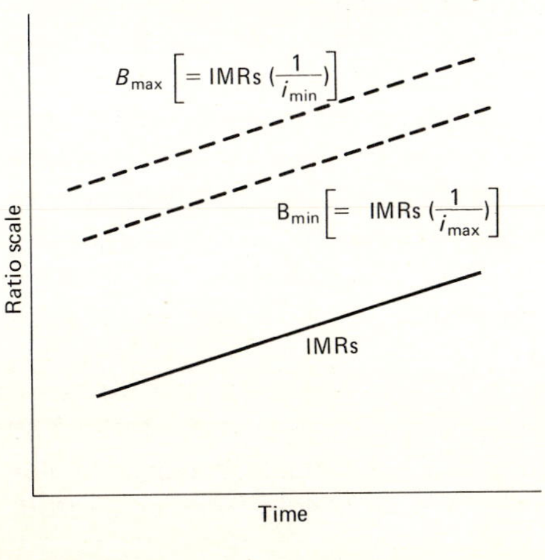

In one interesting type of case, each of these ratios moves in a procyclical manner over a limited range, declining during the economic upswing, next reaching a minimum acceptable position and calling a halt to the expansion, and then rising on the downswing. This behavior of the ratios explains the perverse elasticity of the national monetary system: its characteristic behavior of positive monetary feedback. In explaining the boundary points of national monetary fluctuation—or the width of the corridor of short-run monetary fluctuation—the limitation of the central bank of the range over which its reserve ratio is permitted to vary seems often to play a decisive role. The upswing in the national money supply halts when the central bank decides its reserve position has become precarious and takes actions that reduce the monetary base.

Whatever the short-run performance characteristics of the national monetary system, except insofar as there is a continuing shift in these ratios, the long-run growth rate of the national money supply will be determined by the growth rate of the nation's IMRs. For example, if a nation's international monetary reserves were increasing by 1 percent per year, it could not continue to increase its national money supply by more than 1 percent per year without increasing its composite multiplier, or without reducing in some combination its central-bank reserve ratio, its commercial-bank reserve ratio, and its currency ratio. But there are limits to which this can be done. Moreover, continued reductions in these ratios commonly make the national monetary system more unstable. They raise the hazard that a later increase in the ratio, such as might be caused by a demand of the public for currency or of commercial banks for more reserves, would cause an abrupt decline in the national money supply. The ability of the national monetary system to escape from the influence, or the "discipline," of its holdings of IMRs thus is limited.

Alternative International Monetary Systems

The past has seen several basic changes in the system governing the amount of international monetary reserves. These have importantly affected the performance and the success or failure of national economies throughout the world. The Western nations currently are engaged in a great experiment with a new kind of international monetary reserve asset. As a background for understanding these developments, we shall review the major components of international monetary systems: the commodity money, gold; national currencies used as international monetary reserves; and international monetary reserves created by an international agency.

Gold as international monetary reserves

Under the gold standard, the international monetary reserves consisted of holdings of gold by the central banks. For gold to serve as IMRs required only that each central bank fix the price of its currency in relation to gold. This was done by defining the amount of gold, by weight, in the dollar, the pound, and so on. Another way of looking at the matter is to say that the national governments fixed the price of gold in terms of the national currency. To say that the price of gold is fixed at $35 an ounce and to say that the dollar contains 1/35 oz of gold is to say the same thing. If each national currency is fixed in relation to gold, they are fixed in relation to one another, defining a set of fixed exchange rates.

If international monetary reserves consist of gold, their performance is governed by the general principles applying to commodity moneys. The amount of IMRs then depends on the production function for gold: on technological progress and depletion in the gold-mining industry. The following can be said about the behavior of gold as international money: (1) It is not potentially as unstable as a token money, since its amount cannot decline abruptly and there is some limit to the rate at which new output can add to the stock of gold. (2) The rate of growth of the world stock of monetary gold varies, however, depending upon the discovery of new gold fields and new techniques for mining and refining gold. (3) The long-run expectation is that the stock of gold will not increase rapidly enough to maintain stable prices in a world of rising population and productivity, since in the long run gold mining is subject to depletion and subject to rising production costs.

If the price of gold in terms of all national currencies is kept fixed, the behavior of the world's gold stock depends on the state of gold-mining technology, but there is a possibility of some management of gold as international money if the central banks can agree to change the price of gold in terms of national currencies. What would happen, for example, if all the central banks got together and agreed to double the price of gold? Exchange rates would not be altered. Each national currency would be worth the same amount in terms of each other national currency. But each of them would be worth only one-half as much as before in terms of gold. Looking at the matter from the other side, the world's stock of monetary gold in terms of its command over national currencies now is twice as great as it was earlier. The world's stock of international monetary reserves has been doubled. The central banks by agreement could alter the value of gold in terms of national currencies and thereby adjust the volume of international monetary reserves. In addition to its direct effect in increasing the value of the stock of monetary gold, such an action by increasing the value of gold would encourage an expansion of the current output of gold by making profitable the working of marginal gold mines. In this way also, an increase in the world price of gold would act to increase the world's stock of monetary gold.

A conscious program of managing gold as an international money by changing its value as needed was never really carried out in the past. On the contrary, what chiefly brought the gold standard to ruin in the 1930s—and brought much else to ruin along with it—was a perverse effort of the central banks to reduce the real price of gold, an action taken because its implications were not foreseen.

During the First World War, the major nations experienced inflation that reduced the purchasing power of their national currencies by at least one-half. During the war, they went off the gold standard, no longer maintaining a fixed relation between the national money and gold. The question then arose of how to get back on the gold standard after the war.

What might seem the obvious thing to do—and what was done by Great Britain and the United States—was simply to go back to the gold standard at the old price of gold. This, it seems, simply means going back to the situation that existed before the war. But something important has changed. The value of the British pound in terms of goods and services now is less than half what it was before the war. Therefore, to say that the price of gold in terms of pounds is unchanged—when the price of goods and services in terms of pounds has more than doubled—is to say that gold is worth less in terms of goods and services. Since higher levels of prices throughout the world mean higher money values of income and world trade, the amount of international monetary reserves desired by central banks as measured by their command over national currencies will be increased proportionately.

In other words, in order to have gone back to the situation that existed before the war, the various nations should have increased the price of gold in terms of national currencies proportionately with the increase in prices of goods and services in terms of national currencies. Failing to do this, in effect, involved a reduction in the price of gold in terms of goods and services. It reduced the effective supply of international monetary reserves. To compensate for this, the world supplemented gold by adopting a potentially unstable system, the gold-exchange system, to which we now turn.

The gold-exchange system

Before the First World War, some nations had found it advantageous to hold their international monetary reserves not in the form of gold but rather in the form of assets invested in the London money market. Gold is expensive to transport and to store in safety. Funds held in London earned interest, and so long as the British pound was convertible into gold at a fixed rate anything that could be done with gold itself could be done more economically with British pounds. The gold-exchange system thus arose out of practical experience and the advantages it offered to nations on the periphery of the international monetary system.

The impetus to extending this practice and making it an important part of the international monetary system came from the First World War and the decrease in the real value of the world's gold reserves that—for the reasons we have just reviewed—stemmed from it. Given the decision to go back on the gold standard with the pound, somewhat unrealistically, fixed at the same gold value, there was a shortage of gold. It was necessary to economize gold. How could this be done? By extending the gold-exchange system and inducing nations to hold a portion of their international monetary reserves in the form of currencies of other countries rather than in gold. The Genoa Conference of 1922 by conscious decision took the world to the gold-exchange system, a choice that had great and unfortunate consequences.

Under the gold-exchange system, international monetary reserves consisted of two components: gold and holdings as IMRs of the key currencies, mainly the British pound. The British pound as an IMRs was an inferior money in the sense that its value depended upon its presumed convertibility into gold. This gives rise to a two-level monetary system of the same class that we discussed at the national level. The superior money, analogous to the high-powered money of the national monetary system, is gold. The inferior money, analogous to bank deposits, is balances in the key currency. Holders of international monetary reserves have a choice whether to hold them in the form of gold or in the form of balances in the key currency.

The behavior of the amount of international monetary reserves under a key-currency or gold-exchange system can be interpreted in terms of the expression

$$\text{IMRS} = G\frac{1+c_i}{c_i+r_i}\dagger$$

The world stock of monetary gold is G. Analogous to the currency ratio is c_i, the ratio of gold to key currencies in the system. Analogous to the reserve ratio is r_i, the gold holdings of the key currency country in relation to its foreign liabilities. What can be said about the probable performance of IMRs under this system?

† If G is the stock of monetary gold, IMRs is the total amount of international monetary reserves, I_g is gold held as IMRs by non-key-currency countries, I_k is holdings of IMRs in the form of the key currency, and R_g is the gold reserves held against its foreign liabilities by the key-currency country, we have:

$$\begin{aligned} \text{IMR} &= I_g + I_k \\ G &= I_g + R_g \\ R_g &= r_i I_k \\ I_g &= c_i I_k \\ G &= r_i I_k + c_i I_k = I_k\,(r_i + c_i) \qquad \text{and} \qquad I_k = G\frac{1}{r_i+c_i} \end{aligned}$$

But

$$\text{IMR} = I_k + I_g \qquad \text{and} \qquad I_g = c_i I_k$$

Thus,

$$\text{IMR} = G\frac{1}{r_i+c_i} + c_i\,G\frac{1}{r_i+c_i} \qquad \text{or} \qquad \text{IMR} = G\frac{1+c_i}{c_i+r_i}$$

1. The growth rate of the stock of monetary gold G, as we have noted, is not under any effective control. It depends upon developments in the gold-mining industry.

2. The value of the international reserve ratio r_i is governed by the balance of payments position of the key-currency country. When the key-currency country runs a deficit, its ratio declines, and vice versa. From our review of the subject in Chap. 16, you are aware that we have not as yet devised any fully effective way of controlling the balance of payments position of any nation. The position of a key-currency country is especially difficult, since if foreigners are to hold this currency this precludes putting substantial restrictions on the uses that can be made of it or permitting it to depreciate in terms of gold.

3. The value of the international currency ratio c_i depends upon the proportion of their international monetary reserves that other nations are willing to hold in the form of the key currency rather than gold. This depends upon their confidence that the key currency will continue to be convertible into gold at a fixed price, or that it will in any case not depreciate in terms of gold or lose its value as a means of making international settlements. The behavior of c_i, thus, depends upon the state of international cooperation and political conditions. In this case as in the case of the potentially unstable banking system, if a run on the key currency develops it may spread and the value of the currency ratio may rise until the key-currency country is unable to meet its obligations and the system fails. A run on a key currency is strictly analogous to a run on a bank.

4. If the use of the key-currency system is to provide over a period of years a rate of growth of international monetary reserves greater than the rate of growth of the world gold stock, this requires continuing declines in the system's reserve ratio and currency ratio. But the lower these ratios are pushed, the more precarious the system becomes, the weaker becomes the position of the key currency, and the greater the hazard of a collapse of the system. If there is some minimum level below which the system's reserve ratio and currency ratio cannot fall, the gold-exchange system has only a limited capacity to economize gold or to stretch the world's gold base.

An international token money

A quite different approach to the supply and control of international monetary reserves is to establish an international institution that will create an international token money, a paper asset that will serve as the international monetary reserves of the various nations. The agency can create financial instruments in the form of notes or certificates, like circulating bank notes, or in the form of bookkeeping entries like demand deposits. These will be acceptable as international monetary reserves to any particular central bank so long as it is confident that they will be accepted by other central banks and that for the purpose of supporting its national currency in the foreign exchange market they will serve as well as gold or a key currency such as the dollar. What is necessary to assure that this condition will be met? All that is required is a firm agreement among the central banks to accept the new international money and to hold a proportion of their monetary reserves in this form sufficient to assure that the asset will not depreciate in relation to gold or key currencies.

The international agency could go about creating the international token money by *banking*, acting as an international central bank. To do this, it would engage in open market operations or otherwise acquire debt, say, in the form of government securities of the various nations. It would pay for these securities with its own paper liabilities, notes, certificates, deposits, or whatever. So long as the central banks that get these can use them to support their currencies because other central banks will accept them as international monetary reserves, the system is in business. The amount of the international token money under this arrangement can be varied by the international central bank engaging in open market operations. Thus, this system has a potential controlability that does attach to the kinds of international monetary system discussed above.

It would not be necessary for the international agency to go through the formalities of banking. While there would be some advantage in doing so in that its interest earnings would provide the agency with a source of income to cover its operating expenses, there are also problems in deciding which nation's securities are to be purchased in open market operations. The agency need not even pretend to be a bank. It can simply create paper assets in appropriate amounts and assign them to the various central banks according to a formula. Since what makes these acceptable to central banks is their acceptability to other central banks and since, presumably, this system would never be liquidated in the future, it is not necessary for the international agency to have any assets. Under this system also, the amount of international monetary reserves created is potentially quite controllable by the international agency and in principle can correspond to any rule we define.

It is not necessary, of course, that the international monetary system should include only one of these types of international monetary reserve asset. In fact, for better or worse, the existing system includes all three types. In interpreting the behavior and prospects of this system, it is useful to have some background on the adventures and misadventures that brought it into being.

Historical Development of the International Monetary System

The precursor of the modern international monetary system was the gold standard system that gradually developed during the latter part of the nineteenth century. Before that, some nations held their international monetary reserves in the form of gold, some in silver, and some had the bimetallic system in which either gold or silver served as reserves. Under these institutions, the metals that served as the ultimate means of international settlement also circulated from hand to hand as coins. The relation between the international monetary reserves and the national money supply under these institutions depended on the existing arrangements for creating a national token money. With a system of bank-created token money such as that of the United States, it depended upon the legislation that defined the operating characteristics of the national banking system. Gold and silver were the high-powered money of that day, and thus an international movement of the money metals tended to cause more than a dollar-for-dollar change in the money supply. The practice of coinage of the same metals by the various nations led to a coherent system that performed, albeit imperfectly, the same functions as the modern international monetary system.

The development of the gold standard

The informal international monetary system based upon both gold and silver was potentially unstable. If nations began to shift from silver to gold, for example, this would tend to increase the value of gold and reduce the value of silver. Therefore, nations that continued to use silver as the basis for their monetary system would suffer inflation, providing an incentive for yet additional nations to demonetize silver. As a consequence, there was the hazard of a flight from whichever metal threatened to decline in value.

England headed down the road that others finally followed by adopting gold as the basis of its currency in 1816. In 1872, Germany adopted the gold mark, halted free coinage of silver, and began buying gold and selling silver in world markets on a large scale. By reducing the value of silver in relation to that of gold, these sales implied that nations on the bimetallic system would be forced onto a de facto silver standard unless they took some action. Silver was becoming cheaper in relation to gold, and according to Gresham's law, it would drive out gold in countries on bimetallism. Faced with this challenge, Holland, Sweden, Norway, Denmark, and soon France suspended free coinage of silver. Austria-Hungary joined the gold club when its inconvertible paper money was made convertible in 1892. When William Jennings Bryan—and silver—lost the election of 1896, the United States went on the gold standard in 1900. The only leading nation remaining on silver was China.[2]

[2]For a more detailed treatment of the material of this section see Leland B. Yeager, *International Monetary Relations*, part II, Harper & Row, New York, 1966; Robert Triffin, *Our International Monetary System: Yesterday, Today, and Tomorrow*, part I, Random House, New York, 1968.

The heyday of the gold standard was short, from the 1890s to 1914. Because of new gold discoveries and improvements in gold-refining techniques, the world stock of gold increased rapidly after the early 1890s. Under gold in this period, the world experienced full employment and some inflation. The package of gold, free trade, free capital movements, individualism, and internationalism was a happy one. In the words of Keynes, who was a critic of the restoration of the gold standard after the war: "What an extraordinary episode in the economic progress of man that age was which came to an end in August, 1914!"[3]

World War I and the reconstruction that failed

The First World War destroyed this happy world, and it proved impossible to rebuild it. The nations involved in the war financed their war effort, in part, by creating token money and using it to pay for soldiers and munitions. To permit such policies, the belligerent nations suspended the convertibility of the national currencies into gold, going to a "paper standard" and imposing direct controls on international transactions. Financing the war in substantial part through the creation of paper money led to rapid inflation, more than doubling the price levels in these countries. The war left the world with inflated currencies, a resurgence of nationalism, and a habit of greater control over economic affairs by national governments.

The goal at the end of the war, naturally enough, was to return to the prewar world. But how to do that? How was the gold standard to be restored? Because of the wartime inflation, the amount of world income and trade as measured in terms of national currencies had grown enormously, while the physical stock of monetary gold had grown little. If the gold content of the dollar and the pound, or the price of gold in terms of dollars and pounds, was restored to the prewar level, the stock of international monetary reserves in relation to world trade and income would be something like one-half of what it had been. Moreover, the value of gold in relation to other goods and services would have been reduced by about one-half, thereby reducing the attractiveness of gold mining and the expected future output of gold. This seems a shaky basis for restoration of the gold standard.

What should have been done, no doubt, was to increase the price of gold in terms of national currencies commensurately with the reduction in the purchasing power of the national currencies. If the price of goods and services in terms of the pound had doubled, the price of gold should also have been doubled, to restore the earlier relation between the value of gold and those of goods and services. This would have restored the

[3]John Maynard Keynes, *The Economic Consequences of the Peace*, p. 10, Harcourt, Brace, New York, 1920.

earlier relation between the value of international monetary reserves in the form of gold and world trade and income as measured in terms of national currencies. But while this may seem very reasonable in terms of monetary theory, it was not the way the matter was viewed by political leaders and businessmen. They thought that honor required the nations, which had incurred heavy debt obligations during the war, to return to the earlier gold parity, to pay off their debts in currency worth as much in gold as the currency they had borrowed.

Therefore, the world headed down another road. It was recognized that instituting the gold standard at the old parity for the leading currencies, the pound and the dollar, meant that international monetary reserves were inadequate, so gold had to be economized or stretched. This was done in part by adopting a gold-bullion rather than a gold-coin system. With the gold kept in the vaults of the central bank in large bars rather than circulating from hand to hand as coin, it was more readily available for international payments needs, and the world could do a given business with less of it. The other strategem adopted was to expand the use of the gold-exchange or key-currency system. At the Genoa Conference of 1922, representatives from the European nations, Japan, and the British Empire decided to make increased use of the British pound as international monetary reserves.

England resumed convertibility of the pound in 1925, under precarious circumstances. Reserves of gold were small and the English balance of payments was weak. It was estimated that the English balance of payments needed prices and wages in England to be 10 percent lower than they were, and the reductions did not come easily.

Still, there was a set of rules that would have preserved the system had the nations played by them. The nations gaining pounds because of the English balance of payments deficit should have held the pounds as international monetary reserves, rather than demanding the gold that was in such short supply. But the French, most notably, failed to follow these rules. The franc was stabilized in late 1926 at a gold value only one-fifth of the prewar level. This exchange rate led to French balance of payments surpluses and the acquisition by the Bank of France of large holdings of British pounds. In 1927, and more forcefully at the beginning of 1929, the Bank of France used its claims on the pound, and to a lesser extent the dollar, to pull gold from the reserves of the key-currency countries. The potentially unstable system could not long survive such behavior. Its collapse came in the fall of 1931.

A spreading international financial panic originating in Austria and Germany led to pressure on the pound. Efforts for cooperative action by other central banks to support the pound had limited success. The British losses of gold were such that on September 21 the Bank of England suspended gold payments. The pound no longer was convertible into gold. As a result, it was no longer an acceptable key currency or a fully satisfactory form of international monetary reserves. The demonetization of the pound as international monetary reserves reduced the supply of international monetary reserves at a time when world financial and political uncertainties led national governments and central banks to desire to have substantial holdings of reserves.

We have noted that if central banks in general want more international reserves than they have, they will on balance follow contractionist or deflationary policies, leading to world depression. The extraordinary destruction of international monetary reserves by the collapse of the gold-exchange system in 1931 is the outstanding historical example of such a malady. Interpretations of the Great Depression that emphasize the monetary factor can point specifically to the collapse of the international monetary system as—in a meaningful sense—the major cause of the Depression. Had the international monetary system been one that increased the supply of international monetary reserves steadily year by year in the latter part of the 1920s and the 1930s, surely national governments and central banks would not have followed the policies that they did, national money supplies would not have contracted as they did, and total demand in the nations involved in this international monetary system would not have so behaved as to produce this unparalleled world depression.

The role of the failure of the gold-exchange system as a cause of the world depression has never received great popular attention, partly because of the victory of the stagnationist interpretation of the Great Depression. With the recent growing emphasis among economists upon the role of monetary factors in determining economic developments, further reconsideration of the Great Depression is to be expected.

Among facts that conspicuously fit this interpretation are the timing and distribution of recovery from the Great Depression. Countries involved in the gold-exchange system generally began their recovery from the date when they cut loose from gold and thus freed themselves from the constraint of the system: England in 1931, The United States in 1933, and France in 1935. China, which was still on silver and not involved in the gold-exchange international monetary system, did not encounter depression until 1931, when it began to lose its silver reserves because of the bizarre silver purchase policy of the United States.[4]

World War II, restoration, and reform

Despite limited efforts at monetary cooperation in the 1930s, no new international monetary system was constructed during that period. When countries left the gold standard they increased the price of gold in terms of national currencies or devalued their currencies. Thus, belatedly, the value of the world's stock of monetary gold was increased substantially through revaluation of gold. This plus reduction in prices in the early

[4]These important points are made in the major historical study of monetary policy, Milton Friedman and Anna J. Schwartz, *A Monetary History of the United States: 1867—1960*, pp. 359–362, Princeton University Press, Princeton, 1963.

1930s and proliferating controls on international trade and capital movements provided a workable though far from satisfactory basis for international economic dealings during the latter part of the 1930s.

The Second World War again involved inflationary monetary policies of war finance, the suspension of gold payments, and the imposition of controls on international payments. By this time the spirit of international cooperation fortunately had risen to a new high and ambitious plans were laid while the war was still going on for the planned reconstruction at the end of the war of the international monetary system and for a program to return the world to freer international trade and capital movements. The 1944 conference in the village of Bretton Woods, New Hampshire, built a system that happily has proved more durable than that of the Genoa Conference of 1922.

The Present International Monetary System

Following the expression of determination to seek international economic cooperation in the Atlantic Charter of 1941 and the Declaration of the United Nations of 1942, officials of the United States and Great Britain actively discussed the reconstruction of the international monetary system during the war years. In 1942, early in the United States' participation in the war, the two plans that formed the basis of discussion at Bretton Woods were exchanged. The British plan was the Keynes Plan prepared by the eminent economist; and the American plan, the White Plan prepared by an official of the Treasury Department.[5]

The Keynes Plan was bold and brilliant. It called for an "international clearing union" that was essentially a world central bank. Facing the problem in terms of monetary theory, it proposed an international token money, called "bancor," to be created by the international clearing union in amounts designed to meet the world needs for international monetary reserves. But while intellectually very satisfying, the plan was too daring for the times and was subject to some substantial criticisms of detail.

By contrast, the White Plan was uninspired, but politically realistic and fortunately proved workable. As an application of monetary theory, it was a total failure, quite evading the question of providing an appropriate amount of international monetary reserves. Essentially, it involved a credit approach rather than a monetary approach, emphasizing the importance of the availability of loans to central banks in need of assistance to support their currencies. Theoretically unpromising as this approach seemed, a very high order of international cooperation and competence of the world's central bankers made it work successfully for decades. When in the 1960s it seemed that the problem of creating an orderly mech-

[5]For more information on this important set of negotiations see W. M. Scammell, *International Monetary Policy*, 2d ed., chap. 5, St. Martin's, New York, 1961; Richard N. Gardner, *Sterling-Dollar Diplomacy*, Oxford University Press, Oxford, 1956.

anism for supplying international monetary reserves must be faced or catastrophe threatened, the challenge was met.

The International Monetary Fund

The Articles of Agreement of the International Monetary Fund were signed in July 1944 by the representatives of 44 nations at Bretton Woods. The Board of Governors first met in March 1946, and the organization began operations in 1947. Voting power in the organization is on the basis of national quotas, the quota also measuring the nation's contribution to the IMF's assets, and the amount of assistance it can request from the fund. Quotas are determined by the economic size and role in international trade of the various nations.

The management machinery involves three levels. Each member government selects a governor who attends the annual meeting of the fund, this Board of Governors constituting the highest governing body. A Board of Executive Directors exercises authority on behalf of the Board of Governors. This presently consists of 19 members, 5 representing the 5 nations with the largest fund quotas and the other 14 elected by the other member nations grouped geographically. Actual operations of the fund are conducted by a managing director and professional staff.

The activities of the International Monetary Fund are of three main types. First, as a means of dealing with the disorganized and competitive changes in exchange rates of the 1930s, the IMF officiates over the adjustable-peg system of exchange-rate adjustments, which was defined in the Fund's Articles of Agreement. Despite some imperfections, the system has achieved the goal of avoiding disorderly adjustments of exchange rates and their use in a narrowly nationalistic manner. As we noted in Chap. 16, there is presently discussion of the desirability of moving toward greater flexibility of exchange rates. However, in building an orderly system of exchange rates from the chaotic situation of the 1930s and operating it successfully, the International Monetary Fund, by any ordinary standard of international cooperation, has been a great success.

The second activity of the Fund, especially important during the transition period, has been to work for reductions in restrictions on international trade and international capital movements. In this function, the IMF collaborated with the national governments that were contracting parties to the General Agreement on Tariffs and Trade (GATT) of 1947. The IMF has concentrated particularly on efforts to reduce restrictions on international payments while GATT has focused especially upon trade restrictions such as discriminatory tariffs and quantitative limitations on imports. Efforts to eliminate exchange controls and make the major European currencies freely convertible early in the postwar years failed, and in retrospect seem premature. Thereafter, it was only after a prolonged period of transition and adjustment that general convertibility of the major currencies was achieved at the end of 1958. That it was achieved at all is a testimonial to the untiring efforts of the IMF and the spirit of international cooperation that has been sustained in the 25 years since the Second World War.

The third function of the International Monetary Fund is the one that ties into our discussion of the International Monetary System. The American officials who played the leading role at Bretton Woods did not see a monetary problem of a need for a defined rate of growth in international monetary reserves. Rather, they saw a credit problem, that a nation with a balance of payments deficit might need short-term loans from other nations to tide it over until it could correct its balance of payments deficit—by devaluing its currency if other means failed. Thus, the IMF as originally formulated did not contribute to the growth of international monetary reserves. Rather, it provided international machinery for making short-term loans to nations having balance of payments difficulties.

The Fund's lending operations work in this way. Each member nation is assigned a quota based upon its national income and role in international transactions. It contributes to the Fund 25 percent of its quota in gold and the other 75 percent in its own currency. A nation needing resources to support the external value of its currency can buy from the Fund a convertible foreign currency that it can then use in the foreign exchange market to support the value of its own currency. The nation thus "buying" a foreign currency with its own currency must later reverse the transaction, "buying" back its own currency with convertible foreign currency. It may be more meaningful to view the transaction as a loan by the IMF of convertible foreign currency with the borrowing nation's own currency used as collateral for the loan.

Such borrowing of foreign currencies from the IMF is limited to an amount equal to 25 percent of a nation's quota in any one year and in total may not be so great as to increase the Fund's holdings of a particular currency to more than twice that country's quota. The privilege of borrowing also is conditional on the borrowing nation's satisfying the IMF that it has adopted domestic policies designed to cure its balance of payments deficit.

The overall logic of the system then is this. A nation experiencing a balance of payments deficit would attempt to maintain its exchange rate, supporting it by the use of its holdings of international monetary reserves and taking action to correct the deficit, mainly through domestic stabilization policies and limitation of total demand and inflation in its own economy. If the nation did not have enough international monetary reserves to support its exchange rate, it could borrow additional resources from the IMF so long as it was adopting policies that would correct the payments deficit. If despite the nation's effort the deficit continued, it would be adjudged a "fundamental" imbalance for which an adjustment of the nation's exchange rate would be appropriate.

Since the possibility of borrowing from the IMF was conditional on satisfying the Fund as to the appropriateness of its policies, the nation could not be entirely confident it could borrow and could not treat these borrowing rights as a part of its international liquidity or its international monetary reserves. Partially in response to criticisms that it should make a contribution to increasing the volume of unconditionally available or "owned" reserves, the Fund adopted policies under which a certain amount of borrowing could take place unconditionally, so that these borrowing rights could reasonably be counted as part of a nation's international monetary reserves. Thus, a nation was permitted unconditionally to call on the Fund for foreign currencies not in excess of its "gold tranche position," which is normally the 25 percent of its quota that it paid in gold. As a consequence, this gold tranche position has come to be counted as a part of the international monetary reserves of the various nations. In addition, a nation is given "the overwhelming benefit of the doubt" in drawings so long as the total drawings do not exceed its quota, or its quota plus the amount of outstanding loans the Fund has made in the nation's currency, if any.

The IMF also enters into special standby agreements with nations, permitting them in advance to satisfy the conditional requirements of the Fund and to know how much they can borrow from the Fund if they need it. A supplementary source of resources to the Fund to meet unusual problems is borrowing of the Fund from its members. In 1962, a standby agreement to lend to the Fund up to $6 billion was made by 10 major nations. This arrangement involved special limitations on the purposes for which the funds provided could be used. It was intended to deal with the threat to major currencies associated with expectations of changes in exchange rates and speculative movements of capital among the major nations.

The Fund also has special policies to deal with nations that run excessive balance of payments surpluses. If a nation's excessive balance of payments surpluses lead to depletion of the Fund's holdings of its currency, the Fund can declare it a "scarce currency." Then the Fund may borrow additional currency from the country whose currency is scarce or, if the member is unwilling to lend it, can buy this currency for gold to lend to other members. The Fund also can ration its holdings of the scarce currency among members seeking to borrow and can authorize members to impose exchange restrictions in relation to the scarce currency.

The behavior of international monetary reserves

In the postwar period until 1965, as you see from Fig. 17–3, increase in world monetary reserves came mainly from increase in the world gold stock and from the use by foreign central banks of national currencies as monetary reserves. Despite this expansion, the growth of world monetary

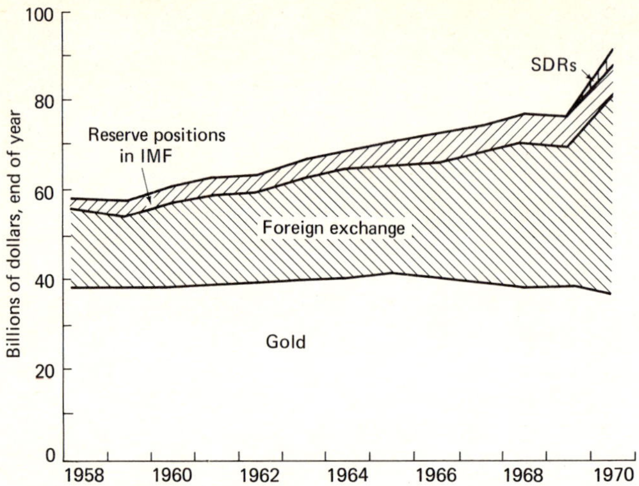

Fig. 17-3 International monetary reserves. (International Monetary Fund.)

reserves was at a slower rate than growth in world incomes and trade, so that the reserve ratios of central banks on balance declined. As a result, the hazard of a general inadequacy of world monetary reserves that would cause a pressure for deflationary and restrictionist policies was raised.

This hazard was much more severe than it otherwise would have been because the sources that had until 1965 provided for the growth of world monetary reserves appeared unable to continue to do so. The world stock of monetary gold reserves stopped rising and showed some decline after 1965. There were several reasons for this. World inflation in terms of national currencies had reduced the real purchasing power of gold, since its price was pegged in terms of national currencies, and thus reduced the attractiveness of producing gold. It became widely believed that the shortage of gold and inability to provide other means of increasing world monetary reserves would require the IMF and the national governments to devalue national currencies in general or to permit a worldwide increase in the price of gold. This led to speculative holdings of gold in the expectation of an increase in its price, thereby keeping a part of the existing stock of gold out of the hands of central banks and thus out of world monetary reserves.

A suggestion made at this time was, Why not provide the needed increase in world monetary reserves by adding more rapidly to the supply of United States dollars available to foreign central banks? This could be done simply by the United States running a large balance of payments deficit. The United States payments deficit would provide foreigners with unneeded dollars, which they would sell to their banks and thus to their central banks. If foreign holdings of dollars grew sufficiently rapidly, an increase in world monetary reserves could be provided even though the gold component of reserves was declining.

But the difficulty with this approach is that the continued increase in foreign holdings of dollars, while United States holdings of gold were stable or declining, would make the dollar look increasingly weak to foreign central bankers. The future convertibility of the dollar into gold would increasingly be called into question. A devaluation of the dollar would imply losses for foreign central banks that were holding dollars, rather than gold, when such a devaluation occurred. It seems that providing dollars in the required *quantity* would so lower the *quality* of the dollar as international reserve asset as to raise the hazard of a run on the dollar—a flight from dollars to gold—that could bring about a collapse similar to that of 1931.

Some other way of increasing international monetary reserves had to be found.[6] Consequently, in the latter part of the 1960s, world economic policy faced a critical challenge. Some fundamental reform of the international monetary system was required.

There were two main directions in which reform of the international monetary system could have gone. One course was to move away from increased reliance on token assets as international monetary reserves and back toward gold. This could have been done by agreeing on a worldwide increase in the price of gold in terms of national currencies. Increasing the value of gold in terms of national currencies would immediately increase world gold reserves, say, by as much as one-half if that were desired. Moreover, the higher value of gold would have a continuing effect in increasing the profitability of gold mining and so annual increases in the world stock of gold. Such a movement back toward gold would be subject to both the advantages and disadvantages of commodity moneys, which we have discussed in earlier chapters. At best, gold could not be managed as closely as a token asset, but at worst, it could not disappear abruptly as could a token asset in the event of a failure of international cooperation.

The other major course was to create a token asset as an international monetary reserve that would command sufficient confidence to permit continued growth in its volume in relation to gold. This is the course that was explored and negotiated beginning in 1962, accepted at Rio de Janiero in 1967, given final approval in 1969, and implemented in January 1970. The initial decision was to create $9.5 billion in the new IMF Special Drawing Rights between 1970 and 1972. In addition, during 1969 the Executive Board of the IMF agreed to recommend an increase in IMF quotas by a total

[6] The problem can be interpreted in terms of the gold multiplier as defined in the footnote on p. 387. To achieve the required rate of growth of international monetary reserves when monetary holdings of gold were declining would require a continued increase in the multiplier. This would require continued reductions in the gold reserves of the United States (r_i), or in the proportion of their international monetary reserves held in the form of gold by foreign central bankers (c_i), or both. It did not seem that potential confidence in the dollar was great enough to permit continued reductions in these ratios.

of $7.6 billion, or 35.5 percent. For the foreseeable future, the threatened logjam in international monetary reserves was broken. As events worked out in 1970 and the spring of 1971, the very large balance of payments deficit of the United States led to an extraordinary increase in holdings of dollars by foreign central banks and, thus, to an abrupt increase in IMRs in the form of foreign exchange. However, foreign central bankers did not desire such an increase in the proportion of their IMRs in the form of dollars. A target for the future development of the international monetary system was reduction in foreign holdings of dollars, with future needs for growth in IMRs met largely through expansion of SDRs.

The gold crises and the two-tier gold market

The maintenance of the fixed price of gold in terms of national currencies while the prices of other things continued to rise naturally created expectations that the price of gold might be permitted to increase—or that national currencies would be devalued in relation to gold. The gold price of $35 an ounce had prevailed since 1933, but from 1933 to 1960 the value of the dollar in terms of goods and services had fallen about 60 percent. The belief that the central banks might be unable to prevent a large increase in the price of gold led to a series of gold crises from 1960 to 1968 reflecting speculative flights from national currencies to gold.

A focus of these crises was the free market in gold that had reopened in London in 1954. The first "gold rush" in the fall of 1960 sent the price of gold temporarily to $40 an ounce, $5 above its pegged official value. Opening a tug-of-war between the central banks and the speculators, the U.S. Treasury reportedly sold gold in the free market, through the Bank of England, in an effort to reduce its price and to prove wrong those who were speculating on devaluation of the dollar. In 1961, a "gold pool" was formed by the central banks of the United States, Great Britain, France, Germany, and four other nations to limit fluctuations in the free-market price of gold. In 1961 also the Federal Reserve Bank of New York, acting as the agent of the Treasury, began dealing in foreign exchange as a way of stabilizing exchange rates. In 1962 it began operations also on behalf of the Federal Open Market Committee.

The close cooperation of the major central banks extended beyond operations in the gold market and the foreign exchange markets. The major resource against a speculative attack on a currency (an outflow of speculative funds in anticipation of a devaluation) was a complex set of standby arrangements for loans (some in the form of currency swaps) among the major nations. These made available to a central bank whose currency was being sold by speculators, loans in other major currencies that could be used to buy the threatened currency and keep it at its par value. In 1962, supplementary borrowing arrangements through the International Monetary Fund arranged by a group of 10 major nations provided a pool of up to $6 billion of their currencies to be used to deal with a crisis. Without such close cooperation among the world's central bankers, it is doubtful that the international monetary system would have survived the troubled 1960s.

By the late 1960s, however, the central banks had to abandon their efforts to stabilize the free-market price of gold. They successfully adopted basically new tactics. The devaluation of the British pound in late 1967 led to expectations of a dollar devaluation and to huge speculative purchases of gold. After providing about $3 billion in gold to the London gold market in an effort to hold the price of gold near $35 an ounce, the nations of the gold pool threw in the towel—or staged a strategic withdrawal:

> The Governors believe that henceforth officially-held gold should be used only to effect transfers among monetary authorities and, therefore, they decided no longer to supply gold to the London gold market or any other gold market. Moreover, as the existing stock of monetary gold is sufficient in view of the prospective establishment of the facility for Special Drawing Rights, they no longer feel it necessary to buy gold from that market.[7]

This bold action created the "two-tier gold marketing agreement" and at a stroke reduced the role of gold in the international monetary system to a trivial one. It severed the link between the value of national currencies and gold—which is the crux of the gold standard. Under the new arrangement, central bankers would trade among themselves a fixed amount of gold—since it was to be neither bought from nor sold to the private market—at the arbitrary price of $35 an ounce, and the price of gold in the private market could rise or fall as it would.

The prospect that no more gold would be bought for international monetary use had a chastening effect on speculative expectations; the gold price settled down for a time to a level modestly above the official $35 an ounce. If the central bankers of the major gold-holding nations could thus agree to assign gold a purely nominal role in the international monetary system, the possibility was raised that they would take the further step of demonetizing gold as international monetary reserves. This they could do by agreeing among themselves gradually to sell their gold holdings in the free market, finally disposing entirely of their gold and replacing it with another agreed asset, such as SDRs, as international monetary reserves. The prospect of some $41 billion worth of gold (at the present official price) being unloaded onto the free market by central bankers is one to give pause to the gold speculator.

This drastic action to reduce the role of gold in the international monetary system was part of a package including the creation of a new token monetary reserve unit, the SDRs. Given the ability to create SDRs in whatever volume is desired, further additions to the stock of monetary gold are not needed. Without the SDRs, however, and given the dubious acceptability of large increases in foreign holdings of dollars as international monetary reserves, an increase in IMRs through an increase in the price of gold was the major alternative course. The tree the speculators barked up turned out

[7] "Meeting of Governors of Central Banks Contributing to Gold Pool: Communique," *Fed. Reserve Bull.* p. 254, March 1968.

to be the wrong one, but it was not an improbable one. Thus, in 1967–1969 was made one of those great decisions that took the international monetary system down one road rather than the other, SDRs rather than increase in the gold price—like the gold-exchange system rather than increase in the gold price in the 1920s. The next question is how this system will work.

The role of gold in the international monetary system continues to be a matter of debate and uncertainty. In December 1969, the IMF announced a plan by which it would buy gold from South Africa, the leading producer, under certain conditions.[8] Those who wished to reduce the role of gold in the international monetary system viewed this with disfavor.[9]

In August 1971, the United States halted gold sales to central banks. Its goal was to resume gold sales to central banks at the old gold price as soon as the dollar was strong enough. But in response to pressure from other nations, President Nixon in December 1971 agreed to devalue the dollar in relation to gold by increasing the price of gold from $35 to $38. When the United States would resume gold sales to central banks and what role gold would have as IMRs remained to be clarified in 1972.

The expanded IMF and SDRs

The discussion and negotiation that led to creation of a new token unit of international monetary reserves occupied most of the 1960s. Attention was first limited to arrangements for borrowing among central banks to provide resources to defend exchange rates against short-term capital movements. But the Group of Ten nations that agreed on the supplementary lending arrangements in December 1961 continued to function and became the key movers in the more basic international monetary reform.[10]

In 1963 the International Monetary Fund commissioned studies by the Group of Ten and by the IMF staff on "the outlook for the functioning of the international monetary system." Having recognized in its report in 1964 the possible need for a new international monetary reserve asset, the Group of Ten pursued the matter until in a communique published in 1966 it set forth alternative means of achieving this and expressed the preference of the Group for an arrangement involving only the major nations.

Faced with this challenge of a possible creation of a new reserve unit

[8] *Fed. Reserve Bull.* pp. 107–110, January 1970.

[9] For one expression of such a viewpoint, see "The Pedigreed Gold System: A Good System—Why Spoil It?" U.S. Congress, Subcommittee on International Exchange and Payments. Joint Economic Committee, December 1969.

[10] An important contribution to awakening awareness of the problem was Robert Triffin, *Gold and the Dollar Crisis,* Yale University Press, New Haven, Conn., 1960 (rev. ed. 1961). For descriptions of the process leading to the agreement, see Fritz Machlup, *Remaking the International Monetary System: The Rio Agreement and Beyond.* Johns Hopkins, Baltimore, 1968; Robert Triffin, *Our International Monetary System: Yesterday, Today, and Tomorrow,* Random House, New York, 1968; and Robert V. Roosa, *Monetary Reform for the World Economy,* Harper & Row, New York, 1965.

outside the IMF, at the 1966 Annual Meeting of the International Monetary Fund many speakers expressed a preference for incorporating any new arrangement within the IMF and permitting all member nations to participate. A series of meetings between representatives of the IMF and the Group of Ten resulted in a draft Outline that was then accepted by the Board of Governors of the IMF in a momentous decision in Rio de Janeiro in 1967. The required revisions of the IMF Articles of Agreement were drafted, ratified by three-fifths of the member governments having among them four-fifths of the total voting power, and the new system went into operation at the beginning of 1970.

This successful outcome was by no means a foregone conclusion. Initially, the United States government and the IMF were cool to the idea of a new reserve asset, preferring conventional extensions of credit arrangements among central banks. The French government until late in the day opposed the new arrangement, and its ultimate assent required skillful diplomacy, goodwill, good luck, and a dash of judicious ambiguity in the documents agreed to.[11] History includes both improbable failures and improbable successes. This is one of the latter.

The Special Drawing Rights (SDRs) involve entries in a special account at the International Monetary Fund. They will be passed among central banks in making international settlements much as gold and dollar balances have in the past. A nation's holdings of SDRs is included as a component of its international monetary reserves. A reduction in a nation's holdings of SDRs is one means of settling or financing a balance of payments deficit. Since SDRs will be only exchanged among central banks and not used in the foreign exchange market—as gold has not been—the operating arrangements provide for a country wanting to use (or spend) some SDRs to exchange them for a "currency convertible in fact," which then can be used in the foreign exchange market.

The rules determining which convertible currency is to be received by the nation wishing to use its SDRs, and which nation is to provide it, are somewhat complex. SDRs may be used by bilateral agreement among two nations, as when the United States uses them to buy dollars that have been accumulated by a foreign central bank. Otherwise, the IMF will designate which countries are to receive the SDRs and provide convertible currency in exchange. Moreover, the revised Articles provide a special category of "interconvertible" currencies, consisting of the United States dollar, the United Kingdom pound sterling, and the French franc. If a nation receiving one of these interconvertible currencies as a result of its use of its SDRs wishes to exchange it for one of the other ones, the country involved is obligated to exchange its currency for the designated other interconvertible currency at a rate of exchange specified by the IMF. For example, if Italy

[11]Machlup, *op. cit.*, pp. 8–12. This is a useful reference for detailed information on the new system, possible future problems, and alternative ways of dealing with them.

spent some of its SDRs and by IMF designation received United States dollars but preferred to have British pounds, the United States is obligated to exchange the dollars for pounds at the exchange rate specified by the IMF, which is based on the market exchange rate.[12]

SDRs differ somewhat from accustomed forms of money. They lack the tangible character of gold, and are not exchanged through payments orders or checks presented to the payee as are demand deposits. Rather, arrangements for the transfer are made directly with the IMF. In this sense, the SDRs are like the giro systems of payments offered by the postal departments of some European countries. In these systems, the payer notifies the post office to make the payment, and it then notifies the payee that the funds have been transferred to his account. In their mechanics, the SDRs have been set up in a thoroughly modern way: they are accounted for by a computer program at the IMF.[13] A money that exists in the memory of a computer is a long step from the tradition-backed and tangible gold.

The role of SDRs in the monetary system of the United States is very similar to that of gold. The newly created SDRs allocated to the United States by the IMF as well as those acquired from other countries are held by the U.S. Treasury, as are the nation's monetary gold reserves. SDRs acquired from other countries will be paid for by the Treasury in dollars or other convertible currencies. This will pull down the Treasury's balance at Federal Reserve banks or its holdings of foreign currencies unless the SDRs are monetized. They are monetized by issuing SDR certificates (which are bookeeping entries rather than physical certificates) that become assets of the Federal Reserve banks, the offsetting item being an increase in the Treasury balance with the Federal Reserve banks.[14]

Newly created SDRs are not paid for by the recipient nations but are distributed, as it were, as a free gift or dividend. Thus, the Treasury is not under financial pressure to monetize SDRs acquired in this way. Their monetization provides a means of financing the Treasury's expenditures—just as would the printing by the government of an additional amount of the national money. The United States was allocated $867 million in SDRs January 1, 1970 and $717 million in 1971. At the end of September 1971, it held $1,097 million, only $400 million of which had been monetized by the issue of SDR certificates.[15] Any change in outstanding SDR certificates affects the reserves of United States banks and the monetary base, unless it is offset by other factors or by Federal Reserve open market operations.

[12]For details, see "SDR's in Federal Reserve Operations and Statistics," *Fed. Reserve Bull.* p. 423, May 1970.

[13]Candelario Trujillo, Jr., "Special Drawing Rights: The Computer Approach to the New Reserve Asset," *Financ. Dev.*, 54–59 (1970).

[14]"SDR's in Federal Reserve Operations and Statistics," pp. 421–424.

[15]Federal Reserve holdings in the SDR certificate account are shown in the table on Member Bank Reserves, Federal Reserve Bank Credit, and Related Items in the *Fed. Reserve Bull.* United States holdings of SDRs are shown in the table on U.S. Reserve Assets.

Limitations on the use of SDRs

The applicability of monetary theory to international monetary reserves is strikingly illustrated by the creation of the new token international monetary unit, the SDR. The dependence of the amount of money on political decisions as to what is to serve as money could scarcely be more clearly illustrated than by this case. At the same time, we noted that international monetary reserves differ in some ways from a national money. Because of these differences, the modification of the Articles of Agreement of the IMF providing for the SDRs defined explicit rules as to the uses that could be made of them and the obligations of nations to accept them and to hold them.

The acceptability in payment of a domestic money is not subject to any well-defined limitations, though the acceptability of checks drawn on demand deposits is, in practice, subject to a number of limitations. What protects an individual from having to accumulate more dollars than he wants to hold? Basically, that the sales of other things by which he acquires dollars are voluntary on his part. Moreover, he can always limit his sales, and his intake of dollars, by increasing the price at which he is willing to sell whatever he sells.

International monetary reserves, however, are acquired by a central bank in pursuance of an unlimited obligation to buy its national currency at a fixed price. As a result, some participants in the discussion have seen a need to limit the liability of central banks to accept SDRs. This view may arise in part from viewing the arrangement—perhaps improperly—as an arrangement for extending credit rather than a monetary system, as characterized the French view and the earlier United States view. The fact that the game is played by a small number of central banks and that one may want to limit his obligations to the others is perhaps also a part of the picture.

Just as the basic defense of an individual against unwanted accumulation of a domestic money is his ability to limit his sales, the basic defense of a nation against unwanted accumulation of international monetary reserves, including SDRs, is its ability to limit its net sales to other nations, i.e., to limit its balance of payments surplus. This can be done, we recall, by appreciating the national currency (increasing its external value), easing restrictions on imports and on the outflow of capital, and increasing total demand or inflation. That these adjustment tools work imperfectly and involve substantial side effects is a reason for a desire of central banks for additional protection against the accumulation of IMRs, especially in their less attractive forms. The basic limitation in the revised IMF Articles of Agreement on the maximum obligation of a nation to acquire SDRs is that it is not obligated to accept SDRs from other nations once its holdings are three times its cumulative allocations of newly created SDRs.[16]

[16]Machlup, *op. cit.*, p. 18; and *Annu. Rep. Board Governors Fed. Reserve Syst.* pp. 328–330, 1968.

There also exist limitations of the opposite kind, on the nation's minimum holdings of SDRs. These have two basic functions: (1) By limiting the extent to which any nation can spend down its SDRs, they limit the extent to which other nations will be called upon to accumulate them. (2) They create a demand for SDRs in relation to other forms of international monetary reserves—particularly gold—that limits the hazard that SDRs will acquire a second-class status relative to gold and the possibility of a flight of central banks from SDRs to gold.

Major provisions operating to this effect are somewhat complex: During the initial basic period of 5 years, each participating nation's *average* holdings of SDRs must be at least 30 percent of its average cumulative allocations. Moreover, SDRs are to be used only for specified purposes, to meet a balance of payments deficit or a decline in reserves resulting from shifts by other countries in the composition of their reserves. The SDRs, thus, are not to be used simply to acquire and hoard gold. The use of SDRs through voluntary agreement with other countries—in contrast to those used by application to the IMF—is to be only to acquire the nation's own currency held by other central banks or for other objectives enumerated in the agreement. These arrangements reflect a careful effort to devise a set of rules under which the new form of international monetary reserves will not be subject to the potential instability that afflicted the gold-exchange system. The initial experience with the new system was judged successful.[17]

Future Problems and Directions for Reform of the International Monetary System

Maintaining an effective international monetary system requires the meeting of new challenges in each decade. What may be some of the major challenges of the 1970s?

Inflation versus price stability: Nationalism versus economic integration

Throughout the world during the 1950s and 1960s inflation has been the rule rather than the exception. Moreover, the inflation of this period is widely interpreted as involving wage-price push factors and, therefore, as not controllable quickly or without serious side effects through limitation of total demand. This raises the question as to how vigorously the effort to slow inflation and gain a closer approximation to price stability is to be pushed in the 1970s. At the 1970 Annual Meeting of the IMF, a number of governors of central banks expressed concern over continuation of inflation and a desire to deal more forcefully with it in coming years.[18]

[17]Comments made at the Annual Meeting of the IMF in Copenhagen in September 1970 are summarized in Larry Helm and John Kay, "The Fund Meeting," *Financ. Dev.*, 41-42 (1970)
[18]*Ibid.*, pp. 40-42.

Different nations, however, will exhibit different degrees of willingness to combat inflation and of effectiveness in doing so, and this will creat tensions within the international monetary system. The nations that want to curb inflation will want the rate of growth of IMRs limited to an amount consistent with noninflationary growth in national total demand and the nominal value of world trade. Some of them will want restriction of IMRs to play a role in disciplining the national governments and putting them under pressure to adopt anti-inflationary policies. But national governments that assign a lower priority to price stability or that in any case find themselves unable to achieve it will argue for a higher growth rate of IMRs.

Moreover, harking back to our discussion of flexibility of exchange rates, if inflation continues to predominate, the nations achieving greater price stability will want to be able to insulate themselves from inflation abroad by limiting their balance of payments surpluses and their accumulation of IMRs. Thus, differences of viewpoint among nations will arise both with respect to targets in anti-inflationary policy and with respect to the amount of pressure that the international monetary and economic system should apply to each nation to keep in step with the average performance of the others.

The composition of IMRs: The hazard of instability

We have discussed the potential instability of the gold-exchange international monetary system. This arises from the hazard of a flight from key currencies—national currencies used as IMRs—to gold, which is associated with loss of confidence in the one or more key currencies. This happened in 1931. The creation of SDRs and the building of a three-part international monetary system—gold plus key currencies plus SDRs—does not necessarily solve this problem. There remains the hazard of a flight from one to another component of IMRs, such as the hazard of a flight from both the dollar and the SDRs to gold. This could destroy the international monetary system.

So long as the various kinds of IMRs are not equally secure in their future value and acceptability as a means of making international settlements, this hazard of a flight from the inferior to the superior form of IMRs will remain. Well aware of this problem, the designers of the new system attempted to deal with it by defining rules that impose on central banks an obligation to hold a certain volume of SDRs, to use them for only certain purposes, and to accept them from other central banks under defined conditions. Furthermore, the major central banks have agreed to acquire gold only from one another and only at the fixed price of $35 an ounce.

The viability of this system depends on its rules being followed by the central banks. If because of general political animosities or accidents of leadership the central bank of one or more major countries began to violate the rules, would the system survive or would it collapse? If one major nation, for whatever reasons of its own, began directly or deviously to use its holdings of dollars and SDRs to acquire gold and expressed fears that the system would fail and central banks holding dollars and SDRs would suffer serious losses on them, would other central banks join the rebel in a cumulating flight to gold, or would they stand firm and preserve the system? A system, after all, that requires every major nation to agree or to behave in violation of what it sees as its own interests is a risky one.

Some observers believe that the danger of a flight to gold is fictitious and that belief in the long-run value of gold is anachronistic or superstitious. Others, however, point out that gold is the one international monetary asset whose value does not depend upon a successful political performance at the national or international level. In addition, they argue that continued world inflation will make the fixed gold price of $35 an ounce increasingly unrealistic, thereby raising the possibility that under some unusual pressure a central bank will kick over the traces and begin a flight to gold.[19]

Quite different strategies can be applied in further modifying the international monetary system to deal with this potential challenge. One approach is to take the bull by the horns and fully demonetize gold as international monetary reserves. This would be done by an agreement of central banks gradually to sell their gold holdings on the free market and thenceforth to hold as IMRs only SDRs and whatever national currencies were assigned this role by mutual agreement—or, indeed, to go all the way and demonetize national currencies also, holding IMRs only in SDRs. For the foreseeable future, this would make gold unattractive as a speculative asset. Agreement among central banks not to accept gold in settlements would—if credible—destroy the position of gold as the safest port in a storm. The agreement of the major central banks to halt transactions in gold with outsiders and establish the two-tier gold market was viewed favorably by some people as a long step toward adoption of this strategy.

The other strategy, which goes in quite the opposite direction, is to maintain gold in an important role in the international monetary system, increasing its official value from time to time so that its price will not become "unrealistic" and tempt a flight to gold. Proponents of this approach believe that the agreed demonetization of gold as IMRs is a radical political policy that will not be workable for want of sufficient agreement among national governments and central banks. Opponents reply that the proposed half-way position guarantees the continued acceptability of gold in international settlements, while continued increases in its price in relation to reserve units tied to national currencies preserves the temptation to a flight to gold. Unfortunately, there may be an element of truth in the pessimistic observations of both schools.

[19]For a discussion of alternative viewpoints on this subject, see Thomas E. Davis, "Gold and the International Monetary System," *Fed. Reserve Bank Kansas City Mon. Rev.*, pp. 11–20, March 1970.

The events of the second half of 1971 left the future of the international monetary system in a state of unusual uncertainty. The planned devaluation of the dollar in relation to gold weakened the dollar's future position as international monetary reserves, although it may facilitate future adjustment of dollar exchange rates. The changes proposed in December 1971 raised the price of gold in terms of dollars, but reduced it in terms of strong currencies such as the mark and the yen. The agreement of December 1971 did not necessarily foreshadow an increased role of gold in the international monetary system.

The direction of future development of the international monetary system that at the end of 1971 seemed most likely was a continued shift from gold and the dollar toward international token money in the form of SDRs as the central element in the system. Further change in this direction seemed to require creation of an international monetary unit in which SDRs could be denominated and in terms of which the price of gold in central-bank transactions could be stated. With gold and other currencies no longer pegged to the dollar and SDRs no longer denominated in dollars, the United States could adjust its exchange rates in the same way as other countries. The unique status of the dollar then would have been outgrown. The international monetary system would have been basically reformed and thoroughly internationalized.

SUMMARY

1. International monetary reserves are like a national money in that (*a*) given the behavior of central banks there is only some single behavior of the amount of international monetary reserves that is consistent with effective operation of the international economic system; and (*b*) the behavior of the amount of international monetary reserves depends upon institutions determined by political decisions.

2. Deficient growth of international monetary reserves leads to a combination of (*a*) deficient growth in national money supplies, leading to deflation and unemployment; (*b*) additional restrictions on international trade; (*c*) additional restrictions on international capital movements; and (*d*) competitive devaluations of national currencies.

3. Where the central bank holds international monetary reserves systematically related to the monetary base, as in IMRs = zB, the formula for the national money supply can be expanded to

$$M = \text{IMRs}\frac{1+c}{z(c+r)}$$

4. The major types of international monetary system involve (*a*) the commodity money gold; (*b*) national currencies used as international monetary reserves—the gold-exchange or key-currency system; and (*c*) a token unit of international monetary reserves created by an international agency. The existing international monetary system includes as components all of these arrangements.

5. The gold-exchange system is potentially unstable because national currencies used as international monetary reserves are not certain to be maintained convertible into gold at a fixed price. The collapse of the gold-exchange system in 1931 was a major factor explaining the depth and duration of the Great Depression.

6. A token unit created by an international agency as international monetary reserves is the most controllable kind of IMRs, if the political conditions for effective management of such a system can be assured.

7. Historically, the world has moved from gold and silver as international monetary reserves to gold, to the gold-exchange system, and to the existing system, involving gold, key currencies, and SDRs created by the International Monetary Fund. The gold-exchange system was established after the First World War in an effort to "stretch gold" and avoid the necessity of either world price deflation or devaluation of national currencies in terms of gold. The experiment failed.

8. The international monetary system established at Bretton Woods was only a stopgap system in that it did not provide a means for the long-run expansion of international monetary reserves. The system of SDRs that went into operation in 1970 has the potentiality of meeting such needs through the controlled creation of token units as IMRs.

9. A series of gold crises during the 1960s led initially to operations of the United States and then to the gold pool in the London gold market to keep the free market price of gold near $35 an ounce. In 1968, however, the central banks of the gold pool agreed to halt dealings in gold with outside parties, maintaining the official $35 an ounce price in dealings among themselves. This created the two-tier gold marketing system, which cut the international monetary system off from any important influence from gold.

10. The continuing role of gold in the international monetary system is one of the major questions for the 1970s. Alternative courses are (*a*) maintenance of the existing two-tier system and the fixed official price of gold; (*b*) further steps toward the demonetization of gold as IMRs; (*c*) an increase in the role of gold in the international monetary system by greater dealings in gold by the IMF or the central banks with outsiders and a possible increase in the price of gold; and as an improbable extreme position (*d*) a large increase in the price of gold coupled with demonetization as IMRs of key currencies, SDRs, or both.

11. Another basic issue for the 1970s is the degree to which international monetary factors should impose "discipline" on national governments to combat inflation, and the terms on which individual nations are to be able to insulate themselves from such factors.

QUESTIONS FOR REVIEW AND DISCUSSION

1. Who uses international monetary reserves and for what purpose? In what ways are IMRs like and unlike a national money? Explain how policy, or political factors, affect the international monetary system.

2. What are the effects of a deficiency of IMRs? Of an excess? Roughly what is the optimal time path for the volume of IMRs?

3. Explain how the volume of IMRs affects the behavior of the money supply in the nations of the international monetary system.

4. Discuss the factors affecting the volume of IMRs and their expected time path under each of the major types of international monetary system. Explain why the gold-exchange system is potentially unstable, pointing out any parallel to an unstable national monetary system.

5. Summarize major developments in the international monetary system during this century. Describe the circumstances that gave rise to the International Monetary Fund, and the international monetary system initially established under that organization.

6. Characterize the sources of growth in IMRs since World War II. Explain why it was not possible for gold and the dollar to continue to provide the needed growth in IMRs.

7. Explain why the free market gold prices during the 1960s sometimes rose above the official price. What problem did this pose for the existing international monetary system? Explain how the two-tier gold marketing arrangement was relevant to dealing with this problem.

8. Explain SDRs, their function and how they are used. What major rules were established for the use of SDRs. To what potential problems were these rules addressed? What is the expected future role of SDRs in the future growth of IMRs?

9. What potential problems are associated with the future role of gold in the international monetary system? What alternative strategies might be adopted to deal with them? What is your own recommended program for the international monetary system?

10. "Growth of international monetary reserves should be limited to the rate consistent with noninflationary increase in world income and trade. Only in this way can the international monetary system play its proper role in disciplining the economic policy of national governments." Define and discuss theoretical and policy issues raised by this statement.

PART 5

monetary and financial policy

18
evaluating monetary and financial policy

For a nation to avoid inflation or deflation and unemployment, its total demand must grow along a time track defined by its rate of growth in labor force and productivity. But the actual rate of growth of total demand and its short-run fluctuations about its growth path depend importantly on the money supply function and other factors defined by government actions. Much historical variation in economic performance seems explainable in terms of changes in government policy. A framework within which we can interpret and evaluate such government policies is therefore necessary in order to interpret past economic developments and to define policies that will yield a better performance in the future.

The Theory of Economic Policy

As in so many other areas of money and banking, the 1960s have brought important new tools for the evaluation of stabilization policy. The related subjects of game theory, control systems theory, and operations research have provided tools that by the late 1960s were being increasingly applied to stabilization policy. A familiar concept given a new precision by game theory is the concept of a strategy, or decision rule.[1] This leads naturally to the idea of defining the best-possible or optimal decision rule and to the application of this approach to monetary and fiscal policies.

Optimal decision rules

A strategy or decision rule involves a coherent set of responses to outside variables. In deciding whether or not to offset factors

[1]An introductory treatment of the concept of a strategy and related topics is given in Henri Theil, John C. G. Boot, and Teun Kloek, *Operations Research and Quantitative Economics*, McGraw-Hill, New York, 1965.

affecting the monetary base, the Federal Reserve, unless it behaves randomly, implements some explicit or implicit decision rule. Alternative Federal Reserve decision rules can be associated with alternative money supply functions. If we can define the money supply function that is best for the economy, we can make it effective by writing out the corresponding decision rule for the Federal Reserve and inducing it to follow this rule.

Application of rigorous analysis to the definition of optimal decision rules for government and business actions has clarified what is involved in the rational making of policy choices.[2] The basic components are two: (1) a precise statement of the satisfactoriness of various possible outcomes, which can be thought of as defined by a social preference function; and (2) a model defining the constraints subject to which the goals are sought or defining the outcomes of alternative policy actions. The analytical problem then is to maximize the value of the preference function subject to the economic model—or to get the most desirable outcome that is available given the limitations of the available policy tools.[3]

This approach unfortunately cannot be implemented as rigorously as it can be formulated, since we cannot now provide an accurate statement of either the social preference function or the relevant economic model.[4] Nevertheless, posing the problem of policy choice in this way makes several important points:

1. In a scientific approach, policy goals and policy actions must be stated in a definite and quantitative way. It is not scientific to discuss policy, as has been common in the past, in terms of the intentions or motives of the policy makers or in undefined terms like "tight money."

2. Rational formation of policy strategy takes into account the side effects of policy actions and limitations on the ability to use certain kinds of policy actions. Such limitations and side effects have proved to be especially important in the case of fiscal policy.

3. Rational formation of policy depends in a systematic way on economic theory, which must provide estimates of the effects of alternative

[2]A relatively simple statement of this approach is Henri Theil, "Linear Decision Rules for Macrodynamic Policy," in Bert G. Hickman (ed.), *Quantitative Planning of Economic Policy*, The Brookings Institution, Washington, D.C., 1965.

[3]In Theil's simple expository formulation of the problem, this involves maximizing the social preference function $U(Y,G) = -w_1(Y - Y^*)^2 - w_2(G - G^*)^2$ subject to the economic model $Y = a + bG$, in which U is utility, or welfare, Y is GNP, and G is government expenditures (the only policy variable included in the illustration). The w's are weights defining the utility loss attached to deviations of Y and G from their desired values Y^* and G^*. These deviations are squared to express the idea that the utility loss increases more than proportionately with the error. Simplified models can be solved for an actual decision rule defining the optimal value of G for any value of Y, Y^*, and G^*.

[4]Illustrative of recent exploratory studies are Gregory C. Chow, "Optimal Stochastic Control of Linear Economic Systems," *J. Money, Credit Banking*, **2**:291–302 (1970); and E. Phillip Howrey, "Stabilization Policy in Linear Stochastic Systems," *Rev. Econ. Stat.*, **49**:404–411 (1967).

actions. Thus, formation of policy, whether explicitly or implicitly, in terms of an erroneous theory will lead to a policy strategy that is systematically defective, that consistently causes undesired effects.

4. The public probably desires a risk-avoiding policy strategy—one that minimizes the likelihood of really serious errors such as a bad depression or inflation. In view of the existing uncertainty as to the exact effects of various policy actions, this implies that an attempt should be made to find policy strategies that will not work out extremely badly whichever theory turns out to be the true one.

Control systems theory

Once we remove the vagueness from our thinking about stabilization policy and reduce the problem to quantitative terms, it becomes a problem of "control," analogous to the problems of controlling temperature, pressure, and industrial processes in automated factories. A well-developed body of thought on the subject of "control systems theory" has been worked out, originating mainly in electrical engineering. An early application of this literature to the problem of stabilization policy was that of A. W. Phillips in 1954.[5] Also relevant is a broader literature on cybernetics and the study of internal control in ongoing systems.[6] These approaches provide background and analogies that help define the class of decision rule or policy system that may be approximately optimal. Such a decision rule will act as an optimal control system analogous to the optimal system for controlling an industrial process.

Monetary policy can be viewed as a control system rather like the temperature control system in a house, consisting of the thermostat and the furnace. This temperature control system keeps the house temperature close to the target value set into the thermostat by cutting in when the temperature gets too low and cutting out when the temperature reaches some higher value. This corresponds closely to our everyday idea of an anticyclical monetary policy as one that cuts in to drive total demand upwards when we experience a recession and that shifts gears to slow down the growth rate of total demand when we have an inflationary problem. Just as for a house where there are temperature control systems that would be totally ineffective, others that would work but poorly, and some small group that would be approximately optimal, so for monetary policy we have in principle the possibility of choosing among a large number of potential systems and should seek to define the optimal one.

The central idea of control systems theory, and of the broader subject of cybernetics, is the principle of error-controlled negative feedback. A very complex system can be kept approximately on target, even given

[5]A. W. Phillips, "Stabilization Policy in a Closed Economy," *Econ. J.*, **64**:290–323 (1954).
[6]See, for example, Stafford Beer, *Decision and Control*, Wiley, New York, 1966.

but limited knowledge of the way the system works, by a control mechanism that responds to the error—the amount by which the system is off target—and pushes it in the right direction. Actually, to define a precise thermal model for any house would be extremely difficult. The heat loss depends upon the severity and direction of the wind, the intensity of the sun, the outside temperature, the number of times people open the door, and so on. If a comfortable temperature in the house could be achieved only by first defining precisely the thermal model for the house, we should all be too hot or too cold most of the time.

Application of the principle of error-controlled negative feedback, however, permits the problem to be approximately solved in all houses without even an attempt to define the relevant thermal model. Given a working thermostat and a furnace that is large enough to raise the temperature even on the coldest day, the feedback control principle can keep the temperature approximately on target.

These ideas carry over to stabilization policy. We do not have perfect models of the behavior of total demand, any more than we have perfect thermal models for houses. Thus, we need an approach to the problem of control that will work even though we lack perfect knowledge of the behavior of the system being controlled. We need a strategy of control that is *robust,* in the sense that it will produce a satisfactory performance under a wide variety of circumstances. The principle of error-controlled negative feedback seems to meet these needs.

Applying to monetary policy the basic principle of error-controlled negative feedback, stabilizing systems of monetary policy are those in which a *positive* error in total demand has a *negative* effect on the money supply. In our earlier discussion, this was termed negative monetary feedback. If this class of monetary policy is stabilizing, tending to keep total demand on target, the opposite class must be destabilizing. Therefore, monetary policies involving positive monetary feedback are destabilizing. The same principles apply also to other branches of stabilization policy.

The performance standards for the monetary system defined in Chap. 2 thus reflect basic ideas of control systems theory that apply to all branches of stabilization policy. These standards provide that the controlled variable:

1. Should show an average or long-run behavior consistent with the desired rate of growth of total demand
2. Should not vary erratically
3. Should show zero feedback or a justified negative feedback—but not positive feedback—in response to deviations of the economy from its desired time path

The use of error-controlled negative feedback may not work out well if (1) the response lags are too long in relation to the period of fluctuation of the system, or (2) there are large erratic errors or noise in the data to which policy actions respond.[7]

These possible problems are a reason for not choosing a feedback coefficient much larger than the one that was implicitly involved in the more successful past uses of stabilization policies.

The Formation of Stabilization Policy

The term "stabilization policy" is used in a narrower sense to refer to policies affecting the behavior of total demand, and in a broader sense to include also policies affecting wage-price push and the balance of payments. In the latter sense, it includes a number of different types of action taken in pursuit of a number of immediate objectives.

Drawing on ideas developed earlier, the major elements in the puzzle of stabilization policy fit together as depicted in Fig. 18–1. The three major target variables of the control system are:

[7]The existence of a long and variable lag in the effect of monetary policy as well as fiscal policy was earlier asserted by Milton Friedman. Some recent studies seem to indicate a rather short lag for monetary policy but a longer one for fiscal policy. Precise knowledge of such lags is lacking, but Friedman's view that they are so long and variable as to preclude anticyclical use of monetary and fiscal policy has not been widely accepted. Another hazard is that errors in the data being used to guide stabilization policy could lead to the choice of policy actions having adverse effects. Apart from the effects on GNP of incidents such as major strikes, for which special allowance should be made, the errors in the estimation of GNP do not seem to have been of such a nature as would cause serious problems for stabilization policies involving error-controlled negative feedback on a modest scale.

Fig. 18–1 Stabilization policy.

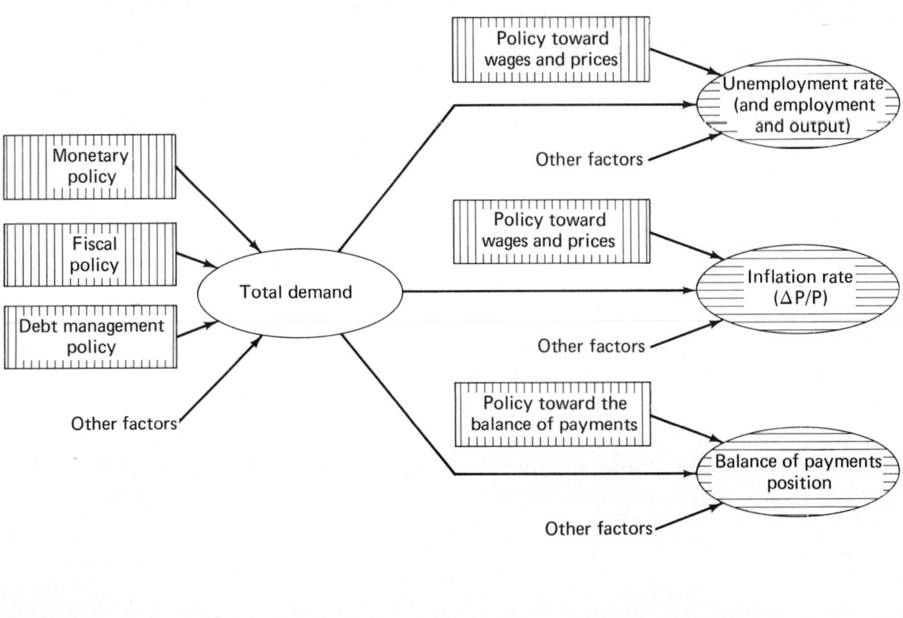

1. The unemployment rate (used as a measure also of the employment rate and of real output)
2. The behavior of the price level, or the inflation rate
3. The nation's balance of payments position

All these target variables are affected by the behavior of total demand. Increasing the growth rate of total demand will reduce the unemployment rate (and perhaps later shift the Phillips curve), increase the inflation rate, and worsen the balance of payments position. Because the behavior of total demand thus has several important effects, the choice of the best available time path for total demand involves a compromise and depends on the available trade-offs among the target variables. For example, it depends on *how much* the inflation rate and the balance of payments will be hurt by a given acceleration of growth of total demand taken to improve the unemployment rate.

The trade-off between unemployment and inflation is defined in the short run by the relevant Phillips curve (and over longer periods by long-run Phillips curves or by the way the Phillips curve shifts over time). Among the factors determining the Phillips curve, some can be affected by government actions. Thus, one branch of stabilization policy involves actions to shift the Phillips curve and improve the trade-off between unemployment and inflation. Relevant actions were discussed in Chap. 15.

The relation between the balance of payments position and the other target variables is another trade-off on which government actions have some influence. For example, the balance of payments position that accompanies a given time path for total demand, and unemployment and inflation, might be improved by imposition of restrictions on imports or devaluation of the nation's currency. Such actions to affect the balance of payments trade-off constitute another branch of stabilization policy. They were considered in Chap. 16 and 17.

These sets of actions affecting the trade-offs among target variables can be thought of as stage I in the formation of overall stabilization policy. Once the best-available set of trade-offs has been achieved and estimates made as to what the relevant trade-offs are (for example, what the relevant Phillips curve now is), the consequences for the target variables of alternative time paths of total demand are defined. Each time path for total demand now can be defined as "buying" a certain package of time paths for unemployment, inflation, and the balance of payments position. This set of alternative packages is the best achievable set, since it reflects the adjustments that already have been made in stage I of policy actions.

The government can choose among these alternative packages by affecting the behavior of total demand. A more rapid growth rate of total demand implies a package involving less unemployment, more inflation (and thus a less favorable Phillips curve in later periods), and a larger balance of payments deficit. The government chooses what it judges to be the best-available package from among this set. This choice defines the target time path for total demand.

Stage II of the decision process involves choosing the best-available time path for total demand and the best-available set of policy actions that will achieve this time path for total demand.[8] Three major kinds of policy are relevant to controlling total demand—monetary policy, fiscal policy, and debt management policy—and many alternative sets of actions may be available within each of these. The costs of taking various kinds of action must be weighed against their effects in limiting deviation of total demand from its desired path. These effects, of course, must be estimated in terms of the theory of total demand. In practice, what is done is to follow certain accustomed patterns of policy, except when a decision is made to make a change—which keeps the complexity of the decision process within tolerable proportions.

Success with stabilization policy not only requires an orderly solution of this complex decision problem, but also depends on the knowledge or theory that is used to estimate the consequences of alternative action programs. Errors in the theory on which policy planning is based will lead to false estimates of the results that will follow from the various possible actions. Thus, an error in theory is to be expected to lead to the failure of policy actions to hit their targets. In stage I of stabilization policy, the knowledge problem involves estimating the behavior of unemployment, inflation, and the balance of payments that will be combined in the packages associated with various growth rates of total demand and estimating the effects of policy actions aimed at improving the Phillips curve and the balance of payments position. In stage II, the knowledge problem is estimating the time path of total demand that will be associated with various possible combinations of monetary, fiscal, and debt management policy. Since existing knowledge is far from perfect, errors of both types must be expected. Diagnosing such errors in past stabilization policy is a way of improving knowledge and procedures for forming stabilization policy and, thus, achieving an improved record in the future.

Branches of policy toward total demand

Exactly how monetary policy and fiscal policy are to be defined and measured are questions considered in the chapters that follow, but a preliminary definition of the three branches of policy toward total demand is needed at this point. Monetary policy as interpreted in terms of monetary theory involves government actions affecting the nation's money supply

[8]This division of the decisions into two stages is a simplifying device for expository purposes. Each stage of the decision actually depends to some extent on the options available in the other stage, so the two are not independent. In practice, the decision can be handled in two stages, with cross checking between the two, and an answer found through a series of successive approximations.

function and the behavior of the money supply. Accordingly, it includes discontinuous acts such as changes in banking legislation and Federal Reserve regulations, as well as day-to-day actions such as Federal Reserve open market operations. Although many factors other than such government actions potentially affect the money supply, the policy actions available can offset these and cause the money supply to behave in a specified way. Consequently, it is meaningful to interpret monetary policy as measured by the behavior of the money supply.

Fiscal policy involves the government actions affecting government receipts and expenditures, mainly changes in tax rates and in government expenditures programs. The concept of fiscal policy is usually limited to actions of the federal government, excluding those of state and local governments. Fiscal policy is measured by government expenditures and receipts, as a first approximation by the net receipts (surplus) or net expenditures (deficit) of the federal government. A shift toward a government deficit tends to increase total demand and a shift towards a surplus tends to reduce it. Since a government deficit is financed by selling government securities and a surplus is used to retire government securities, fiscal policy determines the net borrowing of the government and the change in the outstanding government debt.

Debt management policy involves federal government actions determining the term structure or maturity structure (and other features) of the securities sold and retired by the government. Therefore, it determines the characteristics of the outstanding government securities held by the public. It is measured mainly by measures of the maturity structure of government debt. Selling short-term debt and shortening the maturity of outstanding government securities is economically expansive, while shifting to long-term government securities has a contractive effect on total demand.

Complex interrelations may exist between these types of government action, but the nature of such relations depends upon the policies themselves. Each of the branches of policy can be conducted quite independently of the others. Thus, it is reasonable to consider and evaluate each of them independently. For example, if the monetary policy being followed is one of stabilizing interest rates, an increase in the government deficit would tend to increase the money supply (by increasing the demand for credit and raising interest rates).

But a government deficit does not necessarily increase the money supply. If the monetary policy being followed involves increasing the money supply along a predetermined growth path, the money supply would be quite unaffected by fiscal policy. Under still other monetary policies, an increase in the government deficit would tend to reduce the money supply (since it would reduce the money supply that is consistent with any given path of total demand). Interaction among monetary, fiscal, and debt management policy does not take any predetermined form, but itself depends on the policies being followed.

Alternative Approaches to Policy toward Total Demand

In reading the economics literature and the financial press, one may be puzzled to find, say, monetary policy being described by different people in ways that are quite inconsistent with one another. One economist may describe monetary policy in a particular year as expansive, another as contractive; one may see it as stabilizing, another as destabilizing. There are many possible bases for these differences in viewpoint, but several are so pervasive in their influence as to merit discussion before we turn to discuss the branches of policy toward total demand.

Objective versus subjective approaches to policy

An interpretation and evaluation of monetary policy within a scientific framework as a control system for total demand naturally defines "monetary policy" as those *actions* of the government that affect total demand through the money supply. Policy thus refers to actions that can and must be measured quantitatively and objectively.

An approach that has been more prevalent in the past relates policy rather to the *motives* and *intentions* of the policy makers, not to what they did but to what they say they were trying to do. Nontechnical discussions perhaps take this approach as a way of simplifying the subject. The makers of policy naturally have a preference for this approach, for while their performance by objective criteria might be found faulty, their motives and intentions as they describe them are ordinarily above reproach. Clarity, therefore, requires care to distinguish policy in the sense of the intentions of the policy makers from policy in the sense of the actions that were actually taken. In some cases, there is little relation between the two.

Bias in the characterization of policy

The major source of information on stabilization policy is the publications of the makers of policy: the annual reports of the Council of Economic Advisers and the publications of the Federal Reserve System. Probably we do not really expect the policy makers to advertise their mistakes, or even publicly to admit them. It would not be surprising if they reported their activities in such a way as to show them in the best possible light. But this may be a source of great confusion. By choosing the time periods over which comparisons are made and the particular policy actions to emphasize, the policy makers may give a very misleading picture of what was done—and this without outright dishonesty or violation of any defined rules of the game. Critics of policy, of course, may play an opposite game, leading to another kind of biased picture of policy. A very cautious attitude is needed in evaluating characterizations of policy—for in some cases the picture presented is almost the opposite of the one that emerges from an objective examination of the data.

Alternative theoretical frameworks

Another source of differences in viewpoint and possible confusion in discussion of stabilization policy is that different economists and government spokesmen implicitly apply theories that involve different ideas on the effects of policy actions and even on the way policy actions are to be measured. In recent decades, three major approaches to the theory of total demand will be found underlying discussions of stabilization policy: the Keynesian theory, monetary theory (also called the neoclassical or monetarist approach), and the credit approach. The differences among these approaches are especially marked in connection with monetary policy.

We have noted in earlier chapters that the credit approach measures monetary policy in terms of nominal interest rates and related measures of credit conditions. Monetary theory, however, measures monetary policy in terms of the money supply. The Keynesian theory in a formal sense measures monetary policy by the money supply, but since monetary policy in this theory affects total demand only by changing the interest rate, it has become common for those applying the Keynesian theory to measure policy by interest rates and to disregard the money supply as a measure of monetary policy.

Consequently, in a typical economic upswing in which the money supply is increasing rapidly but interest rates are rising (because of increases in demand for credit associated with rising expected profit rates and inflation), those who are applying monetary theory will describe monetary policy as expansive and destabilizing because the money supply is rising rapidly while those applying the credit approach and the prevalent version of the Keynesian theory will describe monetary policy as restrictive because the nominal interest rate is rising. As our earlier discussion pointed out, there are grave theoretical objections to measuring monetary policy by nominal interest rates, but this approach has nevertheless been widespread. Thus, one must expect to find the monetary policy of a given period being interpreted by different people in ways that are just about the opposite of one another.

Errors of Stabilization Policy Programs

In recent years, the goals and expected outcome of stabilization policy have been stated fairly definitely in the annual reports of the Council of Economic Advisers. As a consequence, the respects in which the policy program failed to achieve the expected results can be defined, and in some cases the particular error in theory or information underlying the error in policy analysis can be identified. For example, at the beginning of 1969 the administration expected the monetary and fiscal policies that were in effect to bring about an increase in total demand of about 7 percent. In fact, the increase turned out to be 9 percent. The goal of 7 percent was a reasonable one, given the prevailing trade-offs among unemployment, inflation, and balance of payments position. The growth of a total demand of 9 percent, while it did result in a favorable unemployment rate, led to an acceleration of inflation and deterioration of the balance of payments position, the heavy costs of which were still being felt in 1971. The major error in this case was not in defining the target path for total demand but rather in estimating the behavior of total demand that would result from a given set of monetary and fiscal policies. It seems to have reflected mainly a misinterpretation of the monetary policy that was being followed and an overestimation of the effects of fiscal policy.

The new Nixon administration aimed at a marked deceleration of growth of total demand in 1970 in order to slow down inflation and limit further deterioration in the United States balance of payments. The goal was an increase in GNP of about 5.7 percent from 1969 to 1970.[9] The actual increase in this case was below the target, at 4.8 percent. The error of less than a percentage point is favorable by past standards, though still large enough to do substantial damage. It implied, of course, a greater increase in unemployment than the administration expected.

This error in stage II of stabilization policy, however, was joined with an error in stage I. The Phillips curve underlying the administration's planning was more favorable than the one that proved to apply. The administration expected the price level to rise by 4.4 percent; it actually rose by 5.3 percent. The unemployment rate increased by 1.4 rather than the expected 0.8 percentage points.

The administration's policy program for 1971 and 1972 aimed to reduce unemployment, cut the inflation rate, and improve the balance of payments. Stage I of the policy package that was to accomplish this involved a number of orthodox actions to improve the Phillips curve and the balance of payments. Stage II aimed at a speed-up in the growth rate of total demand to close to 10 percent.

This policy program failed dramatically in the summer of 1971 when unemployment remained close to 6 percent, inflation was virtually undiminished, and the balance of payments deteriorated explosively. Since the failure was mainly in stage-I policies, the new policy program adopted in August 1971 included radical actions toward the Phillips curve: a wage-price freeze followed by wage and price controls. It also involved radical policies toward the balance of payments: the import surtax and large requested changes in exchange rates. Moreover, the growth rate of total demand was below target, causing a shift to a very expansive fiscal policy. Given the failure of the earlier policies to have the expected effects, the outcome of these drastically new policies was unusually uncertain.

[9]This interpretation is based on Keith M. Carlson, "The 1971 National Economic Plan," *Fed. Reserve Bank St. Louis Rev.* pp. 11–18, March 1971.

SUMMARY

1. The theory of economic policy provides a framework for approximating the optimal decision rule for monetary policy, the rule implying the best possible money supply function for the economy. To estimate the optimal decision rule requires definition of social preferences regarding the variables affected by monetary policy and an economic model or theory that defines the effects of alternative actions.

2. Control systems theory and cybernetics emphasize the ability of error-controlled negative feedback to keep a controlled system close to its target, even when little is known about the response patterns of the controlled system. In terms of this approach, monetary systems and systems of monetary policy involving positive monetary feedback are seen as destabilizing, while the optimal policy system is some specific one involving error-controlled negative feedback.

3. The formation of stabilization policy can be divided into two stages. Stage I makes any desirable adjustments in government actions affecting wage-price push (the Phillips curve) and those affecting the balance of payments position. Given the trade-offs then existing between inflation, unemployment, and the balance of payments position, and given estimates of the rate of growth of the labor force and productivity, Stage II chooses the best-available time path for total demand and defines actions of monetary, fiscal, and debt management policy that will cause total demand most advantageously to approximate this time path.

4. Inconsistencies among interpretations of monetary and fiscal policy arise largely from three factors: (*a*) Some interpretations are based on the government actions that are taken that affect total demand (the approach taken here), while others relate to the motives and intentions of the policy makers. (*b*) Discussions of policy by those responsible for it naturally undertake to represent it in a favorable light, which leads to bias in the way policy is measured and the comparisons that are made. (*c*) Interpretations of monetary policy in terms of monetary theory or the "monetarist approach" evaluate it in terms of the behavior of the money supply (or nominal interest rate in relation to the natural rate of interest), while those using the credit approach and the prevalent version of the Keynesian approach have evaluated it in terms of the behavior of the nominal rate of interest.

5. Stabilization policy in recent years has involved a defined target path for total demand and estimates of the unemployment rate and inflation rate (and less precisely, the balance of payments position) that would be consistent with this. Stabilization policy in 1969 erred in producing a growth of total demand of 9 percent rather than the planned 7 percent, which led to acceleration of inflation and deterioration of the balance of payments position. In 1970, stabilization policy undershot its target for growth of total demand, achieving 4.8 percent as against a planned 5.7

percent. Moreover, the trade-off between unemployment and inflation in 1970 was less favorable than expected by the administration. The administration program for 1971 and 1972 called for marked acceleration of growth of total demand, decelerating inflation, and declining unemployment. The policy program failed in the summer of 1971 because of extreme deterioration in the balance of payments, accompanied by continued high unemployment and inflation. The new policy program adopted in August 1971 included radical actions to improve the balance of payments and reduce wage-price push, and a shift to a very expansive fiscal policy to speed growth of total demand.

QUESTIONS FOR REVIEW AND DISCUSSION

1. Give some illustrations of strategies or decision rules from areas other than stabilization policy. Show how defining the optimal decision rule in each case requires a preference function and a model that defines the constraints to which the actions are subject. Give some hypothetical decision rules for monetary policy and comment on the expected performance and the shortcomings of each.

2. Think of illustrations of control systems from areas other than economic policy. In each case, define the target variable that is to be controlled and the instrument variable that is being manipulated, and characterize the mechanism that governs and transmits the feedback. Discuss parallels and differences between these control systems and the Federal Reserve, viewed as a control system for the nation's monetary system.

3. Discuss the nation's current economic situation and policy in terms of the two-stage process for determining stabilization policy. What changes would you make in policies relating to wage-price push and the balance of payments? Given these, what target would you set for the rate of growth of total demand?

4. Define monetary policy, fiscal policy, and debt management policy.

5. "Monetary policy cannot be independent of fiscal policy, because if the government is going to make more expenditures it has to have some way of financing them." Discuss critically.

6. With relation to a recent period, describe and evaluate monetary policy as this might be done in terms of (*a*) monetary theory, (*b*) the Keynesian theory, and (*c*) the credit approach to central banking.

7. Define the targets of stabilization policy for the current year. Discuss respects in which the policy program seems likely to fail to achieve the expected results. Try to define the errors in theory or information that underlay the failure of policy to hit its targets.

19

United States monetary policy before the federal reserve

Before 1913, monetary policy could not take the form of a decision rule for Federal Reserve actions, since there was no Federal Reserve System. Rather, changes in the nation's money supply function reflected changes in legislation affecting the coinage and the conditions under which banks were chartered and regulated. Such decisions importantly affected the behavior of total demand and economic conditions in the country. Indeed, the inflations, periods of decline in price level, financial crises, and depressions resulting from peculiarities of the nation's monetary system loom large in the economic and political history of the United States.

The United States monetary system always has involved at least two kinds of money. One of these was a superior money and the other an inferior one, or one was high-powered money and the other ordinary money. The high-powered money in early times was gold and silver coin and the ordinary money was circulating paper notes created by commercial banks. In recent times, the high-powered money is created mainly by the Federal Reserve System and the ordinary money is demand deposits of commercial banks. A historical review of monetary policy thus divides into two branches. One set of questions relates to the behavior of the high-powered money, its definition and its relation to international transactions and the balance of payments. The other branch of the story relates to the ordinary money, which has been created mainly by commercial banks.

Only in recent decades have data on the money supply and total demand permitted us to apply monetary theory and to evaluate monetary policy in a quantitative way. Earlier thinking and discussion about policy centered about large decisions and basic adjustments of the monetary mechanism.

Mr. Hamilton's System: Its Building and Its Destruction

After the success of the Revolution and the adoption of the new government under the Constitution of 1789, the nations's leaders faced the most basic decision of monetary policy, the choice as to what kind of a monetary system to establish. The architect of the nation's monetary system was Alexander Hamilton, its first and greatest Secretary of the Treasury. The choice was for a monetary system that was orthodox for the times. It was patterned after that of England, throughout the century the leader in monetary affairs.

The superior money of the new monetary system and its international monetary reserves were to be gold and silver coins under a bimetallic system of coinage modeled after that of England and based on Hamilton's "Report on the Establishment of a Mint." Quite avoiding government creation of paper money, the system provided for creation of paper money by state banks and by a bank chartered by the national government and analogous to the Bank of England. The system embodied the best thought of the times. The reasons why it worked poorly and was gradually dismantled make up a fascinating story.

The bimetallic system

The Coinage Act of 1792 placed the nation on a bimetallic monetary standard. The basic monetary unit of the nation was the United States dollar, derived from the Spanish dollar that had been the principle coin of the colonies. The United States dollar was defined by law as 371¼ grains of pure silver or 24¾ grains of pure gold. Thus, the relation between the gold and the silver dollars involved a mint ratio of 1:15. The choice was made in a curiously scientific manner. The weight of the silver dollar was determined by weighing a random assortment of circulating Spanish dollars. The mint ratio of 1:15 was derived from the famous report on the coinage by Isaac Newton, the Director of the Mint in England.

The legal monetary unit, the dollar, was tied to these coins by the maintenance of free coinage by the government. Anyone with gold could take it to the mint and have it made into coins denominated in dollars at the rate of 24¾ grains per dollar. This free coinage prevented the value of coins from rising above the value of the specified amount of gold. On the other hand, since coins could readily be melted down and sold as metal, neither could the value of coins fall appreciably below the value of the specified amount of metal. The dollar was rigidly tied to the value of gold and silver.

In our discussion of bimetallic monetary systems in Chap. 10, we pointed out that ordinarily coins of only one of the metals remain in circulation. Except under the rare condition that the ratio between the values of the money metals on the bullion market quite corresponds to their legally determined mint ratio, it will be possible to get a dollar more cheaply by bringing one metal to the mint than by bringing the other. The metal that declines in relative market value, thus, comes to make up the circulating coins and effectively defines the value of the dollar. Since it costs more than a dollar's worth of the other metal to coin a dollar from it, such coins are not struck and the outstanding ones are hoarded or melted down and sold as metal.

In retrospect, it seems that this could have been figured out in advance and the operating characteristics of the bimetallic monetary system realistically anticipated. Surprisingly, however, this was not done. It was widely expected that both coins would circulate, and taken as an astonishing failure of the system when they did not. It took a century of experience before the downfall of the bimetallic system in the face of the continuing ravages of Gresham's law finally was conceded.

While the original 1:15 gold-silver ratio of the Coinage Act of 1792 seems to have been about as good a choice as could have been made at the time, later the relative value of silver declined, and silver drove gold from circulation. Another unanticipated problem arose. The United States silver dollars proved to be of excessively good design and quality. They were valued abroad at more than their monetary value in the United States. As a result, they were exported, largely to the Spanish West Indies, where they were hoarded. In return, abraded and underweight Spanish coins were shipped to the United States, where they formed a large part of the circulating coinage. A secondary policy mistake was to make these foreign coins legal tender, thereby permitting Gresham's law largely to drive from circulation in the United States not only gold coins but United States silver coins.

In 1834, Congress took action to cure this problem—and caused a worse one. It reduced the gold content of the gold dollar, changing the mint ratio to 1:16. Unfortunately, this proved to be an overcorrection, as the relative value of gold in the bullion market declined. Now, gold coin drove silver from circulation. This was made very troublesome by the intriguing technical characteristic of gold coins: that they are very small for their value and cannot be made in small denominations. There were now no coins in circulation with which small purchases could be made or change made.

There is a perfectly simple solution for this problem. Produce silver coins sufficiently adulterated with metals of smaller value so that it will not be profitable to melt them down and they will stay in circulation to meet the essential need for durable, small monetary units. The solution is to use "subsidiary coins" containing metal of less than the monetary value of the coin, a kind of metallic token money. In the 1960s, the United States faced a similar problem as increase in the value of silver began to cause disappearance of coins containing silver. The bull was taken by the horns and silverlike coins containing no silver and of small value as metal were coined in replacement. But in the 1830s, subsidiary coinage was an invention of the future—curious, again, though this seems in retrospect. Thus, people struggled along with a technically deficient and quite inconvenient system of coinage.

The great expansion of gold production in the United States resulting from the California gold rush led to what might be termed a "gold inflation." Domestic production of gold rose from about $900,000 in 1847 to about $10 million in 1848 and ranged from $20 million to $60 million for decades beginning in 1849. This produced a great and abrupt increase in the growth rate of gold coin in circulation, illustrating the potential instability of commodity-money systems based upon metals.

The Civil War brought the issue of paper money, the greenbacks, by the national government and their designation as legal tender. Thus, Gresham's law naturally identified "the dollar" with the greenbacks, which depreciated in relation to gold. Although the bimetallic system and the coinage of silver were great political issues through the rest of the century, as we see below, as the story turned out the coinage of silver never again played an important role in the monetary system. When the nation returned to the commodity-money system by making the greenback convertible into gold dollars, silver was out of the picture and the nation was on the gold standard.

This part of Mr. Hamilton's system, therefore, based though it seemed to be on the best thought of the times, proved to be a substantial failure. The fault, if we may put it so, was one of poor theory. The expectations of its proponents as to the way a bimetallic monetary system would perform were unrealistic. They did not understand the implications of Gresham's law.

Paper money: The bank and wildcats

Paper money had caused great mischief during the colonial period and —though perhaps it was necessitous mischief—during the Revolutionary War. What was to be its role in Mr. Hamilton's system? The Constitution prohibited the states and their subsidiaries from coining or creating money. This blocked off the hazardous road of creation of money by state governments. But the Constitution did not explicitly prohibit, and was not interpreted as prohibiting, the indirect creation of money by state governments through the chartering of money-creating banks and even by banks operated by the state governments. In terms of monetary theory, this was perhaps an inappropriate policy. If the federal government was to have responsibility for the performance of the nation's monetary system, it ought to have had full control over the chartering and supervision of money-creating banks. But in the thinking of the times, the dominant role of government was limited to the coinage, banking belonging to the province of ordinary business. As matters worked out, the monetary misadventures of the nation arose largely from the lack of control over state-chartered banks, and it continues troublesome down to the present day.

Until the Civil War, not only the state governments but the national government stayed out of the paper-money business. The War of 1812 and the Mexican War were financed without the use of paper money. Funds were raised by selling interest-bearing obligations that did not circulate as money and were not given the legal-tender privilege. The funds were borrowed from the public rather than created though the use of paper money. The Civil War, however, took us down a new road on this matter.

Hamilton's provision for paper money consisted in the chartering by Congress of a national bank, which was to have branches throughout the country. The charter of the Bank of the United States began in 1791 and ran for 20 years. The capital of the bank was fixed at $10 million, $2 million of which was subscribed by the federal government. The bank was authorized to issue circulating bank notes, or paper money. These were acceptable in payments to the federal government, so long as they continued to be redeemed by the bank in silver or gold coin, but they were not made legal tender.

The bank opened its head office in Philadelphia and gradually established eight offices in other cities. It was conservatively managed, invariably maintaining convertibility of its notes into coin. It was a commercial success, paying high dividends to its stockholders, many of whom were foreigners, especially Englishmen. In addition to its functions in providing a part of the money supply of the nation and in supplying credit to finance commercial operations, the bank served the function of agent for the Treasury in making payments and—which proved to be very important—in maintaining a discipline over the creation of paper money by state-chartered banks.

Let us consider this last function of the Bank of the United States and its implications for the performance of the monetary system. From the viewpoint of a state-chartered bank, the way to maximize profits was to put into circulation the largest possible volume of circulating bank notes. The funds available to the bank to invest, on which it could earn interest, depended on the volume of notes it could keep outstanding.

The basic discipline or constraint limiting the ability of banks to expand paper money was their legal obligation to redeem their notes in coin upon demand. If this constraint did not work adequately, overissue by banks of paper notes would cause inflation. Moreover, an inflationary expansion of bank notes could lead to a reversal and an economic contraction in which banks failed, losses being imposed upon the holders of their notes. Furthermore, even though there was no general inflationary creation of bank money, an individual bank could profit its owners by creating a large volume of notes, using the funds in shady dealings, with the insiders getting away and leaving the note holders in the lurch.

That the requirement for state banks to redeem their circulating notes in coin did not automatically impose a sufficient restraint on their note issue was abundantly illustrated later, when the Bank of the United States no longer operated. The individual or business receiving the notes of a bank in the ordinary course of transactions usually had no knowledge of the financial position of the bank and whether its note issue was excessive. Even more importantly, the individual receiving some notes of a bank had no incentive to take the time and expense to return them to the bank for redemption in coin. It was quicker and easier simply to pass the notes on to someone else. This was especially the case when the notes circulated at some distance from the office where they could be redeemed. Accordingly, unscrupulous banks would locate their redemption office in out of the way places or introduce their notes into circulation in a distant city. No one had an incentive to gather up these dubious notes and take them back for redemption. As a result, the legal obligation of banks to redeem their notes in specie did not prevent the notes from continuing to circulate even when suspicion as to their authenticity led them to pass in trade at only a fraction of their nominal value.

The Bank of the United States provided the missing link in the chain. It assumed the responsibility of collecting the notes of state banks, especially those of doubtful repute, and presenting them for payment in coin. These continuing demands for payment in coin limited the amount of bank notes that a state bank could keep in circulation. It brought to an early end the operation of fraudulent banks. It made the two-level monetary system perform somewhat as its theory said it should perform.

The role of this disciplining mechanism in the behavior of the total money supply can be interpreted in terms of our familiar expression $M = B\,(1 + c)/(c + r)$. In this system, the monetary base B was the gold and silver coin. The inferior money and the token money of the system was the circulating notes of the commercial banks. For any given amount of gold and silver coin, the money supply was the greater, the larger the base-money multiplier, or the lower the currency ratio c and the reserve ratio r. The existence of poorly run and unscrupulous banks caused the reserve ratio to fall as the banks did not hold as many reserves as prudence or sound banking practice required them to hold. Such banks also attempted to reduce the currency ratio by making it difficult to redeem their notes. This loose banking practice could cause inflation by leading to reductions in the reserve ratio and the currency ratio and to an increase in the amount of the bank-created paper money. The Bank of the United States limited this by itself retaining a proper reserve ratio and by limiting the reserve ratio and the currency ratio applying to state-chartered banks through presenting their notes for redemption in coin.

So long as the Bank of the United States performed its functions, the banking system as a whole functioned adequately. The overall monetary system was economically rational. Politically, however, it was a fragile system. The Bank of the United States was a Federalist institution coming up for renewal in a Republican administration. It was understandably unpopular with the state banks over which it exercised discipline, with their owners, and with those who wanted easy credit from the state banks. It was generally antagonistic to the easy-money West. Its profitability and the large dividends it paid, along with the substantial proportion of its stock being owned by Englishmen, did not make it any the more popular.

When the Bank's charter was not renewed in 1811, the dire consequences predicted by its proponents rapidly occured. As it has been put, "seldom have party politics been refuted so fast by subsequent events."[1] The number of state banks grew rapidly, about 120 being chartered and put into operation within 3 years. The volume of notes of state banks increased rapidly. The excessive note issue led most state banks in 1814 to suspend the redemption of their notes in coin, an extralegal tactic that was to become habitual for the United States banking system.

This state of affairs severely embarrassed the national government. Its funds were mainly held in the suspended banks, the notes of which came to circulate at discounts of 10 to 30 percent in relation to coin. In states where its funds were thus tied up, the government lacked the means to meet the interest payments on the government debt, which had to be paid in coin or in notes of banks that were meeting their legal obligation to redeem their notes in coin. This plight of the government, which obviously derived from the undisciplined behavior of the banking system, led Mr. Dallas, the Secretary of the Treasury, only 1 month after the bank suspension to recommend the reestablishment of a national bank.

It was a widely accepted lesson of the experience that a national bank was needed. But although Congress and President Madison both favored the bank, it was 1816 before agreement on the terms of legislation was reached. The new bank, the Second Bank of the United States, was similar to the earlier one, also being limited to a 20-year charter—a fateful feature of the legislation. Although seriously mismanaged in its early years, this bank later performed effectively the functions assigned to it and the nation's banking system had another period of reasonably effective performance.

Had the bank been granted a perpetual charter or had its charter somehow been renewed in 1836, this would have taken United States monetary history down a road quite different from the one it followed. However, the bank's political liabilities this time were aggravated by conflict between its able and indiscreet president, Nicholas Biddle, and that embodiment of the spirit of the West, Andrew Jackson. Once Biddle associated the bank's cause with the election of Jackson's opponent in the presidential race, Henry Clay, the Bank and Clay went down together.

What followed was surprisingly predictable. The number of state banks increased from 330 in 1830 to 704 in 1835. Rapid expansion in the money

[1]Arthur Nussbaum, *A History of the Dollar*, Columbia University Press, New York, 1957.

supply stemming from expansion of notes of the state banks (based upon an increase in the base-money multiplier of the kind discussed above) led to a classic boom, complete with speculative fever. The expansion hit its ceiling in 1837. The crisis of May 1837 led again to suspension by banks of their obligation to redeem their notes in coin. By 1843 when the banking system returned temporarily to normal, the $149 million of bank notes outstanding had shrunk to $59 million.

The depression following 1837 was one of the most severe in the nation's history. Other factors were involved, but in most interpretations the crux of the story was the excessive monetary expansion and the subsequent violent reduction of the money supply.[2]

In the brief period until it was reconstructed during the Civil War, the banking system did not cause another major panic. It continued to be characterized, however, by the circulation of notes of a great many state banks of uncertain soundness and value, many circulating at various discounts from their nominal value. That is, a bank note for $5 might really be worth $5, or might circulate at $3.75, and might rather suddenly be discovered not to be worth anything at all. Banking in this period was in some cases little more than a peculiar kind of fraud. To get a bank charter, print up and introduce into circulation—preferably in a distant location—as many bank notes as possible and then abscond with the proceeds might be viewed as a kind of legal counterfeiting. The burden placed by the system on ordinary people is illustrated by the following example:

> The Towanda Bank of Pennsylvania established its credit and gained a large circulation by having an agent to redeem its notes in Philadelphia. Suddenly the agent stopped redeeming them. "Hundreds of poor laborers," said the *Public Ledger*, "were to be seen running in every direction with their hands full of the trash and not able to induce a broker to give a sixpence on the dollar for them. We passed in the market a woman who makes her living by selling butter, eggs, and vegetables, who had almost all she was worth, about $17, in Towanda Bank notes. When appraised that it was worthless, she sank in agony upon her stool and wept like a child."[3]

The paper-money branch of Mr. Hamilton's structure had failed in performance. In this case, his economics had not been faulty. Had the national bank been continued in existence, the system presumably would have continued to work satisfactorily and our subsequent banking history would never have taken the turn that it did, but Mr. Hamilton's system did not prove to be politically viable. Creating banking institutions that perform as the economy requires and that are also politically acceptable is a problem, however, not limited to Mr. Hamilton's time.

[2] Among these other factors were crop failures in 1835 and 1837, an English financial panic, and the Specie Circular of 1836 requiring payment for public land in specie or convertible notes. This contributed to causing the upper turning point by calling attention to the dubious convertibility of the overissued bank notes.

[3] Horace White, *Money and Banking*, 4th ed., p. 324, Ginn, Boston, 1911.

Monetary Aspects of the Civil War and Its Aftermath

The outbreak of the Civil War faced the national government with one of those great decisions on monetary policy, a choice among quite different roads. The most basic question was whether to finance the war in part through the creation of paper money: legal-tender notes. Should the war be financed through taxation and the sale of interest-bearing securities as had the War of 1812 and the Mexican War? Or should the government create paper money, declare it to be legal tender, and use this as a means of meeting its expenditures, in other words, create a counterpart of the continental currency of the Revolutionary War?

The decision contained a large element of accident, Secretary of the Treasury Chase providing little leadership and leaving Congress to fill the gap. With the initial opposition and subsequent approval of Mr. Chase (and later in retrospect his violent disapproval in his capacity as Chief Justice of the Supreme Court), the first legal-tender bill passed Congress early in 1862. The nation was headed down the paper-money road.

The response to the war involved also other fundamental changes in the monetary system. The paper money in the form of United States notes—popularly called greenbacks—was decreed to be legal tender. The government did not attempt to keep the greenbacks convertible into gold at par. Naturally, the value of the greenback dollar fell below that of the gold dollar. Thus, by the operation of Gresham's law, "the dollar" came to mean the greenback. Gold dollars became worth more than a dollar in terms of greenbacks. By making the dollar a paper dollar not convertible into gold or silver, the United States departed from the bimetallic system. No longer was it on a commodity-money system that tied the dollar to the currencies of other nations but rather on a "paper standard." This was viewed as a temporary situation, but the question how to get from the paper standard back to a commodity money proved to be a very important one.

At the same time, Congress adopted a basic and far-reaching reform of the banking system and the token-money component of the national monetary system. A part of the justification for this action was that it would aid the financing of the war. Although it is doubtful that the action would otherwise have been taken, in practice, the banking reform had little effect upon the financing of the war. Its major implications were for the later performance of the monetary system, and we shall consider it below in that connection.

War finance and the greenback

Congress was not unmindful of the hazards of financing the war with paper money. Its theory was that the greenbacks would not depreciate unduly or have disruptive side effects if the volume issued was sufficiently limited. Accordingly, the maximum amount authorized by Congress, which was to be a definite limit, was $450 million. The amount actually issued reached about $433 million. Unfortunately, the available data do not permit accurate definition of the increase in the money supply that this involved—a problem complicated by the splitting of what had been the United States into two units. The value of the greenback in terms of the gold dollar never fell below 44 cents. In terms of inflation as measured by available price indexes, the value of the dollar (now the paper dollar) does not seem to have declined more than about 50 percent during the Civil War. This is an inflation of roughly the same order of magnitude as those involved in the First and Second World Wars. In thus avoiding runaway inflation, the use of paper money in financing the Civil War was a success, the same order of success as achieved in more recent episodes.

In contrast to recent wartime experiences, the use and trading of gold was not prohibited during the Civil War. The New York gold market remained open, providing daily figures on the value of greenbacks in terms of gold. The paper dollar, viewed in relation to the international money gold, behaved like a speculative commodity. Its value depended upon the likelihood that the number of greenbacks issued would be limited and that the government eventually would again make the greenback convertible into gold dollars having the old gold content. The value of the greenback thus moved up and down in response to the success of the Union armies and the probability that the gold value of the greenback eventually would increase from its low of 44 cents back up to 100 cents.

The legal-tender status of greenbacks implied that debtors repaid in them fared badly. Interest on the United States government debt was interpreted to involve an obligation to pay in gold and, therefore, continued to be paid in gold. Yet more curiously, in California the greenback was never accepted as worth "a dollar," whatever the law of the land said on the subject. California remained on the gold standard. Creditors in California required payment in gold, accepting greenbacks not at their nominal value of a dollar but rather at their market value of substantially less than a dollar.

The redemption issue

At the end of the war, the government faced another basic decision of monetary policy—one especially important because it foreshadowed the even more fateful decisions taken after the First and Second World Wars. This was the question of how to get back to the commodity-money system that was the standard of the times. At the end of the war, the dollar meant greenbacks and paper money created by banks that was convertible into greenbacks (except for the gold dollar applying in California, on interest payments on the government debt and in limited other uses). Fig. 19–1

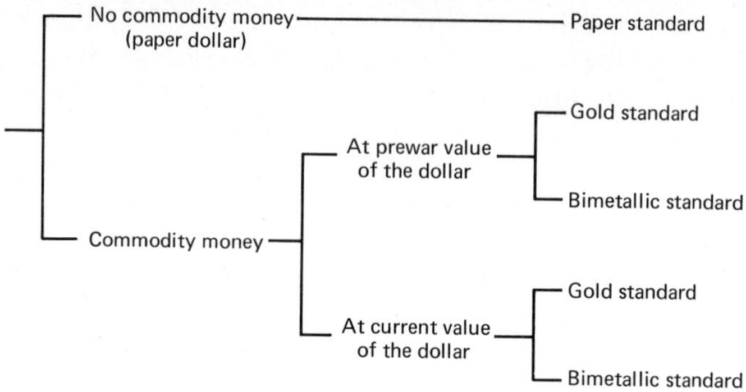

Fig. 19-1 Monetary policy choices at the end of the Civil War.

maps five different directions in which this basic choice of monetary policy might have gone.

The United States might have remained on the paper dollar, the dollar being defined by the greenback and bank money convertible into the greenback. If, more conventionally, the nation had returned to a dollar tied to gold or silver, the basic question would have been whether to go to a commodity dollar of the prewar value or to adopt one at about the existing value of the greenback dollar. The first course implied a large increase in the value of the dollar, or a period of deflation. But the second course implied, or was interpreted as implying, a partial repudiation of the government's obligation after the war to redeem greenbacks in gold dollars of the prewar value.

Whichever choice was made on this score, the nation could return to its bimetallic system, perhaps adjusting the mint ratio in another effort to achieve circulation of both gold and silver coins, or could demonetize silver and legalize the de facto gold standard that had prevailed in the years before the war. Each of these courses would have implied a different monetary system, a different behavior of the money supply, and a different performance of the economy in the decades after the Civil War.

The Movement to the Gold Standard

The policy finally adopted was option 2 in Fig. 19-1. The nation went back to the prewar gold dollar. In a series of steps, it demonetized silver, shifting from the bimetallic to the monometallic gold standard. The effects of this decision were momentous. To return the dollar to its prewar value required one of history's great deflations, an experience that left its mark on our economic and political thought. Moreover, it tied the United States into the international monetary system based on gold that collapsed in 1931 and made this country a full partner in the Great Depression.

Steps back to gold

The movement of the nation to the gold standard involved important elements of historical accident. The predominance of the Republican party, which was associated with hard money, underlies the general movement. By a curious reverse logic, the depression of 1873, which was blamed by the public on the Republicans' hard-money policy, led to the decisive action in the movement to gold. When the Congressional elections of 1874 were won by the Democrats, the lame-duck Republican Congress was moved to take a final action for the sound-money cause. In its last session in January 1875, it passed The Resumption Act.

This important action of monetary policy provided that the Treasury beginning in January 1879—five years in the future—was to begin redeeming greenbacks at par in gold dollars of the prewar content. This was a schedule to bring the nation back to the commodity-money standard. Strangely, the Democratic Congress did not overturn this action. In part this reflected another accidental factor, the inflow of gold from abroad beginning in 1875, which mollified critics of resumption. The combination of a temporarily favorable economic climate and the skill of President Hayes's Secretary of the Treasury, John Sherman, permitted resumption to be achieved without serious incident.

How was it that the nation moved to the gold dollar rather than back to the bimetallic system? The operation of Gresham's law had made the silver dollar a dead issue until about 1873, after which the price of silver began to decline in an unusual manner. This reflected the increase in silver output and the beginnings of the demonetization of silver by other nations, referred to in Chap. 17. Because of its current unimportance, the Coinage Act of 1873 did not mention the standard silver dollar. It provided for a "trade dollar" intended for export and use abroad that was declared to be legal tender in the United States in sums not exceeding $5 and that was not to be freely coined. Three years later the legal-tender status of this coin was removed.

The cause of silver continued to be supported by silver producers, easy-money interests, and others opposing the deflation resulting from the resumption of gold. In 1878, these interests succeeded in passing the Bland-Allison Act, which reinstated the standard silver dollar and gave it unlimited legal-tender status. By this time, however, the depreciation of silver was so great that its proponents could not gain passage of the privilege of the free coinage of silver. The silver dollar now had a bullion value of only 89 cents, thus being at a discount in terms of gold as great as had been the greenbacks for some years before resumption. The act authorized the Treasury to purchase $2 million to $4 million worth of silver per month, coining it or retaining it and creating a new kind of paper money, "silver certificates" which were essentially warehouse certificates for silver dollars.

In 1890, this act was replaced by the more drastic Sherman Silver Purchase Act, which required the Treasury to buy 4.5 million oz of silver per month to be paid for with Treasury notes (paper money) that were given legal-tender status. This act led to doubts as to the future of the gold dollar and to speculation against the dollar and a drain upon the nation's gold reserves. In this way, the act contributed to the panic of 1893. The act was repealed in 1893.

In 1896, monetary policy was the principal issue in the presidential election. The Democratic nominee, William Jennings Bryan, was an extreme silverite, while the Republican McKinley supported the gold standard. Bryan's "cross of gold" speech to the Democratic national convention was the emotional high-water mark of the silver cause. With the election of McKinley and continued depreciation of silver on the bullion markets, the movement to the gold standard was made final. The Gold Standard Act of 1900 placed the nation firmly on the gold standard, opening a new chapter in United States monetary policy.

The great deflation

The decision to return to the prewar gold dollar implied that for decades the nation must experience declining prices, which were gained only at the expense of hardship for debtors and large unemployment. At the end of the Civil War, the paper dollar was worth about 70 cents in terms of the gold dollar. By 1879, its value had to be increased to 100 cents. The value of the gold dollar in terms of goods and services was not declining during this period. Therefore, increasing the value of the paper dollar in terms of gold also meant increasing it in terms of goods and services. It meant a reduction in the general price level measured in terms of the paper dollar, or an era of price deflation.

This was one of the great deflations of history. The Wholesale Price Index of the United States declined from its wartime high by the early 1890s by almost two-thirds. The deflation and the economic hardships it imposed were central facts of life in the United States during this era and a central focus of the political debate and thought of the times. There is little doubt that the deflation reflected the basic decision of monetary policy to return to the prewar gold dollar, rather than to stay on the paper dollar, to move to a cheaper gold dollar, or—as was so vigorously advocated—to go to a cheap silver dollar.

Let us see how these developments are to be interpreted in terms of the analytical tools developed above. The growth path of total demand consistent with full employment and price stability during this period was steeply upward-sloping because of the rapid increase in population and in productivity. To increase the value of the paper dollar relative to the gold dollar and to achieve the balance of payments position consistent with accumulation of the required gold reserves called for large reductions in the price level. These were achieved by providing a growth corridor for the money supply that was consistent with a growth corridor for total demand that was much less steeply upward-sloping than the one consistent with full employment and price stability.

On the average, the economy suffered a combination of price reductions and unusually large unemployment. Thus, on the average during the period it inhabited a position on its Phillips curves that was unusually far to the right, one that involved large unemployment and reduction in the price level. As this situation generated expectations of price reductions, it led to Phillips curves much lower than otherwise would have prevailed; the deflation was achieved with unemployment rates that, although burdensome, proved not to be unbearable.

The golden era

After the depressed 1870s and early 1890s, second only to the 1930s in severity, the nation had little patience for more deflation and unemployment. Had the gold standard implied continued deflation, it doubtless would not have survived long. But a favorable accident intervened to save the gold standard and, indeed, to make the decades around the turn of the century, in retrospect, a period that was a golden age figuratively as well as literally. After 1890, the world output of gold began to grow at a greatly increased rate because of gold discoveries in South Africa, Alaska, and Colorado, and improvements in mining and refining methods. As a result of this accelerated growth of the leading international money, and the superior money of the United States monetary system, corridors of monetary growth became more steeply upward-sloping. The gold standard became consistent not only with full employment but, until the First World War, with an appreciable rate of inflation. As a result, the world entered the First World War thinking well of the gold standard and was anxious after the war to restore it.

The Banks Again: The National Banking System

We now return to the other branch of our story and see what was going on with the banking system and its contribution to the nation's money supply function. Before the Civil War, the banking system was in an unhappy state. Its instability was demonstrated by its contribution to the boom leading to the banking panic of 1837, and the subsequent depression. Moreover, the monetary system was inefficient in including the notes of innumerable state banks, many of which were worth less than their face value and of uncertain and changing value.

The national banking system

Doubtless banking reform would have come soon in any case, but the outbreak of the Civil War posed the problem in an unusual context and led to an action that probably could never have been taken under other circumstances. Apart from political considerations, the most obvious course perhaps was a return to Mr. Hamilton's system of chartering a single national bank to ride herd on the unruly state banks. The economic logic of this approach, however, was overruled by its political unattractiveness, and the nation went off in a new direction. This led to a kind of banking system that does not exist elsewhere in the world, one that explains peculiarities of the money supply function of the United States and the performance of the United States economy until the First World War.

Rather than adopt the politically unpopular action of chartering a monopoly national bank, the National Bank Act of 1863 adopted the principle of "free banking." This involved the granting of a national charter for a bank to any group meeting certain defined standards, primarily involving the size of the bank's capital and the rules under which it was to operate. That the notes (paper money) of the national banks would be safe and pass at par was to be assured by requiring these banks to hold reserves against notes equal to more than 100 percent of their value in the form of United States government securities.

With reference to their note issue, the national banks were taken out of the banking business in the usual sense and made custodians of government securities. The radical nature of this reform is clear if we recognize that the special issues of government securities eligible to support national bank notes can be viewed as simply interest-bearing bank reserves. This makes the system essentially identical with the 100 percent reserve systems proposed as radical reforms in the 1930s.

Making the notes of the national banks (which means privately owned but nationally chartered banks) safe by basing them on government securities had a side effect that explains the passage of this radical legislation. The purchases by the national banks of the government securities to back their notes would, it was thought, contribute substantially to providing a market for the government bonds that would have to be issued to finance the Civil War. As matters worked out, the delay in implementing the act was such that the national banks made no important contribution to the financing of the war. With reference to control over the amount of national bank notes, the government had a special lever by its control over the amount of government bonds identified as eligible for this purpose, as well as by its control over the interest rate paid on these bonds and, thus, the attractiveness to the national banks of creating additional circulating notes.

It was expected that the attractiveness of note issue under national charters would lead existing state banks to shift to national charters. When this expectation was disappointed, the Congress in 1865 imposed a tax of 10 percent on notes other than those of national banks, effectively putting the state banks out of the bank-note business. Since at the time money creation by banks was almost entirely in the form of circulating bank-notes, these actions seemed to imply—and at the time were taken to imply—the final solution to the problem of ill-disciplined creation of money by state-chartered banks. In thus imposing a rigorous system of control on money creation by banks, it seemed that the National Bank Act had finally brought the United States monetary system under effective control and eliminated a major source of instability of the economy.

Thwarted again: The resurgence of state banks

The legislation of 1863 and 1865 failed to put state banks out of the money-creation business because of a technical development that was not foreseen when it was passed. This was the rise of checkbook money, or bank-created money in the form of demand deposits subject to check.

As the act was written, the tax on state banks applied only to their notes and not to their demand deposits, although functionally the latter had almost the same significance. The growth of checkbook money required only some technical developments: city clearing houses to make check collection efficient and improved mail service for collection of out-of-town checks. The growth of checkbook money in retrospect probably was inevitable in any case, but the ability of state banks in this way to retain most of their earlier prerogatives despite the National Bank Act surely accelerated the development. The nullification of this aspect of the act was complete. By 1890, bank deposits (including time deposits) were more than 10 times as great as national bank notes.

The accidental element in history is again striking. Had the National Bank Act applied the 10 percent tax also to demand deposits of state banks or had it simply required all banks to operate under a national charter—United States monetary history and economic history from this point would have followed a different road than the one we know.

This development undercut the improvement in the soundness and stability of banking that had been hoped for by federal chartering and the supervision of banks by a federal agency, the Comptroller of the Currency. So long as banks could continue to operate successfully under state charters and thus escape federal supervision, the inclination of the Comptroller of the Currency to enforce rigorous banking standards was limited by the threat that banks would give up their national charters and escape to the more lax supervision of state banking authorities. The "dual banking system" gave rise to a "competition in laxity" that has continued to be a problem.

In curing the victimization of members of the public by worthless bank notes, the reform was entirely successful. This security, however, did not extend to checkbook money. This may be less objectionable from an equity point of view, since if a bank fails the loss is borne mainly by the depositor—who has some opportunity to protect himself. However, from another point of view the new system was worse than the old. This is with reference to its potential instability and its proneness to phases of expansion, banking panic, and contraction.

Instability under the national banking system

The National Banking System proved to be distinctive among the historical banking systems of the world for its susceptibility to banking panics. Major banking panics involving numerous bank failures and followed by depression occurred in 1873, 1893, and 1907. The panics and depressions were widely interpreted as deriving from provisions of the banking system as this was defined by the National Bank Act. This dissatisfaction led after the panic of 1907 to a set of political steps culminating in the establishment of the Federal Reserve System in 1913.

Its susceptibility to panic seems to have been built into the national banking system. The money supply now comprised a class of perfectly safe money, consisting of gold coins and national bank notes, and another class of money, that was quite unsafe, in the form of checkbook money or demand deposits. If a bank failed, those holding deposits in the bank would have their funds tied up and upon liquidation of the bank might lose a major part of them. Even a soundly managed bank might fail if it was forced to liquidate its assets under pressure, as when its depositors descended upon it en masse in a bank run. However, many banks were not soundly managed, for supervision by state banking authorities was ineffective and the national banking authorities—in part limited by competition with state charters—also had shortcomings.

General application of the principle of "free banking" and limitations on branch banking meant that the individual bank had to stand on its own resources. A means by which banking systems in other countries avoided banking panics and bank failures was by development of large branch banking systems. In these, a local run could be met by bringing cash from other branches, thereby using the resources of the whole branch system. The political opposition to branch banking in the United States led to the unit banking system that underlay the susceptibility to banking panics.

The development of deposit banking in replacement of the earlier bank notes of state banks increased the hazard of local banking panics. When bank notes were scattered geographically and held by many individuals and businesses, there was little likelihood of their all being presented to the bank for payment in coin at any particular time. But bank deposits are all held in the locality of the bank. If a rumor developed that a bank was weak, its depositors could descend upon it in force.

Once a run on a bank develops, there is a strong likelihood that the bank will fail, so the interest of the individual depositor is in getting his funds out before it fails. When each depositor follows his interest, however, the failure of the bank may be almost assured. The game becomes one of confidence, the bank attempting to persuade the depositors not to fear, but fear if it persists being self-justifying.

The bank run became a distinctive feature of the life of the times in this country. The frightened depositors lined up in the bank and sometimes far down the street to withdraw their funds from the bank in the form of coin or national bank notes. The bank sometimes would stall, paying out funds slowly, especially if it had additional cash on the way from out of town. A common tactic, however, was to pay out cash quite freely hoping in this way to persuade the depositors that there was no cause for fear. If the lines of fearful depositors disappeared before the bank ran through the cash it had or could borrow, the bank was saved. If the cash ran out first, it was closed, tying up depositors' funds and in many cases involving losses to them.

When a run caused the failure of one bank, this commonly led to runs on other banks. This was partly just because of the spread of fear and the feeling that if one bank was weak the others might be weak also. Partly, it reflected relations among banks such that the failure of one would be known to weaken the position of others. The tendency of bank runs to spread gave bankers an incentive to attempt to cooperate by pooling their available cash to save a bank that was subject to a run. But this could not always be done, for some banks were, indeed, poorly managed and in shaky condition, and the sound bank did not want to risk its cash in a hazardous effort to save a weak bank. The most dramatic such episode was that in which J. P. Morgan in the panic of 1907 in an effort to get cooperative antirun action by leading New York bankers locked them in his library until they signed a cooperation agreement. Curiously, Morgan's lieutenant in this operation was Benjamin Strong, who became the leading figure in the Federal Reserve System during the 1920s and the most notable leader the System has yet produced.

In terms of the money supply function {you recall $M = B(1 + c)/(c + r)$} the effect of bank runs is abruptly to increase the currency ratio and the reserve ratio, thus reducing the money supply for any given amount of high-powered money. Recent research does bring out that instability of the money supply did contribute to economic instability during this period and that this behavior of the money supply was explained in large part by instability of the currency ratio.[4]

Naturally, the existence of bank runs and of misbehavior of the currency ratio led to aggravating variation in the reserve ratio. When some banks were hit by runs, other banks, fearing that they might be next, would begin to accumulate cash. That is, they would increase their reserve ratio. As a result, the same features of the banking system that led to this perverse

[4]Philip Cagan, *Determinants and Effects of Changes in the Stock of Money, 1875–1960*, National Bureau of Economic Research, New York, 1965.

variability of the currency ratio led also to like behavior of the reserve ratio. The short-run instability of the money supply stemmed mainly from this variation of the currency ratio and the reserve ratio rather than from misbehavior of high-powered money.

An unusual feature that gradually evolved under the national banking system was the use of extralegal devices to avoid complete collapse of the banking system (such as did occur in 1933) in the face of spreading bank runs. Commonly, the banks created extralegal "currency" in the form of clearinghouse certificates, which served as additional reserve funds for local banks to see them through an increase in the public's demand for currency. Other measures failing, the banks rather than simply failing under an onslaught of bank runs collaborated in an extralegal suspension of their obligation to redeem their deposits in currency or coin. By simply agreeing not to pay out currency, the banks in cooperation put an end to bank runs. This was far from an ideal monetary system, causing considerable inconvenience as deposits went to a discount in terms of currency—or a dollar deposit was not worth a dollar in currency. However, it did prevent the ultimate catastrophe, which was not prevented by the supposedly reformed banking system of 1933.[5]

Which way next?

After the panic of 1907, the country was ready for banking reform. It had had enough of being, as Irving Fisher put it, "the land of runs and bank failures." But as we have seen already, correcting the shortcomings of the monetary system within the nation's political constraints—or correcting one fault without causing a worse one—was not an easy matter. Much depended upon the diagnosis as to just what was wrong with the system. As we view the matter from a present-day vantage point, benefiting from the important recent work of Friedman and Schwartz, Cagan, and others, the diagnosis seems straight-forward. The instability of the banking system derived from the insecure status of deposits in relation to currency and coin, in conjunction with the prevalence of unit banking in contrast to the branch-banking arrangements prevailing in other nations.

The way to correct the defect was to make bank deposits as secure as bank notes. This could have been done by applying to demand deposits the provision for 100 percent reserves of government securities that applied to bank notes under the National Bank Act. Or the problem could have been solved, as it finally was solved in 1933, by a government guarantee of bank deposits.

But the thinking of the times did not run in this direction. It was heavily shaped by bankers, who at this time played an important role on the

[5]The history of these devices is brought out in the important study, Milton Friedman and Anna J. Schwartz, *A Monetary History of the United States, 1867–1960*, National Bureau of Economic Research, New York, 1963.

stage of affairs. This also was the high-water mark of influence of the commercial loan theory of banking, which was of course sympathetic to the ears of the banking community. The disposition was not to apply to bank deposits a radical reform such as the one that had been applied to bank notes under the impetus of the Civil War. Rather, it was to see the fault in technical aspects of the system such as its arrangements for holding reserves and, most basically, to see the failing as the lack of harmony of the system with the commercial loan theory of banking. Thus, a major theme was the need for an "elastic currency," one that could rise to meet the "needs of trade." The difficulty was diagnosed not as one of excessive creation of deposits by the banking system or of instability in the public's demand for a currency, but rather of an inelasticity in currency that prevented the amount of currency from validating changes in deposits and in the public's demand for currency.

This was the basic thinking that underlay the next reconstruction of the nation's system for the creation of token money. Since the major lesson of the experience is how a faulty diagnosis leads to an ineffective remedy, we should note in advance that the experiment failed. Under the Federal Reserve System, the banking system in 1929–1933 failed to a degree that it had never failed before and was instrumental in causing a depression the like of which had never been seen before.

The susceptibility of the system to banking panics was cured, somewhat inadvertently, as a side effect of the insurance of bank deposits first undertaken in 1933. The principles of the commercial loan theory of banking, by which the Federal Reserve was to overcome the defects of the National Banking System, never worked out in practice and the theory in the form in which it underlay the Federal Reserve System is now virtually defunct, although a broadened version of the credit approach to monetary policy has continued to influence the Federal Reserve. What is interesting intellectually is the manner in which a misdiagnosis of the shortcomings of the national banking system led to reform measures that then caused new difficulties that, in principle, could have been anticipated and avoided by a more adequate theory of money and banking.

SUMMARY

1. The nation's first monetary system used a bimetallic gold-silver standard as its high-powered money and notes of state banks and a monopoly national bank as its token-money component.

2. The bimetallic system did not work as expected because of the operation of Gresham's law and the failure of gold and silver coins to circulate simultaneously.

3. The token-money component of the system performed badly after the failure to recharter the Second Bank of the United States in 1831, as the system lacked a mechanism to prevent overissue of notes by state banks. This led to an excessive increase in the money supply and then to a banking panic in 1837 and a serious depression. The notes of state banks also were deficient in being of changing and uncertain value and involving a hazard of loss to those who accepted them in payment.

4. The decision to finance the Civil War partially with paper money, the greenbacks, contributed to a major inflation, the greenback falling to a low value of 44 cents in terms of the gold dollar. The postwar decision to return to the prewar gold dollar involved a long period of price deflation until the early 1890s, with severe depressions in the 1870s and 1890s. The adoption of the gold dollar, however, integrated the United States into the gold-standard system that flourished from the 1890s to the First World War.

5. The National Bank Act of 1863 corrected the uncertainty of value of bank notes by backing them 100 percent with United States government securities and limiting their issue to national banks. The intent of the act was thwarted, however, by the rise of demand deposits as a means of payment, which revived the state banks. The insecure position of demand deposits in relation to bank notes and coin led to instability of the system. The currency ratio and through it the reserve ratio varied in response to the state of confidence in the banking system. Periods of confidence and decline in the currency ratio were followed by banking panic, rise in the currency ratio and decline in the money supply, and business depression. The inherent instability and panic-proneness of the banking system under the National Bank Act underlay the instability of the United States economy from the Civil War until the Federal Reserve Act of 1913.

QUESTIONS FOR REVIEW AND DISCUSSION

1. Explain how a government can use the creation of paper money to finance its expenditures. How do the privilege of legal tender and other legal provisions affect the government's ability to achieve this? If the government in this way gets a command over resources without using taxes, from whom are the resources taken? Is this an equitable way for the government to get resources to carry out its activities?

2. Explain what kinds of changes in the monetary system would be favored by debtors who were pursuing their own interest; by creditors; and by the producers of a commodity that might conceivably be designated for use as money.

3. Explain the logic of the monetary system established under the leadership of Hamilton. Explain how and why each part of it failed to perform as expected.

4. "Without the Bank of the United States, the United States banking system after 1836 was potentially destabilizing because it lacked a mechanism to discipline its currency ratio." Explain.

5. "After the Civil War, with the greenback dollar depreciated in relation to the gold dollar, no course the government could take would stabilize prices at the new level while fully preserving the rights of creditors." Discuss. Explain what course was followed, and why it necessarily implied a period of price deflation.

6. Explain the major features of the banking system under the National Bank Act, and why they led to a banking system that was exceptionally prone to banking panics. In what alternative ways might this panic-proneness of the system have been corrected?

7. "The money supply function of the United States during the nineteenth century was in many ways altered by unforeseen factors that importantly affected the performance of the economy." Cite major examples and the consequences in each case.

20

Federal Reserve policy through war, depression, and war

The turn of the century found no complaints over the performance of the high-powered money and international-money component of the United States monetary system. The gold standard was in its heyday. But the demand-deposit component of the United States monetary system was in the doghouse. It was widely agreed that "our habit of falling prostrate once in every ten years, and exposing ourselves to to the jeers of mankind, is the worst banking habit we have, and the one which we could most advantageously lay aside."[1] The nation faced another great decision point of monetary policy. Down another road—yet another surprise!

The panic of 1907 led to passage of the Aldrich-Vreeland Act of 1908. This provided immediate resources to use against banking panics. It legalized the creation of emergency currency by groups of national banks and, with permission of the Secretary of the Treasury, by individual banks. The act also laid the groundwork for basic reform of the banking system by providing for a National Monetary Commission. The Commission was to study the banking system and before 1910 to recommend for its reform. The Commission arranged for a number of detailed studies of the banking system. In 1910, the Commission came forth with the Aldrich Plan. This provided for a National Reserve Association located in Washington, D.C., which was to have a branch in each of the 15 districts into which the country was to be divided.

A bill based upon the Aldrich Plan was defeated in Congress in 1912, and banking reform was an issue in the presidential election of that year. The victorious Wilsonian Democrates, in opposition to the Aldrich Plan, cited arguments against banking concentration similar to those that had caused the downfall of the First and Second Banks of the United States and that had led to the practice of free banking, with all its implications. But the time was ripe for banking reform. The Federal Reserve Act passed by the Democratic Congress in 1913 was similar to the Aldrich Plan, except for an emphasis on decentralization

[1]Horace White, *Money and Banking*, 4th ed., p. 436, Ginn, Boston, 1911.

and diffusion of power. In Chap. 8, we reviewed the structure and operations of the Federal Reserve System. Now we view the establishment and later performance and reform of the Federal Reserve System as another stage in the process of trial and error that has shaped the United States monetary system.

Foundations of the Federal Reserve System

There are several classes of effective action that might have been taken against the instability of the United States monetary system, with its proneness to banking panic:

1. The basic reform of the National Bank Act of 1863 might have been belatedly rehabilitated by extending to demand deposits the requirement of 100 percent reserves in United States government securities and by applying the 10 percent tax on the notes of state banks also to the demand deposits of such banks.

2. Demand deposits might have been guaranteed by the federal government, thus removing the incentive for runs from deposits to notes.

3. Consolidation of banks into large branch systems might have been encouraged by the government, so that these systems could on their own resources deal at least to some extent with local bank runs.[2]

"To furnish an elastic currency"

The preamble of the Federal Reserve Act defined its major monetary function as "to furnish an elastic currency"—a curious request, for one might have thought the monetary system being replaced was elastic to a fault, as elastic as a bouncing ball.

But that is the crux of the matter. What was being complained of was not that the volume of demand deposits was unstable—but that their expansion was being hampered by the inelasticity of currency, or high-powered money. Rather than redesigning the institutions so that the growth of deposits stayed more closely in line with that of high-powered money, the idea was that the growth of currency would be adjusted to that of deposits—which were responding to the "needs of trade." The dog was to be wagged by its tail.

[2]It is instructive to note that Mr. Hamilton's remedy for the misbehavior of state banks—a monopoly national bank—would not meet the need in this case. The national bank overcame the key deficiency of the note-issuing state banks by overcoming the geographical dispersion of bank notes and presenting the bank notes for collection. But the problem that caused deposits to make the later banking system unstable was a different one, not susceptible to this remedy. What is needed was a way of preventing abrupt demand for payment in currency of the already geographically concentrated deposits, or else a means of providing additional resources to offset such cash drains to the particular banks involved.

This was not, of course, the way the matter was viewed by contemporary bankers and the economists who took the credit approach to central banking. The implications of elasticity were characterized thus by one contemporary enthusiast:

> By elasticity is meant the capacity to increase or diminish in volume in accordance with the needs of the community, and simultaneously therewith. . . . Where note issues are unrestricted the amount of notes outstanding at any time depends not upon the volition of either the bank of the depositor, but upon the public demand. . . . A flexible currency is one which rises and falls in volume harmoniously and simultaneously with these trade movements.[3]

Applied in relation to economic fluctuations, such a conception of meeting the needs of trade seems to imply positive monetary feedback and the magnification of economic instability. This would not necessarily be the case if the needs of trade were to be met not at constant interest rates but only at interest rates that changed with the expected rate of return on investment and that rose in economic expansion and declined in economic contraction in line with the Wicksellian natural rate of interest. But the Federal Reserve was to meet the needs of trade rather at interest rates that were relatively stable.

The needs-of-trade approach also can be applied to seasonal movements within the year. In this context also, it implies permitting variation in the money supply in an effort to reduce variation in nominal interest rates. The seasonal increase in demand for credit in the fall to move crops to market had led to high interest rates in the fall. Farmers were naturally unhappy that interest rates were high just when they needed to borrow. This case differs from that discussed above in that seasonal changes in the economy are inherently self-limiting. An economic expansion can go on until the economy blows up—but autumn only lasts until winter. Therefore, for the Federal Reserve to combat seasonal variations in interest rates by inducing a seasonal variation in the money supply does not involve the hazard of self-feeding instability that attaches to following the same rule in relation to economic fluctuations.

This type of policy may involve a social cost in accentuating seasonal swings in economic activity, insofar as the seasonal variations in interest rates perform a function in causing seasonally optional activities to be concentrated during slack times of the year. Most economists see this as a minor consideration. The Federal Reserve application of the needs-of-trade approach to reduction in seasonal variation in interest rates has been effective, and its termination probably would not be favorably received by the public.

A final context in which the elastic currency conception must be considered is in relation to banking panic and the associated monetary

[3]White, *op. cit.*, p. 401.

contraction resulting from a sharp rise in the currency ratio. If "meeting the needs of trade" was interpreted to include "meeting demands of the public for additional currency to offset a panic-related increase in the currency ratio," the formula would lead to Federal Reserve action to offset variations in the currency ratio and offset procyclical variation in the money supply. Such actions also would mitigate, though not completely solve, bank runs.

The interpretation predominantly applied by the Federal Reserve was more narrow than this. It related not to the demands of the public for currency but rather to the demands of sound business for loans. Once banking panic and business uncertainty led to economic contraction and a desire of business to liquidate inventories, the demand for such credit fell. Moreover, under such conditions of economic stress some potential business borrowers who earlier looked "sound" would now no longer seem to meet that criterion.

Such a version of needs-of-trade criterion leads to and justifies contraction of the money supply under conditions of banking panic. The failures of businesses and of banks can be interpreted as a healthy cleaning out from the economy of unsound developments, excesses, and maladjustments that crept in because of earlier laxity in not limiting bank credit sufficiently rigorously to short-term loans to sound businesses. During the decline into the Great Depression, this second interpretation of the needs-of-trade approach was more influential than the first.

The thinking underlying the Federal Reserve Act also attributed the panic-proneness of the national banking system in part to the way reserves were held in that system. A part of the difficulty, it was believed, was that bank reserves were diffused, being held in the vaults of the individual banks and in correspondent balances, rather than being pooled or all held in a central location. The instability of the system also was attributed in part to the "pyramiding of reserves," the fact that the reserves of some banks were held in the form of deposits at other banks. Consequently, the performance of the system under panic conditions was expected to be greatly improved by the fact that reserves of member banks were to be held pooled at the Federal Reserve banks.

In the light of modern monetary theory, we can see that this was not a realistic diagnosis. An increase in the currency ratio and in the reserve ratio desired by banks in the face of bank runs would cause forced contraction of the money supply and bank credit no matter where reserves were held or in what form. The belief that revision of the reserve system would greatly improve the stability of the nation's banking system rested on faulty analysis.

The basic revision of the token-money component of the United States monetary system in 1913 rested peculiarly upon the credit approach to banking and central banking. Its success or failure depended upon the accuracy of that approach, which proved wanting.

The Federal Reserve and the gold standard

The thinking underlying the Federal Reserve Act took for granted continued United States participation in the gold standard international monetary system. However, the implications of the gold standard were not in the foreground of discussions leading to the Federal Reserve System. It would be possible to tie the behavior of the national money supply very closely to the international monetary system, providing that the money supply should rise and decline in response to changes in the nation's international monetary reserves. In English monetary history, Peel's Act of 1844 embodied this approach.

The Federal Reserve Act, on the other hand, put its emphasis upon the needs-of-trade approach, leaving the gold standard in the background. The Federal Reserve System was not provided any guidance as to the response it should make to changes in the nation's gold reserves and how in making its policy choices it should weigh changes in gold reserves against changes in credit conditions and the needs of trade.

The First World War and Postwar Adjustment

Ill-instructed as to what it was to do under normal circumstances, the infant Federal Reserve confronted the First World War. Large purchases from the United States by the belligerent nations led to a balance of payments surplus, a large gold inflow, a rapid increase in the money supply, and substantial price inflation. Even had the Federal Reserve desired to sterilize the gold inflow and prevent it from causing a rapid increase in high-powered money, it had no ammunition with which to do so. This would have required reductions in Federal Reserve earning assets, and the Federal Reserve banks had started business with no earning assets that they could sell. They were in a position to increase the monetary base, but not to reduce it or offset other factors that were increasing it.

War finance again

The financing of the First World War involved no explicit printing of paper money like the continental currency and the greenbacks of the Civil War. This time, it was possible to finance the war, in part, through money creation in a less obvious and more respectable-looking manner. Rather than issuing legal-tender notes, the government sold normal interest-bearing securities. These, however, were bought by the Federal Reserve banks, which paid for them by creating Federal Reserve notes and deposits that added to the money supply and the monetary base. By creating excess reserves for member banks, these Federal Reserve purchases provided the means for the commercial banks to buy additional government securities, paying for them by creating money in the form of demand deposits. During the United States participation in the war, from 1917 to 1919,

Federal Reserve earning assets increased from a small amount to over \$2 billion.

The gold inflow halted after the nation's entry into the war in April 1917 as shipments to the new allies now were financed by United States government loans rather than by further payments in gold. Consequently the expansion of the monetary base during this period was entirely accounted for by Federal Reserve activities. The increase in the money supply was less than proportionate, because of a remarkable increase in the currency ratio from the spring of 1917 through late 1918. The causes of this are not understood, although use of currency to avoid taxation and its relation to the increased mobility of wartime living have been offered as possible explanations.[4]

After the armistice in November 1918, there was a modest slowing of economic activity, despite continued increase in the money supply, because of the termination of war orders. The money supply continued to increase rapidly until early 1920. The bases for this were very rapid growth in Federal Reserve credit, especially in the latter part of 1919, and the reversal of the earlier sharp rise in the currency ratio. At this time, the Federal Reserve was not helpless in the face of the rising money supply. It could have taken action to prevent the increases or to force reductions in the borrowing from it of member banks that now ran to more than \$2 billion. The Federal Reserve did not take such action because it thought it necessary to prevent further reductions in prices of government bonds (or further increases in yields on government bonds) until the Treasury had completed some war-related debt sales and banks and their customers were in a less vulnerable position with reference to their holdings of government securities.[5]

For the whole period from mid-1914 through the spring of 1920, the money supply slightly more than doubled. Wholesale prices increased nearly 150 percent and consumer prices showed something less than a doubling. The quantity theory of money gives a good rough explanation of the experience. The inflation was of the same order of magnitude as that of the Civil War and of that later in World War II.

Several lessons drawn from this experience with war finance affected policy in the Second World War and thus were a factor in more recent history:

1. The war was fought at rising interest rates, the large and continuing sales of government securities pushing interest rates up to unusually high levels. It proved embarrassing to the U.S. Treasury, which was selling its bonds in part through public rallies and emphasis upon patriotism, that the prices of government bonds continued to fall. For those who had

[4]Milton Friedman and Anna J. Schwartz, *A Monetary History of the United States, 1867–1960,* pp. 218–219, Princeton University Press, Princeton, 1963. This chapter draws heavily on this source and on Phillip Cagan, *Determinants and Effects of Changes in the Stock of Money, 1875–1960,* National Bureau of Economic Research, New York, 1965.

[5]Friedman and Schwartz, pp. 223–224.

bought bonds out of patriotism to see the price of the bonds sink lower and lower did not seem a satisfactory arrangement. To prevent this, in World Was II an agreement was made at the outset that the Federal Reserve would peg the prices of government securities. World War II was fought at stable interest rates.

2. The period of rapid inflation immediately after the war in 1919 and early 1920 led to a slow and cautious approach to the dismantling of wartime price controls after the Second World War.

3. Efforts were made to finance the war more largely through taxation and to impose more extensive and rigorous systems of controls in the Second World War. These were effective in the sense that a much longer and more costly war was attended by inflation of only the same order of magnitude.

Postwar readjustment: The glorious deflation

By late 1920, the arguments for continued monetary inflation to support the government securities market were losing their appeal. Moreover, the rapid increase in Federal Reserve liabilities plus an outflow of gold resulting from the inflation were bringing the Federal Reserve holdings of gold certificates close to the minimum reserve ratio defined in the Federal Reserve Act. Federal Reserve credit was almost all in the form of member bank borrowings rather than Federal Reserve holdings of government securities. To check further increases in Federal Reserve credit, Reserve banks began to increase their discount rates in November and in late January and early February increased them by more than a percentage point to the high level of 6 percent. The money supply increased more slowly until the fall of 1920 and then declined until mid-1921.

The economy showed a mild contraction until about the middle of 1920 and then an extraordinarily rapid decline. Production and employment declined sharply, but what was distinctive was the remarkably rapid reduction in the price level. Consumer prices declined by more than one-fifth and wholesale prices by almost one-half. The deflation was concentrated in less than 1 year. Modern experience includes no parallel to it in the speed and relative painlessness of the reduction in the general price level.

Although it reduced its discount rates, the Federal Reserve took no substantial actions to halt the contraction nor to deal with the rapid rise in bank failures: from 63 in 1919 to 506 in 1921. Surprisingly, and a testimonial to confidence in the Federal Reserve System, this rise in bank failures did not lead to a general liquidity panic or a substantial rise in the currency ratio. Opinions within the Federal Reserve System were divided, the influential Governor Strong of the Federal Reserve Bank of New York resisting reductions in Federal Reserve discount rates until a large reduction in the price level had occurred. Although there was a worldwide reduction in prices in 1920—1921, that in the United States was exceptionally great. It was explained in part by the Federal Reserve policy that permitted a very rapid increase in the money supply in 1919 and then reversed it.

The achievement of so great a reduction in the price level in so short a time seemed a source of great satisfaction to some contemporary observers. Looking backward from the prosperity of the 1920s, it seemed possible to argue that the return to a sound price level had laid the groundwork for prosperity. This interpretation contributed to later troubles. The successful deflation reenforced the idea that deflation could be brought about by policy, which probably encouraged England in its ultimately unsuccessful attempt to return the pound to the gold standard at the prewar parity. England was not successful in painlessly deflating, and we recall that the fall of the pound in 1931 brought down the international monetary system. The idea that deflation was desirable and laid the groundwork for prosperity also perhaps influenced policy in the United States in 1929—1933, when the deflation was long and destructive.

For the fledgling Federal Reserve to permit rapid inflation after the war in 1919 and then to permit violent deflation caused much criticism. It is widely agreed that a policy involving more steady monetary growth and more steady growth of total demand would have been preferable. Friedman and Schwartz ask whether the record during this period would not have been better had there been no Federal Reserve and had the country still operated under the National Bank Act. They conclude that the 1919—1920 inflation would not have occurred under this monetary system and that the overall record in this period probably would have been better.[6]

The 1920s

To those who peopled them, the 1920s seemed a great period, a "new era." Economic fluctuations were minor, unemployment was small, prices were stable, living was good. The Federal Reserve System, from which much had been expected, received a great deal of the credit for the economic success of the period. People looked forward to the continuation of this success of the new era. Unfortunately the 1920s were to be as Friedman and Schwartz put it, "the high tide of the Federal Reserve System."[7]

The money supply and its determinants

The money supply grew at a relatively steady rate after the 1920—1921 decline. It grew more slowly after mid-1925, but this seemed appropriate as the rise of optimism, speculation, and interest rates in the lat-

[6] *Ibid.*, pp. 238-239.

[7] *Ibid.*, chap. 6.

ter part of the 1920s led to an increase in velocity and made modest money growth consistent with a satisfactory growth of total demand. Deceleration of growth of the money supply did occur before the mild recessions of 1923–1924 and 1926–1927 and can be interpreted as contributing to them. But monetary growth accelerated early in the recessions and thus contributed to keeping them as mild as they were. By the usual standards of the United States monetary system, this was a first-rate performance of the monetary system, and it led to a first-rate outcome.

This rather steady growth of the money supply reflected offsetting changes among the determinants of the money supply. The reserve ratio declined rather steadily and was one factor making for growth of the money supply through the decade. The currency ratio declined at a substantial rate. It was the major factor providing growth of the money supply and the source of such procyclical variation as it showed. The monetary base showed no cyclical variation, growing slowly and steadily from 1922 through 1925 and then remaining virtually stable until 1929.

This rather steady growth of the monetary base, however, reflected a set of cross currents in its determinants. Changes in Federal Reserve credit outstanding rather systematically offset changes in the gold stock. Since the movements in the gold stock were anticyclical, involving increases in the early phases of the two recessions, the usefulness of this offsetting action may be doubted. Within Federal Reserve credit, Federal Reserve open market operations to a considerable extent offset changes in member bank borrowings. But prior to the recession of 1923–1924, it was member bank borrowings that were rising and Federal Reserve holdings of government securities that were declining. That is, Federal Reserve open market operations, taken by themselves, can be interpreted as destabilizing.

Just how Federal Reserve behavior in the 1920s is to be interpreted remains a moot question, one requiring further study within the framework of present-day monetary theory. It seems clear that during this period, under the predominant leadership of Benjamin Strong, the Federal Reserve was not primarily guided by an attempt to stabilize interest rates. Interest rates were permitted to show substantial cyclical variation, and long-term yields showed a pronounced decline until 1927, which reversed the increases that occurred during the First World War. The Federal Reserve during this period seems to have been attempting to minimize economic fluctuations, sterilizing gold flows when it thought domestic stability demanded this, but it was responding mainly to criteria other than stability of interest rates.

The stock-market boom

In the latter part of the 1920s, the United States was afflicted by that curious disease of economic mob psychology, the speculative boom. The Florida land boom and then the stock-market boom made this the era of the greatest speculative mania in the history of the nation. This presented the makers of Federal Reserve policy with another puzzle to which their instruction kit provided no answers.

There are several different directions that policy might have taken. The Federal Reserve might have broken the stock-market boom, even at the expense of causing an economic contraction, by imposing monetary restriction considerably earlier, say, by early 1928. Or the Federal Reserve might have diagnosed this as an unusual situation calling for new tools of monetary policy and asked by 1928 for something like the control over stock-market borrowing that it finally was given in 1933, after the game had been lost. Finally, the Federal Reserve might simply have ignored the stock-market boom, keeping the money supply and total demand on an appropriate course and letting the stock market take care of itself.

However, committee decision making commonly avoids clear-cut policy choices and ends up with something in the middle. The Federal Reserve reduced its holdings of government securities and increased discount rates, virtually halting expansion of the money supply after early 1928. This action was not vigorous enough to halt the stock-market boom while cyclical economic expansion still was strong, but it gradually produced a condition of modest economic slack, which then interacted adversely with the eventual collapse of the stock-market boom in 1929. In retrospect, probably any of the other courses would have been better than the one the Federal Reserve followed. However, the severity of the Great Depression stemmed not from this error of policy but from the great errors that were to come later.

Roots of doom

On the face of things, it seems astonishing that the period of the Federal Reserve's greatest success should be followed immediately by a period of total and catastrophic failure. With the advantage of hindsight, we can see a number of elements in the approach taken by the Federal Reserve in the 1920s that sowed the seeds of the imminent disaster:

1. The Federal Reserve became accustomed to a very large number of bank failures, attributing these to bad bank management and special factors. As a consequence, when bank failures rose even higher after 1929, an extension of this attitude explains why the Federal Reserve never did the one thing it had been confidently expected to do—take vigorous action to prevent banking panic and wholesale bank failures.

2. Although it does not seem to have followed during the 1920s policies based upon the commercial loan theory of banking, the Federal Reserve System did formalize its attachment to that approach. The 1923 Annual Report of the Board of Governors of the Federal Reserve System is the all-time classic statement of this approach by a central bank. Thus, the basis was laid for a policy after 1929 that was geared to the credit approach and not at all responsive to monetary theory.

3. There emerged no clear pattern of authority and no reliable system of capable leadership within the Federal Reserve System. The temporary predominance of the Federal Reserve Bank of New York and the relative competence of Federal Reserve performance through 1927 both derived from the personal abilities and persuasiveness of Benjamin Strong, the Governor of the Federal Reserve Bank of New York. His withdrawal from the scene due to illness in 1927 left a gap in terms of ability at the top level and an organizational gap as the Federal Reserve Bank of New York, the Board of Governors, and the Governors (now called presidents) of the other Federal Reserve banks disagreed as to who was running the show.

4. The stock-market boom and the undoubtedly pervasive existence of speculative fever lent support to the view that what was needed was to clean the unsoundness out of the economy by another beneficent deflation like that of 1920–1921. Against this most unusual historical background, permitting deflation to run its course seemed to some responsible officials preferable to encouraging a renewal of speculative sentiment by "easy credit."

5. The Federal Reserve habit of sterilizing gold flows in the 1920s set the stage for sterilization of a gold inflow in 1930 when this action contributed both to continuation of the United States economic contraction and to the destruction of the precarious gold-exchange international monetary system.

Taken together, these factors go some distance toward explaining why the Federal Reserve behaved as it did in 1929–1933, which in turn goes far toward explaining why the money supply and the economy behaved as they did.

The Great Contraction: 1929–1933

Between late 1929 and the spring of 1933, the United States money supply declined about one-fourth and total demand by more than this. The increase in the value of money and very unfavorable returns on real investment assets caused a reduction in velocity of circulation. The general price level declined continuously, but much less than proportionately with the decline in total demand and less rapidly than in 1920–1921—as the economy showed a less favorable Phillips curve in the face of deflationary pressure. Thus, a large part of the decline in total demand was reflected in reduction in real output and employment. Unemployment rose to about one-fourth of the labor force, a figure unheard of in other modern experience.

The decline in the money supply reflected the same mechanisms that had caused it to decline during the banking panics under the National Banking System, though these operated over a much longer period of time. The decline in the money supply reflected an unprecedented rise in the currency ratio and a substantial rise in the reserve ratio. The monetary base declined only slightly in 1930 and thereafter showed some increase. During the early phase of the contraction through the fall of 1931, the nation's gold stock was rising, so that a gold-based monetary system would have provided increases in the money supply. The gold inflow, however, was more than offset by a reduction in Federal Reserve credit. As a result, reduction in Federal Reserve credit sterilized the gold inflow and increases in the currency ratio and reserve ratio translated a stable monetary base into a contraction in the money supply.

In broad terms, what differentiated this monetary contraction from that of the panic of 1907 was that it lasted about five times as long, including a series of banking panics, and therefore led to a much greater decline in the money supply and in total demand. The contraction of 1929–1933 was not unusually rapid or abrupt, less so than that of 1920–1921. Had the economy turned around in 1930 or 1931, this would have looked much like any other contraction associated with the panic-prone banking system of the nation. What sets it apart is that the banking and monetary contraction hit no lower boundary until 1933, the destructive interaction continuing until the nation's banking and economic system was brought to a state of complete demoralization.

The monetary system in the contraction

The stock-market crash in late 1929 did not directly trigger any monetary difficulties. The Federal Reserve bought some government securities, causing a temporary increase in the monetary base. Through late 1930, the money supply declined slightly because of reduction in the monetary base associated mainly with reductions in member bank borrowings from the Federal Reserve System. During this phase, the currency ratio actually declined somewhat. The continued modest reductions in the money supply in the face of growth of labor force and productivity led to a recession, with reductions in output and in prices. To this point, however, it seemed that things were well under control. The absence of banking panic was a testimonial to the public's confidence in the Federal Reserve System.

In late 1930, however, a banking crisis did arrive. In November and December 1930, more than 600 banks failed and both the currency ratio and the reserve ratio began to rise, reflecting the loss of confidence in the banking system. Of special symbolic significance was the failure in December of the Bank of the United States with over $200 million of deposits, the largest commercial bank that had ever failed in United States history and a member bank of the Federal Reserve System. The fact that efforts of the Federal Reserve Bank of New York to save this bank were not supported by the clearinghouse banks and failed undermined the prestige of the Federal Reserve System and confidence in its ability to deal with bank failures and banking panic.

This was a decisive turning point for policy. If the Federal Reserve was to take effective action against cumulative banking panic, this was the time to do it. Friedman and Schwartz offer the judgment that had the Federal Reserve System not been created and the prior institutions still existed, the banks at this point would have suspended payments of currency and brought into play the extralegal defenses that had been developed against banking panic. They argue that this would have prevented the subsequent waves of bank failures of 1931–1932 and 1933 and the continued monetary contraction associated with them.[8] Under these conditions, it is conceivable that the economic decline would have hit bottom by 1931 and seemed only a garden-variety recession.

This banking crisis had scarcely subsided when another one began in March 1931. The currency ratio now began to rise sharply and the money supply declined rapidly.

Up to this point, the monetary contraction had been entirely caused by domestic factors, the United States had been reducing its domestic money supply in the face of a gold inflow, had been oversterilizing gold. In the face of this and other misbehavior of national governments, the fragile gold-exchange international monetary system based upon the British pound approached its demise. A deepening financial crisis in Europe led to a run on the British pound, mainly by France and the Netherlands, and on September 21 Britain detached the pound from gold, removing itself from the gold standard and destroying the basis of the pound as an international monetary reserve asset.

This led to an abrupt reversal of the gold inflow into the United States, as the dollar came under pressure. The immediate effect on the monetary base of the gold outflow was fully offset by a large increase in Federal Reserve credit, reflecting both member bank borrowings and Federal Reserve purchases of bills. Accordingly, the monetary base never declined, continuing steadily upward at a modest rate until early 1933, when it increased sharply.

With most monetary systems, this would have sufficed to produce an increase in the money supply, but the inherent instability of the United States monetary system was reflected in another spurt of bank failures and continued increase in the currency ratio and the reserve ratio. The continued decline in the money supply through 1932 and early 1933 reflected entirely these factors.

In 1932, the money supply continued to decline as increases in the

[8] *Ibid.*, pp. 167–168 and 311.

currency ratio and the reserve ratio more than offset modest increase in the monetary base. In early 1933, the final banking crisis led to another wave of bank failures, a sharp rise in the currency ratio, and abrupt contraction of the money supply despite substantial open market purchases of government securities by the Federal Reserve.

In early March, New York and then several other states declared banking holidays, putting the nation's banking system temporarily out of business. A nationwide bank holiday was declared on March 7 by President Roosevelt, and for more than 1 week the nation's monetary system was at a standstill. Never before had it failed so completely or brought the national economy so low.

What went wrong?

In one interpretation that was extremely influential from the latter part of the 1930s through the 1940s and has had diminishing influence since then, the Great Depression derived not from the unusual instability of the monetary systems of the time but rather from deep-seated anomalies in Western economies, the stagnation of aging capitalism. Those who approached the subject in terms of monetary theory, however, pointed out that (1) the monetary collapse was not a matter of historical necessity but stemmed specifically from the peculiar institutions and policies of the time and that (2) the monetary collapse appears to be a sufficient explanation of the depression.

Irving Fisher stated this view at the time, and it is developed at length in the important recent study of Friedman and Schwartz. If one sees the monetary collapse as not reflecting historical necessity, he is naturally moved to ask how the United States monetary system can have completely fallen apart just over a decade after its faults were supposed to have been corrected by the Federal Reserve Act. It is natural to ask, What went wrong? or as Friedman and Schwartz do, "Why was monetary policy so inept?"[9]

Of course, any story as to how things might have gone differently provides an answer to this question. Since there are innumerable places in the chain of policy choices where different actions might have been taken, a great many such answers can be given. Among factors that various writers have pointed out might have made the story come out very differently are these: If Benjamin Strong had retained his health and continued to dominate Federal Reserve policy, decisive action might have been taken by 1930 against the first banking crisis. If the world in the 1920s had established a stable international monetary system rather than the fragile gold-

[9]Their answer to this question depicts the collapse as resulting largely "from the shift of power from New York to the other Federal Reserve Banks and from personal backgrounds and characteristics of the men nominally in power," i.e., from leadership deficiencies within the Federal Reserve System, *ibid.*, 407–419.

exchange system so that the United States was alone in its economic contraction, the gold inflow induced by deflation might have put a floor under the contraction by 1931. If the Federal Reserve Act had never been passed, as we noted, cooperative action by banks to implement their extralegal defenses against a banking panic probably would have gone into effect in 1930, precluding the catastrophic liquidation of the next 2½ years. And, of course, since the monetary contraction derived from the internal instability of the panic-prone United States banking system, had the Federal Reserve Act dealt with this in some effective way—such as insurance of bank deposits or 100 percent reserves of government securities behind bank deposits—the increase in the currency ratio and the reserve ratio that immediately explain the monetary contraction would not have happened and the story would have been different. Perhaps the Great Depression, far from being dictated by historical necessity, is among history's most improbable episodes.

A decisive factor in the debacle was bad monetary theory. If the Federal Reserve officials had been trying to control the money supply, they could hardly have let it decline by one-fourth. But what they were trying to do was to provide credit to accommodate commerce and business on reasonable terms. Whether "reasonable terms" existed they judged by the level of nominal interest rates. Thus, once nominal short-term interest rates (on high-grade debt) declined to low level, they inferred that they had done all it was proper for them to do:

> There was substantial opposition to the proposed program of additional open market purchases, based largely on the theory that the depression was the result mainly of nonmonetary causes such as overproduction and excess capacity in a number of industries. Therefore, cheaper and more abundant credit would not stimulate business recovery. Instead, more ease might encourage increases in productive capacity, defer essential readjustments, and retard recovery.[10]

Monetary Reform Pell-Mell

In a matter of months after the banking holiday there was passed an action of basic monetary reform that was probably more important than the establishment of the Federal Reserve System. This was the establishment of federal insurance of bank deposits. It was this that finally made bank deposits as safe as currency, put an end to bank runs, and removed the basis for cumulative increases in the currency ratio and the reserve ratio such as had just caused a reduction of the money supply by one-fourth. Were it not for this action, we presumably still would be "the land of runs and bank failures." The element of political accident in key decisions of monetary policy is again illustrated by the fact that the amendment to the Banking Act of

[10]Clay J. Anderson, *A Half-Century of Federal Reserve Policymaking, 1914–1964*, Federal Reserve Bank of Philadelphia, Philadelphia, p. 63, 1965. The passage refers specifically to the fall of 1930.

1933 embodying the insurance system that became effective in 1934 was introduced by a Senator of the minority party and at least initially opposed by President Roosevelt as well as by leading bankers and some of the major figures in the Federal Reserve System.[11]

Another basic decision of monetary policy was the devaluation of the dollar or the increase in the price of gold in terms of dollars from $20.67 to $35 an ounce. This was carried out in a series of steps from April 1933 to the fixing at the end of January 1934 of the price of gold that was in effect until 1971. This led immediately to a rapid inflow of gold which continued—later increasingly derived from political deterioration in Europe and Hitler's persecution of Jews—until 1940. This inflow of gold was the major basis of the rapid increase in the money supply that underlay the rapid rise of total demand beginning in 1933. A companion policy to this large increase in the price of gold was a program to purchase silver at a price about 75 percent above the prior market price.

While the domestic effect of these policies was to increase the money supply by increasing the monetary base, the money supply could have been increased without such actions by institutional changes that reversed the earlier decline in the base-money multiplier. The nation's actions toward gold and silver did great damage to the rest of the world and the prospects for reconstruction of the international monetary system.

The avalanche of gold and silver that the United States gained by raising its prices for the metals came largely from the monetary reserves of other nations. Since the inflow of metals was largely sterilized by an increase in the reserve ratio in the United States, from the point of view of the world monetary system the United States actions were seriously destructive. These actions and the torpedoing by President Roosevelt of the World Monetary and Economic Conference that convened in London in June 1933—a necessary counterpart of this extremely nationalistic policy—were major factors contributing to the continuation of international economic anarchy during the 1930s.

Other reform measures passed during this period lie behind the present-day institutions that we described earlier. The Banking Act of 1935 officially established the Federal Open Market Committee, gave the Board of Governors the power to change reserve requirements within a specified range and to fix the maximum interest rates that banks may pay on time deposits. Control over stock-market credit also dates from this time.

The Depression: Recovery Phase

Economic recovery began in the spring of 1933. In the first year it reflected more largely increase in velocity of circulation than in the money supply.

[11]Friedman and Schwartz, *op. cit.*, pp. 434–435.

Rapid growth of total demand continued into the Second World War, interrupted only by the recession of 1937–1938. The result was unsatisfactory in the sense that in 1941 the unemployment rate was still above 10 percent. Understanding of why the rapid increase in money supply and total demand left large unemployment requires a quantitative analysis. Major reasons why full employment was not reached for a decade after the Depression hit bottom in 1933 were as follows:

1. The contraction phase was very much longer than usual and carried the economy very much further below its full employment track. Therefore, a recovery at the customary rate would be expected to take several times as long as it normally did to regain full employment.

2. The serious recession of 1937–1938 set the recovery back about 3 years. It was 1940 before the unemployment rate got back down to where it had been in 1937.

3. A substantial part of the increase in total demand went into increased prices rather than increased output and employment. This reflected an extraordinarily unfavorable Phillips curve, since these price increases were occuring at a time when enormous excess capacity existed and unemployment was at unheard-of levels. It largely reflected policies of the federal government deriving from the belief that prosperity would be encouraged by pushing up wages and prices.

4. The existence of this inflation, inflation within depression, discouraged policies that would have caused a yet more rapid growth of total demand and probably was the major factor leading to the policies that caused the recession of 1937–1938. Policy makers of the times took seriously the inflation and the speculative unsoundness they saw lurking behind it.

Some interpretations of the Great Depression that do not rest upon a detailed review of the facts involve an argument like this: "Monetary policy was easy but full employment was not regained until the war years; therefore, monetary policy must be ineffective." Such a loose and nonquantitative approach is misleading. The rapid growth in money supply beginning in 1933 was fully reflected in growth in total demand. The increase in the money supply was not offset by decline in velocity of circulation. Thus, monetary policy was completely effective in doing what it could be expected to do, increasing total demand. The slowness of achievement of prosperity was due not to any demonstrated impotence of monetary policy but rather to the factors listed above.

For monetary policy, the period 1933–1941 was a unique one. Except for its ill-fated intervention in 1936–1937, the Federal Reserve did practically nothing. The enormous inflow of gold and the purchases of silver led to a very rapid and continued increase in the monetary base. The Federal Reserve sat back and watched "monetary policy" shaped by forces outside its control. During most of the period, Federal Reserve policy makers were worried that monetary policy was too easy and bank reserves too large. Thus, we may infer that had it not been for the golden avalanche and had monetary expansion depended upon positive Federal Reserve action, the recovery movement would have been slower than it was.

Growth in the money supply did not fully reflect the growth in high-powered money. The currency ratio declined from 1933 to 1935 and then leveled off, but the reserve ratio rose throughout the period. This reflected a continued increase in excess reserves and the doubling of reserve requirements by the Board of Governors in 1936–1937. Thus, the United States monetary system was reducing its base-money multiplier and partially sterilizing the gold it was pulling from the rest of the world, which was scarcely helpful to economic recovery abroad.

In 1937–1938 there was a depression within a depression, an economic contraction that dwarfs any we have experienced since and rivals in severity that of 1920–1921. A number of factors, including a change in fiscal policy associated with inaugeration of the social security system, can be cited as contributing to the recession. However, monetary policy may have been its main cause.

The Board of Governors of the Federal Reserve System announced in 1936 a set of increases that from August 1936 to May 1937 would double reserve requirements. The excess reserves of the banks were large enough for the banks to meet these higher reserve requirements without halting the expansion of the money supply if (1) there were no problems associated with the distribution of reserves among banks, (2) there was no adverse psychological reaction to this enormous shift in policy, and (3) the banks regarded these reserves as truly "excess" in the sense of *superfluous* rather than constituting in part a liquidity reserve that they needed under the existing circumstances.

The Federal Reserve interpreted the excess reserves as being truly redundant, but as posing a threat of future inflationary developments. Its theory was that removal of most of the excess reserves would safeguard the future without damaging the present.

The theory turned out to be wrong. Interest rates rose sharply as banks sold government securities, indicating that they did not regard their excess reserves as entirely superfluous. The money supply declined slightly from early 1937 through spring 1938, in contrast to its earlier rapid expansion. From the spring of 1937 through the spring of 1938, the economy again went into decline and the achievement of prosperity receded again into the future.

There is little doubt that the Federal Reserve action was a very costly mistake. Voices within the Federal Reserve System at the time argued that it would be time enough to worry about monetary restriction when the need for it arose rather than acting in anticipation of future needs. They also argued that gradual and exploratory action would be more appropriate than a huge change in an untried policy the implications of which could only be uncertain. Unfortunately, these were not the voices that prevailed.

The Second World War and Postwar Adjustment

The Second World War was longer and more costly than its predecessor, but its effects upon the money supply and the price level were roughly similar. Both about doubled. A larger proportion of the government's expenses were financed through taxation and a smaller proportion through money creation; wartime controls over prices and spending were more extensive and more effectively enforced; and the nation went into the war with a large cushion of unused resources because the recovery from the Depression was still incomplete. In relation to monetary policy, these are important respects in which the financing of the Second World War was unusual and had implications for the future:

1. The fact that the unemployment rate was still around 10 percent at the outbreak of the war implied that the nation had a substantial volume of excess capacity that could be put to war work. This made inflationary pressures in the early stages of the war much less severe than they otherwise would have been. Perhaps even more important was the psychological legacy of the Great Depression. The predominant belief of the times was that the war would be followed by a return to conditions of large unemployment and economic stagnation. This deterred people from bullish speculation such as had agitated the 1920s. Their pessimism led them to maintain large holdings of money and liquid assets through the war and early postwar periods, only gradually returning to "normal" ratios of cash and liquid assets to expenditures as the Depression-induced pessimism was gradually worn away by events.

2. As a matter of conscious policy in response to a lesson that had been drawn from the financing of the First World War, interest rates were not permitted to rise during the war. The Federal Reserve was assigned the job of freezing them at the level that existed at the beginning of the war. During this period, thus, the Federal Reserve conducted open market operations with the reverse of the rationale it has in monetary theory. Rather than buying and selling government securities to affect the money supply and letting the interest rate be set by supply and demand, the Federal Reserve bought and sold government securities to fix the level of interest rates and let the money supply be determined as the dependent variable.

During the war this did limited mischief because of the existence of economic controls and of pessimism, but it could have been an explosive formula if continued after the war, as it had been in 1919. The government, under President Truman, was reluctant for the Federal Reserve to depart from its role as stabilizer of the prices of government securities. The early postwar years did not see an upsurge of inflationary demand, presumably because of the hangover of Depression-related pessimism. The outbreak of the Korean war in mid-1950, however, created a situation in which continued stabilization of interest rates could have led to rapid expansion of the money supply and a self-feeding inflation like that of 1919. At this point, the Federal Reserve refused to continue to support prices of government securities and monetary policy entered a new phase.

In contrast to the experience after the First World War, there was not only no postwar inflation but also no postwar deflation. The economy moved smoothly, much more smoothly than anticipated by the pessimistic expectations of the times, through the transition from war to peace. The money supply decelerated in its growth and expansion of total demand depended largely upon increase in velocity of circulation. This reflected the freeing of demand from the wartime restrictions and the gradual building of confidence in the future.

Federal Reserve action in 1948 to control what was taken to be an inflationary situation contributed to causing a mild recession in 1949. Once again, the Federal Reserve used increases in reserve requirements, though these were cushioned by the offsetting use of open market operations. In fact, the offsetting was such that policy changes had little visible effect upon the money supply, and the monetary contribution to the recession stemmed from the failure of the money supply to increase after 1947. As subsequent experience was to illustrate, such a leveling off of the money supply does suffice to weaken total demand and lead to recession.

The Federal Reserve reversed its changes in reserve requirements, cushioning these also with open market operations, and recovery in the economy and resumption of modest expansion of the money supply both seemed to begin at the end of 1949.

The Treasury–Federal Reserve confrontation and the accord

The process by which the Federal Reserve disengaged itself, over the objections of the reluctant Treasury, from its obligation to support prices of government securities was complex and full of disagreement. In the recession of 1949, its policy of pegging yields and prices of government bonds caused the Federal Reserve to sell government bonds to resist the decline in their yields caused by the recession and the reduction in demand for credit. Federal Reserve reluctance to continue this clearly destabilizing pattern of operations led to a somewhat ambiguous statement by the Federal Open Market Committee indicating a less rigid policy of supporting bond prices.

The outbreak of the Korean war in mid-1950 led to increases in interest rates and expectations of inflationary conditions and further rise in interest rates. The Federal Reserve under the leadership of the Chairman of the Board of Governors Thomas McCabe thought an effort to hold down interest rates through Federal Reserve open market purchases of government securities (which would increase the monetary base and the money supply) would be seriously inflationary. The Federal Reserve asserted its independence with resolution, leading to a confrontation with the Treasury, complete with acrimonious bureaucratic infighting. The Federal Reserve won and the administration gracefully accepted the withdrawal of the Federal Reserve from the policy of supporting prices and yields of government securities. This was reflected in the Treasury–Federal Reserve Accord of March 1951.

This introduced a new era in Federal Reserve policy. It freed the Federal Reserve from its lingering war-related obligation to stabilize interest rates. It also led to the resignation of Chairman McCabe and his replacement by William McChesney Martin, Jr. as Chairman of the Board of Governors. Chairman Martin so dominated the Federal Reserve policy until his resignation in early 1970 that it would be appropriate to term this period of almost two decades the Martin era. We turn to it in the next chapter.

SUMMARY

1. The Federal Reserve Act derived from an erroneous diagnosis of the faults of the National Banking System. Its basic proposition that "an elastic currency" whose quantity varied to meet "the needs of trade" would correct these faults was incorrect.

2. During the First World War, the money supply and the price level roughly doubled.

3. Rapid expansion of the money supply based upon growth of Federal Reserve credit caused a severe inflation in 1919; its reversal caused a depression and an extraordinarily abrupt decline in the price level in 1920.

4. Monetary policy was unusually successful during the 1920s, relatively steady growth in the money supply being associated with steady growth of total demand and with high employment and price stability.

5. The great contraction of 1929–1933 involved a complex interaction process in which an essential element was the decline of one-fourth in the money supply. This reflected waves of bank failures leading to increases in the currency ratio and the reserve ratio. That the Federal Reserve did not take decisive action to check the progressive banking panic was contrary to expectations.

6. A basic reform of the United States monetary system was the guarantee of bank deposits, first passed in 1933. This finally halted bank runs and waves of bank failures, thus halting the variation in the currency ratio, the reserve ratio, and the money supply associated with these. This removed the inherent instability that had plagued the National Banking System and had continued under the Federal Reserve System.

7. The rapid growth of the money supply after 1933 reflected the inflow of gold from abroad. The Federal Reserve in 1936–1937 doubled reserve requirements, acting upon a mistaken interpretation of the significance of the existing large excess reserves. This was a principal cause of the major recession of 1937–1938.

8. The rapid increase in the money supply after 1933 was fully effective in the sense of leading to a proportionate rise in GNP. Recovery from the Depression took a long time because (1) the 3-year decline in total demand had carried it very far below the full-employment level, (2) the recession of 1937–1938 set the timetable of recovery back 3 years, and (3) much of the growth of total demand was consumed in increases in prices rather than in output and employment, largely because of government policies to increase wages and prices.

9. During the Second World War, the money supply and the price level roughly doubled, some of the price increases being delayed until the removal of price controls after the war.

10. The postwar transition to prosperity—rather than to the expected return of depression—led to a gradual growth of confidence and a reversal of deflationary expectations.

11. The Treasury Federal Reserve Accord of early 1951 freed the Federal Reserve from its obligation to support prices of government securities, permitting it to use open market operations for stabilization purposes.

QUESTIONS FOR REVIEW AND DISCUSSION

1. Contrast the ideas underlying the new Federal Reserve System with those of monetary theory. On the basis of present knowledge, what kind of reform of the United States monetary system in 1913 would have been desirable?

2. Point out some respects in which the financing of the Second World War differed from that of the First World War and the Civil War.

3. Comment on the deflation of 1920–1921 in relation to (*a*) the Phillips curve it reflected, (*b*) the appropriateness of monetary policy, and (*c*) its implications for the subsequent operation of the international monetary system.

4. Point out ways in which the experience and ideas of the 1920s laid the basis for Federal Reserve policies that worked badly in the 1930s.

5. "If the United States monetary system had been so set up as to have a stable currency ratio and reserve ratio, the money supply would have increased in the first year and a half after the 1929 downturn, and the cumulative economic collapse would not have occurred." Discuss.

6. Show how one following the credit approach to monetary policy could argue that the Federal Reserve had in 1929–1933 done all that could be done to combat the economic contraction. On the basis of monetary theory, what are the flaws in this interpretation?

7. What factors determined the major movements of the money supply in 1933–1940; what role did they have in explaining economic developments during this period.

8. "Since the Federal Reserve followed an easy-money policy after 1929 but the Depression continued to get worse, monetary policy must be ineffective." Comment critically.

9. "Since expansion of the money supply after 1933 did not bring prosperity, monetary policy must be ineffective." Comment critically.

10. Describe the issues that gave rise to the Treasury–Federal Reserve Accord. What do you think would have happened if the Federal Reserve had followed the Treasury's wishes?

21 monetary policy: 1951-1971

In 1951, as in 1920, the Federal Reserve freed itself from domination by the Treasury and got back to its standard business. We cannot say it was a return to normal, for things never seem to be quite normal. The 1920s involved special problems associated with reestablishment of the gold standard and then a period of speculative booms. In the 1950s and 1960s, the task of economic stabilization was complicated by erratic changes in government expenditures associated with the wars in Korea and Vietnam and other defense emergencies. All the same, we find the Federal Reserve after the catastrophic 1930s facing afresh the question what it was to do with its powers.

The Postwar Terms of Reference

During the 1930s, Federal Reserve policy reflected the credit approach to central banking. Critics such as Irving Fisher and Henry Simons interpreted monetary policy in terms of monetary theory or the neoclassical approach. After the Second World War, and to some extent by the latter part of the 1930s, these two approaches were joined by a third, based on the Keynesian theory. This new entrant seems to have had little or no influence on the Federal Reserve, but it dominated academic economics until its position was contested by monetary theory in the 1960s. Moreover, it formed the framework within which stabilization policy was interpreted by the Kennedy and Johnson administrations, i.e., from 1961 to 1969. In the late 1960s, academic opinion swung to some degree from the Keynesian toward the monetary approach. The Nixon administration initially emphasized this approach.

In 1969 and 1970, the Federal Reserve shifted to some extent from the credit-oriented interpretation of its actions that underlay its often procyclical operations in the past. It adopted the pattern of giving major attention to the behavior of the money supply and other "monetary aggregates," and stating a target for the growth rate of the money supply. However, the focus of Federal Reserve open-market operations continued to be conditions in the money market, and the actual growth rate of the money supply sometimes differed widely from the one stated as a goal of policy.

Since the actions of the 1950s and 1960s and the way various people interpreted them can only be understood in terms of the frameworks within which they were viewed, we shall sketch the major differences between the alternative approaches to monetary policy as they operated during this period of history. It is not necessary to elaborate our earlier discussion of neoclassical theory or the monetary approach. The monetary theorists of this period, as we noted earlier, were divided on a number of important issues of theory. But they agreed on a few essential points that provided a rough basis for interpreting and evaluating monetary policy and that clearly distinguished them from proponents of the credit approach and the predominant version of the Keynesian approach.

This core of agreement among monetary theorists included the following ideas: (1) The money supply (or the monetary system, or the monetary policy that determines its behavior) is an important causal influence on total demand. (2) Monetary policy should be measured and evaluated in terms of the behavior of the money supply or in some equivalent manner, and the usual interpretations in terms of nominal interest rates are misleading and erroneous.

These basic ideas sufficed to lead to the diagnosis that actual monetary policy was seriously defective, especially in the late 1960s. Widespread acceptance of monetary theory's interpretation of the role of monetary policy in causing the inflation of 1965–1970 underlay the increase in the acceptance of this approach and its increased influence on the Federal Reserve.

The ideas underlying Federal Reserve actions

For nearly two decades, from 1951 to 1970, the Federal Reserve System was under the leadership of the Chairman of the Board of Governors William McChesney Martin, making the Martin era the longest period of constant leadership and policy in the System's history. The ideas underlying Federal Reserve actions during nearly all of this period continued to be the credit approach to central banking, the view that the goal of the Federal Reserve was the maintenance of sound or appropriate credit conditions. The major framework for characterizing Federal Reserve actions was in terms of the degree of "credit restraint" or of "credit ease" that prevailed. Changes in the degree of credit tightness or ease were attributed to Federal Reserve actions with but little emphasis on other factors affecting the supply of and demand for credit.

The Federal Reserve view was that no single index measured adequately the degree of credit tightness or ease, precluding a quantitative analysis. The major factors taken to indicate credit tightness or ease, however, were the "free reserves" of member banks, interest rates in the money market, and the "tone and feel" of the money market. Other factors to which reference was made were the total volume of credit in the economy, changes in bank credit, and evidence that credit was being used for unsound speculative purposes.

During the earlier part of the period, the measure of credit conditions to which the Federal Reserve gave most of its attention and in terms of which it defined its instructions to the Manager of the Open Market Account was the free reserves of members. Free reserves are defined as excess reserves of member banks minus their borrowings from Federal Reserve banks. Thus, member bank borrowings are interpreted as essentially negative excess reserves, and free reserves as net excess reserves.

The reasoning behind use of free reserves as a measure of credit conditions is this: If banks are in an "easy" reserve position and could make additional loans or acquire additional investments if they *chose* to do so, then assuredly credit conditions must be easy. On the other hand, if bank reserve positions are "tight" so that banks have not the ability to make additional loans and investments then it can be inferred that additional loans and investments will be difficult to get and that credit conditions are tight.

Using interest rates in the New York money market, and the tone and feel of that market, as a measure of credit ease or tightness was rationalized on the basis that "New York is the focal point of pressure or ease in bank reserves throughout the country, regardless of the origin of such pressure or ease."[1]

The difficulty with this approach that is pointed up by monetary theory is a familiar one. Federal Reserve actions are not the only thing that affects money-market interest rates, and the feel and tone of the money market. They also are affected by changes in economic conditions and the demand for credit. An increase in the growth rate of total demand and the development of bullish expectations will increase the demand for credit and tend to increase interest rates and make the money market tight. Moreover, the increase in demand for customer loans and in short-term interest rates (especially when the Federal Reserve discount rate lags behind, as it usually does) will make member banks more willing to borrow from Federal Reserve banks and will reduce the banks *desired free reserves*. Thus, a strengthening of economic conditions will cause "tight money," or what the Federal Reserve could interpret as "monetary restraint," no matter what the Federal Reserve is doing—just as the weakening of economic conditions in 1929–1933 created what the Federal Reserve interpreted as "credit

[1]Albert R. Koch, "An Approach to Monetary Policy Formulation," *Fed. Reserve Bank Phila. Bus. Rev.*, p. 5, February 1965.

ease" even while the money supply was declining in an extraordinary manner.

To avoid this error and give a valid interpretation of Federal Reserve actions in terms of credit conditions requires separating the influence on credit conditions of Federal Reserve actions from the influence of other factors, including changes in economic conditions and expectations. In principle, this could be done by using Wicksell's concept of the natural rate of interest. A shift to more bullish expectations, for example, would increase the natural rate of interest. Federal Reserve actions would be interpreted as restrictive only if they increased interest rates *by more than the increase in the natural rate of interest.* We say that this could be done *in principle,* but in practice we do not seem to have a way of estimating with confidence the changes in the natural rate of interest.

A special difficulty with this approach is that an error will tend to be self-aggravating, leading to cumulative instability. For example, if the Federal Reserve underestimates the increase in the natural rate of interest and does not permit market interest rates to increase by enough (interpreting as "monetary restraint" what is in truth "monetary ease"), it will provide bank reserves that cause an unusually rapid increase in the money supply. This will make for a greater increase in total demand and bullish expectations, increase the natural rate of interest still further, and cause the initial error to be compounded.

These same difficulties attach to the tone and feel of the money market as a measure of Federal Reserve actions. The tone and feel of the market also responds to changes in economic conditions. During an economic upswing, the Federal Reserve should think of itself as causing monetary restraint only if the money market tightens by *more than par,* and since par depends upon unknown expectational factors it is difficult to estimate. Similarly, the amount that member banks want to borrow from Federal Reserve banks (and to a lesser extent the amount of excess reserves they want to hold) depends on the customer demand for loans, the cyclical position of the economy, and the Federal Reserve discount rate in relation to market interest rates. In an economic upswing, the free reserve position should be taken to indicate monetary restraint only if free reserves decline by more than par. Once again, par is difficult to define, and an error in estimating it can be self-aggravating.

These ideas, which are carried forward from our discussion of monetary theory, provide the framework needed to understand the debate over monetary policy in the 1950s and 1960s, and the shift in the Federal Reserve position that occurred in 1969 and 1970. The basic story of monetary policy during these two decades is this: The Federal Reserve in interpreting its actions in terms of credit restraint and credit ease did not make sufficient allowance for changes in credit conditions resulting from changes in business expectations and the demand for credit. This caused it to increase the money supply unusually rapidly when total demand was above target and unusually slowly when it was below target. The Federal Reserve finally acted strongly to reverse such movements, then in some cases appearing to be too heavy-handed or forceful. The argument that a better job of guiding Federal Reserve policy and the economy could have been done in terms of the behavior of the money supply became increasingly persuasive and after 1969, was at least temporarily accepted by the Federal Reserve.

The Keynesian view of monetary policy

The Keynesian theory that predominated among economists in the 1950s and remained important in 1970 (Chap. 12) did not have well-defined implications for monetary policy in the kind of economic environment that existed. Keynes, we recall, had interpreted the Great Depression as the onset of secular stagnation. He expected that maintenance of prosperity through monetary policy would require getting interest rates down to very low levels. He thought that because of impediments to such continuing reductions in interest rates, monetary policy would have but a limited ability to combat economic stagnation.

This picture proved to have little relevance to the 1950s and 1960s. No stagnation problem appeared. Interest rates were not unusually low and were rising rather than falling. Thus, the job Keynes thought monetary policy could not do is not the job with which it was confronted. An economist working with the broad framework of the Keynesian theory could without logical error or inconsistency have interpreted monetary policy in the way that we have associated with monetary theory.

However, most economists associated with the Keynesian theory adopted a different viewpoint. They interpreted monetary policy not in terms of the money supply, but rather in terms of the interest rate. Moreover, they posited that such changes in interest rates as would be feasible and could be brought about by Federal Reserve actions had a relatively small payoff in terms of changing total demand. In this sense, they viewed monetary policy as relatively ineffective. They saw it as perhaps not worth its cost in terms of the unsettling changes in interest rates that would be required if it were to have any substantial effect on total demand.[2]

As the Keynesian economist's fears of economic stagnation were only gradually eroded by experience, he also leaned towards low interest rates. Within his framework these might be badly needed if stagnation did set in and might be desirable in any case because they lowered the relative incomes of interest recipients. Accordingly, the operational con-

[2]In terms of the model reviewed in Chap. 12, this view is consistent with the case in which the *IS* curve is steeply downward-sloping (because the response of investment to the interest rate is small), and the *LM* curve is relatively flat (because the response of the demand for money to the interest rate is large). As you can see by drawing some diagrams, in this case changing the money supply has only a small effect in changing Y relative to its effect on i.

clusions that were drawn from the Keynesian theory by the most influential group of economists using that framework were: (1) The Federal Reserve should direct its attention to the interest rates (rather than the money supply). (2) The interest rate should be kept relatively steady, since the disruptive effect of changes in interest rates were not worth their benefits. (3) The interest rate should be kept low.

The lineup

The economists who interpreted the Keynesian theory in this way had much in common with the Federal Reserve, applying its traditional credit approach. They agreed on the following important points: (1) The tightness of ease of monetary policy was to be measured by nominal interest rates (and other credit indexes that behave in a similar way). (2) Short-run changes in interest rates ought to be limited to moderate or reasonable proportions. Thus, on the crucial points of difference between monetary theory and the Federal Reserve's credit approach, this version of the Keynesian theory sided with the Federal Reserve.

One point of difference between the Federal Reserve approach and this Keynesian approach related to the general level of interest rates. The Federal Reserve was as concerned that interest rates might be too low as that they might be too high, and at the time of the Treasury–Federal Reserve Accord fought the administration on behalf of an increase in interest rates. The Keynesian approach, on the other hand, led to a general preference for low interest rates.

Another point of difference stemming logically from the two theories related to *which* interest rates were taken as the major guide to Federal Reserve actions. The Federal Reserve was oriented mainly to short-term interest rates and conditions in the New York money market, which it interpreted as reflecting bank reserve positions and credit conditions throughout the country, and, therefore, as a focal target in preserving sound and reasonable credit conditions. But within the Keynesian theory monetary policy affects total demand only by affecting investment, and investment—it was argued—is affected not by interest rates in the money market but by long-term interest rates and conditions in the bond market and the mortgage market. This led to the argument that the Federal Reserve not only should be guided in its actions by long-term interest rates but also should conduct its open market operations in long-term securities. If what matters is not the money supply (as the monetary theorists thought) or bank reserves and conditions in the money market (as the Federal Reserve thought) but long-term interest rates and conditions in the bond market, the obvious step is to use Federal Reserve open market operations directly to regulate the bond market—just as during the war they had been used to regulate the government securities markets.

This difference of viewpoints and theories contributed to the "bills-only" controversy that began in 1953. The Federal Reserve was criticized for limiting its open market operations to short-term government securities. It nominally compromised and expressed a willingness to deal in government securities of all maturities, although in practice it continued to operate almost entirely in the short-term market.[3]

This was the basic lineup of competing ideas during the 1950s and 1960s. The Keynesians were allied with the Federal Reserve in interpreting monetary policy in terms of nominal interest rates, though differing from it in generally wanting lower interest rates and in wanting to be guided by long-term rather than short-term rates. In terms of monetary theory, both of these approaches were faulty and potentially hazardous because they failed to deal with the problem posed by Wicksell—and the problem that underlay the catastrophic Federal Reserve performance in 1929–1933. They did not distinguish changes in interest rates that reflected Federal Reserve actions from those that reflected changes in economic conditions, expectations, and the demand for credit. The Keynesian ideas had the additional fault that their bias in favor of low interest rates implied a bias in favor of actions that would prove to be inflationary. We turn now to see what emerged from the contest among proponents of these competing strategies.

Monetary Policy in the 1950s

As a major tool for interpreting economic developments and monetary policy in the 1950s, we use Fig. 21–1. This depicts the *rates of change* in total demand and related variables. Thus, it contains the same information as Fig. 3–6, but cast into a form permitting a somewhat closer interpretation. Checking back and forth between the levels of the variables in Fig. 3–6 (where the slopes of the curves show rates of change) and their rates of change in Fig. 21–1 may be helpful.

In interpreting and evaluating monetary policy, the focal question is whether it contributed to keeping GNP growing along an appropriate time path or whether the behavior of the money supply tended to produce (1) the wrong average growth rate of GNP, (2) erratic variation in GNP, or (3) self-feeding movements of GNP away from its target path. In Fig. 21–1, the money supply can be interpreted as a variable potentially controlled by Federal Reserve actions, and GNP as defining the major target variable of monetary policy. The behavior of velocity reflects all of the factors affecting GNP except the money supply, as well as showing the way in which GNP responded to changes in the money supply. The rates of change in the money

[3]On this point, it was reasonable for the monetary theorists to side with the Federal Reserve. If open market operations are to be used mainly to control the money supply, letting interest rates be set by supply of the demand for credit, it is desirable to minimize the side effects of open market operations on interest rates. This is accomplished by conducting such operations in the largest and most stable of debt markets, the market for Treasury bills.

supply and in velocity can be interpreted as jointly causing the change in GNP, which is roughly their sum:

$$1+\frac{\Delta Y}{Y}=\left(1+\frac{\Delta M}{M}\right)\left(1+\frac{\Delta V}{V}\right) \qquad \frac{\Delta Y}{Y}\approx\frac{\Delta M}{M}+\frac{\Delta V}{V}$$

In the same way, the change in GNP then can be interpreted as causing the combined change in the price level and in output:

$$1+\frac{\Delta Y}{Y}=\left(1+\frac{\Delta P}{P}\right)\left(1+\frac{\Delta O}{O}\right) \qquad \frac{\Delta Y}{Y}\approx\frac{\Delta P}{P}+\frac{\Delta O}{O}$$

These variables are among the important targets of stabilization policy. The extent to which a given change in GNP is reflected in change in the price level as against change in output is determined by the set of factors discussed above in connection with the Phillips curve. Change in output is closely related to change in employment and to change in the unemployment rate. We thus expect a period of small increases in output to be one of rising unemployment.

During 1951 and 1952, the Federal Reserve characterized its policy as restrictive, as maintaining a posture of restraint to limit inflation associated with the Korean war. During this period, interest rates did rise further, continuing the adjustment from their low wartime levels. As measured by the behavior of the money supply, however, monetary policy through mid-1952 was unusually expansive. The money supply in late 1951 and early 1952 grew at one of the most rapid rates of the 1950s. This reflected on increase in the monetary base, largely from increases in Federal Reserve credit. During this period, monetary policy actually contributed to the inflationary growth of total demand, although policy as defined by the Federal Reserve was one of "restraint."[4]

The rapid rise in GNP in early 1951 and the correspondingly rapid increase in velocity reflected scare buying and inflationary expectations arising from the Chinese entrance into the Korean war in late 1950. The spurt in GNP in late 1952, again based on a temporary rise of velocity, also was associated with extreme buoyancy of the economy and the rise of inflationary expectations. The rapid average increase in the money supply in 1951 and 1952—the most rapid for any postwar period until 1958–1959, which also generated inflationary expectations and a lagging rise in velocity—was one factor contributing to this outcome.

The recession of 1953–1954

From late spring of 1953 through mid-1954, the economy experienced a recession. Total demand declined rather than showing its usual growth

[4]The annual reports of the Board of Governors of the Federal Reserve System provide an official characterization of Federal Reserve actions and the thinking behind them. They also provide a report on each meeting of the Federal Open Market Committee, including the directive given to the Manager of the Federal Reserve System Open Market Account and the names of committee members voting for and against the directive that is passed. These reports on meetings of the Open Market Committee have since 1967 also been published with a lag of about 90 days in the *Fed. Reserve Bull.*

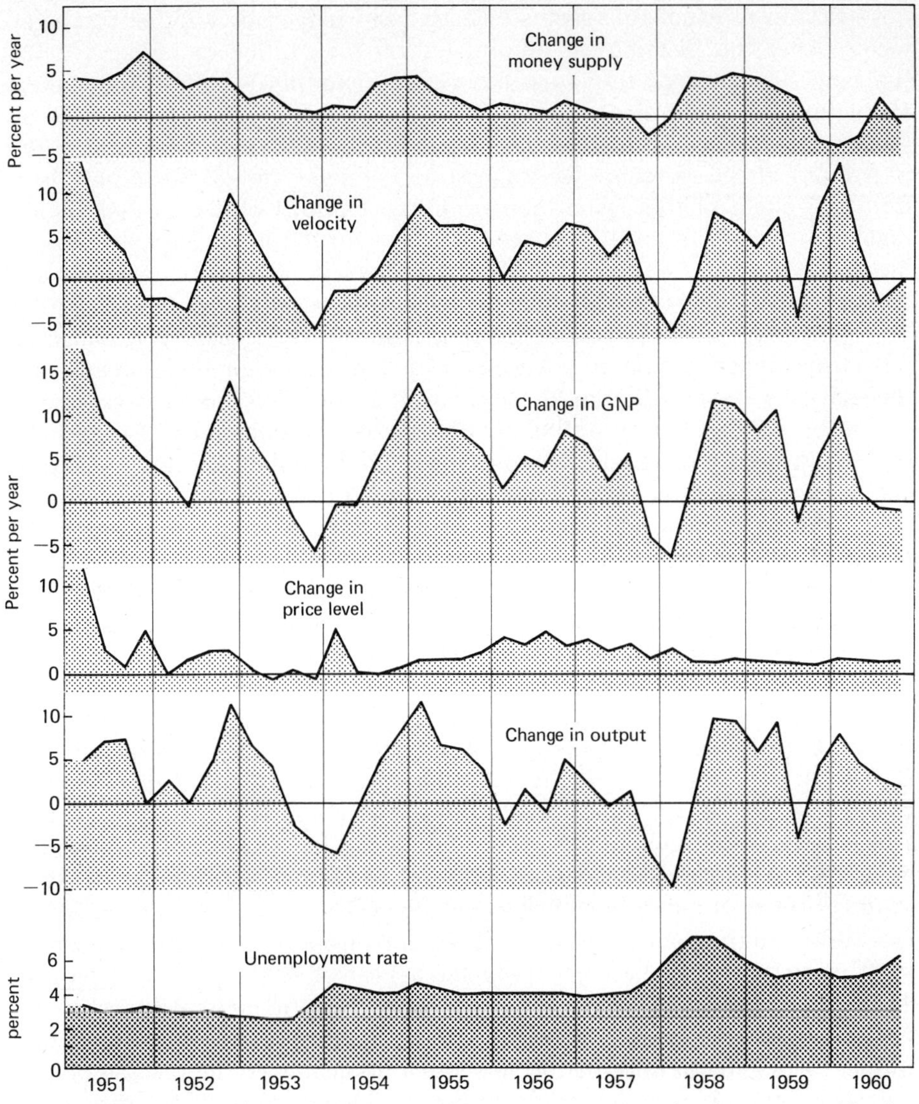

Fig. 21–1 Change in GNP and related variables, 1951–1960. (Price level is measured by the GNP deflator; output by GNP in 1958 prices. All data are seasonally adjusted. Annual rates of change are quarterly percentage changes times 4.) (Money supply, Board of Governors of the Federal Reserve System; GNP, GNP deflator, and GNP in 1958 prices, U.S. Department of Commerce; unemployment rate, U.S. Department of Labor.)

(Fig. 21–1). Its decline below its full employment path (see Fig. 3–7) was reflected in a decline in output and an increase in the unemployment rate from about 3 to over 5 percent.

The reduction of about one-half in the rate of growth of the money supply in early 1953 contributed to the onset of the recession. In this case however, an unusual role seems to have been played by another financial factor. After the Eisenhower administration took office in January 1953, the new Secretary of the Treasury, George Humphrey, made statements about funding the national debt that seemed to imply very large sales of long-term Treasury securities. The Treasury did sell $1.2 billion of a 30-year bond at 3¼ percent, well above accustomed yields. Seemingly less from the effect of this issue than from expectations of the further issues that were feared, interest rates rose sharply and the bond market fell in a near-panic manner. This combination of monetary and debt management actions seems to have been the major cause of the onset of recession.

Why were these policies followed? After nearly 3 years of expansion, reflecting in part the large government expenditures for the Korean war, the economy was at full employment and the price level had increased appreciably. A deceleration of the growth rate of total demand was called for to avoid a period of accelerating inflation. So the policies followed were a step in the right direction. It is just that they turned out to be too large a step. The experience points up the need for a close calculation of the required dosage in changing monetary policy.

Once the recession began, Federal Reserve actions tended to aggravate it. The money supply showed little increase from the second quarter of 1953 through the second quarter of 1954. Thus, monetary policy contributed to making this a full-blown recession, in contrast to the later "pause" or "mini-recession" of 1966–1967. Once the recession was underway, the reduction in incentives to spend and the declines in interest rates led to a shift from increases in velocity to decreases. Most of the decline in the growth rate of GNP reflected this shift in velocity. The reduction in velocity, however, does not seem to have been an independent cause of the recession, but rather to have reflected the whole set of factors that tend to make a swing in the economy—once begun—self-feeding.

Why did the Federal Reserve take actions leading to only an unusually small growth of the money supply for a year after the recession began? This seems to have been one of those cases where the Federal Reserve was misled by viewing itself as regulating nominal interest rates and credit conditions. The Federal Reserve did not intend to aggravate the recession, and changed its nominal policy to one of ease at the very onset of the recession, in the spring of 1953. Its goal seemed to be limiting the economic contraction and quickly turning the economy upward again. However, as in 1929–1933, the easing in credit conditions that the Federal Reserve saw as reflecting its policies was not enough to keep pace with the decline in the demand for credit and the natural rate of interest, as the money supply failed to show its normal growth. Recovery began a year later in the third quarter of 1954, simultaneously with accelerated growth of the money supply.

From mid-1954 through the spring of 1955, monetary policy contributed to rapid growth of total demand, as the money supply increased about as rapidly as in 1951–1952. A rapid rise in total demand did occur, the favorable spending environment bringing an increasing rise in velocity. Inflation accelerated, but remained modest until 1956. Output thus increased at rates of more than 5 percent. The labor force grew unusually rapidly in late 1954 and 1955, however, in part because of the release of men from the armed forces. As a consequence, the rate of growth of output was not rapid enough to bring a sharp reduction in the unemployment rate (like that of 1958–1959). Unemployment remained close to 4 percent, not far below its recession peak and considerably higher than in 1951–1953.

The recession of 1957

The rate of increase in the money supply declined after early 1955 and remained at a low and declining level until late 1957, when it became negative. Velocity increased fairly steadily until late 1957 by about 5 percent per year, producing increases in GNP of more than 5 percent. The economy's Phillips curve appears to have shifted upward, however, and in 1956 the price level was rising by more than 3 percent when unemployment was 4 percent. As a result, most of the increase in total demand in 1956 and 1957 was reflected in increases in the price level rather than in growth in output, which was modest.

In late 1957, after two quarters of negligible expansion of the money supply, the economy again suffered a cyclical downturn. The swing to unfavorable spending incentives brought a decline in velocity and in GNP. This was almost entirely reflected in a decline in output, the behavior of the price level showing no immediate response to the recession. The unemployment rate rose from the 4 percent level that had now characterized it for 4 years to a peak of more than 7 percent.

Again in 1957, deceleration of the rate of growth of total demand may have been on balance desirable. Inflation and balance of payments difficulties might have worsened if the economy had not been reined in. The question to be raised is whether this could have been done without another full recession, with its substantial loss of output and increase in unemployment. Continuation of increases in the money supply in 1956 and 1957 at a more normal rate would have been conducive to this outcome, but the Federal Reserve's use of credit criteria did not permit so fine an adjustment of policy.

Once again, monetary policy acted to amplify the recession, the money supply declining in the fourth quarter of 1957 and remaining at the reduced level in the next quarter. Once again, monetary expansion began simultaneously with expansion of the economy. Rather rapid growth of the money supply contributed to the recovery of total demand during 1958 and the first half of 1959.

Compared to the 1930s and to most earlier United States experience, the 1950s were a successful period of stabilization policy. The fact that the recessions of 1949, 1953, and 1957 were limited in scale; that unemployment except in recessions was at a normal level; and that no tendencies toward secular stagnation appeared led to gradual dissipation of the pessimism regarding the economic future with which the nation emerged from the Second World War.

However, if policy is compared not with past performance but with the best that could have been done, some opportunities for improvement seem to emerge. These became increasingly clear as the sample of experience lengthened in the 1960s, but the Federal Reserve also was criticized at the time for actions that seemed to contribute to initiating and then to prolonging the recessions of 1953–1954 and 1957. These actions seemed to reflect the inability of the Federal Reserve, in directing its operations in terms of interest rates and measures of credit conditions, to judge closely just what changes in these measures were required for economic stability.

As interpreted in terms of monetary theory, thus, the experience seemed to support the propositions that (1) the money supply is an important causal influence on total demand, and (2) guiding Federal Reserve actions by the behavior of the money supply is more accurate and less hazardous than guiding them by indexes of credit conditions.

Economic Slack: 1960–1965

In the summer of 1959, when unemployment remained high, a protracted steel strike substantially affected the output of the economy. Economic expectations remained very optimistic. The catch phrase of the time was the "soaring sixties." The fear was all of inflation.

Growth of the money supply decelerated in the third quarter of 1959 and the money supply actually declined for three quarters thereafter. If the money supply is an important causal variable, we should expect that after some lag the monetary contraction would overcome the bullish expectations and turn the poststrike expansion into a recession. In fact, signs of recession first appeared in early 1960 and GNP declined through the first quarter of 1961. The decline in the money supply in late 1959 at a time when business expectations remained bullish and the demand for credit strong led for a time to sharp increases in interest rates. The recession was quite unexpected. Monetary policy seems to have been its principal cause.

While the role of monetary policy in initiating the 1953 and 1957 recessions can be interpreted as reflecting a dose of needed medicine that proved in retrospect to be an overdose, in 1959 it is not so clear that any dosage of economic restriction was needed or that the Federal Reserve intended to administer one. Perhaps an important element in explaining why the money supply first declined is that the Federal Reserve's credit criteria caused it to be misled by the steel strike. In the recessions of 1953 and 1957, the money supply declined as the Federal Reserve did not permit interest rates to decline by enough to offset the decline in the demand for credit.

The steel strike, by causing large-scale liquidation of businss inventories, also reduced the demand for credit (and the natural rate of interest). Federal Reserve open market operations aimed at stabilizing interest rates and credit conditions in the New York money market led to reductions in the money supply. Such reductions in the money supply, in turn, can explain the unexpected onset of recession a few months later.

This time, the money supply was turned around and began to increase before the recession was far advanced. This may explain why GNP never declined substantially, but only leveled off for a year. In this case the Federal Reserve did not let positive monetary feedback contribute to aggravating the recession as had happened in 1953 and in 1957. But the increases in the money supply, although earlier were also smaller than in the other cases. It was a year and a half after its upturn, or the end of 1961, before the money supply became as large as it had been in 1959. The upturn in GNP lagged behind this weak monetary turnaround and then was not as strong as in earlier cyclical recoveries.

Fig. 21–2 Change in GNP and related variables, 1961–1970. (Price level is measured by the GNP deflator; output by GNP in 1958 prices. All data are seasonally adjusted. Annual rates of change are quarterly percentage changes times 4.) *(Money supply, Board of Governors of the Federal Reserve System; GNP, GNP deflator, and GNP in 1958 prices, U.S. Department of Commerce; unemployment rate, U.S. Department of Labor.)*

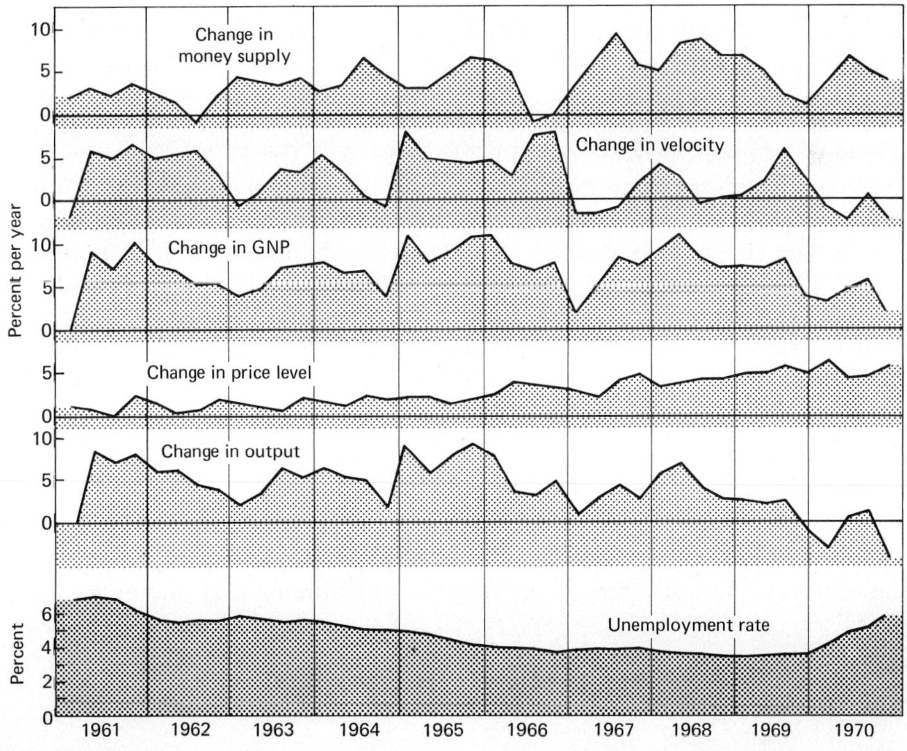

Since the 1960 recession had begun when unemployment was still above prosperity levels, the gap to be covered before full employment was regained was larger in 1961 than it had been in 1958. What was needed at this point was a rapid growth in GNP to close this gap and restore full employment. Unfortunately, the required rapid expansion of GNP did not occur this time. We note from Fig. 21–2 that growth of GNP in 1961 and 1962 was less rapid than in 1955 and 1958 and that unemployment remained high. The growth rate of GNP belatedly accelerated in 1963 and 1965, finally reducing the unemployment rate to the 4 percent level by late 1965.

What was the contribution of the money supply to this story? We find that it fits its usual role as a causal factor. In contrast to the rapid monetary expansion that contributed to the speedy recovery of GNP in late 1954 and in 1958, the money supply in the latter part of 1960 and in 1961 grew at less than its average rate. It made no contribution to prompt recovery of GNP. During 1962, growth of the money supply slowed further, contributing to a weakness of demand in late 1962 that brought fears of another recession. In late 1962, the money supply began to grow more rapidly. After mid-1963, GNP grew more rapidly and unemployment declined, reaching the 4 percent level in late 1965.

Federal Reserve actions thus contributed to the recession of 1960, which occurred before full employment had been reached and initiated the period of economic slack. They also contributed to the slow growth of GNP in 1961 and 1962, as well as to the acceleration of growth of total demand that finally brought full employment and ended the episode of economic slack.

Once again, the Federal Reserve did not intend to cause a recession by its 1959 actions and did not view them as unusually restrictive by the measures of credit at which it looked.[5] Similarly, the Federal Reserve did not view its actions as contributing to slow growth of total demand in 1961 and 1962, explaining this in terms of other factors and saying its actions "continued to encourage credit and monetary expansion."[6] The problem is again the misleading nature of the credit criteria by which the Federal Reserve was guided. An evidence of this is the fact that in 1963 when the money supply finally began to increase more rapidly and to stimulate an accelerated growth of GNP, the Federal Reserve said that it "gradually lessened the degree of credit and monetary ease."[7]

1966–1969: Inflation

The rapid growth of total demand in 1964 and 1965 was useful. It offset the slow average growth of 1960–1962 and brought the unemployment

[5] *Annu. Rep. Board Governors Fed. Reserve Syst.*, pp. 1–4, 1959.
[6] *Ibid.*, p. 8, 1962.
[7] *Ibid.*, p. 10, 1963.

rate back down to a prosperity level. But continued expansion of total demand at this rate after the slack was worked out of the economy and real output could no longer increase so rapidly would lead to inflation. The problem of stabilization policy by late 1965, was to slow the growth of total demand without causing another recession. Monetary theory would prescribe slowing the increase in the money supply moderately from the 4 percent rate that prevailed during 1963 and 1964.

Unfortunately, rather than slowing down, growth of the money supply spurted from the spring of 1965 to the spring of 1966. GNP, rather than slowing down, also spurted ahead at a rate of more than 9 percent per year. As a result, inflation accelerated from about 1½ to about 3 percent by 1966. Thus began an inflation problem that still dogged us in 1971.

The explanation of the accelerated growth of the money supply appears to be the Federal Reserve policy of conducting open market operations with a view to permitting only limited increases in interest rates in the money market. Most meetings of the Federal Open Market Committee during 1965 directed the Manager of the Open Market Account to conduct open market operations "with a view to maintaining about the same conditions in the money market as have prevailed in recent weeks." The meeting of February 2 directed that operations should be conducted "with a view to moving toward slightly firmer conditions in the money market"; that of March 23 called for "attaining slightly firmer conditions in the money market"; and that of October 12 called for "maintaining a firm tone in the money market." On the other hand, the directive of December 14 called for open market operations "directed to moderating any further adjustments in money and credit markets that may develop," i.e., using open market operations to limit increases in interest rates brought about by increases in the demand for credit.[8]

This was 1929–1933 in reverse. By using open market operations to resist increases in nominal interest rates brought about by increases in the demand for credit, the Federal Reserve brought about inflationary increases in the money supply. Its decision rule of combating market-caused increases in interest rates prevented market interest rates from rising equally with the natural rate of interest, or gave rise to positive monetary feedback.

Beginning in May 1966, the Federal Reserve took actions that resulted in no increase whatever in the money supply for 9 months. This was an interesting test of the effectiveness of monetary policy. No other important factors seemed to be making for an economic slowdown. The question was whether the very rapid growth of total demand, in a very bullish economy, would be slowed down by simply leveling off the money supply.

In this severe test of its effectiveness, monetary policy led to a marked slowdown of growth of total demand in the first quarter of 1967. This may not look very striking on the chart, but at the time it seemed to bring the

[8] *Annu. Rep. Board Governors Fed. Reserve Syst.*, pp. 82–153, 1965.

economy to the brink of recession. What next? Down to recession, back up into inflation, or would the happy medium now be found?

We note first that the abrupt cutting off of the contribution to the supply of credit from the creation of money by the Federal Reserve banks and the commercial banks, at a time when bullish expectations made demand for credit very strong, led to an abrupt increase in interest rates. As is usual in such cases, institutional lenders were reluctant to let interest rates rise as rapidly as would have been required to clear the credit markets and did some rationing of credit among potential borrowers. The abrupt increase in the price of credit and the reduction in its availability was called the "credit crunch of 1966." The shortage of credit most severely affected those sectors which are most responsive to changes in interest rates and which derive their funds from financial intermediaries that cannot match the sharply rising interest rates in the open market. Hardest hit was credit for residential construction.

Quite in conformity with the picture presented in our discussion of interest theory, however, the direct effects of the cessation of growth of the money supply in increasing interest rates (by reducing the supply of credit) were shortly followed by its indirect effects in reducing interest rates (by weakening growth of total demand and thus the demand for credit). Interest rates declined sharply in early 1967 (though this also reflected the direct effects of the rapid increase in the money supply that began in early 1967).

Back to the question, "Which way next?" The answer was, "Inflation with a vengeance!" Compared to its 4 percent increase in 1963–1964 and the increase of over 6 percent in 1965 that started the inflation, the money supply was increased during 1967–1968 at the rate of about 7½ percent per year. The Federal Reserve viewpoint that gave rise to this outcome is by now a familiar one. The Federal Reserve saw itself as imposing "restraint" because bank reserves were "under pressure" and interest rates were rising and were high in relation to earlier experience. But in terms of monetary theory—a view supported by the outcome—Federal Reserve actions were what fed the inflation. The inflation rate accelerated from 3 percent in 1966 to about 5 percent by the end of 1968.

1969–1970: Slowing Things Down

The task of stabilization policy in 1969–1970 was essentially the same one that had been dealt with unsuccessfully during 1965–1968. This was to slow the growth of total demand in order to reduce the rate of inflation, without overdoing the restriction and causing a major recession.

Federal Reserve actions in 1969 finally led to a behavior of the money supply that was consistent with this objective. Growth of the money supply was slowed down markedly, though less abruptly and severely than in

1966. The rate of monetary expansion was reduced from about 7½ to about 5 percent in early 1969 and then to less than 1 percent in the second half of 1969. Then, before the effects of this were fully felt, growth of the money supply was resumed in early 1970 at a rate of about 5½ percent, a rate between the extremes of earlier performance.

Once again, growth of total demand responded promptly to the change in monetary policy, slowing in mid-1969 to a rate of about 4½ percent, in contrast to the 8 to 10 percent rates of the preceeding 2 years. Had the price level been stable, growth of total demand at 4½ percent would have been about sufficient to provide normal growth of output and to keep the unemployment rate stable. However, the inflation rate had been accelerating in 1968 and was over 5 percent in early 1969. Thus, the prevailing Phillips curve was one based on experience with and expectations of an inflation rate of some 5 percent. Moreover, unemployment in early 1969 was at the unusually low rate of 3.3 percent. The position of the economy was unusually far to the left on an unfavorable Phillips curve, and inflation continued at about 5 percent through 1969.

With the price level rising by more than 5 percent, an increase in total demand of less than 5 percent implied an absolute reduction in output. Given increasing productivity, it implied a more rapid reduction in employment. Reduction in employment plus continued growth of the labor force implied rising unemployment. By late 1970, the unemployment rate had risen from 3.3 to 6 percent.

The unpleasant surprise of 1970 was that the slowing of growth of total demand and the resulting rise in unemployment did not lead to a greater reduction in inflation. Thinking in terms of the Phillips curve, the rise in unemployment should have led to a slowing of inflation as the economy moved to the right along the prevailing Phillips curve. Furthermore, there should have been favorable indirect effects—after some lag—as the slowing of inflation and reduction in inflationary expectations led to a leftward shift of the Phillips curve, reducing the rate of inflation associated with any given unemployment rate.

Inflation did, indeed, decelerate in 1970. The rate of increase in the various price indexes fell by about one percentage point, or roughly one-fifth, but this was less of a response than had been expected. The extent to which this disappointing outcome reflected lags in the response of the inflation rate to change in demand conditions,[9] shifts in the structure of the labor force that altered the meaning of a given unemployment rate,[10] and other factors required further investigation and discussion.

[9]An empirical study emphasizing expectations is Leonall C. Andersen and Keith M. Carlson, "A Monetarist Model for Economic Stabilization," *Fed. Reserve Bank St. Louis Rev.*, pp.7-25, April 1970. A somewhat different interpretation and estimate of lags is given in Ray C. Fair, "Aggregate Price Changes and Price Expectations," *Fed. Reserve Bank St. Louis Rev.*, pp. 18-28, November 1970.

[10]Such an interpretation is offered in George L. Perry, "Changing Labor Markets and Inflation," *Brookings Pap. Econ. Act.*, **3**: 411-441 (1970).

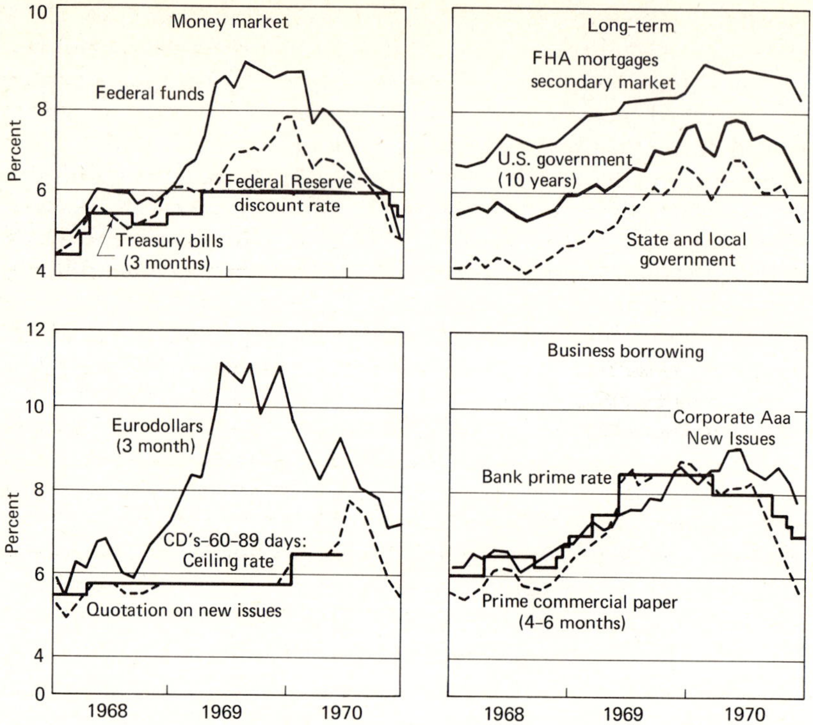

Fig. 21–3 United States interest rates, 1968–1970. *(Board of Governors of the Federal Reserve System.)*

The marked slowing of growth in the money supply at a time when the economy had built up bullish and inflationary expectations led to abrupt increases in interest rates, greater increases even than in the similar episodes of 1953, 1960, and 1966 (see Fig. 3-8). As in the earlier cases, the rise of interest rates was temporary. The monetary restriction caused the usual weakening of total demand and reductions in demand for credit. In 1970 and early 1971, interest rates declined almost as sharply as they had risen.

The role of regulation Q

The sharp increases in interest rates had some far-reaching side effects because the maximum interest rates permitted on time deposits under Federal Reserve Board Regulation Q were not increased commensurately. As Treasury bill yields and other money market interest rates rose above 7 percent while regulation Q ceilings ranged from 4 to 6¼ percent for various types of time deposit (for details see Table 8–1), the public shifted its funds from time deposits to other liquid assets, and the volume of time deposits—especially CDs—declined. From late 1968 through early 1970, the volume of time deposits dropped about $10 billion. Perhaps a more meaningful measure of the impact of regulation Q is how far time deposits by early 1970 were below what they would have been at their prior growth rate, about $40 billion; although the situation probably would have brought some slowing of growth of time deposits in any case (Figs. 21–3, 21–4).

The abrupt drop in their inflow of funds at a time of very strong credit demands set banks to searching for new sources of funds—in effect, for ways of getting around the regulation Q ceilings. Their major find was the Eurodollar market. By paying interest rates above 10 percent in Europe (while limited by regulations to paying 4 percent to the holders of their savings deposits), the banks acquired about $7 billion from this source from late 1968 to late 1969, running their peak borrowings from this source to over $14 billion (Fig. 7-1).

The forced-draft development of the Eurodollar market under the unusual inducement of the regulation Q ceilings provided a new and embarrassingly efficient channel for inflicting American inflationary pressures on European nations. The great inflow of short-term funds seemingly relieved the United States balance of payments problem in 1969, but then deluged European central banks with dollars in 1970 and 1971 when the funds flowed back to Europe because of the declines in United States interest rates and the unwillingness of United States banks to pay high rates for foreign funds. The new institutions for facilitating short-term flows

Fig. 21–4 Interest-bearing sources of bank funds, 1968–1970. (Nondeposit sources include borrowings from foreign branches and, beginning June 1969, bank-related commercial paper, loan repurchase agreements, and borrowings from foreign banks and branches in United States territories and possessions. Time and savings deposits other than CDs exclude those due to domestic commercial banks and the United States government and balances accumulated for repayment of personal loans.) *(Board of Governors of the Federal Reserve System.)*

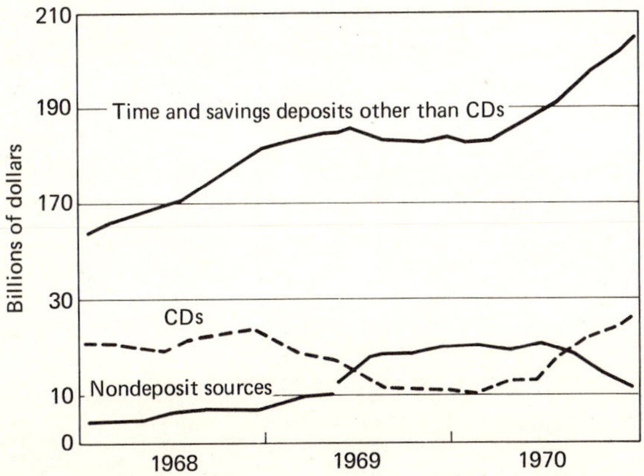

between currencies aggravated the difficulties of the international monetary system.

The second most important discovery of banks in their quest for ways of replacing the funds they were losing because of regulation Q ceilings was borrowing on commercial paper by affiliates of banks owned by holding companies. The temporary availability of this means of avoiding the harsh effects of regulation Q provided an inducement to formation of additional one-bank holding companies, with lasting damage to the United States banking structure.

The Federal Reserve saw the regulation Q ceilings as limiting the growth of bank credit and, thus, contributing to monetary policy's curb on inflationary growth of total demand.[11] Critics saw them as having little effect on total demand—and no effect that could not have been achieved by limiting growth of the money supply—and as causing diversions of credit flows and changes in institutions that involved substantial social costs.[12]

The guidance of Federal Reserve policy

Although the disruptions caused by the regulation Q ceilings may have been unnecessary, monetary policy in 1969 was successful in bringing about a reasonable deceleration of growth of total demand. This was done without permitting the slowdown to snowball into a full-fledged recession, as had been done in 1953–1954, 1957–1958, and 1959–1960. Also avoided was the error of flopping back to an excessively expansive policy, the error of 1967–1968.

This relative success of Federal Reserve policy seems to have reflected a basic change in the ideas by which policy was guided. In response to widespread criticism of the performance of its credit-oriented approach to monetary policy, the Federal Reserve guided its actions during this period to an important extent on the basis of "the monetary aggregates," primarily the money supply.

In 1969, the usual instruction to the Manager of the Open Market Account was to conduct open market operations "with a view to maintaining the prevailing firm conditions in the money and short-term credit markets."[13] But this instruction was not interpreted literally. On the contrary, short-term interest rates from late 1968 to the spring of 1969 were permitted to rise at an unprecedented rate to unprecedented levels—the federal funds rate going from 6 to 9 percent. Meanwhile, bank reserves were provided only at a rate consistent with growth of the money supply

[11] *Ann. Rep. Board Governors Fed. Reserve Syst.* pp. 4–5, 1969.

[12] See Milton Friedman, "Controls on Interest Rates Paid by Banks," *J. Money, Credit, Banking*, **2**:15–32 (1970).

[13] *Annu. Rep. Board Governors Fed. Reserve Syst.* p. 140, 1969.

less rapid than in 1968. Thus, the Federal Reserve did *not* respond to increases in demand for credit by providing additional bank reserves. Late in the year during a period when interest rates were declining, "A number of members expressed the view that operations should not be undertaken to resist tendencies toward lower interest rates that might be produced by market forces."[14] The long-neglected problem of Wicksell was given explicit attention.

A major variable used as a guide to policy operations by the Open Market Committee in 1969 was the behavior of total commercial bank credit. This variable changes roughly with the total of demand deposits plus time deposits of commercial banks. If the Federal Reserve goal had been defined as stabilization of total bank credit, this could have resulted in seriously destabilizing behavior of the money supply. The volume of time deposits declined rapidly for some months after mid-1969, because yields on open market liquid assets were higher than the yields that banks could offer on time deposits.

If the Federal Reserve had undertaken to resist the resulting decline in total bank credit by providing additional bank reserves, this would have resulted in a sharp increase in reserves available to support demand deposits and in the money supply. However, the goal of policy was not taken to be stabilization of total bank credit, but rather only attention to deviations of bank credit from a projected time path. In estimating this time path, allowance was made for market factors affecting the demand for time deposits.[15] Thus, the criterion being applied by the Federal Reserve was not stabilization of interest rates or stabilization of bank credit, but an approach that allowed for feedbacks to these variables from changes in economic conditions. Although it was not used as the variable in terms of which instructions to the Manager of the Open Market Account were defined, the behavior of the money supply seems to have been an important guide to the setting of these short-run targets for Federal Reserve actions.

At its meeting of February 10, 1970, the Open Market Committee explicitly shifted policy in an economically expansive direction. The instruction to the Manager of the Open Market Account was to conduct operations "with a view to moving gradually toward somewhat less firm conditions in the money market; provided, however, that operations shall be modified promptly to resist any tendency for money and bank credit to deviate significantly from a moderate growth pattern."[16] After discussing the importance to attach to alternative guides to policy at its meeting of September 15, 1970, "The Open Market Committe concluded . . . that for

[14]*Ibid.*, p. 195.

[15]For example, the projections used at the Open Market Committee meeting of August 12, 1969, involved reductions in bank credit at an annual rate of 9 to 12 percent. *Ibid.*, p. 169.

[16]"Record of Policy Actions of the Federal Open Market Committee," *Fed. Reserve Bull.* p. 443. May 1970.

the time being the practice should be continued of giving preponderant weight to the money stock in assaying the implications of the behavior of financial aggregates for System operating decisions."[17]

During 1970, differences of opinion continued to exist within the Open Market Committee as to the emphasis to be placed on the money supply (or other monetary aggregates) as against interest rates and conditions in the money market as guides to Federal Reserve actions.[18] The behavior of the money supply was deemphasized from May through July, when attention was centered on reducing interest rates (or "moderating pressure in money and credit markets"). After again being emphasized in the fall, the monetary aggregates were deemphasized late in the year, and their future status at that time seemed uncertain.

Moreover, even when the Open Market Committee referred to the money supply in its decision-making process, open market operations were not conducted as a feedback control mechanism to keep the money supply on the time path defined by the Committee. Rather, open market operations were used, as they had been in the past, as a feedback control mechanism to influence interest rates. What was new was that the operating target set for interest rates now was one that was asserted to be consistent with the defined target for the money supply. Often it proved not to be consistent, and then the money supply did not behave as the Committee had prescribed. The actual growth rate of the money supply, thus, was to some extent accidental, as the view that the primary function of the Federal Reserve is to stabilize interest rates continued to be influential and in some periods dominant in defining Federal Reserve actions.[19] But though the Federal Reserve's reliance on the behavior of the money supply as a guide to its actions in 1970 was far from complete, the use of this measure seems to have been the key to its success in striking a middle course between excessively restrictive and excessive by expansive actions.

One factor responsible for the Federal Reserve's partial emphasis on the monetary approach to its actions—for the first time in its long history—in 1969 and 1970 was the shift of government from the Kennedy-Johnson administrations, whose economic advisers were governed by the Keynesian theory, to the Nixon administration, which interpreted Federal Reserve actions in terms of monetary theory. The difference in interpretations of

[17]"Record of Policy Actions of the Federal Open Market Committee," *Fed. Reserve Bull.* p. 926, December 1970.

[18]For a detailed review, see Jerry L. Jordan and Neil A. Stevens. "The Year 1970—A 'Modest' Beginning for Monetary Aggregates," *Fed. Reserve Bank St. Louis Rev.*, pp. 14–32, May 1971.

[19]These points are made in *ibid*. For a restatement of the money-market approach to Federal Reserve policy, see Paul Meek and Rudolf Thunberg, "Monetary Aggregates and Federal Reserve Open Market Operations," *Fed. Reserve Bank N. Y. Mon. Rev.*, April 1971. Also relevant is "Monetary Aggregates and Money Market Conditions in Open Market Policy," *Fed. Reserve Bull.* February 1971.

An accidental disrupter of Federal Reserve decision making during 1970 was a revision in the latter part of the year of the data for the money supply, which indicated that the money supply throughout the year had grown more rapidly than had earlier been believed, or than had been intended (in relation to the background figures provided by the old series).

monetary policy is strikingly shown in the economic reports of the Council of Economic Advisers. Those of 1962–1969 emphasize fiscal policy and interpret monetary policy in terms of credit tightness or ease, measured by nominal interest rates. Monetary policy is discussed without mention of the money supply. The January 1969 Economic Report of the Council of Economic Advisers represented monetary policy in 1968 as restrictive, found no basic errors or lessons to be learned from prior experience with monetary policy, and explicitly rejected the monetary approach.[20]

The January 1970 Annual Report of the Council of Economic Advisers, the first of the Nixon administration, characterized monetary policy in terms of the behavior of the money supply and noted that it had in 1967–1968 been a source of inflation: "Certainly it was necessary that the money supply grow more slowly than the 7.2 percent increase of 1968."[21] In the contest over whether the Federal Reserve should view itself as regulating interest rates or as controlling the nation's money supply, the administration in 1969 switched from the credit side to the monetary side. Within the Federal Reserve System, the Federal Reserve Bank of St. Louis was the stronghold of the monetary approach, while the Federal Reserve Bank of New York remained a center of the credit approach.

1971: Which Way Next?

Stabilization policy was successful in slowing the growth rate of total demand beginning in late 1969, resulting in some deceleration of inflation and a marked rise in unemployment in 1970. Possible policy programs from this point were to seek a sharp slowdown of inflation by holding the unemployment rate in the 5½ to 6 percent range, or to seek a quick reduction in the unemployment rate to 4 percent, accepting the speedup of inflation this might entail. The administration sought a middle course:

> There is a feasible path between these extremes that would better meet the Nation's present requirements by allowing significant progress to be made against both inflation and unemployment. This is a path that would see the unemployment rate reduced to the 4½ percent zone by the second quarter of 1972 and the inflation rate, as measured by the GNP deflator, declining to approach the 3-percent range at the same time.[22]

The admininstration estimated, perhaps somewhat optimistically, that given its proposed policies toward wage-price push and the lagging effects of earlier high unemployment, the Phillips curve prevailing in mid-1972

[20]See, respectively, pp. 39, 77–78, and 89–93.

[21]P. 33. The error of interpreting changes in interest rates as reflecting monetary policy is noted on p. 68.

[22]*Annu. Rep. Counc. Econ. Advis.*, p. 78, January 1971.

would be one in which 4½ percent unemployment would be consistent with 3 percent inflation, and it chose this as the target point on the curve.

Given estimates of the growth rates of the labor force and of output per worker, this target for unemployment and inflation roughly defined the required target path for total demand. The Council of Economic Advisers estimated the consistent GNP as about $1,065 billion for 1971. This involves a 9 percent increase in the yearly average, which implies about 11 percent growth from the fourth quarter of 1970 to the fourth quarter of 1971.

This target of the Council of Economic Advisers for total demand was widely criticized as (1) excessive and (2) unattainable. The criticism of the target as involving an excessive growth rate of total demand seemed to reflect a failure to make a quantitative analysis of the behavior of total demand that would be required to reduce unemployment, given the rate of inflation that had to be assumed.[23] The assertion that such rapid growth of total demand could not be brought about reflected mainly application of the Keynesian theory, the view that investment expenditures are unresponsive to economic developments and that monetary policy has little influence over total demand.

To translate the target path for total demand into a presumptive target path for the money supply requires an estimate of the behavior of velocity under the economic conditions assumed to prevail. During the 1950s, velocity was rising at rates above 5 percent much of the time (see Fig. 21-1). During economic upswings, large increases in GNP occurred with but moderate growth of the money supply, as velocity temporarily increased at annual rates up to 10 percent. But in the 1960s the average rise in velocity slowed close to zero; even remarkably high interest rates and inflationary expectations brought only a modest rise in velocity.

It seemed reasonable to expect—subject to continual checking against current data—that if the economic situation in 1971 developed as the administration hoped, with declining inflation rates and only gradual reductions in unemployment, only modest increases in velocity would occur. This implied that to achieve the administration's target of about an 11 percent growth rate of total demand would require a rate of growth of the money supply much more rapid than had been common in the past, perhaps something over 8 percent.

In early 1971, a public difference of opinion arose between the administration and the Chairman of the Board of Governors of the Federal Reserve System, Arthur Burns, as to what monetary policy was needed to permit achievement of the administration's target path for GNP. Speaking for the

[23]On the basis of conservative assumptions of inflation of 4½ percent from late 1970 to late 1971, labor force growth of 1½ percent, and increase in output per worker of 2 percent, more than 8 percent growth of total demand would be required just to keep the unemployment rate from rising. If, as was hoped, weekly hours worked and output per hour increased generously in 1971, to reduce the unemployment rate, say, from 6 to 5 percent might require an increase in GNP substantially larger than this.

administration, Paul McCracken, the Chairman of the Council of Economic Advisers, estimated that with the slowed rise in velocity that was to be expected, to hit the administration's target might require an increase in the money supply of more than 7 percent in terms of annual averages (which would require a yet higher rate of increase from February through the end of the year).[24] Mr. Burns discounted the change in the behavior of velocity and the unusually large desired increase in total demand, and emphasized a usual maximum desirable rate of increase in the money supply of 5 to 6 percent. He also deemphasized the behavior of the money supply as a measure of monetary policy, emphasizing the amount of bank credit, the availability of credit, and the role of "confidence to use abundantly available money and credit."[25] Had the Federal Reserve really provided only a 5 percent increase in the money supply and the administrations' estimates of requirements proved to be correct, the outcome would have been rising unemployment during 1971. Such an outcome would have raised some basic questions as to the distribution of responsibility and authority for national economic policy: Should the Federal Reserve be able to tell the elected administration that it cannot carry out its planned program of stabilization policy because the Federal Reserve will not provide the behavior of the money supply that it requires?

A confrontation on this issue in the spring of 1971 was avoided—and the controversy gained a certain comic-opera flavor—when the Federal Reserve, after shying at suggestions that the money supply might be permitted to increase by as much as 7 percent, from late January to late May caused the money supply to increase at an annual rate of 17 percent and provided an average rate of growth of the money supply for the first half of 1971 of 11 percent. The reason for this seemed to be that the Federal Reserve again put aside its money supply criterion and permitted open market operations to be governed by interest rates. After declining rapidly until February 1971, short-term interest rates then began to rise. The Federal Reserve, using open market operations to combat the rise in interest rates, provided the most rapid increase in the money supply for a six months' period since the Second World War.

Beginning in August, perhaps because interest rates moved downward, the money supply declined somewhat; it showed no net increase from July through November. In late 1971, future Federal Reserve actions seemed as uncertain as ever. Whether Federal Reserve actions would support or thwart the new economic policies of the fall of 1971 was unclear. The lack of agreement as to how its powers should be used that had plagued the Federal Reserve from its inception continued to afflict the economy in 1971.

[24]Joint Economic Committee, U.S. Congress, *Hearings, The 1971 Econ. Rep. Pres.*, pt 1, p. 7, February, 1971.

[25]*Ibid.*, pp. 240 and 244. The view that the fault does not lie with monetary policy and the behavior of the money supply but rather with the public, for not bringing about that velocity required to produce the required GNP with the given money supply, has been strongly associated with the Federal Reserve's credit approach to monetary policy.

Monetary Theory and the History of Monetary Policy

The eventful monetary history of the United States illustrates everything that can go wrong with a monetary system: the inefficiency and inconvenience of multiple moneys, lack of small change, and diverse bank notes of uncertain and changing value. It illustrates great deflations in the 1870s and 1880s, in 1920–1921, and in 1929–1933. Inflation had its day in the wars, after the turn of the century, in 1933–1937 and in 1965–1970. In financial panics, the United States was the aknowledged leader of the world; those of 1843, 1873, 1893, 1907, 1931, and 1933 were especially noteworthy. The tendency of the monetary system to increase the money supply in economic upswings and reduce it in downswings is illustrated too often to mention and has been shown as recently as the late 1960s.

These extravagant illustrations of the principles of monetary theory were not mechanistic and impersonal, but were played out in a dramatic set of contests among the actors on the public stage: Alexander Hamilton, Nicholas Biddle, Andrew Jackson, Henry Clay, Salmon P. Chase, J. P. Morgan, Benjamin Strong, and William McChesney Martin—these men marked history through their influence on the nation's monetary system. Divisions of interest as well as personalities influenced the drama: debtors and creditors, bankers—sound and unsound—and the silver producers.

Nor was this empty drama, leaving untouched the course of events and the lives of ordinary people. The economic misadventures arising from the perverse behavior of the monetary system touched all aspects of life, as well as political developments, and even philosophy. How would history have run after 1929 had there been no Great Depression?

The troubles with the monetary system can be associated with the lack of the understanding that could have prevented them. How to get the national and international monetary systems going again after an episode of wartime inflation was a problem never very well handled until the most recent episode, after the Second World War. But the most notable knowledge gap in United States monetary experience was the failure to keep bank-created money under control. For a variety of reasons, most recently because of the credit-oriented approach of the Federal Reserve, this was never satisfactorily done. In 1971, the ideas that were to govern monetary policy remained in dispute, its future performance uncertain.

SUMMARY

1. In the Martin Era of 1951–1969, Federal Reserve policy was formed within a modernized version of the credit approach. Policy was governed mainly by Federal Reserve judgments regarding the appropriateness of the degree of "credit restraint" or "credit ease." These were viewed as measured mainly by member bank free reserves and by money-market interest rates. Since this approach did not deal adequately with the influence upon free reserves and interest rates of factors other than Federal Reserve actions, the degree of credit tightness or ease as interpreted by the Federal Reserve bore no consistent relation to the behavior of the money supply.

2. Leveling off or reduction in the money supply contributed to causing and then aggravating all of the recessions of this period: in 1953–1954, 1957–1958, and 1960–1961. It also caused slow-downs of total demand in 1962, 1967, and in 1969–1970. Slow growth of the money supply after the recession of 1960–1961 contributed to the deficient growth of total demand that led to the high unemployment of 1960–1964.

3. Accelerated growth of the money supply in 1965 and again in 1967–1968 seems to have been the major cause of the excessive growth of total demand that led to the inflationary problem of that period.

4. Monetary policy during this period acted as a positive-feedback system. Holding the money supply to a path of steady growth would have led to steadier growth of total demand and mitigated or avoided the major stabilization problems of these two decades.

5. In 1969–1970, the Federal Reserve paid some attention in forming its policy to the behavior of the money supply. Where interest rates and total bank credit were used as short-run guides to open market operations, the targets set for these variables allowed for changes in market factors affecting them. Thus, the Federal Reserve no longer responded to increases in interest rates and the demand for credit by providing additional bank reserves. During 1971, however, the money supply again seemed to respond to changes in interest rates, increasing sharply from February to August and then declining somewhat. Controversy continued within the Federal Reserve System as to targets for monetary policy and the response to be made to changes in the money supply and in interest rates.

QUESTIONS FOR REVIEW AND DISCUSSION

1. Describe and contrast the three major frameworks within which monetary policy was interpreted within the 1950s and 1960s. Show how the experience of 1967–1968 would be interpreted and evaluated in terms of each approach. What approach governed the Federal Reserve? the Council of Economic Advisers?

2. Explain why the money supply continued to decline after the economic downturn in 1953–1954 and 1957–1958. What effect did this have on economic developments? Cite a case in which a weakening in the economic situation turned out differently because of a different monetary policy.

3. "The initiation, prolongation, and cure of the high unemployment of the early 1960s all are explainable by changes in the growth rate of total demand caused largely by monetary policy." Expand this interpretation.

4. Explain, drawing on our earlier discussion of interest theory, why interest rates rose especially sharply in 1966 and in 1969, pointing up the role of monetary policy. Why did these increases in interest rates not continue longer?

5. "The experience of 1966–1968 is persuasive evidence of the ability of monetary policy both to slow down the economy and to speed it." Explain.

6. "The rapid growth of total demand in 1967–1969 cannot be attributed to monetary policy, since credit during this period was tightening to an unprecedented degree." Comment.

7. If you had been forming policy in 1969 and 1970, what targets would you have set for growth of total demand? What targets would you have set for monetary policy? What criticisms would you make of the actions that were taken?

8. What was the role of monetary policy during 1971? Discuss the contribution of monetary policy to the outcome of the new economic policies initiated in August 1971.

22
fiscal policy

Fiscal policy has in recent decades been regarded as the second major instrument for control over total demand, along with monetary policy. Fiscal policy refers to the government actions determining the expenditures and receipts of the federal government. The same actions on the part of the local governments are not usually termed "fiscal policy," since they are assumed not to be available for use as an instrument for controlling total demand.

Government (again, federal only) expenditures for goods and services have the direct effect of increasing total demand, since they are a component of total demand. On the other hand, government tax receipts are a drain from the expenditures-income stream. They divert to financing government expenditures a flow of money income that otherwise would have been available to finance the spending of individuals and businesses. As a first approximation, thus, fiscal policy can be measured by the net injection of funds into the expenditures-income stream, by government expenditures minus government receipts. This is called the government deficit or, with the opposite sign, the government surplus. The problem of measuring fiscal policy is discussed later.

Government expenditures are made with money, specifically, by writing checks against the government's demand deposit balances at Federal Reserve banks. Like the rest of us, if it is to spend more money than it takes in, the government must raise the money by borrowing. Since its cash balances at Federal Reserve banks are kept stable and those at commercial banks are subject only to limited short-run variation, the government must finance a deficit by borrowing funds from the public through the sale of government securities. Similarly, a government surplus will be reflected in the retirement of outstanding government securities and a reduction in the government debt. The government's fiscal position (its surplus or deficit) is, therefore, only part of a package that includes also the sale or retirement of about an equal volume of government securities.

The expenditures programs and the tax system of the Federal government determine the government surplus or deficit associated with any given set of economic conditions and thus define fiscal policy. Government expenditures increase because Congress passes legislation providing for new programs or expansions of old programs and appropriates the funds to be spent. The President has some limited control over the rate at which expenditures are made under some programs, but basically fiscal policy is determined by Congress. Fiscal policy cannot be changed frequently, and usually cannot be changed on short notice, because Congress is not always in session and does not act rapidly on such matters. Moreover, frequent changes in expenditures programs in most cases would be wasteful, since such programs need to be planned and carried through with continuity. Frequent changes in tax rates are unsettling to taxpayers and involve compliance costs, as the taxpayers must familiarize themselves with the new rules and change their procedures. While monetary policy could, if it were useful, be changed from day to day, the interval between major adjustments of fiscal policy usually runs to several years.

In taking actions on tax and expenditures programs, Congress is not primarily oriented toward bringing about a particular fiscal policy. Expenditures programs are considered primarily on their political merits. Changes in tax rates also are heavily affected by political considerations. Fiscal policy emerges almost as a side effect of congressional actions in which other motives predominate, or at best as one among a set of considerations affecting congressional decisions. Consequently, when we take the historical behavior of government receipts and expenditures as constituting fiscal policy, this does not imply that the actions taken by Congress involve a coherent and conscious fiscal policy.

Measurement of Fiscal Policy

If government expenditures are an injection into the expenditures-income stream and government receipts are a drain or withdrawal from it, the obvious way to measure the combined effect of the two is to net the one against the other. Thus, the net injection of funds is measured by the government deficit, government expenditures minus tax receipts ($D = G - T$), or the government surplus ($S = T - G$). Obviously, these are the same quantity with opposite signs. If the surplus is \$5 billion, the deficit is −\$5 billion. It is conventional to measure the fiscal position by the government surplus—perhaps because surpluses are more respectable, though rarer, than deficits. But we must remember that to increase total demand calls for a *reduction* in the government surplus, since the surplus measures the net *withdrawal* of funds by the government from the expenditures-income stream.

Interpreting fiscal policy in this way is fully correct only if each of the types of expenditures and of tax receipts entering into the totals has substantially the same effect on total demand. There are a number of reasons why this might not be so. Changes in taxes do not directly affect total demand, but affect the income after tax of the taxpayer. If the consumer's marginal propensity to spend is less than 1, changing his disposable income through tax changes should have less than a dollar-for-dollar effect on his expenditures. The effect on total demand of a change in taxes affecting consumers, thus, would be the marginal propensity to consume times the change in tax payments ($b\ \Delta T$).

In the case of taxes paid by business, the question is to what extent an increase in tax payments and a reduction in business income after tax affects business investment expenditures, as well as payments of dividends and other income to owners of the business. In terms of direct effects, it appears that government expenditures for goods and services have a dollar-for-dollar effect on total demand while tax receipts have a smaller effect. It also has been argued that taxes on businesses and on high-income individuals fall more largely on saving and therefore have a smaller effect on total demand than taxes on low-income individuals.

This point applies also to transfer payments such as expenditures for unemployment benefits and welfare payments. These do not enter into GNP directly. They increase the incomes of the recipients and cause them to increase their expenditures. But, again, the increase in their expenditures may be something less than dollar-for-dollar. Thus, for present purposes government transfer expenditures could be treated as negative taxes and viewed as having a less potent per-dollar influence on total demand than government purchases of goods and services.

These considerations imply that the ideal measure of fiscal policy would give a lower weight to changes in tax receipts than to changes in government expenditures for goods and services, and perhaps give different weights to different kinds of taxes and expenditures. However, agreement does not exist as to just what these weights ought to be. In practice, fiscal policy is usually measured by the government surplus, despite widespread belief that a dollar of tax drain from the expenditures-income flow has less effect than a dollar of injection of government expenditures.[1]

The full employment surplus

Using the government surplus as the measure of fiscal policy involves yet another kind of difficulty. Suppose we had an economic recession. The decline in total demand would cause reductions in personal income and business profits. Since most taxes are levied against personal income, business income, and various kinds of expenditures, tax receipts naturally will fall because of the recession. There will also be an automatic increase

[1]This point arose in our discussion of government receipts and expanditures in terms of the nonfinancial Keynesian model (Chap. 12, Appendix A). The asserted difference in effects between government expenditures and tax receipts is what underlay the positive balanced-budget multiplier. In theories that emphasize financial influences on total demand, this point loses its validity.

in expenditures under some programs, such as unemployment insurance. Therefore, even though Congress does nothing whatever to change tax and expenditures programs, the recession leads to a reduction in tax receipts and an increase in expenditures, and so to a reduction in the surplus. (If the government is running a deficit at the outset, we think of this as a negative surplus and reducing the surplus as involving a shift to a larger negative surplus.)

If fiscal policy is interpreted as relating to tax and expenditures *programs*, or to government *actions*, evidently there has been no change in policy. The decline in the surplus reflects not a change in *policy*, but a change in economic conditions. If we are to use the government surplus as a measure of fiscal *policy* in this sense, we must disentangle changes in *policy actions* from those reflecting changes in *economic conditions*.

One way to do this is to compute the hypothetical government surplus that would exist with the prevailing tax and government expenditures programs under a hypothetical, standardized set of economic conditions. This hypothetical government surplus will not be affected by economic conditions, but will measure only changes in tax and expenditures programs. The way this has been done is to define the standardized economic conditions as involving full employment (or high employment), defined as involving 4 percent unemployment. The "full employment government surplus" is thus an estimated, hypothetical surplus that would exist if economic conditions followed a standardized time track.

If tax and expenditures programs remain unchanged, the full employment surplus will not be affected by the occurrence of a recession, though the actual government surplus will decline. If tax rates were reduced to combat the recession, this would lead to a reduction in the full employment surplus. In this case, the actual surplus would decline by a larger amount, since it reflects both the change in tax rates and the effects upon the fiscal position of the changes in economic conditions.

To estimate the full employment surplus requires a number of assumptions that are somewhat arbitrary or debatable. Some economists do not regard the full employment surplus as a satisfactory measure of fiscal policy and have suggested alternative measures, or they take the view that it is impossible to characterize fiscal policy in a single number. One approach that may be developed in the future is to associate alternative fiscal policies with alternative fiscal policy functions analogous to the money supply functions with which we characterized monetary policy. For the present, the full employment surplus is widely used—albeit with reservations—as the best simple, single-valued measure of fiscal policy.[2]

In this approach, an "unchanged fiscal policy" can be interpreted as

[2]For discussion of methodological problems of estimating the full-employment surplus and evaluative comments, see Arthur M. Okun and Nancy H. Teeters, "The Full Employment Surplus Revisited and Comments and Discussion," *Brookings Pap. Econ. Act.*, **1**:77–116 (1970). An alternative approach to measuring fiscal policy, which would raise some new problems, is given in E. Gerald Corrigan, "The Measurement and Importance of Fiscal Policy Changes," *Fed. Reserve Bank N.Y. Mon. Rev.*, pp. 133–145, June 1970.

a set of actions that keeps the full employment surplus constant. More accurately, since the economy and GNP grow from year to year because of long-run factors, an unchanged fiscal policy should be defined as one that keeps that full employment surplus constant in relation to full employment GNP, for example, keeps it equal to 1 percent of full employment GNP. This is one meaningful definition of an unchanged fiscal policy. The main reason for developing the concept of the full employment surplus is to provide a better definition of an unchanged fiscal policy than the actual surplus, since the latter implies that in order to keep fiscal policy unchanged it is necessary to increase tax rates in recessions and reduce them in booms.

An unchanged fiscal policy, in the sense of a constant full employment surplus in relation to full employment GNP cannot be achieved simply by doing nothing. It will not occur automatically. Indeed, to achieve it would require better control over government budgeting than we have ever attained. For it would be necessary for Congress every time it passed new legislation affecting government expenditures also to change tax rates so as to alter tax receipts by exactly the same amount. As Congress is accustomed to operate, its tax-collecting hand is not that familiar with what its expenditures hand is doing.

Moreover, secular growth of GNP increases tax receipts about proportionately—or a bit more than proportionately by shifting people to higher income-tax brackets—if tax rates are unchanged. Unless government expenditures grow at just the same rate, the full employment surplus will drift over time in one direction or the other. Controlling government receipts and expenditures in the traditional manner, therefore, must be expected to result in an erratic fiscal policy, as measured by the full employment surplus. Just to "do nothing" with fiscal policy—but to prevent it from being a disturbing element in the economy—would require major reforms of the governmental budgeting process.[3]

Alternative Interpretations of the Effects of Fiscal Policy

The effects and the effectiveness of fiscal policy are depicted quite differently by different approaches to the theory of total demand. Indeed, before

[3]This point applies also to monetary policy. The Federal Reserve does not keep monetary policy unchanged simply by doing nothing. On the contrary, to cause the money supply (or interest rates) to behave in any defined manner the Federal Reserve must offset changes in factors affecting the monetary base that otherwise would cause erratic or undesired changes in the money supply. In the case of monetary policy, the continual Federal Reserve open market operations required to achieve such an "unchanged monetary policy" cause no great administrative or political problems, as their side effects are small. But taxes cannot be changed without disturbing taxpayers, or without opening the question as to whose taxes should be increased or decreased. The important economic and political side effects of changes in government expenditures programs and taxes thus pose a real impediment to the continual adjustments that are needed to keep fiscal policy under control.

the rise of the Keynesian theory, fiscal policy in the modern sense did not exist. The idea that the federal government should normally vary its receipts and expenditures as a means of controlling total demand was not prevalent before the late 1930s. In part, this may have reflected fears that such a notion of fiscal policy would open the doors to government spending based on irresponsible political motives. More basically, the lack of emphasis on fiscal policy stemmed from a conception of the determinants of economic conditions in which such manipulation of government receipts and expenditures was neither necessary nor likely to be helpful, except perhaps in the case of a severe depression. Booms and depressions were attributed mainly to misbehavior of the banks and the monetary system. Monetary reform, it was thought, would cure them.

In the previous chapter, we noted how Federal Reserve actions are interpreted very differently within the three major approaches that have been applied to them in recent decades: the neoclassical approach, or monetary theory; the credit approach; and the Keynesian approach. In order to see why different people have viewed fiscal policy so differently, we shall apply this same framework to it.

Interpretation of fiscal policy in terms of the neoclassical or monetary approach

One way to estimate the effects on total demand of a change in fiscal policy is in terms of the equation of exchange

$$Y = MV$$

Since a change in the government surplus will not affect the money supply,[4] it can affect total demand only by affecting velocity. How could an increase, say, in government expenditures and a reduction in the government surplus increase velocity?

The government finances its deficit by selling additional government securities, drawing from the credit markets the flow of money required to cover its deficit. These funds come from the pool of sources of loan funds in which the government competes against other potential borrowers. Its additional competition on the demand side of the market tends to make the interest rate higher than it otherwise would be and perhaps makes credit less available (in relation to nonprice terms of borrowing) to other borrowers. Thus, the funds the government raises are diverted from other potential borrowers, businesses, consumers, and state and local governments. We have, therefore, an explanation of how it is that an increase in

[4]The behavior of the money supply, you recall, is interpreted as determined by monetary policy. Whether an increase in the government surplus, for example, causes the money supply to increase more rapidly or more slowly, or leaves it quite unaffected, depends on the monetary policy that is in effect. Moreover, the ability of monetary policy to bring about any desired behavior of the money supply is not contingent on any particular behavior of the government surplus. Thus, it is reasonable to allocate the responsibility for whatever happens to the money supply to monetary policy, and to treat fiscal policy as affecting total demand only through the government surplus and the government borrowing associated with it.

government spending and the government deficit might leave total demand and velocity of circulation of money unchanged. In financing its deficit in the credit markets, the government diverts to financing its expenditures the credit that otherwise would have financed someone else's expenditures. An increase in government expenditures leads to an equal decrease in other kinds of expenditures.[5]

It is not logically necessary that additional deficit-financed government expenditures should crowd out a precisely equal amount of other expenditures, thus leaving velocity of circulation unaffected. By causing an increase in the interest rate, the government deficit might raise velocity by increasing the opportunity cost of holding money. Whether such an effect operates to a significant extent depends on how responsive the demand for money is to interest rates. We recall that this is a matter on which opinion is divided, and research studies remain inconclusive.

Insofar as the demand for money is affected mainly by short-term interest rates, or yields on liquid assets, the effect of the government deficit depends on the kind of government securities sold (or bought) and so on whether the direct impact falls on short-term or long-term interest rates. For fiscal policy to have the greatest effect, the government securities that are sold or retired should be short-term securities, since then the government borrowing will tend to cause a change in the demand for money and velocity of circulation rather than being entirely reflected in the crowding out of nongovernmental spending.

The kind of securities sold or retired by the government we treat as determined by a separate branch of policy, debt management policy, which is considered in Chap. 23. It is reasonable to treat debt management actions as separate, because the volumes of short-term and long-term government securities outstanding can be changed, without altering the government deficit, by replacing existing long-term securities with short-term securities, or vice versa. Thus, insofar as any expansive effect of a government deficit derives from a resulting shift in the composition of outstanding government securities from long-term to short-term forms, we might want to attribute the effect to debt management policy rather than fiscal policy. For in this case the effect could be achieved by shifting the composition of the government debt without running a government deficit, and this might be a preferable way of achieving it.

Another possible mechanism by which a government deficit might increase velocity and total demand is by making for more bullish expectations. Whether this would be the case, however, is an open question. While an expected increase in a certain type of government expenditures or an expected reduction in tax rates would favorably affect expectations, the offset to this is that an expected increase in the government deficit and govern-

[5]It may be useful to refer to Fig. 5-1. In terms of this diagram, the flow of funds to finance a government deficit comes from the credit market, drawing from that market funds that otherwise would have financed some other type of expenditures. Of course, repayment of government debt puts additional funds into the credit market, making them available to finance other types of expenditures.

ment borrowing leads to expectations of increases in interest rates and reductions in credit availability and of reductions in the kinds of expenditures that will be adversely affected by credit stringency. Consequently, it might be expected that government expenditures will rise but that expenditures for residential construction will thereby be depressed. Since the credit markets sometimes overreact to expectational factors (as in the spring of 1953), it is conceivable that they could more than offset other factors and cause an increase in the government deficit to have a depressing effect on total demand.

Monetary theory depicts total demand as constrained by financial factors. In this view, monetary policy can have a powerful effect on total demand because it can enlarge the expenditures-income stream by injecting into it newly created money or can contract it by pulling money from the stream and extinguishing it. Fiscal policy, however, only alters the composition of expenditures by varying the proportion of the funds flowing through credit markets that is borrowed and spent by government. A decline in the government surplus would tend to increase interest rates and reduce availability of credit. It probably would have some effect in increasing total demand, but it might have no appreciable effect and, in some cases, might reduce it.[6]

Fiscal policy in the Keynesian theory

The Keynesian theory (see Chap. 12) depicted an economy in which total demand was not constrained mainly by monetary and financial factors but by limitations of the public's desire to spend, particularly by the limited incentives to invest. If what limits growth of total demand is not limited access to a flow of money from income plus credit markets but rather a limited desire of people to spend, an increase in government spending does seem to strike at the root of the problem. In an economy in which monetary and financial constraints are not important, the financial aspects of fiscal policy in terms of changes in government borrowing also would not be important. This is the kind of economy that is depicted by the Keynesian theory.

The nonfinancial Keynesian model goes all the way in this direction by giving an interpretation of the determination of total demand in which monetary and financial factors play no part whatever. Thus, there is no financial offset to the direct effects of changes in fiscal policy on expenditures and disposable income. A change in government expenditures has the same multiplier effect on total demand (Chap. 12, Appendix A) as does a change in investment. The effect of a change in taxes is slightly smaller, since it falls in part on savings, but is also free of financial offsets and defined by the appropriate multiplier. This model or theory depicts fiscal

[6]A review of alternative interpretations of the financial implications of fiscal policy is given in Roger W. Spencer and William P. Yohe, "The 'Crowding Out' of Private Expenditures by Fiscal Policy Actions," *Fed. Reserve Bank St. Louis Rev.*, pp. 12–24, October 1970.

policy as a reliable instrument for the control of total demand, and as playing a role like investment as a basic determinant of total demand.

The standard Keynesian model does include monetary and financial factors, but has usually been interpreted in such a way as to assign them a minor role as a determinant of total demand. This effect emerges when expenditures are assumed to be but little affected by interest rates, while the demand for money is very responsive to the rate of interest.[7] This implies that a change in fiscal policy will not have much effect on interest rates and its multiplier effects will not to any considerable extent be offset by financial factors.[8]

The Keynesian model does not include the credit markets nor take into account the need of the government to sell securities to finance its expenditures before it can make them. In the Keynesian model, an increase in government expenditures increases the interest rate only through its effect in increasing total demand and, therefore, the amount of money demanded. The structure of the model is such that it could not fully take into account the financial offsets to changes in fiscal policy associated with changes in government borrowing in the credit markets. To do so would require a theory that brings into the picture the sources and uses of credit.

Fiscal policy in the credit approach to central banking

The credit approach to central banking resembles monetary theory in viewing economic conditions as heavily determined by monetary and financial factors. As a result, earlier Federal Reserve ideas assigned no substantial role to fiscal policy as a determinant of total demand. In the 1940s and 1950s when, because of the dominance of the Keynesian theory, fiscal policy was generally accepted as a major factor affecting total demand, the Federal Reserve accomodated itself to this interpretation.

Had the Federal Reserve in applying its credit approach to central banking attempted to estimate the natural rate of interest, or the interest rate that under prevailing conditions was consistent with economic stability, it could logically have tried to take into account the effect of the government deficit on the demand for credit and the natural rate of interest, but it does not appear to have done so. The projections used by the Federal Open Market Committee beginning in 1969 that depicted consistent combinations of interest rates, bank credit, and the money supply presumably

[7]This yields a steeply downward-sloping *IS* curve and a relatively flat *LM* curve. We recall from the last chapter that in this case monetary policy is relatively ineffective in that it must cause a large change in the interest rates in relation to its effect on total demand. The counterpart of this is that fiscal policy is highly effective. Shifts in the *IS* curve brought about by fiscal policy cause little change in interest rates and, thus, little financial offset occurs to the multiplier effects of the change in fiscal policy.

[8]The version of the Keynesian theory used by the Council of Economic Advisers during 1961 – 1968 does not seem to have allowed for a financial offset to the direct effects of fiscal policy. In explaining "the process by which an $11.1 billion tax cut can add as much as $30 billion to total demand," the Council made no reference to such factors. *Annu. Rep. Counc. Econ. Advis.*, p. 171, January 1964.

do bring into the picture the credit implications of fiscal policy. Essentially, the Federal Reserve, at least until 1969, seems to have accepted the Keynesian view of fiscal policy while holding to its credit view of its own activities, although the consistency of these ideas is questionable.

Changing ideas on fiscal policy in the 1960s

The contributions of the 1960s to economic theory and the empirical studies discussed in Chap. 13 involved an increasing emphasis on monetary and financial factors as determinants of total demand. As a consequence, the shift was away from the Keynesian theory's picture of an economy in which total demand was limited by lack of spending opportunities to one in which monetary and financial factors were the deciding factor. This set the stage for the formulation of theories attributing to fiscal policy a much smaller role than it had assumed in the thinking of the preceding decades. This development is still in process. The incorporation of credit markets into economic models is inherently a difficult task, one that may require the work of many more years. Recent work has indicated the kind of adaptation of existing models required for greater realism on this point. Simple models depicting an economy in which total demand is governed by monetary factors, and fiscal policy has little effect, have been found to yield a close fit to the historical data.[9]

The principal piece of evidence that shook confidence in the effectiveness of fiscal policy was the fact that the very large change in fiscal policy represented by the imposition of the income tax surtax in 1968 failed to have any discernible effect on total demand. It had been predicted that this huge dose of fiscal policy would forcefully slow down growth of total demand. There were fears that the dosage was too large, and would cause a recession. When the action failed to have any noticeable effect whatever, many economists and organizations had to take a new look at the theory of total demand. The empirical studies mentioned earlier on the effects of monetary and fiscal policy also support the view that fiscal policy has had limited effects on total demand.[10] Further research and discussion on the subject will be needed, however, before any concensus of views is reached.

The Record of Fiscal Policy

Before the Great Depression, the relative role of the federal government in the economy was so small during peacetime that even large changes in the relation between government expenditures and receipts involved

[9] "A Monetarist Model for Economic Stabilization," *Fed. Reserve Bank St. Louis Rev.*, pp. 7–25, April 1970.

[10] Leonall C. Andersen and Jerry L. Jordan, "Monetary and Fiscal Actions: A Test of Their Relative Importance in Economic Stabilization," *Fed. Reserve Bank St. Louis Rev.*, April 1970.

changes in the government surplus that were small in relation to GNP and, presumably, a minor influence on interest rates and total demand. During the early stages of the Great Depression in 1930 and 1931, fiscal policy was highly expansive. Government expenditures increased in a way that was unprecedented in peacetime, and taxes were not raised. This did not, however, prevent continued reductions in total demand.

After 1931, fiscal policy was erratic.[11] A large increase in taxes and a reduction in government expenditures in 1932 swung it back in the restrictive direction, followed by enormous increases in government expenditures and a swing in the other direction in 1933. It was expansive in 1936 and 1938, restrictive in 1937. For the decade as a whole, fiscal policy —in contrast to monetary policy—was expansive. It appears that the full employment surplus was smaller in the 1930s than in the latter part of the 1920s by an amount equal to about 2 percent of GNP. We have noted how closely events during the decade seemed to follow the behavior of the money supply. Their response to changes in fiscal policy is not evident.[12]

During the Second World War, as in earlier wars, government expenditures increased enormously and tax receipts by much less. At its wartime peak the government surplus was nearly minus $50 billion per year.

As war expenditures were terminated, the federal budget moved to about a balanced position, with both receipts and expenditures much larger than before the war. This was a reasonable fiscal position in which to make the transition from war to peace and from a depression psychology to a rising optimism.

Fiscal policy shifted substantially in an expansive direction from the first half of 1948 to the first half of 1949. With the advantage of hindsight, this appears an inspired use of fiscal policy in an effort to head off the recession of 1949—which, incidentally, it failed to do. The truth is less favorable. It was not known in 1948 that a recession was impending. The prevalent diagnosis was one of inflationary hazards. Thus, President Truman responsibly asked for tax increases, and Congress somewhat irresponsibly rejected his advice—but then turned out to have done the right thing by mistake.

Fiscal policy in the 1950s

The initial response of fiscal policy to the outbreak of the Korean war in mid-1950 was highly creditable. President Truman requested and Congress granted substantial tax increases. Military expenses increased less rapidly than anticipated, so fiscal policy was relatively restrictive in the latter part of 1950 and the first half of 1951, contributing to damping the

[11]A historical review of ideas and actions of fiscal policy is given in Lewis H. Kimmel, *Federal Budget and Fiscal Policy, 1949–1958,* The Brookings Institution, Washington, 1959.

[12]Michael W. Keran, "Monetary and Fiscal Influences on Economic Activity—The Historical Evidence," *Fed. Reserve Bank St. Louis Rev.,* Nov. 1969.

inflationary developments arising from the outbreak of the war. The next chapter in the story is not so favorable. As defense expenditures rose in 1952 and new taxes were not voted, the budget swung sharply in the deficit direction. The economy in 1952 and 1953, thus, received rather a large dose of expansive fiscal policy, which was not suited to the needs of the times. Fortunately, it did not discernibly affect the behavior of total demand.

Thus, the recession of 1953 began with fiscal policy in a highly expansive position, although the end of the Korean war and cutbacks in defense orders were factors operating in a contractive manner. During the recession, fiscal policy moved toward a surplus, in a contractive direction. Again, it did not noticeably hamper the recovery from the recession. Fiscal policy then moved to a position that might be regarded as normal and that was about the average of the period as a whole, the full employment surplus amounting to around 1 percent of GNP. This fiscal position was maintained with unusual stability from 1956 through 1958, fiscal policy by this measure not being substantially involved one way or the other in the recession of 1957.

Fiscal policy in the 1960s

Fiscal policy moved in a restrictive direction in 1959 and 1960. Reflecting a deliberately restrictive fiscal policy instituted by the Eisenhower administration because of its concern with inflation and the balance of payments, the fiscal position in 1960 became the most restrictive in a decade. Thus, fiscal policy is a candidate, along with monetary policy, to explain the recession of 1960. In 1961, now under the Kennedy administration, fiscal policy moved toward a less restrictive position, this being partially reversed in 1963. Taken as a whole, the period from 1960 through 1963 had the most restrictive policy in the postwar period. This we recall was the period when total demand was consistently below the full employment level, the period of persistent economic slack. Thus, fiscal policy in this period was the opposite of what circumstances required. Again, however, the highly restrictive fiscal policy of 1963 (Fig. 22–1) did not prevent the acceleration of growth of total demand that began late in that year.

After 1963, fiscal policy made a great swing to an extraordinarily expansive position. President Kennedy had requested a substantial tax reduction in his economic report of January 1963, but it was not until more than 1 year later that Congress took action. This famous "tax cut of 1964," however, only brought fiscal policy back from its unusually restrictive position to a more usual one. In 1965, second-stage tax reductions that had been passed in 1964 plus accelerated growth of military expenditures did push the fiscal position to an unusually expansive position. The fiscal policy of 1967 was the most expansive of the postwar period.

We recall that total demand had grown to the full employment level by late 1965 and thereafter the problem of stabilization policy was one of excessive total demand and inflationary pressures. As a result, fiscal policy

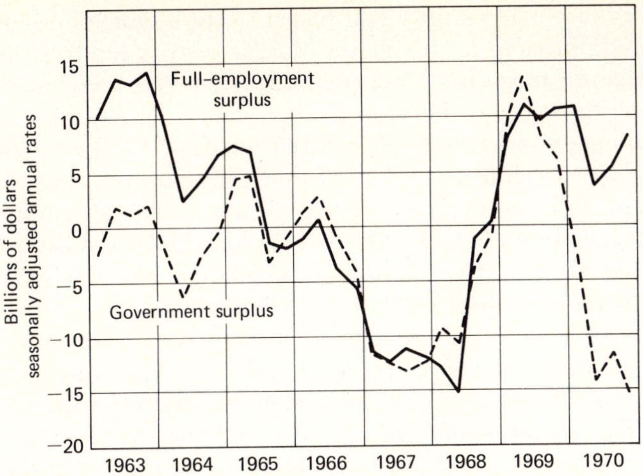

Fig. 22–1 Actual Government surplus and full employment surplus, 1963–1970. (The series shown measure federal government expenditures and receipts as these are included in the national income and product accounts. Alternative measures of federal fiscal position are the administrative budget, the consolidated cash statement, and the unified budget. *(U.S. Department of Commerce, Office of Management and Budget; and Federal Reserve Bank of St. Louis.)*

now was unusually expansive at a time when what was required was a restrictive policy. In other words, if the restrictive fiscal policy of 1960–1963 and the expansive policy of 1965–1968 could have been reversed, they would have been much better suited to circumstances.

Another major and explicit change in fiscal policy, the counterpart of the tax cut of 1964, was the imposition of the income tax surcharge in mid-1968. This brought an extraordinarily abrupt shift in fiscal policy. Within a year, the full employment surplus (on a quarterly basis) increased about $25 billion, or nearly 3 percent of GNP.

This was clearly a shift in the right direction, a belated shift that administration economists and others had been asking for for more than 1 year. However, economists who viewed fiscal policy as a highly potent influence upon total demand feared that the dosage might have been too large. They feared that "fiscal overkill" would lead to a recession. In response to this fear the Federal Reserve in the fall of 1968 took some actions that it interpreted as easing credit in order to limit the hazard of overkill.

The facts proved to be quite inconsistent with these predictions. Total demand continued to increase unabated, showing no effects of fiscal restraint. When total demand finally did slow down, in late 1969, this seemed plausibly attributable not to the tax increase of mid-1968 but to the deceleration of growth of the money supply that began in the spring of 1969. The failure of these predictions as to the effects of fiscal policy led to a reconsideration of the theory and forecasting methods on which they were based, a reconsideration that is still continuing.

Fiscal policy was steady in an average posture from early 1969 through early 1970. The great policy shift of mid-1968 that included the income tax surcharge raised the full employment surplus to about $10 billion, or about 1 percent of full employment GNP. The Nixon administration aimed for a moderate expansive shift in fiscal policy in 1970 and a further one in 1971. These were estimated to reduce the full employment surplus to small proportions. But then the new economic policy of the fall of 1971 called for a large additional expansive change in fiscal policy. The reductions in taxes of the Revenue Act of 1971 implied a shift to an extremely expansive fiscal policy in 1972. The actual budget surplus dropped sharply to a large deficit after early 1969 (Fig. 22–1), reflecting the adverse effects on tax receipts of the economic slack and unemployment that developed.

Experience with fiscal policy during the 1950s and 1960s indicated that under existing political arrangements it is not effectively controlled. As measured by the full employment surplus, fiscal policy was inappropriate during much of the 1960s. The two great changes in fiscal policy came much later than would have been appropriate. The first of them, the tax cut of 1964, proved to be both too late and too much, the problem it was designed to cure having disappeared before the full remedy was given.

Proposals for Reform of Fiscal Policy

Discussion of fiscal policy in the 1930s ranged from proposals to balance the budget in the Depression, through large increases in tax rates, to proposals based on the Keynesian theory for deliberate use of large government deficits as a means to recovery. In the early postwar period, a major focus of discussion was the proposal of the Committee for Economic Development for a systematic program of fiscal policy.[13] In this program, government expenditures programs would be set at a level defined by the desired role of government in the economy. Tax rates then would be set so that under prosperity conditions they would bring in enough receipts to produce a modest government surplus. If the economy got into recession, what would be done? Unless the recession were especially severe or threatened to get out of hand, nothing would be done. The automatic reduction in tax receipts would shift the government from a surplus position to a deficit position. The policy would be simply to let this "built-in flexibility" in the tax system work unimpeded.

[13] *A Postwar Tax Plan for High Employment*, Research Committee, Committee for Economic Development, New York, 1944; *Taxes and the Budget: A Program for Prosperity in a Free Economy*, Research and Policy Committee, Committee for Economic Development, New York, 1947.

This approach contrasts with the balance-the-budget-every-year rule, which would lead to increases in tax rates in recession. This program accepts the desirability of running government deficits during recessions. But the rule that taxes should be set high enough to result in a small surplus under prosperity conditions provides a rather definite decision rule, one that incorporates some defense against erratic changes in fiscal policy and against the use of fiscal policy as a justification for government deficits reflecting ulterior political motives.

The CED decision rule for fiscal policy can be restated in present-day terminology as, "keep the full employment surplus constant (except in unusual conditions) at, say, plus 1 percent of full employment GNP." If it were desired to increase the strength of the dosage of fiscal policy automatically administered to the economy when total demand got off its desired track, this could be done by expanding the decision rule to provide additional error-controlled negative feedback in fiscal policy. For example, the rule could provide that if the unemployment rate rose above 5 percent, taxes would be adjusted to reduce the full employment surplus from 1 percent of full employment GNP to zero—a reduction in taxes of about $10 billion at current levels of GNP. It could also be provided that if, say, unemployment were below 4 percent and prices rose more than 3 percent per year, taxes would be increased to raise the full employment surplus to 2 percent of full employment GNP. Such decision rules for changes in tax rates are termed "formula flexibility."

An alternative way of using fiscal policy more actively than the CED's program of built-in flexibility is for changes in tax rates to be made not under a predetermined formula but by discretionary action. Since it was feared—with some merit, as subsequent events proved—that Congress would not be able to move quickly in changing taxes in response to the desire to change fiscal policy, it was proposed that Congress should delegate to the President certain powers to change tax rates for fiscal-policy reasons. President Kennedy made such a proposal to Congress in his January 1962 Economic Report, but Congress did not adopt it. Thus, adjustments of fiscal policy in the 1960s continued to be made through the regular machinery for control of taxes and government expenditures.

Changing views of fiscal policy in the late 1960s

Several aspects of experience with fiscal policy in the 1960s caused it to be viewed differently in 1970 than it had in the 1950s and 1960s:

1. Contrary to most earlier expectations, monetary policy seemed capable of controlling the rate of growth of total demand. This reduced the need for active variation in fiscal policy to control total demand.

2. The effects of fiscal policy on total demand turned out to be much less than expected, and uncertain in extent and timing.

3. Experience indicated that timely changes in fiscal policy for control of total demand could not be achieved through the existing governmental machinery and that Congress was unwilling to make the far-reaching political changes required to adjust fiscal policy more quickly.

4. Objective interpretations of fiscal policy in the 1960s indicated that rather than operating consistently as a stabilizing factor, it had varied erratically and much of the time had operated in a destabilizing manner.

5. Review of the machinery of control of taxes and government expenditures indicated that even to prevent erratic variations in the government's fiscal position would require closer coordination than had been achieved in the past between tax programs and expenditures programs and would require major and difficult reform of the political decision-making machinery.

The *Economic Report of the Council of Economic Advisers* of January 1970 took account of these lessons: "Fiscal policy should avoid large destabilizing swings occurring at random or contrary to the clear requirements of the economy. The big ursurge of Federal spending . . . after mid-1965, which was unmatched by any general tax increase for 3 years, is a major example of such a destabilizing movement."[14] Its initial program of fiscal policy was to set the full employment surplus at an appropriate level and avoid erratic variations in it. The possible desirability of variations in expenditures and tax rates to influence total demand under unusual conditions was recognized,[15] but the difficulty of doing so was also noted, as well as that "recent experience and analysis suggest that the stabilizing power of temporary income tax changes may not be as great as had been hoped."[16]

In the 1971 policy crisis, the administration adopted an activist approach to fiscal policy, proposing large tax reductions. This time Congress acted quickly, within four months. The result was an extremely expansive fiscal policy, one that would be unsuitable when total demand growth accelerated. A future challenge was posed for discretionary fiscal policy, to increase taxes promptly when circumstances no longer justified large government deficits as a means of stimulating total demand.

SUMMARY

1. Fiscal policy refers to the (federal) government actions determining government receipts and expenditures. The basic measure of fiscal policy is the government surplus, the excess of government receipts over expenditures. A negative surplus is termed a deficit. A government surplus leads to reduction in government borrowing from the public and a deficit leads to an increase in government debt held by the public.

2. A decrease in the government surplus has been thought to increase

[14]P. 67.

[15]*Ibid.*, pp. 67–68.

[16]*Ibid.*, p. 67.

total demand, since it involves a net injection of money by the government into the expenditures-income stream. The Keynesian theory represents the effects of fiscal policy on total demand, which are defined by the multiplier, as reliable and rather large. This outcome occurs because the Keynesian theory omits or deemphasizes the financing implications of changes in the government surplus.

3. A government deficit is financed by additional government borrowing in the credit markets, and the money received from a government surplus is used to reduce outstanding government debt. Thus, the financing of a deficit draws from the credit markets money that would have been borrowed and spent by others, while a surplus makes available additional funds that others can borrow and spend. When these financing implications of the fiscal policy are taken into account, it appears that a change in fiscal policy may have little effect on total demand, since it will be largely offset by changes in private expenditures.

4. A widely used measure of fiscal policy is the full employment surplus. This distinguishes between the effects on the government surplus of changes in economic conditions (and tax receipts) and the effects of changes in tax rates and expenditures programs, measuring only the latter.

5. Experience does not support the Keynesian view that fiscal policy has a large and reliable effect on total demand. The lack of evident effect from the large increase of taxes in 1968, along with a number of statistical studies, support that view that the effects of fiscal policy may be small. Further studies will be required to define more closely the amount, reliability, and promptness of the influence of fiscal policy on total demand.

6. Fiscal policy in the 1950s and 1960s was erratic and often inappropriate. The restrictive fiscal policy during the slack years of 1960–1963 and the unusually expansive fiscal policy of inflationary 1965–1967 are striking cases in point.

7. A minimum program for fiscal policy would stabilize the full employment surplus at some value like 1 percent of full employment GNP, avoiding erratic variations and letting the built-in flexibility of the tax system contribute to combating deviations of total demand from its desired track. To achieve this program, however, would require major improvements in the machinery for coordination and control of government expenditures programs and tax decisions. Such reforms have substantial political implications and will be difficult to accomplish.

QUESTIONS FOR REVIEW AND DISCUSSION

1. Define fiscal policy. What should be meant by "keeping fiscal policy unchanged"?

2. Define the full employment surplus. What is the major purpose of this concept? How will the full employment surplus differ from the regular surplus during a recession?

3. "When the government increases its expenditures without increasing taxes, this is bound to increase total demand, because the government is putting more money into the expenditures-income stream but is not taking any more out." Comment.

4. Explain why the effect of fiscal policy on total demand is depicted as large and reliable by the Keynesian theory but uncertain by the neoclassical or monetary approach.

5. "Under adverse conditions, an increase in the government deficit could reduce total demand." Explain.

6. "1967 illustrated the uncontrollability of fiscal policy, 1968 its ineffectiveness." Spell out the argument.

7. Describe the CED program of fiscal policy. What difficulties would be encountered in implementing it? Do you think it would have been better or worse than the actual fiscal policy of the 1960s?

8. What program of fiscal policy do you recommend for the United States?

23 debt management and liquidity policy

The final member, and junior member, of the team of instruments for control of total demand is debt management policy. This relates to the kinds of securities the United States government sells to finance its deficits and to replace maturing securities. The government at the end of 1970 had outstanding debt in the amount of about $389 billion. About $62 billion was held by Federal Reserve banks and $97 billion more by other government agencies and trust funds. Thus, about $230 billion of government debt was held by the public.

The *amount* of outstanding government debt, we recall, is determined by fiscal policy. Accordingly, debt management policy relates to government actions defining the form of government securities held by the public, while fiscal policy determines their amount. As you can see from Fig. 23-1, the government's debt has increased almost continuously, growing most rapidly during periods of large government deficits caused by wars and depressions.

The significance of the government debt as an element in the economy's liquidity structure depends on the size of the public's holdings of government debt in relation to total demand and total financial assets. In these terms, the importance of the government debt has declined sharply since 1945. The role of the government debt as a factor affecting economic stability, however, depends not so much on the *amount* of outstanding government debt as on short-run *changes* in the amount and form of this debt.

The size of the government debt as this affects the tax burden arising from its interest payments depends on the size of the government debt in relation to GNP and the incomes from which the taxes must be raised. It also depends on the general level of interest rates. Since 1945, the size of the government debt in relation to GNP has declined, but the level of interest rates has risen sharply. The net effect of these has been to reduce the interest payments of the federal government in relation to GNP.

The reduction in the government debt and in government interest

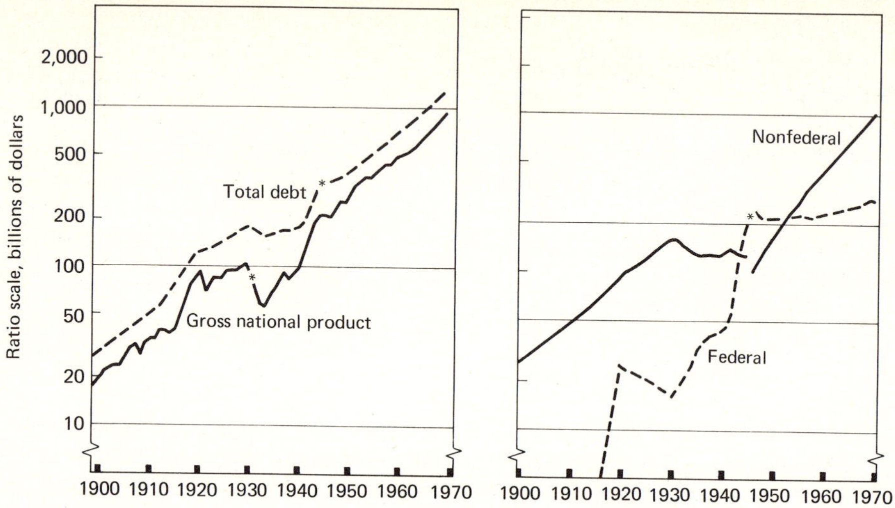

Fig. 23-1 United States debt in relation to GNP. U. S. Department of Commerce; Board of Governors of the Federal Reserve System; John W. Kendrick, *Productivity Trends in the United States*, Princeton University Press, Princeton, N.J., 1961; and Raymond W. Goldsmith, *A Study of Savings in the United States*, 3 vols., Princeton University Press, Princeton, N.J., 1955, 1956.

payments in relation to GNP is not entirely an economic achievement. A large part of it reflects inflation, which has doubled the price level (in terms of the GNP deflator) since 1946 and tripled it since 1939. This inflation reduces the real burden and significance of the debt by reducing the value of the dollars in which it is denominated. Another way of saying the same thing is to say that inflation increased the dollar value of GNP and total debt in the economy, thus reducing the relative importance of the government debt that was defined in terms of dollars. The reduction in the real value of the government debt has occurred largely at the expense of the holders of the debt.

How the Government Debt Is Managed

In getting a picture of just what is involved in debt management operations, it is useful first to distinguish between refunding operations and offerings of government securities to raise new cash. If the amount of outstanding government debt did not change at all—say, remained fixed at precisely $390 billion from month to month and from year to year—there would still be a task of debt management. The securities that the Treasury Department sells in the name of the United States government have a limited term to maturity. Most Treasury bills come due in 91 days. Most government securities have an initial maturity of less than 5 years, and only a few run for more than 20 years. As a result, each year and, indeed, each week, some of these securities come due and the Treasury must be prepared to pay their owners the money it has promised to pay.

Ordinarily, the Treasury pays off the holders of maturing securities through refunding operations. It sells a new security to get the money to pay off the maturing one. In many cases, this is done through an exchange offering. Holders of the maturing security are offered the opportunity to exchange it for a new security. In conducting a refunding operation through such an exchange offering, however, the Treasury cannot hope to entice all of the holders of the maturing security to exchange it for the new one. Thus, there is some *attrition*, some proportion of the holders of the maturing security who wish to be paid off in cash rather than with a replacement security. To pay them off, the Treasury must raise cash in some other way. Unless it happens to have some excess cash because of a budget surplus, it must do this by selling another security for cash.

Of course, if the government is running a surplus, it will wish to reduce the size of the outstanding debt. This can be done by not fully replacing outstanding securities in refunding operations, using the Treasury's excess cash to make up the difference.

The other general category of debt operations is cash offerings, sales of securities not in exchange for maturing securities but to raise new cash. When the government is running a deficit, it must make such cash offerings to get the money to finance the excess of its expenditures over its tax receipts.

In connection with each of its offerings of securities in an exchange operation or for cash, the Treasury must make a decision as to what kind of security to sell. The types of securities held by the public at any time reflect simply the cumulative effect of such decisions made by the Treasury in the past.

Debt management policy relates to the government debt held by the *public*. (Fig. 23–2) The government securities held by government agencies and trust funds are largely special issues tailored by the Treasury to their particular needs. In any case, the behavior of these agencies is not significantly affected by the nature of the government securities they hold. We treat the debt operations of such agencies as being within the governmental family but not as having the economic significance that attaches to the composition of government securities sold to the public.

The Treasury as manager of trust funds and special accounts sometimes does use these funds to buy government securities in the market. Both these operations and the open market operations of the Federal Reserve System affect the composition of the government securities held by the public. If from an existing total stock of outstanding Treasury securities the government agencies buy some short-term securities, the short-term

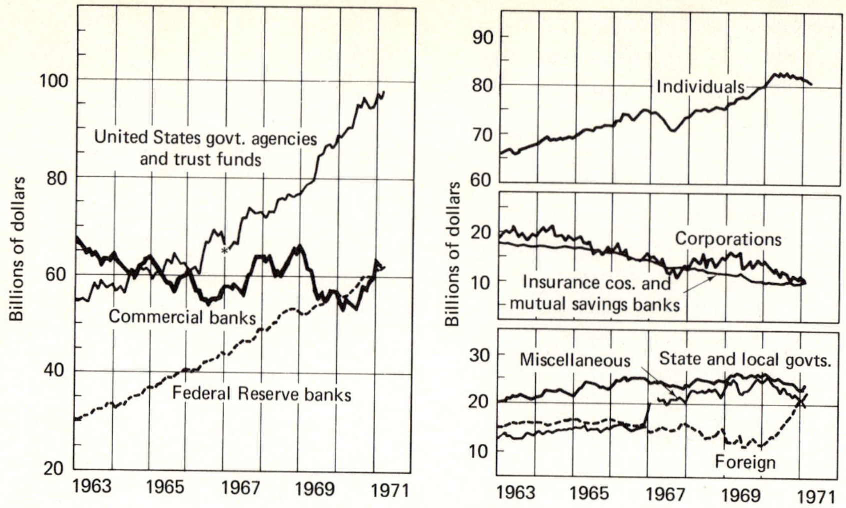

Fig. 23-2 Ownership of the United States public debt. *(U.S. Department of the Treasury and Board of Governors of the Federal Reserve System.)*

securities held by the public are thereby decreased. If we think of debt management as including all activities of agencies of the federal government that affect the composition of government securities held by the public, thus, we must include in debt management policy the actions of the Treasury on behalf of trust funds and the actions of the Federal Reserve System.

The government debt increased rapidly in 1967 and 1969–1970, as Fig. 23-3 shows, because of the large government deficits of those years. Takings of government securities by the Federal Reserve banks and by United States government agencies and trust funds were about as large (Fig. 23-2), so that the public's holdings of government securities have changed little in the past decade. There has been some switch of such securities from businesses to individuals. Commercial banks follow a cyclical pattern, absorbing government securities during periods of economic slack when business demand for credit is weak and selling them during periods of business expansion. Foreign holdings of government securities showed an unusual expansion in 1970.

Kinds of United States government securities

In classifying United States government securities, we are primarily concerned with their term to maturity or the duration of the debt contract. Short-term securities, those that mature within less than 1 year, qualify as liquid assets, or secondary reserve assets. To their holders, they serve the same functions as time deposits, commercial paper, and other liquid assets. At the other extreme, Treasury securities running for 10 or 20 years are very dissimilar to money-market instruments, competing rather with residential mortgages, corporate bonds, state and local bonds, and to some extent high-grade common stock.

In discussing Treasury securities, it is useful to distinguish between "coupon issues" and "discount issues." A coupon security has a par value and a specified rate at which interest payments are made in relation to this par value. This is illustrated by a government bond of $1,000 par value paying interest semiannually at the rate of 4¼ percent per year.

Fig. 23-3 Composition of United States public debt. U.S. Department of the Treasury, and Board of Governors of the Federal Reserve System.

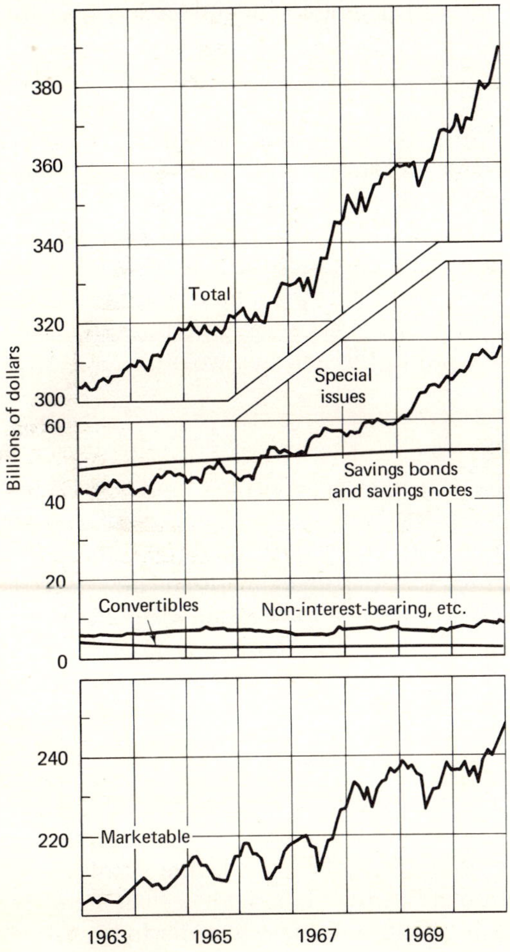

The discount issue has no explicit interest rate, indicating only the amount that will be paid at maturity. Thus, the Treasury bill only specifies that, say, $1 million will be paid on the maturity date of the bill. If such a bill were sold by the Treasury for $1 million, of course, it would earn no interest. Discount issues are sold for less than their redemption value, the interest earned being determined by the difference between the price paid for the security and its redemption value.

The question sometimes is raised as to how the Treasury decides to whom to sell its securities, whether to sell them to the Federal Reserve banks, the commercial banks, or other groups of holders. The answer is that the Treasury does not make any such decisions. It is the buyers of securities who decide whether or not they will buy. The Treasury has no power to decide that the Federal Reserve System shall buy government securities or that the commercial banks shall buy government securities, and so it cannot decide to sell securities to the Federal Reserve or the commercial banks. What the Treasury decides is only what kind of securities it will offer for sale, the various classes of buyers then deciding whether or not or how much they will buy.

Thus it is not meaningful to think of the Treasury as selling its securities to particular types of buyers. The Treasury simply sells to the market, just as the individual grower of wheat sells to the market. The market for United States government securities is a very large and active one, transactions running to billions of dollars each day. Accordingly, the reception accorded Treasury offerings of securities is not dependent upon the decisions of any small groups but arises from a market in which are involved investors disposing of a large proportion of the nation's wealth.

Treasury debt management operations

Refunding operations involving the coupon securities—notes or bonds—ordinarily are handled through an exchange offering of new coupon issues. Commonly, the holder of the maturing security will be offered the opportunity to exchange it for either of two, or even three, new issues. Ordinarily, the new security is available only in exchange for the maturing one. Thus, an investor who wants to receive the new security when it is issued but does not hold the maturing issue seeks to buy the maturing issue from a holder who does not want the new issue. Because the maturing issue involves the right of exchange for the new issue, the maturing securities are called "rights."

As the exchange date approaches, trading in rights involves two groups: (1) Investors desiring the new security and not holding rights who are in the market to buy them. (2) Investors holding rights who do not want to exchange them and who have the option of turning them in for cash at maturity or of selling them to someone who wants to buy them in order to exchange

TABLE 23-1 United States Government Debt, December 31, 1970 (Par value, in billions of dollars)

By Type of Security		By Holder	
Total	$389.2	Total	$389.2
Special issues	78.1†	United States government agencies§	97.1
Total public issues	309.1	Federal Reserve banks	62.1
Nonmarketable	59.1‡	Total held by public	229.9
Convertible bonds	2.4	Commercial banks	63.2
Total marketable	247.7	Mutual savings banks	2.8
Bills	87.9	Insurance companies	7.0
Notes	101.2	Other corporations	10.6
Bonds	58.6	State and local governments	22.9
		Individuals: savings bonds	52.1
		Individuals: other	29.8
		Foreign and international	20.6
		Other investors	21.1

†Held only by United States government agencies and trust funds and Federal Home Loan Banks.

‡Includes $52.4 billion in savings bonds and notes.

§Includes United States government trust funds.

SOURCE: Fed. Reserve Bull.

them for the new issue. A government securities dealer may buy them for his own account or for a customer. Investors holding rights who want the new issue will simply hold them for exchange.

If the attrition rate on the exchange operation is to be kept low, holders of rights who do not want to exchange them must be given an incentive to sell them to people who do want to exchange them. To achieve this, the market price of rights in the days before the exchange must be above par. How does the Treasury contrive to bring this about? The market value of the rights, of course, depends upon the attractiveness of the new securities for which they can be exchanged.

In defining the terms of the new securities, and particularly the interest rate offered on them, the Treasury must make a careful calculation. It wants the new securities to be attractive enough to create a demand sufficient to bring the price of rights slightly above par so that holders of rights will sell them to others rather than turning them in for cash. However, it does not want to make the issue so attractive as to cause an excessive premium on rights and a windfall gain to their holders—at the expense of the taxpayer who foots the bill for interest payments. Add the complication that interest rates and securities prices may change between the time when the Treasury makes its announcement and the crucial last days before the exchange, and it becomes clear that such refunding operations as now handled are a delicate business.

A variant of this approach that somewhat increases the flexibility of the Treasury is the "advance refunding." In this case, the Treasury offers new securities in exchange for outstanding securities that have not yet reached their maturity date. In this case, holders of the old securities who do not want to exchange them for the new ones simply continue to hold the old securities. There is no immediate problem of attrition and cash drain on the Treasury, which can still approach the holders of the outstanding issue later with another exchange offering.

Treasury bills, the shortest-term United States government securities, are handled in quite a different way. The outstanding stock of Treasury bills has been designed in such a way that they mature regularly, a block maturing each week. The maturing bills ordinarily are "rolled over" each week. However, this is done not through an exchange offering but simply by selling new bills for cash and using the cash to repay holders of outstanding bills. The Treasury, thus, is free to raise some additional cash by offering to sell a volume of bills larger than the week's maturing issue. It also can reduce outstanding government debt when it has available cash to do so by in any week selling a volume of bills smaller than the maturing issue.

In addition to regular Treasury bills, there are sold some tax-anticipation bills designed to mature at corporate tax-payment dates. These are a convenient instrument for investment by corporations of the funds they are accumulating for tax payments. The securities are accepted in payment of taxes. Since the Treasury has ample funds on tax-payment dates it has no need to replace the maturing securities.

The other major respect in which the handling of Treasury bills differs from that of most other Treasury securities is that they are sold at auction. Rather than deciding what interest rate it will pay on the security and then offering to sell the public a specified amount on those terms, the Treasury simply announces the volume of Treasury bills it wishes to sell and accepts competitive bids, accepting those bids involving the lowest interest cost. Since the Treasury bill is a discount issue, the bids are in the form of the price to be paid for a bill of given redemption value. The auction approach saves the Treasury the difficulty and possible embarrassment of determining in advance what interest rate it will offer on a particular issue, and permits the interest rate to adjust to market conditions on the day of the auction. The bidding in the weekly auction for Treasury bills is done largely by government securities dealers and financial institutions with a high degree of money-market expertise.

The other major category of security offering is the sale of coupon issues to raise new cash (in contrast to exchange offerings). In this case, the Treasury does announce the terms of the security or securities being offered, including the interest rates. It also announces the volume of securities it will sell. In setting the terms of the new securities, the Treasury's goal is to make them attractive enough to assure that it has buyers for the full volume of securities it wishes to sell without making the issue excessively attractive and thus wasting the taxpayers money on unnecessarily high interest payments. For the Treasury to find itself without takers for the full amount of securities it offered to sell is viewed as a "failure" of the offering. At some times in the past this has been viewed as a catastrophe reflecting on the public credit of the nation, but perhaps today it is more realistically viewed as simply a matter of the Treasury having miscalculated the interest rates it was necessary to pay on the issue.

Sales of coupon issues for cash are almost entirely taken in the first instance by commercial banks and then sold by the banks to others. The reason is this. When the Treasury sells a large security offering, it will not want the use of most of the money right away. We recall that it keeps its balance at the Federal Reserve banks constant. Therefore, the money raised by a sale of securities for cash is mainly left at commercial banks until the time comes to run it through the Federal Reserve banks to make payments of the government's obligations.

The Treasury follows the practice of placing these deposits in commercial banks, in "tax and loan accounts," with the particular commercial banks that originated them. Consequently, a commercial bank that buys $1 million of government securities in a cash offering knows that it will thereby receive a $1 million deposit of the United States government. Its expert on government finance, or the government securities dealer advising it, can make an estimate as to the period of time it probably will have this government balance before it is drawn out. During this time, the bank must, of course, hold additional cash as required reserves for this deposit, but the rest of the funds it can invest in earning assets. From its estimate of the number of days it will keep the deposit and of the rate of return it can earn on the portion of the funds that need not be kept in the form of reserves, the bank can estimate what it is worth to acquire the deposit.

Since by buying the government security the bank is essentially buying this temporary government deposit, the transaction is attractive to the bank even though it resells the security at less than it paid for it, so long as its loss on the security is smaller than the interest it earns on the temporary government deposit. Since the special incentive to buy the government securities applies only to banks, they naturally outbid other purchasers and act as a channel for distributing securities sold under these arrangements.

A general impression that perhaps emerges from this brief characterization of debt management operations is that they involve considerable technical difficulties. This is important because these technical considerations have affected the kind of debt management operations conducted in the past, and they put some kind of limits on what can be done in the future.

In this, debt management policy contrasts with monetary policy, where as we have indicated the Federal Reserve is able to conduct almost any kind of operation it might want to conduct unhindered by technical problems. In the case of fiscal policy, the constraints on the use of policy are not so much technical as political and are connected with costs of changing tax rates and expenditures programs. Debt management policy differs from both of these in that technical considerations do affect what can be done, and therefore, suggestions for procedures to overcome these technical problems may be an important contribution to reform of debt management policy.

Debt management operations and the money supply

What is the direct effect on the money supply of debt management operations such as we have been discussing? The general answer is that there is no such effect. The money that the Treasury borrows when it sells securities is not newly created money but is money given up by those who buy the securities. The basic transaction on the books of the commercial banks is a reduction in the demand deposits of the purchasers of securities and an increase in the Treasury balance.

But what if the securities are purchased by commercial banks? This still does not necessarily imply any effect upon the money supply. For the bank that maintains a given reserve position, the purchase of an additional government security means the bank will acquire less of some other earning asset.

Another channel through which Treasury debt management operations could affect the money supply is by causing the Federal Reserve to change the monetary base. The Federal Reserve assumes some responsibility to prevent instability in the credit market during those days most crucial to a Treasury financing operation. Thus, if interest rates began to rise abruptly at just the wrong moment the Federal Reserve would engage in open market purchases of government securities to stabilize the market, and this would increase the monetary base and the money supply. However, such Federal Reserve operations to maintain an "even keel" in the government securities markets ordinarily are limited to a matter of days. Thus, on the average over a period of weeks the Federal Reserve—so long as it is not required to maintain any particular level of interest rates on government securities —can closely achieve its objectives, such as a desired rate of growth of the money supply, and the money supply is not affected by debt management operations.

Debt Management, Liquidity, and Economic Stability

Let us consider the effect on total demand of debt management operations and other factors affecting the liquidity structure of outstanding investment assets. As was true of the other branches of stabilization policy, the effects of debt management actions are depicted differently by different approaches to economic theory.

Debt management in monetary theory

In terms of monetary theory, debt management actions affect total demand by affecting velocity. Either money or liquid assets (also called secondary reserve assets) can be held against some liquidity needs involving possible expenditures in the near future. An increase in the amount of liquid assets causes a part of the additional liquid assets to be held for purposes in which they substitute for the holding of money. This reduces the ratio of cash to expenditures of the economic units acting in this way. Consequently, it reduces the average cash ratio of the economy and increases the velocity of circulation of money. The substitution of liquid assets for cash balances is motivated by the increase in yields on liquid assets that tends to be caused by an increase in their supply.

Similarly, a reduction in the supply of liquid assets and a reduction in their yields causes cash balances to be held in uses earlier met by the holding of liquid assets. As a result, it increases holdings of money in relation to expenditures and reduces velocity of circulation.

In considering debt management operations, we deal only with changes in the *kinds* of government securities outstanding, since the amount of outstanding government securities is determined by the government surplus and by fiscal policy. Thus, a debt management action designed to increase total demand would shift government securities from long-term to short-term forms. The short-term securities are liquid assets and, as just indicated, would substitute in some degree for money holdings and tend to increase velocity of circulation.

Reducing the outstanding volume of long-term government securities would release long-term investment funds for the purchase of mortgages, corporate bonds, state and local government securities, and other securities that would finance nongovernmental expenditures, as investors with reduced holdings of long-term government securities reinvested their funds in functionally similar assets. The net effect of such a shift of government debt from long-term to short-term forms, it seems quite clear, is to increase total demand. The quantitative size of this effect, however, is uncertain and a matter on which judgments differ.

Unusual liquidity developments arising from debt management operations or other factors should be evidenced in an unusual term structure of interest rates. The unusual decline in short-term interest rates relative to long-term rates in the early 1930s and the sharp rise in long-term rates relative to short-term rates in the spring of 1953 seem explainable, in part, in terms of restrictive liquidity conditions that contributed to a decline in velocity and in total demand. Past developments seem to support the view that a large dose of debt management or other factors affecting liquidity conditions can significantly affect total demand.

A minimum program of debt management policy would guard against erratic or procyclical variations in liquidity on a scale that might contribute significantly to pushing total demand away from its desired path. More ambitious programs would use debt management policy systematically to combat other factors causing undesired liquidity developments or to cause liquidity changes that would operate as a negative-feedback mechanism to dampen deviations of total demand from its target path.

The stabilizing class of debt management policy shifts the government debt toward short-term forms and increases the supply of liquid assets when total demand is deficient; and shifts the government debt toward long-term forms and reduces the relative supply of liquid assets when total demand is excessive. Such debt management operations operate in the direction of limiting fluctuations in short-term interest rates, and thereby limiting variation in velocity. The direct effect of such a program is to amplify variations in long-term interest rates and the terms on which credit is available to private borrowers. However, insofar as the program contributes to limiting economic fluctuations, its indirect effects would reduce variations in demand for credit and fluctuations in interest rates in general.

Debt management in the credit approach to central banking

The credit approach to central banking as applied by the Federal Reserve before 1969 did not emphasize debt management or liquidity conditions. Indeed, to do so would have raised difficulties for the credit approach. The reason for this is that once liquidity developments are taken into account, low short-term interest rates and easy conditions in the money market may not reflect general credit ease in the sense in which the Federal Reserve interpreted it to exist, but rather a shortage of liquid assets. Thus, the low short-term interest rates may reflect not an expansive monetary policy but a restrictive liquidity situation. Moreover, if unavailability of secondary reserve assets and low short-term yields caused banks to hold reserves in uses in which they earlier held secondary reserve assets, the Federal Reserve interpreted this also as a sign of easy credit or even redundant reserves and moved to withdraw reserves from the banking system. The credit approach as applied by the Federal Reserve during the 1930s led to systematic misinterpretation of liquidity developments, which contributed to the destabilizing monetary policy.

Debt management in the Keynesian theory

The Keynesian theory did not explicitly deal with liquidity, but focused on money and the long-term rate of interest. The approach might have been expanded to deal with liquid assets, but it appears that this would have caused it substantial difficulties, and in any case it was not done. In relation to the influential version of the Keynesian theory in which financial variables in general were deemphasized, it was logical to deny the significance of changes in the structure of interest rates, and this was the approach taken.[1]

But if the Keynesian theory did not emphasize liquidity developments as such, its focus on the long-term interest rate saved it from the error attaching to the Federal Reserve's misinterpretation of the short-term interest rate. A shift in outstanding debt from short-term to long-term forms that increased long-term interest rates and reduced short-term rates, for example, would be interpreted by the Federal Reserve as easing of credit; but in terms of the Keynesian theory it would be interpreted as credit tightening. In this case, it is the Keynesian theory that points in the right direction and, at least in extreme cases, leads to the same general diagnosis as monetary theory.

An important difference between the two approaches, however, is that the monetary approach would develop an interpretation in terms of the supply of and demand for liquid assets (paralleling its interpretation in terms of the supply of and demand for money), thus avoiding the hazard of misinterpretation arising in an interest-rate-oriented approach because of inability to estimate changes in the natural rate of interest.

Alternative Programs of Debt Management Policy

The different frameworks within which debt management policy has been viewed have led to a number of different conceptions as to what would be a reasonable program of debt management policy. An idea influential in the early 1930s—relating to the Federal Reserve's notion of maintaining "sound credit conditions"—was that canons of "sound finance" required government debt to be mainly in long-term securities. This reflected the idea that the government should maintain itself in a liquid position just as should individuals and businesses. But if the government is to play the role of stabilizing the economy, it must not act as if it were just another business. When others are scrambling for liquidity, it should create liquidity for them, rather than joining in the scramble. While the view that the federal government is not subject to the rules of finance that apply to private borrowers is now almost universally accepted, this was not the case in the early 1930s. It explains why the government sold a large volume of intermediate and long-term securities at a time when the economy had an unusual shortage of liquid assets.

[1]"Since it is doubtful whether within moderate limits an increase in the general level of interest rates has strong effects, it becomes even more dubious whether the net effect of raising one rate and lowering another would amount to much." Warren Smith, *Debt Management in the United States*, Study Paper No. 19, Study of Employment, Growth, and Price Levels, U.S. Congress, Joint Economic Committee, 1960, p. 8.

Economists applying the Keynesian theory have usually adopted low and stable long-term interest rates as a goal. This leads to the conclusion that debt management policy should offer mainly or entirely short-term securities, thus avoiding upward pressure on long-term interest rates. If long-term securities are to be sold, this should be mainly during periods when long-term interest rates are temporarily depressed. This is usually in periods of weak demand for credit, which are in recessions. This results in—as interpreted in terms of monetary theory—a destabilizing debt management policy.

Applying monetary theory leads to the conclusion that debt management policy ought to avoid being a source of erratic or procyclical variation in total demand and perhaps should be a stabilizing influence on total demand. Perhaps, more ambitiously, it ought to try to offset other factors making for undesired changes in the supply of liquid assets. Thus, although debt management operations were the main instrument of policy, it would be a *liquidity* policy—just as we have a *monetary* policy that is conducted mainly through Federal Reserve open market operations.

The behavior of the amount of liquid assets in the economy, just as is true of the amount of money, depends upon certain aspects of the prevailing institutions and certain kinds of government actions, or policies. Three sets of factors importantly affect the economy's liquid asset supply function and the behavior over time of the amount of liquid assets: (1) short-term securities provided from securities speculation, (2) liquid assets provided by financial institutions (the behavior of which is itself heavily influenced by government regulations applying to the institutions), and (3) debt management operations. In the modern world, government regulations affect all three of these determinants of the economy's liquid asset supply function. Only in the case of debt management, however, does the government engage in operations that can serve as a continuous control system.

The decision rules for debt management emerging from this approach involve the following elements:

Sales by the Treasury of long-term securities should not be concentrated in periods of economic contraction or economic slack. As a minimum, they should be spread rather evenly over time (a zero-feedback debt management policy). More ambitiously, they should offset undesirable changes in liquid assets supplied by speculation and financial institutions, and should shift the government debt from long-term to short-term forms during periods of deficient total demand.

If debt management operations are conducted with a view to minimizing the administrative problems of the Treasury or minimizing interest cost of the government debt, this will lead to a pattern of operations that is the opposite of the one just described. Short-term securities are easier to sell—at least under the procedures the Treasury has used in the past. On the average, they also involve a lower interest rate, although during periods of generally high interest rates this has not been true. Accordingly, the path of least resistance would be to sell mainly short-term government securities, and to concentrate sales of whatever long-term securities are sold during periods of economic contraction or economic slack when the capital market is receptive to additional bond offerings and when long-term interest rates are relatively low.

Thus there are a number of different directions in which debt management policy could go. The sound-finance approach calls for selling only, or mainly, long-term securities. The Keynesian and the path-of-least-resistance approach call for selling mainly short-term securities and concentrating any sales of long-term securities during periods of deficient total demand. As viewed in terms of monetary theory, concentrating sales of long-term securities in periods of economic weakness makes debt management contribute to economic fluctuations. Selling only long-term securities implies that any favorable effects of fiscal policy—say, from the built-in flexibility of the tax system—are minimized or nullified. Thus, unless debt management is governed by a program designed to prevent this, it may contribute to economic instability.

The Record of Debt Management

The government debt in the years before the First World War was so small as to make debt management operations of minor importance, and our knowledge of liquidity developments in this period is limited. In the latter part of the 1920s, a combination of economically expansive liquidity factors seem to have contributed to the substantial increase in velocity of circulation that occurred. The extensive financing of securities speculation by short-term loans provided an extraordinary expansion in the supply of liquid assets and drove yields on liquid assets to very high levels. The extremely optimistic view of the future that prevailed seems to have reduced the demand for liquidity and thus to have made the effect of this increase in the supply of liquid assets greater than it otherwise would have been.

These developments might not have been so interesting and important except that they were then abruptly reversed, and the extraordinary reversal of liquidity developments contributed to the economic contraction of 1929–1933. The collapse of the stock-market boom meant an abrupt decline in the supply of short-term debt from this source. The decline in business investment implied a similar disappearance of short-term debt created by financially secure businesses. The decline in the supply of liquid assets made them very scarce, and investors seeking secondary reserve assets bid the yield on them down close to zero.

We should have expected this to lead banks and financial institutions to create additional liquid assets in the form of savings accounts and time deposits, taking advantage of this opportunity to get funds to lend for the payment of only nominal interest. The reason this did not happen is that the banks and financial institutions were themselves failing, their collapse also extinguishing liquid assets. It was not a part of the thinking of the times that the Treasury should offset this disappearance of liquid assets, and it did not do so to any substantial extent.

This led to a most unusual liquidity situation. From being extraordinarily abundant and so having their yields driven high, liquid assets became extremely scarce and their yield was driven virtually to zero. This implied that individuals and businesses had to hold money for purposes for which they would normally have held liquid assets. This, of course, contributed to the decline in velocity of circulation of money. The unavailability of liquid assets also implied that the commercial banks had to hold cash, or reserves, where they would normally have held short-term debt or secondary reserve assets. This, of course, increased the reserve ratio of banks and contributed to explaining the decline in the money supply. These perverse liquidity developments, occurring on an extraordinary scale, may have contributed significantly to the Great Depression.

The insurance of banks and financial institutions after 1933 somewhat relieved the shortage of liquid assets, but the liquidity situation remained relatively unfavorable during the latter part of the 1930s. The low yields on liquid assets contributed to explaining the failure of velocity of circulation to rise. In the Second World War the structure of interest rates was pegged, but there was a great increase in the supply of liquid assets in the form of short-term government securities, United States savings bonds, and time deposits and liquid assets of financial intermediaries. People were willing to accumulate liquid assets because of the current unavailability of goods and the desire to carry wealth forward to finance spending after the war.

The nation emerged from the war, therefore, in a liquidity condition favorable to expansion of total demand. The buildup of liquid assets during the war was one of the factors explaining why short-term interest rates when they were unpegged at the end of the war jumped up from their low depression levels before long-term rates rose appreciably. The fact that the public during the war had accumulated liquid assets beyond what it regarded as its normal holdings is indicated by the circumstance that the ratio of liquid assets to gross national product declined by about one-third from the end of the war to 1951. Thereafter, it showed only modest further decline. The position of the economy with reference to liquidity, thus, seems to have been again fairly normal by 1951 after an eventful period, in which liquidity greatly expanded in the latter part of the 1920s, shrunk from 1929 to 1933, expanded enormously during the Second World War, and then was worked back down to a relation to GNP that persisted for a decade.

Liquidity conditions and debt management in the postwar period

Several broad generalizations can be made about liquidity developments in the two decades after 1950. In the first decade, the volume of liquid assets held by the public increased about in line with GNP, but from 1961 through 1968 it rose more than proportionately. There was a broad shift in the relative importance of different kinds of liquid assets. At the end of the Second World War, a major and unusual role was played by liquid government securities. The decades since the war have seen a major shift toward an increased importance of liquid assets provided by financial institutions and a decline in the relative importance of short-term government securities. This has occurred despite a continued shift toward shorter maturities for government securities. It has reflected the fact that total government securities have grown less than proportionately with GNP and that a large part of the growth in government securities has been absorbed by government trust funds and Federal Reserve banks so that the total volume of United States government securities held by the public has shown no increase in a rapidly growing economy.

The provision of liquid assets by commercial banks in the form of time deposits and by financial intermediaries has included an anticyclical element. That is, the volume of liquid assets provided has grown most rapidly during periods of recession. At the height of economic expansions it commonly has declined. The reason for this is the mechanism discussed earlier. The volume of time deposits and other such savings obligations depends in a direct sense on the amount the public wants to take. This depends on the relation between interest rates on such obligations and interest rates on short-term debt available in the money market. Since interest rates on the obligations of savings institutions show less cyclical variation, these obligations are most attractive in recession when yields on money-market instruments decline sharply and least attractive during boom periods. While this mechanism operates in an anticyclical direction, it is somewhat abrupt and erratic because it depends in part on legal ceilings on the rates savings institutions can pay on their obligations.

Debt management operations, on the other hand, have been somewhat procyclical in nature. We indicated above that this would be a natural way for the Treasury to operate unless it had a positive instruction to behave in some other way. The natural tendency of the Treasury to concentrate its sales of long-term securities during periods of recession and low interest rates has been reinforced by a legislative prohibition against offering Treasury bonds at interest rates above 4¼ percent. This often made it impossible for the Treasury to sell bonds, especially during boom periods and at any time during the latter part of the 1960s. The legislation is a historical anachronism dating from the First World War, but political sentiment against high interest rates made its repeal impossible. The legislation prevented any kind of reasonable debt management program.

The nature of debt management policy varied considerably with the change in administrations and the ideas of the Secretary of the Treasury. Under the Truman administration, Secretary of the Treasury Snyder believed that interest rates should be low and stable and sold virtually no long-term

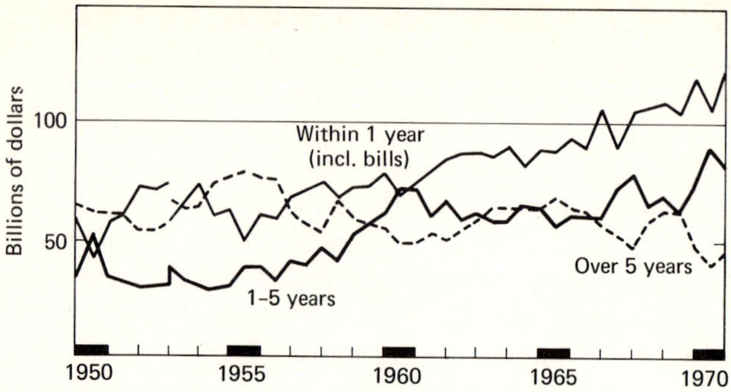

Fig. 23-4 Maturity of outstanding United States Government securities. (Includes marketable and convertible securities outstanding at the end of June and December.) *(U.S. Department of the Treasury and Board of Governors of the Federal Reserve System.)*

securities. The Eisenhower administration and Secretary Humphrey had very different ideas and arrived in Washington with bold talk of funding the federal debt by shifting it on a large scale from short-term to long-term securities. The bold talk seems to have so frightened the debt markets that the administration's first effort at selling long-term securities caused a near panic in the bond market, with sharply rising interest rates, and contributed to causing the recession of 1953–1954. After thus burning its fingers, the administration put its principles of debt funding aside and sold nearly all short-term securities. Consequently, the shortening of the average maturity of the government debt that had occurred under the previous administration continued, not as a matter of intention but in deference to the practical difficulties of selling long-term securities (Fig. 23-4).

The Kennedy administration was not dedicated to debt funding, but in Under Secretary of the Treasury Robert Roosa it commanded an unusually skillful and imaginative debt manager. This administration was the only one that sold a substantial volume of long-term government securities. The rising level of interest rates, in conjunction with the anachronistic 4¼ percent limitation on interest rates on government bonds, made it impossible after 1965 to do anything other than let the maturity of the government debt drift shorter.

Two episodes in postwar debt management merit special mention. The first of these is the effort at a rather substantial and abrupt lengthening of the debt in the spring of 1953. It is difficult to separate the effects of the debt management operations from the effects of the somewhat alarming statements of public officials with which they were accompanied. However, the combined package seems to have had a substantial role in explaining the recession of 1953–1954. There had been some retardation of growth of the money supply before the onset of this recession, but of all the postwar recessions it was the one most largely reflecting reduction in velocity rather than in the money supply. Consequently, the episode can be taken as supporting the belief of the financial community that the bond market is a somewhat delicate institution and sales of long-term government securities must be managed with some finesse and moderation. The episode also can be taken as supporting the interpretation that financial factors other than the money supply can have a significant effect upon the behavior of total demand.

The second debt management operation meriting comment was "operation twist" of 1961–1962. What was in question in operation twist was an application of anticyclical debt management policy in a period of economic slack. There existed a special incentive to such a policy. The balance of payments position of the United States was weak, and it was feared that if short-term interest rates fell to low levels this would cause a capital outflow and make the balance of payments situation even more. Debt management operations shifting the government debt from long-term to short-term forms would tend to bring down the long-term interest rates while preventing an excessive decline in short-term rates.

Operation twist was supposed to have been conducted by the Federal Reserve System, illustrating that Federal Reserve open market operations can be used to achieve debt management objectives. The Federal Reserve in its purchases of government securities shifted from its usual short-term securities to somewhat longer-term securities, mainly short intermediates. Other things being equal, this would have left the public holding somewhat shorter term securities than if Federal Reserve buying had been done at the extreme short end.

Other things were not entirely equal, however, since in this period the Treasury in *its* debt management operations was doing more to sell long-term securities than at any other time in the postwar period. Thus, if one looks at the combined operations of the Federal Reserve and the Treasury there was no large movement of the government debt toward short maturities. Operation twist existed more largely in name than in fact.

Proposals for Reform of Debt Management

There is not at present any wide agreement among economists as to the necessity or direction of reform of debt management. The shift in economic thought in the past decade toward greater emphasis upon monetary and financial factors as determinants of total demand would support an increased concern with liquidity developments and debt management. Such a development may occur in the 1970s. The hamstringing of debt management by the 4¼ percent interest rate limitation and the technical and political difficulties that seem to attach to this instrument of policy may have discouraged economists from giving it much attention. We must remember, however, that some organized program of debt management is necessary to assure that it is not a contributor to economic instability; therefore, attention to debt management is appropriate even though one does not foresee making it a major tool for positive stabilizing actions.

One major issue for consideration in connection with the economy's liquid-asset supply function is the major shift that occurred in the postwar period from the provision of liquid assets through government securities to their provision through time deposits and obligations of financial institutions. If debt management were effectively controlled and available as an instrument of stabilization policy, it might be argued that it would be better to provide the economy's liquid assets in the form of government securities rather than through financial institutions, which cannot be so accurately controlled. However, if one accepts the pessimistic view that debt management cannot politically be brought under control he may want to make the opposite argument, that since debt management operations will continue to be erratic and commonly procyclical the smaller their role in the economy's liquid-asset supply function the better off we are.

A program to make debt management more responsive to considerations of economic stabilization would involve two parts. The first would be the official adoption of this goal and of some general guides as to the way the maturity structure of government securities should behave. This would appropriately be done through legislation.

The second phase would be development of debt management techniques that would increase the ability of the Treasury to carry out such a program. The main problem is the development of techniques whereby long-term securities can be sold as called for by considerations of economic stabilization without causing panic or undue reaction in the debt markets. The technique of advance refundings developed by Mr. Roosa is one relevant technical achievement. Another suggestion is that long-term government securities should be sold at frequent intervals, or continuously, in small amounts rather than only rarely in large amounts. It is argued that to go for a long period without selling any long-term Treasury securities and then expect to enter the bond market with a number of billions of dollars worth of them to sell during a period of rising interest rates and falling bond prices is to take a very crude and heavy-handed approach to debt management.

Another suggestion, which could be combined with that of frequent offerings of Treasury bonds, is that these securities should be sold at auction, like Treasury bills, rather than through a method that requires the Treasury, in defining what interest rate to put on the security, to anticipate market conditions on the day of the sale. If there were a strong interest in making active use of debt management, doubtless technical improvements could be made that would permit the Treasury to do more good, or less mischief, than it characteristically has in the past.

A further point of discussion has been the political arrangements for the conduct of debt management operations and the agency to which this function should be assigned. The view reflected in the Treasury–Federal Reserve Accord of 1951 was that the Treasury should conduct debt management policy, the Federal Reserve limiting itself—and being free to limit itself—to monetary policy. This is accomplished by restricting Federal Reserve activities to very short-term securities. With Federal Reserve activities so defined, the Treasury would have the responsibility for determining the structure of government securities held by the public.

It would be possible to go in quite the opposite direction by assigning to the Federal Reserve responsibility for both monetary and debt management policies. The Treasury could borrow all its funds from the Federal Reserve, the Federal Reserve then selling to the public securites of the kinds that the Treasury now sells and thus assuming full responsibility for debt management operations. It is argued that this approach achieves full coordination, or consolidation, of government monetary and financial policy.

On the other hand, it can be argued that there is a place for the division of functions among agencies—a principle widely applied in our government. If the Federal Reserve were assigned responsibility for debt management and given no instruction as to how to use this power, the outcome would be uncertain. If a clear instruction or decision rule for debt management policy existed, the required operations could be carried out by the Treasury, preserving a separation between government financing and central banking that may still be useful.[2]

SUMMARY

1. Debt management determines the types of United States government securities held by the public. The amount of outstanding government debt is determined by fiscal policy, by the cumulative effect of government deficits and surpluses. The relative importance of government debt in the economy has declined greatly since 1946, as the government debt has increased only modestly while CNP and private debt have risen sharply. As in increasing proportion of government debt has come to be held by government agencies and trust funds, the decline in the economic role of government securities held by the public has been even more rapid.

2. Debt management operations are of two types: Refunding operations are conducted to replace maturing securities with new ones. Cash offerings involve an increase in outstanding government securities, such as is required to finance a government deficit. For securities other than Treasury bills, refunding operations ordinarily involve offerings of new securi-

[2]Here are some sources for different viewpoints on debt management policy: Milton Friedman, *A Program for Monetary Stability*, chap. 3, Fordham University Press, New York, 1959; Warren Smith, *op. cit.*; James Tobin, "An Essay on Principles of Debt Management," in *Fiscal and Debt Management Policies*, Commission on Money and Credit, Prentice-Hall, Englewood Cliffs, N.J., 1963; John M. Culbertson, *Macroeconomic Theory and Stabilization Policy*, chap. 21, McGraw-Hill, New York, 1968.

ties in exchange for the maturing ones. Securities sold in cash offerings ordinarily are bought in the first instance by commercial banks, since payments commonly are permitted in credits to tax and loan accounts, and such government deposits have a value to the bank gaining them.

3. Treasury bills differ from other government securities in being sold on an auction basis, being sold for cash and repaid in cash, and being a discount issue rather than a coupon issue.

4. Debt management operations that shift the government debt from long-term to short-term forms increase short-term interest rates and reduce long-term rates, and increase velocity and total demand. The quantitative importance of this relation is depicted differently by different theories of total demand and is uncertain.

5. An anticyclical debt management policy would shift government debt toward short-term forms during periods of deficient total demand and toward long-term forms during periods of excessive total demand. Debt management operations also might be used to offset undesired changes in liquid assets arising from securities speculation or the activities of financial intermediaries.

6. Unless conducted under such an instruction, debt management is likely to be procyclical, since confining sales of long-term securities to periods of recession eases the technical management problems of the Treasury, minimizes political complaints, and may also save something on the interest cost of the government debt.

7. Unusually adverse liquidity developments appear to have contributed to the Great Depression. During the postwar period, debt management has varied with the changes of administration but has been somewhat procyclical, such long-term debt as was sold having been concentrated in periods of recession. The relative importance of short-term United States government securities among the economy's liquid assets has greatly diminished in recent decades, a growing role being assumed by time deposits and savings and loan shares.

8. The economy is not now subject to any coherent government policy with regard to liquidity, and none is likely in the foreseeable future.

QUESTIONS FOR REVIEW AND DISCUSSION

1. What determines changes over time in the amount of outstanding United States government debt? Characterize changes in the size of the government debt and its importance in the economy since 1946.

2. Distinguish "refunding" and "cash offering," "coupon security" and "discount security." Explain the problems that arise when the Treasury undertakes to sell coupon issues during a period of rising interest rates.

3. "The obligation of the Federal Reserve to maintain an 'even keel' in the government securities market during Treasury financing operations implies that debt management decisions affect the money supply and that the Federal Reserve cannot effectively control the money supply." Comment.

4. Explain in terms of neoclassical or monetary theory how a debt management operation affects total demand.

5. Define a set of alternative programs of debt management that can be justified in terms of one set of ideas or another.

6. Explain how unfavorable liquidity developments contributed to economic instability in the late 1920s and early 1930s.

7. Give a brief characterization of debt management policy in the 1950s and 1960s.

8. What do you believe should be done about debt management and liquidity policy?

24 the future of monetary policy

Since it was designed by Alexander Hamilton, the United States monetary system has failed to perform adequately and has been basically revised a number of times. Major changes were the shift from bimetallism to gold in the latter part of the nineteenth century, the insurance of bank deposits in 1934, and—if it proves lasting—the replacement in 1969–1970 by the Federal Reserve of its traditional credit approach to central banking by an application of monetary theory. What are some of the basic choices regarding monetary policy that we may face in the 1970s?

The Context of Monetary Policy

The role of monetary policy has changed over time in response to four factors:

1. The potency or importance attributed to it.
2. Whether monetary policy was determined administratively or defined automatically by institutions that were set up by law.
3. The predominance of international considerations in the determination of monetary policy.
4. The significance of wage-price push as an influence on monetary policy.

Before the First World War, the importance of monetary policy was taken for granted. The idea that it did not make any difference whether the banking system was expanding or contracting the money supply would have been viewed as absurd. In the United States, monetary policy was largely automatic, determined by mechanisms defined by banking and monetary legislation, with some intervention by the United States Treasury. International considerations dominated monetary policy, except in the very short run; devaluation of the dollar or the imposition of restrictions on trade or capital movements to protect the balance of payments was out of the question. Finally, wage-price push did not enter the picture. When total demand was deficient, the price level declined.

How have the terms of reference of monetary policy changed in recent decades, and what is the context within which monetary policy will operate in the 1970s and 1980s? In the 1920s, the Federal Reserve entered the picture. Its discretionary or administratively determined monetary policy had special implications because of its application of the credit approach to central banking. The dominance of international considerations in monetary policy was not emphasized by the Federal Reserve Act, and the sterilization of gold flows by the Federal Reserve in the 1920s and 1930s was an important shift from an international towards a national monetary policy.

By the latter part of the 1930s, monetary policy was operating in quite a new context, which carried forward into the 1940s and 1950s. It was widely assumed that monetary policy had little power, emphasis having shifted to fiscal policy. Economic policy was nationalistic in its orientation. Wage-price push became a reality in the United States after the early 1930s and attracted increasing attention by the 1950s.

What further changes had occurred by 1971 and what seemed to be the context within which monetary policy would be interpreted in the 1970s? The period in which monetary policy was believed to be impotent seemed to be past with the 1960s. Monetary policy was again a major, or *the* major, instrument for controlling total demand. In the United States, monetary policy continued to be set by the Federal Reserve, but whether policy would be governed by monetary theory or the credit approach was a disputed question. The idea of applying an explicit decision rule for the behavior of the money supply was regarded as within the realm of reasonable discussion, as it would not have been a decade earlier.

The degree of nationalism versus internationalism in economic policy was the subject of active discussion, but the issue remained to be faced up to by (1) providing additional means of accommodating national differences in economic policy, as by providing greater flexibility of exchange rates or *else* (2) accepting the necessity of making monetary policy and the behavior of national total demand more closely responsive to balance of payments considerations. This dilemma, difficult enough at best, was aggravated by the seeming predominance of wage-price push, which implied that in the short run limitation of total demand for balance of payments reasons would involve a large cost in unemployment in relation to its benefits in influencing the price level.

This is a new environment or context for monetary policy. In this setting, monetary policy assumes a quite different appearance than it did within the terms of reference of the 1950s, the 1930s, the 1920s, or the days of gold. Thinking of monetary policy in this context may permit us to deemphasize some ancient controversies that have become irrelevant and to emphasize the choices and trade-offs that will matter in the 1970s.

Decision Rules for Monetary Policy and Instructions to the Federal Reserve

The credit approach to central banking that governed the Federal Reserve System during nearly all of its history rejected the idea of any quantitative instruction to the Federal Reserve. In this approach, we recall, the Federal Reserve is viewed as regulating *credit conditions*. The factors defining appropriate credit conditions are asserted to be too complex to permit of any explicit definition. Consequently, the matter is to be left to the discretion of the committee of Federal Reserve decision makers. In principle, the credit approach could be reflected in an explicit rule, such as "keep the market interest rate equal to the natural rate of interest, which is to be estimated in this manner. . . ." But this approach has never been developed.

The credit approach not only avoids a defined decision rule for the Federal Reserve but also precludes a quantitative analysis of the effects of monetary policy. As a result, it is inconsistent with the approach of defining a target path for total demand and then defining the particular set of Federal Reserve operations that are consistent with the realization of this target. It has been argued that the Federal Reserve can maintain sound credit conditions or discourage the development of unsound credit conditions, but if this does not result in the desired economic performance, the outcome is not to be blamed on monetary policy and must be the fault of some other policy or institution. This approach thus sets only loose criteria for guiding monetary policy and disclaims the ability and the responsibility to hit any closer target. The government has no other policy instrument with which it could hope to keep the year-to-year growth of GNP close to a defined target path, given the lack of close control over fiscal policy and the lack of evidence of its effectiveness.

If monetary policy is thus permitted to withdraw to the sidelines, disclaiming responsibility for the growth rate of GNP, the government will be left without any effective control instrument to bring about a growth of GNP that best reconciles the competing claims of high employment, price stability, and a satisfactory balance of payments. The government will have to retreat to some less demanding strategy of stabilization policy that does not require close control over the growth rate of total demand. It is not clear that any such strategy would meet the political and economic needs of the 1970s. Therefore, much depends on avoiding a relapse of the Federal Reserve into its traditional credit approach to central banking. This is the more true, of course, in that this approach not only avoids responsibility for controlling GNP but may contribute to perverse swings in GNP, as it did in 1965–1968.

A decision rule for negative monetary feedback: The Joint Economic Committee approach

A basic instruction for a negative-feedback monetary policy is illustrated by the approach suggested in 1967 by the Joint Economic Committee of Congress. The proposed decision rule was that the money supply should ordinarily increase by not less than 2 percent per year nor more than 6 percent per year, that large or erratic variations in the growth rate of the money supply should be avoided, and that the money supply should grow more rapidly during periods of economic slack and unemployment and less rapidly during periods of inflationary pressures.[1]

Such an instruction leaves the Federal Reserve to decide exactly how the money supply should respond to any given situation, but it puts significant constraints on the behavior of the money supply. The Federal Reserve did not follow this instruction, but continued the pattern of behavior that the instruction was intended to correct, increasing the money supply at a rate of more than 8 percent in the inflationary year of 1968 and then dropping down to a growth rate of 0 percent in the latter part of 1969. Past monetary policy would have been in violation of this rule much of the time. Thus, the adoption by Congress of such an instruction to the Federal Reserve would bring about a monetary policy importantly different from the one that has prevailed.

An even less specific instruction would limit itself to charging the Federal Reserve to cause *the money supply* to behave in a way that would contribute to the achievement of full employment and price stability. This would leave even greater latitude to the Federal Reserve, but it once again implies a monetary policy quite different from the one the Federal Reserve has produced, which emerged from Federal Reserve efforts to control credit conditions rather than the money supply. If the Federal Reserve is instructed that its business is to control the money supply rather than interest rates, this clearly implies that the money supply should not be permitted to increase more rapidly than usual during an inflationary period. Thus, even so general an instruction would have prevented the inflationary monetary policy of 1965–1968.[2]

Such instructions to the Federal Reserve could readily be embodied in new legislation, if Congress could agree on such a matter. Viewing Federal Reserve actions in terms of monetary theory, it seems clear that such instructions would have prevented the seriously destabilizing Federal Reserve actions that have been common in the past and would offer insur-

[1]Joint Economic Committee, *Jt. Econ. Rep.*, 1967 and 1968. A somewhat more detailed set of provisions for carrying out the instruction is suggested by Representative Henry S. Reuss, 1968 Jt Econ. Rep., pp. 44–46.

[2]Within the Federal Reserve System, the view that Federal Reserve policy should be governed by the behavior of the money supply was espoused by Darryl R. Francis, the President of the Federal Reserve Bank of St. Louis. See "The New, New Economics and Monetary Policy," *Fed. Reserve Bank St. Louis Rev.*, p. 6, January 1970. This implies a self-instruction to the Federal Reserve of the kind discussed above.

ance against their repetition in the future. Such an approach, however, would not impose on the Federal Reserve a responsibility to conduct its operations in a way consistent with a target path for total demand defined by the President. Thus, reliably to integrate the Federal Reserve into the approach to stabilization policy that has been attempted in recent years would require more basic or far-reaching reform of the existing institutions.

Responsibility for stabilization policy

If stabilization policy is to be formed in an integrated and coherent way, the responsibility for defining the target path for total demand must be assigned to the President and the executive branch of the government, including the Council of Economic Advisers. For it is the administration that must propose actions relating to wage-price push and the balance of payments, must assess the social costs of the trade-offs involved in the policy choices, and must decide fiscal and debt management policies.

Once a target path for total demand is defined, the definition of a set of Federal Reserve actions that will tend to realize this goal is a technical problem. That is, it involves knowledge and technique, rather than choices involving important trade-offs among social goals. If an accurate econometric model defining the dynamic properties of the economy and the effects of alternative money supply functions existed, monetary policy could be chosen simply by simulating the model with alternative monetary policies and choosing the one that brought GNP the closest to the target path. Unfortunately, present knowledge on this matter is imperfect, and responsible experts disagree as to what kind of model most accurately estimates the consequences of alternative sets of Federal Reserve actions.

But if the task assigned to the Federal Reserve in this system of decision making involves only knowledge and technique, the present structure of and instructions to the Federal Reserve System are ill-suited to fulfill it. The members of the Board of Governors of the Federal Reserve System are not chosen for their ability to perform this task. The task does not call for a diffuse decision-making structure run by a group of men appointed on political criteria.

The Federal Reserve System was set up to maintain a decentralized control over the quality of credit, applying the commercial loan theory of banking. The fact that it is organizationally well suited to that task and very poorly suited to defining the behavior of the money supply required to effectuate the administration's stabilization policy encourages Federal Reserve officials to continue to play their historical role.

But if the Federal Reserve does not so act as to effectuate the administration's target path for total demand but chooses different targets for total demand or reverts to its old game of "sound credit conditions," this makes a shambles of the approach to formulation of stabilization policy that has been attempted—with but little success—in recent years.

Within these terms of reference, the existing set of institutions is anomalous and requires reforms more far-reaching than those discussed above. To effectuate the approach being attempted, the Federal Reserve should be instructed to bring about that behavior of the money supply that will—on the basis of the best available estimates of the effects of alternative Federal Reserve actions—most closely achieve the administration's target path for total demand. Since the present organization and structure of the Federal Reserve is so ill suited to this task, it would be reasonable within this approach radically to simplify the Federal Reserve System, to centralize control and responsibility within it, and to assure its adherence to its instruction. It may be that achievement of an integrated and responsible stabilization policy in the modern context requires terminating the independence of the Federal Reserve and making it directly responsible to the President.

Professor Friedman's rule

A quite different strategy of stabilization policy is illustrated by the decision rule for monetary policy proposed by Milton Friedman.[3] The approach discussed above involves adapting the growth rate of total demand, and thus adapting monetary policy, to the best-available trade-off between unemployment and inflation and to the balance of payments situation. But Friedman proposes an overall approach in which the growth rate of the money supply and of total demand are permanently fixed, and the balance of payments and the wage-price push problems are then taken care of within that framework.

The balance of payments problem is handled within Friedman's program by the adoption of flexible exchange rates. It is taken—though this is debatable—that with flexible exchange rates it will be unnecessary to consider variations in the growth rate of total demand in deference to balance of payments considerations, which will be taken care of automatically and relatively painlessly by adjustments in exchange rates.

What, then, of the problem of wage-price push? Friedman's view is that this arises in large part from past inflation caused by excessive and erratic expansion of the money supply, and that after an adjustment period the improved behavior of total demand arising from his decision rule for the money supply would lead to expectations of price stability and to reductions in wage-price push. Insofar as the upward pressure on wages and prices arises from a self-seeking exercise of power by economic interest groups, Friedman advocates revisions of the legal framework to correct such abuse of economic power.[4]

With the problems of wage-price push and the balance of payments

[3]Milton Friedman, *A Program for Monetary Stabilization*, Fordham University Press, New York, 1960; and "The Role of Monetary Policy," *Am. Econ. Rev.*, **63**:1–17 (1968)

[4]*Capitalism and Freedom*, The University of Chicago Press, Chicago.

thus taken care of, a steady growth of total demand from year to year at a predefined rate would never be very far from the rate consistent with full employment and price stability. In view of the hazard—so abundantly illustrated by past monetary policy—that a discretionary monetary policy would work capriciously or in a destabilizing manner and destroy the framework of stable expectations on which the performance of the economy depends, Friedman favors the risk-avoiding approach of a simple decision rule for monetary policy: that the money supply should grow at the same fixed rate every year, for example, at 4 percent.

The Friedman rule is often stated with reference to "the money stock" defined to include not only money in the medium-of-exchange sense but also time deposits at commercial banks. Because of erratic, but roughly anticyclical, variation in the growth rate of time deposits, this particular rule would have led to procyclical variation in the money supply defined in the medium-of-exchange sense. When inflationary conditions cause high interest rates in the money market and so a decline in time deposits, the Federal Reserve would have to provide reserves as needed to get an accelerated growth of demand deposits and currency. If the increase in demand deposits and currency has a greater effect on total demand than the decline in time deposits, the automatic response will aggravate the inflation and be systematically destabilizing. Restatement of the Friedman rule in terms of the money supply would correct this problem.

A further point is that Friedman's defense of his rule rests in part on his view that monetary and fiscal policies affect total demand only with a long and variable lag, so that an effort to use these instruments of policy actively to combat fluctuations in total demand is hazardous and may aggravate instability. The doctrine of the long and variable lag has not been widely accepted nor borne out by subsequent empirical studies. However, Friedman's rule may make a useful reference point for discussion of alternative policy programs even if this particular argument in its favor is not accepted.

Rationalizing the Instruments of Monetary Policy

Neither the Federal Reserve Act nor the banking reform measures of the 1930s were designed to establish a system for the control of the nation's money supply or of total demand. The Federal Reserve Act specifically reflected the view of the Federal Reserve as a credit-regulating institution. If the Federal Reserve now is to be interpreted as the controller of the nation's money supply, this calls for a reassessment of the instruments through which it operates.

Open market operations are the major instrument of Federal Reserve policy. Moreover, they are a sufficient instrument for Federal Reserve control over the money supply. The rest of the machinery can be set up in such a way that the Federal Reserve through open market operations can offset anything else affecting the money supply and thus keep the money supply very close to any defined target path. It is interesting to note that open market operations were not among the instruments assigned to the Federal Reserve in the Federal Reserve Act. On the contrary, the relevance of this power was discovered only during the 1920s, somewhat by accident. If the Federal Reserve possessed only the powers conferred upon it by the Federal Reserve Act, it would have very limited ability to control the money supply.

Member bank borrowing and the discount rate

In the credit approach to central banking reflected in the Federal Reserve Act, the major instrument of Federal Reserve policy was to be the Federal Reserve discount rate and the conditions attached to the privilege of member banks to borrow from Federal Reserve banks. It was thought that by lending to member banks only on commercial loans the Federal Reserve would encourage bank behavior consistent with the commercial loan theory of banking. The Federal Reserve discount rate was to permit the Federal Reserve to influence interest rates and conditions in credit markets.

Member bank borrowing from Federal Reserve banks never worked out in conformity with this theory, and since the 1930s the theory has been a dead letter. Member bank borrowing now has no connection with commercial loans or the quality of credit. Since borrowing by member banks from Federal Reserve banks adds to Federal Reserve credit and the monetary base, it poses a potential threat to Federal Reserve control over the money supply. It would not be surprising if member banks wanted to borrow more from Federal Reserve banks when interest rates were high and economic conditions expansive. As a consequence, unless changes in member bank borrowing are offset by other factors they would lead to positive monetary feedback and a destabilizing monetary policy. From the point of view of monetary control, member bank borrowing from Federal Reserve banks is at best a nuisance and at worst a threat to the effectiveness of monetary policy.

The amount that member banks want to borrow from their Federal Reserve banks depends on what they must pay for the money in relation to what they can earn on it. That is, it depends on the Federal Reserve discount rate in relation to other interest rates. To provide the banks with a constant inducement to borrow, the Federal Reserve should continually adjust its discount rate to keep it in line with market rates. The Federal Reserve has not done this. Rather, it has changed discount rates only infrequently and during economic fluctuations has changed them by less than the change in other interest rates. This implies that the inducement to member banks to borrow (1) varies erratically depending on the timing of changes in Federal Reserve discount rates and (2) varies in a procyclical manner, borrowing being most attractive to member banks when interest rates are high and Federal Reserve discount rates are increased less than proportionately.

A further source of mischief from the discount apparatus attaches to the announcement effects of changes in Federal Reserve discount rates. The view is widespread that any increase in Federal Reserve discount rates should be viewed as a move toward "tight money" or a "restrictive monetary policy." Because of this, the Federal Reserve sometimes does not change discount rates as required to keep them adjusted to other interest rates because of the confusion or political or psychological response of the public.

Yet an additional complication is that the Federal Reserve is not free to increase its discount rates immediately before a Treasury financing operation, which further reduces its flexibility of action. When all these considerations are added together, the conclusion is drawn by many economists that the whole discounting apparatus should be regarded not as an instrument of monetary policy so much as an impediment to monetary policy. From this point of view, it would be appropriate to neutralize or sterilize the discount apparatus somehow, if not to eliminate it entirely.

One way to correct the erratic and procyclical element in member bank borrowings is by an institutional reform that keeps the Federal Reserve discount rate continuously adjusted to market rates of interest. The major proposal for doing this is to provide that the Federal Reserve discount rate automatically is set each week—or even each day—in a defined relation to a money-market interest rate, probably the rate on Treasury bills. To provide banks with a sufficient disincentive to borrow, the discount rate in these proposals could be a "penalty rate," say, one percentage point above the yield on Treasury bills. This arrangement would keep the borrowing privilege available to member banks, but the penalty rate would keep member bank borrowings small, and the continuous adjustment of the discount rate would limit their variation and get rid of undesired announcement effects. A good many economists would support a change of this type.[5]

A committee of the Federal Reserve System in 1968 published a proposal for reform of the discount mechanism that would go in the opposite direction to these proposals.[6] This would define a complex set of conditions under which member banks are privileged to borrow from Federal Reserve banks. While the proposal recommends that "the discount rate be changed considerably more frequently, to keep it reasonably closely in line with the

[5]Professor Friedman proposes a more radical approach in which member bank borrowing from Federal Reserve banks simply is eliminated. He proposes, however, that banks be penalized for holding less than their required reserves by a fine on the deficiency that is higher than the market rate of interest. Unless this fine were set so high as to effectively prohibit reserve deficiencies, the reserve deficiencies would be equivalent to member bank borrowing. The amount of such reserve deficiencies would have to be added to high-powered money to explain the behavior of the money supply. In this event, it may be preferable to preserve the existing arrangements. See Friedman, "A Program for Monetary Stabilization," pp. 44–45.

[6]"Reappraisal of the Federal Reserve Discount Mechanism," Board of Governors of the Federal Reserve System, Washington, D.C., 1968; and Reappraisal of the Federal Reserve Discount Mechanism, *Fed. Reserve Bull.*, pp. 545–551, July 1968.

movements in other money market rates,"[7] the discount rate is not to be changed continuously and presumably is not to be higher than the market rates of interest. This reform is intended not to reduce the amount of member bank borrowing but rather to increase it. Given continued looseness of Federal Reserve control over member bank borrowing, policy changes that increase its absolute amount may increase undesired variation in the monetary base from this source. From the viewpoint of monetary theory, the proposed change would seem to be a step backward.[8]

Changes in reserve requirements

Changes in member bank reserve requirements can be used to change the volume of deposits and the money supply and, in this sense, are an alternative to open market operations. Rather than increasing the money supply by buying government securities and raising the monetary base, the Federal Reserve can have a similar effect by reducing reserve requirements, thereby reducing the reserve ratio and increasing the base-money multiplier.

As an instrument of monetary control, such changes in reserve requirements have some important side effects. An increase in reserve requirements, for example, in addition to acting to reduce the money supply (1) reduces bank profits by requiring replacement of bank earning assets by nonearning assets in the form of reserves; (2) requires greater Federal Reserve holdings of government securities to achieve a given money supply, thereby increasing the income of Federal Reserve banks and reducing the net interest cost on the United States government debt; (3) reduces the base-money multiplier and the amount of leverage in the system through which monetary policy is effectuated; and (4) imposes on all member banks simultaneously the necessity of adjusting to a change in the rules of the game with reference to their holdings of reserves.

If it is possible to control the money supply in a manner that does not involve these side effects, this seems the preferable system. It appears that open market operations do constitute a sufficient means for controlling the money supply. Therefore, within the framework of the monetary approach a reasonable reform is to terminate the Federal Reserve power to change reserve requirements. An alternative is to continue the power in existence but instruct the Federal Reserve that it is to be used only in unusual circumstances. The danger in this is that if used only rarely and in large doses (the most likely unusual circumstance), changes in reserve requirements will have an effect that connot be fully anticipated, raising the possibility of another great error like that of 1936–1937.

[7] *Ibid.*, p. 546.

[8] Some different interpretations and evaluations of the Federal Reserve proposal are given in "The Federal Reserve Discount Policy: A Symposium," *J. Money, Credit Banking*, **2**:135–165 (1970).

As an instrument of monetary control, it would be desirable not only to eliminate changes in reserve requirements but also to make reserve requirements the same for all banks. In 1971, different reserve requirements were in effect for four classes of member banks and for many categories of nonmember banks in various states. Changes in the location of demand deposits thus cause a change in the average required reserve ratio and so in the average reserve ratio, altering the amount of money for any given amount of high-powered money. While such variation in the average reserve ratio of the system is not quantitatively an important impediment to effective monetary control, it surely is a liability rather than an asset. The situation would be corrected, so far as Federal Reserve member banks are concerned, by imposing the same reserve requirements upon all member banks.

A further reform that would require new legislation and politically would be very difficult to achieve is to impose on all nonmember banks the same reserve requirements that apply to Federal Reserve member banks. While such legislation would be resisted by state banks and doubtless by state banking authorities, it would be more attainable if reserve requirements were permanently fixed than while they remain variable at the option of the Board of Governors with no instruction or rules as to what either the level or the structure of reserve requirements may be in the future.

Consequently, imposing standard reserve requirements on all commercial banks not only would standardize the base-money multiplier of the system but also would have a important effect in removing one of the incentives for banks to leave membership in the Federal Reserve System. Some economists believe that some Federal Reserve actions that seem detrimental to the cause of monetary control are taken in an effort to deter banks from giving up their membership in the Federal Reserve System. While in other respects the Federal Reserve System may have excessive powers, in this ability of banks to escape the System by becoming state nonmember banks it may be argued that the Federal Reserve needs more power than it has.

A final change that might be undertaken in the system of reserve requirements is to abolish legal reserve requirements for time deposits of commercial banks. If the rationale of the reserve mechanism is as an instrument of monetary control, and if time deposits are treated as liquid assets rather than as a part of the money supply, legal reserve requirements for time deposits are inappropriate. They are not needed, just as legal reserve requirements are not needed in connection with the liquid assets created by savings and loan associations and mutual savings banks. We indicated above that the volume of such assets created by savings institutions is controlled by the price system. It is only in the case of a medium of exchange that the price system does not limit supply and thus a reserve mechanism is necessary.

If special legal reserve requirements for time deposits are not needed for monetary control, they become another factor complicating the task of monetary control. To preserve growth of the money supply along any defined path, the Federal Reserve must through open market operations offset all changes in required reserves behind time deposits associated with changes in the volume of time deposits. We have noted that failure to do so, given the way time deposits characteristically behave, will contribute to procyclical variation of the money supply.

In opposition to the abolition of legal reserve requirements for time deposits of commercial banks, it may be argued that (1) this would inappropriately increase bank profits and (2) it would unduly improve the competitive position of commercial banks in relation to mutual savings banks and savings and loan associations. While the merit of these points is debatable, it seems reasonable to reply that if the social interest calls for the imposition of some competitive disadvantage on commercial banks in their time deposit activities, this is best done by imposing on them a tax or other regulation that does not confuse and reduce the efficiency of the nation's mechanism of monetary control.

While these proposals for changing the role of reserve requirements in the monetary system derive logically from the monetary approach, it is equally logical that the Federal Reserve in the 1960s was led by its application of the credit approach in quite a different direction. The Federal Reserve continued to make use of changes in reserve requirements, viewing them within the framework not of continuous control over the money supply but as a means of bringing about changes in credit conditions when large changes in such conditions were thought to be necessary. The Federal Reserve also in 1968 added an additional dimension of complexity to the system of reserve requirements by imposing higher requirements on banks with deposits of over $5 million. This stems from the Federal Reserve emphasis upon the allocation of credit and its attempt to favor or subsidize the provision of credit in rural areas and through small banks. Once again, the merits of such intervention into the system of credit allocation are debatable, but if such action is to be taken it can be done in a way that does not confuse and weaken the mechanism of monetary control.

The logic of the reserve mechanism was further undermined when the Board of Governors of the Federal Reserve System assessed reserve requirements against certain kinds of borrowings from abroad in connection with the Eurodollar market in October 1969 and against bank-related comercial paper in August 1970. This, once again, is not inconsistent with the Federal Reserve's view of itself as controlling the availability of credit and the level of interest rates—although in this connection it has the effect of discriminating against certain types of capital inflow into the United States. This extension of reserve requirements, however, undermines their logic as a system of monetary control. This action by the Federal Reserve provides an additional basis for proponents of the monetary approach to call for removing from Federal Reserve hands the ability not only to change reserve requirements but to assess reserve requirements against various forms of credit.

Regulation Q

Whether ceilings on the interest rates paid on time deposits seem essential, useful, or harmful depends on one's theory of monetary policy. Focusing on credit conditions and the amount of bank credit, the Federal Reserve has viewed as a significant tool of monetary restraint its ability to prevent banks from paying competitive interest rates on their time deposits. But, on the other hand, if the Federal Reserve's basic job is making the money supply grow along a path consistent with the desired growth path of total demand, this power is not needed. Rather, such actions are to be avoided because of their extensive side effects.

Prohibiting banks from procuring funds through their ordinary activities sets them to looking for ways to evade the regulations, leading to such things as development of bank-related commercial paper and development of the Eurodollar market. This then puts the Federal Reserve to imposing new regulations to limit evasion of the old ones, such as new reserve requirements on bank-related commercial paper and Eurodollar borrowings. Whether further escalation of this game would contribute to the efficiency of the economy is debatable.

Ceilings on interest rates paid by commercial banks on time deposits also are supported as needed to limit the competitive advantages of banks over savings institutions and as needed to prevent credit from escaping from socially desirable areas such as housing. It seems arguable that insofar as either of these objectives merits government regulations on its behalf, itself a matter on which opinions may differ, other modifications of the framework of laws and regulations can achieve the goals more efficiently than ceilings on bank interest rates.[9]

In the past few years a group of economists, following Milton Friedman,[10] have criticized the prohibition of payment of interest on demand deposits. A quite different set of considerations are at issue in this case. Since the prohibition of payment of interest on demand deposits applies all the time, its effects do not cut in and out abruptly as do those of the ceilings on time-deposit interest rates, which become effective only as interest rates generally rise above the ceilings. Moreover, since institutions other than banks are prohibited from creating demand deposits in any case, this restriction does not affect the terms of competition among financial institutions so forcefully as do ceilings on time deposits and savings accounts.

[9]Recommendations that regulation Q should not ordinarily be used, but should by placed on a standby basis for use in exceptional circumstances were made by all of the major independent investigations of the financial system in recent years, the Commission on Money and Credit in 1961, the Advisory Committee on Banking to the Comptroller of the Currency in 1962, and President Kennedy's Committee on Financial Institutions in 1963. Lawrence S. Ritter, *Regulation Q: Issues and Alternatives*, p. 12 Association of Reserve City Bankers, Chicago, 1965. For completeness, Ritter recommends likewise.

[10]"The Optimum Quantity of Money," in his *The Optimum Quantity of Money and Other Essays*, Aldine, Chicago, 1969.

The major argument offered in favor of permitting payment of interest on demand deposits is that it would increase the efficiency of the economy. The legal prohibition of such interest, it is argued, causes a distortion of the price system. By divesting demand deposits of the interest they otherwise would earn, the law causes people to hold fewer demand deposits than they otherwise would hold, which makes their economic satisfactions less than they could be. Indeed, the argument's basic proposition is that since token money costs practically nothing to produce, people should treat money to hold as a free good, which they will do only if money pays as much interest as the other assets people would hold in its place. A number of objections have been raised against this argument, and it is not yet clear whether it finally will be accepted or rejected by professional opinion.

Control over the allocation of credit

Qualitative credit controls are those involving the allocation of credit, or the relative terms on which credit is available to different classes of borrower or to different regions of the country. Such credit controls represent an intervention in or overriding of credit allocation among competing uses by the price system. The general message of economics is that such overriding of the market mechanism should be engaged in only where there is some clear showing of a net social benefit. There is a hazard that actions on behalf of particular groups will be taken as a result of political pressures without due regard for the indirect consequences of the action for the economy as a whole and for outsiders who do not realize their interests are being damaged. Special measures to make credit particularly easy or particularly expensive for some kind of use, thus, we should consider within the same framework as special subsidies to encourage or support some activities and special taxes to discourage others.

A special point emphasized by the monetary approach to central banking is that any selective credit controls engaged in should not override the cause of monetary control and economic stabilization. For example, if it is desired to favor housing in the credit market, this should be done by diverting credit to housing from other sources and not by supporting housing credit with newly created money, thereby leading to general inflation. More broadly, the point should be emphasized that any instruments of selective credit control should not interfere with the nation's control over its money supply function and its pursuit of full employment and price stability.

One selective credit control that meets these criteria is that relating to credit to finance securities speculation. If this is regarded not as a device for Federal Reserve control over stock prices but primarily as a standby measure to be invoked in the event of an incipient speculative boom, probably most economists support this instrument of control. A speculative boom can be damaging. Although administered by the Federal Reserve, the existing margin requirements in no way intrude into the mechanism of monetary control. Indeed, the setting of margin requirements could be shifted to a different agency such as the Securities and Exchange Commission without loss of effectiveness.

A number of other actions taken by the Federal Reserve with reference to allocation of credit do, however, potentially interfere with the effectiveness of control over the money supply. This does pose a significant question in monetary reform, the more so since the Federal Reserve in the latter part of the 1960s aimed at extending its selective credit controls in ways that seemed to threaten the effectiveness of the system of monetary control.

A kind of qualitative credit control not based upon powers conferred by legislation was engaged in by the Board of Governors in 1966. A letter was sent to all member banks requesting the limitation of business loans, particularly loans for "nonproductive" purposes. The letter indicated that banks judged not to be cooperating by complying with this request would receive less favorable treatment if they undertook to borrow from the Reserve bank.

Discriminatory use of the privilege of borrowing could be used by the Federal Reserve as an enforcement sanction for other requests regarding the way credit is to be allocated among competing users. In this connection, the revision of the administration of Federal Reserve loans to member banks proposed by the Federal Reserve System in 1968 would increase the importance of this power. If member banks generally became dependent upon the Federal Reserve bank for a part of their operating funds, they should be less able to resist any Federal Reserve requests as to the kinds of credit to be extended. Regardless of its merits in other connections, such a policy reduces the effectiveness of monetary control by making the amount of member bank borrowing subject to side considerations having to do with the allocation of credit rather than with the behavior of the money supply.

An additional proposal for a qualitative credit control not made by the Federal Reserve was the proposal in 1970 by the Joint Economic Committee that the Federal Reserve should not limit its open market operations to Treasury securities but should buy the debt of federally supported agencies that contributed funds to the housing market. This poses a threat that depressed conditions in the housing market would lead to Federal Reserve open market purchases of such debt, increase in the money supply, and general inflation.[11]

In principle, perhaps the Federal Reserve could do all these other things and still keep the money supply on the defined path. It would do this by conducting open market operations in such a way as to offset variations in all other factors affecting it, now including such new factors as Federal Reserve special open market operations in support of the housing

[11]Joint Economic Committee, *1970 Jt. Econ. Rep.*, p. 16, 1970.

market. In practice, it is most unlikely that the Federal Reserve can occupy itself with supporting the housing market, encouraging small and rural banks, discouraging certain kinds of short-term capital inflow, and instructing the banks on what kinds of loans to make—all of this on top of its historic goal of keeping general credit conditions suited to the "needs of trade"—and at the same time come up with an acceptable behavior of the money supply. The likely outcome of such further emphasis upon selective credit controls is that the behavior of the money supply in the future would be more erratic and destabilizing than in the past.

Radical Reform: 100 Percent Banking

If it may still be true of the existing monetary system that the credit tail wags the money dog, then it is still useful to discuss a reform of the nation's monetary system that Irving Fisher proposed 35 years ago: "The essence of the 100% plan is to make money independent of loans; that is, to divorce money from banking."[12] While such a proposal is not likely to be adopted, it defines an illuminating alternative to the existing institutions.

The transition to 100 percent reserves

How should we get from what we now have to the 100 percent reserve system? Let us assume that we wish to do this while keeping growth of the money supply on a predetermined track. What is needed is gradually to increase reserve requirements behind demand deposits, while at the same time providing the additional reserves required so the commercial banks can meet these increased requirements while the money supply grows along its predetermined track. In other words, the Federal Reserve System through open market operations would increase the monetary base by enough fully to offset the effects of the increase in the reserve ratio. This process would continue until reserve requirements on demand deposits reach 100 percent.

This process would involve a three-way shift in debt or earning assets. The commercial banks would be selling all the earning assets associated with their demand-deposit activities. In replacement, they would be acquiring additional reserves. To provide the additional reserves, the Federal Reserve banks would be acquiring a large volume of United States government securities, which would come from commercial banks and other investors. Other investors would have to pick up the earning assets of commercial banks other than United States government securities, selling United

[12]Irving Fisher, *100% Money*, p. viii, The Adelphi Company, New York, 1935. This approach was advocated at the same time by Henry Simons, "A Positive Program for Laissez Faire: Some Proposals for a Liberal Economic Policy," in his *Economic Policy for a Free Society*, pp. 62–65, The University of Chicago Press, Chicago, 1948. For a recent argument on behalf of this approach see Milton Friedman, *A Program for Monetary Stability*, pp. 65–76.

States government securities that would be picked up by the Federal Reserve banks. The specialized lending functions of commercial banks in consumer credit and business loans also would be taken over by these other institutions. Existing commercial banks could continue to carry out their time-deposit activities.

If banks were not paid interest on their reserves, they could earn income to support their checking account activities only by increasing their service charges. The counterpart of this loss of income by the commercial banks is the increase in income of the Federal Reserve banks that have essentially taken over earning assets formerly held by the commercial banks. Since the interest earnings of the Federal Reserve banks are returned to the Treasury, this would reduce the interest cost on the government debt.

Alternatively, it might be decided that the public welfare would be served by paying interest on reserves held by the demand-deposit institutions. If very high service charges caused the public to shift from using demand deposits to using currency, this might involve a social cost by increasing the incidence of robbery and requiring additional expenses for police protection. By setting the rate at which interest is paid on these reserves, the government can choose the extent to which it wishes to subsidize the use of checkbook money. Thus, the question of the level of service charges on demand deposits can be separated from the leverage and credit-creation aspects of the reform, to which we now turn.

Operation of the 100 percent reserve system

The new system, in contrast to the old one, has these characteristics: (1) There is no leverage in the system. A $1 million open market purchase by the Federal Reserve results immediately in a $1 million increase in the money supply. (2) The commercial banks are not involved in the creation of either credit or money. They are only bookkeeping offices handling the transfer of checks. (3) The demand-deposit institutions are not extenders of credit. They make no loans and hold no earning assets. The demand-deposit institutions are not "banks" as we have used that term, since they do not create a token money and inject it into the economy by lending it.

In the new system, the banking functions that earlier had been divided between the Federal Reserve banks and the commercial banks are shifted entirely to the Federal Reserve banks. This now is a one-level monetary system, involving no leverage. Money creation, credit creation, and the extension of credit all occur entirely at the level of the Federal Reserve banks. If further expansion of the money supply is brought about by Federal Reserve open market operations in government securities, the credit associated with the creation of new money is injected into the economy entirely through the market for United States government securities. Thus, money creation is divorced from credit creation by private banks and from the extension of credit to private borrowers. Money still is created by banking, however, and money creation has not been separated from credit creation.

Thus, a question is raised as to whether the reform would accomplish what has been expected of it by its proponents down through the years. If the Federal Reserve used its enlarged powers to bring about an appropriate behavior of the money supply, all would be well, but the Federal Reserve could, if it chose, bring about such an outcome with its existing powers. Would the fact that money creation and the associated creation of credit was concentrated in the Federal Reserve banks ease the political pressures to use these powers to influence interest rates—or might it make them worse? Even this radical reform does not necessarily solve the problem.

The ultimate reform, back to commodity money

To separate money creation from credit creation a still more radical reform is needed. Newly created money can be injected into the economy not by being loaned, but by being used to buy a commodity or commodities. A useful intellectural reference point in this connection is the multiple-commodity money with circulating warehouse certificates, which was discussed in Chap. 10. In this system, a fixed money price is set for a defined package of commodities. The monetary authority is instructed to buy these commodities whenever it can get them at that price or below it, creating new money to pay for them. It also is instructed to stand ready to sell the commodities whenever their price rises above the fixed price.

Under this system, the money supply would respond negatively to changes in the average price of the package of commodities and would thus tend to so vary as to stabilize the price level. If the international economic system were such that price stability was consistent with a satisfactory balance of payments and if the economy's institutions for determining wages and prices were such that price stability was consistent with acceptably full employment, this monetary system would do the job.

Other more elegant monetary systems could be defined that would do the job more efficiently, if their implementation were politically feasible. But implementing rational and efficient policies in a world of imperfect knowledge, prejudice, and special interests is not easily done, or often done. These proposals for radical monetary reform provide useful intellectual benchmarks against which to measure the pretensions and the performance of existing institutions.

Monetary Policy and the Future

The Federal Reserve Act in 1913 established a monetary system controlled not by the government but by an independent agency carefully insulated from control of the government. The Federal Reserve System was established as a highly decentralized independent agency to control credit and enforce the commercial loan theory of banking.

The terms of reference of 1913 do not fit the political realities and the ideas of the 1970s, but the implied revisions of the Federal Reserve System remain to be made. The peculiarities of the existing decision system were illustrated by the formation of a stabilization policy in 1971. The Nixon administration formulated a target path for total demand that it considered to be a reasonable response to the trade-offs between unemployment, inflation, and the balance of payments situation that were expected to emerge from circumstances and the planned actions of the administration. Federal Reserve Chairman Burns declined to accept the administration's targets as well as its interpretation of the behavior of the money supply that would be consistent with the achievement of its targets. This situation in which the administration is held responsible by the public for the effects of the stabilization policy but lacks the power to carry out its policy program is not likely prove satisfactory or sustainable.

SUMMARY

1. The way monetary policy was viewed has changed over time because of changing ideas as to its potency, whether policy was determined administratively or was automatic; the predominance of international considerations; and the role of wage-price push.

2. In recent years, the President has formulated a program of stabilization policy responsive to the available trade-offs among inflation, unemployment, and balance of payments deficits. This defines a target path for total demand. The President can propose a fiscal policy consistent with the target path of GNP, but prompt and responsive congressional action on such requests is rare. Since monetary policy is controlled by the Federal Reserve, it need not be consistent with the President's program of stabilization policy.

3. A decision rule for monetary policy suggested by the Joint Economic Committee is that the money supply should grow not less than 2 or more than 5 percent per year, large or erratic variations in its growth rate should be avoided, and growth should be at the high end of the range when economic slack prevails and at the low end under inflationary conditions. This is a simple decision rule for a monetary policy incorporating error-controlled negative feedback. Federal Reserve actions have often been inconsistent with this decision rule.

4. To assure consistency of Federal Reserve actions with the administration's overall program of stabilization policy requires new legislation so instructing the Federal Reserve or more basically changing its responsibilities and structure.

5. A decision rule for monetary policy proposed by Milton Friedman involves a constant rate of growth in the money supply at a predetermined rate estimated to be consistent with price stability. Friedman's overall program contemplates correction of balance of payments imbalance by flexible adjustments in exchange rates. He believes wage-price push would diminish if monetary policy assured stable prices and if abuses of market power were reduced through changes in legislation.

6. Existing arrangements for member bank borrowing from Federal Reserve banks at the Federal Reserve discount rate are an impediment to effective control over the money supply. Erratic and procyclical influence on the economy of changes in member bank borrowing and in the discount rate could be reduced by continuous adjustments in the discount rate to keep it in line with market rates of interest.

7. Changes in reserve requirements affect bank profits, the interest cost of the government debt, and the base-money multiplier and amount of leverage in the monetary control system. Since the money supply can be controlled through open market operations without such side effects, a case exists for legislation terminating the authority of the Federal Reserve to change reserve requirements.

8. The assessment of reserve requirements against time deposits of commercial banks, Eurodollar borrowings, and bank-related commercial paper increase the complexity of the system of monetary control. Maintenance of the money supply on any given time path requires changes in such required reserves to be offset by Federal Reserve open market operations.

9. A radical reform intended to overcome the long-standing performance failures of the United States monetary system involves the gradual increase in reserve requirements against demand deposits to 100 percent. This would dissociate the creation of money from the creation of private credit and give Federal Reserve open market operations an immediate, dollar-for-dollar effect on the money supply. However, it would not prevent the Federal Reserve from conducting its open market operation with reference to interest rates or other such criteria and would not separate money from credit.

10. Money creation would be completely separated from credit by a return to a commodity-money system, in which new money is injected into the economy through purchase of specified commodities rather than through the purchase of debt. A system using as money warehouse certificates for a defined group of commodities would cause the money supply to so vary as to stabilize the price level.

QUESTIONS FOR REVIEW AND DISCUSSION

1. Contrast the context within which monetary policy is considered in the 1970s with that of the late 1930s; of the years before World War I.

2. Explain how in 1971 a stabilization policy program was formulated that integrates the various aspects of the problem. How does monetary policy relate to this program?

3. Describe the decision rule for monetary policy proposed by the Joint Economic Committee. Characterize this rule in relation to control systems theory. Evaluate monetary policy during the 1950s and 1960s in relation to this rule. Discuss the pros and cons of legislation instructing the Federal Reserve to follow this decision rule.

4. "The existing arrangements for monetary policy need basic reform. They give the administration responsibility without power and the Federal Reserve power without responsibility." Discuss the problem and the way you would recommend handling it.

5. "Friedman's rule for the money supply belongs to a logical and coherent package but implies basic changes in the rules of the national and international economic system." Discuss this proposition.

6. "Differences in viewpoint as to the use to be made of the various instruments of Federal Reserve policy arise mainly because some see the task as control of the money supply while others see it as regulation of credit conditions." Illustrate with reference to each policy instrument.

7. "Had the 100 percent reserve system been in effect after 1929, the money supply would not have declined as it did." "The existence of the 100 percent reserve system would not necessarily have prevented the inflationary increase in the money supply in 1965–1968." Discuss these two propositions. Attempt to define what problems of monetary misbehavior would be cured by 100 percent reserves and what problems might remain.

8. "One's prescription for monetary reform depends on his monetary theory and his degree of political optimism or pessimism." Categorize alternative approaches within this framework. Define and justify your program of reform of United States monetary policy.

index

index